£30=

R

# Sri Lanka

The British Documents on
the End of Empire Project
gratefully acknowledges
the generous assistance of
the Leverhulme Trust.

The Project has
been undertaken
under the auspices
of the
British Academy.

BRITISH DOCUMENTS ON THE END OF EMPIRE

General Editor S R Ashton
Project Chairman A N Porter

Series B Volume 2

# Sri Lanka

## Editor
## K M DE SILVA

## Part II
# TOWARDS INDEPENDENCE
# 1945–1948

Published for the Institute of Commonwealth Studies
in the University of London

London : The Stationery Office

ISBN 0 11 290559 5

British Library Cataloguing in Publication Data
A CIP catalogue record for this book is available from the British Library

If you wish to receive future volumes from the British Documents on the End of Empire project, please write to The Stationery Office, Standing Order Department, PO Box 276, LONDON SW8 5DT, or telephone on 0171 873 8466, quoting classification reference number 040 30 017

Printed in the United Kingdom for the Stationery Office Ltd
Dd. 303023, 6/97, 2100, 29858

*The* Stationery
Office

Published by The Stationery Office and available from:

**The Publications Centre**
(mail, telephone and fax orders only) PO Box 276, London SW8 5DT
General enquiries 0171 873 0011
Telephone orders 0171 873 9090
Fax orders 0171 873 8200

**The Stationery Office Bookshops**
49 High Holborn, London WC1V 6HB (counter and fax orders only) Fax 0171 831 1326
68–69 Bull Street, Birmingham, B4 6AD   0121 236 9696   Fax 0121 236 9699
33 Wine Street, Bristol BS1 2BQ   0117 9264306   Fax 0117 9294515
9–21 Princess Street, Manchester M60 8AS   0161 834 7201   Fax 0161 833 0634
16 Arthur Street, Belfast BT1 4GD   01232 238451   Fax 01232 235401
The Stationery Office Oriel Bookshop, The Friary, Cardiff CF1 4AA   01222 395548   Fax 01222 384347
71 Lothian Road, Edinburgh EH3 9AZ (counter service only)

Customers in Scotland may mail, telephone or fax their orders to:
Scottish Publications Sales, South Gyle Crescent, Edinburgh EH12 9EB
0131 479 3141   Fax 0131 479 3142

**Accredited Agents**
(see Yellow Pages)

*and through good booksellers*

# Contents

| | page |
|---|---|
| Sri Lanka: Schedule of contents: parts I–II | vii |
| Abbreviations: parts I–II | ix |
| Principal holders of offices: part II Apr 1945–Mar 1948 | xiii |
| Glossary: parts I–II | xvii |
| Chronological table of principal events: parts I–II | xix |
| Summary of documents: part II | xxiii |
| Documents: part II | 1 |
| Biographical notes: parts I–II | 371 |
| Bibliography 1: Public Record Office sources searched | 381 |
| Bibliography 2: Official publications, unpublished official material, unpublished private papers, published documents and secondary sources | 383 |
| Index: parts I–II | 389 |
| MAP Sri Lanka: Provincial Divisions and Principal Towns | vi |

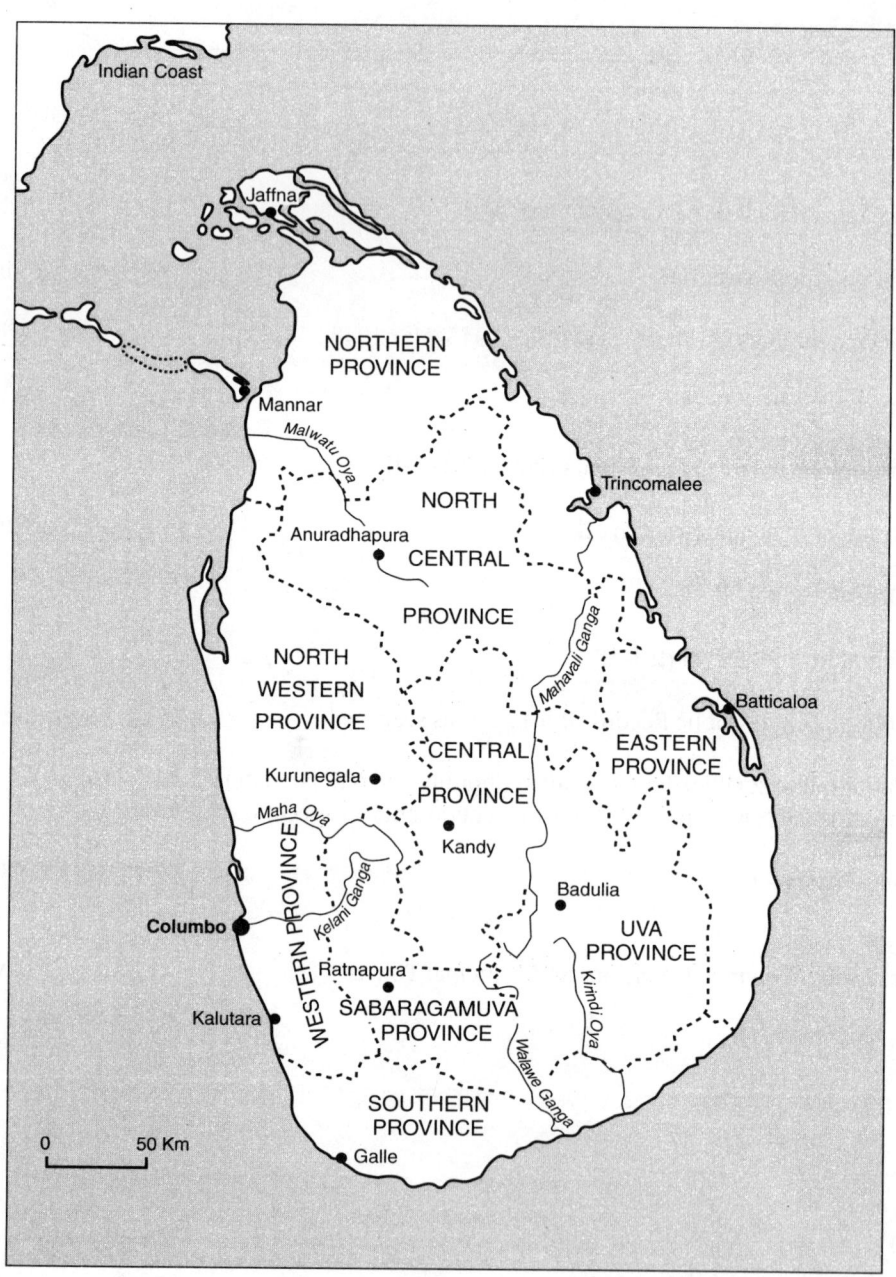

Sri Lanka: Provincial Divisions and Principal Towns

Sri Lanka

# Schedule of Contents: Parts I–II

PART I     THE SECOND WORLD WAR AND THE SOULBURY COMMISSION 1939–1945

Chapter 1    The war and postponement of constitutional reform; Indo–Ceylon relations, Sept 1939–Apr 1941
(*Document numbers 1–93*)

Chapter 2    Wartime conditions and the revival of pressure for constitutional reform; Ceylon and wartime supplies: the case of rubber production (1), Apr 1941–July 1943
(*Document numbers 94–174*)

Chapter 3    The ministers' draft constitution and the Soulbury Commission: Ceylon and wartime supplies: the case of rubber production (2), Sept 1943–Apr 1945
(*Document numbers 175–239*)

PART II    TOWARDS INDEPENDENCE 1945–1948

Chapter 4    Senanayake at the Colonial Office; the negotiating team; the Soulbury Report, Tamil protests and the white paper, Apr–Nov 1945
(*Document numbers 240–329*)

Chapter 5    The Indian problem, post-war reconstruction and the communist challenge, Nov 1945–Nov 1946
(*Document numbers 330–376*)

Chapter 6    India, Burma and Ceylon; the defence agreement, sterling balances and citizenship, Dec 1946–Mar 1948
(*Document numbers 377–446*)

# Abbreviations: Parts I–II

| | |
|---|---|
| ACTC | All-Ceylon Tamil Congress |
| AFPFL | Anti-Fascist People's Freedom League (Burma) |
| ARP | air raid precaution |
| BSI | Burma: Struggle for Independence (Burma documents series) |
| CB | Companion of the Order of the Bath |
| CBE | Commander of the Order of the British Empire |
| CCS | Ceylon Civil Service |
| CD | coast defence |
| CDF | Ceylon Defence Force |
| CGA | Ceylon Garrison Artillery |
| c-in-c | commander-in-chief |
| CIC | Ceylon Indian Congress |
| CICLU | Ceylon Indian Congress Labour Union |
| CID | Criminal Investigation Department |
| cif | cost in freight |
| CIWF | Ceylon Indian Workers' Federation |
| CLI | Ceylon Light Infantry |
| CMG | Commander of the Order of St Michael and St George |
| CNC | Ceylon National Congress |
| CNVF | Ceylon Naval Volunteer Force |
| CO | Colonial Office; commanding officer |
| Con | Conservative Party (UK) |
| COS | Chiefs of Staff |
| COSSEA | Chiefs of Staff, South-East Asia |
| CPRC | Ceylon Planters Rifle Corps |
| CRO | Commonwealth Relations Office |
| corrupt gp | corrupt group (undeciphered word or words in telegram) |

| | |
|---|---|
| DFC | Distinguishing Flying Cross |
| DO | Dominions Office |
| DSC | Distinguished Service Cross |
| DSO | Companion of the Distinguished Service Order |
| EPT | excess profits tax |
| Ex Co | executive committee/committees |
| FAA | Fleet Air Arm |
| fob | free on board |
| GA | government agent |
| GB | Great Britain |
| GCMG | Knight Grand Cross of the Order of St Michael and St George |
| GOC | general officer commanding |
| GOI | Government of India |
| gov | government; governor |
| gov-gen | governor-general |
| HE | His Excellency |
| HM | His Majesty |
| HMG | His Majesty's Government |
| HQ | headquarters |
| ICS | Indian Civil Service |
| IGP | inspector general of police |
| ILO | International Labour Organisation |
| IO | India Office |
| IRRC | International Rubber Regulation Commission |
| KBE | Knight Commander Order of the British Empire |
| KC | King's Counsel |
| KCMG | Knight Commander of the Order of St Michael and St George |
| kt | Knight |
| Lab | Labour Party (UK) |
| LSSP | Lanka Sama Samaja Party |
| MC | Military Cross |
| MP | member of parliament |

| | |
|---|---|
| MSC | member of State Council |
| OAG | officer administering the government |
| OBE | Officer Order of the British Empire |
| PM | prime minister |
| PRO | Public Record Office |
| QMG | quarter master general |
| RAF | Royal Air Force |
| RN | Royal Navy |
| RNVR | Royal Naval Volunteer Reserve |
| RTC | round table conference |
| SAC | supreme allied commander |
| S of S | secretary of state |
| SACSEA | supreme allied commander, South-East Asia |
| SEAC | South-East Asia Command |
| SMS | Sinhala Maha Sabha |
| TOPI | Transfer of Power in India (India documents series) |
| UK | United Kingdom |
| UN(O) | United Nations (Organisation) |
| UNP | United National Party |
| VP | vital point |

# Principal Holders of Offices: Part II
# Apr 1945–Mar 1948

## UNITED KINGDOM

1. *Ministries*

(a) *Caretaker government 23 May–26 July 1945*

| | |
|---|---|
| Prime minister | Mr W S Churchill |
| S of S foreign affairs | Mr A Eden |
| Chancellor of Exchequer | Sir John Anderson |
| S of S colonies | Mr O F G Stanley |
| S of S dominion affairs | Viscount Cranborne |
| S of S India and Burma | Mr L S Amery |

(b) *Labour government 26 July 1945–26 Oct 1951*[1]

| | |
|---|---|
| Prime minister | Mr C R Attlee (26 July 1945) |
| Lord president of the Council | Mr H S Morrison (27 July 1945) |
| Lord chancellor | Lord Jowitt (27 July 1945) |
| Lord privy seal | Mr A Greenwood (27 July 1945)<br>Lord Inman (17 Apr 1947)<br>Viscount Addison (7 Oct 1947) |
| S of S foreign affairs | Mr E Bevin (27 July 1945) |
| Chancellor of Exchequer | Dr H J N Dalton (27 July 1945)<br>Sir Stafford Cripps (13 Nov 1947) |
| President of Board of Trade | Sir Stafford Cripps (27 July 1945)<br>Mr J H Wilson (29 Sept 1947) |
| S of S colonies | Mr G H Hall (3 Aug 1945)<br>Mr A Creech Jones (4 Oct 1946) |
| S of S dominion affairs<br>(Commonwealth relations<br>from 7 July 1947) | Viscount Addison (27 July 1945)<br>Mr P J Noel-Baker (7 Oct 1947) |

---

[1] Details to Mar 1948, the concluding date for this volume.

| S of S India and Burma | Lord Pethick-Lawrence (3 Aug 1945)<br>Earl of Listowel (23 Apr–14 Aug 1947 for India; to 4 Jan 1948 for Burma) |
|---|---|
| S of S defence | Mr C R Attlee (27 July 1945)<br>Mr A V Alexander (20 Dec 1946) |

(c) *Colonial Office: junior ministers*

| Minister of state | Earl of Listowel (4 Jan 1948) |
|---|---|
| Parliamentary under-secretary<br>of state | Duke of Devonshire (1 Jan 1943)<br>Mr A Creech Jones (4 Aug 1945)<br>Mr I B Thomas (4 Oct 1946)<br>Mr D R Rees-Williams (7 Oct 1947) |

2. *Civil servants*

(a) *Secretary to the Cabinet*

Sir Edward Bridges (1938–1946)
Sir Norman Brook (1947–1962; additional secretary, 1945–1946)

(b) *Colonial Office*

| (i) Permanent under-secretary<br>of state | Sir George Gater (1942–1947)<br>Sir Thomas Lloyd (1947–1956) |
|---|---|
| (ii) Deputy under-secretary<br>of state | Sir Arthur Dawe (1945–1947)<br>Sir Sydney Caine (1947–1948)  ⎫<br>Sir Charles Jeffries (1947–1956) ⎬ joint |
| (iii) Assistant under-secretary<br>of state, responsible for<br>the Ceylon and Pacific<br>Department | G E J Gent (1942–1946)<br>C J Jeffries (1947–1948) |
| (iv) Assistant secretary, head<br>of the Ceylon and Pacific<br>Department | J B Sidebotham (1943–1948) |

## CEYLON

| 1. *Governor* | Sir Henry Monck-Mason Moore (3 Dec 1944) |
|---|---|
| 2. *Officers administering<br>the government* | Sir John Howard (20 July 1945–2 Feb 1946)<br>Sir Robert Drayton (14–21 Apr 1946) |

3. *Board of Ministers*

| | |
|---|---|
| Chairman | The chief secretary (*ex-officio*) |
| Vice-chairman | D S Senanayake |
| Minister of home affairs | A Mahadeva |
| Minister of agriculture and lands | D S Senanayake |
| Minister of local administration | S W R D Bandaranaike |
| Minister of health | G E de Silva |
| Minister of labour, industry and commerce | G C S Corea |
| Minister of education | C W W Kannangara |
| Minister of communications and works | J L Kotelawala |

4. *Officers of State*

(a) *Chief secretary*

Sir Robert Drayton (3 Dec 1944–13 May 1945)
C H Collins (13 May–10 Dec 1945, *acting*)
Sir Robert Drayton (10 Dec 1945–14 Apr 1946)
E Jones (14–21 Apr 1946, *acting*)
Sir Robert Drayton (21 Apr 1946–1 Apr 1947)
C H Collins (from 1 Apr 1947)

(b) *Legal secretary*

M W H de Silva (5 Apr–4 Oct 1945, *acting*)
J H B Nihill (4 Oct 1945–25 Jan 1946)
C Nagalingam (25 Jan–6 May 1946, *acting*)
J H B Nihill (6 May 1946–15 Oct 1947)
A E P Rose (from 15 Oct 1947, *acting*)

(c) *Financial secretary*

C E Jones (30 Jan–1 May 1945, *acting*)
Sir Oliver Goonetilleke (1 May–24 June 1945, *acting*)
Sir Oliver Goonetilleke (24 June 1945–8 Jan 1946)
C E Jones (8 Jan–13 Apr 1946, *acting*)
C J D Lanktree (14–21 Apr 1946, *acting*)
C E Jones (21 Apr–5 May 1946, *acting*)
Sir Oliver Goonetilleke (5 May–11 June 1946)
C E Jones (11 June–4 Nov 1946, *acting*)
Sir Oliver Goonetilleke (4 Nov 1946–8 March 1947)
C E Jones (from 8 March 1947, *acting*)

## 5.  Cabinet (from 26 Sept 1947)

| | |
|---|---|
| Prime minister and minister of defence and external affairs | D S Senanayake |
| Minister of health, local government and leader of the House of Representatives | S W R D Bandaranaike |
| Minister of industries, industrial research and fisheries | G E de Silva |
| Minister of home affairs and rural development | Senator Sir Oliver Goonetilleke |
| Minister of labour and social services | T B Jayah |
| Minister of finance | J R Jayewardene |
| Minister of transport and works | J L Kotelawala |
| Minister of education | E A Nugawela |
| Minister of justice | Senator L A Rajapakse (23 Oct 1947) |
| Minister of food and co-operative undertakings | A Ratnayake |
| Minister of agriculture and lands | Dudley S Senanayake |
| Minister of posts and telecommunications | S Sittampalam |
| Minister of commerce and trade | C Suntheralingam |
| Minister without portfolio | L A Rajapakse<br>R S S Gunawardena |

# INDIA

| | |
|---|---|
| *Governors-general and Viceroys* | Field Marshal Viscount Wavell (20 Oct 1943)<br>Earl Mountbatten of Burma (24 March–14 Aug 1947) |

# Glossary: Parts I–II

| | |
|---|---|
| conductor | a minor supervisory officer on a plantation |
| estate | plantation |
| government agent | administrative head of a province |
| *Kachcheri* | provincial or district secretariat |
| Kandyan | pertaining to the old Kandyan kingdom which occupied the central highlands and much of the north central and south eastern plains; Sinhalese from the Kandyan region |
| *kanakapulle* | a minor official in a plantation, generally with some responsibility over maintenance of accounts, especially those relating to wages of workers |
| *kangany* | organiser or head of a group or gang of workers on plantations; on the larger estates there were several kanganies of whom one or more would be given the title of head-kangany |
| *Korale* | administrative unit within a district |
| *Perahera* | a famous ritual ceremony associated with the Temple of the Tooth in Kandy. Generally for ten days in July or August there is a magnificent procession of elephants and dancers which attracts thousands of people to the town. The head of state is traditionally the guest of honour on the last day – hence the presence in British times of the governor |
| *Pongal (also Thaipongal)* | Hindu harvest festival, observed early in January |
| rupee | coin in use in Ceylon; worth about 1s 6d or 7½p (UK) or 30 cts (US) in the 1940s. Ceylon had and has a decimal currency of 100 cents to a rupee |
| *sangam* | a trade union on a plantation |
| *suriya mal* | *thespesa populnea*; marxist groups in Ceylon began selling this flower on memorial day as an anti-imperialist gesture, and in opposition to the sale of poppies |
| visiting agent | a senior planter, overseeing work of several plantations |

# Chronological Table of Principal Events: Parts I–II

## 1939

| | |
|---|---|
| 3 Sept | War declared between Great Britain and Germany |
| 3 Oct | CO decides that constitutional reform in Ceylon should be postponed until after the war |

## 1940

| | |
|---|---|
| 10 Jan | Police shooting of Indian plantation worker at Mool-oya, Hevaheta |
| 27 Feb | Resignation of Board of Ministers on constitutional issues arising from Mool-oya incident |
| 6 Mar | Ministers re-elected by executive committees |
| 12 July | Arrest and detention of Lanka Sama Samaja Party leaders |
| 4 Nov | Exploratory talks between delegations representing the governments of India and Ceylon in New Delhi |
| 12 Nov | GOI reports failure of Indo–Ceylon talks |

## 1941

| | |
|---|---|
| 11 Jan | A contingent of the Ceylon Garrison Artillery, the first batch of Ceylon servicemen sent for overseas service in Second World War, leaves the island |
| 14 Mar | Major G StJ Orde Browne, CO labour adviser, arrives in Colombo to report on labour conditions in Ceylon |
| 4 Sept | Indian delegates arrive in Colombo for Indo–Ceylon talks |
| 21 Sept | Delegates at Indo–Ceylon talks conclude their sittings on reaching 'agreed conclusions' on all subjects |
| 28 Oct | Governor Caldecott submits reform proposals to CO |
| 17 Nov | Ceylon placed under the command of the c-in-c, India. Major General R D Inskip appointed general officer commanding troops in Ceylon |
| 8 Dec | Declaration of war between Great Britain and Japan |

## 1942

| | |
|---|---|
| 15 Feb | Singapore surrenders |
| 25 Feb | Senanayake leaves for India to negotiate food supplies |
| 5 Mar | Vice Admiral Layton appointed c-in-c, Ceylon |
| 9 Mar | Dutch forces in Java surrender |
| 23 Mar | Japanese occupy Andaman islands |
| 24 Mar | War Council established in Ceylon |
| 5 Apr | 75 sea-borne Japanese aircraft attack Colombo in morning raid |

8 Apr      Escape of Lanka Sama Samaja Party leaders from jail
9 Apr      American forces in Bataan, Philippines, surrender. Japanese raid on
           Trincomalee
6 May      Surrender on Corrigedor ends American resistance in Philippines
1 July     Establishment of University of Ceylon with Dr W Ivor Jennings as first
           vice chancellor
8 Aug      Indian National Congress adopts 'Quit India' resolution
9 Aug      Indian National Congress leaders arrested and interned
2 Dec      Senanayake chosen as leader of house and vice-chairman of Board of
           Ministers. A Mahadeva elected minister for home affairs in place of Sir
           D B Jayatilaka
18–20 Dec  Ceylon National Congress, in annual session at Kelaniya, adopts resolu-
           tion that its objective is 'the attainment of Freedom for Ceylon'

## 1943

26 May     Official announcement from Whitehall on future constitution for Ceylon.
           Speaker reads message to State Council
8 June     Senanayake makes statement in State Council on ministers' response to
           declaration of 26 May; announces ministers' resolve to draft a constitu-
           tion
6 July     M S Aney appointed agent for GOI in Ceylon
9 July     Clarification of policy statement of 26 May
25 Aug     Admiral Mountbatten appointed supreme allied commander, SEAC
6 Nov      Publication of report of special committee on education
21 Dec     Senanayake resigns from Ceylon National Congress

## 1944

3 Feb      Ministers' draft constitution despatched to London
15 Apr     Mountbatten arrives in Ceylon; headquarters of SEAC transferred from
           New Delhi to Kandy
6 June     Allied landings in Normandy (D-Day)
15 June    Whitehall announces decision to appoint a commission to visit Ceylon
           and report on constitutional reform
15 July    Appointment of commission to report on social services
25 Aug     Paris liberated
18 Sept    CO announces appointment of Sir Henry Moore as new governor of
           Ceylon
17 Oct     Caldecott relinquishes office and leaves island
29 Oct     All-Ceylon Tamil Congress established
19 Nov     Official announcement of appointment of commission on constitutional
           reform in Ceylon chaired by Lord Soulbury
4 Dec      Arrival of Sir Henry Moore in Colombo
22 Dec     Arrival of Soulbury commission

## 1945

| | |
|---|---|
| 8 Jan | Admiral Layton relinquishes post of c-in-c, Ceylon; succeeded by Lt-Gen E de R Wetherall |
| 22 Jan | Soulbury Commission begins public sittings |
| 13 Mar | Soulbury Commission concludes public sittings |
| 10 Apr | Soulbury commissioners return to London |
| 20 Apr | Sir Oliver Goonetilleke, civil defence and food commissioner, appointed financial secretary |
| 23 Apr | Japanese evacuate Rangoon |
| 9 May | End of hostilities in Europe |
| 17 May | White paper on Burma published |
| 23 May | Coalition government dissolved in Britain |
| 11 July | Senanayake leaves for London for discussions at CO on constitutional reform |
| 26 July | Labour Party victory in British general election |
| 14 Aug | Japanese surrender |
| 11 Sept | British Cabinet decides to accept Soulbury Report as basis of Ceylon's future constitution |
| 12 Sept | Japanese forces in S E Asia surrender to Mountbatten in Singapore. Publication of Senanayake's note on Ceylon's claim for dominion status |
| 1 Oct | Free education introduced in Ceylon from primary school up to university, with Sinhalese and Tamil as medium of instruction |
| 9 Oct | Soulbury Report published |
| 1 Nov | White paper on constitutional reform in Ceylon published |
| 8 Nov | State Council accepts motion introduced by Senanayake on white paper proposals by 51 votes to 3 |

## 1946

| | |
|---|---|
| 25 Jan | J H B Nihill, legal secretary, leaves for London for consultations on drafting of new constitution |
| 23 Mar | Cabinet Mission arrives in India |
| 16 May | Cabinet Mission plan for India announced |
| 17 May | Order-in-Council promulgating new Ceylon constitution published |
| 18 July | Senanayake introduces 16th and last budget under the 1931 constitution |
| 6 Sept | United National Party established |

## 1947

| | |
|---|---|
| 6 Jan | R Aluvihare appointed first Ceylonese inspector-general of police |
| 27 Jan | Attlee-Aung San agreement on Burma |
| 20 Feb | British government announces intention to transfer power in India by a date not later than June 1948 |
| 12 June | Official statement on dominion status for Ceylon |
| 1 July | Last meeting of State Council |
| 15 Aug | Polling commences for election to new parliament of Ceylon. Indian independence (14 Aug for Pakistan) |
| 20 Sept | Parliamentary elections concluded in Ceylon |

24 Sept    Senanayake becomes Ceylon's first prime minister
8 Oct      First formal meeting of new Cabinet
14 Oct     First meeting of House of Representatives
11 Nov     White paper on new constitutional status of Ceylon published. Agreements on Ceylon independence signed in London and Colombo
12 Nov     First meeting of Senate
13 Nov     Ceylon Independence Bill introduced in House of Commons
25 Nov     Ceremonial opening of parliament
26 Nov     Senanayake moves independence motion in House of Representatives
1 Dec      First national budget presented in House of Representatives by J R Jayewardene, minister of finance
5 Dec      Independence motion passed in House of Representatives by 59 to 11
10 Dec     Ceylon Independence Bill receives Royal Assent. Sir H Moore appointed first governor-general

## 1948

4 Jan      Burma becomes independent republic
4 Feb      Ceylon Independence Day

# Summary of Documents: Part II

Chapter 4
Senanayake at the Colonial Office; the negotiating team;
the Soulbury Report, Tamil protests and the white paper
Apr–Nov 1945

| NUMBER | | SUBJECT | PAGE |
|---|---|---|---|
| | | *1945* | |
| 240 | Sir H Moore to Sir G Gater | 29 Apr | Tel on date for Mr Senanayake's visit to London | 1 |
| 241 | Mr Stanley to Sir H Moore | 1 May | Tel (reply to 240) | 1 |
| 242 | Admiralty | 10 May | Minute on 239, on defence reservations under new constitution [Extract] | 2 |
| 243 | Sir H Moore to Mr Stanley | 15 May | Despatch on re-opening negotiations with India on rights & status of Indians in Ceylon, + *Enclosures* | 3 |
| 244 | Mr Stanley to Sir H Moore | 15 May | Tel on timetable for publication of Soulbury Report | 5 |
| 245 | Sir H Moore to Mr Stanley | 21 May | Tel conveying Mr Senanayake's views on publication of Soulbury Report | 5 |
| 246 | Mr Stanley to Sir H Moore | 23 May | Tel (reply to 245) | 6 |
| 247 | Sir H Moore to Mr Stanley | 29 May | Tel on question of Mr Bandaranaike acting for Mr Senanayake during latter's absence in London | 7 |
| 248 | H N Morrison & I M R Campbell (Admiralty) | 11–21 June | Minutes on defence portfolios under new constitution | 8 |
| 249 | Sir H Moore to Mr Stanley | 13 June | Tel transmitting message from G G Ponnambalam requesting equal opportunities with Mr Senanayake in discussions with secretary of state | 9 |
| 250 | Sir H Moore to Mr Stanley | 13 June | Tel suggesting a reply to G G Ponnambalam's message in 249 | 10 |
| 251 | Sir H Moore to Mr Stanley | 14 June | Tel explaining why resumption of negotiations with India on Indians in Ceylon must await clarification of position on constitutional reform | 10 |

NUMBER                                SUBJECT                                PAGE

*1945*

252    Mr Stanley              15 June   Tel (reply to 249 & 250)            11
       to Sir H Moore

253    Sir H Moore             9 July    Letter on disallowance of Free Lanka   12
       to Mr Stanley                     Bill, + *Enclosure*: minutes of special
                                         meeting of Board of Ministers, 8 July

254    Sir R Drayton (London)  13 July   Tel on question of second chamber    15
       to Sir H Moore

255    C H Collins (acting     [18 July] Memo on debate in State Council on   16
       chief secretary)                  Mr Bandaranaike's motion protesting
                                         against rejection of Free Lanka Bill

256    G E J Gent              21 July   Note on reception to be accorded by  18
                                         secretary of state to delegations from
                                         Ceylon

257    Trafford Smith          23 July   Minute on points raised by Lord Soul-  19
                                         bury in discussion with Mr Senanayake

258    J B Sidebotham          23–24     Minutes on 251                       21
       to G E J Gent           July

259    Sir H Moore             25 July   Letter conveying governor's personal  22
       to Mr Stanley                     views on Soulbury Report

260    Mr Stanley              25 July   Memo, 'Ceylon constitution', on Soul-  24
       for Cabinet Ceylon                bury Report
       Committee

261    Sir H Moore             26 July   Letter conveying governor's further   28
       to G E J Gent                     personal views on Soulbury Report

262    Sir H Moore             28 July   Tel explaining why Sir O Goonetilleke  30
       to Mr Stanley                     has seen Soulbury Report before Mr
                                         Senanayake

263    Admiral Layton          31 July   Letter on defence requirements & atti-  31
       to Admiralty                      tude of CO towards Ceylon    [Extract]

264    Sir G Gater             1 Aug     Notes of discussion with Mr Stanley &  31
                                         interview with Mr Senanayake on
                                         Soulbury Report

265    Trafford Smith &        7 Aug     Joint minute on 259 & 261, + *Annex*   33
       J B Sidebotham

266    Mr Senanayake           16 Aug    Letter stating case for dominion status  37
       to Mr Hall

267    Sir H Moore             17 Aug    Tel on Soulbury Report, on risk of    47
       to Mr Hall                        leakage

268    Sir H Moore             27 Aug    Tel on general support in Ceylon for  48
       to Mr Hall                        dominion status

| NUMBER | | SUBJECT | PAGE |
|---|---|---|---|
| | | *1945* | |
| 269 | Mr Hall<br>to Sir H Moore | 27 Aug | Letter on Mr Senanayake's claim for dominion status | 48 |
| 270 | Mr Greenwood<br>(lord privy seal) | 29 Aug | Cabinet memo on Soulbury Report, submitting a report from the Colonial Affairs Committee | 49 |
| 271 | Cabinet meeting<br>CM 26(45)3 | 30 Aug | Conclusions on 270 | 53 |
| 272 | Mr Hall<br>to Sir H Moore | 30 Aug | Tel on Mr Senanayake's claim for dominion status | 54 |
| 273 | Cabinet meeting<br>CM 24(45)2 | 3 Sept | Conclusions authorising Mr Hall to open discussions with Mr Senanayake on recommendations of Soulbury Report | 55 |
| 274 | CO | 4 Sept | Record of discussion between Mr Hall & Mr Senanayake on Soulbury Report | 56 |
| 275 | Trafford Smith | 5 Sept | Minute on proposed timetable for action on Soulbury Report | 60 |
| 276 | R N Gilchrist<br>(India Office)<br>to J B Sidebotham | 5 Sept | Letter on communication of Soulbury Report to viceroy, + *Enclosure*: India Office note for Lord Wavell | 61 |
| 277 | G E J Gent | 5 Sept | Note on 276 | 63 |
| 278 | Mr Hall<br>to Mr Attlee | 7 Sept | Minute on consultation with Lord Wavell on Soulbury Report | 64 |
| 279 | CO | 7 Sept | Record of discussion between Sir G Gater & Mr Senanayake on Soulbury Report | 65 |
| 280 | Mr Hall | 10 Sept | Cabinet memo on procedure for disclosure of Soulbury Report & advocating that HMG are not prepared to grant any form of dominion status | 70 |
| 281 | Sir E Bridges (Cabinet secretary)<br>to Mr Attlee | 10 Sept | Minute on procedure for publication of Soulbury Report | 71 |
| 282 | CO | 10 Sept | Record of discussion between Sir G Gater & Mr Senanayake on Soulbury Report | 72 |
| 283 | Cabinet meeting<br>CM 30(45)3 | 11 Sept | Conclusions on publication of Soulbury Report & dominion status | 77 |
| 284 | C H Thornley (private secretary to Mr Hall) | 11 Sept | Minute on discussion between Mr Hall & Mr Creech Jones & G G Ponnambalam on Soulbury Report | 79 |

| NUMBER | | | SUBJECT | PAGE |
|---|---|---|---|---|
| | | *1945* | | |
| 285 | C H Thornley | 12 Sept | Minute on discussion between Mr Hall & Mr Senanayake on Soulbury Report | 80 |
| 286 | Mr Hall to Sir H Moore | 12 Sept | Tel on publication of Soulbury Report | 82 |
| 287 | Sir G Gater | 13 Sept | Note of interview with Mr Senanayake on Soulbury Report | 83 |
| 288 | Sir G Gater | 13 Sept | Note of interview with H M Desai on enfranchisement & citizenship rights of Indians in Ceylon | 84 |
| 289 | Sir H Moore to Mr Hall | 14 Sept | Tel (reply to 286) | 85 |
| 290 | Mr Senanayake to Mr Hall | 14 Sept | Letter on revised draft of constitution | 85 |
| 291 | C H Thornley | 17 Sept | Minute of interview between Mr Hall & H M Desai on Indians in Ceylon | 88 |
| 292 | CO | 17 Sept | Record of discussion between Mr Hall & Mr Senanayake on Soulbury Report | 89 |
| 293 | Mr Hall to Sir H Moore | 19 Sept | Tel on discussions with Mr Senanayake on Soulbury Report & text of announcement | 93 |
| 294 | Mr Hall to Mr Senanayake | 19 Sept | Letter on conclusion of discussions on Soulbury Report | 95 |
| 295 | Sir H Moore to Mr Hall | 25 Sept | Tel on Mr Senanayake's return & need for HMG to make a 'generous and spontaneous' gesture to Ceylon | 96 |
| 296 | E E Sabben-Clare (CO) | 26 Sept | Minute on Ceylon defence expenditure | 96 |
| 297 | G E J Gent to Sir H Moore | 28 Sept | Letter explaining that immigration question & status of Indians in Ceylon had not been raised in discussions with Mr Senanayake | 99 |
| 298 | Mr Senanayake for Board of Ministers | 29 Sept | Letter on his discussions with Mr Hall on Soulbury Report | 99 |
| 299 | Trafford Smith | 1 Oct | Minute briefing Mr Hall for his interview with G R Motha on Indians in Ceylon | 104 |
| 300 | Lord Soulbury to Mr Hall | 5 Oct | Letter arguing case for grant of greater measure of self-government to Ceylon than recommended by Soulbury Commission | 106 |
| 301 | Mr Senanayake to Lord Soulbury | 5 Oct | Letter expressing fear that he might lose his majority | 113 |

| NUMBER | | SUBJECT | PAGE |
|---|---|---|---|

*1945*

| 302 | Sir H Moore to Mr Hall | 12 Oct | Tel on response of Board of Ministers to Soulbury Report | 113 |
|---|---|---|---|---|
| 303 | Sir H Moore to Mr Hall | 12 Oct | Letter supporting Mr Senanayake's assessment of local political situation | 114 |
| 304 | Cabinet Colonial Affairs Committee meeting | 15 Oct | Minutes recommending a review of new constitution after six years | 115 |
| 305 | F F Turnbull (India Office) to C H Thornley | 15 Oct | Letter on wording of statements of policy in regard to Burma | 117 |
| 306 | Mr Hall to Sir H Moore | 16 Oct | Tel explaining proposals considered by Cabinet Colonial Affairs Committee (304) | 118 |
| 307 | Admiral Layton to G E J Gent | 16 Oct | Letter on difficulties with regard to defence requirements | 119 |
| 308 | Sir H Moore to Mr Hall | 17 Oct | Tel (reply to 306), proposing a more explicit statement with regard to dominion status | 119 |
| 309 | Sir H Moore to Mr Hall | 17 Oct | Tel transmitting a resolution on Soulbury Report by Working Committee of Ceylon Indian Congress | 121 |
| 310 | Lord Wavell to Lord Pethick-Lawrence (India Office) | 18 Oct | Tel forwarding comments of his Executive Council on Soulbury Report | 122 |
| 311 | Trafford Smith | 22 Oct | Minute of a meeting with Lord Soulbury on latter's opposition to HMG's policy | 124 |
| 312 | Mr Greenwood (lord privy seal) | 23 Oct | Cabinet report on behalf of Colonial Affairs Committee, + *Annex*: paras 10–12 of draft statement of policy | 125 |
| 313 | G E J Gent to Sir H Moore | 24 Oct | Letter on draft statement of policy | 131 |
| 314 | Sir H Moore to Mr Hall | 25 Oct | Tel transmitting a resolution on Soulbury Report by European Association of Ceylon | 131 |
| 315 | Admiral Layton to Sir H Markham (Admiralty) | 25 Oct | Memo, 'Defence policy for Ceylon', urging consideration of all defence implications of proposed reforms | 132 |
| 316 | Cabinet meeting CM 46(45)4 | 26 Oct | Conclusions on draft statement of policy | 133 |
| 317 | Cabinet Office | 29 Oct | Note of meeting of ministers on draft statement of policy, + *Annex*: revised paras 10 & 12 | 135 |

NUMBER                                          SUBJECT                                          PAGE

*1945*

318   G E J Gent                       30 Oct   Minute on meeting between Mr Hall &     137
                                                Lord Soulbury on latter's views &
                                                HMG's policy statement

319   Mr Hall                          31 Oct   Tel transmitting a personal message to  137
      to Sir H Moore                            Mr Senanayake on HMG's statement

320   Sir H Moore                      2 Nov    Tel (reply to 319) transmitting text of 138
      to Mr Hall                                Mr Senanayake's reply & resolution to
                                                be moved in State Council

321   P J Gibson                       3 Nov    Letter on views of GOI on Soulbury      139
      (India Office)                            Report, + *Enclosures*
      to CO

322   G G Ponnambalam                  3 Nov    Letter on Tamil minority case, + *Encl-* 141
      to Mr Hall                                *osure*

323   H M Desai                        5 Nov    Letter urging HMG to reconsider on      157
      to Mr Hall                                issues of franchise and status of Indi-
                                                ans in Ceylon

324   Sir H Moore                      9 Nov    Letter on reforms debate in State       158
      to G E J Gent                             Council

325   Sir H Moore                      10 Nov   Letter on reforms debate in State       159
      to G E J Gent                             Council

326   Sir H Moore                      12 Nov   Tel transmitting result of reforms de-  160
      to Mr Hall                                bate in State Council

327   Sir H Moore                      13 Nov   Tel transmitting message from joint     161
      to Mr Hall                                secretary, All-Ceylon Tamil Congress,
                                                on vote in State Council

328   W Dahanayake                     13 Nov   Letter stating case for a general elec- 162
      to R W Sorenson,                          tion in Ceylon
      T E N Driberg &
      T Reid (MP's)

329   Mr Senanayake                    13 Nov   Letter on vote in State Council &       163
      to Mr Hall                                drafting of new constitution

# Chapter 5
## The Indian problem, post-war reconstruction and the communist challenge
### Nov 1945–Nov 1946

330   J B Sidebotham                   14 Nov   Note on drafting of new constitution    164
      to Sir G Gater

NUMBER                              SUBJECT                              PAGE

                                     *1945*

331    K Natesa Aiyar (CIWF)    18 Nov   Tels protesting against white paper    166
       & S Thondaman (CICLU)
       to Mr Hall

332    Sir H Moore             20 Nov   Tel transmitting message from joint    167
       to Mr Hall                       secretary, All-Ceylon Tamil Congress,
                                        repudiating action of Tamil members
                                        in State Council in voting for white
                                        paper

333    Trafford Smith          [Nov]    Briefing note for Mr Hall's meeting    168
                                        with deputation from Ceylon Associa-
                                        tion in London

334    Trafford Smith          27 Nov   Note of interview between Mr Hall &    170
                                        deputation from Ceylon Association in
                                        London

335    R R Powell (Admiralty)  13 Dec   Letter (reply to 315) on defence ques- 172
       to Admiral Layton                tions

336    Mr Hall                 14 Dec   Letter on Indo-Ceylon relations, on    173
       to Sir H Moore                   re-opening of negotiations, + *Enclo-
                                        sure*: CO note of discussion between
                                        Mr Hall & Sir R Mudaliar

337    Admiral Layton          17 Dec   Letter (reply to 335) on the need for  175
       to Sir H Markham                 'unceasing vigilance' over defence mat-
                                        ters in peacetime

                                     *1946*

338    Sir H Moore             8 Jan    Tel conveying Mr Senanayake's posi-    176
       to Mr Hall                       tion on resumption of negotiations
                                        with India

339    S Sivasubramaniam       15 Jan   Letter, 'The proposed constitution of  177
       to Mr Attlee                     Ceylon', on behalf of All-Ceylon Tamil
                                        Congress

340    Sir H Moore             22 Jan   Tel transmitting a message from Mr     185
       to Mr Hall                       Senanayake to Sir R Mudaliar on re-
                                        sumption of negotiations with India

341    Sir H Moore             25 Jan   Letter on defence, the public services 186
       to Sir G Gater                   and the post of attorney-general

342    Sir R Mudaliar (GOI)    11 Feb   Letter urging HMG to make a decision   187
       to Mr Creech Jones               on franchise question

343    Lord Pethick-Lawrence (In- 15 Feb  Letter supporting Sir R Mudaliar on  189
       dia Office)                      franchise question
       to Mr Hall

| NUMBER | | SUBJECT | PAGE |
|--------|--|---------|------|
| | | *1946* | |
| 344 | Sir H Moore to Sir G Gater | 18 Feb | Letter on definition of defence & appointment of attorney-general + *Enclosure*: note by Sir R Drayton (7 Feb) | 189 |
| 345 | Mr Creech Jones to Lord Pethick-Lawrence (India Office) | 26 Feb | Letter (reply to 343) explaining why it would not be appropriate for HMG to intervene on franchise question, + *Enclosure*: letter from Creech Jones to Sir R Mudaliar (26 Feb) | 191 |
| 346 | J B Sidebotham & Sir C Jeffries | 26 Feb –23 Mar | Minutes on drafting of constitution | 193 |
| 347 | S Sivasubramaniam to Mr Attlee | 13 Mar | Letter suggesting that Cabinet Mission to India should visit Ceylon | 194 |
| 348 | CO for COS Committee | 16 Mar | Note on definition of defence clause in Ceylon constitution, + *Enclosure* | 196 |
| 349 | Sir G Gater to Sir H Moore | 29 Mar | Tel on different interpretations of franchise recommendations of Soulbury Commission | 198 |
| 350 | Sir H Moore to Sir G Gater | 30 Mar | Tel (reply to 349) stressing 'the danger of throwing Senanayake over now' | 199 |
| 351 | Sir D Monteath (India Office) to Lord Pethick-Lawrence (Cabinet Mission) | 30 Mar | Tel requesting clarification of Indian viewpoint on franchise question | 201 |
| 352 | Sir H Moore to Mr Hall | 1 Apr | Tel transmitting personal message from Mr Senanayake to Sir O Goonetilleke on franchise question | 202 |
| 353 | Sir G Gater to Mr Hall | 1 Apr | Tel (reply to 350) | 202 |
| 354 | CO | 1 Apr | Note on All-Ceylon Tamil Congress | 203 |
| 355 | Sir H Moore to Sir G Gater | 2 Apr | Tel (reply to 353) | 204 |
| 356 | Sir H Moore to Mr Hall | 7 Apr | Tel on HMG's attitude on franchise question | 205 |
| 357 | Cabinet Colonial Affairs Committee meeting | 11 Apr | Minutes, 'Ceylon constitution', endorsing positions adopted by Mr Senanayake | 206 |
| 358 | Mr Henderson (India Office) to Lord Pethick-Lawrence (Cabinet Mission) | 12 Apr | Tel reporting recommendations of Colonial Affairs Committee on franchise question (357) | 209 |

| NUMBER | | SUBJECT | PAGE |
|---|---|---|---|
| | | *1946* | |
| 359 | Lord Pethick-Lawrence to Mr Henderson | 16 Apr  Tel (reply to 358) on safeguards for Indian population | 210 |
| 360 | Mr Henderson to Lord Pethick-Lawrence | 18 Apr  Tel (reply to 359) | 211 |
| 361 | M S Aney (GOI representative in Ceylon) to Sir H Moore | 22 Apr  Letter citing acquisition by Ceylon govt of Knavesmire Estate in Kegalle District as an example of discrimination against Indian plantation labour | 212 |
| 362 | Sir R Drayton to M S Aney | 25 May  Letter (reply to 361) refuting claim of discrimination | 213 |
| 363 | Sir H Moore to Sir G Gater | 7 June  Letter on proposals to inaugurate new constitution | 215 |
| 364 | M S Aney to Sir H Moore | 12 June  Letter conveying further representation from GOI on matters connected with Knavesmire Estate | 216 |
| 365 | Sir H Moore to Mr Hall | 17 June  Despatch on conditions of service of European civil servants, + *Enclosures* 1 & 3 | 217 |
| 366 | Mr Senanayake to State Council | 1 July  Report on Knavesmire acquisition & related matters | 220 |
| 367 | Mr Hall to Sir H Moore | 30 July  Despatch (reply to 365) | 224 |
| 368 | Sir O Goonetilleke for Mr Hall | 5 Sept  Memo, 'Purchase of Ceylon products' | 225 |
| 369 | Mr Hall to Sir H Moore | 10 Sept  Tel explaining implications of recent rapid increase of rubber production in Malaya & suggesting that Sir O Goonetilleke should proceed to Washington with UK representatives for discussions with Americans | 244 |
| 370 | G L M Clauson (CO) | 18 Sept  Memo on Sir O Goonetilleke's discussions with State Dept in Washington | 245 |
| 371 | S Caine (CO) | 18 Sept  Memo on 368 | 247 |
| 372 | CO | 22 Oct  Note of meeting between Mr Creech Jones & Sir O Goonetilleke (14 Oct) on purchase of Ceylon products | 251 |
| 373 | Board of Ministers | 28 Oct  Minutes (item 17) of meeting on strikes of Oct 1946 and Mr Senanayake's criticism of public service | 255 |
| 374 | Mr Creech Jones to Sir O Goonetilleke | [30 Oct]  Letter (reply to 368) on purchase of Ceylon products, + *Minutes* by Creech Jones & Sir G Gater | 255 |

NUMBER                                    SUBJECT                                    PAGE

                                          *1946*
375    Sir J Howard (OAG)        18 Nov   Tel on Mr Senanayake's campaign for      258
       to Sir G Gater                     termination of contracts of three Euro-
                                          pean police officers

376    Sir J Howard             25 Nov   Tel on Mr Senanayake's proposal to       259
       to Mr Creech Jones                 establish a permanently mobilised
                                          Battalion of Volunteers

# Chapter 6
## India, Burma and Ceylon; the defence agreement sterling balances and citizenship, Dec 1946–Mar 1948

                                          *1946*
377    J B Sidebotham           16–18    Minutes on political implications for     260
                                 Dec      Mr Senanayake of impending promise
                                          by HMG of independence to Burma


                                          *1947*
378    Sir J Howard (OAG)        4 Jan    Despatch on public service forwarding    262
       to Mr Creech Jones                 correspondence with Mr Senanayake,
                                          + *Annexes* I–V

379    Sir J Howard             4 Jan    Letter on 378, on Mr Senanayake's        269
       to Sir C Jeffries                  criticisms of public service

380    A B Acheson &            7–8      Minutes on question of Ceylon's repre-   271
       G F Seel (CO)             Jan      sentation at British Commonwealth
                                          Conference   on   Nationality   &
                                          Citizenship

381    Mr Senanayake            28 Feb   Letter asserting that Ceylon cannot      275
       to Mr Creech Jones                 accept a lower status than that of India
                                          or Burma

382    Sir H Moore              7 Mar    Letter   supporting   Mr   Senanayake    276
       to Mr Creech Jones                 (381)

383    Mr Creech Jones          19 Mar   Tel (reply to 382)                        278
       to Sir H Moore

384    Mr Creech Jones          22 Mar   Minute on Mr Senanayake's proposals      279
       to Mr Attlee                       for dominion status

385    Sir H Moore              24 Mar   Tel conveying Mr Senanayake's views      280
       to Mr Creech Jones                 on timing of an announcement by
                                          HMG about dominion status

386    S Caine                  24 Mar   Letter on management of Ceylon's         281
       to Sir H Moore                     sterling balances

| NUMBER | | SUBJECT | PAGE |
|---|---|---|---|

*1947*

| 387 | Sir H Moore<br>to Mr Creech Jones | 4 Apr | Tel transmitting a message from Mr Senanayake to Sir O Goonetilleke on an announcement by HMG & proposals for defence & foreign affairs | 282 |
| 388 | Mr Creech Jones<br>for Cabinet Colonial<br>Affairs Committee | 29 Apr | Memo recommending that HMG should support Mr Senanayake over dominion status | 283 |
| 389 | COS | 5 May | Cabinet report, 'Ceylon constitution' on strategic importance of Ceylon & UK defence requirements | 286 |
| 390 | Cabinet meeting<br>CM 44(47)2 | 6 May | Minutes, 'Ceylon: constitutional development' to effect that a decision on dominion status should not be rushed | 288 |
| 391 | Sir H Moore<br>to Mr Creech Jones | 8 May | Tel conveying his initial reaction to Cabinet's decision (390) | 290 |
| 392 | Mr Creech Jones<br>to Sir H Moore | 12 May | Tel transmitting drafts of a message to Mr Senanayake about dominion status & announcement by HMG | 291 |
| 393 | Sir H Moore<br>to Mr Creech Jones | 14 May | Tel (reply to 392) suggesting amendments to message & announcement | 293 |
| 394 | Mr Creech Jones<br>to Sir H Moore | 16 May | Tel (reply to 393) suggesting further amendments | 294 |
| 395 | Mr Creech Jones | 1 June | Cabinet memo, 'Ceylon constitution', on message to Mr Senanayake & announcement by HMG, + *Annexes* | 296 |
| 396 | Joint Planning Staff<br>for COS Committee | 3 June | Report, 'Ceylon defence requirements', + *Annex*: draft report from COS to Cabinet | 299 |
| 397 | Sir H Moore<br>to Sir C Jeffries | 4 June | Tel on attitude of Board of Ministers to strikes & possible introduction of emergency powers | 306 |
| 398 | Mr Creech Jones<br>to Sir H Moore | 6 June | Tel on Cabinet's amendment of terms of announcement about dominion status | 307 |
| 399 | Mr Creech Jones<br>to Sir H Moore | 6 June | Tel transmitting a message to Mr Senanayake about dominion status and text of announcement approved by Cabinet | 307 |
| 400 | Sir H Moore<br>to Mr Creech Jones | 8 June | Tel (reply to 399) reporting Mr Senanayake's surprise at 'retrograde nature of announcement' | 309 |

NUMBER                                     SUBJECT                                     PAGE

                                            *1947*

401   Sir H Moore              8 June   Tel supporting Mr Senanayake's con-   309
      to Mr Creech Jones                cern & transmitting an amendment to
                                         announcement

402   Sir C Jeffries           9 June   Tel (reply to 401) explaining that gov-   311
      to Sir H Moore                     ernor's amendments would be un-
                                         acceptable to Cabinet & transmitting
                                         text of points suggested by Sir O
                                         Goonetilleke

403   Sir H Moore             10 June   Tel (reply to 402) explaining that Mr   312
      to Sir C Jeffries                  Senanayake is anxious for early
                                         announcement & emphasising two
                                         points of overriding importance

404   Mr Creech Jones         10 June   Minute explaining case for revised   313
      to Mr Attlee                       announcement, + *Minute* by T L
                                         Rowan (principal private secretary to
                                         PM)

405   Mr Creech Jones         12 June   Tel transmitting text of revised   314
      to Sir H Moore                     announcement

406   Sir H Moore             13 June   Tel transmitting a message from Mr   315
      to Mr Creech Jones                 Senanayake suggesting alternatives to
                                         the phrase 'fully responsible status
                                         within the British Commonwealth of
                                         Nations' in the announcement

407   Mr Creech Jones         14 June   Tel (reply to 406) on the wording of the   315
      to Sir H Moore                     announcement

408   Sir H Moore             19 June   Tel on heads of agreement, on issues to   316
      to Sir C Jeffries                  be decided

409   CO                       9 July   Note of discussion with Sir H Moore on   317
                                         draft agreement on minorities

410   K O Roberts-Wray        14 July   Minute on changes proposed by Sir O   318
      (legal adviser, CO)                Goonetilleke in Order-in-Council, +
                                         *Annex*

411   J B Sidebotham,         14–16    Minutes on Ceylon's right to secede   319
      K O Roberts-Wray,        July     from Commonwealth
      J J Paskin, Sir C Jeffries
      & Sir T Lloyd

412   CO                      15 July   Note of discussion with Sir H Moore &   322
                                         Sir O Goonetilleke on third draft of
                                         defence agreement

413   CO                      15 July   Note of inter-departmental discussion   323
                                         with Sir H Moore & Sir O Goonetilleke
                                         on reciprocal treatment of nationals

| NUMBER | | | SUBJECT | PAGE |
|---|---|---|---|---|

*1947*

| 414 | CO | 17 July | Note of discussion between Mr Creech Jones & Sir H Moore & Sir O Goonetilleke on draft agreements | 325 |
| 415 | Mr Creech Jones for Cabinet India & Burma Committee | 21 July | Memo, 'Ceylon constitution', on draft agreements | 327 |
| 416 | Lord Addison (CRO) to UK high commissioners | 21 July | Tel on draft agreements & consultation with dominion governments | 330 |
| 417 | J S Bennett (CO) to J B Sidebotham | 22 July | Minute, 'Ceylon defence agreement' on responsibility for maintenance of internal security | 331 |
| 418 | F Strahan (Cabinet secretary, Govt of Australia) to UK high commission | 28 July | Letter communicating views of Australian govt on agreements for defence & external affairs & suggesting that relations between Ceylon & UK & dominions should be discussed at Commonwealth meeting | 332 |
| 419 | Cabinet India & Burma Committee meeting | 28 July | Minutes on 415 | 334 |
| 420 | CO | 29 July | Note of inter-departmental discussion with Sir H Moore on defence agreement | 336 |
| 421 | Lord Addison (CRO) to UK high commissioner, Australia | 2 Aug | Tel transmitting reply to views of Australian govt (418) | 337 |
| 422 | Mr Creech Jones to Sir H Moore | 3 Sept | Tel on Australian proposal for Commonwealth conference | 339 |
| 423 | Sir H Moore to Mr Creech Jones | 5 Sept | Tel (reply to 422) arguing against proposal | 339 |
| 424 | Lord Addison (CRO) to UK high commissioner, Australia | 17 Sept | Tel transmitting reply to proposal for Commonwealth conference | 340 |
| 425 | Sir H Moore to Mr Creech Jones | 24 Sept | Tel on election results in Ceylon | 342 |
| 426 | Sir C Jeffries to Sir H Moore | 6 Oct | Letter on British practice in respect of control of permanent secretaries | 342 |
| 427 | Sir H Moore to Mr Creech Jones | 17 Oct | Tel transmitting a message from Lord Addison on Ceylon's citizenship negotiations with India & the British Nationality Bill | 343 |

| NUMBER | | SUBJECT | PAGE |
|--------|--|---------|------|

*1947*

| 428 | A H Stainton (Office of Parliamentary Counsel) to J A Peck (deputy legal adviser, CO) | 24 Oct | Letter, 'Ceylon Bill – armed forces' on legal position of UK forces in Ceylon | 344 |
| 429 | Sir H Moore to Sir C Jeffries | 27 Oct | Tel transmitting statement by Mr Senanayake explaining grounds upon which he considers that British Nationality Bill might prejudice his negotiations with India | 345 |
| 430 | Sir H Moore to Sir C Jeffries | 28 Oct | Tel on provisions to be made for UK service requirements in Ceylon Independence Bill | 346 |
| 431 | Sir H Moore to Mr Creech Jones | 29 Oct | Tel explaining that Ceylon Cabinet is anxious to have independence bill passed before 20 Nov | 346 |
| 432 | Sir H Moore to Mr Creech Jones | 29 Oct | Tel on 431, explaining Mr Senanayake's views on timetable | 347 |
| 433 | Mr Rees-Williams (CO) to Sir H Moore | 30 Oct | Tel (reply to 432) | 347 |
| 434 | Mr Creech Jones to Sir H Moore | 4 Nov | Tel (reply to 429) on British Nationality Bill | 348 |
| 435 | Mr Creech Jones to Sir H Moore | 6 Nov | Tel expressing grave concern over extent of proposed further reduction of Ceylon's sterling balances | 349 |
| 436 | Cmd 7257 | 11 Nov | Text of white paper, 'Proposals for conferring on Ceylon fully responsible status within the British Commonwealth of Nations', + *Appendices* I–III | 350 |
| 437 | *Times of Ceylon* | 19 Nov | 'External affairs', editorial comment on Ceylon Independence Bill | 354 |
| 438 | C E Thorogood (UK trade commissioner, Colombo) to Board of Trade | 21 Nov | Despatch on local reactions to agreements between UK & Ceylon | 355 |
| 439 | Mr Creech Jones to Sir H Moore | 28 Nov | Tel transmitting a message from Sir E Machtig (CRO) on procedure for appointment of governor-general | 357 |
| 440 | Sir H Moore to Mr Creech Jones | 5 Dec | Tel on Mr Senanayake's request that appointed day should be 4 Feb 1948 | 357 |
| 441 | Sir H Moore to Mr Creech Jones | 13 Dec | Tel on independence day ceremonies & symbolic significance of Kandyan throne | 358 |

| NUMBER | | | SUBJECT | PAGE |
|---|---|---|---|---|
| | | *1947* | | |
| 442 | Sir H Moore<br>to Mr Creech Jones | 20 Dec | Tel (reply to 435) explaining that Ceylon govt cannot accept proposed limit on sterling withdrawals | 359 |
| | | *1948* | | |
| 443 | Mr Gordon Walker (CRO)<br>to Mr Creech Jones | 21 Jan | Letter on administrative arrangements for Maldive Islands | 360 |
| 444 | CO Finance Dept<br>for Mr Gordon Walker<br>(CRO) | 26 Jan | Briefing memo, 'Ceylon sterling balances' on current position | 361 |
| 445 | War Office | Mar | Memo, 'Ceylon defence contribution' | 363 |
| 446 | Mr Gordon Walker<br>(CRO) | 17 Mar | Cabinet memo, 'Report on Ceylon', on independence celebrations & political situation in Ceylon | 365 |

**240**  CO 54/986/6/1, no 34                                         29 Apr 1945
[Reforms]: inward unnumbered telegram from Sir H Moore to Sir G Gater on the date for Mr Senanayake's visit to London

Your secret and personal telegram of 27th April.
Following for Gater. *Begins.*
I I am arranging to see Senanayake probably on Thursday next but, from conversations with Goonetilleke, following, subject to confirmation, appears to be the position.
II Senanayake realises that the date for discussions cannot be fixed now, but would like an invitation before the middle of May to attend the discussions at date to be fixed later. Reason is that he does not want to introduce Estimates into the State Council, if he is not going to see them through, and would like some time (?on leave) in London for medical treatment before the discussions begin.
III He would welcome Drayton's presence to assist him in the discussions. It would be quite impossible for both Drayton and Goonetilleke to be absent as suggested, nor would Goonetilleke's presence be necessary. Goonetilleke is quite definite on this point himself, and is quite prepared to work with Collins as Acting Chief Secretary.
IV I should propose to keep proposals in my personal custody and, as no one except the Governor's Secretary and Officers of State, where necessary, would see them, there ought to be no possibility of public (?disclosures).
V I have just heard that Ponnambalam, I.X. Pereira and one other, at present unknown, but probably Tamil, are likely to apply for priority flying passages in May to proceed to the U.K., so as to be in London on publication of the Report. Strongly recommend that I be authorised to say you are not prepared to receive any deputations in London from persons in Ceylon who have already had fullest opportunity of stating their cases to the Commission and that no special priority can, therefore, be granted.
VI I will wire after Thursday in confirmation and (?suggest) date for Drayton's leave. In the meantime I would be grateful for your views on paragraphs II and V above. *Ends.*


**241**  CO 54/986/6/1, no 35                                          1 May 1945
[Reforms]: outward unnumbered telegram (reply) from Mr Stanley to Sir H Moore on Mr Senanayake's visit to London

Your secret and personal telegram of 29th April to Gater, paragraph I.[1]
1. On the assumption that Senanayake will fully understand that it is impracticable for me to commit myself to any particular date at which I shall be ready to discuss constitutional proposals with him I am agreeable to your giving him now on my behalf invitation to do so in London in due course.
2. For your strictly personal information however, I should like to explain that if

---

[1] See 240.

he leaves Ceylon towards the end of May, it seems likely that he will have to spend some considerable time in this country before I shall be ready for any discussions and it might prove embarrassing to me if his visit here were unduly prolonged, owing to a possible upset of the timetable or for other reasons. I trust therefore, that you may be able to persuade him to postpone his departure from Ceylon until as late a date as possible.

3. Your paragraph V. I accept your proposal that you should be authorized to reply on the lines you suggest to applications for priority to visit the United Kingdom. While it is not, of course, possible to prevent such individuals coming to this country I entirely agree that no special facilities should be granted, and that I should not contemplate any good purpose would be served by my consenting to receive deputations here of the character you mention.[2]

---

[2] Moore replied on 4 May:

'I. I saw Senanayake today and gave him the invitation on your behalf, for which he is most grateful. He fully understands that you can commit yourself to no particular date, and that the last week in July is possibly optimistic. He does not feel able now to fix a definite date for his own departure, but thinks it will probably be in the second or third week in June. This will enable him to go into nursing home if necessary for observation, and have some leave before the talks begin. I advocated, but felt it unwise to press for a later date than this as he reiterated his readiness to wait and meet your convenience in the matter of the actual date. He does not propose to announce his intended visit immediately, but will await a suitable opportunity and give me timely notice so that I may inform you first.

II. I confirm paragraph III of my secret and personal telegram of 29th April. Drayton will proceed on leave by sea with wife and family by first opportunity, probably in about 12 days' time.

III. Your paragraph 3 noted. I now learn that persons named require priority sea, not air passages. I am informing them in sense authorized' (CO 54/986/6/1, no 36).

## 242  ADM 116/5546                                      10 May 1945
## [Defence]: Admiralty minute on defence reservations under a new constitution[1]                                              [Extract]

. . .

3. It will be observed that it appears to be the Commission's intention to confine the portfolios of defence within special limits though precisely what is intended in this respect is not very clear.

4. There is no reason to suppose that a further extension of self-government to Ceylon would be likely to weaken either their attachment to this country or their general interest in defence matters. However, if H.M.G. is to remain responsible for defence in its widest aspects, H.M.G. must as a last resort be armed with the necessary authority to carry out its responsibility. If a future war were to affect the Indian Ocean it would almost certainly be necessary to deal with all sorts of matters, for example, lighting, communications, navigation, requisition, etc., which would not fall within the scope of a Defence Minister. It seems hopeless to deal with points of this kind piecemeal. . . . [A]ll we can do is to make a bid to secure that H.M.G.'s Defence Representative, presumably the Commander-in-Chief, at a time of declared emergency has the legal authority to make defence regulations on all these matters.

---

[1] This minute was written in response to Trafford Smith's letter of 25 Apr 1945, see part I of this volume, 239.

5. We must leave it to the Colonial Office so to hedge this reservation round as to make it palatable to politicians in Ceylon and to our own people.

6. At present we know very little about what the Commission intends. Provided we succeed in making the broad reservation . . . indicated, we will probably have done the best we can.

## 243   CO 54/988/2, no 20                                    15 May 1945
## [Indo–Ceylon relations]: despatch from Sir H Moore to Mr Stanley on the re-opening of negotiations on the rights and status of Indians in Ceylon. *Enclosures*

I have the honour to refer to my secret despatch of 13th January[1] enclosing correspondence with the Government of India relating to the re-opening of negotiations regarding the rights and status of Indians in Ceylon.

2. I enclose a copy of a further message from the Government of India which was received by me at the hands of Mr. Aney, the Representative in Ceylon, on 15th April.

3. The Board of Ministers considered the message and concurred in the reply dated 11th May, a copy of which is enclosed.

**Enclosure 1 to 243: Government of India reply to Ceylon government's letter, 11 Jan 1945**

The Government of India thank the Government of Ceylon for their letter of the 11th January, 1945. They are happy to note that if an agreed basis can be found the Government of Ceylon would be willing to resume negotiations at a date convenient to both Governments. The Government of India must however confess to a sense of disappointment to find that the Government of Ceylon should be unable to consider any basis other than the Joint Report of 1941, if that basis rejected in advance any of the agreed conclusions contained in that Report, or if it precluded an agreement at least as acceptable to the Ceylon Government as that contained in that Report.

2. The Government of India would urge that when the Joint Report was signed by the delegations appointed by the two Governments it was clearly understood that it only set out certain proposals for consideration by the Governments concerned. It was agreed that the report should be published and that after public opinion, particularly the reactions of the Legislature, in both countries had been elicited, the two Governments would arrange for a final exchange of views on the Report. The Government of Ceylon are aware that public opinion in India expressed itself very definitely against the Report and that, after full consideration, the Indian Central Legislature declared the conclusions embodied in the Report to be totally unacceptable.

3. The serious turn which events arising out of the war with Japan took early in 1942, precluded the two Governments from embarking on the "final exchange of views" originally envisaged. Had such an exchange of views taken place, the

---

[1] See part I of this volume, 233.

Government of India would have suggested substantial modifications to the proposals contained in the Report. In fact, as noted in the Ceylon Government's letter, on
two subsequent occasions, in February, 1943, during the negotiations for the
recruitment of additional labour for rubber plantations in Ceylon and in December,
1943, when it was reported that the Ceylon Ministers were framing a draft
Constitution for the Island, the Government of India found it necessary to signify
their inability to agree to the conclusions of the Joint Report governing matters
arising between the two countries.

4. In these circumstances when public opinion in India has so unequivocally
expressed itself against the acceptance of the Joint Report it is hoped that the
Government of Ceylon will appreciate the Government of India's difficulty in
agreeing to that Report as forming a basis for further negotiations. At the same time,
the Government of India feel that now that the war clouds are beginning to disperse,
a renewed and earnest endeavour should be made to resolve the outstanding
questions and not permit them to continue prejudicing the relations between the
two countries. They feel further that such an effort to arrive at an agreement should
not be allowed to be handicapped from the outset and the prospects of its success, to
be marred by insistence on the outcome of a previous unsuccessful attempt. The
Government of India feel that it should not be impossible to frame an agreed basis for
the resumption of negotiations, without reference to the Joint Report, acceptable to
reasonable opinion in both the countries and affording the best prospects of a final
understanding being reached.

The Government of India would therefore earnestly request the Government of
Ceylon to assist in creating an atmosphere most favourable to a successful outcome
of the resumed negotiations by withdrawing their insistence on the Joint Report
forming the basis and by agreeing to a fresh search being made for such a basis.

Enclosure 2 to 243: letter from Sir R Drayton to M S Aney, 11 May 1945

I have the honour to refer to the message of the Government of India regarding the
resumption of negotiations in the matter of Indo–Ceylon relations which you handed
to His Excellency the Governor at Nuwara Eliya on the 15th April, 1945.

2. The Board of Ministers note that the Government of India decline to accept the
agreed conclusions of the Joint Report of 1941 as the basis for the resumption of
negotiations. They regret that this is so, but it was with this possibility in mind that
they endeavoured to make it clear in their letter of the 11th January, 1945, that, if
the Government of India felt compelled to suggest another basis for the resumption
of negotiations, such an alternative basis would only be acceptable to the Board of
Ministers if:—

(i) it did not reject in advance any of the agreed conclusions of the Joint Report of
1941;
(ii) there was the possibility of the resumed negotations resulting in an agreement
at least as acceptable to Ceylon as the agreement contained in the Joint Report of
1941.

3. The Board of Ministers fully appreciate the difficulty of the Government of
India which arises from the attitude of the Central Legislature and the public of India

towards the Joint Report of 1941 but they wish to draw attention to the fact that they also are in a similar difficulty, namely, that there was considerable opposition in Ceylon to the agreed conclusions of 1941 on the ground that they did not adequately safeguard the legitimate interests of Ceylon.

4. The Board of Ministers trust that this further explanation of their attitude as described in my letter of the 11th January, 1945, will be of assistance to the Government of India.

## **244**   CO 54/986/6/1, no 39                                      15 May 1945
## [Reforms]: outward unnumbered telegram from Mr Stanley to Sir H Moore on the timetable for the publication of the Soulbury Report

My secret and personal telegram of 8th May.

Timetable in your secret and personal telegram (2) of the 23rd March[1] has been reconsidered between myself and Lord Soulbury, and I incline to the conclusion, with which Lord Soulbury agrees, that the Commission should complete their Report, submit it to me, and that it should be printed and published as soon as possible without waiting for any Government conclusions on its recommendations or for transmission to yourself in draft form for your comments and possible consequent revision by the Commission before final signature. Under this arrangement publication would be likely early in July. Copies would be sent by air for simultaneous publication in Ceylon.

2. The Report would not be the last word, but His Majesty's Government would then have to consider its own eventual decisions on the Commission's recommendations. It would, of course, be my intention that before these final decisions were taken I should have the advantage of discussions with Senanayake.

3. I have not definitely decided on the above course, but should wish you and Senanayake to know at once that this is likely, and I will confirm as soon as possible. Please communicate the above in strict confidence and personally to Senanayake.

---

[1] See part I of this volume, 235.

## **245**   CO 54/986/6/1, no 45                                      21 May 1945
## [Reforms]: inward unnumbered telegram from Sir H Moore to Mr Stanley conveying Mr Senanayake's views about the publication of the Soulbury Report

My secret and personal telegram of 19th May.[1]

Following are Senanayake's reactions:—

(a) Proposed procedure will considerably increase his difficulties, and yours, if it is still your intention that Commission's report, as finally accepted or modified by His Majesty's Government, should be approved by Ceylon State Council.

---

[1] cf 244.

(b) Interval between publication of Report and announcement of His Majesty's Government's decisions, will be utilized by nearly all sections in Ceylon from Freedom and Dominion Status groups to extreme reactionaries, to launch violent attacks on Soulbury Commission.

(c) If Constitution, as finally approved by His Majesty's Government, constitutes little if any advance on 1943 declaration, his task of carrying it through State Council, in the teeth of agitation referred to in (b), will be impossible.

(d) While, therefore, he is prepared to take his share of responsibility, whatever may be your final decision, he strongly urges that report, and His Majesty's Government's decisions upon it, should be published simultaneously. If this is done, he and his supporters will be in a position, from date of first announcement, to throw their whole weight into influencing local opinion in favour of His Majesty's Government's decision.

2. I am, of course, unaware of considerations which have led Lord Soulbury and yourself to reconsider procedure originally agreed upon. On the grounds of Ceylon, as opposed to United Kingdom political expediency, on which I am of course not in a position to speak, I have no doubt that Senanayake's appreciation is right. If His Majesty's Government were prepared to impose a forced Constitution in Ceylon, the position would be different but since policy appears to be to secure for it the maximum local support possible through the good offices of Senanayake, he will be placed in impossible position vis-à-vis the State Council, and his freedom of action seriously impaired if he is not consulted till after the report has been published and become subject of controversy.

3. He is anxious to make an announcement to begin the Council at 5.30 p.m. on Tuesday, 29th May, and suggests the following:—

> "His Excellency the Governor has informed me that it is the hope and intention of the Secretary of State for the Colonies that, after Soulbury Commission's report has been received (or decisions are taken by His Majesty's Government), the Secretary of State should have advantage of an opportunity for personal discussion of all issues involved [with myself] as leader of the House. I have agreed to make myself available to Secretary of State for these discussions". He hopes that in the light of this telegram the word "receive" can be substituted for "published" in agreed enactment."

# 246   CO 54/986/6/1, no 46               23 May 1945

## [Reforms]: outward unnumbered telegram (reply) from Mr Stanley to Sir H Moore on the publication of the Soulbury Report

Your Secret and Personal telegram of the 21st of May.[1]

I am in full sympathy with Senanayake's difficulty and for the reason of policy stated in your second paragraph I want to give him such help as I can. Therefore on further consideration I am willing to agree that discussions which I envisage with him should take place before the Report is published.

2. In these circumstances, I propose to communicate a copy of the Report to

---

[1] See 245.

Senanayake, for his personal and confidential consideration only, when he reaches this country and I should prefer that no reference should be made to the matter of publication of the Report in the contemplated announcement on Tuesday, the 29th May.

3.  This should, I suggest, read as follows:—*Begins.*

> "His Excellency the Governor has informed me that it is the hope and intention of the Secretary of State for the Colonies that before decisions on the revision of the Constitution are taken by His Majesty's Government the Secretary of State should have the advantage of an opportunity for personal discussion of all issues involved with myself as Leader of the House. I have readily agreed to make myself available to the Secretary of State for these discussions". *Ends.* Please telegraph if you agree.

4.  I may add that I shall of course send a copy of the Report, after it has been submitted to me, to you under Secret and Personal cover for your personal observations.

5.  Eventual decisions as to procedure must in any case take account of security considerations in Ceylon so long as it is important base of S.E.A.C. operations, and I should accordingly be glad if after consultation with Commander in Chief you would let me know whether you and Commander in Chief agree that from defence aspect procedure now suggested is the least likely to risk deterioration of Ceylonese morale and efficiency for war purposes.

# 247  CO 54/986/16/1, no 7                                   29 May 1945
## [Reforms]: inward unnumbered telegram from Sir H Moore to Mr Stanley on the question of Mr Bandaranaike acting for Mr Senanayake during the latter's absence in London

My secret and personal despatch of 11th April, 1945.

Senanayake is considering question of who should act for him when he leaves for the United Kingdom. He would prefer to put in Bandaranaike, rather than Kotalawala, provided he can get a satisfactory assurance, that Bandaranaike will not intrigue against him during his absence, on line that he has betrayed Ceylon by agreeing with you to something less than Dominion status, before His Majesty's pleasure has been announced in respect of the Sri Lanka Bill.[1] He has no doubt in his own mind, nor, he says, has anyone else, that the Bill will eventually be disallowed, in view of the 1943 Declaration and terms of reference given to the Soulbury Commission. In these circumstances, he would much prefer that disallowance should be notified at once.

From local point of view, I agree that this is desirable, as it would prick the Sri Lanka bubble and force Bandaranaike to define his attitude towards Senanayake, but I am, of course, unaware whether this would be politically embarrassing to you in London.

Senanayake proposes to tackle Bandaranaike in the near future, but before doing so, he would welcome any information you can give, as to when decision on Sri Lanka Bill is likely to be announced.

---

[1] See part I of this volume, 236.

## 248   ADM 116/5546        11–21 June 1945

## [Defence]: minutes by H N Morrison[1] and I M R Campbell[2] on defence portfolios under a new constitution

The draft transmitted in the enclosed semi-official letter of the 17th May from the Colonial Office was considered at a further conference on the 4th June at the Colonial Office, presided over by Lord Soulbury, with representatives of the Colonial Office, Treasury, Admiralty, War Office and Air Ministry. The Admiralty was represented by Colonel Spraggett of Plans Division and the undersigned.

2.   The main item discussed was the proposal on page 6 of the draft, that there should be a Portfolio of Defence in the new Constitution for Ceylon, and that it should be held by the Prime Minister. It will be noted that in Article 44 of Sessional paper XIV—1944 reference is made inter-alia to the appointment of a Minister of Defence. The Admiralty representatives stated that the draft had only so far been examined on a Staff level, and expressed some doubt whether the creation of such a Portfolio was in accordance with the 1943 statement of Government policy, whereby matters relating to the defence of the Island and of the Commonwealth were reserved as the responsibility of the Imperial Government. In view of this reservation, the institution of a local Minister of Defence might give rise to anomalies and confusion of responsibility, and embarrassment to the Governor and to the Commanders of the Imperial Forces. They thought it well, therefore, that the reasons which prompted this proposal should be fully ventilated.

3.   It was also pointed out that while the Commission were about to recommend that Ceylon should make an equitable contribution to the contribution [sic] to the cost of local defence, care should be taken to ensure, when deciding upon the responsibilities assigned to a Minister of Defence, that responsibility should be real and not such as might be regarded as a sinecure, and thus tend to jeopardise the success of our intentions to enlist wholehearted co-operation. It was thought that there might be room for an adequate measure of responsibility in the sphere of local defence.

4.   In reply Lord Soulbury stated that the requirements of the defence of the Island and of the Commonwealth would give rise to many demands upon the Island's resources, financial and otherwise, emanating either from the Governor or from the Commanders of the Imperial Services. It would be a great convenience, if not indeed essential, to the Imperial Authorities that there should be a Minister of Defence in the local Government, through whom all these defence requirements could be canalised. There were also the requirements of the Island's local defence which would need to be co-ordinated under one Minister, and the administration of such local forces as were contemplated in the Report. All these requirements indicated the need for a Minister of Defence in the Island, and it seemed much the most appropriate arrangement that this Portfolio should be held by the Prime Minister. Lord Soulbury promised to clarify the Report in the light of the discussion.

5.   The representatives of the War Office and Air Ministry saw no objection to the proposal, subject to the necessary safeguards of Imperial responsibility for defence which were proposed elsewhere in the draft.

---

[1] Principal assistant secretary, Admiralty.      [2] Deputy director of naval intelligence, Admiralty.

6. Various other amendments to the draft paragraphs were discussed and agreed to, and it was arranged that a copy of the revised draft should be sent to each of the three Service Departments, when they would have another opportunity to examine and remark upon it before it went to press.

H.N.M.
11.6.45

1. From the Naval point of view, the strategical significance of Ceylon is of a high order. Apart from the Ceylon R.N.V.R. referred to in para 2 of Hd. of M.'s 26th May, the efficiency of Naval defence measures may rest in large measure on the loyal cooperation of officials in harbour and other local establishments.

2. For these reasons it may be highly desirable that the Governor General should be vested with powers to authorize the dismissal of officials in Ceylon Government service. It is proposed that the Colonial Office should be advised accordingly.

I.M.R.C.
21.6.45

## **249**   CO 54/986/6/2, no 55                                    13 June 1945
[Reforms]: inward telegram no 1102 from Sir H Moore to Mr Stanley transmitting a message from G G Ponnambalam requesting equal opportunities with Mr Senanayake in discussions with the secretary of state

Following is sent at the request of G.G. Ponnambalam.

*Begins.* The All Ceylon Tamil Congress, representing the cause of over 1½ million Tamils in Ceylon, notes with great misgiving the exclusive opportunity given to Mr. Senanayake to hold ex parte discussions with the Secretary of State in the absence of any representative of the Opposition.

Mr. Senanayake, though in name the Leader of the House, cannot claim to speak for five out of six communities in the Island.

He is an interested partisan and advocates for the Sinhalese against Tamil and other minorities on matters of vital constitutional importance. He, as Leader of the State Council and Vice-Chairman of the Board of Ministers, led a boycott of the Soulbury Commission, which boycott signally failed, owing to united and determined opposition of Tamil and other minorities and eventually of considerable sections of Sinhalese.

The Tamil community and Congress, by virtue of their contributions to political and constitutional progress of the Island, ask for equal opportunities of discussions with the Secretary of State. Such discussions will, we are sincerely convinced be essential for the evolution of a constitution suitable and acceptable to all sections of the population.

Mr. Senanayake has refused to obtain a mandate from the State Council or even to afford an opportunity to debate the scope of his mission. His individual presence in London will, we fear, seriously undermine the confidence of large sections of the people and make them deeply apprehensive of their future. *Ends.*

**250**   CO 54/986/6/2, no 56                                    13 June 1945

[Reforms]: inward unnumbered telegram from Sir H Moore to Mr
Stanley suggesting a reply to G G Ponnambalam's message

Reference my confidential telegram No. 1102.[1]

I have had two interviews with person named, and explained to him that
Senanayake has received invitation by virtue of his special position as Vice-Chairman
of the Board of Ministers and Leader of the House, but he is not prepared to accept
that argument. Message, though it does not specifically ask for it, is intended to be a
request for a similar invitation to himself.

2. Senanayake has made it plain that he is not prepared to sit round a table with
person named and yourself, and that, if person named were to receive an invitation
from you, he would have respectfully to beg you to excuse his attendance, though he
appreciates you cannot prevent person named coming to London.

3. I doubt if person named has the wide Tamil backing he claims. Hence his
looking to I.X. Pereira for support. He has made it clear to me—see paragraph 5 of
my secret and personal telegram of 29th April—that whether you receive him in
London or not, they both want to renew House of Commons contact (?rather
omitted) than to secure implementations of Macdonald's and Dufferin's pledge in
1938 that Parliament would be consulted in the matter. I am not aware of exact form
of pledge given.

4. I would therefore suggest your replying something on the lines that you regret
that the invitation tendered to Mr. Senanayake should have given rise to misgivings
in the mind of person named, which you believe to have no substance in fact, that
you are not prepared to issue similar invitation or to afford any Government priority
passage facilities to himself or to the representatives of any majority or minority
groups, as you do not contemplate any good purposes would be served by such an
arrangement.

---

[1] See 249.

**251**   CO 54/988/2, no 30                                    14 June 1945

[Indo–Ceylon relations]: letter from Sir H Moore to Mr Stanley
explaining why a resumption of negotiations must await clarification
of the position on constitutional reform

In your letter of 4th June you ask me whether I think there is anything you could
usefully say to Senanayake to remove obstacles in the way of the resumption of
Indo–Ceylon negotiations.

I find some difficulty in advising as the Board of Ministers, including Drayton,
appear to hold the view strongly that it is no use going round the table without some
formula for discussion and that such formula should not rule out in advance
consideration of the terms of the 1941 Bajpai agreement, although it is appreciated
that they were not and are still not likely to be accepted by the Government of India.
Bandaranaike is probably the most die-hard of the lot on this subject and in view of
the uncertainty as to whether he will or not give support to Senanayake in accepting

anything less than the status provided in the Sri Lanka Bill, I doubt if Senanayake, even if he wished to, could afford to make any move in the Indian franchise question which is really the crux of the whole question—which might weaken his position in the country at a time when he is negotiating with you over the recommendations of the Soulbury Commission Report.

I think there is no doubt that India wants to get round the table. Aney's attitude at his last interview with me indicated this, and Sir T.B. Panabokke, who has not been too well in Delhi and has come back here for a spell primarily on health grounds, confirms this. Indeed he believes a reply to our last note is in course of preparation and may be received shortly. When I referred to this question in conversation with Senanayake a day or two ago, he expressed the view that there was very little chance of the Government of India ratifying any local agreement that Ceylon could accept so long as the Indian National Congress had the last word at Delhi.

I might add that Sir Arthur Hope[1] wired me the other day asking if I thought an unofficial visit to me, if the Government of India were agreeable, would help matters, but I replied that I thought such a visit at the present time might be embarassing, though it might be useful later. Senanayake's casual reaction, when I referred to the possibility of such a visit, was that he would much prefer to have discussions conducted between the Governors of Bombay and Madras, who had shewn both understanding and goodwill in the solution of common problems, rather than with a team of politicians appointed by Delhi.

I'm afraid all this is not very helpful but I doubt if we can hope to make much progress till the Constitutional Reform position is more clarified.

Drayton has strong views on the subject and you may care to discuss it with him, if you have not already done so. I think you will find that he will react strongly against any step that could be construed as surrendering the Ceylon case in advance.

---

[1] Governor of Madras, 1940–1946.

## 252   CO 54/986/6/2, no 57                                    15 June 1945
### [Reforms]: unnumbered telegram (reply) from Mr Stanley to Sir H Moore on G G Ponnambalam

Your Secret and Personal telegram (2) of the 13th June, and your telegram No. 1102.[1]

I am grateful for your endeavours to make Ponnambalam realise the position, and you may assure Senanayake for his personal information that it is not my intention to send any invitation to any of his countrymen other than himself to come to this country for discussions, but that I am glad that he realises that I cannot prevent individuals coming to London if they are determined to do so. They would not, however, be invited to take part in the discussions which I propose to hold with him personally.

2. If you see no objection, I should be grateful if you would inform Ponnambalam that I have received his message, but that, as I understand you have already explained to him, the invitation which has been issued to Senanayake has been issued to him in

---

[1] See 249 & 250.

his capacity as Vice-Chairman of the Board of Ministers and Leader of the House: that all parties in Ceylon have had full opportunity of placing their views before the Ceylon Constitution Commission: that I regret that the invitation tendered to Mr. Senanayake should have given rise to misgivings which are, I believe, without foundation: and that I am not prepared to issue a similar invitation or to provide Mr. Ponnambalam or the representative of any majority or minority groups with any Government priority passage facilities, since I do not consider that any useful purpose would be served thereby. Please telegraph whether you agree.

3.   As regards pledge referred to in paragraph 3 of your Secret and Personal telegram under reply, I assume that reference is to Question and Answer in House of Commons on 7th December, 1938, copy of which was sent to you under Despatch Form M.3 of 12th December, 1938, and to statement during Debate in House of Lords by Lord Dufferin on 20th December that "it is not the intention of His Majesty's Government to prevent a full discussion of any proposed changes in the Constitution of Ceylon".

## **253**   CO 54/986/16/1, no 20                                 9 July 1945
## [Reforms]: letter from Sir H Moore to Sir G Gater on the disallowance of the Free Lanka Bill. *Enclosure*: minutes of a special meeting of the Board of Ministers, 8 July 1945

I am writing to confirm my Secret and Personal telegram of to-day's date in which I informed you that Bandaranaike has been elected to act as Vice-Chairman of the Board of Ministers and Leader of the State Council during Senanayake's absence.

You will remember my Secret and Personal telegrams which I sent you on Senanayake's request on the subject of notification of Disallowance of the Sri Lanka Bill.[1] Senanayake asked for an early announcement for two reasons:—

1. He wanted it to be made clear that the Act of Disallowance had been made before his arrival in London so that there could be no suggestion that he had advised you in the matter.
2. He hoped that when once the Disallowance was a fait accompli he could use it as an argument with Bandaranaike, whom he wanted to see Acting Leader, to get assurances from him that he would carry on Senanayake's policy during his absence in London.

Actually, for the reasons already reported to you, the Disallowance of the Sri Lanka Bill has not yet been officially communicated to the State Council by the Speaker, but, in the course of a symposium which Senanayake gave to his fellow Ministers a day or two ago, he gave them a broad hint in conversation that the Disallowance of the Bill had in fact been communicated. Bandaranaike took this up at once and confirmation was obtained from the Speaker. As a result of this Bandaranaike managed to stage an emergency meeting of the Board of Ministers yesterday and I enclose, for your information, an uncorrected draft of the Minutes of that meeting. The terms of the different resolutions and the voting upon them indicate fairly clearly the attitude of the different Ministers concerned. You will see that except in

---

[1] See part I of this volume, 236, and 247.

the case of Motions numbers 2, 4 and 5, Senanayake declined to vote. On Motion number 2 I am glad to see that he had registered his vote though I suppose he could hardly have been expected to reveal to his fellow Ministers the part he had played in securing an early communication of Disallowance. I think the real feelings of the Board are reflected in Motion number 5 which was actually, I believe, drafted by Mahadeva though moved by Kotelawala, and, except for Bandaranaike, who has been fighting for position throughout, and to a less extent, Kannangara, I do not believe the Disallowance of the Sri Lanka Bill is being taken very seriously. This does not mean, however, that when Council meets some Private member may not table a resolution of protest or censure of the Secretary of State, but I understand there is no question of any such motion being actually moved by a Minister.

The result of all these manoeuvres was that Kotelawala, Corea and Bandaranaike all wished to be considered for the Acting Leadership and it was finally decided that they should draw lots for it since it was considered desirable that the general public, at any rate, should be led to believe that the nomination was an unanimous one. The lot has fallen upon Bandaranaike and he will, I understand, be officially represented as having received the unanimous support of the Board. I am writing this to catch the mail and so have had no time to see Senanayake but I am informed by Collins that both he and Goonetilleke are quite happy with this result since, owing to the manner in which Bandaranaike has obtained nomination, he will not be in a strong enough position to act independently during Senanayake's absence, and I understand he has given a general promise to his brother Ministers that he will be a good boy and create no constitutional crises during the next three months. He is coming to see me this evening but I am afraid the bag will have closed before I can report to you on his attitude.

## Enclosure to 253

1. The Chairman read to the Board letter dated 5th July, 1945, from the Hon. Mr. Bandaranaike, Minister of Local Administration, requesting that an emergency meeting of the Board be summoned to consider the situation arising out of the disallowance of the Sri Lanka Bill on the ground that it did not conform with the Declaration of His Majesty's Government of 1943, with particular reference to the proposed visit of the Leader of the State Council to England in response to an invitation to him by the Secretary of State for consultations on Constitutional matters.

The Chairman also read to the Board a telegram from Mr. W. Dahanayake, M.S.C. to the effect that the Leader should be authorised to oppose a Second Chamber in accordance with the provisions of the Sri Lanka Bill.

2. The Hon. Mr. Bandaranaike explained to the Board the reason why he considered it necessary to ask for a special meeting of the Board.

A discussion then ensued.

After discussion, the following motions were moved and decisions taken thereon, viz.,

*Motion No.1 moved by the Hon. Mr. Bandaranaike*
The Board protests against the action of the Secretary of State in disallowing the Sri Lanka Bill.

*Decision.* The motion was agreed to—the Hon. Mr. Kannangara, the Hon. Mr. Corea, the Hon. Mr. Bandaranaike and the Hon. Mr. de Silva and the Hon. Col. Kotelawala voting for the motion: the Hon. Mr. Mahadeva and the Hon. Mr. Senanayake declining to vote.

*Motion No.2 moved by the Hon. Mr. Bandaranaike*
The Board protests against the conduct of the Secretary of State in making the decision (refered to in Motion No.1 above) on the Sri Lanka Bill before the Leader of the State Council who had been invited by him to England to discuss with him all the issues connected with the Reform of the Constitution had an opportunity of expressing his views to the Secretary of State.
*Decision.* The motion was negatived. The Hon. Mr. Bandaranaike and the Hon. Mr. Kannangara voting for it; the Hon. Mr. Mahadeva, the Hon. Mr. Corea, the Hon. Mr. Senanayake and the Hon. Col. Kotelawala, voting against and the Hon. Mr. de Silva declining to vote.

*Motion No.3 moved by the Hon. Mr. Bandaranaike*
In the new circumstances that have arisen as a result of the disallowance of the Sri Lanka Bill on the ground that it does not conform with the Declaration of 1943 (which makes it clear that the Secretary of State is not prepared to depart from the terms of the Declaration of 1943) the Board does not consider that the Leader of the State Council should proceed for discussions with the Secretary of State. The Board considered further that it is now at least necessary for his visit to England to be postponed until the Soulbury Report is available and the Ministers and the State Council have had a chance of considering it.
*Decision.* The motion was negatived. The Hon. Mr. Bandaranaike voting for it, the Hon. Mr. Mahadeva, the Hon. Mr. Kannangara, the Hon. Mr. Corea, the Hon. Col. Kotelawala voting against it and the Hon. Mr. Senanayake and the Hon. Mr. de Silva declining to vote.

*Motion No.4 moved by the Hon. Mr. Bandaranaike*
If the Leader of the State Council were to go now for discussions with the Secretary of State (which the Board considers unwise) it should at least be after full discussion with the other Ministers and with some general indication of the attitude he should adopt in the discussion with the Secretary of State.
*Decision.* The motion was negatived. The Hon. Mr. Bandaranaike and the Hon. Mr. Kannangara voting for it, the Hon. Mr. Mahadeva, the Hon. Mr. Corea, the Hon. Mr. Senanayake, and the Hon. Col. Kotelawala voting against it and the Hon. Mr. de Silva declining to vote.

*Motion No.5 moved by the Hon. Col. Kotelawala*
The Board is of opinion that the Hon. Mr. Senanayake should accept the invitation of the Secretary of State for consultation on all matters connected with the Reform of the Constitution on the understanding that any action of his at those discussions would not be considered as binding on the country.
*Decision.* The motion was agreed to. The Hon. Mr. Mahadeva, the Hon. Mr. Corea, the Hon. Mr. Senanayake, the Hon. Mr. de Silva and the Hon. Col. Kotelawala voting for it and the Hon. Mr. Kannangara and the Hon. Mr. Bandaranaike declining to vote.

   3.   The meeting then adjourned until 9 a.m. on Monday July 9, 1945.

# 254   CO 54/986/6/2, no 78A                         13 July 1945

## [Reforms]: outward unnumbered telegram from Sir R Drayton (London)[1] to Sir H Moore on the question of a second chamber

Your secret and personal (2) telegram of the 9th July. Following from Drayton.
*Begins.* Following is result of conference with Soulbury:—

1.   Your paragraph 2 (b). Soulbury also agrees.

2.   Your paragraph 2 (c) and (d). We have agreed with Soulbury on certain amendments designed to give effect to our proposals regarding legislation by Order in Council which also in our opinion meet your criticisms.

3.   Your paragraph 2 (a) regarding life of Senate. We have discussed very fully this problem which is as difficult as it is important. As to last sentence of your comments, Ministers, whether in Second or First Chamber will have to retain office in interval between dissolution and meeting of new Parliament. Difficulty is to find middle course between Second Chamber which is so independent and permanent as to be regarded by bulk of majority community and some others as a constant threat to First Chamber, and one which is so impermanent and subject to fear of dissolution and vagaries of election as to be, in the opinion of those who desire a real safeguard against hasty or discriminatory legislation, practically indistinguishable from First Chamber and therefore not worth supporting. The limited powers proposed for the Second Chamber and the principle of election of 50 per cent by the First Chamber ought to mitigate the fears of the former body of opinion but will undoubtedly arouse the apprehension of the latter. If fear of dissolution exists at all times and vagaries of election apply to 50 per cent at the time of the General Election, i.e., when political temperature is at its highest as will be the case if the lives of the two Chambers are coterminous, it is more than likely that latter body of opinion will not regard Second Chamber as any safeguard at all. Soulbury is therefore proposing to his colleagues that five elected and five nominated members should retire every three years and be eligible for re-election or re-nomination. This will avoid dissolution of the Second Chamber as a whole and at the same time ensure reasonably frequent opportunities for changes in personnel and for the Governor-General not only to make essential readjustments but also to make them at a time when the political temperature will not be at its highest. We think this proposal is not only right but best from the point of view of negotiations with Senanayake.

4.   We trust that we have enabled you to form your final opinion. *Ends.*

---

[1] Drayton was in London in preparation for the visit by the delegations from Ceylon.

**255**   CO 54/986/16/2, no 24, annex                    [18 July 1945]

[Reforms]: memorandum by C H Collins[1] on the debate in the State Council on Mr Bandaranaike's motion protesting against the rejection of the Free Lanka Bill

Mr. Bandaranaike, Acting Leader of the State Council, with the approval of the House for the suspension of all relevant Standing Orders to enable him to do so, moved the following resolution this afternoon in the State Council:

> "This Council protests against the rejection by His Majesty's Government of the Ceylon Constitution Bill as such rejection is a denial of the right of the people of Lanka to freedom and to determine their own Constitution".

The discussion on the motion occupied the whole afternoon and evening and was completed at 6 p.m. when the Council rose for the day.

The whole debate had a feeling of unreality and play acting about it. No one really took the matter seriously, and there was a great deal of joking and laughter all through the debate.

Mr. Bandaranaike opened the debate in a short speech. He gave a brief history of the matter from the time of the declaration, gave credit to the Minorities who had supported "freedom" and said all must work together for freedom. The "protest" is only a start. The Leader is now in England and the motion will strengthen his hands in explaining the position, and in indicating to the Secretary of State what the House is likely to accept or not accept. When we get the Constitutional proposals in a concrete form, and only then, can we consider them. Meanwhile he made an appeal for Unity. After a brief speech by *Wille, Mr. Dahanayake* spoke. He said the motion did not go far enough. The proper course was for the issue to be taken to the country. They should press for a dissolution, and a new election on this issue. He moved an amendment to the motion, to add the words "and to request dissolution of the Present Council to enable issue to be raised at a general election". There was nothing however violent in this speech. *Black* then spoke, saying that the motion, like the Sri Lanka bill itself, was an irrelevancy.

He was followed by *Mr. Aluwihare*, Acting Minister for Agriculture & Lands who made a good short speech, saying that he had stated that the Bill itself was premature, as the Board of Ministers had at first accepted the Declaration. He still thought the whole business including the motion premature as even the Mover admitted that we should wait for negotiations to be completed.

*Henry Amarasuriya* followed in a rather lengthy speech, in which he first blamed the Board of Ministers for what had occurred; for framing a Constitution without coming to the House. He agreed with Mr. Dahanayake that a protest was not enough but further action was necessary. He did not agree however that a dissolution was the proper course. He urged that the Council should *either* send a deputation to England

---

[1] Acting chief secretary. Bandaranaike's motion was debated on 18 July 1945 and carried by thirty-one votes to seven, with four declining to vote. Reporting the result to the CO on 19 July in tel no 1332, Moore did not consider 'that any serious notice need be taken of this protest' (CO 54/986/16/1, no 19). The governor forwarded Collins's memo as an annex to his savingram no 479, 23 July 1945 (CO 54/986/16/2, no 24).

to "work up reforms" there, *or* give a definite Mandate to the Leader Mr. Senanayake containing the views and instructions of the House. Mr. *Jayawardena* [sic] (Kelaniya) supported Mr. Dahanayake's amendment, as being the proper Constitutional method of procedure.

Mr. *Nalliah*, Member for Trincomalee then delivered what was by far the most objectionable speech of the day—in fact it was rank sedition, though held to be in order when Mr. Black raised a question of order. His remedy was to give notice to the British Government that on and from a particular date Ceylon will function as an independent State. Ceylon had received a kick in the pants from the Secretary of State just as the Indian Congress had received a kick from the Governor General. We should join all freedom loving people, and get the help of Russia and put an end to British Imperialism. Mr. *Ratnayake* supported Mr. Dahanayake. He was followed by Mr. *Ponnambalam* who was in very good form and made a most amusing speech, criticizing most of those who preceded him. He ended by saying that what we really should do now was all to get together, and work together.

Mr. *Mahadeva* who spoke next attacked Ponnambalam, as proposing unity but likely to be a second Jinnah. The Member for *Ruanwella* said that the protest was too mild and what was wanted was a strong lead and sacrifices. Mr. *Thyagarajah* pressed for unity and said it was futile to pass such a resolution till they knew what the Leader would bring back. Mr. *George de Silva* then made a long speech, adding little, but supporting the motion as a "dignified protest". He raised laughter by such phrases as "you cannot govern a country by learning Classics alone" and by warning Mr. Black against "dabbling in things he did not understand". *Dr. de Zoysa* referred to the legal aspect, saying that our Constitution does not give us power to decide our new Constitution, and as we haven't the right we have no reason to protest. Moreover the Secretary of State has done only what a responsible Secretary of State would be expected to do. Refusal to agree to the Bill does *not* mean that the Secretary of State denies the right of the people to Freedom. Mr. *Jayah* said Leader was too cautious. The protest must be regarded as only a first step otherwise it is meaningless. He said that those who proposed resignation should resign—but he himself supported Mr. Amarasuriya's suggestion for a delegation to England, *or* a Mandate to the Speaker.

Mr. *Bandaranaike* then replied and closed the debate in a good speech, in which he said that he had it on good authority that the Secretary of State would *not* impose an Order-in-Council on us but his proposals would be sent out for the approval of the House. He did not accept either the amendment of Mr. Amarasuriya's proposals. He went on to say that the Sri Lanka bill was a *start* not an end in itself. It was something round which we can rally. The Protest is also only a beginning. We must attain salvation through our own efforts and the bill and Protest are steps in the way. What is wanted is unity particularly among progressive units.

The amendment was then put to the vote and lost by 37 votes to 5. Those who voted for the amendment were Messrs. Dahanayake, Jayawardena, [sic] Nalliah, Ratnayake & Siriwardena. The motion was then put and carried by 31 votes to 7, 4 declining to vote. Those who declined to vote were Messrs. Mahadeva, Aluwihare, de Zoysa and Natesan. Those against were Messrs. Black, Griffith, I.X. Pereira, Ponnambalam, Thyagarajah, Whitby and Wille.

## 256  CO 54/987/1, no 22                                    21 July 1945

## [Reforms]: note by G E J Gent on the reception to be accorded by the secretary of state to the delegations from Ceylon

The Secretary of State has made it clear to us that his primary purpose is to assist Mr. Senanayake in getting through the State Council the constitutional proposals which H.M.G. may decide upon after the Secretary of State has had his discussions with Mr. Senanayake. Accordingly, the Secretary of State intends to sound Mr. Senanayake before definitely deciding on his attitude towards the minority representatives who are on their way to London.

The Governor of Ceylon has advised the Secretary of State that Mr. Senanayake is likely to offer no objection to courtesy interviews being accorded by the Secretary of State to the individual representatives, but would strongly object to anything in the nature of a round-table conference.

The delegation from the Indian Mercantile Association are coming with a mandate to supplement the representations made to the Soulbury Commission on behalf of the Indian community in general and of mercantile interests in particular.

The others, including Mr. Ponnambalam,[1] are coming as delegates from a special Conference of Minorities for the purpose of conferring with the Secretary of State on the proposals for constitutional changes in Ceylon before any conclusions are reached by H.M.G.

The Burgher community is not sending a delegation but has telegraphed a request that the Soulbury Report should be published before H.M.G. takes decisions so that they may be able to submit representations if they feel it necessary.

In our view the Secretary of State could consider according a personal interview to these visitors under the following heads:—

(a)  To receive the delegations altogether.

(b)  To receive the delegations separately.

(c)  To receive all or some of the particular visitors individually.

We offer the following comments on each course.

(a) could be misrepresented as a round-table conference in London—with only those represented from Ceylon who have ignored the Secretary of State's opinion and have sent delegates to London. We believe that Mr. Senanayake would strongly object to this course as a breach of faith.

(b) As delegations, these visitors have a mandate only for the purpose of conferring with the Secretary of State, or making representations to him, on constitutional proposals. Until the Report is published they do not know what the proposals are, but they can be expected to demand the same facilities for this purpose as Mr. Senanayake. Other communities and interests would claim a similar opportunity to send a delegation to London.

---

[1] Ponnambalam had written to Gent on 8 July on the eve of his departure from Ceylon: 'You are doubtless aware that Mr. Senanayake has been afforded an opportunity for personal discussions with the Secretary of State on the question of Constitutional Reform. Some of us propose to make ourselves available even though we have not received any invitation. Senanayake cannot claim to speak for us and does not enjoy our confidence. I hope that no conclusions will be reached before an opportunity is also afforded to us. I am hoping that you will be good enough to secure for us this opportunity' (CO 54/987/1, no 20C).

We believe that Mr. Senanayake would strongly object to this course.

(c)  Since these visitors are coming as delegates sent by Tamil and Indian interests for a particular purpose, they will feel bound at any interview with the Secretary of State to speak to their brief and to telegraph to their constituents in Ceylon that they have done so.

If they are to be received by the Secretary of State and are able to speak to him personally on constitutional proposals on behalf of their special interests, other interests e.g. Burghers, Muslims, Europeans, Kandyans (who have not sought to send uninvited delegations to London) would claim a similar opportunity.

If the Secretary of State receives them personally, for the purpose of courtesy as distinguished visitors from Ceylon, it would be undesirable to make a distinction between the 4 Members of the State Council and the other 3. In that event it would be advisable for the Secretary of State to see them singly & individually (to avoid the semblance of a delegation), and to let each of them know that while he will be glad to see them, it must be on the clear understanding that he cannot discuss constitutional proposals with them. A reassurance to this effect should, we suggest, be given to Mr. Senanayake. Failing such an understanding, it is likely that they will confront him at once with their special disabilities as compared with the opportunity given to Mr. Senanayake and the presumed disclosure to him alone of the Soulbury proposals.

The above paragraphs relate to a situation *before* the publication of the Report. Mr. Senanayake's desire is that the Report should not be published until H.M.G.'s conclusions can be published simultaneously and that this publication should be followed with the least possible delay by a debate in the Ceylon State Council on a motion introduced by himself. It would be inadvisable to give any encouragement to these delegates to stay in London to make their speeches here rather than in the State Council (where we are advising that a three-fourths assenting vote should be required as a condition of the approval of the constitutional proposals.)

Our advice would therefore be that, whether before or after the publication of the Report:—

(1)  the delegations, as such, should not be received either together or separately

(2)  that the visitors, if personally received, as a matter of courtesy, should come singly and under the clear understanding that the Secretary of State cannot discuss constitutional proposals with them.

## 257   CO 54/986/6/2                                    23 July 1945

### [Reforms]: minute by Trafford Smith on points raised by Lord Soulbury in discussion with Mr Senanayake

It will, I think, be advisable to have on record a note of what was said to Mr. Senanayake about the Soulbury report during his week-end with Lord Soulbury from July 20th to 23rd.

There was discussion after dinner on the 20th (i.e. before the arrival of Lord Swinton) during which Lord Soulbury outlined to Mr. Senanayake the recommendations made by the Commission in regard to (1) the Second Chamber, method of election, duration, etc., (2) the reserve powers remaining to the Governor for use in an emergency, and (3) the Public Services Commission.

This was not in response to any direct enquiry by Mr. Senanayake, but was simply in the nature of a continuation of similar conversations held on several occasions in Colombo during the concluding weeks of the Commission's stay. Lord Soulbury has always taken the line that, since Mr. Senanayake is the only Ceylon politician who can undertake the launching of a new constitution with any prospect of success, it is necessary to secure his concurrence throughout and to be reasonably sure that the scheme recommended by the Commission goes as far as possible to meet his wishes. It was indeed on that basis that the recommendation for a Second Chamber was made, it having been agreed in discussion that Mr. Senanayake was quite prepared to accept it.

Lord Soulbury explained in some detail the various alternatives which the Commission had considered as regards the duration of the Second Chamber. Mr. Senanayake seemed quite prepared to accept the 3–3–3 proposal under which a third of the membership will retire every three years: his only doubt was whether embarrassment would be caused if at the end of year three (when a third chosen by lot would have to retire in order to start the scheme moving) the lot fell upon one of the Ministers or deputy Ministers in the Second Chamber. Lord Soulbury pointed out that if this happened and the Minister concerned failed to secure a re-election, it would be up to the Governor-General to nominate the Minister in question if the Prime Minister were able to convince him that the Government would be embarrassed if he were left out.

The only other possible difficulty Mr. Senanayake saw in the portions of the schemes outlined to him was this: he seemed to fear that if the Governor-General were armed with radical overriding powers for use in an emergency, he would be tempted to use the threat of them to interfere in matters of ordinary administration. Lord Soulbury explained that the whole tenor of the Commission's recommendations is in favour of a "constitutional" Governor-General who will remain more or less in the position of the Crown in the United Kingdom except when circumstances force him out of it. Mr. Senanayake seemed satisfied—or at least as satisfied as he will ever be while overriding emergency powers continue to exist.

As regards the Public Services Commission, he was quite prepared to accept the necessity for one in order to secure impartiality and agreed that the success or failure of the Commission will depend greatly on the calibre of its members. His only anxiety on this score seemed to be lest the Colonial Office retained any power of interference in Ceylon public service matters. Lord Soulbury pointed out that, in the scheme proposed in the report this was not so.

The only question Mr. Senanayake addressed to me concerned the date when he might expect to have a copy of the report to read. He seemed to expect one about the first week in August and I said that if all went well he ought certainly to get one in the first or second week.

(In this connection I should perhaps record that Mr. Muston informs me that the production of a further proof after the present corrected one is sent in will take about a fortnight. All being well, it should be possible to send in the corrected proof by the end of this week.)

**258**  CO 54/988/2                                                    23–24 July 1945

[Indo–Ceylon relations]: minutes by J B Sidebotham to G E J Gent on the governor's assessment of the position

*Mr. Gent*

In the light of (30),[1] I think that the best thing would be to have a talk with Sir R. Drayton. It seems very doubtful whether there is anything we can do to advance this matter much further at the moment.

We have, as you know, in (29) recently sent out some information about the position of Indians elsewhere in the Colonies. Sir T.B. Panabokke has now retired from the post of the Ceylon Representative at Delhi owing to ill-health, and the Governor has promised us a further despatch about who is to be his successor.

There is some duplicating action outstanding with regard to (29), but this does not press, and it is more important to get any discussion arranged quickly with Sir R. Drayton before he goes out of Town, which I understand he will be doing shortly.

J.B.S.
23.7.45

*Mr. Gent*

This matter was discussed with Sir R. Drayton this morning by yourself. Sir R. Drayton's views are briefly as follows.

The reference to the franchise is not the only thing that matters to India.[2] Sir R. Drayton took the opportunity of asking Mr. Aney directly what he thought, and got the impression that Mr. Aney is much more concerned about the economic and commercial interests of Indians in Colombo, e.g. the possibility of quota legislation against Indian employment by Indian firms in Colombo, who at present use solely Indian labour in their offices, etc., and at present, by this means, the Indians are able to undercut the Ceylonese trader all the time on account of the higher standard of living of the Ceylonese. The reference to the question of franchise is to some extent window-dressing on the part of India.

Sir R. Drayton thinks a great error was made by the Government of India in agreeing to publication of the 1941 agreement if they were not going to ratify it. In Ceylon it was regarded as a considerable surrender by Mr. Senanayake, and Mr. Senanayake could not go into a conference room if that agreement was going to be ruled out of consideration beforehand.

Whatever basis for negotiation is found, it must not exclude the 1941 agreement conclusions, e.g. the Immigration Bill which is before a Standing Committee of the State Council (though temporarily in cold storage) is based on that agreement. The Ceylon Government is not going to tear up that Bill. India has agreed to it, see Sessional Paper XXVII of 1941. Ceylon are not moving on that Bill until agreement has been reached on a basis for the resumption of negotiation.

The Ceylon Government have made their attitude perfectly clear to India, see the Chief Secretary's letter of the 11th May to the Representative of the Government of India, (second enclosure in No. 20).[3] All Ceylon want is a basis which will not reject

---

[1] See 251.                          [2] Sidebotham noted in the margin: 'or the thing that really matters'.
[3] See 243, enclosure 2.

in advance the conclusions of the 1941 agreement.

I still feel that the conclusion at $X^4$ in my minute is probably correct, and that there is nothing we can usefully do until, as the Governor says, "the constitutional reform position is more clarified".

J.B.S.
24.7.45

---

[4] A reference to the second sentence of para 1 of Sidebotham's minute of 23 July.

## 259   CO 54/986/6/2, no 97                          25 July 1945
## [Soulbury Report]: letter from Sir H Moore to Mr Stanley conveying his personal views on the report

As requested by telegram I forward my personal observations on the Soulbury Commission's Report.

In the enclosure[1] to this letter I have commented in detail under the relevant Chapter or paragraph of the Report on certain of the recommendations made, and will therefore confine myself here to some general observations on the Report as a whole. If, however, some of my detailed comments appear to be critical, I should like to make it clear that they have been deliberately so framed, not in any sense of disparagement of the work of the Commission, but in the hope that such criticisms may contribute to a full appreciation of the points at issue.

2.   In my view the Report is a most valuable contribution to the solution of the problem which the Secretary of State has clearly set out in the terms of reference given to the Commission, and its recommendations must be read in the light of the historical background which is so ably described in Chapters IV and V of the Report. In short, to quote from paragraph 95 of the Report:—

> "Although the Ministers' Scheme was not technically before the Commission, it naturally provided a most valuable basis for discussion, and was of great assistance in focussing attention on the salient features of constitutional reform."

3.   It is, I submit, a fair commentary on the Report to suggest that the Commissioners, after a full hearing of all possible points of view in Ceylon, have addressed their minds to the task of deciding how far the proposals contained in S.P. XIV or 1944 by modification or elimination can be utilized to provide a constitution for Ceylon which, while conforming to the general policy laid down by H.M.G. in the 1943 Declaration, and providing reasonable safeguards for the minorities, is at the same time likely to prove acceptable to Ceylonese public opinion as a whole. For it is implicit in the appointment of the Commission that an imposed constitution, even if practicable, would be politically undesirable.

4.   On arrival, the situation which confronted the Commissioners was of some difficulty and delicacy, since the Ministers had officially withdrawn their own scheme (S.P. XIV), and very shortly after their arrival the Sri Lanka Bill (a modified edition of S.P. XIV designed to confer full Dominion Status on Ceylon) was introduced into the

---

[1] Not printed but see 265.

State Council with the approval of the Board of Ministers, passed, and subsequently disallowed by yourself. While, as I have separately reported, the country as a whole has regarded the pantomime as a piece of political play acting, the voting on the third reading reveals that the representatives of some of the minority communities conveniently forgot the apprehensions, to which they had given expression on the original publication of the Ministers' scheme, and voted for the Bill. In my view their attitude is to be attributed to the fact that they knew the Bill would be disallowed, and so could safely vote for it, since by so doing they could subscribe to the ideal of Dominion Status, without any risk of incurring the disabilities inherent in the Bill itself.

5.   I have referred to this at length because I suggest it is of some importance in evaluating the reception which the Report may be expected to receive on its publication. It can, I think, be safely assumed that the Report as drafted, with such modifications as may result from its further consideration here and in London, should represent the limit of concessions which you and your advisers feel able to make, regard being had to the interests of the minorities and the general policy of H.M.G., in order to assist the Leader of the State Council in carrying through the House an agreed and settled policy of constitutional advance. Viewed from that angle I consider the Report should go a long way to effecting such a settlement. It must be remembered that Mr. Senanayake has by no means the unqualified support of the Sinhalese majority community, some of whom are opposed to a second chamber, while others profess to be content with nothing less than Independence. I shall be surprised, therefore, if he is prepared to sponsor anything less than the main recommendations of the Report, and he may well ask for some further concession— e.g. the removal of currency from the reserved subjects—as a token reward for his pilgrimage to London.

6.   What then will be its reception by the minority communities? Ponnambalam and his followers will, I'm afraid, regard it as partisan and a victory for the Sinhalese majority, and will, I anticipate, subject the Chapter on discrimination to detailed recrimination. Since the question of Indian immigration and franchise is left in the air and the results of the Delimitation Commission cannot be officially predicted— though if the intentions of the Commission are realized the critics would be largely answered—I fear you may expect pressure from the Government of India. The Europeans will, I think, be satisfied with the Second Chamber, but will not feel sufficiently safeguarded over the question of immigration unless the definition of "ordinarily resident" and the powers of the Governor with reference thereto are clarified. The Moors should be reasonably content.

7.   My personal view is that for administrative, quite apart from political reasons, the present state of affairs cannot be allowed to continue, and that concessions, where necessary, must be made and some risks run in the effort to evolve a more efficient form of Government. I believe that communal differences have been exploited for political ends, and that where there has been discrimination it has been due rather to local or personal causes than deliberate communal feeling. Corruption is undoubtedly rife, and personal ambitions and perquisites rank higher than communal causes. We should hear much less of communal feeling if we could secure a reasonable representation of community interests in the Upper House and in the Cabinet. For that reason I have suggested for consideration though I would not press the suggestion *à l'outrance*—that the Governor might receive some directions in the

Royal Instructions on the subject in making his nominations to the Upper House, even if he is to exercise no discretion in the appointment of Ministers.

8. It remains to consider the question of the Public Service. In my detailed comments I have dealt at length with the proposed relationship between the Governor and the Public Services Commission. I fear that in any case there will be a considerable exodus of European senior officers on the inauguration of the new constitution. That being so, if Ceylon is to be granted internal self-government it would be a contradiction in terms to give the Governor a sort of watching brief over their interests when in fact he will be powerless both in law and practice to protect them. He has held such powers in theory in the past. In practice they have become increasingly difficult to exercise, and have proved one of the most fruitful causes of controversy between the local legislature and the Secretary of State. Ministerial interference with the Public Service is inevitable particularly in the initial stages of the Constitution, as the bad old habits will die hard. But in my opinion a strong and independent Public Services Commission should provide a much surer protection than any illusory powers vested in the Governor.

9. To sum up, I consider that if the Leader of the State Council is prepared to sponsor the Report substantially in its present form it will be in the best interests of Ceylon to support him in his efforts to secure its adoption by the State Council. But I am doubtful if he will be able to secure for it the three quarters majority stipulated in the 1923 [sic: 1943] declaration.

# 260   CO 54/986/11, no 8, CC(45)2                    25 July 1945

## 'Ceylon constitution': memorandum by Mr Stanley for Cabinet Ceylon Committee on the Soulbury Report[1]

1. My colleagues on this Committee will recollect that the question of constitutional reform in Ceylon was under reference to the War Cabinet in W.P. (44) 299 of the 7th June, 1944,[2] and it was then decided that a Commission should be appointed to examine proposals for constitutional reform in Ceylon, on the understanding that this did not entail for His Majesty's Government any further commitment than that contained in the Declaration made by His Majesty's Government in 1943, set out in Annexure I to W.P. (44) 299.

2. Since then the Commission, of which Lord Soulbury was Chairman, have visited Ceylon and have now submitted their recommendations to me after full opportunity had been given during their visit for all interested parties to express their views. I have already circulated to the members of this Committee proof copies of the Commission's Report for my colleagues' information.

3. The Commission studied the various memoranda submitted to them in Ceylon

---

[1] The Cabinet Ceylon Committee appointed in July 1945 to consider the Soulbury Report consisted of the secretary of state for the colonies, the service ministers, the secretary of state for India, the chancellor of the Exchequer and the president of the Board of Trade (CAB 66/67, CP(45)73, Cabinet memo by Stanley, 'Ceylon constitution', 11 July 1945). The committee was not reappointed after the Labour victory at the election in the UK in July–Aug 1945. Under the new Labour government, consideration of the Soulbury Report was referred to the Cabinet Colonial Affairs Committee (see 270).

[2] See part I of this volume, 202.

and also a scheme of constitutional reform prepared by Ceylon Ministers (Appendix I to the Commission's Report); and I have invited Mr. Senanayake in his capacity as Vice-Chairman of the Board of Ministers and Leader of the State Council to visit this country to confer with me on the Soulbury Commission's proposals, and he has now arrived in London.

4. Before proceeding to these discussions with him, I feel that I should seek, at this stage, the concurrence of the Cabinet Committee in basing these discussions upon certain main provisions which have emerged from the Commission's recommendations. These may be briefly summarised as follows, the references in brackets being to paragraphs of the Soulbury Commission's Report:—

(a) The Government of Ceylon would consist of a Governor-General with the reserve powers set out in the 1943 Declaration and a Cabinet with an Upper and Lower House.

(b) Universal adult suffrage would be retained on the present basis. (Paragraph 223.)

(So far as suffrage of immigrants into Ceylon is concerned, the Commission regards this as a matter of internal civil administration, and proposes that the Ceylon Government should be granted the right to determine the future composition of its population with full powers of control in respect of immigration).

(c) A Delimitation Commission would be appointed by the Governor-General in his discretion to define new electoral districts. (Paragraph 279.)

(d) The Lower House would be designated the House of Representatives and would consist of 95 elected members together with six members who would be nominated by the Governor-General to represent the European and Burgher communities. (Members of the Lower House would be known as Members of Parliament.) (Paragraph 319.)

(e) The Upper House would be designated the Senate, and would consist of 30 Members of whom 15 would be elected by the Lower House and 15 nominated by the Governor-General acting in his discretion. (Paragraph 308.)

The Senate would have no power to reject, amend or delay beyond one month a Finance Bill, and if a Bill other than a Finance Bill is passed by the House of Representatives in two successive sessions and is rejected by the Senate in each of those sessions the Bill shall on its second rejection be deemed to have been passed by both Chambers. (Paragraph 308 (vii).)

(f) There would be a Cabinet with Ministers possessing full Cabinet responsibility in all matters of internal affairs in Ceylon, subject to the reservations contained in paragraphs 2, 3 and 5 of the 1943 Declaration. (Paragraph 328.)

(g) There would be a Prime Minister appointed by the Governor-General. The Prime Minister would hold the portfolios of External Affairs and Defence. (Paragraphs 324, 328, 357).

(h) Appointments to the Public Services would be made on the recommendation of a Public Services Commission to be nominated and appointed by the Governor-General in his discretion (*i.e.*, after consultation with the Prime Minister, but without being bound to follow his advice). (Paragraph 391.)

(i) There would be a Judiciary in which the Chief Justice and Judges of the Supreme Court would be appointed by the Governor-General acting in his discretion with a Judicial Services Commission to advise him in regard to subordinate judicial appointments. (Paragraph 406.)

5.  The safeguards for minority communities include the proposals for a Second Chamber and for the Public Services Commission. The first can be expected to provide an instrument for impeding precipitate legislation and for handling inflammatory issues in a cooler atmosphere (paragraph 299); while the Public Services Commission is designed as an impartial and authoritative body, free from the taint of partisanship, on whose advise the Governor-General will exercise his powers of appointment to the Public Service and the promotion and discipline of Public Officers. (Paragraphs 373, 378, 388.)

If the recommendations of the Soulbury Commission's Report are accepted, the following safeguards for minority interests (European and Asiatic) will appear in a new Constitution:—

(a)  Classes of reserved Bills under the new Constitution will include any Bills which relate to the Royal Prerogative, the rights and property of His Majesty's subjects not residing in the Island, and the trade and shipping of any part of the Commonwealth. (Paragraph 330.)

(b)  The classes of reserved Bills will also include any Bill which has "evoked serious opposition by any racial or religious community and which, in the Governor-General's opinion, is likely to involve oppression or unfairness to any community." (Paragraph 330.)

(c)  In regard to immigration into Ceylon, the Report recommends that Bills relating to the prohibition or restriction of immigration will not be regarded as coming into the category of Bills which the Governor-General will reserve for the signification of His Majesty's pleasure, but if any such Bill contains a provision restricting or prohibiting the re-entry of persons who should be regarded as belonging to Ceylon or of persons, other than the destitute and undesirable, ordinarily resident in Ceylon at the date when the Bill becomes law, the Governor-General must be required to reserve that Bill. (Paragraphs 330 and 236.)

(d)  The Soulbury Commission's Report further recommends that in relation to the further class of Bills relating to external affairs which are to come within the category of reserved Bills, there shall be excluded from the category of Bills relating to external affairs "any Bill relating solely to the prohibition or restriction of the importation of or the imposition of import duties upon any class of goods, provided that such legislation is not discriminatory in character". (Paragraph 330.)

(e)  The Report further recommends that the Order in Council shall provide that the Ceylon Parliament "shall not make any law to prohibit or restrict free exercise of religion; or to alter the constitution of any religious body except with the approval of the governing authority of that religious body," and "shall not have the power to make any law rendering persons of any community or religion liable to disability or restrictions to which persons of other communities or religions are not made liable or to confer on the persons of any community or religion any privileges or advantages which are not conferred on the persons of other communities or religion." (Paragraph 242 (iii).)

6.  The powers reserved by His Majesty's Government under the 1943 Declaration are to be secured in the Commission's proposals in the following ways:—

(a) Defence. Any Bills on this subject must be reserved by the Governor-General. (Paragraphs 330 (i) and 348 *et seq*.)

(b) External Affairs. Bills in this category are also to be reserved. (Paragraphs 330 (ii), 335 and 336.)

In both these subjects the Governor-General will have power himself to enact any measures necessary to comply with the directions of His Majesty's Government. (Paragraph 335.)

(c) Currency. Legislation must be reserved by the Governor-General. (Paragraph 330 (iii).)

(d) Trade, transport and communications affecting any part of the Empire. Any Bill of an extraordinary nature or importance which may prejudice these interests must be reserved. (Paragraph 330 (iv).)

7. This is in outline the new form of Constitution which the Commission recommends for adoption, and one which I am satisfied will provide a suitable measure of constitutional progress within the terms of His Majesty's Government's 1943 Declaration, and which also conforms in broad outline to the scheme which the Ceylon Ministers themselves originally put forward, save as regards the creation of a Second Chamber.

8. It will be remembered that, in their 1943 Declaration, His Majesty's Government laid it down that the final acceptance of any scheme of constitutional reform formulated by Ministers was conditional *inter alia* on its acceptance by three-quarters of the Members of the State Council. The Ministers drafted a scheme, but withdrew it. That scheme does, however, form the background of many of the Soulbury Commission's recommendations, but any constitution based on the Commission's proposals is likely to differ materially in detail, as well as in the important point of a two-Chamber Legislature, from that framed by the Ceylon Ministers.

9. I am given to understand that Mr. Senanayake will claim that the three-fourths proviso could reasonably be insisted upon for a locally devised scheme, but since any recommendations of the Commission, even if based on the Minister's published scheme, will now result in a Commission-made, and not a Ceylon-made, constitution, His Majesty's Government should be free to approve of it provided that they are satisfied that minority interests are adequately safeguarded, whether or not it obtains a three-fourths majority on presentation to the State Council. There is a great deal of substance in this claim, but, on the other hand, His Majesty's Government has publicly stated that, in the interests of the minorities, two safeguards were provided in respect of any scheme formulated by the Ceylon Ministers, viz., (1) examination by a Commission or Conference and (2) subsequent approval by three-fourths of the voting members of the State Council. As the Ministers' scheme is, in fact, the basis of the Soulbury Report, the Minority interests might claim a breach of faith by His Majesty's Government if the second of the two safeguards were in these circumstances abrogated.

10. I should therefore propose to start my discussions with Mr. Senanayake on the basis that His Majesty's Government regard this second requirement as applying to the proposals of the Soulbury Commission. If he can convince me that insistence on this view is a question deserving to be reconsidered, I shall consult my colleagues again on the matter. The voting strength of the different elements in the State

Council is 57 and is analysed in the Annex.

11.  I will of course place the details of a new constitutional scheme before this Committee for fuller consideration when my discussions with Mr. Senanayake have taken place, and ultimately seek the approval of the Cabinet and that of Parliament to such proposals as I may then find myself able to recommend for adoption.

**Annex to 260: State Council voting strength**

| | *Elected* | | *Nominated* |
|---|---|---|---|
| 40 | Sinhalese | 4 | European |
| 6 | Ceylon Tamils | 1 | Burgher |
| 2 | Indians | 1 | Indian |
| 1 | Muslim | 2 | Muslims |
| 49* | | 8 | |

Total  ...  ...  57

\* Excludes Speaker of the State Council, who has a casting vote only.

# 261  CO 54/986/6/2, no 98                    26 July 1945
## [Soulbury Report]: letter from Sir H Moore to G E J Gent conveying further personal views on the Soulbury Report

I'm sending to-day my comments on the Soulbury Report addressed to the S. of S.,[1] but you may like to have a little more private dope for your own consumption and discreet communication to Higher Authority.

Only Collins, Goonetilleke, Mulhall[2] and Sudbury have read the whole Report. I gave Howard the Judicial and Prerogative of Pardon part and Wetherall[3] the Defence part to read. Some of my detailed comments are based on their comments, but I have not always agreed with them so that the views expressed are essentially my own. I think with the possible exception of Goonetilleke we are all a little disappointed with the Report. It introduces no new or original solutions, the Indian question and immigration are left in the air, the minority Representation and Delimitation results will only be effective, if they are cooked in advance and the Chairman told what finding to bring in, while none of us like the Discrimination Chapter in form while broadly accepting its conclusions. All this is on the belittling side, which is always so easy to do. But the fairer approach, I think, is to ask oneself what else could they have produced on their terms of reference and in the light of past events. Goonetilleke's comment that, if he had written the Report for them himself out here, it would have been substantially the same, is probably the shrewdest verdict on the sort of reception it will receive locally. It is, I think, bound to be regarded as a victory for Senanayake. Provided you can get him to sponsor it substantially in its present form

---

[1] See 259 where the date is recorded as 25 July.

[2] J A Mulhall, secretary to governor.

[3] Lt-Gen Sir H Edward de Robillard Wetherall, c-in-c, Ceylon, 1945–1946.

and to stake his political future on getting it through out here, that in a sense is all to the good. But the proposals differ so little from the original Ministers' scheme, which the S. of S. was not prepared to accept without an independent enquiry, that the criticism may be made: Why have a Commission at all? Or even, why not give them Dominion Status outright and be done with it? Provided the S. of S. is prepared to consider the Second Chamber as an adequate minority safeguard, the greatest risk of a breakdown appears to me to be over the Indian question. You will find Senanayake pretty sticky over that, though actually he is less bigoted on the subject than Banda. If the India Office beats the big drum and Ponnambalam gets the House of Commons interested, I would not like to prophesy the results. I suppose much will depend on whether the failure of the Wavell Conference[4] has alienated sympathy with Indian politicians for the moment.

According to Goonetilleke Senanayake's technique will be:—

(a) A demand for Dominion Status. He won't expect to get this, but wants to be able to say he asked for it.

(b) A demand to "unreserve" currency. Nothing sinister about this, but he wants to be able to say he's got "something more" out of his London visit, and they seem to think the C.O. will regard this as least important.

(c) Transfer of Ceylon from C.O. to D.O. I think he will press for this. it would certainly be good window dressing from his point of view, and if they are going to get all the Report recommends, Ceylon will be much more like Southern Rhodesia or Newfoundland than any Colony. I should hate to think that by such an arrangement we should lose you, but I should hope you'd take the whole boiling across the passage and double the part in some way!

Apart from the above 3 points he may press a bit for the Supreme Court to adjudicate on reserved bills and may not like the new proposals re the life of the Second Chamber. He's sensitive and vulnerable on this point, and may feel this may give him added difficulty over here. Since I presume it is unlikely that he will agree to, or the S. of S. press for, any proposal which would enable the Governor to secure a limited number of seats in the Cabinet for the Minorities, the Second Chamber will in effect be almost their only safeguard. That being so, I favour the Drayton proposals, but as I've said in my letter, I think it would be wiser to make no change at all, if there is any risk of conceding again "coterminous life" on local pressure. Goonetilleke has emphasised this, as likely to be the last straw to the minorities.

I've let myself go a bit on the subject of the Public Services Commission and the Judicial Services Commission. Between ourselves I don't think the Public Services Commission is doing its job properly or to the satisfaction of the service at the present time. As explained in my letter there are good excuses for this, apart from the fact that both Collins and Drayton are both complete Colombo wallahs and are regarded as entirely "chair-borne". I'm pretty sure that a Judicial Services Commission composed as proposed would be unsatisfactory. The Judges would not go into details, even if they had the time, and the Secretary of the Commission would exercise an influence quite disproportionate to his status. Howard, Drayton, Nihill, all lawyers, are of course flat out for special terms of service, control, etc. for the legal and Judicial services. Except for the Supreme Court (and possibly the District

---

[4] A reference to the Simla Conference which is documented in *TOPI*, vol V.

Court) Bench I see no reason why appointments and conditions of service in the legal and Judicial services should not be subject to the same Governmental authority as the rest of the public service. You will see that Nihill has gone one further and wants a special Judicial clerical service as well. I think it may well be that under the new Constitution posts may tend to become more departmentalised on the U.K. model, but this will be gradual, and for that reason there is all the more reason for a comprehensive Public Services Commission. I appreciate there may be legal and constitutional difficulties over the appointing authority, but there must surely be ample Dominion precedent, which I should have thought the Commission ought to have found out for themselves. If the Governor has technically to appoint, then I want all his other Powers delegated to a Public Services Commission, so that it is clear from the outset that they have the last word on all service matters. Under Ceylon conditions I don't particularly like the idea of the Governor sitting in Cabinet, as I believe the Governor-General does in South Africa, when considering murder cases or performing such other few functions as "the Governor-General-in-Council" is required to exercise, but it is a little anomalous that under the proposed Constitution the Governor-General in Ceylon will have no body of that kind to turn to in the exercise of the few functions left him. I suppose there is no sort of Dominion or West Indian precedent for some form of Privy Council, who could advise the Governor on the exercise of the Royal Prerogative, or even perhaps on the reservation of Bills on policy as apart from legal points. A sub-committee of the Cabinet, consisting of 3 Ministers including the P.M. and appointed by the Governor in his discretion, might be a possibility, if constitutionally realisable, but I should not like to take the advice of the full cabinet on such questions.

This letter is already long enough, but I hope it may be of some assistance.

## 262    CO 54/986/6/2, no 94                                    28 July 1945
[Soulbury Report]: inward unnumbered telegram from Sir H Moore to M Stanley explaining why Sir O Goonetilleke has seen the report before Mr Senanayake

Your secret and personal 25th July.
   Soulbury Report.
   I confirm that Goonetilleke has read and discussed with me in strictest confidence first proof. In my secret and personal telegram of 29th April to Gater, I indicated that Officers of State would be consulted, where necessary, and when Gent informed me in his secret and personal letter of 22nd June that copies were being furnished to Drayton and Nihill, I considered it would be highly invidious if Goonetilleke alone of three Officers of State was excluded. I consulted him in that capacity and the reference to his membership of the Board of Ministers in Ceylon is not understood.
   2. I expressly waited for Senanayake's departure before showing proof to person named. He could not, therefore, communicate substance to Senanayake except by letter. He has, in fact, just submitted a letter to Senanayake for me to read before transmission by bag, which would indicate that he has a proper sense of responsibility in this matter. In it, he discusses the attitude of the State Council as reflected in Bandaranaike's budget speech and the reception given to it, and expresses the view

that a halfway house between the Minister's scheme and the Sri Lanka Bill is likely to secure a majority, and hopes that Senanayake will examine with (? patients) any proposals which differ from the views which he expressed to the Commission out here. The letter appears to me to be intended to be helpful and I propose to forward it and to secure that any further communications he may have to make to Senanayake are similarly submitted to me.

**263**  ADM 116/5546                                                    31 July 1945
[Defence]: letter from Admiral Layton to the Admiralty on defence requirements and the attitude of the CO towards Ceylon          [Extract]

. . . It has occurred to me that I should draw your attention in case no one else has done so, to some of the possible dangers attaching to the new Constitution which the Colonial Office are I believe about to confer on Ceylon.

I talked to Brendan-Bracken[1] about it when he was here about a fortnight ago and he was well alive to the dangers and had no intention of being a party to surrendering any of the rights and powers in Ceylon which are essential to the Imperial Government for defence purposes.

As you know it is the intention in the new Constitution to reserve defence and external affairs to the Imperial Government, but what I think is most important is to ensure that the limits of these subjects are not drawn too narrowly: the most vital aspect of this is that of communications. It is essential that we should retain some control in regard to railways, roads, posts, telegraphs (land line and W/T) and above all the ports and harbours. If we don't do this we shall never be able to rely on the Naval bases in Ceylon or its commercial harbours being any use to us in any future trouble. The present war has given us a very good example of what happens. The position of Ceylon in 1942 was deplorable as a base for the operations of the Fleet and this was due mainly to the organisation and communications being practically non-existent.

I mention this as I have a feeling (with some reason) that the permanent staff at the Colonial Office are only too anxious to rid themselves of the island and its troubles at any cost and so avoid having to deal with another Indian problem. . . .

---

[1] First lord of the Admiralty, 1945, in Churchill's caretaker government.

**264**  CO 54/986/6/2                                                    1 Aug 1945
[Soulbury Report]: notes by Sir G Gater of a discussion with Mr Stanley and an interview with Mr Senanayake

I told Colonel Stanley [on 31 July] that I had agreed to see Mr. Senanayake at 3.30 today. I asked him whether, in the course of his interview with Mr. Senanayake, he had mentioned that an advance copy of the Soulbury Commission Report would be handed to him. Colonel Stanley said that he had no precise recollection of having mentioned the matter. It was, however, possible that he might have referred to giving him an advance copy of the Report. Colonel Stanley said he thought it was desirable to deal with Mr. Senanayake with the greatest possible frankness. He authorised me at my interview to tell him that he would be supplied with an advance copy of the Report of the Soulbury Commission which would be available about the 7th or 8th of August. I reminded Colonel Stanley of the difficulty arising from the fact that Mr. Goonetilleke had seen the first rough draft of the Report which had been sent to the Governor.[1] He would, therefore, have seen the Report in advance of Mr. Senanayake. The Secretary of State said that while it would perhaps be inadvisable to mention directly that Mr. Goonetilleke had seen a copy of the first draft of the Report, he thought it might be wise for me to mention in the course of conversation that there had been an earlier draft of the Report, a copy of which had been sent to the Governor.

Mr. Senanayake asked me whether I could give him any indication as to future plans for dealing with the Ceylon Constitution. I replied that I had no information in regard to the appointment of a new Secretary of State. As soon as the appointment is made I should, at the earliest convenient opportunity, put the whole position regarding the Ceylon Constitution and Mr. Senanayake's visit to the Secretary of State. I should explain the plans which Colonel Stanley had made. It would be for the Secretary of State to decide how matters should proceed. I felt bound, however, to emphasise that some interval would be necessary as the Secretary of State would wish to study the subject, and the matters involved were of such importance that it would be necessary for him to consult his Cabinet colleagues. I enquired how long Mr. Senanayake proposed to stay here. He said that it was his desire to return to Ceylon about the middle of September, as he thought it would be unwise for his absence to continue longer as he must keep control of affairs there. In particular the budget would fall to be dealt with at the end of September. He did not know whether the length of his stay, which seemed to be sufficient for discussions with Colonel Stanley, would cover what might be required by the new Secretary of State. On this I replied that I could give him no clear indication now. It would be desirable for him to keep in close touch with me and I would, as far as possible, let him know how matters were developing.

In one respect I told Mr. Senanayake it would be possible to make some progress. Colonel Stanley had authorised me to inform him that I would supply him with an advance copy of the Soulbury Report in a few days time, probably about the 7th or 8th of August. This was an unusual procedure and I felt sure he would understand that the copy would be for his own private and strictly confidential information. I indicated that the actual date of publication of the Report would be a matter for the Secretary of State to decide. Mr. Senanayake seemed to be very pleased to hear that he would receive an advance copy of the Report so soon, and he agreed that he would require a few days to examine its contents.

Mr. Senanayake asked me whether a copy of the Report had been sent to the Governor as he realised it would be necessary for us to have the Governor's views before decisions were taken here and he thought that if the Governor had not yet received a copy there might be delay on this account. His enquiry gave me a good opportunity for mentioning that the Governor had received an early rough draft of the Report, which required some revision, on which he could indicate his views. I

---

[1] See 262.

explained that the copy which Mr. Senanayake would be given was a revised copy. In the circumstances, as Mr. Senanayake made no enquiry, I did not feel it necessary to mention that the Officers of State had seen the Report.

I asked Mr. Senanayake whether he had had any news from Ceylon. He said he had heard very little except that representatives of the minorities had left Ceylon and would shortly be arriving here. He said that he fully understood that whereas he had been invited by H.M.G., no invitation had been issued to them. I said that the position in this respect would be explained to the Secretary of State.

The interview was most friendly and cordial. I asked Mr. Senanayake to approach me at any time if there was any matter on which I could help him. I also invited him to spend a Sunday with me in the country on August the 26th.[2]

---

[2] In outward tel no 990 to Moore, Gater referred to the misunderstanding which had arisen over Goonetilleke having seen a copy of the Soulbury Report and conveyed the substance of his interview with Senanayake (CO 54/986/6/2, no 95, 2 Aug 1945).

# 265   CO 54/986/6/2                                          7 Aug 1945
## [Soulbury Report]: joint minute by Trafford Smith and J B Side-botham on the governor's comments. *Annex*

We have discussed Sir H. Moore's letter to the Secretary of State giving his personal observations on the Soulbury Commission's Report.[1] Apart from a number of criticisms of the Report, some political and some on factual grounds, we do not feel that there is anything in it to call for reconsideration of the terms of the Report, especially at this stage when the "revised proof" has gone to press: nor do we think that any of the points made by the Governor need alter the terms of the draft Cabinet Committee paper with which it is suggested H.M.G.'s consideration of the recommendations should be begun.

In his covering letter to the Secretary of State, the Governor makes it clear that he appreciates the Commission's attitude towards the Minister's scheme. From the first the Commission has taken the line that it was necessary to make recommendations which would stand some chance of being passed by the existing State Council under its existing leadership, hence the framing of the Report so as to provide a Constitution as near as possible on the lines of the Minister's scheme while containing the minority safeguards deemed necessary by the Commissioners and the provisions required to meet in full the terms of H.M.G.'s Declaration of 1943. In considering Mr. Senanayake's possible reaction to the Report, the Governor takes the view that he will be content with nothing less than its main recommendations, possibly with the addition of certain concessions which he will take home from London as the achievement of his mission.

As regards the reception of the Report by the minority communities, the Governor's view is that it will be regarded especially by the Tamils, as biased in favour of the Sinhalese. Especially the chapter on discrimination will rouse their wrath and they will subject it "to detailed recrimination". The Governor-General [sic] also considers that the Government of India will exert pressure as regards Indian

---

[1] See 259.

immigration and franchise and the work of the Delimitation Commission. The Europeans and Moors will be reasonably content, though the former may feel some doubts as to the definition of "ordinarily resident".

In summing up, the Governor's view is that, if the Leader of the State Council is prepared to sponsor the Report in its present form, it will be "in the best interests of Ceylon to support him in his efforts to secure its adoption by the State Council". He doubts, however, whether Mr. Senanayake will be able to secure the three-quarters majority stipulated in the 1943 Declaration.

We attach a note on the Governor's detailed comments containing our views thereon.

## Annex with 265

(N.B. The chapter & paras referred to below follow the references in the Governor's secret & personal letter. This numbering corresponds with the galley proof up to & including para 222 but after that para, the galley proof paras are one in advance.)

*Chapter VIII.* The Governor dislikes the Chapter dealing with discrimination and which he feels may lay the Commissioners open to a charge of a special pleading. There is no reason, however, to consider amendment to this Chapter which was incorporated in the Report after very full consideration of views submitted to the Commission by both sides.

*Report Chapters X and XI.* We think that there is force in the Governor's contention that it is desirable to define carefully in the Constitutional Instruments "who should be regarded as belonging to Ceylon or ordinarily resident in Ceylon". It is a matter which will effect both the British and the Indian immigrant minorities. It is understood that the Commission deliberately omitted to express any views on the Indian franchise issue since this is a matter of negotiation in connection with the general question of Indian immigration into Ceylon between the Governments of Ceylon and India and they felt that it would be undesirable for the Commission to intervene in this matter.

*Report Chapter XII.* Mr. Senanayake will, we conclude, prefer the adoption of the Commission's recommendation viz., that the existing arrangements in regard to the ballot system should be maintained but it is a matter which can be discussed with him in due course.

*Report Chapter XIII.* The Governor comments on the apparent inconsistency of certain paragraphs of this Chapter but there can be no doubt that the recommendations of the Commission are a deliberately designed compromise between the alternatives of communal and territorial representation. The Governor expresses doubts whether the minority communities will regard the safeguards proposed in the form of a special Delimitation Commission to be reappointed after each decennial census as satisfactory. (In fact, of course, the only thing that would be likely to satisfy the minority would be communal representation).

*Report Chapter XIV.* The Governor supports the proposal for his Second Chamber.

*Paragraph 306.* The arrangements as regards the life of the Second Chamber have now been redrafted and the Report will provide for five elected and five nominated members retiring every three years. There is, we think, force in the Governor-General-General's [sic] contention that if a provision on these lines appears in the

Report as published it *must* be adhered to as great importance will be attached to it by the minorities.

*Paragraph 307.* The Governor comments on a number of points which will require consideration in drafting the Instruments. As regards his comment on (vi.) the Commission's Report at the present time merely suggests that he should sit in the Senate but the definite recommendation to that effect included in the first draft of the Report which the Governor received was subsequently deleted. The Governor would like to see this restored.

*Report Chapter XV.(i).* The Report now provides that six nominated members shall be appointed "from the European and Burgher communities". There is now no question of nominated Malay representatives.

*Paragraph 323.(vii).* This point has already been met in the corrected proof of the Report. The Report provides that at the setting up of the new Constitution the Governor-General shall appoint permanent Secretaries on the advice of the Prime Minister, as a temporary measure pending the setting up of the new Public Services Commission. Whether Mr. Senanayake would agree to the Governor's suggestion is a matter which may be open to considerable doubt. It is one which, however, can be discussed with him in due course.

*Paragraph 327.(ii).* The intention of the Report is as stated by the Governor i.e. that the Governor-General will appoint Ministers on the recommendation of the Prime Minister on the United Kingdom precedent. The point can, of course, be made clear beyond doubt in the drafting of the Instruments. If there were any question of the Governor-General making Ministerial appointments to satisfy minorities, this would of course bring him into the forefront of political controversy—a situation which it is understood the Commission considered most undesirable.

*Report Chapter XVII.* We do not see how the Governor-General can seek adequate advice as regards the proper reservation of Bills other than, in the last resort, from H.M.G. since the Bills in question relate to subjects, the control of which is retained by H.M.G. and H.M.G. must be in the last event the proper authority to decide whether a Bill ought to be reserved or not. As regards (b) in these matters, the Governor-General must if necessary refer to H.M.G. if he is in doubt otherwise he will clearly have to act on his own responsibility with the benefit of such local advice as may be available. (d) In his semi-official letter to Mr. Gent[2] the Governor has raised the question whether anything in the nature of a Privy Council could be established to advise him inter alia on such matters as the exercise of the Prerogative of Pardon. Mr. Roberts Wray has referred to the provisions of the Jamaica Constitution on this matter and the question is one which might be looked into in greater detail. There would be obvious difficulty in the formation of a Privy Council of ordinary type in Ceylon owing to the communal problem, though if some sort of Judicial Committee were formed to advise the Governor-General on the exercise of the Royal Prerogative, these difficulties might not be so great. It appears from his covering letter that the Governor does not relish the idea of being advised only by a Minister Justice and in his subsequent comment under (d) he appears to press for certain of his functions being discharged by the Governor-General in Council i.e., the Governor-General sitting in Cabinet for the purpose. We feel that such arrangement would be likely to give rise to very real difficulties.

---

[2] See 261.

*Paragraph 335.* Reservation now covers 'communications' generally.

*Paragraph 339.* The Governor recommends the establishment of a Statutory Local Defence Committee. There are no doubt precedents which can be consulted.

*Paragraph 341.* Independent judgment in all cases. The Governor['s] doubts appear to be disposed of by the definite recommendation in paragraph 339 of the recommendations which sets out the Commission's intentions quite clearly.

*Paragraph 342.* As regards the Governor-General's staff, a point will arise here which we do not think has been dealt with in the Commission's Report, viz., by whom that staff is to be paid. If it is to be paid from Ceylon funds the Assistant Secretary may well be drawn from the Ceylon Civil Service; if the cost is to be borne by H.M.G. then the question will arise whether appointments should be made from outside Ceylon.

*Paragraph 337 etc.* Paragraphs dealing with Defence will appear in amended form in the final version of the Report.

*Report Chapters XVIII and XIX.* The Governor appears to dislike the idea of control of the Public Services being exercised in his name, but on the advice of the Public Services Commission. The same applies in the case of the Judicial Services Commission. This proposal was no doubt made quite deliberately by the Commission in order to keep the control of the Public Services free from any interference by Ministers. And it is difficult to see how this could be done except under some such arrangement as the Commission contemplates. It is to be noted that the Ministers' scheme makes very similar provisions. The Governor refers in this connection to the ladder by which Petitions to the King must pass and suggests that powers of appointment and dismissal might be vested in the Public Services Commission direct. If this were so it would presumably mean eliminating the Governor-General from that ladder. Apart from the constitutional aspect it seems doubtful whether such a proposal would meet with approval of Ceylon. Nor indeed does it seem likely that apart from the question of Petitions the Ceylon Civil Service would appreciate having the Public Services Commission as the final arbiter in all decisions.

*Paragraph 370.(v).* The Governor has suggested that once cadres, salaries etc. for the Public Services have been settled they might be incorporated in an Act of the legislature which will be valid for say five years. It is understood that the Commission considered this possibility (which is based on New Zealand practice) but rejected since New Zealand found it did not work in practice.

As regards the Judicial Services Commission the Governor suggests that appointments other than that of the Chief Justice and Judges of the Supreme Court should be made by the Public Services Commission to which one or more Judges serving or retired could be added when Judicial appointments had been made. He realized that this is likely to be strongly opposed by members of the legal and judicial profession but advocates it as a corrective to the demand that service questions affecting the legal and judicial departments should be regarded as a thing apart. We suggest that there is little merit in the Governor's proposal.

# **266**  CO 54/986/6/2, no 113                                    16 Aug 1945

# [Soulbury Report]: letter from Mr. Senanayake to Mr Hall stating the case for dominion status

[It was widely known that Jennings drafted this letter for Senanayake. Pages 90–92 of Jennings's unpublished typescript—*Donoughmore to independence*—provide a detailed explanation of how and when this letter came to be drafted and the form it took. Senanayake was given a final proof copy of the Soulbury Report on 9 Aug 1945 when he met George Hall, the new secretary of state. Hall invited Senanayake to send him a note on 'the points which he wished to have discussed'. Jennings, who was in the UK at the time, was informed of this conversation by telephone and he joined Senanayake at Grosvenor House on 11 Aug. Jennings's typescript described the report, on first reading, as 'very favourable'. The typescript continued: 'It did not in any way affect Mr. Senanayake's decision to press for Dominion Status, but neither did it affect his general policy of accepting anything that was offered provided it was a genuine advance on the Donoughmore Constitution. We were therefore presented with the difficult task of framing a case for Dominion Status which was at the same time an effective criticism of such parts of the Soulbury Report as appeared inconvenient within the framework of the declaration of 1943. . . . Emphasis should be laid on the purposes of this letter. It was essentially an attempt to persuade the Government of the United Kingdom to accept Dominion Status. . . . Advantages to the United Kingdom had to be stressed; the advantages to Ceylon had to be mentioned only incidentally. Concessions had to be made in order that the advantages might prove more attractive than the disadvantages. The arguments which might lead to refusal or delay had to be met before they were used; thought had to be given to what the Colonial Office would say in its own memorandum and to state their case in such a manner as would lead to the conclusion desired by Ceylon. What is more, when the document was drafted the chance of obtaining Dominion Status was not good. In case the main proposal was not accepted it was necessary to provide for a second argument which could justify as large a departure as possible from the declaration of 1945. The Soulbury Commission had just reported, and it was thought that the answer would be that the ministers' draft with Soulbury amendations, should be tried for a while. Hence the efforts in Part II of the letter to squeeze a little more out of the Soulbury Report. . . .']

At our meeting on the 9th August, 1945 you were good enough to hand me an advance copy of the Report of the Soulbury Commission and to ask for my observations. I am most grateful for this opportunity of expressing my views before any decision is taken by His Majesty's Government. I should state frankly, however, that opinion in Ceylon has shifted since the early months of 1944. On the 26th March 1942 the State Council passed a resolution requesting that Dominion Status be conferred on the Island. The Declaration of May 1943 did not go so far, but it would have enabled us to get rid of the Donoughmore Constitution and to place ourselves in an advantageous position for pressing for Dominion status. Accordingly, the ministers accepted the Declaration as interpreted in my statement of the 9th June, 1943. The Ministers' draft Constitution has, however, been before the public since September 1944 and, with the restrictive clause removed, it has been debated and passed by the State Council as the Sri Lanka Bill. It is now generally agreed that the restrictive clauses are unsatisfactory. Meanwhile, too, His Majesty's Government has promised full self-government to Burma. There does not seem to be anything in the social or economic conditions, or in the recent history of the two countries, to justify the placing of Ceylon in an inferior position. Accordingly the case that I should like to put before you is the case for Dominion status.

2. It is the expressed policy of His Majesty's Government, and especially of His Majesty's present Government, to enable the peoples of the Commonwealth to

achieve self-government. Ceylon is sometimes described as the "premier Colony", and if there is anything in that description it can mean only that it should be the first to receive self-government. If it is not yet ripe for this status, there must be some reason for it, and we have so far been given no such reason. The statistics quoted in the appendix to the Soulbury Report seem to me to prove our case. We have a population of 6 million; our annual revenue is over 200 million rupees and our trade is nearly a thousand million rupees; we had a surplus of 15 million rupees in 1942–43 and this year we are budgeting for a surplus of 100 millions; over 4,000 ships, amounting to 10 million tons, use our harbours in a normal year; we have over 6,000 schools with nearly 25,000 teachers and more than 850,000 pupils. The Report draws attention to the progress achieved since we assumed some measure of responsibility in 1931, "particularly in the sphere of social improvement, despite the shortcomings of the form of government" (paragraph 100).

3. A possible reason for the reluctance of the late Government to accord us Dominion status was indicated in a Declaration made in 1941. It referred to proposals for reform "concerning which there has been so little unanimity". There was little evidence of unanimity in Canada a hundred years ago when self-government was first given; there was no unanimity in South Africa in 1906 when the Liberal Government made its noble gesture; there was little unanimity in India at the time of the offer made by Sir Stafford Cripps; there was no unanimity in Burma when the recent White Paper was issued. Indeed, we might ask whether progress towards democracy in Great Britain was achieved by unanimity. In fact, however, Ceylon has approached nearer to unanimity than any. Not a single Ceylonese voted against the resolution for Dominion status in 1942: the Sri Lanka Bill was passed by 40 votes to 7, and only three Ceylonese were in the minority. This vote, be it remembered, was not merely a vote for Dominion status, it was a vote for a complete Constitution whose main principles have also been accepted by the Soulbury Commission.

4. The State Council's resolution of 1942 was inspired by the offer made to India by Sir Stafford Cripps in that year. It is far from my purpose to deprecate that offer: what we hope is that a similar offer will be made to Ceylon. I shall not be thought to disparage our great neighbour if I say that our educational progress has been much greater and our standard of living much higher. We have had partial self-government based on adult franchise for fourteen years. Ceylonese Ministers have had the sole responsibility for finance and have held seven of the ten portfolios of government during a period which included a major depression and a great war. We have taken our full share in the defence of the Island in circumstances of danger as acute as that which threatened Great Britain in 1940. At the end of the Japanese war we take pride in remembering that Ceylon made the first successful resistance to the Japanese advance, and that it was a joint resistance by the Imperial forces and the people of the Island. For over three years the Ceylonese Ministers and the Ceylonese Civil Defence Commissioner have sat in the War Council and shared with the Commander-in-Chief and the Service Commanders the responsibility for defence and the prosecution of the war against Japan. We provided the headquarters and the facilities required by the South-East Asia Command and the East Indies Fleet. We have supplied ninety per cent of the raw rubber available to the United Nations. For a long period we provided all the plumbago required for the manufacture of munitions of war. For years we have negotiated for the purchase and sale to the United Kingdom of our whole output

of tea, rubber and copra. Nearly all the members of the public services, including the Financial Secretary, the Auditor-general, many of the Government Agents, and most of the Heads of Departments are Ceylonese. More than half the judges of the Supreme Court, all the judges of inferior courts, and both law officers, are Ceylonese. We have a University with over a thousand students staffed as to 90 per cent by Ceylonese. All the medical officers in the Island are Ceylonese. The Bank of Ceylon, one of our major financial institutions, is wholly controlled by Ceylonese. We have raised a Ceylon Defence Force and a Ceylon Royal Naval Volunteer Reserve with Ceylonese officers. Our Civil Defence Service, 64,000 strong, was raised and controlled by Ceylonese.

5. The Constitution which we have worked with such success during the past fourteen years was one of the most difficult ever invented. As long ago as 1933 my predecessor, the late Sir Baron Jayatilaka, drew your predecessor's attention to its many defects and asked that they be removed. The Soulbury Commission says very truly that the Donoughmore Constitution "had little to commend it". Opinion in Ceylon would entirely agree with this condemnation. I will spare you a survey of its defects, but one must be mentioned particularly because its consequences may be used as an argument against Dominion status. The Soulbury Commission draws attention to the absence of party divisions on social and economic lines. It does not, however, explain why they are absent. The explanation is that such divisions would have been impracticable under the Donoughmore Constitution. We are divided on social and economic issues as strongly as you are in the United Kingdom: but the Donoughmore Constitution has compelled us to have a perpetual Coalition. The Board of Ministers is not selected for the homogeneity of its social and economic opinions. It consists of the seven chairmen of the seven executive committees. When a committee of seven or eight persons meets to elect a chairman the division of opinion is often very close. The result is that the Board of Ministers is a heterogeneous collection of Ministers, often differing widely in opinion and speaking and voting against each other in the State Council. It is as impossible to work on party lines as it was in Great Britain from 1940 to 1945. The essence of the party system, a homogeneous Cabinet responsible to a parliamentary majority, was forbidden by the Constitution itself. I cannot think, therefore, that the absence of this party system can be an argument against giving us complete self-government with a Cabinet system which will allow parties to develop.

6. Nor can communal divisions be regarded as an argument against Dominion status. They have not prevented the offer of that status to India, where they are much more important. They are in fact less important even than the Soulbury Commission made them, for in large measure they arise out of constitutional discussions. They are of small importance in ordinary political matters, and the Commission shows that a charge of racial discrimination cannot be sustained: but when constitutional advancement is under discussion each community is inspired by its ancestral loyalties to stake out a claim. Accordingly a Commission conducts its investigations in an atmosphere of artificial heat and, though it generally sees the light behind, it cannot but be affected by the atmosphere. We objected to a Commission in 1941 and again in 1944 precisely for that reason. Once the constitutional question is settled, communal questions will cease to be relevant. What is more, they are in themselves an argument for self-government. The Ceylonese as a whole are accustomed to these differences of race, creed, caste and language and know how to avoid offending

susceptibilities: the Englishmen who are sent to govern us do not always possess this advantage. The Soulbury Commission has approved our proposals for representation and the Bill in which they were included was passed by 40 votes to 7, more than half of the minority Ceylonese voting with the Sinhalese and only three Ceylonese voting against. We have thus produced a reasonable compromise which promises a Constitution under which, with complete self-government, we could proceed to tackle our social problems.

7. These social problems are urgent and important. I need do no more than to quote the Soulbury Report:—

> "There are not nearly enough schools to accommodate all the children, and a large number of the pupils do not attend long enough to gain any real profit from the instruction" (paragraph 106);
>
> "Housing conditions, water supplies and proper sanitation urgently demand attention. The death-rate remains unduly high and the infant mortality rate in particular is being only slowly reduced". (paragraph 110);
>
> "The main problem is that of raising the standard of life . . ." (paragraph 112)
>
> "in the rural areas depression means a lowering of the standard of life of the peasant cultivators, and the only real solution is to be found in the maintenance of agricultural prosperity. This raises questions of technical improvements in cultivation, co-operation in purchasing and marketing, and—since the population is steadily increasing—the reclamation of land" (paragraph 113).

Any Ceylonese could add to the list. Nothing is said, for instance, of the problem of establishing industries, to raise the standard of living and provide for our growing population. So long as we are disrupted by constitutional discussions we cannot deal adequately with these questions. The only solution is to place the whole responsibility fairly and squarely on the shoulders of the representative[s] of the people, as in Great Britain.

8. The real conflict over constitutional issues is not between the Sinhalese and the minorities but between the Ceylonese and His Majesty's Government. That conflict arises only because His Majesty's Government refuses to accord to us the complete self-government which almost every Ceylonese, without distinction of race, caste or creed, believes to be his due. It is a conflict which has been kept wholly within constitutional limits. We have not sought to force British opinion to agree with us. We have endeavoured to persuade by argument and to demonstrate by co-operation that Ceylon might be the first of the tropical Dominions, the first of the oriental peoples to be admitted to complete equality, the first to benefit by that policy of raising dependent people which British parties announce in their election programmes. There has been no rebellion in Ceylon, no non-cooperation movement, and no fifth-column: we were among the peoples who gave full collaboration while Britain was hard-pressed. Ireland obtained Dominion status; India has been promised it; Burma is being offered full self-government within the Commonwealth; but Ceylon gets none of these. The inevitable conclusion would be as unwelcome in Ceylon as in Great Britain.

9. The Declaration of May 1943 promised internal self-government with restrictions relating to defence and external affairs. Burma, on the other hand, has been

promised complete self-government subject to the making of an agreement about defence. We cannot understand why the distinction should be drawn. It surely cannot be said that we have proved less competent or trustworthy than the Burmese during the war against Japan. We do not grudge the award to Burma, but we are tempted to ask whether any restrictions would have been imposed on Ceylon if some of the Ceylonese Ministers had assisted the Japanese and a Ceylonese National Army had fought against British troops. We prefer to give an interpretation more creditable to the late Government and to assume that the difference lies in the importance of Ceylon as a base and as a link in the chain of Imperial communications. If this is so, it is our misfortune and not our fault. We are, however, fully aware of the fact. We have not sat in the War Council for three years without learning the implications of Ceylon's strategic position. We are also aware that it is or may be a position of some danger to ourselves. We should be ready and anxious to give all the assistance and all the facilities that His Majesty's Government might require provided that we were also given control of our own country. We are at least as anxious as His Majesty's Government to have the Island properly defended. We know that we cannot defend it alone; on the other hand, we know that it cannot be adequately defended without our assistance. I am ready to pledge my colleagues and the State Council to any reasonable agreement about defence as an integral part of an agreement for Dominion status.

10.   This method would assure Great Britain of a friendly people and a friendly Government, another Dominion, on the sea and air routes to Australia and New Zealand. It would assure Great Britain of naval and air bases that would dominate the Indian Ocean. I submit, with all the earnestness at my command, that the method prescribed by the Declaration of 1943 will not. The limitations imposed by that document were clearly inspired by distrust. In paragraph 357 of its Report the Soulbury Commission makes this plain. It speaks of the possible contingency of the non-co-operation of the Ceylon Government in the defence policies of His Majesty's Government. In the case of the Dominions, His Majesty's Government meets that contingency by providing them with full information and consulting them whenever their interests are specially affected. That, I submit, is the only method likely to be effective for securing full collaboration from Ceylon and making use of the facilities which Ceylon offers. The method prescribed by the Declaration will not, unless the same information is provided and there is full consultation. In Part IV of our draft Constitution we tried to provide a system which would work with the least possible friction. The Soulbury Commission has modified it in such a way that not merely friction but even opposition is much more likely to arise. Your advisers will surely tell you that it would be difficult to have two Governments in Ceylon in wartime, the one concerned with defence and the other with civil government. Either you must have collaboration from the civil government or you must treat Ceylon as hostile territory and impose upon it a military occupation. The process of governing by Governor-General's Ordinance will work only if they dealt with such unimportant matters that nobody thought it worth while to bother about them. In all normal cases a Governor-General's Ordinance would produce a constitutional crisis of the first magnitude. This would certainly be so under the Soulbury scheme. No responsible Minister would remain in office while a Governor-General was giving orders to subordinates behind their Minister's back; nor could responsible Ministers retain office while the Governor-General was spending Ceylon funds, raised by them,

in order to carry out a policy of which they disapproved.

11. Our scheme is certainly better than the Soulbury scheme, but the only satisfactory arrangement—satisfactory to either Government—would be one in which the Ceylon Government was collaborating with the Imperial Government. This can be achieved only by making the Ceylon Government fully responsible and entering into an agreement for the provision of mutual assistance in time of war and of such facilities in time of peace as might be required to that end. It would be, in short, a defensive alliance between the United Kingdom and a self-governing Ceylon. If His Majesty's Government still feels that we cannot be trusted, the simple solution is to give self-government but to provide for the taking over of the administration of the Island in the event of default on our agreement.

12. It is, however, not legal powers that will be needed, but the full collaboration of a free people. If you provide the freedom, the people will provide the collaboration. In 1906 the new Liberal Government took a much greater risk. They gave complete self-government not to a people which had been helping British troops against a common enemy, but to a people which had been waging war against His Majesty. Ten years later there was a South African "rebel" general in the War Cabinet; and a quarter of a century later the Union of South Africa, under the same rebel general, was an essential link in the communications of the army that marched from Egypt to Berlin. We cannot offer you a rebel general—the experience of South Africa and Burma seems to suggest that it would be easier if we could—but we do suggest that an act of faith and generosity, such as the Liberal Government was inspired to do in 1906, will cement the bonds between our peoples. It will indeed do more. It will add to the powers of the British Commonwealth of Nations. It will place another Dominion in a most important strategic position, half-way between England and Australia. It will complete the triangle in the Indian Ocean. Nor is this all. It will show the dependent peoples all over the Empire that your professions are not mere professions, and that it is possible for a people which, a hundred years ago, was almost completely lacking in educational facilities and was compelled to live on a very low standard of life, to achieve the status of a Dominion within the British Commonwealth of Nations.

13. I doubt if I have put my case in all its strength. I am oppressed with the difficulty of stating it adequately. The problem of Ceylon is one only of the many problems which will face the Government of which you are a member. For us, however, it is the fundamental problem. Until it is solved we cannot begin to face the many questions that confront us in that other Island, Milton's "Utmost Isle". I should welcome an early opportunity to reinforce my argument personally. The Constitution which was submitted to you in February 1944 requires only a little alteration to convert it into a Constitution for a fully self-governing Ceylon. It would be easy for me to have a revised draft prepared and at the same time to incorporate the amendments suggested by the Soulbury Commission. If after discussing the matter with me you agree that it would be worth while, I should be glad to have such a draft prepared. I appreciate that any decision to confer Dominion status on Ceylon would require legislation by Parliament: but if it were decided to consider this question I should not wish to have self-government held up. If, therefore, His Majesty's Government was not prepared to confer Dominion status on Ceylon without further consideration, I should suggest that our draft Constitution, as amended, be put into operation by Order in Council and the general responsibility transferred to the

Dominions Office. While the new constituencies were being delimited, the question of Dominion status could be raised with the Secretary of State for the Dominions.

II.

15. I turn now to the specific recommendations of the Soulbury Commission. I have no objection to any of them except as detailed below.

(1) *Franchise* (Chapter X.) There is no difference of opinion as to the desirability of maintaining adult franchise. The Commission also agrees with the Ministers that the present Order in Council, as interpreted, does not carry out the intention of its framers. The fault, we consider, lay in the drafting as well as in the administration, and I agree with the Commission that the administration should be improved. I do not think it is necessary to discuss the revision of the Elections Order in Council at this stage. We are anxious to get rid of the Donoughmore Constitution as soon as possible, and it is already 18 months since we submitted our scheme. Numerous amendments to the Elections Order, on the lines of S.P. XIV of 1938, are required. I suggest that the first elections be held under the 1931 Order. The matter can then be fully considered by the new Legislature. Nobody, as far as I know, denies that "there is a body of Indians in Ceylon, who, by birth and by long association have so identified themselves with the affairs of this country that their interests are no different from those of the indigenous population" (paragraph 239).

(2) *Immigration.* (Chapter XI). I see no objection to the proposed power of reservation in respect of British subjects who are normally resident in Ceylon, provided it is in the form proposed in paragraph 236 and not in that proposed in paragraph 242. Also, it should not apply to those who have entered the Island unlawfully, nor to persons who have been lawfully deported.

(3) *Representation.* (Chapter XIII). I have no objection to the proposal in paragraph 272 provided that it is not carried to extremes. This might be done by prescribing either a minimum or a maximum. In view of the fact that some of the constituencies in the sparsely-populated provinces will be small, I suggest the fixing of a maximum of 75,000 population.

(4) *Second chamber* (Chapter XIV). The question of the Second Chamber is as highly controversial in Ceylon as it is in Great Britain. The vote on the Sri Lanka Bill showed that there is a majority in the State Council against a Second Chamber and we know that we could never secure a three-quarters majority for a Constitution containing a Second Chamber. We therefore followed the example of Southern Rhodesia. It should perhaps be pointed out that, in addition to Southern Rhodesia, some of the Provinces of Canada and of the States of Australia follow the unicameral system. In view of the State Council vote, it would seem desirable to leave the matter to the new legislature, as we proposed. If, however, a Second Chamber were provided, I should have no objection to the type proposed. With regard to its powers, the precise language of the Parliament Act should be used. In view of the interpretation given to the definition of "Money Bill", however, it would be desirable to broaden it somewhat so as to bring ordinary taxing Bills, including Bills relating only to customs and excise, within its provisions. The term of office of a Senator seems to me to be far too long. It might involve us having a high proportion of aged Senators. I suggest a term of six-years, one third retiring every two years. There might be difficulty in forming a government (as with the

Labour Party in 1924 and 1929) if two Ministers and two Parliamentary Secretaries had to be in the Senate. I suggest four Ministers or Parliamentary Secretaries.

(5) *First chamber.* (Chapter XV). There appears to be some discrepancy between Chapter XV and Chapter XIII. It would, in my view, be undesirable to fix the number of members at 101, for then, on a redistribution some seats would be extinguished, and these might be seats normally filled by minority members. I suggest, therefore, that Articles 13 and 15 of S.P. XIV be allowed to stand. This may be the Commission's intention, but it is not clear. I also prefer our wording of Article 17. While we anticipate that normally the nominated members would be Europeans and Burghers, we are anxious not to draw racial distinctions, and we hope that (as in 1931 and 1936) Europeans and Burghers will not think themselves precluded from standing as candidates for territorial constituencies, nor such constituencies precluded from electing them. The opportunities will be greater under the new Constitution. This is one of the many cases where the Commission overemphasises communalism. It may be pointed out that constituencies mainly Sinhalese by racial composition have three times elected Europeans. Further, it would be difficult for the courts to interpret "European" and "Burgher". They are incapable of legal definition.

(6) *The executive.* (Chapter XVI). I should prefer Article 43 of S.P. XIV to remain as it stands so as to leave the number of Ministers under the control of Parliament. The State Council would not wish to leave the number at the discretion of the Prime Minister, and there might be a tendency to increase the number for party or personal reasons.

(7) *The governor-general.* (Chapter XVII). I am not sure what is meant by the phrase "discriminatory in character" in clause (ii)(d) of paragraph 332. Any tariff is necessarily discriminatory against overseas producers. If the phrase is intended to cover "differential duties", as in the present Instructions, I suggest that experience has shown it to be undesirable. In any case it is inconsistent with the Declaration of 1943. I also disagree with clause (vi) of paragraph 332. Article 10. of S.P. XIV requires a two-thirds majority for constitutional amendments and, with the new system of representation, thus provides ample protection for minorities. I see no other reason, why His Majesty's Government should be concerned with the form of Government in Ceylon. I am unable to agree with the recommendation at the end of paragraph 334. It would prevent the legislature from taking the initiative in reforming an organisation which had become inefficient or corrupt. It is surely enough to require "approval".

I should be prepared to deny the statement in paragraph 336. The matter was considered by the Conference on the Operation of Dominion Legislation in 1929, and it was agreed that the Dominions should have the powers to legislate extra-territorially. Confusion arises not so much where the express power is given as where only the power to legislate for peace, order and good government is given; for under the latest decisions of the Judicial Committee of the Privy Council this includes a power to legislate extra-territorially, but of uncertain extent. This is a lawyer's point, but we do not want to spend money on litigation.

I have already discussed Defence and External Affairs in general terms. We do not like Part IV of our draft, which seems likely to lead to endless difficulties unless it became a complete dead letter. However, I like the Commission's version even less.

We had a clear idea as to the manner in which the system would work if His Majesty's Government insisted on it. The Governor-General would have the necessary powers, but he would exercise them through Ministers, above all through the Prime Minister, who would hold the portfolios of defence and external affairs. His legislative power would enable him to impose the necessary obligations on Ministers. There would, however, be no dyarchy. The provision of funds out of the revenues of the Island would be made by the Ministers and the Legislature, not by the Governor-General. The Ceylon Defence Force and the Ceylon Royal Naval Volunteer Reserve would be provided by Ceylon in agreement with His Majesty's Government. The officers of the Ceylon Government, including the naval, military and Air Force Officers, would be under the control of Ministers as in Great Britain. The Commission proposes to upset this comparatively simple scheme, and to substitute a complicated scheme which I am not able to follow in some of its details and with which I am quite unable to agree. Apart from my general objections to the whole scheme, I have no objection to a power being reserved to His Majesty in Council for the following purposes:—

(1) To legislate on External Affairs or Defence as defined for the purposes of Governor-General's Ordinances;

(2) To revoke or amend the Constitution where, owing to the inability of the Governor-General to secure a Government responsible to the House of Representatives, it appears to His Majesty that there has been a break-down of the constitutional machinery.

I accept the former because, if there is to be legislation which is not passed by the Legislature, I would prefer to have it enacted by the King in Council rather than by the Governor-General. I accept the latter because it will enable the Ceylon Ministers to resign if the Governor-General abuses his powers.

I am unable to agree on the following points:—

(i)   The removal of the definition of External Affairs (paragraph 337). I should be glad to discuss this definition if it appears unsatisfactory. I should add that the qualification of "External Affairs" for the purposes of reservation is not extended by the Commission to legislation by the Governor-General, who can apparently legislate by Ordinance on any matter excluded from reservation by clause (ii) of paragraph 332. I am quite unable to agree with this enormous extension of the Governor-General's power.

(ii) The reservation to His Majesty in Council of an unlimited power of constitutional amendment (paragraph 337). The Commission appears to be in error in stating that this is "usual" where powers of self-government are conferred by Order in Council.

(iii) Consultation of officers of the Ceylon Government by the Governor-General behind the backs of their Ministers. (paragraph 341).

(iv) The general power to legislate during wartime or any national emergency other than inability to obtain responsible Ministers (paragraph 351). We have just had experience of war conditions, and I see no reason why self-government should be destroyed in wartime.

(v) The removal of the Ceylon Defence Force and the Ceylon Royal Naval Volunteer Reserve from the definition of "Defence". (paragraph 353). If His Majesty's Government wishes to wage war in Ceylon against the wishes of the

Legislature, it should provide its own troops, not use Ceylonese forces.

(vi) The imposition of a charge upon Ceylon funds by Ordinance (paragraph 354). I see no purpose in making an agreement for allocating cost unless it is assumed that both sides will carry out the agreement. The Commission does not recommend that Ceylon have the power to compel the people of Great Britain to pay under the agreement.

(vii) The power of the Governor-General to appoint or dismiss officers and to issue instructions to officers (paragraphs 354 and 355).

(viii) The withdrawal of Article 39(4), (paragraph 356). The Commission appears to have misunderstood this clause, and I am quite willing to consider the drafting, provided that the principle (which is correctly stated by the Commission) is retained.

Generally the Commission assumes as it admits in slightly different words (paragraph 357), that the Ministers will not "play the game". It would be much simpler, I think, if His Majesty's Government would assume that we are reasonable beings, grant full self-government, and make an agreement about External Affairs and Defence as in Burma. I do not know any reason which leads His Majesty's Government to suspect that we are less trustworthy than the Burmese.

There are certain other points in this Chapter:—

(a) I am unable to agree that Article 40 (d) is inconsistent with the Declaration (paragraph 338). We understood the Declaration to refer to merchant shipping legislation and to ships registered outside Ceylon. Is there any reason why we should not have our own shipping services?

(b) I do not see any serious objection to allowing the question of reservation to be submitted to the Supreme Court. This would surely be a better solution than the Commission's solution of having a general election (paragraph 339).

(8) *The Public Services*. (Chapter XVIII). The Commission appears to me not to realise the difference in the attitude to the public services which will be produced by the removal of the control of the Secretary of State. At present a public officer is responsible to a "foreign" Government. In future he will be responsible to the Ceylon Government. The Commission has also misunderstood the draft Constitution (see paragraph 379). Article 64 is limited in its terms because the powers relating to the public services will be governed by Article 36. I have, however, no other comments to make on this Chapter except on the suggestion in paragraph 383 that the administration of the public services should be transferred to the Ministry of Finance. I suggest that this be left to be decided under Article 44. The analogy drawn with Great Britain breaks down owing to the fact that the Prime Minister, as First Lord of the Treasury, and the Chancellor of the Exchequer are both Treasury Ministers. We shall presumably have nothing comparable in Ceylon. I should also point out that there have been abuses of Article 88 of the Order in Council of 1931 and that its provisions should be modified. This is a question which I will take up when the question of drafting is raised.

### III.

16. You will see from the above comments that the differences which are likely to be fundamental relate to Defence and External Affairs. I am sure that your advisers will agree that the Commission's scheme would work in wartime only if we gave full

collaboration, in which case these powers would be unnecessary, or if the whole civil government were taken over by the Governor-General or the Commander-in-Chief. It is a scheme which assumes a break-down. Indeed, the break-down may occur immediately, for I doubt if the State Council will accept this scheme. On the other hand, I am sure that the Council would agree to any reasonable scheme for the defence of Ceylon and the security of Imperial communications if it were accompanied by a grant of full self-government leading to Dominion status as soon as the necessary discussions had taken place. The Commission's scheme is based on distrust of the Ceylonese or, as they call it, the contingency of the "non-cooperation of the Ceylon Government in the Defence policies of His Majesty's Government." The way to secure our cooperation is to ask us to cooperate and to give us a Constitution, framed by us, under which we can cooperate. It was not by imposing limitations on the powers of their governments that the cooperation of Canada, Australia, New Zealand and South Africa was obtained. We know how essential is Imperial assistance in defence: but we suggest that our active assistance was also valuable. It happens that these words are being written while the whole Commonwealth, and indeed the whole civilised world, is celebrating the victory over Japan. I hope it will not be forgotten that the orders for the surrender of Japanese troops in Malaya and Burma are being sent from the capital of the last Sinhalese kings, that the fleet which will steam into Singapore steamed out of Trincomalee, and that the aircraft which patrol the skies of Malaya and Sumatra are based on Ceylon. Is it worthwhile to force on us a Constitution which assumes that the cooperation which has been so readily forthcoming during the past five years will in future be replaced by non-cooperation? Is it not better to establish a new Dominion on the sea and air routes to Australia and New Zealand, in an Island which guards the whole Indian Ocean? Burma and Malaya and British North Borneo will be freed, in one sense, in a few days. Will not His Majesty's Government, in another sense, free Ceylon also? The conversion of Ceylon into a Dominion would show that this was was not a war between Imperialist powers anxious to maintain their domination but that, on the side of the United Nations, it was a war to enable all the peoples of the world, including all those which have hitherto been dependent on them, to achieve freedom and self-respect.

## 267   CO 54/986/6/2, no 106                              17 Aug 1945
[Soulbury Report]: inward unnumbered telegram from Sir H Moore to Mr Hall on the risk of leakage

Your secret and personal of 15th August.

Glad to know if revised proofs represent recommendations of Commission in final form in which you require any further comments I have to make, or whether they are susceptible of further modification in the light of my detailed comments on first proof, which I presume you have now had time to consider.[1]

2.  If latter is the case, I may wish to consult Collins and Goonetilleke as before, but see no reason why this should become known to other Members of the board of Ministers. Greatest risk of leakage appears to be in London, in view of arrival of Ponnambalam and Desai,[2] who are reported to be already very active.

---

[1] See 265.                    [2] H M Desai, representing the Indian Mercantile Chamber of Ceylon.

**268**   CO 54/986/6/2, no 112                                   27 Aug 1945

[Soulbury Report]: inward unnumbered telegram from Sir H Moore to Mr Hall on general support in Ceylon for dominion status

Your secret and personal telegram of 25th August.

Senanayake's reply[1] has already been shown to me by Goonetilleke to whom he sent a copy direct.

2.   It is manifestly the work of Jennings, whose assistance Senanayake appears to have invoked to the exclusion of Drayton, despite paragraph III of my secret and personal telegram of 29th April.[2]

3.   The end of the war and the change of Government at home coupled with developments in India and Burma, have changed the atmosphere here considerably in the last few weeks. My contemporary comments at the time of the passing of the Sri Lanka Bill, therefore, require some modification. At the time, as already reported, its passage could be broadly construed as indicating general support of Dominion Status as the ultimate constitutional goal, but was not taken very seriously in view of the 1943 Declaration. To-day that goal is regarded as within immediate grasp and, despite the generally favourable nature of the Soulbury Report, Senanayake will, I fear, be regarded as having failed in his mission unless he brings back with him some form of Dominion Status, involving transfer to the Dominions Office. If an award is presented in that form he should get support for a negotiated agreement on defence and external affairs, and possibly a Second Chamber, if that is insisted upon as the price of this agreement and the grant of Dominion Status.

Without it I believe he has no chance of obtaining a three-forths [sic] majority for a Second Chamber, even if some further concessions are made to meet his views on the Soulbury Report. The resultant political situation here might be very serious and give full rein to the extremist Independence Groups.

I should, therefore, be glad to be informed if the possible grant of Dominion Status is to be seriously discussed. If it is, I consider Drayton's presence at such discussions would be most desirable, and I have no doubt I could arrange from this end for Senanayake to ask for him.

---

[1] See 266.                                                              [2] See 240.

**269**   CO 54/986/6/2, no 110A                                  27 Aug 1945

[Soulbury Report]: letter from Mr Hall to Sir H Moore on Mr Senanayake's claim for dominion status

I do not think that I have ever had the pleasure of meeting you personally, but one of the first questions which came before me on my assumption of office here was that of the reform of the Ceylon Constitution and with it I found Senanayake "on my doorstep".

I am writing to send you for your personal information a copy of the letter from Senanayake[1] referred to in my secret and personal telegram dated the 25th August

---

[1] See 266.

which he sent me in response to the request I made to him to put any points he would like to make on the report of the Soulbury Commission in writing, when I handed a copy of it to him for his personal study. As you will see, most of his letter is occupied with a claim for Dominion status. This is, I assume, a political move to enable him on his return to Ceylon to tell his colleagues that he did in fact make this request as strongly as he could, and to enable him to produce evidence that he did so. This request is outside the terms of the 1943 Declaration and as such is not a basis upon which I can usefully initiate discussions with him, as he himself no doubt very well appreciates. I shall have to make this clear to him.

I will keep you informed from time to time as to the progress of the discussions, and if there are any particular points which occur to you, please to not hesitate to send me your comments, which I shall welcome.

## 270   CAB 129/1, CP(45)132                                    29 Aug 1945
## 'Ceylon constitution': Cabinet memorandum by Mr Greenwood[1] on the Soulbury Report, submitting a report from the Colonial Affairs Committee

At the request of the Prime Minister the Colonial Affairs Committee have examined the proposals for constitutional reform in Ceylon submitted by Lord Soulbury's Commission. I now submit the Report of the Committee.

2.  The Cabinet will remember that the Soulbury Commission was appointed by the War Cabinet on the 7th June, 1944, to examine the question of constitutional reform in Ceylon on the understanding that this did not involve any commitment by His Majesty's Government further to those contained in the Declaration made by His Majesty's Government in 1943, the text of which is appended to this Report.[2]

3.  The recommendations of the Commission (the Report of which has been separately circulated to the Colonial Affairs Committee) are briefly summarised below. We are informed that they are based on extensive investigations in Ceylon, in the course of which full opportunity has been given to all interested parties there to express their views on the future of the constitution.

4.  It is a matter of urgency to reach conclusions on these recommendations since Mr. Senanayake, the Vice-Chairman of the Ceylon Board of Ministers and Leader of the State Council, is at present in London for discussions with the Secretary of State for the Colonies on the Ceylon constitutional position.

*Recommendations of the Soulbury Commission*
5.  The recommendations of the Soulbury Commission may very briefly be summarised as follows:—

(a) The existing system of Government in Ceylon, which dates from the Donough-more Commission of 1931 and of which the most prominent feature was the establishment of certain Executive Committees under Ministers, has not worked well, and should come to an end.

---

[1] Mr Arthur Greenwood, lord privy seal and chairman of the Cabinet Colonial Affairs Committee.
[2] Not printed; see part I of this volume, 169, annex.

(b) It should be replaced by a system under which the Government of Ceylon would consist of a Governor-General with the reserved powers set out in the Declaration of 1943, a Cabinet and a bi-cameral legislature. The Lower House would be elected as to 95 members of its house by universal suffrage, its further members being nominated to represent those communities (principally the European and Burgher) which have failed to secure adequate representation in the elections. The Upper House would consist of 30 members, of whom 15 would be elected by the Lower House and 15 nominated by the Governor-General in his discretion. Its powers would be broadly similar to those of the House of Lords. In particular, it would not be able to check, amend or delay any finance bill beyond one month, and it could delay any other bill for not more than two successive sessions.

(c) The constitution would operate subject to the reservation to His Majesty's Government of special powers in respect of defence, external affairs, currency, and trade, transport and communications affecting any part of the Empire.

(d) Special safeguards are contemplated for the minority communities, the principal of which are European, Ceylon Tamil, Indian Tamil, Muslims and Burghers.

(e) The Public services and the subordinate judiciary would be appointed on the recommendation respectively of a Public Services Commission and a Judicial Services Commission. These bodies would be so composed as to ensure complete impartiality.

6. We are in general satisfied, in the light of full discussions with the Secretary of State for the Colonies, that, subject to the points which are discussed below, the new constitution appears to provide a suitable measure of constitutional progress for Ceylon within the terms of the Declaration made by His Majesty's Government in 1943. We think it unnecessary to trouble the Cabinet with a review of its details.

7. There is, however, one substantial point of policy which merits close examination. In their Declaration of 1943, His Majesty's Government laid it down that the final acceptance of any scheme of constitutional reform formulated by Ministers would be conditional, *inter alia*, on its acceptance by three-quarters of the members of the State Council. Ministers in fact formulated a scheme which they subsequently withdrew. That scheme, while it no longer has the avowed support of Ministers, is in effect the declared background to many of the Soulbury recommendations. The question for decision is whether in these circumstances we shall insist on a three-quarters majority for the new constitutional proposals in the State Council or not.

*Arguments for holding to a three-quarters majority in the State Council*
8.—(a) The principal argument for holding to the three-quarters majority envisaged in the Declaration of 1943 is its great importance from the point of view of the minorities. The minorities are the problem of crucial significance in Ceylon. They will undoubtedly apply a critical scrutiny to the effect on their position of any constitutional proposals. The requirement of a three-quarters vote in the State Council is one of the principal safeguards for them. While the other safeguards embodied in the proposed constitution are substantial (chiefly the reserve powers of the Governor), they would not by themselves be likely to reassure minority feeling.

(b) Much public attention has been attracted to the figure of three-quarters since it figured in the Declaration of 1943. Minority opposition to its withdrawal and suspicion of the reasons underlying that withdrawal may be expected to be correspondingly sharp.

*Arguments in favour of abandoning the three-quarters majority*

9. In favour, on the other hand, of abandoning the three-quarters majority and of substituting some smaller but sufficient majority, *e.g.*, two-thirds, coupled with a requirement that that majority should include the largest practicable number of members of the minority communities, the following considerations have been urged upon us.

(a) His Majesty's Government are in terms not bound by the Declaration of 1943 in this regard since the scheme under consideration is one devised by an independent Commission and not by Ministers in Ceylon. There is no reason why His Majesty's Government should not approve a constitutional scheme such as that now before the Cabinet so long as they are satisfied that it represents adequate safeguards for minority interests and is in other respects satisfactory.

(b) The scheme put forward by Ministers for which alone under the 1943 Declaration a three-quarters majority would have been requisite, was devised, we are informed, without consultation with the minorities. The Soulbury Commission, on the other hand, has been at special pains to acquaint itself with minority feeling. They have informed the Secretary of State for the Colonies confidentially that in their view it would be quite impracticable to insist upon a three-quarters majority for the constitutional scheme which they have proposed. We understand in this connection that the Sinhalese majority in the State Council is unlikely to vote solidly in any circumstances in favour of the Soulbury proposals. A minority of the Sinhalese members, which might be as much as one-third, would probably oppose those recommendations on the grounds that they did not go far enough towards Dominion status.

(c) Mr. Senanayake, whose assistance is, we are advised, essential if the Soulbury recommendations are to secure the approval of the State Council, has made it clear that he would not be prepared to support those proposals if we insist on the three-quarters majority. Failing his support and that of the majority party, there would be no prospect of general acceptance in Ceylon for these proposals. In such circumstances any scheme to replace the Donoughmore constitution would have to be imposed from outside. The unhappy impression which this would be likely to create needs no emphasis.

(d) It would be most regrettable if insistence on our part on a three-quarters majority were to result in the rejection of the present recommendations and the imposition (even if this were easily practicable) of a constitution from outside. Sinhalese pressure for still more extensive concessions is reported to be growing. Time is running against us, and the example of India and the constitutional undertakings recently given to Burma have stimulated this demand, all the more so since the Sinhalese contrast their whole-hearted co-operation in the war with the failure to co-operate of certain elements in India and Burma.

*Our recommendation*

10. We have carefully weighed the arguments on either side. The balance is a nice

one. In the result we think it most important that His Majesty's Government should not themselves appear of their own volition to jettison the three-quarters majority contemplated (though in different circumstances) by the Declaration of 1943. We understand, however, that it is likely that Mr. Senanayake will himself raise this matter in his discussions with the Secretary of State for the Colonies. We recommend that the Secretary of State be given a discretion in that event to inform Mr. Senanayake that it should be his object to secure the maximum possible majority in the State Council for the Soulbury proposals; that that majority should preferably include the largest possible element of minority representation; and that on this understanding His Majesty's Government would not necessarily insist on holding to the three-quarters majority of the Declaration of 1943.

## Miscellaneous points

11. We have in addition considered certain other miscellaneous points. Our recommendations are as follows:—

(1) *Consultation with the Government of India.* We think that advantage should be taken of Lord Wavell's presence in this country to acquaint him with the general position in regard to the recommendations of the Soulbury Commission and the action proposed on them.

We recommend that the text of the Soulbury Report be made available to the Governor-General of India and his Executive Council confidentially at the same time as it is made available to the members of the Board of Ministers in Ceylon, and that an appropriate interval, to be adjusted between the Secretary of State for the Colonies and the Secretary of State for India, be given the Government of India to formulate their conclusions.

(2) *Defence.* The Service Ministers inform us that they regard the provisions for defence embodied in the Soulbury Report as generally adequate and satisfactory.

(3) *Question of a change in the style of the governor of Ceylon.* Sinhalese Ministers, actuated by considerations of prestige, have urged that His Majesty's representative in Ceylon should in future be styled Governor-General and not Governor. The scheme put forward by Ministers but subsequently withdrawn by them contemplated that the Governor of Ceylon should in future be a Governor-General. The Secretary of State for the Dominions has drawn our attention to the embarrassing consequences which this might have. We accept the force of the considerations he has urged and we do not support the suggestion that the title Governor-General should be substituted for that of Governor.

(4) *Channel of communication between the Ceylon Government and His Majesty's Government.* The Soulbury Commission, with a view to meeting Sinhalese susceptibilities, have recommended that communications passing between the Ceylon Government and His Majesty's Government should in appropriate cases be addressed to the Prime Minister of His Majesty's Government in the United Kingdom. Given general practice throughout the Empire and the constitutional position of the Governor and of the Secretary of State for the Colonies, we do not support this recommendation. We consider that as in the case of territories of comparable status communications should be addressed to His Majesty's Government through the channel of the Governor of Ceylon and the Secretary of State for the Colonies.

12.   Subject to the points taken in paragraphs 10 and 11 above and to such further consideration of the details of the proposed constitution as may in due course be called for, we recommend that the Secretary of State for the Colonies be authorised to enter into confidential discussion with Mr. Senanayake on the basis of the Soulbury Report as modified by our present proposals. It is, of course, understood that after these discussions have taken place the Secretary of State for the Colonies will again report to the Cabinet and obtain approval to constitutional scheme which he may then wish to recommend before steps are taken to lay it before Parliament for consideration.

## **271**   CO 54/986/11, no 12, CM 26(45)3                              30 Aug 1945
## 'Ceylon': Cabinet conclusions on the report from the Colonial Affairs Committee on the Soulbury Report

The Cabinet had before them a Report (C.P.(45)132) from the Colonial Affairs Committee on the Report of the Soulbury Commission on constitutional reform in Ceylon.[1]

The Committee were in general satisfied that the new constitution proposed, a summary of which was contained in their Report, appeared to provide a suitable measure of constitutional progress. On the question whether the final acceptance of any scheme of constitutional reform should be confidential on acceptance by three-quarters of the members of the State Council, they considered that in the discussions which he was proposing to hold with Mr. Senanayake, Leader of the Ceylon State Council, the Secretary of State for the Colonies should be given a discretion, if Mr. Senanayake raised this matter, to inform him that it should be his object to secure the maximum possible majority in the State Council for the Soulbury proposals; that that majority should preferably include the largest possible element of minority representation; and that on this understanding His Majesty's Government would not necessarily insist on holding to the three-quarters majority contemplated in the Declaration of 1943.

It was proposed to make suitable arrangements for consulting the Government of India and also the Ceylon State Council before final conclusions were reached on the Report.

*The Secretary of State for the Colonies* said that if authorised to enter into confidential discussions with Mr. Senanayake on the basis of the Report as modified by the proposals of the Committee, it would be his intention again to report to the Cabinet after those discussions had taken place and to obtain their approval of any constitutional scheme which he might then wish to recommend, before steps were taken to lay it before Parliament for consideration. All he asked at the moment, however, was authority to enter into these discussions without in any way committing the Cabinet.

A general discussion followed. In the result the Cabinet felt unable to reach conclusions on the important matters covered by the Report or to authorise the Secretary of State for the Colonies to proceed even with the tentative and

[1] See 270.

non-committal discussions with Mr. Senanayake which he had in mind, until the Report as a whole had been circulated to the Cabinet and there had been opportunity to discuss its recommendations in closer detail.

The Cabinet:—

Invited the Secretary of State for the Colonies to circulate the Report of the Soulbury Commission and the minutes of the meeting of the Colonial Affairs Committee at which it had been considered, with a view to resuming their discussion at a meeting early in the following week.

## 272  CO 54/986/6/2, no 114                                          30 Aug 1945
## [Soulbury Report]: outward unnumbered telegram from Mr Hall to Sir H Moore on Mr Senanayake's claim for dominion status

Your Secret and Personal telegrams (1) and (2)[1] of the 27th August.

Thank you for your revised estimate of trends of local political thought, which I shall keep in mind in the course of my discussions with Senanayake.[2]

2. While I fully realise that Senanayake will press the question of Dominion Status I intend in these discussions to adhere to the basis laid down in His Majesty's Government's 1943 Declaration.

3. Senanayake was invited to this country to discuss all issues involved in the reform of the Constitution, including of course the recommendations of the Soulbury Commission. He has no doubt arranged through his own channels to be kept fully informed of local political trends, and should he refuse to agree to a Constitution on the basis recommended in the Soulbury Commission's Report on the ground that he could not hope to carry it successfully through the State Council, a fresh situation will have arisen which it will then be for His Majesty's Government to consider.

4. I cannot at this stage anticipate what His Majesty's Government's attitude will be, but I should, of course, consult you should such a situation arise.

5. In the meantime, Drayton is being informed of your conclusions as to his return to Ceylon, making it clear that his arrangements will be dependent on the progress of the discussions.

---

[1] See 268.

[2] Moore submitted a further assessment in a semi-official letter to Gent on 30 Aug 1945: '. . . I see breakers ahead. The Board of Ministers, despite continued badgering, have been taken quite unprepared by the Jap collapse and nothing is ready for absorbing surplus army civil labour in the local labour market. There was a deputation of 1,000 workers to the State Council yesterday for no reason at all, and I'm afraid Corea, who is weak, may get stampeded. There's a big swing to the left and Senanayake, if he fails in London, may find the Sama Samajists in command. He ought not to linger in London, unless he's going to bring back Dominion Status or something very like it. . . .' (CO 54/986/6/2, no 119).

**273**   CO 54/986/11, no 16, CM 27(45)2                    3 Sept 1945
'Ceylon': Cabinet conclusions authorising Mr Hall to open discussions
with Mr Senanayake on the recommendations of the Soulbury Report

At their meeting on the 30th August[1] the Cabinet had invited the Secretary of State
for the Colonies to circulate the report of the Soulbury Commission and the minutes
of the meeting of the Colonial Affairs Committee at which it had been considered,
with a view to their resuming the discussions of the report by the Colonial Affairs
Committee (C.P.(45) 132)[2] on the Ceylon Constitution.
    The Cabinet now had before them:—

(i)  a memorandum by the Secretary of State for the Colonies (C.P.(45), 138)
circulating copies of the Soulbury Report and of the minutes of the relative
meeting of the Colonial Affairs Committee (C.(45) 1st Meeting);
(ii)  a revised version of the report by the Colonial Affairs Committee on the Ceylon
Constitution (C.P.(45)132 (Revise)).

It was explained that in 1943 a declaration had been made by His Majesty's
Government with regard to Constitutional Reform in Ceylon in the terms of the
Annex to C.P.(45) 132 (Revise). This declaration had invited the Board of Ministers to
formulate a constitutional scheme, on the understanding that acceptance of the
scheme would depend on its being in full compliance with the terms of the
declaration and on its subsequent approval by three-quarters of all the members of
the State Council of Ceylon. The Ministers had formulated a scheme but when the
Soulbury Commission was appointed they had withdrawn their scheme and had
refused to give evidence to the Commission. The Commission had, however, had
private discussion with Mr. Senanayake, the Vice-Chairman of the Ceylon Board of
Ministers and Leader of the State Council, and had reached the conclusion that his
co-operation would be essential in securing acceptance of their proposals for reform.
Mr. Senanayake had accordingly been invited to come to this country for discussions
on the Ceylon constitutional position, and had been furnished with a copy of the
Soulbury Report. He had now been in this country for over a month and it was
desirable that the discussions with him should now be undertaken. Advantage should
also be taken of the Viceroy's presence in this country to acquaint him with the
general position in regard to the recommendations in the Report and the action
proposed on them.
    A special point arose in regard to the condition in the 1943 declaration that the
acceptance of any constitutional scheme would depend upon its subsequent approval
by three-quarters of the members of the State Council of Ceylon. This stipulation had
been made because it was feared that the Ministers in formulating their scheme
would ignore the views of minorities. What His Majesty's Government now had
before them, however, was a scheme formulated by the Soulbury Commission after
full consultation with the minorities and it was accordingly suggested in paragraph
10 of C.P.(45)132 (Revise) that in the discussions with Mr. Senanayake it should be
open to the Secretary of State for the Colonies to indicate that His Majesty's
Government would not necessarily insist on this condition.

---

[1] See 271.                                                            [2] See 270.

In discussion the question was raised whether, if the Secretary of State for the Colonies undertook conversations with Mr. Senanayake, the Government would be regarded as being committed to the proposals in the Soulbury Report. It was pointed out that the Cabinet had not yet had a full opportunity of considering these proposals and that some of the recommendations—in particular the proposals for the selection of the Second Chamber—seemed open to criticism.

*The Secretary of State for the Colonies* said that the recommendations with regard to the Second Chamber were similar to those put forward in His Majesty's Government's statement of policy with regard to Burma (Cmd.6635)[3] and that the Second Chamber was primarily designed in order to safeguard the position of minorities. He would, however, make it clear in his conversations with Mr. Senanayake that the Government were not committed to the conclusions in the Soulbury Report and that they were to be regarded merely as a basis for discussion.

The Cabinet:—

(1) Authorised the Secretary of State for the Colonies to enter into confidential discussions with Mr. Senanayake on the basis of Soulbury Report, on the understanding that it would be made clear that His Majesty's Government were not committed to the proposals in the Report and that after the discussions had taken place the Secretary of State for the Colonies would again report to the Cabinet.

(2) Agreed that the Secretary of State for the Colonies should have discretion to inform Mr. Senanayake that His Majesty's Government would not necessarily insist on holding to the three-quarters majority in the Declaration of 1943.

(3) Agreed that Lord Wavell should be acquainted with the general position in regard to the recommendations of the Soulbury Commission and the action proposed on them.

---

[3] Published in May 1945, reproduced in BSI, I, 153.

# 274  CO 54/987/2, no 1                                    4 Sept 1945
## [Soulbury Report]: CO record of discussion between Mr Hall and Mr Senanayake[1]

*The Secretary of State* opened the meeting by welcoming Mr. Senanayake and apologizing for the delay which had taken place in beginning the discussions on the Constitution. He made the basis of the discussions clear: that His Majesty's Government had not yet reached conclusions on the Soulbury recommendations and that he was empowered only to hear what Mr. Senanayake had to say and to elucidate his point of view for a further report to the Cabinet. In the light of the discussions between the Secretary of State and Mr. Senanayake, the Cabinet would then reach its decisions.

*Mr. Senanayake* thanked the Secretary of State for the opportunity afforded him to discuss the constitutional position. The views he expressed, he said, were those of the people of Ceylon. He must make it clear that the situation in Ceylon had

---

[1] Also present: Mr Creech Jones, A G Ranasinha (secretary to Mr Senanayake), Sir G Gater, G E J Gent, J B Sidebotham and Trafford Smith.

materially changed since the 1943 Declaration. Ministers had accepted the 1943 Declaration as a basis for a better Constitution under which it would be possible for Ceylon to put forward her maximum war effort with the least difficulty. Finding the Donoughmore Constitution increasingly unworkable, the Ministers wanted a change for war purposes and accepted the 1943 Declaration with that in mind.

Since then the war situation had changed; and there had also been changes in the attitude of H.M.G. cf. the recent Declaration in regard to the future constitutional status of Burma.[2] Having before them this declaration made to Burma, the people of Ceylon felt that something at least as generous was their due.

In regard to the limitations which would have to be placed on full Dominion status, they felt that limitations accepted by agreement were infinitely preferable to restrictions imposed. His Majesty's Government should show to Ceylon the consideration they had shown to former enemies whose constitutional rehabilitation they were assisting.

Social conditions in Ceylon left much to be desired and the Executive Committee system was a serious handicap in dealing with them. The political leaders of Ceylon wanted self-Government in order that they might further the well-being and happiness of the people. They quite realised that in order best to secure the Island's future safety and advancement, it was necessary that Ceylon should be associated with the British Government. Future conflicts on the constitutional issue must be avoided, as progress was impossible without stable Government. Thus, *Mr. Senanayake* maintained, it was wiser to give Dominion status forthwith limited by agreements safeguarding defence and External Affairs.

In answer to a question by the Secretary of State whether Ceylon desired *full* Dominion status forthwith, *Mr. Senanayake* made it clear that he intended Dominion status restricted by agreement between H.M.G. and the Ceylon Government on Defence and External Affairs. He emphasized that these restrictions would be accepted *by agreement*. He would not object to a limitation as to External Affairs, provided that the term were defined to mean something which did not impinge on internal affairs. He would suggest that such agreements as Ceylon desired to reach with other members of the Commonwealth might be reached by Ceylon herself. Agreements outside the Commonwealth would of course be negotiated through the Home Government and agreements with Colonies through the Secretary of State for the Colonies.

The *Secretary of State* replied that this question of possible Dominion status for Ceylon was a matter of very high policy on which he was not empowered to take decisions himself. He would however submit Mr. Senanayake's views to his colleagues in the Cabinet for sympathetic consideration. *Mr. Senanayake* pointed out how disappointed Ceylon would be if Burma and India were offered what she was denied.

The *Secretary of State* then suggested that the meeting should turn to the second part of Mr. Senanayake's letter of the 16th August[3] containing his detailed comments on the Soulbury recommendations. He explained that it might be desirable for Mr. Senanayake to meet the Ceylon Department and the Legal Advisers subsequently in order to deal with a number of points of legal interpretation which arose. Mr. Senanayake agreed and it was arranged that a meeting should be held at 2.30 on

---

[2] See 273, note 3.                                                    [3] See 266.

Friday, 7th September, under Sir George Gater's Chairmanship.

Turning to the various points raised in part II of Mr. Senanayake's letter.

## (1) Franchise

Mr. Senanayake reiterated the point made in his letter that the present interpretation of the existing Order in Council operates contrary to the agreement reached with Sir Herbert Stanley. All he asked was that the proper effect should be given to the present law—a point on which the Soulbury Commission were in agreement.

## (2) Immigration

The difference he saw between paragraph 236 and paragraph 234 of the Report was that the word "normally" was in paragraph 236 but not in the latter. It was explained that the attention of the Commission had already been drawn to this point and that arrangements had been made for the word "normally" to be inserted where necessary, as this was in accordance with their intentions.

## (3) Representation

Mr. Senanayake explained in greater detail the point made in his letter that difficulties will arise if the Soulbury recommendation of 101 Members for the House of Representatives still operates when the population of Ceylon has materially increased. There is no objection to the figure of 101 applied to the present population, but with an expanding population, the system of weightage for area would be compromised.

## (4) Second chamber

Mr. Senanayake said that he personally was in favour of a Second Chamber. But the younger generation in Ceylon especially of the educated classes were all against it. He did not wish to force it through against the wishes of the people. If he took the proposal to Council, he would not obtain support: and indeed in the Board of Ministers only two other Members were in favour of the Second Chamber. What he would like to do would be to take the point to the Electorate, where he thought he could succeed. If, however, a Second Chamber were imposed, even the people would be against it.

He accepted the general make-up of the Second Chamber proposed by the Commission. The method of selection and the powers laid down were satisfactory. He was, however, not clear as to the definition of a "money bill", and it was arranged that this point should be cleared up in consultation with the Legal Advisers at the meeting to be held under Sir George Gater's Chairmanship.

As regards the term of office of Senators he thought that if the membership turned out to be, as was desirable, "elder statesmen" of about 50 years of age, the 9 year period was too long. At 35, the lower limit laid down by the Commission, members would be too inexperienced. He preferred the 6 year period. The Secretary of State suggested that the point might be further discussed at the subsequent meeting on Friday.

## (5) The first chamber

The point as regards the number of seats had already been discussed under (3), Representation. As regards the limitation of the 6 nominated seats to European and

Burgher members provided in the Commission's Report, *Mr. Senanayake* said that he would not mind such a provision in the Royal Instructions but did not want it in the Constitution, as it might prejudice the election of Europeans and Burghers in territorial Constituencies in the normal way. Moreover, there were great difficulties in interpreting the word "Burgher". The Secretary of State accepted Mr. Senanayake's point. (Note: The Secretary of State has now ruled that the phrase in question shall be omitted from the Commission's Report.)

## (6) *The executive*
*Mr. Senanayake* reiterated the point made in his letter that he would prefer, as a beginning at least, 10 Ministers and 10 Under Secretaries, it being left to the Ceylon Parliament to decide whether or not a variation of this figure was necessary.

## (7) *The governor-general*
A number of points arose which it was decided to defer to the Friday meeting when Legal Advice could be taken. These points are principally:—

(a) the interpretation of the phrase "discriminatory in character" in clause (ii) (d) of paragraph 332 of the Report.
(b) the revision of bills repealing or amending the Constitution.
(c) the Governor-General's powers to act *proprio motu* in a defence emergency.
(d) the definition of External Affairs.
(e) the question of extra-territorial legislation.
(f) the reference to the Supreme Court of a dispute whether a Bill has been properly reserved.
(g) the question of the Governor-General's power to impose expenditure in defence matters without the approval of the Ceylon Government.

As regards (e), extra-territorial legislation, *Mr. Senanayake* made clear that the Ceylon Government did not wish to legislate for other countries or other people. They wanted simply the power to legislate for their own people outside Ceylon territorial waters, for use, for example, in case of liquor smuggling, etc.

*Mr. Senanayake* developed the line taken in his letter that the whole system of giving the Governor-General special powers in certain circumstances is bound to lead to serious conflict with the Council. He stressed the difficulties of a system of diarchy under which subordinate officials would receive orders from both Ministers and from the Governor-General direct. It would be infinitely preferable, he suggested, that in the case of a conflict with the Ceylon Government, His Majesty's Government should take over the Government by Order in Council. The *Secretary of State* said that this difficult question should perhaps first be elucidated in discussion with the Legal Advisers at the Friday meeting.

As regards the reservation of coastal shipping, to which Mr. Senanayake objected, the *Secretary of State* said that he would consult the President of the Board of Trade as to whether a concession could be made on this point.

## (8) *The public services*
Referring to the Commission's recommendations that the system of "Donoughmore retirements" should be continued, *Mr. Senanayake* pointed out certain abuses that had arisen. The scheme of retirements provided that, in view of the change in terms

and conditions of service resultant on the new Constitution, an officer had an option to retire with compensation for loss of career at any time during the remainder of his service. Cases had been known in which officers had retired with compensation for loss of career in this manner, and then forthwith taken up posts in business, etc. or indeed elsewhere in the Colonial Service. The new Constitution should, he suggested contain some provision to prevent this abuse. It was pointed out that the Donoughmore and Soulbury Commissions had given careful consideration to this point, but that the latter had come to the conclusion that it was impossible to frame a restrictive provision which would not operate unfairly in the case of officers who after retirement with compensation for loss of career, might desire to take on *bona fide* employment in some sphere. There would be no objection to a provision designed to prevent the abuse, provided that it could be properly drafted so as to avoid injustices.

The *Secretary of State* decided that this, again, was a point to be referred to legal advice at the Friday meeting.

# 275    CO 54/986/6/2                                        5 Sept 1945
## [Soulbury Report]: minute by Trafford Smith on the proposed timetable for action

I have sent over the revised proof of the Soulbury Report to Mr. Muston for final printing to-day (September 5th). The procedure at present envisaged is, as I understand it, that set out in paragraph 14 of the Secretary of State's paper for the Colonial Affairs Committee C.I.(45)2, which reads:—

> "Mr. Senanayake will then (i.e. after his discussions with the Secretary of State) be free, if he wished to return to Ceylon taking with him for disclosure to his Ministers, but not for formal publication, copies of the Soulbury Commission's Report, and copies would also be made available to the India Office, for transmission to Field Marshal Lord Wavell who would disclose them to his Executive Council at the same time as Mr. Senanayake furnished them to the Board of Ministers. Thereafter I suggest that a period, say ten days, would be given for consideration and for the submission of any representations by the Government of India, and after a further period of ten days for the consideration of such representations, His Majesty's Government would then convey to Mr. Senanayake their approval of the lines of a new Constitution for Ceylon in the light of any decisions reached. The matter would then be debated in the Ceylon State Council. Arrangements would be made for the Soulbury Commission's Report to be published a few days before the debate."

The timetable is thus:—

*September 17th*
Date provisionally fixed for Mr. Senanayake to leave this country by air for Ceylon. As it is intended that he shall take with him for disclosure, in confidence, to the Board of Ministers copies of the Report, it will be necessary for final copies to be ready on that date, and I have arranged this with Mr. Muston. By this date, also, copies must

be in the hands of the India Office for transmission to the Viceroy, who is to consult his Executive Council in confidence at the same time and on the same basis as Mr. Senanayake consults the Ceylon Board of Ministers.

*September 23rd*
Latest date on which Mr. Senanayake must be back in Ceylon in order to carry the adjournment of the State Council. This is also the date on which he will give the copies he has taken with him to the Board of Ministers, and on which the Viceroy will simultaneously give copies to his Executive Council.

*October 7th*
End of the first period during which (in accordance with para 14 of the Secretary of State's paper for the Colonial Affairs Committee c.I.(45) 2 quoted above) the Ceylon Board of Ministers and the Viceroy's Executive Council are to consider the Report and the latter are to submit representations.

N.B. I have allowed a fortnight instead of ten days as stated in the Colonial Affairs Committee Paper referred to, as it is understood that the Secretary of State for India considers that the Executive Council might require rather longer than ten days to make their representations in view of the incidence of Hindu holidays.

*October 17th*
End of the second ten day period during which H.M.G. is to consider any representations from the Government of India, & to reach their decisions.

*October 18th* (say)
H.M.G. convey their decisions to Mr. Senanayake and at some date thereafter to be arranged the debate begins in the Ceylon State Council. The Report is to be published "a few days before the debate". Since simultaneous publication in the United Kingdom, Ceylon and India will be necessary, copies will have to be sent out to Ceylon and India (by air, if necessary) in time to arrive some. days before publication date.

# 276   CO 54/986/11, no 17                                    5 Sept 1945
[Soulbury Report]: letter from R N Gilchrist (India Office) to J B Sidebotham on the communication of the report to the viceroy.
*Enclosure*: India Office note for Lord Wavell

In continuation of our telephone conversation of yesterday evening, I enclose a draft of a note prepared for Lord Wavell. Will you kindly let us have your comments with the least possible delay as it is expected that he will be leaving for India in a few days?

The Cabinet decision[1] does not make it clear whether a summary of the report should be given to the Viceroy or not, and we should like your views on this point. If the answer is in the affirmative, the summary might be on the lines of the fourth and fifth paragraphs of the Cabinet paper C(45)2 of the 23rd August.

---

[1] Of 3 Sept, see 273, conclusion 3.

**Enclosure to 276: India Office note for Lord Wavell**

1. On the 29th May, it was agreed in discussion between Mr. Amery, Lord Wavell and Colonel Stanley that the Soulbury Report should be made available for Lord Wavell's personal information, and that he should ask his Council orally to frame such representations as they might wish to make on the basis of various alternative possibilities. These alternatives were not to disclose precisely the contents of the Report, but one of them was to be near enough to it to enable the Government of India to feel subsequently that they had had a full opportunity of representing their views.

2. In the interval between Lord Wavell's visits the Government of India have continued to insist that they should be given an opportunity to offer their views before H.M.G. reach their conclusions, and representatives of some minority communities, including Indians in Ceylon, have arrived in this country to place their views before the Secretary of State for the Colonies.

3. The visits of these delegates are the outcome of an invitation issued by Colonel Stanley to Mr. Senanayake, the Leader of the State Council in Ceylon, to come to this country for consultation before H.M.G. reached their conclusions. As soon as this invitation became known in Ceylon, some of the minority communities decided to send delegations to London. At the request of the Colonial Office, the Government of India were asked to refuse [priority][2] transit facilities to the Indian delegates on the ground that Colonel Stanley [had told them that he could see no purpose in their journey to London];[3] but the Viceroy did not think it was possible to deny such facilities as the invitation to Mr. Senanayake had led Indians to believe that the Ceylon ministers might be permitted to negotiate a settlement on which Indians would have no opportunity of expressing their views. In Lord Wavell's view refusal to see the Indians would cause suspicion in both Ceylon and India in respect to the attitude of the Colonial Office to the Indian case.

4. In consequence of these developments, H.M.G. have now reconsidered their attitude towards the manner in which the Government of India may be given an opportunity to express their views on the Soulbury recommendations. They have now decided that the text of the Soulbury Report should be made available to the Governor-General and his Executive Council confidentially at the same time as it becomes available to the members of the Board of Ministers in Ceylon. The Secretary of State for the Colonies will also adjust with the Secretary of State for India the period within which the Government of India will be asked to formulate their views on it.

5. The Secretary of State for the Colonies has also been authorised to enter into confidential discussions with Mr. Senanayake on the basis of the Soulbury Report on the understanding that it will be made clear that H.M.G. are not committed to the proposals, and that after the discussions have taken place the Secretary of State for the Colonies will again report to the Cabinet.

6. In the Declaration issued by the Colonial Office in 1943 on Constitutional Reform in Ceylon H.M.G. undertook to examine either by a Commission or Conference such detailed proposals as the Ceylon Ministers might in the meantime

---

[2] Words throughout in square brackets represent amendments made by the CO, see 277.

[3] At this point the original read 'would not see them'.

formulate, subject to the understanding that acceptance by H.M.G. of such proposals would depend, amongst other things, on approval by three-quarters of all Members of the State Council of Ceylon, excluding the Officers of State (i.e. the permanent officials) and the Speaker or other presiding Officer. The Cabinet have now agreed that the Secretary of State for the Colonies should have discretion to inform Mr. Senanayake that H.M.G. will not necessarily insist on holding to this three-quarters majority [since the present proposals are those of the Soulbury Commission formulation after consultation with all (including Minority) interests in Ceylon.]

7. The Cabinet have agreed that Lord Wavell should be acquainted with the general position in regard to the recommendations of the Soulbury Commission and the action proposed on them.

# 277   CO 54/986/11                                    5 Sept 1945
## [Soulbury Report]: minute by G E J Gent on the India Office note for Lord Wavell[1]

. . . Subject to the pencil amendments, we have no comments on this draft note, but the important point is what precisely the Cabinet intended should be told to Lord Wavell (see Conclusion No.3)[2] is uncertain. The India Office ask for our views on the point. My own interpretation of that conclusion is that Lord Wavell is to be told of

(1) the recommendations in the Soulbury Commission's Report;
(2) the action proposed on those recommendations;
(3) the general position as regards timetable of confidential disclosure to the Board of Ministers in Ceylon and the Viceroy's Executive Council and the timetable as to publication, etc.

In fact, this interpretation would mean that Lord Wavell should be taken into H.M.G.'s full confidence, and I do not myself see how we can expect him to react satisfactorily unless he is so treated. In that case, the simple thing to do is to give him personally and confidentially a copy of the Report with the necessary explanation of all the circumstances attending it.

But the Cabinet conclusion is obviously capable of another interpretation, to wit, that he should only be told the "general position" viz. that there is a Report in existence, that the Secretary of State's discussions with Mr. Senanayake are entirely without H.M.G. being committed to the recommendations in the Report and, finally, that he should be consulted as to the action proposed in the matter of eventual confidential disclosure to the Board of Ministers and to the Viceroy's Council simultaneously, and that thereafter H.M.G. will reach conclusions and eventually the Report will be published and a debate held in the State Council in Ceylon.

We need a direction from the Secretary of State as to which interpretation we are to adopt.

---

[1] See 276, enclosure.                                    [2] See 273.

**278**   CO 54/986/11, no 18                                    7 Sept 1945

[Soulbury Report]: minute by Mr Hall to Mr Attlee on consultation
with Lord Wavell

*Prime Minister*

At their meeting on the 3rd September[1] the Cabinet considered certain questions
arising out of the recommendations of the Soulbury Report in reference to the
Ceylon Constitution, and in Item (3) of their Conclusions "agreed that Lord Wavell
should be acquainted with the general position in regard to the recommendations of
the Soulbury Commission and the action proposed on them" (C.M.(45) 27th
Conclusions). The procedure in regard to the proposed consultation with the
Government of India on the Soulbury recommendations was discussed, and my
understanding of the general sense of the meeting was that the Cabinet approved the
procedure proposed in paragraph 11 (1) of C.P.(45)132 (Revise), of which I attach a
copy,[2] viz. the text of the Soulbury Report should be made available to the
Governor-General and his Executive Council confidentially, and at the same time to
the Board of Ministers in Ceylon. As however no reference is made to this matter in
the Conclusions, I seek your authority to carry out the procedure in question, which
means, of course, a confidential disclosure of the Soulbury Commission's recommendations to those two circles prior to general publication of the Report and its
presentation to Parliament as a Command Paper. Both in Ceylon and in India this
means a risk of course of leakage to a wider circle of people.

If this procedure is approved, the copies of the text of the report sent to Ceylon and
India for confidential consideration will be in *proof* form, and it has been ascertained
from the appropriate authorities of the House of Commons that no question of
breach of privilege will arise from this prior submission of *proof* copies notwithstanding the fact that the Report is subsequently to be laid as a Command Paper.

It will be clear from the above that, in acquainting Lord Wavell with the "general
position in regard to the recommendations of the Soulbury Commission and the
action proposed on them", as approved by the Cabinet, it will be necessary to inform
him of:—

(i)  the Commission's recommendations;
(ii) the procedure to be adopted in obtaining the views of the Ceylon Board of
Ministers and the Governor-General's Executive Council, prior to general publication and presentation to Parliament, in order that His Majesty's Government
might reach decisions on the Report and their decisions be made public at the
time of the publication of the Report.

I should be glad to have your authority to proceed in accordance with proposals
outlined above.[3]

---

[1] See 273.                                    [2] Not printed but see para 11 (1) in 270.
[3] Attlee consulted Sir E Bridges, the Cabinet secretary, on this issue, see 281.

**279**  CO 54/987/2, no 2  7 Sept 1945

[Soulbury Report]: CO record of a discussion between Sir G Gater and Mr Senanayake[1]

*Sir George Gater* opened the discussion by setting out the basis on which the talks were to be held. At the previous meeting between the Secretary of State and Mr. Senanayake,[2] the former had referred to a number of questions arising out of Mr. Senanayake's letter to the Secretary of State of the 16th August,[3] to the present meeting for further elucidation. The results of the meeting would, of course, be reported back to the Secretary of State.

*Mr. Senanayake* said that before proceeding to the Agenda, he would like to hand in a draft he had prepared of a possible Agreement between His Majesty's Government and the Government of Ceylon in conformity with his proposal to the Secretary of State that Ceylon should be granted Dominion status limited by an Agreement covering Defence and External Affairs.

*Sir George Gater* accepted the document for transmission to the Secretary of State. The meeting then proceeded to the Agenda.

1. *Definition of a "Money Bill" (see Section (4), Second Chamber, on page [43][4] of Mr Senanayake's letter)*

*Mr. Roberts-Wray* cited the definition contained in Section 1(2) of the Parliament Act, 1911. *Mr. Senanayake* pointed out that, while from his point of view this definition suitably adapted for Ceylon would be satisfactory, his understanding was that the definition was narrowly interpreted in England and the Speaker did not certify as a "Money Bill" any Bill involving also questions of administration. For the purposes of Ceylon it would be desirable to broaden the definition. It might also perhaps be possible to insert the words in the Ceylon constitution to cover the point he had in mind—i.e. that a Bill should not be excluded from the definition by reason only of the fact that it contained administrative clauses.

After some discussion of the point, it was decided to note the fact that Ceylon had special desiderata as regards the definition of a Money Bill, which should be taken into account when the new Constitutional Instruments came to be drafted.

2. *The term of office of members of the Senate (end of Section (4) on page [43] of the letter)*

The Soulbury Commission had recommended a nine-year term for each Senator, a third of the House retiring every three years. *Mr. Senanayake's* view was that this was too long, especially for the "elder Statesman" type of Senator who might join the Upper House at, say, fifty years of age or more. He preferred a six year life, a third retiring every two years. *Sir George Gater* said that this was essentially a political matter on which the meeting could take no final decision. *It was decided* to note Mr. Senanayake's views.

---

[1] Also present: A G Ranasinha, J H B Nihill, G E J Gent, K O Roberts-Wray (legal adviser, CO), J B Sidebotham, Trafford Smith.
[2] See 274.                                            [3] See 266.
[4] Numbers in square brackets represent the page numbers of Senanayake's letter as reproduced in this volume.

*Mr. Senanayake* observed as a matter of interest, that the procedure for the retirement of Senators on the lines of the Soulbury provisions was set out in the instruments of Indian Provincial Councils and some Australian States. It might be possible to adapt these provisions in drafting the Ceylon instruments.

3. *Interpretation of the phrase "discriminatory in character" in Clause (ii)(d) of paragraph 332 of the Soulbury Report (see Section (7), the Governor-General, on page [44] of the letter)*
*Mr. Senanayake* made two points: first, that the inclusion of this proviso was inconsistent with the 1943 Declaration: second, that he was anxious that the proviso should not be interpreted so as to limit Ceylon's freedom in imposing general duties, or to prohibit the imposition of such duties as, for example, Imperial Preference duties which might be interpreted as discriminatory.

As regards the 1943 Declaration, it was pointed out that Section 5(a) of that Declaration reserved Bills which relate to ". . . the trade and shipping of any part of the Commonwealth", and that the Declaration also reserved in Section 5 External Relations, in general terms. The recommendation in question of the Soulbury Commission (paragraph 332 (ii) (d)) had the effect of removing from Bills relating to External Affairs, which were, of course, already reserved, "any Bill relating solely to the prohibition or restriction of the importation of, or the imposition of import duties upon, any class of goods, provided that such legislation is not discriminatory in character". *Mr. Senanayake* argued that since the reservation in Section 5(a) of the 1943 Declaration referred to "the trade and shipping of *any part of the Commonwealth*", the Soulbury Commission's general reservation of discriminatory tariff legislation went beyond the 1943 Declaration. In answer to this contention, it was explained that the imposition of general duties would apparently have come under the External Affairs reservation if the Soulbury Commission had not specifically excepted such legislation from the definition of External Affairs. The inclusion of the proviso had the effect of re-inserting discriminatory tariff legislation only back into External Affairs. Thus the Soulbury proposals allowed, if anything, a wider freedom to Ceylon in tariff matters than would have been given by strict interpretation of the 1943 Declaration.

*Mr. Senanayake* pointed out that, none the less, he felt that he would have political difficulties in Council over this restriction if it were maintained.

*It was agreed* that an explanatory statement should be prepared for Mr. Senanayake's use, setting out the basis and dimensions of the restriction, and making the point that the Soulbury recommendation was more liberal than the 1943 Declaration. In order, as far as possible, to meet Mr. Senanayake, who had pointed out that his objection attached chiefly to the word "discriminatory" which had special significance in Ceylon, *it was agreed* that the possibility of drafting this provision of the Constitution in somewhat different terms, avoiding the word "discriminatory" and possibly including the expression "differential duties" should be explored.

4. *Reservation of Bills repealing or amending the Constitution—Clause (vi) of paragraph 332 of the Report (see Section (7) and also (ii) on pages [44–45] of the letter)* Mr. Senanayake at first maintained that the Soulbury recommendation in question had the effect of removing from the Ceylon Legislature a power it already

possesses—that of amending its own Constitution, but it was pointed out that under the present Constitution, while the Ceylon Legislature may debate and pass Bills amending the Constitution, they must be reserved by the Governor and cannot become law until His Majesty's assent has been signified. *Mr. Senanayake* accepted this but added that his main contention was the following: His Majesty's Government proposed to give Ceylon full self-government in matters of internal civil administration. In his view, the form of the Constitution, *except where the subjects reserved to His Majesty's Government were concerned*, was a matter of internal civil administration and should be within the competence of the Ceylon Government. Minorities would be safeguarded by the provision of the Ministers' Scheme (Article 10(2)(b)) requiring a two-thirds majority of the Council for amendment of the Constitution.

A general discussion followed in which the Colonial Office representatives endeavoured to make the point that, so long as the grant of a Constitution to Ceylon lay within the power of His Majesty's Government, and so long as such a Constitution granted by His Majesty's Government fell short of full Dominion status, the power of amending such Constitution logically remained with His Majesty's Government.

*Sir George Gater* summed up the discussion by expressing the doubt he felt whether there was any solution to the problem raised by Mr. Senanayake short of full Dominion status. Mr. Senanayake's request was in essence a political matter on which a decision by His Majesty's Government was required, rather than a point of drafting. He (Sir George Gater) could only report the sense of the discussion to the Secretary of State, and in any case the discussion had served the very useful object of elucidating Mr. Senanayake's point of view.

5. *The provision in the Soulbury recommendations that the Ceylon Parliament shall not make any law to alter the Constitution of any religious body except at the request of that religious body—paragraph 334 of the Report (see Section (7) on page [44] of the letter)*

*Mr. Senanayake* explained that if all religious bodies in Ceylon had been formally organised, he would have had no objection to the recommendation. But a number of the Buddhist sects in Ceylon had no clearly established organisation, and there might be doubt whether they came within the term "religious body". Having in mind this peculiarity of some of the Buddhist Temporalities he felt that it might make for smoother administration if the wording of the Ministers' Scheme "with the approval" of the governing authority of the religious body were retained, rather than "at the request" of the governing authority.

*Sir George Gater* thought that from the point of view of His Majesty's Government there would be no objection to meeting Mr. Senanayake's wishes. *Mr. Nihill* suggested that it might be possible to make the proviso applicable only to religious bodies incorporated by statute. This would meet Mr. Senanayake's point. *It was agreed* that this suggestion should be noted for further examination.

6. *The power of the Ceylon Government to legislate extraterritorially—paragraph 336 of the report (see the fourth paragraph on page [44] of the letter)*

*Mr. Senanayake* explained that what the Ceylon Government wanted was power to legislate for Ceylonese outside the territorial limits of Ceylon. He saw no reason why such powers should not be granted in matters which did not prejudice the

Commonwealth or "External Affairs". He cited the instance of ships smuggling outside the three-mile limit.

*Mr. Roberts-Wray* explained the existing legal position. He pointed out that the Soulbury Commission had been careful to provide that the existing situation as regards extraterritoriality should be maintained. The Ceylon Government already had certain powers to legislate for Ceylon citizens wherever they might be. For example, if the Ceylon law laid down that a Ceylonese should marry only one wife, any polygamous marriages by Ceylonese anywhere in the world would be illegal under international law as administered by British Courts, because capacity to marry was determined by the law of the party's domicile. In regard to smuggling outside the three-mile limit, he instanced the case of Croft v Dunphy (1933) A.C.156 in which the Privy Council had held that the power possessed by the Canadian Parliament to legislate "for the peace, order and good government" of Canada extended (before the Statute of Westminster) to enacting provisions operating outside the territorial limits of Canada in respect of smuggling vessels. By Section 3 of the Statute of Westminster it is provided that a Dominion has full power to legislate with extra-territorial effect, but a similar provision in an Order in Council for Ceylon would be *ultra vires* and would therefore be inoperative.

*Sir George Gater* said that this was another question on which it would be best for an explanatory note to be prepared by the Legal Advisers.

7. *Points arising out of the Defence sections of the Soulbury Report—paragraphs 349 to 358 of the Report (see pages [44–45] of the letter)*

(a) *The Governor-General's power to act on his own authority in Defence matters—(see (iv) on page [45] of the letter)*
*Mr. Senanayake* reiterated the principal argument set out in his letter—that the system of diarchy in Defence matters recommended by the Soulbury Commission was bound to prove most unsatisfactory in practice. In certain circumstances the ultimate authority in Defence matters must rest clearly with either His Majesty's Government or the Ceylon Government. It would be an impossible situation if a head of Department were in the position of receiving contradictory orders on the same matter from the Governor-General and from a Minister. In his (Mr. Senanayake's) view it would be greatly preferable to abandon the diarchy, and to provide that His Majesty in Council should have power to legislate for Ceylon in matters of Defence and External Affairs.

A general discussion followed in regard to Defence measures which His Majesty's Government might wish to carry out in Ceylon, but in which the Ceylon Government were not willing to co-operate. *Agreement was reached as follows:—*

I. *The case of a Defence measure which His Majesty's Government felt it was necessary to carry out in peace-time, quite apart from any question of emergency*
*It was agreed* to note for further examination of Mr. Senanayake's proposal that such cases could be covered by *ad hoc* Orders in Council, thus obviating the necessity for Governor-General's Ordinances as proposed by the Soulbury Commission. Ceylon Ministers, he said would be more willing to comply with an order received from the Imperial Government in this way than from the Governor-General, and the political difficulties which a Governor-General's

Ordinance would cause in Ceylon would largely be averted. *Mr. Roberts-Wray* pointed out that this procedure would have the disadvantage that rapid action in case of urgency would not be practicable, but it was thought that this difficulty was not likely to arise in practice.

II. *The case of a Defence measure which His Majesty's Government might wish to carry out in Ceylon in an emergency*

In this case, *it was agreed* to explore further the suggestion made by Mr. Senanayake that the Governor-General should be armed with powers, to be brought into force by proclamation in a Defence emergency, to take such steps as he might deem necessary on his own authority to deal with that emergency. Here again, the Soulbury provision would be avoided. *Mr. Roberts-Wray* explained that it was quite possible to have an Order in Council providing that, on proclamation in an emergency, the Governor would make Defence Regulations, etc.

III. *Breakdown of the Constitution*

Here again, *it was decided* to explore further Mr. Senanayake's suggestion that in the event of breakdown of the Constitution, His Majesty's Government should suspend the Constitution.

In regard to these three matters, *it was agreed* that the proposals should be considered further by the Legal Advisers in order to ascertain whether they provided a suitable means of safeguarding His Majesty's Government's position in regard to Defence as laid down in the 1943 Declaration, and also of meeting the political objections held by Mr. Senanayake to the Soulbury Commission's recommendations as regards Governor-General's Ordinances. In this connection it was pointed out that, in paragraph 360 (ii)(c), the Commission had already recommended that His Majesty in Council should have power to legislate for Ceylon by Order in Council in regard to External Affairs and Defence, and that this recommendation might on examination prove sufficient without the additional recommendation of Governor-General's Ordinances.

(b) *The removal of the Ceylon Defence Force and the Ceylon R.N.V.R. from the definition of Defence—pargraph 353 of the Report (see (v) of page [45] of the letter*

It was explained to Mr. Senanayake that the Commission's recommendation in this respect was in accordance with the 1943 Declaration, and that the Commission's intention was simply that His Majesty's Government should retain (1) operational control of the Ceylon Forces and (2) such control of training, etc, as might be necessary to enable those Forces to conform with the general scheme of Imperial Defence, leaving administration and all other matters connected with the Forces to the Ceylon Government. Mr. Senanayake said that he would have no objection to such an arrangement.

(c) *The Governor-General's power to impose a charge on Ceylon funds by Ordinance—paragraph 354 of the Report (see (vi) on page [46] of the letter)*: and

(d) *The power of the Governor-General to appoint or dismiss officers and to issue instructions to officers—paragraphs 354 and 355 of the Report (see (vii) on page [46] of the letter)*

*It was agreed* that these two points were covered in the general decision at (a) above.

8. *The definition of External Affairs—paragraph 357 of the Report (see paragraph (i) on page [45] of the letter)*
*Mr. Senanayake* said that he did not see what was wrong with the definition of External Affairs—Article 39 (1)(a) of the Ministers' Draft Constitution—"any matters other than a matter affecting internal administration . . . contained in any treaty between His Majesty and a Foreign State or Power, or in any agreement . . . between the Governor of Ceylon and the Government of any other part of His Majesty's dominions or of any Foreign State or Power". *Mr Roberts-Wray* pointed out that there was a large corpus of "External Affairs" outside the category of inter-Governmental Treaties and Agreements and that the definition thus broke down on this point. It was also observed that measures taken in the field of foreign affairs must, of necessity, often affect internal matters. *Mr. Senanayake* said that his only anxiety was that "External Affairs" should be defined so as not to give His Majesty's Government power to encroach on the Internal Affairs of Ceylon. *Sir George Gater* pointed out that the Commission's recommendation that External Affairs should not be defined, but that certain specified subjects should be excluded from the definition, gave His Majesty's Government in effect a discretion to decide in any case that might arise whether or not a particular matter should be regarded as External Affairs. He thought that the Ceylon Government should trust His Majesty's Government not to use this discretion unfairly. Mr. Senanayake's point of view was quite clear, however.

*It was agreed* to explore further the possibility of finding a form of words defining External Affairs which might meet Mr. Senanayake's point, and *Sir George Gater* undertook that the Colonial Office would examine sympathetically any draft Mr. Senanayake might put forward.

The meeting decided to defer the remaining items on the Agenda to a further meeting at 4.30 on Monday, September 10th, for which an Agenda would be circulated.

## 280   CAB 129/2, CP(45)164                                    10 Sept 1945

## 'Ceylon constitution': Cabinet memorandum by Mr Hall on the procedure for the disclosure of the Soulbury Report and advocating that HMG are not prepared to grant any form of dominion status

In the conclusions of their meeting on the 3rd September (C.M. (45) 27th Conclusions)[1] the Cabinet's approval is not recorded as covering the procedure set out in paragraph 11 (1) of the Report by the Chairman of the Colonial Affairs Committee (C.P. (45) 132 (Revise)) of the 31st August, which contemplated that on Mr. Senanayake's return to Ceylon he should take with him for confidential disclosure to his Ministers, but not for general publication, copies of the Soulbury Commission's Report, and that copies would also be made available to the India Office for transmission to Field-Marshal Lord Wavell, who would disclose them confidentially to his Executive Council at the same time as copies were given to the Ceylon Board of Ministers. Thereafter, a suitable period would be arranged between the Secretary of State for India and myself during which the Government of India

---
[1] See 273.

would formulate their conclusions, and after a further period of ten days, for the consideration of the Government of India's views, His Majesty's Government would then convey to Mr. Senanayake their approval of the lines of the new Constitution for Ceylon as they might then decide upon. The matter would at a convenient date thereafter be debated in the Ceylon State Council, and arrangements would be made for the Soulbury Commission's Report to be published a few days before the Debate.

2.  Mr. Senanayake feels it necessary to return to Ceylon on the 17th September for his political functions there, and I am anxious to let him know before he leaves what procedure is proposed. I desire, therefore, to have my colleagues' approval of the procedure set out above.

3.  In accordance with the decisions reached by the Cabinet at their meeting on the 3rd September, I have had a discussion with Mr. Senanayake on constitutional reform in Ceylon.[2] This discussion was entirely non-committal, but Mr. Senanayake made it plain that his particular purpose, now that he has come to England, is to request the grant to Ceylon of Dominion status, limited by agreement between the Ceylon Government and His Majesty's Government as to the control which His Majesty's Government would require to exercise in relation to Defence and External Affairs. This of course is not the purpose for which His Majesty's Government invited him here. The invitation was concerned with the proposals which would result from the Soulbury Commission's visit.

4.  The time is not ripe to concede any substantial constitutional advance on that adumbrated in the 1943 Declaration, and I shall leave Mr. Senanayake in no doubt, when he consults his ministerial colleagues on his return to Ceylon, that His Majesty's Government adhere to the 1943 Declaration as the basis for the grant of a new Constitution, and are not prepared to grant any form of Dominion status.

5.  I therefore seek my colleagues' approval of the procedure set out in paragraph 1 of this Memorandum.

---

[2] See 274.

# 281   CO 54/986/11, no 18A                                    10 Sept 1945
## [Soulbury Report]: minute from Sir E Bridges (Cabinet secretary) to Mr Attlee on the procedure for publication of the report

*Prime Minister*
1.  You asked me this morning whether anything was stated about publication of the Commission's Report when the Commission was set up.[1] The answer is that no undertaking was given.

2.  You asked why it was proposed to send out copies of the report before publication here to be made available to the Viceroy's Executive Council and to the Board of Ministers in Ceylon.

The reason for the proposed procedure is:—

(a)  that the Report concerns the treatment of minorities, of whom the most important is an Indian minority; and that it is felt that H.M. Government could

---

[1] See 278, note 3.

not reach a decision on the Report without knowing the views of the Government of India;

(b) that as a communication to the Viceroy's Council is attended by a risk of leakage the Board of Ministers in Ceylon should have the report also.

3. Discussion with the Colonial Office suggests that following procedure might be adopted:—

(a) H.M. Government should proceed with their consideration of the Report and should reach decisions in principle on it, subject always to the views of the Government of India on the minority problem;

(b) The Viceroy should be asked for his view on this point. If he feels it necessary to consult some of his colleagues he should do so at the latest possible moment before the Report and the Government's findings on it are published;

(c) The Government's findings on the Report and the Report itself should be published simultaneously. I am told that there will be no chance of getting the Report through the Ceylon Legislature by consent unless this is done.

I think that a procedure on these lines could be worked out, which would not be open to objection.

# 282   CO 54/987/2, no 3                                        10 Sept 1945
## [Soulbury Report]: CO record of a discussion between Sir G Gater and Mr Senanayake[1]

After *Sir George Gater* had opened the meeting, *Mr. Senanayake* said that, before proceeding to the Agenda, he would like to hand in drafts he had prepared of:—

(1) a proposed section of the new Constitution dealing with the reservation of Bills amending the Constitution, and
(2) a definition of External Affairs.

He trusted that, on examination, these drafts would be found to meet the points raised at the previous meeting.

*Sir George Gater* said that the Colonial Office would give careful consideration to these drafts. *Mr. Roberts Wray* pointed out that, if the new Constitution did not contain a general power of the Governor-General to reserve Bills, it would be difficult to consider this question of reservation of the power to amend the Constitution without knowing the general framework of the Constitution as a whole.

*Sir George Gater* said that the essential point to be noted by the meeting remained that determined at the previous meeting, i.e. Mr. Senanayake's desire that His Majesty's Government's power to amend the Constitution should be limited only to the reserved sections, and that the Ceylon Government should have unrestricted power to amend other parts of the Constitution. *Mr. Senanayake* explained that he had cited the Southern Rhodesia Constitution as containing provisions similar to those he had in mind, but Mr. Roberts Wray pointed out that, even in the case of

---

[1] This meeting continued the discussion on 7 Sept, see 279. With the exception of Gent, the same personnel were present.

those parts of the Southern Rhodesia Constitution which the Southern Rhodesia Government could amend of their own initiative, the Bill had still to be reserved.

After some discussion *Mr. Senanayake* agreed that Southern Rhodesia was not a precedent for the type of provision which he had in mind. *Mr. Nihill* observed that, since the Ceylon Government may now of their own initiative introduce Bills amending any part of the Ceylon Constitution, subject to reservation when the Bill was submitted to the Governor, Ceylon under its existing Constitution was in this respect better off than Southern Rhodesia.

*It was decided* that the meeting should take careful note of Mr. Senanayake's point in order to examine whether it can be met in any way.

The meeting then proceeded to the AGENDA.

1. *The reservation of shipping (see (a) of page [46]² of Mr. Senanayake's letter and Article 40(d) of SP XIV)—paragraph 338 of the Soulbury Report*
*Sir George Gater* said that the Colonial Office quite understood Mr. Senanayake's point of view that there was no reason why Ceylon should not have full control of her own shipping services. He understood that enquiries had been made of the Ministry of War Transport to ascertain their views.

*Mr. Trafford Smith* said that he had been in touch with Major General Money of the Ministry of War Transport on that point. The latter had explained that the Ministry of War Transport's policy was that free movement of shipping in all parts of the world should be encouraged as far as possible, and they were anxious primarily to safeguard the rights of shipping of other parts of the Commonwealth to use Ceylon ports without restriction. Provided that complete reciprocity between Ceylon and other parts of the Commonwealth were maintained, there appeared to be no objection to Ceylon having full control of her own shipping services.

*Mr. Senanayake* thought that Ceylon would undoubtedly have no wish to place restrictions on complete reciprocity, and expressed the hope that, this being so, it would be found possible to meet his point.

2. *The reference to the Supreme Court of Disputes whether a Bill has been properly reserved (see (b) on page [46] of the letter and Article 41(1) of SP XIV)—paragraph 339 of the Report*
*Mr. Senanayake* said that in his view, under the Soulbury Recommendation which left the Governor-General's power to reserve Bills within his unfettered discretion, with no appeal, the Governor-General was virtually in the position of acting as Judge in his own case. He (Mr. Senanayake) thought that there should be some outside authority to whom disputes on the question of proper reservation could be referred, and the Supreme Court seemed to be the proper body, though he would have no objection to the Privy Council.

*Mr. Nihill* explained that if the Soulbury Constitution were adopted, but a power of reference to the Supreme Court in cases of disputes as to proper reservation were included, the Supreme Court would be put in an extremely difficult position, as the question of proper reservation was largely a political one, not a question of fact or law. He did not see, moreover, how the Supreme Court would arrive at a decision. In

---

² See 266. Numbers in square brackets represent the page numbers of Senanayake's letter as reproduced in this volume.

the case of many Bills it might be necessary for the Court to take evidence. Clearly such a procedure applied to the Governor-General's exercise of his discretion would be impracticable. It would also be most unfortunate if the Supreme Court were in any way brought into politics, as would be inevitable if they were asked to adjudicate on disputes as to proper reservation.

*Mr. Roberts Wray* agreed. He said that the question of proper reservation was not one of law but a question of constitutional propriety depending on the practice and precedents established in the course of time.

*Sir George Gater* thought that in most instances the Governor would have to reach a decision whether or not to reserve at short notice, and there could be no question of a long dispute lasting possibly for a period of weeks during which the question of proper reservation was decided. As no grounds for compromise appeared to have emerged from the discussion, he very much hoped that since, in any case, the contingency in question was extremely remote, Mr. Senanayake would agree to drop the point.

*Mr. Senanayake* said that his only anxiety was to prevent certain abuses of the Governor-General's powers which had occured in the past. He agreed that with the political development of Ceylon it would hardly be possible for such abuses to take place in present conditions, and since the possibility was so remote, he would agree to drop the point.

## 3. *The Public Services (Section (8) on page [46] of the letter)*

*(a) The Powers of the Public Services Commission—paragraph 379 of the Report and Articles 64 and 36 of SP XIV*
On this point *it was agreed* that there was no substantial difference of opinion between Mr. Senanayake and the Soulbury Commission as to the proper exercise of the powers of the Public Services Commission. *Mr. Senanayake* explained that he had merely wished to point out that what the Commission had written in paragraph 379 of the Report indicated a certain misunderstanding of the terms of Article 64 of the Ministers' Scheme, which was designed to be read in conjunction with Article 36.

*(b) The proposed administration of the Public Services by the Ministry of Finance—paragraph 383 of the Report*
In his letter, *Mr. Senanayake* had made the point that since under the new Constitution a Prime Minister of Ceylon would not be First Lord of the Treasury, as in the United Kingdom, it was not logical that the Permanent Secretary of the Ministry of Finance should be Head of the Public Services on the analogy of the system in the United Kingdom.

*Sir George Gater accepted* Mr. Senanayake's point. The Commission had, in any case, not made a definite recommendation on the subject, but had merely put forward the suggestion that the United Kingdom model might be followed.

*(c) Abuse of the system of Donoughmore retirements—paragraph 372 of the Report*
*Sir George Gater* said that he had given much thought to the point raised by Mr. Senanayake in his letter, and in his view the problem could be divided into two aspects:—

(1) The position of Officers appointed before the publication of the Donoughmore Report (17th July 1928),

(2) the position of Officers appointed subsequent to the publication of the Donoughmore Report and before the publication of the Soulbury Report.

As regards (1), a commitment with no limitation of time had been entered into in regard to pre-Donoughmore Officers, and it would be difficult to vary this commitment in any way without a breach of faith.

*It was agreed* that there could be no question of altering the retirement terms in force for Officers appointed before the publication of the Donoughmore Report.

As regards (2), the Soulbury Commission had proposed (in para 370) a limit of 3 years during which Officers were to make up their minds whether or not they wished to retire under the special arrangement. If this period were reduced, there would be, of course, a risk of a large number of Officers retiring at once, with consequent embarrassment to the Ceylon Government.

*Mr. Senanayake* said that he had no wish that a large number of Officers should retire. On the contrary, it was important for Ceylon to retain many of the Officers concerned. He was only anxious that abuses of the kind that had occurred in the past should not take place in the future. As regards the time limit, he thought the best compromise was to split the difference and allow a 2 year period for Officers to make up their minds.

He drew attention to the Ceylon (State Council) Amending Order of 1934 which had brought certain classes of Officers appointed by agreement within the Donough-more retirement terms. He fully realised that this privilege could not be taken away from them now, but he was anxious that Officers appointed on agreement should not be included in the category of Officers eligible for "Soulbury retirements".

*Sir George Gater* said that this point could no doubt be cleared up in the drafting of the Instruments.

*Mr. Senanayake* then went on to cite various cases of abuses of the Donoughmore Retirement Scheme in which Officers had accepted the special terms giving compensation for loss of career, only to take up immediately further employment elsewhere. In fact, these Officers had obtained compensation for loss of career from Ceylon and then continued their careers elsewhere. He cited the cases of Messrs. Spicer, Newnham and Strong.

*Sir George Gater* said that he thought it necessary to make a distinction between Officers who retired in the full knowledge that they were to obtain further employment forthwith, and Officers who might quite legitimately after a period of retirement wish to undertake some paid post. The former case would ordinarily be regarded as a transfer; and he quite agreed that the application of Donoughmore retirement terms to a transfer was unjustified. The Colonial Office would have to bear this point carefully in mind in future cases which might possibly be criticised on this ground. He nevertheless thought that it was difficult to establish in precise terms the distinction between what might be described as "open" and "collusive" cases.

*Mr. Senanayake* suggested that it might help if the Ceylon Government were consulted in the case of all contemplated transfers of Ceylon Officers. *Sir George Gater* undertook that the Colonial Office would consider whether means could be found of tightening up the procedures so as to avoid abuses as far as possible.

*Mr. Senanayake* then went on to say that he felt particularly strongly about the abuse of Donoughmore retirement terms by Ceylonese on whose training, etc., the

Ceylon Government had spent considerable sums of money. He very much hoped that it would be possible to exclude such Officers from the special retirement terms.

*Indian franchise in Ceylon*
*Mr. Senanayake* said that, before leaving, he would like to raise a point which had given him much concern for some years—the administration of the existing law in regard to the franchise (Articles 7, 8 and 9 of the Ceylon (State Council Elections) Order in Council 1931). As was brought out in paragraphs 202 to 222 of the Soulbury Report, the original recommendations of the Donoughmore Commission in regard to the franchise had been modified by agreement between the then Governor, Sir Herbert Stanley and the Secretary of State, for the reason that the Donoughmore recommendation that the franchise of Indian immigrants should depend solely on the condition of 5 year's residence in the island would have precluded acceptance of the Donoughmore Constitution by the former Legislative Council. In the event, the present franchise provisions, i.e. that an applicant may qualify for the franchise

(i)   by domicile,
(ii)  by literacy, property and income qualifications, and
(iii) by the "certificate of permanent settlement"

were a variation from the Donoughmore recommendations which had been agreed upon between Sir Herbert Stanley and the Secretary of State.

He (*Mr. Senanayake*) had collaborated with Sir Herbert Stanley at the time of the introduction of the Donoughmore Constitution in securing the acceptance of these franchise terms by the Kandyans, in whose territory most of the Indian labourers live. As the franchise provisions had been interpreted in the past, however, a far larger number of Indians had been allowed to qualify for the franchise than was proper according to the strict interpretation of the law, and he felt very strongly that he had let the Kandyans down in persuading them to accept franchise provisions which had resulted in their vote being counter-balanced by a disproportionately high Indian immigrant vote. The fault lay, not in the provisions of the law, but in the way they were administered.

*Sir George Gater* wished to be quite clear that Mr. Senanayake was referring to the administration of the Election Law under the present Donoughmore Constitution, and not to the Soulbury recommendations. *Mr. Senanayake* agreed, but again emphasised that the unfortunate effect of his having sponsored the present franchise provisions on the balance of voting in the Kandyan areas had been on his conscience for some time, and he felt that he should take the present opportunity of making his position clear and of entering a plea that the future operation of the existing franchise law, until such time as it came to be changed under the new Constitution, should be more closely controlled, so that the provisions of the Law were strictly adhered to.

*Mr. Nihill* explained that he, as Legal Secretary, was responsible for the conduct of elections and that the provisions of the Order in Council referred to by *Mr. Senanayake* had given considerable trouble to his Department, owing to the difficulty of administering them. He accepted the contention that in the early years of the Donoughmore Constitution too many Indians had been admitted to the franchise, but pointed out that the recent very considerable drop in the number of Indians registered showed that the measures his Department had been taking to tighten up the procedure had been effective. The Registration Officers had in Article 7 an extremely difficult Article to administer and it must be borne in mind that Indian interests in Ceylon constantly maintained that the Article was being administered to their detriment.

A general discussion followed in which *Mr. Senanayake* and *Mr. Nihill* made clear the great difficulties surrounding the interpretation and administration of the franchise articles of the Order in Council.

*Sir George Gater* suggested that the matter might be summed up as follows:—

(1) The Law as it stood, although difficult to administer, was not objectionable in principle: and in any case its amendment at the present stage was impracticable on account of the opposition that would be forthcoming from India.
(2) Sir Robert Drayton's interpretation of the Law (the text of which interpretation was not available) did not appear to be contested.
(3) The instructions given to Registration Officers attempted to set out the way in which the interpretation should be administered as clearly as possible: but
(4) The administration of these instructions nevertheless gave difficulty and it was here that the cause for complaint arose.

Before the question could be gone into properly it would be necessary to obtain copies of the documents in question, but it did not appear that very much could be done at present other than to consider all possible means of tightening up the procedure of administration. *Mr. Nihill* said that he had repeatedly drawn the attention of the Registration Officers to the importance of strict compliance with the terms of the Order in Council, the interpretation by Sir Robert Drayton, and the instructions issued to them: and he felt sure that, during the registration now in progress, an honest attempt was being made to administer the Order in Council fairly. But while Article 7 remained as it did there would always be complaints.

*Mr. Senanayake* said that he would have liked to have asked the Secretary of State to come to an agreement with him on this point and to take some action to have it put right. He understood, however, the difficulties which a move by the Secretary of State in the present situation would create, especially vis à vis the Tamils in Ceylon and the Government of India. He would not wish, therefore, that the Secretary of State should take any action but would content himself with the assurance that everything possible was being done by the Legal Secretary to enforce strict adherence to the Law.

**283**  CO 54/986/11, no 19, CM 30(45)3                            11 Sept 1945
'Ceylon': Cabinet conclusions on the publication of the Soulbury Report and dominion status

At their meeting on the 3rd September[1] the Cabinet had authorised the Secretary of State for the Colonies to enter into confidential discussions with Mr. Senanayake on the basis of the Soulbury Report.

The Cabinet now had before them a Memorandum by the Secretary of State for the Colonies (C.P.(45) 164)[2] proposing that on Mr. Senanayake's return to Ceylon he

---

[1] See 273.                                                        [2] See 280.

should take with him for confidential disclosure to his Ministers, but not for general publication, copies of the Soulbury Report, and that copies should also be made available to the India Office in order that the Governor-General might disclose them confidentially to his Executive Council at the same time as copies were given to the Ceylon Board of Ministers.

*The Secretary of State for the Colonies* said that he had nearly completed his discussions with Mr. Senanayake who would be leaving for Ceylon on the 17th September. It seemed clear that the proposals in the Soulbury Report would have a better chance of acceptance if it were shown confidentially to the Ceylon Board of Ministers before its publication, while, so far as the Government of India was concerned, a definite pledge had been given by his predecessor that in view of their interest in minorities in Ceylon, they would have an opportunity of considering the proposals before His Majesty's Government accepted them.

In the course of the discussions which had taken place Mr. Senanayake had made it plain that the primary purpose of his visit was to request the grant to Ceylon of Dominion status. This was not the purpose for which he had been invited to come to this country and it was proposed to make it clear to him that His Majesty's Government adhered to the 1943 Declaration as the basis for the grant of a new constitution and were not prepared to grant any form of Dominion status.

In discussion the view was expressed that if the Soulbury Report were shown confidentially to the Ceylon Board of Ministers and the Governor-General's Executive Council, its contents would be bound to leak out. For this reason it was felt that it would be better to publish the report simultaneously in this country, in Ceylon and in India. The publication of the Report did not mean that its recommendations had been accepted by His Majesty's Government and would not be inconsistent with the pledge that the Government of India would be given time to formulate their conclusions before His Majesty's Government reached a final decision.

With regard to the question of Dominion status for Ceylon, it was pointed out that, while there could be no question of accepting the claim put forward by Mr. Senanayake, it would be undesirable to make any pronouncement at all on this matter before the Cabinet had considered the recommendations in the Soulbury Report. In any event it did not lie with His Majesty's Government to grant or withhold Dominion status.

The Cabinet:—

(1) Invited the Secretary of State for the Colonies to arrange that the Soulbury Report should be published simultaneously in this country, in Ceylon and in India on the date on which copies were given to the Ceylon Board of Ministers and the Governor-General's Executive Council.

(2) Agreed that the Secretary of State for the Colonies should refrain from making any statement with regard to Dominion status for Ceylon in the course of his discussions with Mr. Senanayake.

**284**   CO 54/987/1, no 62                                    11 Sept 1945

[Soulbury Report]: minute by C H Thornley[1] on a discussion between
Mr Hall and Mr Creech Jones and G G Ponnambalam

Mr. Ponnambalam called yesterday by arrangement to see the Secretary of State and
Mr. Creech Jones. He remained for half an hour.

He started by saying that he had not come to make any representations in
connection with the Soulbury Report. He did feel it necessary to say that great
surprise was caused to members of the minority groups in Ceylon when the
announcement was made that H.M.G. had invited Mr. Senanayake, in his capacity as
Leader of the State Council, to come to England for consultations with the Secretary
of State *before H.M.G. reached decisions in the matter of constitutional reform*. It
was these last words which I have [italicised] which gave rise to anxiety in the
minority groups. He explained that there could be no possible objection to Mr.
Senanayake being consulted in his capacity as Leader of the State Council. The
Secretary of State intervened at this point to point out that this was previously what
his predecessor had in mind when issuing his invitation to Mr. Senanayake to come.
Mr. Ponnambalam said that he quite appreciated this, but he and his friends could
not close their eyes to the fact that Mr. Senanayake had no mandate whatsoever to
represent the views of all five groups in Ceylon, and could not be expected in the
course of these consultations to put forward views held by the minority groups with
which he was not in sympathy. On the other hand it was reasonable to expect that
H.M.G. would be influenced by the views he would put forward which would in fact
be the views only of the Sinhalese who were in a numerical majority in the Island.
The Secretary of State intervened to say that this point would not, of course, be
overlooked and surely Mr. Ponnambalam and his friends could trust H.M.G. to take
the fact properly into account in reaching their decisions. Mr. Ponnambalam quickly
replied that he did not wish to be misunderstood as in any way showing any lack of
confidence in the faith of H.M.G. in this matter. He did, however, stress that it was
very difficult for his friends and himself to appreciate why H.M.G. had invited the one
man who instigated and led the boycott by the Board of Ministers of the Soulbury
Commission—and the one man who desired in the first place to restrict the terms of
reference of the Commission to an examination of a constitutional scheme prepared
by the Board of Ministers without any consideration of the views held by the
minorities. He maintained that Mr. Senanayake's whole purpose in adopting this
attitude was to prevent the Soulbury Commission hearing the views of the
considerable minority groups in the Island.

At this point Mr. Creech Jones enquired whether Mr. Ponnambalam represented
the four minority groups. He replied that in theory he did not; he did, however, hold
a mandate from about 1½ million Tamils and thought that in fact correspondence
was on record here which showed that in the Governor's opinion the views which he
would put forward could be generally accepted as the views of all the minorities.

Mr. Ponnambalam then went on to express the view that the greatest obstacle to
progress in any democratic form of Government was the fact that during the past 15
years no party alignments have emerged in Ceylon. In fact race, religion and cast

---

[1] Private secretary to Mr. Hall.

[sic] continued to dominate the political scene. The minorities strongly favoured the development of party politics as we understand them in this country, the Sinhalese on the other hand strongly favoured the continuation of communal groupings which assured for them a preponderant majority in the State Council. The Secretary of State intervened to suggest that now that they had adult suffrage in Ceylon surely the remedy was in their own hands. Mr. Ponnambalam, while not opposing adult franchise pointed out that it did in fact operate heavily in favour of the racial group in a numerical majority. He pointed out that under the restrictive franchise that held the field between 1834 and 1931 the Sinhalese never on any single occasion held more than 50% of the seats in the State Council; since, however, communal representation had given way to adult suffrage in 1931 the Sinhalese had always, and under the present constitution would continue, to have a preponderant majority in the Council.

Both the Secretary of State and Mr. Creech Jones enquired how, in view of the fact that Mr. Ponnambalam approved of adult suffrage, he thought that the position could be remedied to the advantage of the minority groups. He replied that in his view the only way would be by weighting the representation of the minorities at the centre on some such lines as were proposed by Lord Wavell for meeting the Moslem claims in India. The Secretary of State pointed out that it was the Moslems themselves in India who had turned down this very suggestion which he had mentioned. Mr. Ponnambalam agreed, but added that this was due, in his view, solely to Mr. Jinna's [sic] claim that the Moslems would insist on having their own nominees in the seats reserved for them on the Viceroy's Executive Council. This he realised was an impossible condition owing to the considerable numbers of Moslems already residing in the Congress provinces whom the Moslem League did not in fact represent.

At this point the Secretary of State was compelled to bring the discussion to a close as he had another engagement, and I understand that Mr. Creech Jones had some further discussion with Mr. Ponnambalam before he left. Perhaps he will be good enough to add a note of what transpired during this further conversation.[2]

---

[2] Creech Jones minuted (11 Sept): 'I had only a few further words with Mr. Ponnambalam—they got nowhere & I promised to have another chat with him when I will make a note.'

## 285    CO 54/987/2, no 4                                        12 Sept 1945
## [Soulbury Report]: minute by C H Thornley on a discussion between Mr Hall and Mr Senanayake

Mr. Senanayake called to see the Secretary of State at 6.15 p.m. today. I was present during the talk which followed.

Mr. Hall said how much he had enjoyed the dinner which Mr. Senanayake gave him earlier in the week and he did hope that Mr. Senanayake himself had had an enjoyable time while he was over here. In replying that he had certainly done so, Mr. Senanayake stressed the particular interest with which he had studied our methods of handling our agricultural problems over here. He had been greatly struck with the excellent and effective relations which existed between Government on the one hand

and farmers on the other. He remarked that Ceylon had a great deal to learn in this respect.

The Secretary of State mentioned that he hoped Mr. Senanayake was satisfied with the reply which he had sent yesterday to his letter about the future of the tea and rubber industries in Ceylon. Mr. Senanayake thanked the Secretary of State for his letter and said that what the people of Ceylon really hoped for was some undertaking that they would have an assured market for their tea and rubber unhampered by controls before the present conditions of short supplies entirely disappeared. During the war the farmers had worked hard and produced much, but the necessary war-time controls had naturally operated to restrict profits. They did hope that there would be a further period during which they could sell all their produce under short supply conditions and reap the profits unrestricted by controls.

The Secretary of State said he hoped that there was no ambiguity about the discussion which they had had together after dinner last Monday. Mr. Senanayake said that his great hope was that some form of constitution would be settled which would help them to improve conditions in Ceylon and which would at the same time save Ceylon from any sort of agitation with H.M.G. in this country. He was entirely clear that the future prosperity of Ceylon depended absolutely on the maintenance of the closest possible ties with the United Kingdom. There were, of course, some who were thinking of the future in terms of association with India. He was not one of those.

The Secretary of State enquired whether he did not think that reforms on the lines proposed by the Soulbury Commission would meet with these desiderata. Mr. Senanayake was dubious; he emphasised that it would have been very much easier to put across in Ceylon the recommendations of the Soulbury Commission under war-time conditions and went on to explain that Ceylon had gone through a very difficult and trying period after the last war. He gave a short account of this unhappy period for Ceylon.

The Secretary of State then said that he thought he ought to make it clear that there was no possibility of reaching Dominion status for some time. Mr. Senanayake repeated that what he and his people desired was to be put in a position to improve conditions in Ceylon for themselves. He pointed out that the words "Dominion status" made a very strong appeal to his people—so much so that any suggestion that the attainment of such status was still far distant would cause despair in the Island. Given the facts, as he knew them, that on the one hand there was no desire on the part of H.M.G. to hamper progress in Ceylon, and on the other that there was no general desire in Ceylon to part company with H.M.G. in this country, he did not think that it should be a difficult matter to draw up a suitable constitution for them. He did not think that it would be reasonable now, after the victorious conclusion of the present war when surely it was not beyond the wit of men to ensure that peace should not again be disturbed within the next 50 years or so, to make our defence needs the major consideration in planning for the future prosperity of Ceylon. He thought that any suggestion that Dominion status must necessarily be withheld from Ceylon for a long period because of our defence requirements in the Far East would undermine the people's belief in the sincerity of H.M.G.

The Secretary of State then suggested that the last few years had been years of prosperity for Ceylon. Mr. Senanayake replied that this was so for some of the people, but definitely not so for others. He explained that, owing largely to overpopulation, living conditions for many of the people had in fact progressively declined. In some places the death rate was higher than the birth rate. For instance, in one Moorish village which he had occasion to visit not so very long ago, he was shocked to find that 8 out of every 10 expectant mothers died in childbirth. He repeated yet again that what Ceylon wanted was the opportunity now themselves to plan for their own prosperity. They feel at present frustrated. He asserted that they had not made any progress under the Donoughmore Constitution. Dominion status was the ideal; he would not, however, press for this but emphasised that the recommendations of the Soulbury Commission as they now stand *would not* be acceptable in Ceylon.

The Secretary of State then reverted to his discussion with Mr. Senanayake after dinner last Monday and said that he would not wish Mr. Senanayake to return to Ceylon with any idea that either H.M.G. or indeed he himself had held out any promise that Dominion status would now or at any time be given to Ceylon. He hoped that Mr. Senanayake was under no impression from anything which he might have said on that occasion that he himself had any idea in his mind that Dominion status would be granted now or at any stated time in the future. Mr. Senanayake replied that he would regard nothing which had been said to him over here as in any way binding upon the Secretary of State or H.M.G. He had been invited over here for private conversations with the Secretary of State. He would always regard everything which had been said during the course of those conversations as private. He did confess to having had some hope after that party but fully understood that no promise or commitment of any kind had been made either by the Secretary of State personally or on behalf of H.M.G.

The Secretary of State then closed the interview with an invitation to Mr. Senanayake to dine with him on Tuesday evening, which he understood would be the eve of his departure, and said that he was proposing to invite Lord Soulbury also as a guest. He thought that this would be better than inviting Lord Soulbury to be present at the final talks which, as now arranged, he was to have with Mr. Senanayake on Monday afternoon. Mr. Senanayake agreed and said that he would be delighted to accept the Secretary of State's invitation.

# 286   CO 54/986/6/2, no 118                        12 Sept 1945
[Soulbury Report]: outward unnumbered telegram from Mr Hall to Sir H Moore on the publication of the Soulbury Report

My Secret and Personal telegram of 6th September.

At my first meeting with Senanayake he pressed for grant to Ceylon of some form of Dominion status limited by agreements in respect of Defence and External Affairs. This request has now been considered by H.M. Government who have decided that while there can be no question of accepting claim now put forward by person named it is undesirable that any statement with regard to Dominion status should be made by me in my discussions with him.

2.  At the same time H.M. Government considered the question of publication of the Report, having regard to the need for giving Senanayake an opportunity to consult his Ministerial colleagues in Ceylon and of giving the Government of India the promised opportunity of expressing their views also on the Report before H.M.

Government's decision on the recommendations of the Report are made known. His Majesty's Government has decided that in view of the grave risk (which Senanayake has himself emphasised in discussion with me) of leakage of the contents of the Report before its presentation to Parliament, which would create a situation highly embarrassing to H.M. Government, it is essential that the Report should be published simultaneously in United Kingdom, Ceylon and India, on the date on which copies are given to the Ceylon Board of Ministers and the Governor-General's Executive Council. Separate telegram will be sent regarding publication date but final printing off here likely to take three weeks to which must be added period of conveyance to Ceylon and India by air.

3. Publication of the Report would not (repeat not) (a) mean that H.M. Government had accepted its recommendations (b) be inconsistent with promise that Government of India would be given time to formulate their conclusions before H.M. Government reached final decisions.

4. I fully appreciate that this decision may not be welcome to Senanayake for the reasons explained in your Secret and Personal telegram of the 21st May,[1] and before informing him of them at my next meeting with him on Monday 17th September, I should be grateful for best further estimate you can make of likely effect of these decisions on the political situation in Ceylon.

---

[1] See 245.

## 287  CO 54/987/2, no 5                                          13 Sept 1945
## [Soulbury Report]: note by Sir G Gater of an interview with Mr Senanayake

Mr. Senanayake came to see me this morning quite unexpectedly without previous notice. He said that the purpose of his visit was to thank me and all those in the Colonial Office who had taken so much trouble to make suitable arrangements for him during his stay. He was most grateful and had greatly enjoyed his visit. I replied in appropriate terms and said that I was hoping to see him again at the meeting on Monday, and that the Secretary of State had invited me to a farewell dinner which he was giving to Mr. Senanayake on Tuesday evening.

Mr. Senanayake, in the course of conversation, asked whether it would be possible for him to have a record of the discussions which had taken place. I said that I would note his wishes and would report them to the Secretary of State who would no doubt let him know his decision on Monday. Nearly the whole of the rest of the conversation, which lasted half an hour, was spent in Mr. Senanayake giving me once more an account of his past life from the days when he left school at the age of 17. He stressed the fact that throughout his political life he had never been opposed in his constituency and that he had been elected Leader without opposition. He was hoping to crown his career by achieving a settlement of Ceylon's constitutional problems. He could then retire in good heart. He very strongly stressed his view that Ceylon's future was linked with the United Kingdom and that it was in Ceylon's interest that this should be so. There were some people in Ceylon who did not agree with him. He himself was regarded as an anti-Indian, but this was not true. He was most appreciative of the benefits of Indian culture in Ceylon. He wished to be friendly with

Indians but he would not be dominated by them. At the end of his confession of faith I asked him whether there was anything else we could do for him. He then replied that he understood that his conversations here were confidential and that he could be relied upon to preserve the confidence reposed in him. It would, however, be helpful to him to know what exactly he would be at liberty to say on his return to Ceylon. Could he, for instance, refer to the representations that he had made to the Secretary of State? I indicated that consideration would be given to his request on this point between now and Monday's meeting.

The interview terminated in the most friendly fashion, Mr. Senanayake expressing the hope that he might be able to welcome me in his own home in Ceylon. I took the opportunity, on my side, to express the hope that even if disagreements should arise between H.M.G. and Ceylon in the future, the friendship established between Mr. Senanayake and us in the Colonial Office might remain unaffected. He most cordially agreed.

## **288**  CO 54/987/2, no 66                                      13 Sept 1945
## [Soulbury Report]: note by Sir G Gater of an interview with H M Desai[1]

I saw Mr. Desai on Tuesday last.[1] He stated his case with clarity and moderation. It consisted of three main points:—

(1) He asked for the enfranchisement of the thousands of Indians who are now voteless. Out of about six hundred thousand who, in his opinion, should be enfranchised, only a hundred thousand were so far permitted to vote. Whatever else might be done, it seemed to him to be essential that this wrong should be put right in any new Constitution.
(2) He complained that the Indians who were refused the vote were also refused the citizenship of Ceylon and thus were deprived of their civic rights. He pressed for full civic rights for all those whom he regarded as entitled to citizenship.
(3) He was anxious to make it plain that he agreed with the Sinhalese majority in their request for a new Constitution. He did not wish to thwart them in their endeavours provided satisfaction was given to Indians under the two previous headings.

In conclusion he said that he would have the advantage of a short interview with the Secretary of State but he might not have the opportunity to put the above points and he would be grateful if I would bring them to the notice of the Secretary of State. For the most part I was able to confine myself to listening to his statement. He did ask me one direct question which was whether I could tell him when the report of the Soulbury Commission would be published. I was able to answer that I did not know, and so could not tell him.

---

[1] See 267, note 2.

**289**   CO 54/986/6/2, no 120                                    14 Sept 1945
[Soulbury Report]: inward unnumbered telegram (reply) from Sir H
Moore to Mr Hall on the publication of the report

Your secret and personal telegram of 12th September.[1]

I anticipate that local reaction to these decisions will be as already forecast by
Senanayake in paragraph 1(b) of my secret and personal telegram of 21st May,[2] and
that, as regards paragraph 1(c) of that telegram, his task here will be impossible
unless you can agree with him a communiqué for simultaneous publication in U.K.
and Ceylon on or after his departure, as to the course and results of his
conversations, which should be drafted in such terms that the procedure now
decided upon would appear not to have been dictated by India, but to enable him to
consult his ministerial colleagues.

2.   In his secret and personal telegram of 10th July, your predecessor assured me
that I would be fully consulted before any decision as to simultaneous publication of
Report, and decisions thereon of H.M.G. were taken. While I fully appreciate now
that that decision has been taken by H.M.G., that the general policy must be
regarded as settled, I feel, none the less, that it is my duty to point out that the
proposal to publish the Report simultaneously in India will create a most unfortunate impression in Ceylon, and be likely further to inflame anti-Indian feeling. No-one
could reasonably dispute the propriety of allowing sufficient time for as many copies
as are required by the Governor General's Executive Council to reach them, but
there is, I believe, in the whole history of Ceylon reforms, no precedent for
simultaneous publication of Ceylon State Papers in India, and such a step will
undoubtedly create the impression that the future of Ceylon is being subordinated to
the exigencies of the present political situation in India.

3.   I do not know if Senanayake is still leaving on 17th September and if meeting
referred to will be the last before his departure. If so, I consider it all the more
important that some action on the lines suggested in my paragraph 1 should be
taken. If not, I believe there is a real risk that he may join forces with Bandaranaike
and force a General Election on the Dominions Status issue, the Secretary of State
and Government of India being made the whipping boys.

---

[1] See 286.                                                                [2] See 245.

**290**   CO 54/986/6/2, no 122                                    [14] Sept 1945
[Soulbury Report]: letter from Mr Senanayake to Mr Hall on a revised
draft of the constitution

[Jennings returned to Cambridge after completing Senanayake's letter of 16 Aug (see
266). At Senanayake's suggestion, he prepared the letter reproduced here for presentation
to Hall. On page 94 of his *Donoughmore to independence* Jennings explains: 'Mr.
Senanayake considered that it would be helpful if he could give the Secretary of State a
draft of the proposed Constitution and the Agreement relating to Defence and External
Affairs. I therefore made a thorough revision of the ministers' draft, my tenth draft,
deleting all provisions inconsistent with complete self-government but inserting such of
the Soulbury amendments as Mr. Senanayake was prepared to accept. Necessarily it did
not include the provisions which would have to be enacted by the Parliament of the

United Kingdom, but it recited in the preamble "the intention of His Majesty's Government in the United Kingdom to recommend to the Parliament of the United Kingdom as soon as it may be practicable that the status of a Dominion be conferred on the island of Ceylon". The Soulbury senate was included but the provisions were to come into operation only after a resolution to that effect had been passed by the House of Representatives. . . .' The draft constitution (not reproduced here) and the letter below were presented to Hall on 13 and 14 Sept respectively. The letter is undated on the CO file but there is a copy of it in the Jennings Mss carrying the date 14 Sept.]

I handed to you yesterday a revised draft of the proposed Constitution for Ceylon, and I should now like to explain what it contains. Its fundamental assumption is that His Majesty's Government will in due course recommend that Dominion status be conferred on Ceylon and that in the meantime full self-government will be established by Order in Council with an agreement about defence, external affairs, and the general relations between the United Kingdom and Ceylon. This implies the removal from the Ministers' draft of 1944 (Sessional Paper XIV of 1944) of all the restrictions on self-government. The opportunity has been taken of incorporating these suggestions of the Soulbury Commission which I feel able to recommend, and to meet criticisms which have been made in the course of my discussions in London.

*The form of the constitution*

2.   The main branch of the legislature, which was entitled "The Council of State" in the Ministers' draft, is described as "the House of Representatives" as the Soulbury Commission recommended and the modifications in the disqualification suggested by the Soulbury Commission have been incorporated. The scheme of representation is that recommended by the Soulbury Commission, with the additional requirement that no constituency may exceed a population of 80,000.

3.   The Ministers left the question of a Second Chamber to be settled by the new legislature. The Soulbury Commission, on the other hand, recommended a Senate of 30 members, of whom half were to be elected by the House of Representatives and half were to be appointed by the Governor-General acting in his discretion. The Commission's scheme has been incorporated with the modification that the term of office has been reduced from nine years to six years. The State Council has, however, recently rejected by a large majority a resolution for a Second Chamber moved by a private member, and it would seem to be a question for Ceylon whether it should or should not have a Second Chamber. Accordingly, the revised draft postpones the creation of the Senate until a resolution to establish it has been passed by the House of Representatives. The matter can thus be settled after a general election.

4.   The franchise and the rules for elections are at present contained in a separate series of Orders in Council based upon the Ceylon (State Council Elections) Order in Council, 1931. They are very defective in some of their details, and amendments have been recommended by a Select Committee of the State Council. The Ministers therefore left the matter to be dealt with in a separate Order in Council. In view of the termination of the war and of the fact that the present State Council has been in existence for nearly ten years, it would be undesirable further to delay the reforms pending new legislation. Accordingly, the present franchise and election law has [sic] been incorporated with the revised draft with merely consequential amendments. The reform of the law will thus be a task for the new Parliament of Ceylon, as the Soulbury Commission recommended.

5.   The recommendations of the Soulbury Commission, that the usual power for

His Majesty in Council to amend the Constitution should be reserved, has been the subject of discussion in the light of the new proposal to confer Dominion status on Ceylon in due course. The revised draft retains the full right of the Ceylon Parliament to amend its own Constitution, but provides for the reservation for the Royal Assent of any Bill amending certain Articles, particularly those in which minority groups might be specially interested. It is therefore unnecessary to reserve to His Majesty in Council any powers of constitutional amendment except in the case, contemplated by the Soulbury Commission, in which the Constitution broke down owing to the inability of the Governor-General to obtain responsible Ministers. Though in all probability such a power would never be necessary under full self-government, it has been incorporated in Article 5, and power to amend that Article has been reserved to His Majesty in Council.

*Defence and external affairs*

6.   The draft of an agreement intended to govern the relations between the United Kingdom and Ceylon and to provide the facilities relating to defence required by His Majesty's Government has already been presented to the Permanent Under-Secretary of State for the Colonies for consideration by His Majesty's Government. In deference to possible objections suggested in the course of discussion, the agreement has now been scheduled to the Constitution and a provision has been inserted in Article 5 reserving to His Majesty in Council the power to take such steps as he may deem necessary and expedient for giving effect to this agreement. In view of the assistance towards the war effort so readily given by the people of Ceylon during the past six years, it seems unlikely that the use of this power will every [sic] be necessary; but it seems a suitable means of providing His Majesty's Government with the necessary guarantees without derogating from the independence of Ceylon as a Dominion. Since Article 5 also contains a reservation to His Majesty in Council of power to amend that Article, any subsequent agreement could similarly be given legal effect.

*Other amendments*

7.   Generally speaking, the other proposals of the Soulbury Commission have been incorporated in the draft. These relate especially to the composition and powers of the Public Services Commission, and the protection of the pension and other rights of existing officers. The composition of the Judicial Services Commission has also been modified. The Articles relating to the Governor-General have of course been considerably amended since they contained the restrictions on self-government imposed by the Declaration of May 1943. In the present draft these matters are now covered by the agreement in the First Schedule. The Governor-General's power to reserve Bills which have evoked serious opposition from minorities has, however, been retained, and the suggestion that the Governor-General's salary should be provided free of income tax has been incorporated. Speaking generally, therefore, the revised draft incorporates nearly all the amendments suggested by the Soulbury Commission in so far as they were consistent with the principle of complete responsible government. It is, of course, that complete responsible government which makes the draft Constitution attractive to Ceylon; and it is on that basis that I am prepared to recommend it to my colleagues and to the State Council. I suggest that, when the draft has been agreed by His Majesty's Government and published, the question of its acceptance should be put to the State Council and, if a resolution to

that effect is passed, that the draft should be embodied in an Order in Council with such drafting amendments as might be agreed between the two governments. The process of delimiting constituencies could then be begun in order that the next election might be that of a House of Representatives instead of a State Council.

# 291  CO 54/987/2, no 65                                    17 Sept 1945
## [Indians in Ceylon]: minute by C H Thornley on an interview between Mr Hall and H M Desai

Mr. Desai called to see the Secretary of State by appointment at 11.15 this morning and had a 16-minute conversation with Mr. Hall. I was present.

Mr. Desai started by thanking the Secretary of State for agreeing to receive him and saying that he entirely appreciated the reason why Mr. Hall had felt unable to receive his official Indian Delegation. He then described the Indian Community of Ceylon as being quite indispensable to progress in the Island, and as such should be regarded as settlers entitled to equality of franchise and full rights as citizens of Ceylon. He complained that ever since the inauguration of the Donoughmore Constitution encroachments had been made on their rights although they in no way stood in the way of the freedom of the people of Ceylon.

Mr. Senanayake had no mandate whatsoever from Ceylon. He had been invited and had come to give *personal* views. The whole purpose of Mr. Desai's visit was to plead for full rights of citizenship and absolute equality of franchise for Indian settlers who could prove five years more or less continuous residence in Ceylon and furnish evidence of an abiding interest in Ceylon. The facts were that their status had been progressively worsening over these last few years.

The Secretary of State enquired in what respects, apart from the franchise point, the Indian settlers were worse off now than they were. Mr. Desai replied that they lost the franchise in 1935 and have no right of participation in colonisation schemes. He also instanced an occasion a year or two ago when the services of some 6,900 Indian labourers were dispensed with at short notice on the pretext that their continued employment would mean unemployment for Ceylonese.

Summing up Mr. Desai said that he quite appreciated that the question of future immigration of Indians into Ceylon was one for discussion and decision by the Governments of India and Ceylon, but he strongly pleaded that H.M.G. should insist upon recognition by the Ceylon Government as citizens of Ceylon in every sense of the word, of the old and long established Indian residents of Ceylon. Mr. Hall said that he could be assured that proper attention would be given by H.M.G. to these and the many other representations which he pointed out had all been made and faithfully recorded by the Soulbury Commission.

Mr. Desai then asked when the Report of the Soulbury Commission would be published, whether it would be published in the form of a White Paper, and if so whether it would be published before or after H.M.G. had reached decisions upon its recommendations. The issue as seen by his association was whether H.M.G.'s decisions would be taken after discussion with Mr. Senanayake alone or whether there would be an opportunity of debate in the Council Chamber in Ceylon between publication of the Report and the final decision by H.M.G. The Secretary of State replied that it was impossible for him to say at present when the Report would be published. As to the other questions raised by Mr. Desai he could only say that naturally these were questions which were under consideration by H.M.G., as were all the many representations which had been made to the Soulbury Commission during their visit to Ceylon at the beginning of the year. Mr. Desai must understand that although H.M.G. regard the question of constitutional reform in Ceylon as one of the greatest importance, the present Government, in the short time that it has been in office, has had to deal with a number of other extremely urgent and important matters, in particular problems which had arisen through the sudden termination of the war against Japan. Nevertheless, he did want to assure Mr. Desai that the whole question was now under active consideration by the Government.

Mr. Desai thanked the Secretary of State for seeing him and wondered whether he would be prepared to give a few moments to Mr. Motha, another member of his Delegation. He knew how pressed the Secretary of State was for time and would quite understand it if this were not possible. He did, however, feel that in fairness to Mr. Motha he should make this request. Mr. Hall replied that if he could possibly find the time he would be glad to see Mr. Motha, but he was so pressed that he could give no promise that he would be able to do so.

## 292   CO 54/987/2, no 10                                              17 Sept 1945

## [Soulbury Report]: CO record of a discussion between Mr Hall and Mr Senanayake[1]

1. *Mr. Senanayake's request for records of his talks here*
*The Secretary of State* handed to *Mr. Senanayake* the records of his two talks with Sir George Gater on September 7th and 10th,[2] together with notes on two technical points, (a) the interpretation of the phrase "discriminatory in character", in the proviso to the recommendation of the Soulbury Report which excepts bills dealing with import duties etc., from reservation and (b) on extraterritoriality.

2. *Sir George Gater* observed that Mr. Senanayake had already been given a copy of an excerpt from Section 1(2) of the Parliament Act 1911 dealing with United Kingdom definition of a money bill, and read out from the record of the meeting on the 7th September the passage in which it was decided to note Ceylon's special desideratum as regards the definition of a money bill to be taken into account in the drafting of the new Constitutional Instruments. (See Section 1 on the first page on the record of the meeting of the 7th September).

3. *The Secretary of State* then went on to say that under cover of a letter he would be sending Mr. Senanayake on his departure copies of the record of his discussion with Mr. Senanayake on September 4th[3] and the notes of to-day's discussion.

4. *The communiqué to be issued on Mr. Senanayake's departure*
*Mr. Senanayake* pointed out that he would have to report to his colleagues on the Ceylon Board of Ministers the representations he had made to the Secretary of State

---

[1] Also present: A G Ranasinha, J H B Nihill, Sir G Gater and Trafford Smith.
[2] See 279 & 282.                                                              [3] See 274.

and any understanding that may have been reached as a result of them. He would also like if possible to say something to the general public, but he was not clear in his own mind exactly what stage had been reached as a result of his discussions here.

5. *The Secretary of State then showed Mr. Senanayake the draft communiqué*
After glancing through it, *Mr. Senanayake* said that it seemed satisfactory to him. With regard to the second paragraph of the communiqué in which publication of the Soulbury Report was mentioned, he asked how matters stood, and *Sir George Gater* explained the present position that it was now impossible for publication of the Report and the announcement of H.M.G.'s decisions to be simultaneous.

6. *Mr. Senanayake* then explained his position. His idea had been, he said, that after his discussions here had reached an agreed conclusion, he would be able to put that conclusion to his colleagues and to the Ceylon State Council. The communiqué in its present form, announcing no decision, relieved him from any commitment as to the course he would have to adopt in Ceylon, and thus the result would be that he would be freer in his choice of the proper course of action after returning to Ceylon than if he had been tied by an agreement reached in London. He would, however, wish to be able to give an indication of the representations he had made to the Secretary of State in London at the time when the Report was published. His understanding the whole time, however, had been that the procedure of publishing decisions at the same time as the Report was to be followed, and he felt the greatest regret that it had been felt necessary to abandon it.

7. *The Secretary of State* explained that the present procedure was an inevitable consequence of the change of Government, and the end of the Japanese war, which had not left H.M.G. time to complete its decisions before Mr. Senanayake's departure. He very much hoped that what Mr. Senanayake had said about complete freedom of action after returning to Ceylon did not mean that he had given up all intention of co-operating with H.M.G. *Mr. Senanayake* assured the Secretary of State that he would continue to do anything he could to help Ceylon. He agreed with the communiqué and to its being cabled to Ceylon.

8. Later in the discussion the text of the last paragraph of the communiqué was again referred to, and it was agreed that, since the phrase "study of the Report by all concerned" might be interpreted as "by the minorities", the Secretary of State would consider redrafting the last paragraph so as to remove this impression, and to bring out the fact that H.M.G. would announce decisions after studying both the Report and Mr. Senanayake's representations (a redraft of the communiqué on the lines proposed is attached to this record).[4]

9. *Mr. Senanayake* then reverted to the question of publication of the representations he had made to the Secretary of State while in England. *The Secretary of State* explained that, in his letter which would send records of the discussions to him he would make it clear that there was to be no public reference to these documents or public quotation from them until the Report had been published, unless the terms of the matter to be published had been previously agreed upon with the Secretary of State.

10. *Mr. Senanayake* said that he would certainly honour the confidential character of the records given to him. The question which he wished to raise,

---

[4] Not printed.

however, was that of publication of his letter of representations to the Secretary of State dated August 16th, 1945[5] and of the draft constitution for Ceylon and the draft agreement between the United Kingdom and Ceylon on general relations, external affairs and defence, which he had handed to the Secretary of State at their meeting on September 12th.[6] He read a letter he had received from Mr. George de Silva, the Minister of Health, about the meetings being organized in Ceylon to press for Dominion Status. The movement was going on all over the country, supported not merely by the Ceylon National Congress but also by Sama Samajists. Reference had been made at these meetings to his visit to England and he could not go back and say nothing at all. He must be in a position to give a general idea of what he had said in London, and if possible, of what he hoped to get.

11. *Sir George Gater* pointed out that if the documents referred to by Mr. Senanayake were published the question would immediately be asked "what answer did you get?" *Mr. Senanayake* again stressed his desire to respect the confidential nature of his talks in London and that he would answer that his representations were receiving attention. His object throughout was to be of service to Ceylon and he did not want it to be said after his return "the sooner they drop him the better".

12. *The Secretary of State* asked whether Mr. Senanayake thought that publication of his plea for Dominion Status might not help the position in Ceylon of the minorities and make the institution of a reasonable constitution more difficult. To this *Mr. Senanayake* replied that if he could hold out no prospect that Dominion Status would be granted in a reasonable time, his prospects of getting through anything less would indeed be difficult. H.M.G. had always said that the ultimate goal of their Colonial policy was that the Colonies should attain full self-Government. His goal was Dominion Status and if he could not have it fulfilled, he would willingly take the next best thing—a Constitution which brought him nearer to that goal. He felt he must make it clear that he had never expected Dominion Status within the next two years and had always thought that it would be at least five years. If H.M.G. were unwilling to grant it or to make a promise about it now, he would accept as an interim stage a constitution on the lines of that he had suggested to the Secretary of State—i.e. the Soulbury Constitution modified as in draft Order in Council drafted by Mr. Senanayake and by agreement between H.M.G. and Ceylon on external affairs and defence. In such a constitution H.M.G. would still have full rights of revocation and specification and to that extent it would fall considerably short of Dominion Status.

13. *Mr. Nihill* observed that this was of course a considerable revocation of the Ceylon recommendations. To this *Mr. Senanayake* said that since his draft constitution gave H.M.G. the over-riding authority what else did they want.

14. *Sir George Gater* pointed out that H.M.G. were working on the 1943 declaration and that Mr. Senanayake's proposals went a great deal further. *Mr. Senanayake* explained that the circumstances of to-day were radically different from those in which the 1943 Declaration had been drawn up. As early as 1941 the State Council had passed an *unanimous* resolution in favour of full Dominion Status. When the war situation grew worse, they accepted the 1943 Declaration as an important war-time advance. At that time the restrictions as regards defence etc., were understandable. Now no one in Ceylon felt them to be necessary since their

---

[5] See 266.                                    [6] The date should read 13 Sept; see 290, note.

possible future application was remote. *The Secretary of State* interjected that no one knew and that it was necessary that H.M.G. should be prepared against a risk: but *Mr. Senanayake* felt sure that the people of Ceylon would never believe that there was any hope for them in the future if it was necessary to retain these restrictions for a mere risk. The people of Ceylon were anxious to co-operate with the United Kingdom but they lacked the authority to be able to do so.

15. *The Secretary of State* pointed to the economic reasons for the maintenance of mutual relations between the United Kingdom and Ceylon, but *Mr. Senanayake* said that even with regard to trade, the people of Ceylon did not know whether they would be permitted to take part in the world economic re-organization now on foot. At the moment, however, they were not consulted and they were kept in the dark as to what way [sic] on foot. They did not want to be a supplier only when goods were in short supply. In the matter of plumbago, to take only one instance, after the re-occupation of Madagascar they had been left to shift for themselves.

16. *Sir George Gater* drew Mr. Senanayake's attention to the way in which H.M.G. had consulted Ceylon and met Ceylon's interests for example in the negotiations as to rice supply and the price of rubber. *Mr. Senanayake* said that there will be no doubt that Ceylon will co-operate in these matters if the people could be sure that H.M.G. regarded Ceylon's interest and the United Kingdom's interest as one.

17. *The Secretary of State* suggested that the meeting should return to the consideration of the present political situation. His understanding of the position was that the Ceylon Government disliked the Donoughmore Constitution and wanted it replaced. He asked Mr. Senanayake if he would regard the Soulbury Constitution as an advance. *Mr. Senanayake* replied that he felt the Donoughmore Constitution would break down in any case and the Soulbury Constitution was undoubtedly an advance. *The Secretary of State* then asked if the Soulbury Constitution was not then the next step to be tried out. Would it not give Ceylon the opportunity which would help in the fulfillment [sic] of her desire.

18. To this *Mr. Senanayake* replied that so long as Ceylon felt that she was being kept back she would feel a sense of grievance. Ceylon was like a cow tied to a tree by a rope. A longer rope was better than a shorter one, but still the restriction remained. Ceylon wanted more than a longer rope, the people felt that they deserved better than that and that their efforts in the war would secure it.

19. *The Secretary of State* then summed up by saying that Mr. Senanayake's position was evidently that he still pressed for Dominion Status. *Mr. Senanayake* agreed. He felt that his mission had been a failure. He had come here on the understanding that he was to [? negotiate] communicate an agreement, take it back to Ceylon and get the new Constitution through; now all that had to be abandoned.

20. A discussion followed on the exact nature of the understanding on which Mr. Senanayake had come to this country. He agreed that the Secretary of State was not under obligation to accept his advice. He had seen the cables which, he said, made it clear that if a decision was reached, the Report and the decisions would be published simultaneously. It was for this reason that he had asked for no mandate from the Board of Ministers as he did not wish to embarrass himself in being able to reach agreement in London. Since there was now no agreement, however, the position was quite different.

21. When *Sir George Gater* made the point that Mr. Senanayake's action in

advising the people to ask for Dominion Status had delayed the reaching of decision on the Soulbury Report: Mr. Senanayake agreed. He explained however, that the 1943 Declaration and the Soulbury Report were only an interlude in Ceylon's continued pressure for Dominion Status which had begun in 1941, had been suspended during the consideration of the Ministers' Summary and had been resumed even during the Commission's stay in Ceylon by the passing of the Sri Lanka Bill. He had thought that H.M.G. had summoned him to England in order to consider some compromise between the 1943 Declaration and the Ceylon view that Dominion Status should be given. But now, the fight for Dominion Status would continue.

22. *Sir George Gater* felt that to regard Mr. Senanayake's mission as a failure would be wrong. The talks have been very beneficial to H.M.G. as revealing exactly what Mr. Senanayake had in mind and wished to attain. Mr. Senanayake expressed his gratitude for this statement, but considered that he could not point to anything which indicated the success of his mission. When the Report was published, he added, it would be represented that H.M.G. was hoping for disentions [sic] which would delay reforms. He did not understand why H.M.G. could not decide forthwith. *The Secretary of State* then pointed out the difficulties of the last month, the change of Government, the surrender of Japan, the Conference of Foreign Ministers and all the preparations it had been necessary to make for it. In the midst of this, H.M.G. had found it difficult to reach decisions on Ceylon, not because they did not desire to reach decisions or for ulterior motives but because of the sheer physical impossibility of dealing with all these subjects at one [sic].

23. *Mr. Senanayake* said that he personally understood this but that could not guarantee that it would be understood in Ceylon. He wanted if he could to prevent a wrong impression from being created there, and for this reason felt it necessary to define his attitude after his return. It was then agreed that the draft communiqué should be reconsidered and that Sir G. Gater would show Mr. Senanayake an amended draft on the following day.

# 293    CO 54/986/6/2, no 125A                          19 Sept 1945

**[Soulbury Report]: outward unnumbered telegram in two parts from Mr Hall to Sir H Moore on his discussions with Mr Senanayake and the text of an announcement**

*Part I*
My discussions with Senanayake are now concluded.

2. I have informed him of H.M. Government's decision that Report should be published simultaneously here and in Ceylon before any decisions are reached by H.M. Government.

3. This interval will also give opportunity for Government of India to formulate their views and submit any representations they may wish to make before any decisions are reached by H.M. Government. I have not (repeat not) made any reference, in the course of my discussions with Senanayake to consultation with India.

4. Senanayake emphasised that these decisions leave his hands entirely free on

his return to Ceylon, that he felt his visit here to have been a "failure", to which I replied that that was not my opinion as I regarded discussions as most helpful; I think I made some impression on him. He went on to say that he would continue to press for Dominion status. He could not understand why decisions could not be reached now. The atmosphere throughout the discussion was entirely frank and friendly. I am sending by early air mail record of discussions for your personal information together with copy of letter which I am sending Senanayake before he leaves.

5.  A short press announcement in regard to the discussions was agreed with him for simultaneous publication here and in Ceylon on Friday 21st September. Text will be released here at 12 noon B.S.T. on Friday 21st September and it may be released in Ceylon at equivalent local time. Text of announcement follows in second part of this telegram.

6.  With reference to paragraph 2 of your Secret and Personal telegram of 14th September,[1] I should of course have wished to consult you as contemplated by my predecessor, but the procedure set out in my Secret and Personal telegram of 4th September was decided on by Cabinet in circumstances which gave no opportunity of prior consultation with you.

7.  The decision to publish simultaneously here and in countries interested overseas a Command Paper to be laid before Parliament here cannot I consider, afford any real justification for the impression of the subordination of Ceylon's future to Indian issues which you mention as likely to be created in Ceylon.

*Part II*
Following is text of announcement referred to in Part I, paragraph 5. *Begins.* "It is announced from the Colonial Office that the discussions on the question of the reform of the Ceylon Constitution between the Honourable D.S. Senanayake, Vice-Chairman of the Board of Ministers and Leader of the State Council in Ceylon, and Mr. G.H. Hall, Secretary of State for the Colonies, have now been concluded, and Mr. Senanayake is leaving England this week. These personal conversations have given Mr. Hall the opportunity of ascertaining Mr. Senanayake's views on all aspects of constitutional reform in Ceylon, and have been of great value to the Secretary of State and his advisers.

His Majesty's Government have decided that the Report of the Commission which visited Ceylon under the Chairmanship of Lord Soulbury should be published. After publication His Majesty's Government will complete their consideration of all the issues raised in the Report and of the representations made by Mr. Senanayake and will then reach decisions." *Ends.*

---

[1] See 289.

# 294   CO 54/986/6/2, no 124                                        19 Sept 1945
[Soulbury Report]: letter from Mr Hall to Mr Senanayake on the
conclusion of the discussions

Before you leave I should like to take this opportunity of saying how much I have
appreciated the opportunity which I have had for very frank and cordial discussions
with you on the question of constitutional reform in Ceylon. I am reporting your
views fully to His Majesty's Government for their consideration.

His Majesty's Government have felt bound to require a further period of time
before their final conclusions can be announced, and have decided that during this
period the Report of the Commission which visited Ceylon under Lord Soulbury's
Chairmanship should be published.

As you yourself have emphasized, our discussions here have been conducted on
the basis that they are strictly confidential in character, and we shall both so regard
them until the Report of the Soulbury Commission is published, when you may feel
it necessary to give some exposition to your ministerial colleagues in Ceylon of the
matters which you covered at your meetings with me. If there were any question of
publishing the record of those discussions or making public quotation from them,
you would no doubt, do so after agreement with me.

You have told me that you would wish to be free, on your return to Ceylon, to
make such disclosure as you would think appropriate of the following documents:—

(1) your letter to me of 16th August,[1]
(2) a revised draft of a Constitution for Ceylon which you gave me on the 13th
September,[2]
(3) the notes on two constitutional points which you gave us on the 10th
September.[3]

I readily agree to fall in with your wishes in these matters with the exception that
your letter of the 16th August contained detailed comments of the recommendations
in the Soulbury Commission's Report. From what we agreed at our meeting on 17th
September,[4] I know you will appreciate that it will not be possible for you to disclose
those parts of your letter until the Report of the Commission is itself published. If
you were also thinking of making any other use of your letter to me which
accompanied the revised draft of a Constitution (mentioned in 2 above) the same
comment would apply to parts of that letter also.

It has been a matter of very real satisfaction and value to myself to have had this
opportunity of having these personal discussions with you, and I am personally
conscious of the valuable service which you have rendered by coming to England so
that we could achieve a clear personal understanding and mutual approach to these
affairs.

I wish you a safe journey home to resume your important responsibilities in
Ceylon, and all success and happiness in the future.

I am enclosing notes of our discussions for your confidential and private use.

---

[1] See 266.                [2] See 290, note.                [3] See 282.                [4] See 292.

**295**   CO 54/986/6/3, no 131                                    25 Sept 1945

[Soulbury Report]: inward unnumbered telegram from Sir H Moore to Mr Hall on Mr Senanayake's return and the need for HMG to make a 'generous and spontaneous gesture' to Ceylon

My immediately preceding secret telegram No. 1773.

Senanayake today showed me your letter of 19th September[1] when he explained that he must be free to tell his colleagues at once, in strict confidence, the general substance of his conversations and his own estimate of the resultant position. All of them already knew that he has seen an advance copy of the Report and commented upon it, and he cannot, therefore, decline to discuss with them the attitude he has adopted towards it until the Report is officially published in about a fortnight's time. He wishes, therefore, to be free to refer to the record of discussions he has brought back with him. I consider this request is reasonable and, provided you insist that documents may not be copied or tabled or circulated in advance, but only read or handed round, the risk of leakage would appear to be no greater than that which obtains at present.

2. He appeared most appreciative of his personal reception, but made no secret of the fact that he considered the course of events at home has resulted in the failure of his mission. He will, therefore, launch a campaign immediately after the publication of the Report for full Dominion status and has no doubt that on this cry he will rally the whole Country, including the minorities, to his banner, the general line being that Ceylon's just claims are being sacrificed to the problems of India and Hong Kong.

3. I believe he would accept now a Constitution on the general lines of the Soulbury Report, with a negotiated agreement on Defence and Foreign Affairs, and transfer to the Dominions Office. If this was coupled with a promise of full Dominion status, say in five years time, I believe he would and could get the Country to accept it. If no clear pronouncement of policy is made by His Majesty's Government very early after the publication of the Report, I foresee a further period of acute agitation, not to say political deadlock, and concessions which will inevitably have to be made eventually, will appear to have been obtained by threats and intimidation. His Majesty's Government has a golden opportunity by the exercise of a little courage now, of making a generous and spontaneous gesture to Ceylon, which, in the long run, would pay a handsome dividend.

---

[1] See 294.

**296**   CO 537/1671, no 29                                    26 Sept 1945

'Ceylon defence expenditure': note by E E Sabben-Clare

[Sabben-Clare was on secondment to the CO from Tanganyika. J B Williams, assistant secretary at the CO and head of the Finance Dept, had earlier commented on the issues raised in this note: 'The whole subject of defence contributions is to my mind one of very great potential importance indeed. These contributions nearly always tend to arouse strong political feelings and I think in consequence that it is not too much to say that the wisdom or otherwise of the financial arrangements we make with Colonial Governments

concerning defence expenditure will play a big part in maintaining—or weakening—
Empire unity' (CO 537/1671, minute, 8 Feb 1945).]

1. Up to 1941 the allocation of defence expenditure in Ceylon between the local
Government and H.M.G. in the U.K. was as follows:—

(a) Under the Defence Contribution Ordinance of 1898 (Ceylon Laws Cap.294) the
Ceylon Government paid three quarters of the cost of the Imperial Garrison in
Ceylon, provided that this figure did not exceed 9½ per cent of the Ceylon
Government Revenue. (The sums paid in 1938/9, 1939/40 and in 1940/41 were
£180,614, £201,764 and £229,907 respectively, representing three quarters of the
cost of the Imperial Garrison in each case. For the half year 1 April to 30
September 1941 Ceylon paid £150,000.)
(b) Ceylon paid for and maintained the local military forces, viz. the Ceylon
Defence Force, and the local naval forces, viz. the Ceylon Naval Volunteer Force.
(c) The Ceylon Government "rendered many services to the Navy, Army and Air
Force, including the use of Government buildings, either free or at less than cost."

2. In the last quarter of 1941 the War Office suggested a change should be made
in these arrangements. Their grounds were that the Ceylon garrison was being
heavily reinforced by troops from India and that owing to the nature of the war-time
arrangements between H.M.G. in the U.K. and India in respect of military
expenditure it would not be possible for the War Office to ascertain the cost of these
Indian reinforcements and so to give the Ceylon Government a figure for the sum
which they would be required to pay. The War Office, therefore, suggested a lump
sum should be paid instead. The Ceylon Government readily agreed with the
suggested change since under the arrangements then in force they had had to bear
all the cost of the expansion of the Ceylon Defence Force and the Ceylon Naval
Volunteer Force.
3. In April, 1942, the Commander-in-Chief stated that the rate of defence
expenditure borne by Ceylon was, exclusive of A.R.P. and miscellaneous defence
measures such as censorship, about Rs.23,000,000 against an average for the five
pre-war years of Rs.2,500,000. This was made up of Rs.12,000,000 on the Ceylon
Defence Force, Rs.3,000,000 on the Ceylon Naval Volunteer Force, Rs.2,000,000 for
land and buildings for the garrison and Rs.6,000,000 defence contribution.
4. The Board of Ministers suggested a new financial arrangement to operate from
the 1st of October, 1941, until the "armistice", whereby Ceylon would contribute a
lump sum to the Imperial Government in respect of active defence, naval, military
and air measures, including the cost of the Ceylon Defence Force and the Ceylon
Naval Volunteer Force. The position after the "armistice" was to be reviewed in the
light of post-war circumstances. Full control of the C.D.F. and C.N.V.F. was to pass
to the War Office and Admiralty, but no change of policy was to take place without
prior consultation with the Board of Ministers. The Ceylon Government would
accept liability for pensions and gratuities for these forces under their existing
regulations. The Ceylon Government and the Imperial Government would charge
each other for stores, services and rent of buildings, but no charge would be made for
Crown land required by forces, except expenses consequential on vacation. Expenditure on buildings for the Ceylon Defence Force and Ceylon Naval Volunteer Force
should be met from Imperial Funds and if financial responsibility for those forces was

to revert to Ceylon at the end of the war payment would be made by Ceylon for buildings erected from Imperial Funds required for post-war use. The inclusive contribution the Board of Ministers offered in respect of these charges was Rs.30,000,000 per annum.

5.  This offer was accepted by H.M.G., except that, owing to Admiralty representations, the cost of the Ceylon Naval Volunteer Force was borne directly for a time by the Ceylon Government and the Ceylon contribution reduced accordingly from Rs.30,000,000 to Rs.27,000,000. This was changed in August 1943, when the Admiralty agreed to take over financial responsibility for the Ceylon Royal Naval Volunteer Reserve, as it was now called, in return for a contribution from Ceylon of Rs.3,000,000 less any payment for non-effective benefits. This brought the Ceylon total up to Rs.30,000,000 originally suggested by the Board of Ministers.

6.  The Governor of Ceylon stated in his telegram No. 1276 of 15 September 1942 that steps were being taken to suspend by Defence Regulation the operation of the Defence Contribution Ordinance (see para 1(a) above). "The Ordinance will revive after the war and constitute a basis for fresh negotiations."

7.  As mentioned above, this settlement was to last only to the "armistice" and, though it was not clear what was meant by this when the Board of Ministers made their offer, it was thought better to leave the point in the air for the time being. The Ceylon Government suggested in January 1945 that, if the "armistice" occurred before fresh financial arrangements regarding the defence of Ceylon were concluded under a new Constitution for the Island, they should pay, from the date of the "final armistice" to the date when such fresh arrangements come into force, a defence contribution on a peace-time basis bearing some relation to pre-war payments under the Defence Contribution Ordinance of 1898, viz. Ceylon's payment should be limited to three quarters of the cost of the garrison or 9½ per cent of her revenue whichever is the less.

8.  In our telegram No.1084 of the 27th of August we agreed that the undertaking by the Ceylon Government to pay 30,000,000 rupees per annum as a defence contribution ceased on the 15th of August, the date of the cessation of hostilities against Japan. We asked, however, that as it would not be possible for some months to decide the composition of local or Imperial forces in Ceylon, the Ceylon Government should continue to pay at the rate of 30,000,000 rupees per annum without prejudice to later adjustment when a final settlement had been reached.

9.  The Ceylon Ministers have refused and are proposing instead to provide a sum of Rs.5 million and to tell the Ceylon State Council that further negotiations are proceeding. This is more than Ceylon paid before the war—average for five pre-war years being Rs. 2½ million; but at that time Ceylon paid for and administered her own local military and naval forces, which she now does not. No details are given of the way in which the figure of 5 million rupees has been arrived at or is to be spent, nor is it clear whether this sum will meet the statutory obligations of the Ceylon Defence Contribution Ordinance as soon as the Defence Regulation suspending that Ordinance is revoked.

**297**   CO 54/988/2, no 38                                    28 Sept 1945
[Indo–Ceylon relations]: letter from G E J Gent to Sir H Moore explaining that the immigration question and the status of Indians in Ceylon had not been raised during discussions with Mr Senanayake

May I refer to your personal and confidential letter to the Secretary of State of the 14th June,[1] on the question whether there was anything we could usefully say to Senanayake while he was here which would smooth the way for a resumption of India–Ceylon negotiations on the immigration question and the status of Indians in Ceylon.

He has asked me to let you know that he gave this matter very careful consideration, and indeed had hoped that it would be possible to raise this matter with Mr. Senanayake before he left, but that our discussion developed along lines which made it unwise for us to bring up any question affecting India. The particular question referred to in your letter was not therefore mentioned to him.

---

[1] See 251.

**298**   CO 54/986/6/3, no 145                                    29 Sept 1945
[Soulbury Report]: note by Mr Senanayake for the Board of Ministers on his discussions with Mr Hall

The Board of Ministers should, I think, be informed of the general nature of my representations to His Majesty's Government during the course of my recent visit. I informed the Secretary of State that opinion in Ceylon had shifted since the early months of 1944. I pointed out that on the 26th March, 1942, the State Council had passed a resolution requesting that Dominion Status be conferred on the Island. The Declaration of May, 1943, did not go so far, but it would have enabled Ceylon to get rid of the Donoughmore Constitution and to be placed in an advantageous position for pressing for Dominion Status. I explained that it was mainly for this reason that the Ministers accepted the Declaration as interpreted in my statement of the 9th June, 1943. The Ministers' draft Constitution had, however, been before the public since September, 1944, and, with the restrictive clauses removed, it had been debated and passed by the State Council as the Sri Lanka Bill. It was now generally agreed that the restrictive clauses were unsatisfactory. Meanwhile, too, His Majesty's Government had promised full Self-Government to Burma. There did not seem to be anything in the social or economic conditions, or in the recent history of the two countries to justify the placing of Ceylon in an inferior position.

I called attention to the fact that it was the expressed policy of His Majesty's Government, and especially of His Majesty's present Government, to enable the peoples of the Commonwealth to achieve self-government. Ceylon was sometimes described as the "Premier Colony" and if there was anything in that description, it could mean only that it should be the first to receive self-government. If it was considered that it was not yet ripe for this status, there must be some reason for it, and I said we had so far been given no such reason. We had a population of 6 million;

our annual revenue was over 200 million rupees and our trade was nearly a 1,000 million rupees; we had a surplus of 15 million rupees in 1942–43 and this year we were budgeting for a surplus of 100 millions; we had over 6,000 schools with nearly 25,000 teachers and more than 850,000 pupils.

A possible reason for the reluctance of the late Government to accord us Dominion Status was indicated in a Declaration made in 1941. It referred to proposals for reform "concerning which there has been so little unanimity". In answer to this, I pointed out that there had been little evidence of unanimity in Canada a hundred years ago when self-Government was given; that there had been no unanimity in South Africa in 1906 when the Liberal Government made its noble gesture; that there had been little unanimity in India at the time of the offer made by Sir Stafford Cripps; that there had been no unanimity in Burma when the recent White Paper was issued. I asked whether progress towards democracy in Great Britain had been achieved by unanimity. In fact, however, Ceylon has approached nearer to unanimity than any other country. Not a single Ceylonese voted against the resolution for Dominion Status in 1942; the Sri Lanka Bill was passed by 40 votes to 7, and only three Ceylonese were in the minority. This vote was not merely a vote for Dominion Status, it was a vote for a complete Constitution.

The State Council's resolution of 1942 was inspired by the offer made to India by Sir Stafford Cripps in that year. The reasons which would justify the conferment of Dominion Status on India would apply with even greater force in Ceylon. We have had partial self-government based on adult franchise for fourteen years; Ceylonese Ministers have had the sole responsibility for finance and have held seven of the ten year portfolios of Government during a period which had included a major depression and a Great War; we had taken our full share in the defence of the Island in circumstances of danger as acute as that which had threatened Great Britain in 1940. At the end of the Japanese War, we take pride in remembering that Ceylon made the first successful resistance to the Japanese advance, and that it was a joint resistance by the Imperial forces and the people of the Island. For over three years the Ceylonese Ministers and the Ceylonese Civil Defence Commissioner had sat in the War Council and shared with the Commander-in-Chief and the Service Commanders the responsibility for defence and the prosecution of the war against Japan. We had provided the Headquarters and the facilities required by the South East Asia Command and the East Indies Fleet. We had supplied ninety per cent of the raw rubber available to the United Nations. For a long period we had provided all the plumbago required for the manufacture of munitions of war. For years we had negotiated for the purchase and sale to the United Kingdom of our whole output of tea, rubber and copra. Nearly all the members of the Public Services, including the Financial Secretary, the Auditor-General, many of the Government Agents, and most of the Heads of Departments were Ceylonese, and more than half the Judges of the Supreme Court, all the Judges of the lower Courts, and both Law Officers, were Ceylonese. We have a University with over a thousand students, with a 90% Ceylonese staff. All the Medical Officers of the Island were Ceylonese. The Bank of Ceylon, one of the major financial Institutions, was wholly controlled by Ceylonese. We had raised a Ceylon Defence Force and a Ceylon Royal Naval Volunteer Reserve with Ceylonese officers. Our Civil Defence Service, 64,000 strong, had been raised and controlled by Ceylonese.

The Constitution which we had worked with such success during the past fourteen years had been one of the most difficult ever invented. As long ago as 1933 my predecessor, the late Sir Baron Jayatilaka, had drawn attention to its many defects and asked that they be removed. I pointed out that the Board of Ministers was not selected for the homogeneity of its social and economic opinions, that it merely consists of the seven Chairmen of the seven Executive Committees. When a committee of seven or eight persons met to elect a Chairman, the division of opinion was often very close. The result was that the Board of Ministers was a heterogeneous collection of Ministers, often differing widely in opinion and speaking and voting against each other in the State Council. It was as impossible to work on party lines as it was in Great Britain from 1940 to 1945. The essence of the party system, a homogeneous Cabinet responsible to a parliamentary majority, was forbidden by the Constitution itself. The absence of this party system could not be an argument against giving us complete self-government with a Cabinet system which would allow parties to develop.

Nor could communal divisions be regarded as an argument against Dominion Status. When constitutional advancement is under discussion each community is inspired by its ancestral loyalties to make out a claim. Accordingly a Commission conducts its investigations in an atmosphere of artificial heat, and, though it generally sees the light behind, it cannot but be affected by the atmosphere. We had objected to a Commission in 1941 and again in 1944 precisely for that reason. Once the constitutional question was settled, I asserted that communal questions would cease to be relevant. What was more, I urged that they were in themselves an argument for self-government. The Ceylonese as a whole were accustomed to these differences of race, creed, caste and language and knew how to avoid offending susceptibilities; the Englishmen who were sent to govern us did not always possess that advantage. The Bill in which our proposals for representation had been incorporated had been passed by 40 votes to 7, more than half of the minority Ceylonese voting with the Sinhalese and only three Ceylonese voting against. We had thus produced a reasonable compromise which promised a Constitution under which, with complete self-government, we could have proceeded to tackle our social problems.

I emphasized that these social problems were urgent and important. So long as we were disrupted by constitutional discussions, we could not deal adequately with these questions. The only solution was to place the whole responsibility fairly and squarely on the shoulders of the representatives of the people, as in Great Britain.

The real conflict over constitutional issues was not between the Sinhalese and the minorities but between the Ceylonese and His Majesty's Government. That conflict arose only because His Majesty's Government refused to accord to us the complete self-government which almost every Ceylonese without distinction of race, caste or creed, believes to be his due. It was a conflict which had been kept wholly within constitutional limits. We had not sought to force British opinion to agree with us. We had endeavoured to persuade by argument and to demonstrate by co-operation that Ceylon might be the first of the tropical Dominions, the first of the oriental peoples to be admitted to complete equality, the first to benefit by that policy of raising dependent peoples which British parties announce in their election program-mes. There had been no rebellion in Ceylon, no non-co-operation movement, and no fifth column; we had been among the peoples who had given full collaboration while Britain was hard pressed. Ireland had obtained Dominion Status. India had been promised it; Burma was being offered full self-government within the Common-wealth; but Ceylon was apparently to get none of these.

The inevitable conclusion would, I said, be as unwelcome in Ceylon as in Great Britain.

The Declaration of May, 1943, had promised internal self-government with restrictions relating to defence and external affairs. Burma on the other hand, had been promised complete self-government subject to the making of an agreement about defence. We could not understand why the distinction should be drawn. It surely could not be said that we had proved less competent or trustworthy than the Burmese during the war against Japan. We did not grudge the award to Burma, but we were tempted to ask whether any restrictions would have been imposed on Ceylon if some of the Ceylonese Ministers had assisted the Japanese, and a Ceylonese National Army had fought against British Troops. I said that we preferred to give an interpretation more creditable to the late Government and to assume that the difference lay in the importance of Ceylon as a base and as a link in the chain of Imperial communications. If this was so, it was our misfortune and not our fault. We were fully aware of the fact; we had not sat in the War Council for three years without learning the implications of Ceylon's strategic position. We were also aware that it was or might be a position of danger to ourselves. We should be ready and anxious to give all the assistance and all the facilities that His Majesty's Government might require provided that we were also given control of our own country. We were at least as anxious as His Majesty's Government to have the Island properly defended. We knew that we could not defend it alone; on the other hand, we knew that it could not be adequately defended without our assistance. I said I was ready to pledge my colleagues and the State Council to any reasonable agreement about defence as an integral part of an agreement for Dominion Status, and indeed I went to the length of preparing the draft of such an agreement to govern the relations between Ceylon and the United Kingdom, particularly in matters of defence and external affairs on lines which would be acceptable to the State Council.

This method would, I suggested, assure Great Britain of a friendly people, and a friendly Government, another Dominion on the Sea and Air routes to Australia and New Zealand. It would assure Great Britain of naval and air bases that would dominate the Indian Ocean. I submitted with all the earnestness at my command that the method prescribed by the Declaration of 1943 would not. The limitations imposed by that document had been clearly inspired by distrust. In the case of the Dominions, His Majesty's Government met a possible contingency of non-cooperation by providing them with full information and consulting them whenever their interests were specially affected. That, I submitted, was the only method likely to be effective for securing full collaboration from Ceylon and making use of the facilities which Ceylon offers. The method prescribed by the Declaration would not. In part IV of our draft Constitution we had tried to provide a system which would work with the least possible friction. The Secretary of States' advisers would have informed him that it would be difficult to have two Governments in Ceylon in wartime, the one concerned with defence and the other with Civil Government. Either there must be collaboration from the Civil Government or Ceylon must be treated as hostile territory and have imposed upon it a military occupation. The process of governing by Governor-General's Ordinances would work only if they dealt with such unimportant matters that nobody thought it worth while to bother about them. In all normal cases a Governor-General's Ordinance would produce a constitutional crisis of the first magnitude.

The only satisfactory arrangement—satisfactory to either Government—would be one in which the Ceylon Government was collaborating with the Imperial Government. This would be achieved only by making the Ceylon Government fully responsible and entering into an agreement for the provision of mutual assistance in time of war and of such facilities in time of peace as might be required to that end. It would be, in short, a defensive alliance between the United Kingdom and a self-governing Ceylon. If His Majesty's Government still felt that we could not be trusted, the simple solution was to give self-government but to provide for the taking over of the administration of the Island in the event of default on our agreement.

It was not legal powers that would be needed, but the full collaboration of a free people. If the British Government provided the freedom the people of Ceylon would provide the collaboration. In 1906 the new Liberal Government had taken a much greater risk. They had given complete self-government not to a people which had been helping British troops against a common enemy, but to a people which had been waging war against His Majesty. Ten years later there was a South African "rebel" General in the War Cabinet; and a quarter of a century later the Union of South Africa, under the same rebel General, was an essential link in the communications of the Army that marched from Egypt to Berlin. We could not offer a rebel General—the experience of South Africa and Burma seemed to suggest that it might have been easier if we could—but I suggested that an act of faith and generosity, such as the Liberal Government had been inspired to do in 1906, would tend to cement the bonds between our peoples. It would indeed do more. It would add to the power of the British Commonwealth of Nations. It would place another Dominion in a most important strategic position, half way between England and Australia. It would complete the triangle in the Indian Ocean. Nor was that all. It would show the dependent peoples all over the Empire that the professions of the British Government were not mere professions and that it was possible for a people which, a hundred years ago, had fallen into evil days, had been almost completely lacking in educational facilities, and had been compelled to live on a very low standard of life, to achieve the status of a Dominion within the British Commonwealth of Nations.

I told the new Secretary of State that the problems of Ceylon was one only of the many problems which would face the Government of which he was a member. For us, however, it was the fundamental problem. Until it was solved we could not begin to face the many questions that confronted us in Ceylon. The Constitution, which had been submitted to his predecessor in February, 1944, required only a little alteration to convert it into a Constitution for a fully self-governing Ceylon. I appreciated that any decision to confer Dominion Status on Ceylon would require legislation by Parliament; but if it were decided to consider this question, I should not wish to have self-government held up. If, therefore, His Majesty's Government was not prepared to confer Dominion Status on Ceylon without further consideration, I suggested that our draft Constitution, as amended, be put into operation by Order in Council and the general responsibility transfered to the Dominions Office. While the new constituencies were being delimitted [sic], the question of Dominion Status could be raised with the Secretary of State for the Dominions.

I said I felt sure that the Council would agree to any reasonable scheme for the defence of Ceylon and the security of Imperial Communications if it were accompanied by a grant of full self-government leading to Dominion Status as soon as the necessary discussions had taken place. The way to secure our co-operation was to ask us to co-operate and to give us a constitution, framed by us, under which we could co-operate. It was not by imposing limitations on the powers of their Governments that the co-operation of Canada, Australia, New Zealand and South Africa was obtained. We knew how essential Imperial assistance was in defence; but our active assistance was also valuable. The discussions were taking place while the whole Commonwealth, and indeed the whole civilized world, was celebrating the victory over Japan. I hoped it would not be forgotten that the orders for the surrender of Japanese troops in Malaya and Burma were being sent from the capital of the last Sinhalese Kings, that the fleet which would steam into Singapore steamed out of Trincomalee, and that the aircraft which patrolled the skies of Malaya and Sumatra were based on Ceylon. I asked whether it was worthwhile to force on us a Constitution which assumed that the co-operation which had been so readily forthcoming during the past five years would in future be replaced by non-cooperation. Was it not better to establish a new Dominion on the sea and air routes to Australia and New Zealand, in an Island which guards the whole Indian Ocean? Burma and Malaya and British North Borneo would be freed, in one sense, in a few days. Would not His Majesty's Government, in another sense, free Ceylon also? The conversion of Ceylon into a Dominion would show that this war was not a war between Imperialist Powers anxious to maintain their dominion but that, on the side of the United Nations, it was a war to enable all the peoples of the world, including all those which had hitherto been dependent on them, to achieve freedom and self-respect.

These representations in writing were followed by personal discussions with the Secretary of State. As has been announced by the Colonial Office, His Majesty's Government proposes, after the publication of the Soulbury Report, to complete their consideration of the issues raised in the Report and of the representations made by me. In the meantime, I fear I am not at liberty to disclose even to my Ministerial Colleagues the full details of the discussions I had with the Secretary of State and his advisers. Since it would be embarrassing both to my colleagues and to myself to attend meetings of the Board while such a prohibition was in operation, I feel that it would be more convenient if I remained on leave until after the publication of the Report, which would not, I understand, be long delayed.

I propose to send copies of this letter to the Press.

## 299   CO 54/987/1, no 78                                1 Oct 1945
## [Indians in Ceylon]: minute by Trafford Smith briefing Mr Hall for his interview with G R Motha[1]

Mr. Sidebotham is on leave.

The question of the rights and status of Indians in Ceylon, about which Mr. Motha will wish to talk to the Secretary of State, is a very difficult and complicated one, and

---

[1] Motha represented the Indian Mercantile Chamber in Ceylon and he was also joint secretary of the All-Ceylon Tamil Congress. Trafford Smith comments in his minute on a memo submitted by Motha to the CO which is not printed here.

my advice is that the Secretary of State should, as far as possible, refuse to be drawn into argument and confine himself to giving a sympathetic hearing to what Mr. Motha has to say.

The facts about the Indian Tamils are given in half a page on page 39 of the Soulbury Report, and the difficult questions of the Indian Franchise and Immigration are dealt with in the Chapters under those titles on pages 53 and 60 respectively.

It must be borne clearly in mind that the Indians who Mr. Motha is talking about are not the "Ceylon Tamils" permanently based in Ceylon. They are, on the one hand, the immigrant labour force amounting with dependants to about 900,000, and on the other, a much smaller body of Indian traders, etc., who for commercial reasons have found it advantageous to take up semi-permanent residence in the Island.

Mr. Motha is quite right in saying that the economic prosperity of Ceylon very largely depends on the immigrant estate labour concerned with the production of tea and rubber. The essence of the difficulty, however, is the unwillingness of the great majority of these Indians to renounce their ties with the mother country and attach themselves permanently to Ceylon. They all go back to their Indian villages at varying periods—usually I believe once every three or four years—and quite frequently stay for a period of months. They are in touch with their relatives and friends in India, and many send remittances back to India. This being so, the Sinhalese very naturally say that they are not real "citizens of Ceylon" and thus should not have equal franchise and citizenship rights with people whose home and only connection is in Ceylon.

The present franchise qualifications provide that any person in Ceylon may have the vote if he has Ceylon domicile of origin, or has certain property and income qualifications, or is prepared to make a declaration of "permanent settlement". A good many of the Indian traders get the vote on the property and income qualification, while the labourers can get the vote either by domicile (if their families have been in Ceylon for some time and they can establish it), or by making a declaration of permanent settlement, which is tantamount to saying that they now regard Ceylon as their home and renounce their ties with India. The number of labourers possessing the vote, however, is relatively small, precisely because the labourers will not renounce their ties and make the declaration.

There is no doubt that, in the face of great difficulties, the Ceylon Authorities do their best to apply this law fairly, and it may be remembered that one of Mr. Senanayake's main points was that any unfairness in its operation had been in favour of the Indians and against the Sinhalese, in that more Indians had been admitted to the franchise than would have been admitted under strict interpretation of the law. Thus Mr. Motha's point in paragraph 7(a) on page 3 that "the restriction of the franchise has resulted in an Indian population of over 900,000 being able to return only 2 Indians . . ." is based on mis-representation, and it seems to me that the Sinhalese contention that Indians, if they are going to have full citizenship rights, must plump for Ceylon and renounce India, is a fair one.

Mr. Motha rather gives the game away at the end of (e) in the same paragraph (on page 4) where he says that the Government of India's ban on the emigration of unskilled workers "stopped an influx of men whom Ceylon was not prepared to treat in a human way". Surely the labourers would not have wanted to emigrate from India to Ceylon if conditions in Ceylon had not been attractive to them. They were in no way bound to emigrate except by the pressure of bad conditions in India, and the fact that they did not in practice get such a bad deal in Ceylon is proved by the necessity of the Government of India to place a ban on their departure before they could be stopped from going to Ceylon.

So far as the Soulbury Commission was able to gain an insight into the question, their conclusion was, I think, that this question of the Indian vote is, like so many other questions in Ceylon, largely a politicians' point. One of the principal reasons why the labourers do not take the trouble to qualify for the vote is simply apathy.

The later part of the memorandum deals with the grievances of Ceylon Indians, and indeed some of the grievances in paragraph 8 on page 5 are, judging from the evidence supplied to the Commission, very real ones, especially the restrictions placed on labourers living in lines receiving their friends within those lines which always remain the property of the Companies.

Mr. Motha's plea in paragraph 9 on page 6 that "complete equality of political, economic and civic status should be restored to the Indians . . ." is obviously unjustifiable. It is clearly not fair that they should have complete equality unless they are prepared to make Ceylon their home in the full sense of the word. So long as they insist on retaining a strong connection with India, it is not right that they should have an equal right with any other inhabitants of Ceylon to take part in the government of the country.

Mr. Motha's arguments as to discrimination are somewhat overdrawn. Indeed, the memorandum throughout betrays precisely that "intense narrow and highly objectionable communalism" of which he is accusing the Sinhalese. He finishes up with a plea for the 50/50 Constitution under which the Sinhalese would have half the seats in the Legislature and the minorities the other half, the statutory division of seats between the communities being extended to the Cabinet, in which each community would have an allotted representation. The Soulbury Commission turned this down as it would be tantamount to reducing the Sinhalese majority to a minority in their own country.

# 300   CO 54/986/6/3, no 174                                            5 Oct 1945
[Soulbury Report]: letter from Lord Soulbury to Mr Hall arguing the case for the grant of a greater measure of self-government to Ceylon than that recommended by the commission

During the recent visit of Mr. Senanayake to this country you very kindly allowed me from time to time to give you my views regarding various matters arising out of the Commission's Report on Ceylon and your conversations with Mr. Senanayake. I greatly appreciated this opportunity and I think it might now be worth while putting in writing the opinions which I have formed and have expressed to you since the Commission's Report was presented.

These involve partly questions of tactics and partly questions of principle, and the consideration of—inter alia—the following points:—

1. The publication of the Report prior to the publication of H.M. Government's proposals.
2. The position of India in the negotiations between H.M.G. and Ceylon.

3. Mr. Senanayake's Memorandum to you of the 16th August.[1]
4. Mr. Senanayake's Draft Constitution submitted to you in September.[2]
5. The transfer of Ceylon to the Dominions Office.

*1 and 2*
I understand that H.M.G. has decided to publish the Commission's Report before announcing its own proposals. When I discussed the question of publication and the subsequent time-table with your predecessor I think he was—at any rate provisionally—in favour of publishing the Report and H.M.G's proposals, in the form of a White Paper, simultaneously. This was in accord with the wishes of Mr. Senanayake and was, I believe, designed to avoid the embarrassments of agitation and propaganda which were expected from the more extreme Ceylonese politicians if an interval were permitted between the publication of the Report and the proposals of H.M.G.

The interval which must now ensue will, unless it is extremely short, provide an opportunity for a spate of representations and memorials from both the majority and minority interests in Ceylon with corresponding repercussions in this country, and a repetition in the press and on the platform of much of the evidence already received, examined and assessed by the Commissioners.

The consequence may well be that when H.M.G's proposals are announced, modifications of the Report in the direction of conferring upon Ceylon wider powers of self-government than those which are recommended by the Commissioners will be ascribed to pressure exercised by the majority during the interval, and—if narrower powers are proposed—to the representations of the minorities. In neither case will H.M.G. get much credit or gratitude, and in either case the majority and minority disagreement in Ceylon will be stimulated.

My views as to the result of accepting the Commission's recommenations as they stand or without material alteration will be gathered from what follows.

According to Mr. Senanayake's Memorandum of August 16th opinion in Ceylon on Constitutional Reform has shifted since the early months of 1944. I agree. There has been a growth in the demand for fuller powers of self-government than were proposed in the Ministers' Scheme of September 1944 (S.P.XIV) and I think that Mr. Senanayake's influence in the State Council—though perhaps not yet in the country—has deteriorated. He is faced with competition for his leadership and it seems a pity to give his competitor the chance of weakening him still further and perhaps of forcing him to join hands. Consequently, H.M.G's decision to publish the Report in advance of its proposals is, in my judgment, regrettable.

I understand that this decision has been taken in order to allow time for the Government of India to examine the Report and express its views upon it to H.M.G. and that it was held to be inadvisable to acquaint the Government of India with the contents of the Report before publication, for fear of the risk of leakage. I can well understand that apprehension, but while my colleagues and I were aware of the need to consult the Government of India on points in the Report of common interest to India and Ceylon, we did not envisage the necessity of referring to the Government of India the general layout of Ceylon's new constitution or the extent of the self-government to be conferred upon her.

[1] See 266.                                                                              [2] See 290, note.

It seems to me that there are three chapters in the Report, and three only, which are of direct concern to the Government of India; namely, Chapter 10—Franchise, Chapter 11—Immigration, Chapter 13—Representation. As a matter of fact, the issues raised in those chapters, so far as they affect India, are rapidly becoming of academic importance. Immigration of unskilled Indian labour on any considerable scale seems unlikely in the future; the Indian Government banned it in 1939, and the Ceylon Government shows no sign of wishing the ban to be removed. In regard to Franchise and Representation, the Report indicates that before long the great majority of Indian unskilled workers now in Ceylon will be able, if they so desire, to acquire domicile of choice origin and rights of franchise on precisely the same footing as the Ceylonese.

Bearing that in mind, I should have preferred to confine consultation with the Government of India to the three chapters above mentioned. If there had been leakage from those chapters the damage would not have been serious; by no means so serious as the damage to the relations between Ceylon and Great Britain if the publication of the Report in advance of the proposals of H.M.G. has the consequence which I fear, or the damage to the relations between Ceylon and India, already none too good, if it becomes known or even suspected that the powers of self-government to be conferred on Ceylon are contingent upon the approbation or otherwise of the Government of India.

Of course, if the assent of the Government of India to the Commissioners' recommendations is to be in substance little more than a token assent, then the interval preceding the publication of H.M.G's proposals can presumably be a very short one and not much harm will have been done. But I am apprehensive lest the Government of India may take the opportunity to examine in great detail not merely the contents of Chapters 10, 11 and 13, but the whole plan of the new constitution. In that case it might, I fear, be some months before H.M.G's proposals could be made known and such a delay would, in my opinion, be most unfortunate, not only for the reasons already given but for the effect on the time-table, of which you have a copy. It was, as you know, proposed that a Delimitation Commission should be set up in May, 1946, that the Government should proclaim the new constitution at the Dissolution of the present State Council due to take place in October, 1946, and that a General Election on the basis of an enlarged Legislature should be held in January, 1947. If this programme is to be carried out there is already very little time to spare, for I assume that the acceptance of H.M.G's proposals by the State Council now in being will be an essential preliminary.

*3 and 4*

Although Mr. Senanayake is still the most influential politician in Ceylon, his power has, I think, during the last few months declined. This is to some extent due to the campaign engineered by the more extreme and less responsible members of the Board of Ministers, under the leadership of Mr. Bandaranaike, for Dominion status, culminating in the passing by the State Council by 40 votes to 7 of the Sri Lanka Bill. Mr. Senanayake has studiously refrained from giving overt support to this movement and has in consequence probably lost ground to Mr. Bandaranaike who is obviously manoeuvering to oust him from the leadership of the Council. It remains to be seen whether Mr. Senanayake can hold his own. He has passed the prime of life and does not enjoy the best of health.

In drawing up our Report we took Mr. Senanayake's position into consideration, for we formed the opinion, with which I believe you agree, that if he was unable or unwilling to sponsor H.M.G's proposals the probability of their acceptance by the State Council was doubtful. Consequently, wherever possible we framed our recommendations so as to minimize the criticism and opposition which Mr. Senanayake was likely to encounter from Mr. Bandaranaike's faction.

In the light of the Memorandum of August 16th submitted to you by Mr. Senanayake it would not be wise to exclude the possibility of finding him eventually in the same camp as Mr. Bandaranaike, being driven there in an effort to preserve his own leadership.

His Memorandum is a frank and closely reasoned appeal for Dominion status and I expect that it was prepared not only with the object of inducing H.M.G. to accede to his demands—he may not have expected to attain that—but with a view to its publication in Ceylon as a means of protecting himself against his critics and withstanding charges of having sold the pass and so forth. At the moment, however, it is evident from the new Draft Constitution which he produced to you a few weeks ago, that he is prepared to accept and sponsor certain material limitations on Dominion status.

The argument in the Memorandum rests partly on the fitness of Ceylon for full self-government, and partly on the pledges given by H.M.G. to India and Burma, and the absence of any justification for treating Ceylon less favourably than those two countries. In his own words ". . . If it (Ceylon) is not yet ripe for this status there must be some reason for it and we have so far been given no such reason". His critics will certainly press for the reason and will endeavour to ascertain what, in the opinion of H.M.G., are the criteria which determine fitness for Dominion status or otherwise. If Mr. Senanayake is to obtain the acceptance in Ceylon of the new constitution to be proposed by H.M.G.—assuming that it confers powers of self-government substantially less than those proposed in his Memorandum of August 16th or in his Draft Constitution—he will, in the absence of adequate reasons, find it difficult to persuade his country to accept a constitution which does not give it full legislative and fiscal autonomy and equality of status with other autonomous members of the British Commonwealth.

His Memorandum lays stress on the financial stability of Ceylon, the development of her social services such as education and public health, the exercise of adult franchise for fourteen years, the political and administrative experience gained by Ceylon Ministers over the same period, the part played by Ceylonese in the Civil Service and the Judiciary, and the contribution of Ceylon to the war in close co-operation with Great Britain.

Neither I myself nor my colleagues would be prepared to contest the advance made by Ceylon since 1931 in practically every phase of her social and economic life. Our Report draws attention to many notable features of this progress. Nevertheless, it may well be held that further progress and more experience are desirable before the grant of full self-government and Dominion status can be contemplated. But this contention will be difficult for Mr. Senanayake to support when comparison is made, as it is bound to be made, with India or Burma; for it is apparently now in the power of the political leaders of India, if they so desire, to devise and adopt a constitution proper to Dominion status and eventually to decide whether or not to remain within the British Commonwealth. I understand that Burma has been promised Dominion status as soon as conditions in that country permit.

I have no qualification to make any comparison between India and Ceylon but I should be surprised to learn that the social and economic conditions of Ceylon are inferior to those of India, or that the political and administrative experience and the behaviour of Indian politicians are in any way superior. It is, I think, beyond doubt that the standard of living of the Ceylon peasantry is higher. The Ceylon peasant is still poor but there is little in Ceylon to resemble the abject poverty and destitution commonly reported to be the lot of millions of Indian peasants. The level of education and of literacy amongst the masses in Ceylon is, I believe, much higher than in India.

If considerations of this kind constitute any evidence of fitness for Dominion status, Mr. Senanayake will have a difficult case to meet in the State Council when pledges given by H.M.G. to India and Burma are contrasted with the prospects of Ceylon. The existence of minority and communal problems in Ceylon will not help him to justify differential treatment for his country, for it is well known that these problems are of far more importance and more acute in India, nor will it be easy for him to convince his people that the political leaders of Ceylon have done less than the political leaders of India to win the esteem and confidence of H.M.G.

Frankly, I do not envy Mr. Senanayake his task and if he is unable to present any reasons for the apparent discrimination against his own country beyond the non possumus of H.M.G., he may well fail to carry the Council with him.

In view of the foregoing you may ask me why the Commissioners did not advocate Dominion status or, at any rate, much fuller powers of self-government than are recommended in their Report. The answer will be found in our terms of reference—"To examine and discuss any proposals for constitutional reform in the Island which have the object of giving effect to the Declaration of His Majesty's Government on that subject dated 26th May, 1943". Those terms obviously precluded the Commissioners from dealing with any proposals for Dominion status, and you will observe that our recommendations have been, generally speaking, kept within the compass of the Declaration. Whether we should have recommended the grant of Dominion status had there been no such limitation, I am, of course, unable to say. We did not examine any proposals having that objective but I think that I ought to point out that our recommendations regarding Defence and External Affairs were made in the light of a situation which has vastly changed since our Report was presented to your predecessor. When we reported, the Japanese war was still going on and, so far as we were able to judge, might well continue for another eighteen months or two years. Nor was it possible for us to foresee precisely what the position would be at the termination of hostilities. We were, therefore, not prepared to take any chances and our recommendations on Defence were pretty strictly conceived. But since we reported, Japan has collapsed and it is barely conceivable that any further menace can arise from that quarter for many years.

It would, therefore, seem that the Defence problem of Ceylon must now be reduced in importance and perhaps the advent of the atomic bomb will reduce it still further. Had Japan been defeated before our Report was presented, we should have been bound to take this new situation into account.

I stress this point, because Mr. Senanayake appears to take greater exception to our recommendations on Defence and External Affairs than to any other portion of our Report, for as he says in his Memorandum (para. 16)—". . . You will see from the above comments that differences which are likely to be fundamental relate to Defence and External Affairs".

It is possible that Mr. Senanayake would be prepared to accept and support a new constitution based substantially on our Report, except as regards Defence and External Affairs. If our recommendations on those two subjects remain unamended, he will have to explain to his people why H.M.G. should object to the conclusion of an agreement between Great Britain and Ceylon regarding Defence and External Affairs similar to the agreement which he believes to be contemplated in the case of Burma. The terms of an agreement between Great Britain and Ceylon are suggested in the first schedule to Mr. Senanayake's draft constitution. Paragraph 6 of the schedule seems designed to provide the essential safeguards (see also Part 3, page 18, of his memorandum).

5

If, in the light of the present constitution, H.M.G. were prepared to modify our recommendations on Defence and External Affairs in the direction desired by Mr. Senanayake, I think that his position in the State Council would be improved and his ability to sponsor a new constitution with success strengthened. If, however, H.M.G. is not so prepared, then it remains to be considered whether any other concessions can be made to help him. I suggest two:—

(a) When we were in Ceylon we were pressed by Mr. Senanayake to advise the Secretary of State to transfer Ceylon from the Colonial Office to the Dominions Office. We were favourably impressed by this suggestion, particularly in view of a similar suggestion made by the present Foreign Minister in regard to India. Moreover, we were assured by Mr. Senanayake that the transfer would be a material aid in enabling him to persuade his people to accept H.M.G's proposals. We put forward the suggestion to your predecessor and to yourself and strongly supported it. We did not include it in our Report as it did not seem to us to be strictly relevant to the reform of the constitution or to lie within the ambit of our terms of reference.

I venture to hope that this suggestion will be adopted. It will be a valuable indication of H.M.G's eventual intentions and will go a considerable way towards smoothing Mr. Senanayake's difficulties. It is true that it would be only a gesture, and would have no practical effect on Ceylon's powers of self-government, but, as you are aware, though gestures in politics may have no legal effect, they can be very helpful. At any rate, that seems to be Mr. Senanayake's view, and if his request is refused I doubt if he will understand the reason for the refusal and both he and his countrymen will become more than ever suspicious of the policy of H.M.G.

(b) It would, I think, also be an advantage to Mr. Senanayake if H.M.G. could announce its intention to concede Dominion status to Ceylon at the same time as, and not later than, it is conceded to India or Burma.

Failing any modification of our Report in the matter of Defence and External Affairs on the lines I have indicated, or the adoption of the suggestions (a) and (b) above, it is my opinion that Mr. Senanayake will have a weak hand to play before his Council and may possibly be unwilling to play it, or may play it halfheartedly and so fail to secure the acceptance of H.M.G's proposals. At the best he will put them forward with bad grace and under protest and recommend their acceptance simply on the ground that half a loaf is better than no bread. He may eventually get them through in the face of much acrimony and recrimination and H.M.G. will be subjected to a continuance of the agitation which has been persistently carried on since 1932 against the Donoughmore Constitution. When, in the fullness of time, Ceylon achieves Dominion status—the admitted policy of H.M.G.—there will be little gratitude or good will from the Ceylonese.

My own personal opinion is that H.M.G. should now go considerably further in the direction of giving self-government to Ceylon than the Commissioners recommended. There would, of course, be the risk of mis-government and there would be opposition from the minorities in the State Council, despite the difficulty that some of them would have in explaining away their votes on the Sri Lanka Bill. I should not expect serious protests from the Muslims; and whatever further powers of self-government are conceded to Ceylon, whether to the extent of Dominion status or short of it, there will be antagonism from the leaders of the Ceylon Tamils who profess themselves to be content with nothing less than equality of representation for the minorities, both in the Legislature and in the Executive. The Commissioners found themselves quite unable to agree to that.

Provided that the safeguards which we recommended for the minorities are embodied in any new constitution, I do not myself believe that H.M.G. could do much more to protect them.

I realize that the immediate grant of Dominion status to Ceylon may be premature and the risk too great; and there may be other cogent factors of which I am unaware. It is evident that Mr. Senanayake also realizes this, for in preparing and submitting the draft of a new constitution he has indicated his willingness to accept a good deal less than Dominion status. On the lines of his draft, I have little doubt that he could get a new constitution through the State Council and I am of opinion that H.M.G's proposals should be framed as nearly as possible to meet his views. To do so would admittedly confer upon Ceylon considerably wider powers of self-government than the Commission felt itself able to recommend, but in view of the change in the political atmosphere of Ceylon and in Mr. Senanayake's personal position to which I have alluded, and the defeat of Japan, I think that the wider powers for which Mr. Senanayake asks should be conceded.

As a protection for the minorities H.M.G. might consider the desirability of repeating the condition imposed by the Declaration of 26th May, 1943, i.e. that Mr. Senanayake's proposals should receive the approval of three-quarters of all members of the State Council of Ceylon excluding the Officers of State and the Speaker or other presiding officer.

When we were in Ceylon no reference to this condition was made by any of the witnesses, majority or minority, and we did not think fit to include it in our recommendations because the constitution to be based upon our Report was not a constitution devised and submitted by the Ceylon Ministers. This consideration does not apply with the same force to Mr. Senanayake's draft constitution and I do not think that he could resist the condition.

It seems to me that a great opportunity has now arisen to make permanent the good feelings that exist in Ceylon towards Great Britain and the British Commonwealth, and to cement the loyalty of the Island to the British Crown. It is an opportunity that may not present itself again. Certain parallels can be drawn between Ceylon and Ireland. Many of the Ceylonese resemble the Irish in temperament and intelligence and like the Irish they have long memories. It would be a tragedy to repeat in Ceylon any of the colossal mistakes we have made in Ireland. The treatment of South Africa by the Liberal Government of 1906 is a much happier example. To hit the golden mean between caution and magnanimity is perhaps impossible but I believe that in the long run giving too much and too soon will prove to be wiser than giving too little and too late.

## 301   CO 54/986/6/3, no 176                                    5 Oct 1945
## [Soulbury Report]: letter from Mr Senanayake to Lord Soulbury expressing the fear that he might lose his majority

I ought to have written to you earlier. We were however delayed by bad weather on the return journey and I have been engaged in preparing my statements[1] for the Board of Ministers and the press. I am most grateful for all the assistance that you have given us. As I feared, the postponement of a decision has had the worst possible effect. Already I am being accused of having offered too much and asked too little. The Communists have published a complete rejection of Dominion status, and they may carry the Ceylon National Congress with them. When it becomes known that India is the stumbling-block the Sinhala Maha Sabha is quite likely to take up the running—you know Bandaranaike's attitude to the Indian question—and I shall have lost my majority. A week ago I could have obtained an almost unanimous vote for a reasonable settlement. If there is to be a favourable decision it must come before the State Council meets on November 6th, and the earlier it comes the more chance I have of carrying it. If the decision is unfavourable, I fear that we shall soon be waging "war" on two fronts.

With all good wishes to Lady Soulbury, your daughter and yourself.

---

[1] See 298.

## 302   CO 54/986/6/3, no 145                                    12 Oct 1945
## [Soulbury Report]: inward unnumbered telegram from Sir H Moore to Mr Hall on the response of the Board of Ministers to the report

Your Secret and Personal 4th October. Board of Ministers at two meetings from which Officers of State were excluded have given preliminary consideration to Soulbury Report and to Senanayake's conversations in London, person named having circulated to them in strict confidence copies of the records he brought back with him. I have again urged him to impress upon his colleagues their strictly confidential character in view of the terms of your letter to him of 19th September.[1]

Ministers have now issued a communiqué, which I will send with other press cuttings by fast bag, to effect that they will await final conclusions of His Majesty's Government which they understand will be communicated at an early date before making any pronouncement to State Council.

---

[1] See 294.

Present indications are that Ministers wish to avoid any emergency meeting of State Council before November 6th, but Senanayake has impressed upon me the difficulty in which he will be placed if there is any delay or lack of finality in His Majesty's Government's promised pronouncement. In the Board itself Bandaranaike pressed for immediate pronouncement in favour of full Dominion Status, and Senanayake himself was only just persuaded from making a statement to the same effect in the Press simultaneously with the Report's publication. He is now being courted by Communist and Sama Samajist Parties to form a United National Party for the same object. He has assured me personally that if His Majesty's Government can make an early pronouncement on the lines I suggested in paragraph 3 of my Secret and Personal telegram of 25th September,[2] he would back it and he believes be able to carry the State Council with him. But if there is any equivocation or delay, particularly if arising from objections raised by the Government of India, the opportunity will be lost and he will be forced to join hands with the extremists.

---

[2] See 295.

# 303    CO 54/986/6/3, no 153                                12 Oct 1945
## [Soulbury Report]: letter from Sir H Moore to Mr Hall supporting Mr. Senanayake's assessment of the local political situation

I am most grateful for your letter of 3rd October 1945 in which you say that you will spare no effort to secure a decision as soon as possible after the publication of the Soulbury Report and its consideration by Wavell's Executive Council. I appreciate this all the more as I realize how much you must be preoccupied at the present time by the situation in Palestine and developments in French Indo-China and the Netherlands East Indies.

I enclose some local Press Cuttings[1] which reflect the reactions of the Lake House Press and of the "Times of Ceylon" to the Report. The former are working in close touch with Senanayake and Goonetilleke and have adopted a generally favourable but cautious attitude to the Report in case at a later date Senanayake may be forced to jettison it in favour of full Dominion Status.

In this connection you may be interested to know that he had prepared a press interview for simultaneous publication in the "Daily News" on the day the report was released, denouncing the 1943 declaration, accusing H.M.G. of breach of faith, etc., and generally burning his boats and going bald-headed for Dominion Status. When Goonetilleke informed me of this I pointed out to him the folly of Senanayake's adopting this attitude now, before he had got any local reactions to the Report or H.M.G.'s official attitude to it, and I am glad to say Goonetilleke succeeded in convincing him of this just in time. The script was actually in the printer's hands and had to be recovered! It is, however, being kept in reserve.

The line taken by the "Times of Ceylon" does not, I think, carry weight with anyone, and indeed as Senanayake said to me yesterday, is making his task an easier one.

From my S & P telegram of to-day's date,[2] of which I enclose a copy, you will see

---

[1] Not printed.                                                    [2] See 302.

the attitude the Board has adopted. Actually Bandaranaike wanted to force the issue, but Senanayake, being now convinced, as explained above, that it was wiser to wait and see, managed to carry the day. But he came in to see me after the meeting to stress the point, which he clearly wished me to convey to you, that he did not think he could hold the position very long. The extreme Communist and Sama Samajist groups have already approached him to close ranks on an island wide demand for 'Independence', encouraged no doubt by the press accounts of what is going on in Saigon and Java. At the moment the different groups in Ceylon are jockeying for position and don't quite know what line to take. If the period of political uncertainty is prolonged, the extremist element will seize the opportunity, and he fears the present fluid situation will harden.

I think he is right. My personal difficulty, if I may say so, is ignorance as to the contemplated scope of the "decisions" which H.M.G. proposes to take before November 6th. Senanayake clearly expects a pronouncement by H.M.G. on the Report itself and the representations which he made to you in London for its modification. He hopes for a pronouncement on the lines I have referred to in paragraph 3 of my telegram of to-day's date. If a definite pronouncement of policy, possibly something on the lines of the Burma White Paper, is made, then there are already signs that the less militant section of the Ceylon Tamil Congress would desert Ponnambalam, whose fifty-fifty formula is largely discredited, and that the other minorities would support Senanayake on the grounds that Ceylon had secured a notable constitutional advance, with Dominion Status in the offing. In such a contingency Ceylon's formal transfer to the Dominions Office would have a local political value out of all proportion to its actual effect. This should, in my view, outweigh the departmental objections which are bound to be raised against it on practical administrative grounds.

But if the "decisions" are merely to postpone final judgment pending say, a Round Table conference in London, I have no doubt that not only will Senanayake refuse to attend it, but he may well create a situation under which I shall have no alternative to taking over the Government under emergency powers. I would, therefore, very much appreciate any information you can give me for my strictly personal use, as I wish to prepare in advance for all eventualities.

## 304  CO 54/986/11, no 24, C(45)2                              15 Oct 1945
## [Soulbury Report]: Cabinet Colonial Affairs Committee minutes recommending a review of the new constitution after six years[1]

*The Committee* had before them a memorandum by the Secretary of State for the Colonies (C.(45) 3) covering a draft statement on constitutional reform in Ceylon.

*The Secretary of State for the Colonies* read two telegrams which had been received from the Governor of Ceylon. The first stressed the importance of an early statement of Government policy, in order to strengthen Mr. Senanayake's hand in

---

[1] Present: Mr Greenwood (lord privy seal) in the chair; Lord Addison (DO), Lord Pethick-Lawrence (India and Burma), Mr Hall. Also present: Mr Alexander (first lord of Admiralty), Lord Jowitt (lord chancellor). Secretariat: J A Drew, Trafford Smith.

the Board of Ministers,[2] and the second reported the reaction of the Tamil minority to the Soulbury Commission's Report, which was regarded by them as failing to provide adequate safeguards for minorities: they had registered an emphatic protest against the recommendations.

*The Secretary of State for the Colonies* explained that throughout his discussions with Mr. Senanayake, the latter had reverted time after time to the undertaking as regards eventual Dominion Status which had been given to Burma. He thought, however, that Mr. Senanayake would be quite prepared, for his own part, to accept something less than Dominion status, providing that, in their undertaking, the new Government gave, as far as possible, the new constitution the appearance of that of a Dominion.

There was some discussion about the phrase "some appropriate form of Dominion status". There was general agreement that the phrase was too concrete and might give rise to considerable difficulties, particularly with the Dominions, and in regard to our defence requirements. It was felt that the most satisfactory way of meeting the Secretary of State for the Colonies' point of view would be to adopt some such phraseology as "The review after six years would be directed towards self government under a constitution on Dominion lines, subject to such reservations as may be necessary for defence and foreign affairs." *The Secretary of State for the Colonies* undertook to consider this wording.

*The Lord Chancellor* referred to the proposed undertaking to initiate a review six years after the introduction of the new constitution, and pointed out that, in view of the evident fears of the Tamil and other minorities, it should be made clear in the statement of public policy that our general attitude to further constitutional advancement would be governed *inter alia* by the ability of the Government of Ceylon to prove that it could handle minority questions satisfactorily. He therefore suggested that, in paragraph 10 of the Statement of Policy a sentence on the lines of the three sentences of paragraph 4 of the covering memorandum by the Secretary of State for the Colonies should be introduced in order to bring out the importance attached by His Majesty's Government to a satisfactory handling of minority questions before a further degree of self government was granted.

*The Lord Chancellor* went on to raise a point in regard to paragraph 12 of the Statement of Policy dealing with the question of the three-quarters majority. There appeared to him to be some doubt about the desirability of using the phrase in the second sentence, regarding the "strict interpretation of the Declaration" of 1943. He suggested that the drafting of this should be looked at, as it appeared that the 1943 Declaration had, in fact, been confirmed by the terms of reference of the Commission.

*The Committee* went on to discuss the six-year period laid down in paragraph 10 of the Statement of Policy as the time during which the Ceylon Government was to prove its fitness for further constitutional advance. *The Secretary of State for India* felt that it was unwise for His Majesty's Government to tie itself down to a fixed period, and *The First Lord of the Admiralty* thought that six years was too short. After full discussion, however, and in view of the great difficulty which would undoubtedly be experienced in holding the position for any longer period than six years, *The Committee* decided to accept this provision. During the discussion, *The*

---

[2] See 302.

*Secretary of State for the Colonies* brought out the fact that the six-year period would not, in any case, begin until the introduction of the new constitution, which could not be earlier than 1947. It was agreed that His Majesty's Government's intentions would be clearer if the wording "they will review the constitutional issue" were altered to "they will initiate a review of the constitutional issue".

*The Secretary of State for the Colonies* referred to the discussion in the Cabinet as to the wisdom of providing for an Upper House in Ceylon. Its primary purpose was to provide an additional safeguard for the minorities. With his power of nominating half the membership of the Upper House, the Governor would be in a position to add to the minority representation if the situation required it. *The Lord Chancellor* thought that, in view of its limited power, the Upper House would be little more than a forum in which minorities could express their views. *The Lord Privy Seal* attached importance to its educative effect on public opinion. It was agreed that, in the circumstances of Ceylon, an Upper House was desirable.

*The Committee* then considered the timetable to be adopted. It was decided that:—

> A further meeting of the Colonial Affairs Committee should be held on the afternoon of Monday, 22nd October at 3.45 in the Lord Chancellor's room in the House of Lords, by which time it was hoped that the views of the Government of India would have been received. All being well, the matter would be taken to the Cabinet at its meeting on Thursday, 25th October.

# 305   CO 54/986/11, no 28                                    15 Oct 1945
## [Dominion status]: letter from F F Turnbull (India Office) to C H Thornley on the wording of statements of policy in regard to Burma

My Secretary of State tells me that at the meeting of the Colonial Affairs Committee this morning[1] there was some discussion as to the wording of the statements of policy in regard to Burma and, in particular, how far we had gone in an undertaking that Dominion Status would be granted to Burma.

Lord Pethick-Lawrence desires me to draw your attention to the Statement of Policy contained in Part II of the enclosed White Paper,[2] and in particular to the second sentence of paragraph 1 of the Statement, which reiterates that it is our aim to assist the political development of Burma till she can sustain the responsibilities of complete self-government within the British Commonwealth and consequently "attain a status equal to that of the Dominions and this country".

In the discussion this morning Lord Pethick-Lawrence referred to some further statements on this subject which were to be made in the coming week. What he had in mind are messages from the King, the Prime Minister and himself to the people of Burma on the occasion of the return of Civil Government. None of these, however, uses words which go further than the Statement of Policy referred to above which is the governing one at the present time.

---

[1] See 304.                                    [2] Not printed but see 273, note 3, for the reference.

**306**   CO 54/986/6/3, no 148                              16 Oct 1945

## [Soulbury Report]: outward unnumbered telegram from Mr Hall to Sir H Moore explaining the proposals considered by the Cabinet Colonial Affairs Committee

Your secret and personal telegram of the 12th October.

I am glad to learn that Senanayake has been persuaded to maintain his present attitude.

2.  For your strictly personal information I should like you to know that present position as regards formulation of His Majesty's Government's decisions is as follows:—

A draft statement of policy was considered by the Colonial Affairs Committee of the Cabinet yesterday and will come up for further consideration by that Committee on Monday afternoon next, 22nd October, if, as I hope, views of Government of India on Soulbury Report have been received by that date, with a view to submission to the Cabinet as soon as possible thereafter for final decisions.

3.  I assume from the second paragraph of your telegram under reference, that Ceylon Ministers do not wish, at this stage, to express any views on Report.

4.  As regards assurance given to you by Senanayake referred to in last paragraph of your telegram under reference, it appears unlikely that His Majesty's Government will be prepared to go all the way towards meeting the proposals put forward at the commencement of paragraph 3 of your secret and personal telegram of the 25th September.[1] Proposals laid before Cabinet Committee provide for a Constitution on general lines of Soulbury recommendations with the following modifications designed to meet as far as possible points raised by Senanayake in London:—

(a)  Life of the Upper House would be reduced from nine to six years.

(b)  In place of Soulbury recommendations as regards defence and external affairs, His Majesty's Government would retain power to legislate for Ceylon by Order in Council, the Governor having in reserve an Order in Council for use in public emergency enabling him to make regulations on lines of those specified in Emergency Powers (Defence) Act, 1939.

(c)  Title of Governor and channel of communication with His Majesty's Government would remain unchanged.

(d)  Ceylon Government would be empowered to establish and regulate both coastal and overseas shipping services, provided no action which may be interpreted as discriminatory against shipping of other members of the Commonwealth is taken without concurrence of His Majesty's Government in the United Kingdom.

(e)  Periods specified in paragraph 372 (ii) of Soulbury Report for exercise of right of retirement would be reduced to two years. Special right of retirement with compensation would not extend to officers appointed on agreement.

5.  It is contemplated that an announcement of decisions on above lines would be accompanied by a statement to effect that six years after introduction of the new Constitution His Majesty's Government would initiate a review of the constitutional

---

[1] See 304.                                                    [2] See 295.

issue in consultation with the Ceylon Government; and that this review would be directed towards self-government under a Constitution on Dominion lines subject to such powers as may be necessary for His Majesty's Government to secure in respect of defence and foreign affairs.

6.   I should be glad if you could let me have by Friday noon at latest your own personal estimate of what Ministers' reception of decisions on above lines would be.

## 307   CO 54/986/6/3, no 150                                    16 Oct 1945
## [Soulbury Report]: letter from Admiral Layton to G E J Gent on difficulties with regard to defence requirements

Many thanks for sending me a copy of the Soulbury Commission Report. I have read it with much interest and the Commission have certainly corrected the worst errors of the Ministers' scheme.

From my experience in Ceylon, I foresee that one of the main difficulties is likely to be in dealing with matters which, though primarily concerning internal affairs, have a distinct bearing on defence requirements. An example would be a proposal (which is very likely to come up) to abolish the railway and rely on road transport. I should regard such a measure myself as unacceptable from the defence point of view so long as the Navy contemplates using Colombo and Trincomalee as bases, but the Ceylon Government might well not agree. On the negative side it is comparatively simple for the Governor General to block such a measure by reserving it as coming under the 'Communications' aspect of Defence, but in such a connection it is also possible that he might have to legislate positively by means of a Governor General's Ordinance. In that case, who would advise him on the drafting of such an Ordinance? I quite see the constitutional difficulty of providing the Governor General with a separate set of advisers as regards matters within his discretion, but it does seem to me a fact that he might badly need advice on such matters in their administrative aspect which could not be given by the Defence authorities themselves.

## 308   CO 54/986/6/3, no 149                                    17 Oct 1945
## [Soulbury Report]: inward unnumbered telegram (reply) from Sir H Moore to Mr Hall proposing a more explicit pronouncement with regard to dominion status

Your secret and personal of 16th October.[1]
1.  Your paragraph 2 noted.
2.  Your paragraph 3 confirmed.
3.  I have following comments on your paragraph 4:—

(a) and (b) should assist Senanayake and I see no over-riding objection.
(c) Is logical corollary of Constitutional status now proposed, but I have no doubt for prestige reasons local sentiment would much prefer Soulbury proposals

---

[1] See 306.

combined with transfer of Dominions Office—see paragraph 6 of my secret and personal letter of 12th October.[2]

(d) Local politicians dislike word "discriminatory" suggest "No action which would subject shipping of other members of the Commonwealth to differential treatment" might be more locally acceptable.

(e) I think two years would be fair to public service but since there may be delay between date of enactment of Order-in-Council and actual operation of new Constitution, suggest effective date should be first meeting of new Parliament.

I think this may be what Senanayake intended and, if not, I doubt if he would object, as he is anxious that the better men should not be frightened away before they know what conditions will really be.

4. Your paragraph 5. I appreciate that His Majesty's Government may not be prepared to give Ceylon a blank cheque for full Dominion status in six years time, but I fear proposed text of Statement may come as a cold douche and possibly jeopardize acceptance of His Majesty's Government's decisions on Soulbury Report itself. I do not know, of course, how far His Majesty's Government is prepared to go nor how explicit a pronouncement it is desired to make, but I would respectfully suggest that something more on the lines of the Burma White Paper might be considered. For example:—

> "His Majesty's Government desire to make it clear that they would not regard such a Constitution as the final word in Ceylon's Constitutional development. On the contrary, it will be the consistent policy of His Majesty's Government to assist Ceylon in her political development till she can sustain the responsibilities of complete self-government within the British Commonwealth. His Majesty's Government therefore propose in six years time to review the position in consultation with the Government of Ceylon, in the light of the circumstances then obtaining and the general security requirements of the British Commonwealth, with a view to Ceylon taking her appropriate place beside the Governments of the Dominions in the exercise of full internal self-government."

5. Your paragraph 6. If some variation of the Statement on the general lines suggested in paragraph 4 can be made, my personal opinion is that Senanayake, Kotelawala, Mahadeva would certainly accept it. Corea would probably follow suit. George de Silva's platform is independence but on a show-down he might come in rather than lose his seat. Bandaranaike is an unknown quantity, purely opportunist, but, if to his political advantage, he may accept it, and then agitate for early grant of full Dominion status. Kannangara will probably follow Bandaranaike, but if the door appears bolted and barred now on Dominion status, as they visualize it, in six years time, the Burma argument will be developed and I would not care to prophesy what attitude Senanayake, much less the others, will adopt.

---

[2] See 303.

**309**   CO 54/986/8, no 34                                       17 Oct 1945

[Soulbury Report]: inward telegram no 1933 from Sir H Moore to Mr Hall transmitting a resolution on the report by the Working Committee of the Ceylon Indian Congress

Following Resolution of the Working Committee of Ceylon Indian Congress is sent at the request of their President. *Begins.* The Working Committee of the Ceylon Indian Congress views the Soulbury Recommendations with grave concern and disappointment. The whole Report has been drafted with the idea of getting it accepted by the majority community rather than doing justice to the real grievances of the Ceylon Indian and other minority communities, whereas the primary object of the Commission was to render justice to the minorities. The Recommendations have been formulated with the sole purpose of harmonising with the salient features of the Draft Constitution of the Board of Ministers and, in doing so, the legitimate rights of the minorities, and more particularly those of the Indian community, have been sacrificed.

The Recommendations on the franchise, status and citizenship rights of Indians in Ceylon are unjust and unfair. The Commission have failed to recognise the inherent rights of citizenship further strengthened by the solemn undertakings given by the Government of Ceylon. The Recommendations, if accepted, will keep the Indians in a state of serfdom and isolation and will prevent their assimilation into a single nation, which the Commissioners apparently so devoutly desire. While the Ceylon Indian Congress, in keeping with its aim of independence for Ceylon, unreservedly supports the transfer of power into the hands of the people of the country, it cannot acquiesce in a scheme where the Indian community will be prevented from taking its legitimate place in the body public of the country.

His Majesty's Government, in making their declaration of 1943, recognised the value of Ceylon's war efforts, which mainly came from Tea and Rubber estate labourers, the vast majority of whom are all Indians. Yet the just demands of the Indians are totally ignored by the Commission. The Ceylon Indian Congress reiterates that its legitimate demands should be met by acceptance of:—

(1) full unrestricted adult franchise
(2) the rights of citizenship on the ascertainable test of a residence of five years and a simple declaration of intention and
(3) of representation in the House of Representatives of a number not less than the proportion of Indian population in Ceylon warrants on the basis of 101 seats for the whole population.

The Working Committee of the Ceylon Indian Congress trusts that it will not be driven to the painful necessity of resorting to measures which will be embarrassing to the Government. *Ends.*

**310**   CO 54/986/6/3, no 151                      18 Oct 1945

[Soulbury Report]: inward telegram no 1824-S from Lord Wavell to Lord Pethick-Lawrence forwarding the comments of his Executive Council

Soulbury report.

Following are our comments after consideration in Council.

2.  We welcome intention of report which recommends large measure of internal self government for Ceylon. We believe this to be in keeping with wishes of people of Ceylon as of other peoples of South East Asia.

3.  But we consider recommendations concerning participation in self government of Indians resident in Ceylon most disappointing and unlikely to facilitate their assimilation as part of Ceylonese nation. Repeated assurances have been given of equality of treatment and legal rights as between Indian and local population, so as to encourage immigration of Indian labour. Latest of these assurances was given by Governor in February 1941. His Majesty's Government's declaration of May 26th 1943 made it clear that Ceylon's relations with other parts of British Commonwealth would be subject to control by His Majesty's Government. Now that complete internal autonomy is recommended and particularly in view of Ceylon Ministers attitude and utterances we are convinced that fundamental rights of Indian [sic] in respect of franchise and citizenship must be incorporated in constitution itself. The proposals in succeeding paragraphs are intended merely to ensure this and to safeguard future of Indians already resident in Ceylon.

4.  We consider Commission's recommendation for retention of franchise on present basis unfair to Indians and contrary (? to) view taken in paragraph 238 that franchise is real safeguard. Present basis has never been satisfactory for Indians. As recognized in paragraphs 216, 217 and 2(? 18) it has failed to secure the enfranchisement of large number of illiterate labourers with a permanent interest in Ceylon. (? Representations) submitted to Commission by Indians representatives show how present basis has (? worked) to the detriment of Indian community. "Tightening up" procedure of 1939 has been used to reduce number of Indian voters from 225,000 in that year to 168,000 in 1943. Working of Donoughmore constitution has thus amply demonstrated futility of present basis.

5.  We cannot admit validity of argument of 1929 used (? by) Commission that Sinhalese majority would not accept Indian franchise based on residence only. Reasons which led His Majesty's Government to accept this argument in 1929 no longer hold good. For 16 years Indians have returned only 2 members to State Council. Issue of licences to recruit new labour for losses ceased in 1935. India stopped emigration of labour in 1939 and report recommends that Ceylon Ministry should have full power to regulate (? or) restrict immigration. Fear of Sinhalese that they might be overwhelmed by Indian immigrants thus has no repeat no force. In paragraph 240 Commission recognize that few Indian labourers now in Ceylon can have been resident for less than 5 years. Indian estate labour is largely stabilised. The labourers stayed on estates throughout the war and contributed largely to Ceylon war effort. There is an increasing body of opinion not only among Ceylon Tamils but among left wing Sinhalese (whose emergence is welcomed by the Commission) in favour of full enfranchisement and assimilation of Indian labour.

6. We note from paragraphs 238, 240, 241 and 274 (? that) Commission consider that Indian community should rely for protection more on 14 seats in Parliament than on any special safeguard. Commission recognise that "(? adequate) measure of enfranchisement" and prevention of "harsh or restrictive policy" regarding enfranchisement of Indian labour are essential. We emphasise that representation contemplated cannot be secured unless the strength of Indian electorate is maintained at appropriate level, and that its strength cannot be so maintained unless Indian franchise is put on a sound and easily determinable basis.

7. We therefore urge that while literacy and property qualification may be retained, franchise on equal footing with rest of population be granted to all Indians who have been resident in island for a total period of not less than five years. This would be in consonance with recent declaration by Secretary of State for the Colonies on citizenship in Malaya.[1] Moreover in view of Ceylon Ministers declared intention of reducing existing Indian population and persistent endeavour to reduce Indian electorate we also urge most strongly that provision (? for) fundamental right of Indian franchise be embodied in constitution. We do not repeat not accept recommendation in paragraph 242 (2), and hold that any bill likely to affect Indian franchise adversely must be reserved.

8. Commission has recommended combination of territorial and communal representation to provide 14 seats in Parliament for Indian community. We do not consider that this object will be achieved if left to discretion of Delimitation Commission as contemplated in para 272. We urge Delimitation Commission be directed so to delimit electoral districts as to form necessary number of constituencies with majority of Indian voters. We note recommendation of multi-member constituencies in para 273, but point out its object will not be achieved unless individual voter is permitted to cast all his votes cumulatively in favour of one candidate. We trust that this is the intention.

9. We are most uneasy about safeguards in respect of citizenship rights outlined in paras 237, 238 and 239. We presume safeguard in paras 239 (III) and 242 (III] is intended to protect all persons including resident Indians against discrimination in respect of acquisition, ownership and disposal of property and right to hold public office or carry on any occupation trade profession or business, as in respect of other civic rights. Experience has however shown that a safeguard of this kind can be circumvented by excluding "non Ceylonese" from privileges, the term "Ceylonese" being so defined as to exclude large elements of resident Indians. We strongly recommend the inclusion in the constitution of specific safeguard covering matters (? mentioned) above. We regard this as the minimum guarantee (? of) fair treatment for Indian community, and (? in view of) discriminatory measures against Indians in recent years, of which details have been furnished in the minority representations, we emphasise that constitutional safeguard must cover executive as well as legislative action.

10. In connection with paragraph 242 (I) we regard the right of re-entry of persons normally resident in Ceylon as a fundamental right, and would urge that this right should be formally recognised and included in the constitution.

11. We have confined (? our) comments to those which we consider of

---

[1] A reference to proposals to establish common citizenship in Malaya in a new Malayan Union; cf BDEEP series B, vol 3, A J Stockwell, ed, *Malaya*, part I, 48.

fundamental importance. If modifications we suggest (? are not) made, (? any) constitution based on Commission's proposals would cause profound dissatisfaction amongst Indian community in Ceylon and public in India. We believe that with modifications suggested Commission's proposals may be acceptable, and will not leave legacy of ill-will and bitterness between the two countries.

12.  We have been gravely handicapped by short time allowed for our comments, presume that we will be given further opportunity of (? commenting) on His Majesty's Government's proposals on report before Cabinet decisions are taken or legislation is introduced.

# 311  CO 54/986/6/3                                    22 Oct 1945
## [Soulbury Report]: minute by Trafford Smith of a meeting with Lord Soulbury on the latter's opposition to HMG's policy

I met Lord Soulbury last Friday, October 19th, at a Chatham House discussion at which Mr. Ponnambalam was speaking.

Lord Soulbury said how very anxious he was that further difficulties should not arise in the introduction of the new Ceylon Constitution owing to delay in reaching decisions by His Majesty's Government, and I assured him that the Secretary of State was fully aware of the necessity for the utmost speed in reaching decisions, and that everything possible was being done in that direction.

Lord Soulbury then went on to mention, in reference to his letter to the Secretary of State of 5th October (flagged below)[1] that he had now received the concurrence of both his colleagues of the Commission in the terms of that letter. He felt very keenly the difficulties of the position in which Mr. Senanayake was now placed, and he said that, if the situation developed in a way which would warrant his so doing, he might possibly feel it necessary to release the letter of the 5th October for publication here and in Ceylon.

Lord Soulbury also said that if His Majesty's Government's decisions did not appear to him to be the right ones, he would have no hesitation in expressing his views in the House of Lords, and in putting his knowledge of the subject at the disposal of the critics of His Majesty's Government in the House of Commons.

I asked him whether he wished the conversation to be treated as a purely private one or whether I was to let its general tenor to be known in the Colonial Office. He said that I might give discrete [sic] hints on the lines above. I have reported the conversation to Mr. Gent and should have preferred to have left it at that; but I have now been asked to record it on paper.

---

[1] See 300.

# 312   CAB 129/3, CP(45)244                     23 Oct 1945

## 'Ceylon constitution': Cabinet report by Mr Greenwood on behalf of the Colonial Affairs Committee. *Annex*: paras 10–12 of the draft statement of policy

[Only paras 10–12 of the annex to which Greenwood refers in the first para of his report are reproduced here. Para 11 explains the point made by Greenwood in para 8(i) of his report. Para 10 (on dominion status) and para 12 (on the three-quarters majority) represent the issues arising from the draft statement upon which the Cabinet focused when it considered the recommendations of the Colonial Affairs Committee (see 316, 317).]

At its two last meetings on October 15th[1] and October 22nd, the Committee has had under consideration a draft Statement of Policy on Constitutional Reform in Ceylon submitted by the Secretary of State for the Colonies. The draft Statement (Annex to this Paper) is intended for publication simultaneously in this country and in Ceylon immediately after approval by the Cabinet, as a White Paper announcing His Majesty's Government's decisions on the recommendations of the Soulbury Commission. The Colonial Affairs Committee has carefully considered the terms of the draft Statement in the light of the arguments advanced by Mr. Senanayake, the Leader of the Ceylon State Council, in his recent discussions with the Secretary of State, of the advice tendered to the Secretary of State by the Governor of Ceylon, and of the views of the Government of India on the Soulbury Report now received by the Secretary of State for India. The Committee recommend that the Cabinet should approve the draft Statement as now revised in accordance with the Committee's views, and should authorise its immediate publication as desired by the Secretary of State for the Colonies in time for consideration by the Ceylon Board of Ministers before the meeting of the Ceylon State Council on November 6th.

2.   The following paragraphs explain the genesis of the draft Statement and summarise the views of Mr. Senanayake, the Governor of Ceylon and the Government of India, which have been taken into account in framing its terms.

3.   In accordance with the conclusions of the Cabinet on the 11th September[2] the Soulbury Report was published on the 9th October simultaneously in this country, in Ceylon and in India, and on that date copies were given to the Ceylon Board of Ministers and the Governor-General's Executive Council in India, and released also in the Dominions. In his discussions with the Secretary of State for the Colonies, Mr. Senanayake put forward the plea that Ceylon Ministers had originally accepted the 1943 Declaration as a basis for interim reforms which would enable them to increase the war effort of Ceylon. Now that the war is over, they were no longer prepared to proceed on the basis of the 1943 Declaration, but wished to press for the grant to Ceylon of Dominion Status. Mr. Senanayake made it clear that, although he had no formal mandate from the Board of Ministers to this effect, he was expressing not only his own views, but the views of the great majority of the people of Ceylon in making this plan. In accordance with the conclusion of the Cabinet the Secretary of State refrained from making any statement to Mr. Senanayake on the subject of Dominion Status for Ceylon.

---

[1] See 304.                                                        [2] See 284.

4. Mr. Senanayake was very disappointed at having to leave this country without having been able to reach any decisions or arguments with His Majesty's Government which he could show in Ceylon as the result of his mission. He has made it clear both before and since his return to Ceylon that he now regards himself as free to adopt whatever line of action may seem to him best, and the Governor has reported that Mr. Senanayake has somewhat reluctantly agreed to await the decisions of His Majesty's Government before he decides whether he must align himself with those elements in Ceylon who are determined to press for Dominion Status at all costs. It therefore appears very doubtful whether without some concession by His Majesty's Government by which he can demonstrate that his mission to England has not been fruitless, he will now be willing to sponsor the Soulbury recommendations before the Ceylon State Council as it was at one time hoped.

5. The Committee share the view of the Secretary of State for the Colonies that the time is not yet ripe for the immediate advancement of Ceylon to the Constitutional Status of a Dominion. In the Committee's opinion, there can be no doubt on general grounds that it would be premature for Ceylon to be granted Dominion Status in advance of India and Burma. Moreover, the Sinhalese majority, whose power under a completely self-governing Constitution would be preponderant, have yet to prove their willingness and capacity to operate self-governing institutions in collaboration with the minorities and having due regard to their legitimate rights and susceptibilities. Nevertheless the Committee have been impressed by the arguments advanced by Mr. Senanayake in relation to the constitutional promise made to Burma of Dominion Status; and the Committee agree with the Secretary of State that the chances of acceptance of the Soulbury recommendations by the State Council and people of Ceylon will be remote unless it is possible for His Majesty's Government to give some assurance of reconsideration of the constitutional issue in the not too distant future. The Committee therefore recommend that His Majesty's Government's decisions should

(i) lay down the general lines of a Constitution for Ceylon based on the Soulbury recommendations, and
(ii) also proclaim His Majesty's Government's intention of initiating a review of the Constitutional issue in consultation with the Ceylon Government, six years after the introduction of the new Constitution, in the light of the circumstances then obtaining and subject to such provisions as may be necessary to satisfy the security requirements of the British Commonwealth. The object of this review will be that Ceylon shall take her appropriate place in the Commonwealth with full internal self-government under a Constitution on Dominion lines.

The Committee are satisfied that, unless some such intention is proclaimed, a Constitution on the lines of the Soulbury recommendations is unlikely to be accepted by the people of Ceylon and their leaders: on the contrary, we must be prepared for a period of political unrest in the island which will make efficient Government exceedingly difficult.

6. Before reaching these conclusions, the Committee most carefully examined the views of the Government of India on the Soulbury Report, which are briefly [sic] summarised below:—

(a) The intention to grant a large measure of self-government to Ceylon is welcomed;

(b) The fundamental rights of Indians in respect of franchise and citizenship must be incorporated in the Constitution itself, now that internal autonomy is recommended, and in view of the attitude and utterances of Ceylon Ministers.

(c) The present recommendation for the retention of the existing franchise, which has never been satisfactory for Indians, is unfair;

(d) The arguments which led His Majesty's Government to accept in 1929 the view that the Sinhalese majority would not agree to an Indian franchise based on residence only no longer hold good, since the issue of licences to recruit new labour ceased in 1935 and the emigration of further labour was stopped by India in 1939. Indian estate labour is, therefore, largely stabilised.

(e) The Indian franchise must be put on a sound and easily determinable basis if representation of the Indian community by 14 seats in Parliament is to be secured and maintained.

(f) It is urged that franchise on an equal footing with the rest of the population be granted to all Indians who have been *resident* in Ceylon for a total period of not less than 5 years.

(g) The recommendation in paragraph 242(ii) of the Report is not accepted. Any bill likely to affect the Indian franchise adversely should be reserved. The Delimitation Commission should be directed so to delimit electoral districts as to form the 14 constituencies contemplated in the Report which would have a majority of Indian voters. This should not be left to the Commission's discretion. In multi-member constituencies, individual voters should be permitted to cast all their votes cumulatively in favour of a single candidate.

(h) The Constitution should provide specific safeguards to protect all persons, including resident Indians, against discrimination in respect of the acquisition ownership and disposal of property, the right to hold public office, to carry on any trade, profession, business, etc. especially in view of discriminatory measures against Indians in recent years.

(i) Provision for the right of re-entry of persons normally resident in Ceylon should be recognised and included in the Constitution.

(j) If the above modifications are not made, a Constitution based on the Soulbury Commission's proposals would cause profound dissatisfaction, both in Ceylon and in India.

7.   The Committee consider that the Government of India's point as regards the operation of voting in multi-member constituencies can be met. But, as regards franchise and citizenship rights, they are unable to recommend the acceptance by His Majesty's Government of the variations of the provisions of the Soulbury Report proposed. The Committee attach importance to the conclusion reached by the Soulbury Commission after exhaustive examination of the views of the minorities, that the franchise and citizenship rights dealt with in (b) to (g) above are essentially matters of domestic concern, to be handled by the Ceylon Government if necessary in direct negotiation with the Government of India; and this conclusion is strengthened by the fact that such direct negotiations on these questions have already taken place in the past. The Committee consider that it would be most unwise for His Majesty's Government to attempt to impose a settlement in a matter on which feeling in Ceylon is so strong.

The safeguards requested by the Government of India in (h) above appear to be provided already in general terms under the recommendation in paragraph 242(iii) of the Soulbury Report, and it would appear undesirable to make specific provision in respect of particular categories and subjects.

As regards the right of re-entry of Indians (see (i) above) Bills dealing with this matter are already required under paragraph 242 (i) of the Report to be reserved by the Governor in certain circumstances; and the Committee consider that to deprive the future Government of Ceylon of the right to legislate at all on this subject as desired by the Government of India would be a serious encroachment on the powers of self-government recommended by the Commission.

8. The following paragraphs contain explanations of the remaining points of importance in the draft Statement:—

(i) The modifications of the Soulbury recommendations proposed in paragraph 11 of the draft Statement are the result of the Secretary of State's discussions with Mr. Senanayake. The Committee agree that these modifications represent the limit to which it is possible to go to meet Mr. Senanayake's views.

(ii) Paragraph 12 deals with the difficult question of the three-quarters majority. The Committee understand that, under the terms of the 1943 Declaration, His Majesty's Government is not committed to apply the three-quarters majority stipulation to the recommendations of the Soulbury Commission. On the other hand, there can be no doubt that very great importance is attached to this stipulation by the minority communities in Ceylon, especially the Tamils, who may be expected to protest very strongly if it is not applied. In the circumstances, the Committee consider that the line taken in the draft statement is the only practicable one for His Majesty's Government to adopt. Under the terms of the present draft Statement, His Majesty's Government would be committed to adopt the new Constitution if it were to obtain a three-quarters majority (a most unlikely event). If such a majority were not obtained, it would be necessary to consider in the light of the results of the voting whether or not the degree of support in Ceylon were sufficient to warrant the adoption of the new Constitution with or without modification. Should the Constitution be decisively rejected, however, a General Election in Ceylon (which under the present Constitution is due to take place not later than March, 1947) would follow, unless the life of the present Council (already extended to eleven years) were further extended by Order in Council, which is clearly undesirable. In that event, His Majesty's Government would have to consider how to resolve the difficulties, and might wish to convene a Round Table Conference in London in due course.

9. In conclusion, the Committee cannot stress too strongly the urgency of an immediate decision on this question of the review of the Ceylon Constitution. The interval between publication of the Report and the announcement of His Majesty's Government's decisions is already being used by the extremist parties in Ceylon to conduct an island-wide campaign against the acceptance of a Constitution on the lines of the Soulbury recommendations, and in favour of an uncompromising demand for far more radical concessions. If the State Council were to meet on November 6th without an announcement of decisions by His Majesty's Government, this demand would gather strength among the members, and all hope of the introduction of a Constitution on the lines proposed would have to be abandoned.

10. The Committee therefore urge most earnestly that the Cabinet should give immediate approval to the terms of the attached draft Statement of Policy, the

principal features of which are:—

(i) His Majesty's Government's decision to lay down the general lines of a Constitution for Ceylon based on the Soulbury recommendations; and
(ii) Their undertaking to initiate a review of the constitutional position in six years' time.

### Annex to 312: paragraphs 10–12 of draft statement of policy on constitutional reform

#### Decisions

10. With all these factors in mind His Majesty's Government have reached the conclusion that a Constitution on the general lines proposed by the Soulbury Commission (which also conforms in broad outline, save as regards the Second Chamber, with the Constitutional scheme put forward by the Ceylon Ministers themselves) will provide a suitable measure of constitutional progress for Ceylon at the present juncture. They have carefully considered all the arguments advanced in favour of Dominion Status but they remain convinced that the time is not yet ripe for the grant of such a status to Ceylon. Nevertheless His Majesty's Government desire to make it clear that they would not regard a Constitution on the lines proposed above as the final word in Ceylon's constitutional development. On the contrary, it will be the consistent policy of His Majesty's Government to assist Ceylon in her political development until she can sustain the responsibilities of complete, self-government in the British Commonwealth, and the present decisions are, therefore, regarded by His Majesty's Government as deserving of review after some further experience.

His Majesty's Government have therefore decided that six years after the introduction of the new Constitution they will initiate a review of the constitutional issue in consultation with the Government of Ceylon in the light of the circumstances then obtaining and subject to such provisions as may be necessary to satisfy the security requirements of the British Commonwealth. The object of this review will be that Ceylon shall take her appropriate place in the Commonwealth with full internal self-government under a Constitution on Dominion lines. The further period under a Constitution on the general lines proposed by the Soulbury Commission would provide for the Government of Ceylon an opportunity of proving their ability to undertake increased responsibilities, and would enable that Government to gain experience, denied to them under the present Constitution, of a collective ministerial responsibility to the people of Ceylon. Moreover the Sinhalese majority, whose power under a completely self-governing Constitution will be preponderant, will be enabled during this period to demonstrate their willingness and capacity to operate self-governing institutions in collaboration with the minorities, and having due regard to the latter's legitimate rights and susceptibilities.

11. The main features of the Constitution under which Ceylon will be governed during this period will follow the general lines of the recommendations of the Soulbury Commission, with the following principal modifications:—

(a) *Life of the Upper House.* In view of the proposed reconsideration of the Constitution after six years, the provisions as regards the life of the Upper House will be changed so that one-third of the Membership will retire after two years, and a further third after four years, the arrangements proposed by the Soulbury Commission being followed for their replacement.

(b) *Reserved powers of the governor.* In place of the recommendations of the Soulbury Commission that the Governor shall be empowered to enact special Ordinances dealing with Defence and External Affairs, His Majesty's Government will retain the power to legislate for Ceylon by Order in Council, and the Governor will be provided by Order in Council to be brought into operation by Proclamation in case of a public emergency with powers to make regulations for purposes such as those specified in the Emergency Powers (Defence) Act, 1939. During the operation of the new Constitution the present title of Governor would not be altered, and the channel of communication between the Government of Ceylon and His Majesty's Government in the United kingdom will remain as at present through the Governor and the Secretary of State for the Colonies, who will retain his present ministerial responsibility in regard to Ceylon Affairs.

(c) *Breakdown of the constitution.* Any contingency arising in this respect will be covered by the general power of His Majesty's Government to legislate for Ceylon by Order in Council which will include, if necessary, suspension of the Constitution.

(d) *Shipping.* The Ceylon Government will be empowered to establish and regulate shipping services, both coastal and overseas, provided that no action is taken without the concurrence of His Majesty's Government in the United Kingdom, which may be interpreted as subjecting the shipping of other members of the Commonwealth to differential treatment.

(e) *Public Services.* The period of exercise of the right of retirement of certain classes of officers specified in paragraph 372(ii) of the Soulbury Report shall be reduced from three to two years from the date of the first meeting of Parliament under the new Constitution: and the exercise of the special right of retirement with compensation for loss of career shall not extend to officers appointed to the Public Services on agreement for a limited period of years.

*The question of the three-quarters majority*

12.   In Section 7 of the 1943 Declaration His Majesty's Government made it clear that the acceptance of any constitutional proposals put forward by Ceylon Ministers would depend upon the subsequent approval of such proposals by three-quarters of all the Members of the State Council of Ceylon, excluding the Officers of State and the Speaker or other presiding Officer. This condition attaches only to constitutional proposals put forward by Ceylon Ministers, and cannot expressly be applied to the proposals which have been put forward independently by the Soulbury Commission. The Commission have made it clear throughout their Report, however, that they regarded the Ministers' Constitution as one of the principal basic documents in their investigation, and many of their recommendations follow its provisions. His Majesty's Government have therefore decided that the provisions of the proposed Constitution shall be laid before the State Council of Ceylon with a view to their acceptance, if possible, by a three-quarters majority of the Council on the basis proposed in the 1943 Declaration. They desire it to be clearly understood, however, that they do not regard themselves as bound by this provision in the event of the requisite three-quarters majority not being obtained.

**313**   CO 54/986/6/3, no 158                                      24 Oct 1945
[Soulbury Report]: letter from G E J Gent to Sir H Moore on the draft
statement of policy

With reference to the penultimate paragraph of your secret and personal letter to the
Secretary of State of 12th October, I have been asked to let you have at once *for your
own most secret and most personal information* the attached copy[1] of the draft of the
statement of policy on Constitutional Reform which it is proposed that His Majesty's
Government should make in relation to the report of the Soulbury Commission.

This statement of policy has still to be approved by the full Cabinet and it was only
yesterday that it received the approval of the Colonial Affairs Committee of the
Cabinet.[2] Until it had got to that stage we felt that it would not be of real practical
value to you to have it, especially as a long telegram from the Government of India, a
copy of which I also enclose, containing its representations in regard to the Soulbury
Commission's Report had only very recently reached us and had also to be
considered.

I will not go into details of the proposed Statement of Policy but as you will see:—

(a) no concessions have been made to the Government of India's representations
on any main issue;
(b) we have endeavoured to meet Senanayake as far as possible, and a promise is
included that if a Constitution on the lines set out in the statement is accepted
there shall be a further review of the constitutional issue in six years' time with the
object of providing full internal self-government under a Constitution on Dominion lines.

In their consideration of general issue the Cabinet Committee were quite adamant
on the question of conceding Dominion status now, with the consequent transfer of
the affairs of Ceylon to the care of the Dominions Office and the change of the title of
Governor to Governor General.

If there are any changes in the draft Declaration as the result of its consideration
in the Cabinet, we will, of course, let you know by telegram. We fully appreciate the
urgency of making an announcement at the earliest possible date.

---

[1] Not printed.                                                          [2] See 312.

**314**   CO 54/986/8, no 38                                        25 Oct 1945
[Soulbury Report]: inward telegram no 1995 from Sir H Moore to Mr
Hall transmitting a resolution on the report by the European Associa-
tion of Ceylon

Following sent at request of European Association. *Begins.* European Association of
Ceylon wishes to call attention to representations which they made to the Soulbury
Commission and to inform you that they adhere to these, particularly in the matter
of Statutory safeguards, especially as regards right of entry, not merely of re-entry,
request for former having been completely ignored by the Commission, also of
election, not nomination, of its own representative. If Constitution is framed on lines

laid down in Soulbury Report, European community in Ceylon is threatened with eventual political and economic extinction. Association reluctant to believe that this is His Majesty's Government's considered policy. Memorandum follows in approximately ten days time. *Ends.*

# 315  ADM 116/5546                                           25 Oct 1945
## 'Defence policy for Ceylon': memorandum by Admiral Layton for Sir H Markham[1] urging consideration of all defence implications of the proposed reforms

Be pleased to inform Their Lordships that I have read with great interest the report of the Commission on Constitutional Reform in Ceylon recently published by the Secretary of State for the Colonies.

2.  Having been Commander-in-Chief of Ceylon from March 1942 to January 1945, and responsible for its defence in all aspects, both service and civil, I consider it my duty to bring to the notice of the Board certain particular points in this report which affect defence and which, in my judgment, it is vital to have considered by the Chiefs of Staff before H.M. Government is fully committed to a future constitutional scheme for Ceylon.

3.  It is the expressed policy of H.M. Government that the whole question of defence shall be a "reserved" subject in the new constitutional scheme; that is, it should be under the effective control of the Imperial Government, though it is intended that measures should be taken as far as possible with the full agreement of the Government of Ceylon and through the responsible Ministers.

What is doubtful is how far this policy is or can be made effective through the machinery envisaged in the Commission's report.

4.  It was made perfectly clear between 1942 and 1945 that the value of Ceylon as a factor in Imperial defence policy is very largely a matter of its communications. The ineffective peacetime organisation of its ports and railways was a great handicap to us not only in building it up as a defensive bastion in 1942, but also in converting it to an offensive base subsequently.

5.  Paragraph 350 of the Commission's report rightly emphasises the fact that in modern warfare defence measures involve practically every branch of administration and I quote this particular question of communications merely to emphasise the interest the Imperial Defence Authorities ought to show, as an example, in the development and organisation of Ceylon's harbours, docks, and railways, and also, to an increasing extent in the future, roads and airports.

6.  Our object must be to see that the Imperial Government have, through the Governor General, an effective voice in policy in such matters as these. I am concerned, however, to find that adequate machinery for this is lacking. It is stated in the report (paragraph 341(a)) that the Governor General will have the advice of the Senior Naval, Military and Air Force Officers in the island on matters of defence. This is correct and sufficient so far as strictly local considerations affecting each service are concerned; but it does not seem to me to provide for the larger issues. Very

---

[1] Permanent secretary, Admiralty.

intricate questions may arise as to the defence aspects of proposed legislation. As an example I may quote an old proposal to abolish the railway, which I consider is quite likely to come up again in the next few years, but which from my experience is quite inacceptable so long as we need to use Colombo and Trincomalee for the fleet. Or again legislation in regard to the control of the ports themselves might well have considerable significance from a defence aspect. These are matters which can hardly be fully appreciated by local Service Commanders, and I feel there should be some provision for expert advice to the Governor General on such matters. I see, however, that it is only proposed that the Governor General should have a small secretariat, headed by a private secretary, although the latter is to be a Civil Servant of high standing (paragraph 344). It is contemplated that the Governor General should have power to legislate on defence matters by means of a Governor General's Ordinance, in default of the agreement of the Government of Ceylon (paragraph 350), but I see no provision for expert advice to him on the drafting of such legislation. It seems to me it would not be a practicable proposition in such a case to rely wholly on the impartiality of a "non-political" Ceylonese Attorney General. Such legislation may well concern the possible arrest or detention of figures well-known in local politics.

7.  I am well aware of the constitutional difficulties of providing the Governor General with a second set of advisers in addition to the responsible Ministers, but I cannot help feeling that the interests of Imperial defence can only be fully served if he has some additional advice in this sphere, especially during the difficult period of a newly born constitution and post-war reconstruction.

8.  It may be that H.M. Government may come to the conclusion that such advice should come direct from them. I am personally of the opinion that advice from H.M. Government in London would need to be supplemented locally, but my main object in writing this letter is to ensure that all the defence implications of the new constitutional scheme are fully considered by the Chiefs of Staff in their widest aspect before H.M. Government is committed to them.

## 316   CO 54/986/11, no 32, CM 46(45)4                     26 Oct 1945
### 'Ceylon': Cabinet conclusions on the draft statement of policy

The Cabinet had before them a report by the Chairman of the Colonial Affairs Committee (C.P.(45) 244)[1] on constitutional reform in Ceylon.

*The Lord Privy Seal* recalled that at their meeting on 11th September[2] the Cabinet had approved the publication of the Soulbury Report. The Report had been published on 9th October, and it was desirable that a statement defining the Government's attitude towards its recommendations should be made without delay. The Colonial Affairs Committee proposed that the draft statement annexed to C.P.(45) 244 should be published forthwith as a White Paper in this country and in Ceylon. In his conversations with the Colonial Secretary Mr. Senanayake had made it clear that, now the war was over, the Ceylon Ministers were no longer willing to proceed on the basis of the 1943 declaration on the reform of the Ceylon constitution and wished to press for the grant of Dominion status; and it was doubtful whether, without some concession by His Majesty's Government which would demonstrate that his mission

---

to London had not been fruitless, Mr. Senanayake would be willing to sponsor the Soulbury recommendations before the Ceylon State Council. The Colonial Affairs Committee had accordingly felt that the proposed statement of policy should include a promise that six years after the introduction of the new constitution the Government would initiate a further review of the constitutional issue in consultation with the Ceylon Government. The object of this review would be that Ceylon should take her appropriate place in the Commonwealth with full internal self-government under a constitution on Dominion lines.

In discussion the following points were raised:—

(a) Past experience had shown that a promise to take a further step forward in constitutional reform after a fixed period of years was likely to create unwillingness to give a fair trial to the constitution in force in the interim period. The proper road towards the achievement of Dominion status was by the gradual development of new constitutional practice in the working of existing institutions.

A promise of a review after a period of six years was also open to the objection that the question of constitutional reform would be a major issue in the general election which would be due to be held five years after the present reforms were introduced.

Paragraph 10 of the draft statement annexed to C.P.(45) 244 should be recast so as to make it clear that our objective was to enable Ceylon to attain Dominion status, but that this objective could be reached only through the evolution of the capacity for self government based on the practical working of the reformed constitution now offered. The statement should not imply that a further instalment of constitutional reform would follow after a fixed period, irrespective of the progress made.

*The First Lord of the Admiralty*[3] asked that, in recasting this part of the statement, special attention should be given to the probable need for reserved powers in respect of defence and foreign policy.

(b) The last sentence of paragraph 12 of the draft statement of policy, which made it clear that His Majesty's Government did not regard themselves as bound by the provision in the 1943 declaration that there should be a three-quarters majority of the Council in favour of the reforms, seemed to be inconsistent with the earlier part of the paragraph. If His Majesty's Government did not intend to be bound by this condition there was no point in referring to it, and some other formula to secure the protection of the minorities should be devised.

*The Secretary of State for the Colonies* said that he was willing to omit any reference to the three-quarters majority.

(c) *The Secretary of State for India* drew attention to paragraph 6 of C.P.(45) 244, which set out the views of the Government of India on the Soulbury Report. These views had been fully considered by the Colonial Affairs Committee and he did not feel that he could press them further. At the same time, he was bound to point out that the proposals were looked upon in India with considerable misgiving.

*The Secretary of State for the Colonies* said that he had good hope that, now the war was over, some of the points at issue between the Government of India and the Government of Ceylon would be settled by direct negotiation.

The Cabinet:—

(1) Agreed that the new constitution for Ceylon should follow the general lines proposed by the Soulbury Commission.

---

[3] Mr Alexander.

(2) Invited the Prime Minister, in consultation with the Lord Privy Seal, the President of the Board of Trade, the Secretary of State for Dominion Affairs and the Secretary of State for the Colonies, to reconsider paragraphs 10 and 12 of the proposed statement of policy in the light of the points made in discussion.

## 317 CO 54/986/11, no 36, GEN 99/1 29 Oct 1945
[Soulbury Report]: note of a meeting of ministers on the draft statement of policy.[1] Annex: revised paragraphs 10 and 12

The Meeting had before it a memorandum by the Secretary of State for the Colonies (GEN/99/1) proposing the revision of Paragraphs 10 and 12 of the draft Statement of Policy on Constitutional Reform in Ceylon which incorporated portions of an alternative draft suggested by the President of the Board of Trade.

In discussion the following points were made:—

(a) *The Prime Minister* suggested that in avoiding the danger of too definite a time table for advance to full Dominion status the draft appeared to have gone to the other extreme by suggesting that the coming years were the testing time of Ceylon's ability to govern herself, after which if she emerged successfully from the test, she would automatically attain full Dominion status. He suggested a variation of the last sentence of the proposed paragraph 10 to bring in a reference to the evolutionary character of constitutional development.

(b) *The President of the Board of Trade* pointed out that it was necessary to import into the Statement some reference to the basis on which advancement to Dominion status must depend. At present Ceylon did not possess such a basis and clearly this must be the experience which she would gain in the operation of the new Constitution.

(c) There was general agreement with the suggestion that it would be wiser to bring into the forefront of paragraph 10, His Majesty's Government's sympathy with the desire of Ceylon for further Constitutional progress.

(d) On paragraph 12 it was pointed out that the wording suggested by the Secretary of State for the Colonies did not contain anything in the nature of a minority safeguard, and the *President of the Board of Trade* suggested an addition to it on the lines of the last sentence of (viii) of his draft statement annexed to GEN/99/1.

The Meeting:—
(a) agreed that paragraphs 10 and 12 of the draft Statement of Policy on Constitutional Reform in Ceylon should be revised as shown in the annex hereto;
(b) authorised the Secretary of State for the Colonies to publish the Statement of Policy, as amended, in the form of a White Paper;
(c) noted that a statement as to Constitutional Reform in Ceylon would be made in the course of the present week in the sense of the revised paragraphs 10 and 12 of the Statement of Policy.

---

[1] Present: Mr Attlee in the chair, Mr Greenwood, Sir S Cripps (Board of Trade), Lord Addision (DO), Mr Hall. Also present; Sir E Bridges, J A Drew, Trafford Smith.

**Annex to 317**

*Paragraph 10*
His Majesty's Government are in sympathy with the desire of the people of Ceylon to advance towards Dominion status and they are anxious to co-operate with them to that end. With this in mind, His Majesty's Government have reached the conclusion that a Constitution on the general lines proposed by the Soulbury Commission (which also conforms in broad outline, save as regards the Second Chamber, with the Constitutional scheme put forward by the Ceylon Ministers themselves) will provide a workable basis for constitutional progress in Ceylon.

Experience of the working of Parliamentary institutions in the British Commonwealth has shown that advance to Dominion status has been effected by modification of existing constitutions and by the establishment of conventions which have grown up in actual practice.

Legislation such as the Statute of Westminster has been the recognition of constitutional advances already achieved rather than the instrument by which they were secured. It is, therefore, the hope of His Majesty's Government that the new constitution will be accepted by the people of Ceylon with a determination so to work it that in a comparatively short space of time such Dominion status will be evolved. The actual length of time occupied by this evolutionary process must depend upon the experience gained under the new constitution by the people of Ceylon.

*Paragraph 12*
In Section 7 of the 1943 Declaration His Majesty's Government made it clear that the acceptance of any constitutional proposals put forward by Ceylon Ministers would depend upon the subsequent adoption of such proposals by three-quarters of the members of the State Council of Ceylon, excluding the Officers of State and the Presiding Officer. This provision was inserted because the 1943 Declaration contemplated the adoption of a constitution worked out by the Ministers and did not specifically require that they should consult minority interests.

This condition was thus attached in the past to constitutional proposals to be put forward by Ceylon Ministers and His Majesty's Government have decided not to insist upon the acceptance of the Constitution now proposed by the Soulbury Commission (after full consultation with minority interests) by so large a proportion of the State Council as three quarters, though they earnestly hope that all those with the future interests of Ceylon at heart will co-operate by giving their support to the new Constitution now offered as a foundation upon which may be built a future Dominion of Ceylon. His Majesty's Government will have to take into account the views expressed by the State Council and the number of those in that Council who vote in favour of adopting the new Constitution.

**318**   CO 54/986/6/3                                           30 Oct 1945

[Soulbury Report]: minute by G E J Gent on a meeting between Mr
Hall and Lord Soulbury on the latter's views and HMG's policy
statement

The Secretary of State saw Lord Soulbury this afternoon who at once offered the
Secretary of State an apology for showing to Colonel Oliver Stanley a copy of his
letter to Mr. Hall of the 5th of October.[1] He quickly appreciated that this was a
mistake on his part. Colonel Stanley when he read it immediately observed that the
letter completely superseded the Commission's Report and that since Lord Soulbury
now held these views he should make them public. Lord Soulbury said that he had, of
course, no such intention.

The Secretary of State made it clear to Lord Soulbury that he agreed that Lord
Soulbury's action was a misjudgment at least, and added that when he learnt of it he
had taken an opportunity of ascertaining the attitude of Mr. Burrows to the letter,
and Mr. Burrows had assured him orally that he nowise shared Lord Soulbury's view
and would not in any case have supported a claim by Ceylon for Dominion Status at
the present juncture. The Secretary of State was therefore a little surprised when it
was suggested that the other Commissioners agreed with Lord Soulbury's letter.

Lord Soulbury said that he could only say that he had sent the letter in its present
form to Mr. Burrows after having toned down a previous draft to meet Mr. Burrows'
views, and that he had had a written reply from Mr. Burrows saying that in its
present form he agreed with it.

The Secretary of State told Lord Soulbury that he intended to make a statement in
the House tomorrow which he would like to read to him, and he thereupon read the
draft Statement as now approved. Lord Soulbury's reaction was generally good,
though he doubted whether the deferred promise of Dominion Status would go as far
as Mr. Senanayake would need to secure his influence in getting the present offer
accepted in Ceylon. He thought that it would have been more certain of success with
Mr. Senanayake if it had been possible to promise that Ceylon would have Dominion
Status at least as soon as Burma. Mention was then made of certain points in which
Mr. Senanayake's views had been met, for instance, in the matter of the form in
which the "safe-guards" in defence and external affairs matters had now been
removed from the Governor-General's normal constitutional powers and had been
left to the special exercise of powers by H.M. in Council should the necessity arise.
Lord Soulbury thought that this would materially help Mr. Senanayake.

---

[1] See 300; also 311.

**319**   CO 54/986/6/3, no 180                                 31 Oct 1945

[Soulbury Report]: outward unnumbered telegram from Mr Hall to
Sir H Moore transmitting a personal message to Mr Senanayake

If you see no objection I should like the following message to be given personal from
me to Senanayake. *Begins.* On the conclusion of your visit to London I lost no time
in meeting what I knew to be your wishes, that H.M. Government should reach its

conclusions on the constitutional question with the least possible delay and I am glad to say that I shall be in a position this afternoon in Parliament to announce our conclusions.

I feel confident that you will appreciate that the views that you so ably and clearly made in your discussions with me have been in the foreground of my deliberations with my colleagues here and that you will find in our conclusions firm ground for building the future of Ceylon to which we all look forward. I trust that you will not regard your visit as fruitless. On my side I cannot tell you how much I have valued the personal discussions with you and how I keenly look forward to your success in securing the co-operation of your colleagues and of the Council in attaining our objective. *Ends.*

**320**   CO 54/986/6/3, nos 181–183                              2 Nov 1945

**[Soulbury Report]: inward unnumbered telegram (reply) in three parts from Sir H Moore to Mr Hall transmitting the text of Mr Senanayake's reply to the secretary of state and the resolution to be moved in the State Council**

[*Part 1*]
Your secret and personal telegram of 31st October.[1]

Following is text of Senanayake's reply.

"I am most grateful to you for your personal message which has been conveyed to me by the Governor. The message is the more welcome as it was least expected, and I deeply appreciate the kind thought underlying it.

I particularly express my thanks to you for the speeding up of decisions of H.M. Government at a time when matters of great importance are engaging its attention, both at home and in the Councils of the Nations. This is further evidence of your genuine sympathy with the political aspirations of the people of Ceylon.

You will no doubt appreciate the difficulty of my task. Though there are many who welcome the decision of H.M. Government, there are others who think it goes by no means far enough, and who are disposed to reject it on that ground. It is obviously desirable that there should be as wide a measure of agreement as possible, and the task of achieving it will be by no means easy. I am much encouraged by the message that you have been good enough to send me".

[*Part 2*]
Reference my immediately preceding secret and personal telegram.

Senanayake, as soon as he learnt of the terms of the White Paper, told me that, though it did not meet all his desiderata, he was definitely prepared to accept it himself and to put it before the State Council for acceptance.

It is too early yet to gauge general reactions to the announcement, and Ministers have refrained from publicly defining their attitude till after this morning's meeting. With possible exception of Bandaranaike, I think they are unlikely to oppose it. Daily News and Lake House Press are solidly backing it. Times of Ceylon yesterday, in

---

[1] See 319.

somewhat surprising article, advised its supporters to accept defeat in the right democratic spirit, and work together with the victors for the common good. The Europeans, as you know, belatedly sent cables of protest just before the announcement was released. After I have seen Chairman of Ceylon Estates Proprietary Association tomorrow, I may know more as to their present attitude, but their principal anxiety is undoubtedly lest immigration legislation, discriminating against Europeans, may be introduced.

[*Part 3*]
My secret and personal (2) of 2nd November.

Following is text of resolution which Senanayake proposes to move in State Council on Thursday 8th November. *Begins.* This House expresses its disappointment that H.M.G. have deferred the admission of Ceylon to full Dominion status, but, in view of the assurance contained in the White Paper of 31st October, 1945, that H.M.G. will co-operate with the people of Ceylon so that such status may be attained by this country in a comparatively short time, this House resolves that the constitution offered in the said White Paper be accepted during the interim period. *Ends.*

This resolution is not officially sponsored by the Board, but I understand all Ministers, with possible exception of Bandaranaike, stated this morning their intention to support it in State Council, though reserving their right of individual action. There is a reasonable hope that Bandaranaike also will not actually oppose it, though he is now showing signs of coquetting with the Tamils and may try to stage a pact with Ponnambalam,[2] if the latter returns here in time.

---

[2] Ponnambalam was still in London from where he submitted a memo to the CO on the Tamil case, see 322.

**321**   CO 54/986/6, no 191                                    3 Nov 1945
**[Soulbury Report]: letter from P J Gibson (India Office) to CO on the views of the Government of India.** *Enclosures*

With reference to recent correspondence relating to the Report of the Soulbury Commission on Constitutional Reform in Ceylon I am directed by the Secretary of State for India to forward a copy of a telegram dated 30th October, 1945, from the Viceroy and of the telegram dated 27th October, 1945, to which it refers, and to express his hope that full consideration will be given by the Secretary of State for the Colonies to the points stressed by the Government of India when the time comes for the drafting of the documents required to give effect to the policy of His Majesty's Government.

Enclosure 1 to 321: telegram 1893S from Lord Wavell to Lord Pethick-Lawrence, 30 October 1945

Your telegram No. 23759 of 27th October. Soulbury Report. Government of India regret that His Majesty's Government have done so little to meet their views, and offer the following comments on points in your paragraph No. 3.

(A) Franchise for Indians is the core of the problem and in view of the past attitude of the Ceylon Ministry we see little hope of satisfactory agreement. If His Majesty's Government cannot (repeat not) provide for Indian franchise in the constitution we think they should at least recognize in their statement the fairness of (? granting) the franchise to all Indians with five years residence and that suitable instructions about Indian franchise should be given to the Governor-General. Without pressure from His Majesty's Government Ceylon Ministry will not (repeat not) be reasonable and relations between the two countries will be further impaired.

(B) The paragraphs mentioned are intended to protect the rights and property of British subjects not residing in Ceylon, the pension rights of retired officials and their families and the selection of candidates for the public services. They do not (repeat not) protect resident Indians against discrimination in the matter mentioned in paragraph No. 9 of our 1824S of 18th October.[1] We trust that these matters will be borne in mind when constitution and instructions to Governor-General are drafted.

(C) We understand that this accepts the substance of our points about re-entry.

2.   Your paragraph No. 4 says nothing about direction asked for in paragraph No. 8 of our 1824S of 18th October as to the formation of Indian Electoral districts. We consider that direction of this kind essential.

3.   We trust that safeguards which we consider necessary and which His Majesty's Government regard as implied by report will be included in draft constitution and instructions. Mudaliar[2] is fully aware of our views and we hope they will receive the fullest consideration.

Enclosure 2 to 321: telegram 23759 from Lord Pethick-Lawrence to Lord Wavell, 27 October 1945

Ceylon. Views of your Government as communicated in your telegram of 18th October No. 1824S have been fully before His Majesty's Government in the formulation of their conclusions on the Soulbury Report. My colleagues desire me to express to you their regret for the short time available to yourself and your Council to consider the Report. It was deemed essential that a final decision should be taken this week in order that the timetable arranged with Ceylon which could not be extended should be adhered to. For the same reason it was found impossible to meet request in your telegram of 22nd October, No. 1837S, for postponement till after Mudaliar's arrival in London.

2.   I am asked to point out to you, however, that the final stage will be the framing of the constitution itself and the Royal instructions to the Governor with regard to it. Decision of His Majesty's Government to be announced shortly will do no more than set out the general lines of their conclusions and there will be opportunity for the Government of India to put forward their views on matters of secondary importance

---

[1] See 310.                    [2] Sir A R Mudaliar, member for supply, Viceroy's Executive Council.

not covered in your telegram 1824S when the time comes to draft the new constitution.

3. Discussion of your telegram centred round three points which I stressed to my colleagues, namely:—

(a) The general point relating to franchise for Indians. With regard to this it was felt desirable that negotiations on the subject between India and Ceylon should be resumed, and that His Majesty's Government should meanwhile not intervene, the existing provisions continuing in force (as recommended by the Commission) pending any changes agreed upon between the two Governments. As regards reservation of franchise Bills it is pointed out that the Commission's recommendations for provisions in the new constitution against discrimination were clearly intended to be overriding and in the light of this recommendation (ii) of paragraph 242 should be read as governed by recommendations (iii) and (iv). The foregoing should I feel allay to some extent your anxiety in this matter.

(b) With regard to your paragraph 9 it is pointed out that an attempt has been made to cover this very difficult point in paragraphs 332 (iv), 372 (iv) and 392 (i) of the Report. When the Constitution comes to be drafted, and the instructions to the Governor delivered, these questions and others with which you are concerned will of course have to be decided.

(c) With regard to your paragraph 10 on the subject of re-entry, it is felt that the point is sufficiently covered by pargraph 242 (i) and there can be no doubt whatever that His Majesty's Government will bear the point in mind in the final documents. It may be helpful to you and your Council to appreciate that the safeguard for Europeans will be in precisely the same position as the safeguard for Indians and that the rights of the latter are not therefore very likely to be overlooked.

4. As regards your paragraph B Colonial Office are willing to meet the point you make in regard to voting in multi-member constituencies, viz., that the individual voter should be permitted to cast his votes cumulatively in favour of one candidate.

5. Statement of His Majesty's Government's policy may be issued in the next few days. I will inform you beforehand of exact date and if possible indicate its general contents.

## 322    CO 54/987/1, no 96    3 Nov 1945
### [Soulbury Report]: letter from G G Ponnambalam to Mr Hall on the Tamil minority case. *Enclosure*

The Soulbury recommendations for the Reform of the Ceylon Constitution were disappointing in themselves as they amounted virtually to an acceptance of the Sinhalese Ministerial Scheme except for the addition of a Second Chamber.

The decisions of His Majesty's Government contained in the recent White Paper offering to Ceylon a Constitution on the general lines proposed by the Soulbury Commission have come as a profound shock to the Tamils of Ceylon.

I am submitting the enclosed memorandum[1] of criticism of these proposals in the

---

[1] Dated Oct 1945.

hope that His Majesty's Government may be persuaded even at this stage to effect certain material modifications to make them acceptable to all important sections of the people.

His Majesty's Government has decided to vary an important requirement of its Declaration that constitutional proposals should be accepted by a three quarters majority of the State Council to accept the proposals by an ordinary majority.

This would in fact amount to imposing upon Ceylon a Constitution acceptable only to the majority of the Sinhalese. The wishes of the Tamils and the other minorities amounting to a third of the population could very well be ignored, as the State Council today consists of more than 72% of Sinhalese members.

The present State Council has been functioning for nearly ten years and it is but fair that large constitutional changes affecting the welfare of the people of the Island for generations to come should be considered by a new State Council and accepted by a three quarters majority.

I shall be happy if you will permit me to explain personally any point in the memorandum that requires elucidation.

## Enclosure to 322

*Introduction*
The decision of His Majesty's Government to offer to Ceylon a Constitution on the general lines proposed by the Soulbury Commission, which also conforms generally, except as regards the Second Chamber, with the constitutional scheme put forward by the Ceylon Ministers comes as a shock to the Tamils the most important minority in Ceylon constituting more than a quarter of its population.

This Memorandum which attempts to survey the present political situation in Ceylon and analyse the Soulbury proposals in the light of existing facts is submitted in the fervent hope that His Majesty's Government, and Parliament, in the plenitude of its power, will see that justice is done to nearly two million of the people of Ceylon, by material modifications in regard to the proposed Legislature and Executive. The *Tamil Demand* is that in accord with recognised precedents in other parts of the Commonwealth with a heterogeneous population, the Tamils should receive such *weightage* as will give them 33% of *Representation* and an assured proportion of portfolios which can be held by their trusted representatives in a *composite Cabinet*.

The Soulbury Commission Report is clear in depicting the political scene in Ceylon as it is—the familiar Eastern plural society of antagonistic communities wherein the principal problem of Government is the protection of minorities. Its findings on facts are unexceptional but when it passes from fact-finding, to recommendations, the Commission unaccountably throws over and disregards its own facts and puts forward a Constitution which will result in still further oppressing the Tamils and other minorities.

The Second Chamber which His Majesty's Government considers was designed by the Commission to be one of the principle [sic] minority safeguards will, it is feared, neither in its composition nor in its powers be so in fact. It is a delaying body that might only help to minimise any conflict that might arise between the Governor and the Lower House.

*Historical background*

The British occupation of Ceylon was confirmed by the Peace of Amiens in 1802, by which the Dutch ceded it to Britain. The unoccupied central portions were transferred to Britain by the Convention of 1815. By an Order in Council of 1833 Executive and Legislative Councils were constituted.

With an area of 25,000 square miles and a population of six millions, the Island is peopled by the Singalese [sic] who number four millions, the Tamils (Ceylon and Indian) who number over a million and a half, the Muslims who number about half a million, the Burghers (the descendants of the Dutch settlers) who number about thirty thousand, and the Europeans who number about ten thousand.

It may be noted that of the Indian Tamils numbering over 750,000 more than 80 per cent. have either been born in Ceylon or are permanently settled there.

Of the Minorities, the Tamils form the most important entity; they were the original inhabitants and rulers of the Island who established independent Kingdoms and even exercised sway over the entire Island over a long period of years. They remember with pride that the Kings of the Singalese were largely of Tamil extraction and that for quite a century till the British occupation the ruling dynasty was wholly Tamil. They impressed their culture and policy on the Singalese and have been, in the main, responsible for the political advancement of the country. In the economic sphere it was British capital and Tamil manpower that came over from South India that have contributed very largely to the development of the land in the plantation industries.

Ceylon's contribution to the War Effort in supplying much of the tea consumed in the United Kingdom and a large part of the natural rubber needed by the United Nations can be attributed to the same source.

The fine natural harbour and naval base at Trincomalee situated in one of the Tamil provinces has been the springboard of the S.E.A.C. for the reconquest of Burma, Malaya etc.

*The governmental system*

The form of Government from 1833 to 1931 was the Crown Colony System with executive functions performed by Government Officials.

The Tamils, treated as a major community, had one Tamil member to one Sinhalese member from 1837 to 1889. From 1889 to 1910 there was one Tamil member to two Sinhalese members. From 1910 to 1921, there were two Tamil members to three Sinhalese members, with one elected seat for the educated Ceylonese who also happened to be a Tamil. In 1921 territorial representation was introduced. The Sinhalese nearly swamped the Council. The Tamils protested and the constitution was withdrawn. In 1923, a new constitution reintroduced the ratio of one Tamil to two Sinhalese, and embodied the principle of balanced representation under which no single community could outvote a combination of the others in the Legislature. In the Legislative Council from 1923 to 1931 there were 37 unofficial members of whom 18 were Sinhalese and 19 minorities; the latter never combined against the former, cordiality prevailed among the communities and national unity was being developed.

The principles of representation were based on the realisation that:—

a. The people of Ceylon were not a single entity.
b. The population was heterogeneous.

c. The social strucure was founded upon a communal basis.

d. The needs of the various communities differed widely.

e. Pro forma territorial representation would in fact be communal representation.

f. Under territorial representation important communities would not be represented at all or be most inadequately represented.

g. Under such a system the Sinhalese would obtain an overwhelming proportion of electoral power, even more than their numbers would warrant, and reduce all the other communities severally and collectively to political impotence.

## The Donoughmore Constitution

Sir Hugh Clifford, Governor, felt that the Legislative Council enjoyed a great deal of power without a commensurate responsibility and in 1928 asked for a Commission to examine the working of the Constitution. The Donoughmore Commission was accordingly appointed, and it recommended "the transfer to 'the people' complete control over the internal affairs of the Island" subject to certain safeguards in the background.

The most daring features of the Commission's proposals were negatively:—

(1) The complete abolition of communal representation,

(2) the removal of the ratio of one to two in the representation of the Tamils and the Sinhalese,

(3) the denial of a scheme of Balanced representation between the Sinhalese and the Minorities, and

positively:—

(1) the grant of universal adult franchise, thereby converting a 4% electorate into a 100% electorate,

(2) the inauguration of a system of government by Executive Committees under which the 50 elected and 8 nominated members divided themselves by ballot into seven Executive Committees each of which elected as its spokesman a Chairman who was thereafter appointed a Minister by the Governor. The Committees themselves were to be responsible for the administration of the Ministry in their charge.

To complete the balance of the scheme they suggested as safeguards:—

(1) The appointment and retention of three permanent officials in charge of:—

(a) Defence, External Affairs, and the Public Service,

(b) Law,

(c) Finance,

to be called the Chief, Legal and Financial Secretaries, to be Ministers without vote in council and to be responsible only to the Governor. These three officers along with the seven Chairmen of the Committees constitute the Board of Ministers of which the Chief Secretary is the Chairman. The three Officers of State by themselves form the Public Services Commission to advise the Governor on all questions of appointment, promotion, transfer, and the dismissal of public servants.

(2) The 'pro tanto' increase in the powers of the Governor to be held in reserve.

*The working of the Donoughmore Constitution*

(A) *Communalism.* With the abolition of communal representation which the Commission described as "a canker on the body politic", it hoped that:—

a. Communal tension would disappear.

b. A corporate consciousness and a community of interests would manifest themselves.

c. The fears of the minorities would prove unfounded.

The history of the last 14 years shows an alarming increase of suspicion and distrust between the various communities. The influence of religion on politics is evidenced by the fact that three of the present Sinhalese Ministers are recent converts from Christianity to Buddhism. Direct appeals have been made to arouse communal passions and mass intimidation against Tamil voters have been resorted to. Governor Sir Reginald Stubbs deprecated

> "the spirit of narrow sectionalism rampant in the country . . . and the tendency manifested in most constituencies to pay regard to considerations of race, caste or religion".

His successor, Governor Sir Andrew Caldecott, deplored that "communalism is so unfortunately rampant in the country". Unlike in the pre-1931 Council debate and divisions in the State Council on important issues and on a number of occasions reveal a sharp majority–minority communal cleavage. The fear of the Donoughmore Commission that racial parties would emerge has been speedily realised by the enthronement of one community in power. The most powerful party among the Sinhalese today is the Sinhala Maha Sabha—which is exclusively Sinhalese and predominantly Buddhist, with the Minister for Local Administration who recently acted as Leader of the House as President and commanding the allegiance of more than half the Sinhalese members of the Council. The Ceylon National Congress calling itself "national" is today only an older addition of the Sinhala Maha Sabha; not a single member of any of the minority communities belongs to it.

Our submissions are borne out by the *following conclusions* of the *Soulbury Commission* arrived at after a survey of the working of the Donoughmore Constitution:—

a. "There is abundant evidence to show that the hopes of the Donoughmore Commission that communal tension would eventually disappear as a result of territorial representation have so far not been realised".

b. "The elimination of communalism from political life under the Donoughmore Constitution was purely formal".

c. "When political issues arise the populace as a whole tends to divide not according to social and economic issues . . . but on communal lines".

d. "It is abundantly clear to us that no alignment of the communities on party lines has yet emerged to take the place of communal division".

The *Tamil complaint* is that the Soulbury Commission, having fully appreciated that the hopes of the Donoughmore Commission had not been realised and their fears proved too true, has suggested nothing in its recommendations to remedy or even to mitigate the obvious evils.

(B) *Representation*. In recommending the abolition of communal representation, the Donoughmore Commission hoped that:—

    a. "the election of candidates would be irrespective of communal bias" and that

    b. "a member of one community may be supported for his ability and character by members of other communities".

In fact, today there is not one European or Burgher elected member and only one elected Muslim member, and these three communities have had to obtain representation by nomination by the Governor. The Commission was also "certain" that the Tamils would obtain "a substantial number of territorial seats" when they decided to remove the ratio of one Tamil to two Sinhalese seats. In fact the Ceylon Tamils who returned 7 out of 23 elected members before 1931 continue to return 7 out of 50 elected members in the present State Council.

The Commission based all its expectations on the hope that

> "the consolidation of the people into a single territorial electorate will ultimately militate against the recording of votes merely on communal lines".

The *Soulbury Commission*, however, has come to the *conclusion* that "the electors undoubtedly tend to vote on racial and to some extent on religious grounds".

The extent of the political submergence of the minorities is seen by the fact that while the Muslims with a population of 400,000 and entitled to five members, on Proportional Representation, return one member and the Indian Tamils, with a population of over 750,000 and similarly entitled to ten members, return only two members, the Sinhalese with a population of about 66 per cent, secure 78 per cent. of the elected representatives. This is a case of weightage for the majority. It would be difficult to find a parallel in any other part of the Empire.

Our submission is that Territorial Representation under the Donoughmore Scheme based on geographical divisions carrying a fixed numerical quota of population has amounted in fact to the worst form of communal representation favourable to the majority. This view is supported by the *Soulbury Commission* which *says*:—

> "To call the representation territorial was merely to disguise the fact that it was fundamentally communal".

The *Soulbury Commission* also sums up the situation aright when it *says* that:—

> "territorial representation tends to become simply numerical representation and it seems to us that to that extent and in the light of results, the recommendations of the Donoughmore Commissioners have pressed too hardly upon the minorities".

*The Tamil Complaint* is that the *Soulbury Commission*, while appreciating and assessing the facts clearly and correctly, has failed to devise a scheme of representation of its own which would prevent the permanent enthronement of a racial majority in the seat of power.

*The Sinhalese ministerial scheme of representation*
Under the Declaration of His Majesty's Government of May 1943 the Ministers drew up a Constitution for Ceylon without the approval or knowledge of the minorities,

incorporating therein a scheme of representation with which the one and only Tamil Minister on the Board would not agree.

When the Soulbury Commission was appointed, affording the minorities an opportunity to make their representations, the Ministers withdrew their scheme and did not appear before the Commissioners either to defend or elucidate its numerous provisions. We are told in the *Soulbury Report* that the Commissioners had "several valuable private discussions" with the Sinhalese Leader; what the purport of those discussions were neither the Tamils nor the public knows.

In the explanatory memorandum of the *Sinhalese Ministers* we find two very *valuable admissions*. They agree that:—

a. "no system of territorial representation would ensure that all sections of the community would be adequately represented."

b. "the minorities ought to have additional weightage in representation."

They claim to achieve this purpose by adopting a two-principle scheme of representation; one is purely numerical representation, the other is the allocation of one seat to every thousand square miles of area; the latter they call giving "weightage to areas". As there are large sparsely populated Sinhalese Provinces, their device of giving "weightage to area" applied uniformly throughout the Island, will be found to result in giving more representation to the already over-represented Sinhalese majority.

Under their scheme the Tamil Provinces of the North and East which today return 7 members (all Tamils) in a Council of fifty elected, will return 16 members (12 Tamils and 4 Muslims) in a council of 95 elected; so that the Ceylon Tamils will get relatively less under this scheme than they have even today.

Outside these Tamil Provinces the only minority which can return elected members will be the Indian Tamils who may obtain a maximum of 7 members in the Central and Uva Provinces, although they will be entitled on Proportional Representation to 12 or 13 seats. Similarly the Muslims who would be entitled to 7 seats will return 4 or 5 members.

The net result is that the Tamils (Ceylon and Indian) who are more than a quarter of the population and would be entitled to a minimum of 25 seats in a council of 101 will get only 19, the Sinhalese who are about 66 per cent of the population will get a minimum of 75 per cent of the elected seats and 70 per cent of the entire Legislature.

It will thus be seen that the seemingly generous *device* of the *Sinhalese Ministers* will in operation *result* not in giving the minorities additional weightage nor even in ensuring that all sections of the population are adequately represented, but in assuring to the Sinhalese a continuance of their present overwhelming predominance.

### The Soulbury recommendations on representation

The Soulbury Commission was admittedly aware:—

a. of the growing dissatisfaction of the minorities with the representation they received under the Donoughmore Constitution.

b. that the scheme of Reforms drawn up by Governor Sir Andrew Caldecott proved unacceptable because of the "failure to agree on the question of increased representation for the minorities".

c. "that the problem of representation is of fundamental importance particularly when the electorate is not homogeneous but like the electorate of Ceylon is composed of a number of communities differing from each other in race, religion, tradition, culture, education, customs, habits and language."

The Commission had also come to clear conclusions that:—

a. communal tension has so far not disappeared,
b. on political issues the people divide on communal lines,
c. there is no alignment of the communities on party lines,
d. electors vote on racial grounds,
e. territorial representation today is numerical representation pressing too hardly on the minorities.

The Commission then goes on unerringly to state that "in the present circumstances of Ceylon we see no satisfactory way *of securing a reasonable proportion of seats for the minorities except by a method which combines territorial and communal elements.*"

The *Tamil Complaint* is that the Soulbury Commission has nowhere stated what in its view is "a reasonable proportion of seats for the minorities," and that the Commission has allowed itself to be contented with the hope that "the additional weightage which (The Sinhalese Ministers) proposed to give to the minority communities may reasonably be *expected* to *diminish the present disparity between the majority and minority groups.*"

The Commission instead of making a definite award "to secure a reasonable proportion of seats for the minorities" and "to diminish the present disparity between the majority and minority groups" and thus settle this question of the most vital importance to the minorities, leaves it in a highly unsatisfactory and speculative state, with the professed hope that with slightly wider powers of reference to a delimitation commission:—

> "a figure approximate to the estimated (by the advocates of the Sinhalese Ministerial scheme) result could be achieved."

## Tamil demands on representation

In England by reason of a common nationality, common political traditions and a common language, population is a satisfactory basis of representation; but in a country like Ceylon with the population divided by every form of heterogeneity, this basis of representation will lead to a negation of representative government.

A growing consensus of current political thought holds that in a sharply divided plural society the majority community should not be placed permanently in a position of complete and unqualified dominance over the minorities. It is essential that where unfair policies are pursued, the minorities should be able to obtain some redress. This would not be possible even under a scheme of Proportional Representation in Ceylon as some of the minorities will go completely unrepresented and the others very inadequately so, leaving the Sinhalese to have an absolute majority in perpetuity in the Legislature over the other groups.

Fair and reasonable dealing can be assured only if the minorities receive some *weightage in representation*. This principle in the representation of minorities in a plural society appears to have been accepted by His Majesty's Government in respect of:—

a. the French Canadians under the Act of Confederation of North America, 1867,
b. the smaller original states in the Act of the Union of South Africa,
c. Tasmania vis-a-vis the Commonwealth of Australia,
d. the Maoris in New Zealand,
e. the Muslims in Cyprus,
f. the Muslims in India under the Morley–Minto Reforms 1909,
g. the Muslims and Sikhs under the Montague–Chelmsford Reforms of 1919,
h. the Muslims, Sikhs, Indian Christians and others under the Government of India Act 1935.

Under this Act the Muslim minority in Madras and Bombay gets twice the number of seats it would be entitled to on its numbers, and the Sikh minority in the Punjab also obtains a hundred percent weightage. In the composition of the Federal Assembly for British India it is laid down that the Muslims (who are 22% of the population) are to get 82 out of the 250 seats, i.e. 33% representation, while the Hindus (who are about 72% of the population) are to get 105 out of the 250 seats, i.e. about 43% representation. It will thus be seen that while the minorities in India are given very heavy weightage in representation the representative strength of the Hindu majority is so reduced as to prevent it being an absolute majority in the Legislature.

In Ceylon where communal divisions are as wide and communal antagonisms as deep seated, it is submitted that the *major community* should be given a *"relative majority"* and *not an absolute majority* in the Legislature. The weight of the difference may be distributed among the minorities. *The Tamils (Ceylon and Indian) who are more than 25% of the population may be given such weightage as to receive one-third (33%) of the seats.*

Such a scheme will have the following *advantages*:—

a. the majority community will be deprived of a primary motive to perpetuate communalism,
b. it will encourage and expedite the formation of parties on western lines,
c. it will make an alternative government possible where it is impossible today,
d. it will prevent domination by any particular community, placed in a permanent racial majority and unalterable by any appeal to the electorate,
e. it will free the minorities from feelings of complete subservence and frustration,
f. it will be a natural evolution of the form of government in existence from 1833 to 1931,
g. it will make self-government a reality for 11 communities in the Island.

## The Donoughmore executive

### The committee system
The Donoughmore Commission and His Majesty's Government considered that the Committee System would serve as a protection for the minorities and to some extent compensate for the abolition of communal representation. They hoped that some of the Chairmen of Committees would be minority representatives and that the Board of Ministers would thus be a composite body. They also hoped that the minorities would be present in sufficient strength in every one of the Committees as to

influence its decisions. In order to prevent the Committees from becoming the instruments of a "communal caucus" the Secretary of State, Lord Passfield, devised a scheme of restricted voting, by which each member of the House could vote for only three out of a possible eight members in each Committee. Even this device was of no avail against the Sinhalese numerical preponderance; the worst fears of the minorities were justified when in 1936 after the second General Election, the Sinhalese leaders with 39 out of 50 elected members, packed every one of the Committees with an absolute majority of five or six Sinhalese out of eight members and captured the Chairmanship of every one of the Committees. The Sinhalese leaders proclaimed publicly that they had deliberately planned to exploit the machinery of the Constitution to achieve homogeniety [sic]—racial homogeniety— to the complete exclusion of all the minorities. This All-Sinhalese Board of Ministers has displayed a remarkable unanimity only on one subject—the demand for constitutional reform along lines that would give a further accession of power to the Sinhalese.

This racially homogeneous Board of Ministers functioned from 1936 to 1942 when they secured a pliant Tamil to join them as a Minister, but even he would not support the scheme of representation drawn up by the Sinhalese Ministers.

The Donoughmore Commission while desiring to transfer responsibility for the management of the internal affairs of the country to the representatives of the people recognised that in the complete absence of a Party System, a system of government by Executive Committees would assure to all sections of the people an adequate share in the government of the country.

Their good intentions miscarried because the Sinhalese majority swamped the territorial electorate.

The *Tamil Complaint* is that *the Soulbury Commission* while it professes a desire to give the minorities "an adequate voice in the conduct of affairs" and while it appears to recognise the desirability of a composite executive, recommends the abolition of the Committee System but attempts to devise no substitute to give the minorities an effective and adequate share in the government of the country.

*The future executive*
The Donoughmore Commission transferred responsibility in matters of internal civil administration to the people of Ceylon, but refused to recommend responsible government on the traditional British model because of:—

a. the complete absence of a Party System,
b. the fear that communal and racial parties would emerge,
c. the harm that such parties would inflict on the social structure of the Island.

It's worst fears have been realised by the emergence of an exclusively and predominantly Buddhist body—The Sinhala Maha Sabha—with the Minister for Local Administration and Acting Leader of the House as President. It claims that Ceylon belongs to the Sinhalese and demands the right to rule. The Soulbury Commission adverts to this in the following words:—

> "some of the speeches of the Sinhalese members delivered inside and outside the State Council emphasizing the solidarity of the Sinhalese and threatening the suppression of the Ceylon Tamils strike us as singularly ill-advised."

The *Tamil Complaint* is that the *Soulbury Commission* has suggested nothing for the future that would prevent a racial party so overwhelming in number and unchangeable by any known parliamentary method from carrying out its present declared intentions.

The impossibility of the formation of an alternative government is the chief defect that has revealed itself in the working of the Donoughmore Constitution for the past fourteen years. This factor has made Sinhalese Ministers collectively and individually to be autocratic and irresponsible. The three examples that follow will illustrate this:—

a. *The Bracegirdle episode*: here the Ministers having approved of the personnel and terms of reference of a judicial commission, which subsequently found against the Chief Minister, defied the findings and continued in office without resigning. The motion condemning the Commission's findings was passed by 34 votes (32 Sinhalese and 2 minorities) to 14 (all minority representatives).

b. *The Mooloya incident*: here the All-Sinhalese Board of Ministers conscious that an obedient communal majority would effectively prevent the formation of an alternative government or the functioning of the constitution, brought about a deadlock by resigning in a body on a point of disagreement with the Governor who had anyhow to run the government for nearly a month without Ministers. Thereafter they got themselves re-elected to the Board.

c. *A Minister and War Contributions*: in 1941 on a message from the Governor to the State Council that he would disapprove of any measure which was a denial of any undertaking given by His Majesty's Government to India the Leader of the House moved its adjournment "without transacting any further business"; on a division 30 voted for the motion (29 Sinhalese and 1 minority) 13 voted against (the entire block of minority members present). The Minister for Local Administration and recently acting Leader of the House carried on a campaign of protest by getting his Committee to disapprove of local bodies making war contributions, and by addressing public meetings in which he asked the masses to boycott the Governor and refuse war contributions. On being called upon by the Governor to reconcile his conduct with his oaths of office, he got the motion rescinded in his Committee but continued in office.

These three examples carry their own lesson for those clamouring for parliamentary government on the British model for Ceylon.

The British Parliamentary system, it is submitted, depends for its success, inter alia.

a. the existence of clearly defined parties agreed on certain fundamental concepts of the State but differing on broad lines of policy,

b. the existence of a sound public opinion and the good sense of the party in power which sets a limit to despotic action,

c. the absence of a permanent, irremovable and irresponsive majority in power,

d. the realisation by the Government that the opposition is an alternative government ever on the alert to assume power by constitutional means,

e. the obtaining of a clear mandate from the electorate at a general Election for the political and economic programme of Government,

f. the consciousness of the opposition that the minority of today may become the majority of tomorrow.

In Ceylon everyone of these factors is conspicuous by its complete absence. This view is supported by the following clear *findings of the Soulbury Commission* that:—

a. the hopes of the Donoughmore Commission that communal tension would disappear have so far not been realised,

b. no alignment of the communities on party lines has yet emerged to take the place of communal divisions,

c. "unless and until parties in Ceylon become divided on social and economic in place of racial lines a minority will have no reason to rely on the swings to the right or left that occur in western democracies, and consequently will have little expectation of taking over the reins of government",

d. on political issues the people divide not as in England but on communal lines.

The Commission goes on to observe that:—

"it is this factor more than any other which makes difficult the application of the principles of Western Democracy in Ceylon."

*The Tamil Complaint* is that in the light of these findings and observations it would be very difficult to justify the Commission's endorsement without any modification whatsoever, of the Sinhalese demand for the British Parliamentary system of government.

The very *apex* of the *Executive pyramid* in the scheme accepted by the Commission is the *Prime Minister* who without the check of a party system, but with the obvious backing of a pliant Sinhalese majority, is to have unfettered control in

a. the choice of the other Ministers.

b. the distribution of portfolios.

c. the appointment of Parliamentary secretaries and presumably to have the right to demand a dissolution on the threat of an adverse vote.

The *results* in a plural society such as that of *Ceylon* will be that

a. the Prime Minister would become virtually a communal dictator.

b. all the other Ministers may well be drawn from the same racial group.

c. the same racial group will be in power at every change of Government (if indeed there can be a change of government.)

d. Sinhalese supremacy would become a prescriptive right.

e. the minority representatives would become "mutes and audience" in the legislature.

f. the country would for ever remain divided and national unity will not be achieved.

g. any opposition that might tend to emerge would be stifled by the threat of a dissolution.

h. the creation of Parliamentary Secretaries would artificially buttress a Cabinet in power.

By way of a *solution* the *Soulbury Commission*, merely exhorts the Sinhalese majority not to give cause for any suspicion of unfairness, and strongly advises the leader of the majority group:

"in forming a government to offer a proportion of the portfolios to the representatives of the minorities and in selecting those representatives to consult the elected members of the group or groups to which they belong."

*The Soulbury Commission* thus clearly *concedes* the desirability and necessity for the formation of a composite cabinet to include the trusted representatives of the minorities.

*The Tamil Complaint* is that instead of suggesting a definite solution on which one could rely the Commission merely asks the minorities to rely for the future on "the qualities and attributes of statesmanship" of Sinhalese leaders. These qualities have been singularly hard to seek in Sinhalese Ministers and members in the last fourteen years as is evidenced by the following:—

a. the deliberate planning and formation of an All-Sinhalese Board of Ministers in 1936 which the Soulbury Commission itself describes "as an act of singular lack of statesmanship",

b. the drafting of a constitution for Ceylon by the Ministers without even consulting the minorities,

c. the withdrawal of the Ministerial scheme on the appointment of the Soulbury Commission to afford opportunities for consultation with the minorities and the statement of the Sinhalese Leader in Council that the Secretary of State in doing so "had tricked and by-passed" them,

d. the boycott of the official proceedings of the Soulbury Commission by the Sinhalese Ministers and by the two exclusively Sinhalese bodies viz, the National Congress and the Sinhala Maha Sabha,

e. the rejection by the Sinhalese members of Council of a suggestion by Governor Sir Andrew Caldecott that the future Constitution of Ceylon should incorporate a Royal Instruction to the Governor to "use his best endeavours . . . to appoint . . . those persons including so far as is practicable members of important minority communities . . ." in the cabinet.

## Tamil demands for the executive

Till genuine parties emerge the future Executive must be so constructed as to assure to the minorities an *adequate and effective share in the Government of the country*. In the circumstances of Ceylon minority representation in the Cabinet cannot be left to convention as in Canada or Switzerland. A direction to the Governor by way of Royal Instructions as under the Government of India Act of 1935, has proved to be almost completely futile and ineffective in operation. Hence only a *mandatory provision* in the Constitutional Instrument *reserving for the minorities* a *specific proportion of the portfolios* on equitable lines can secure for them this vital right.

The majority being a permanent communal majority and not a political majority, there can be no justification for an invariable presumption that a Committee of the majority group is necessarily entitled to form the whole government. *The Cabinet should derive its mandate both from the majority and from the minority in the Legislature* and should *reflect the composition of the Legislature*.

This could be effected in the following way:—

a. The Prime Minister to be elected by the House and thus enjoy its confidence.

b. The Ministers to be elected by the House on a system of proportional representation by means of the single transferable vote.

c. The Ministers belonging to the minorities in order to enjoy their confidence to be selected by them in the first instance.

*The franchise*
The elective principle was first introduced into Ceylon in 1911 on a high educational franchise. This was somewhat extended in 1921 by the inclusion of income and property qualifications. It may be noted that from 1911 to 1931 the number of Tamil voters was a fairly close approximation to that of the Sinhalese in spite of the disparity in their populations.

The Donoughmore Commission recommended the introduction of universal adult franchise to Ceylon on a qualification of five years residence as a test of abiding interest. The Sinhalese made the acceptance of the Constitution conditional on the Franchise of the Indian Tamil workers being arbitrarily restricted by the requirement of domicile as a standard test. The suggested discrimination was communal and calculated to increase the numerical preponderance of the Sinhalese majority.

The Soulbury Commission admits that this material alteration regarding the franchise, translated into the Order in Council has had and still has:—

> "an important effect on the enfranchisement of a substantial section of the population" (Indian Tamil).

The Elections Order in Council of 1931 was amended in 1936 by removing the requirement of an application by a voter for registration. This amendment which was intended to increase the numbers on the Electoral Rolls has been manipulated against the Indian Tamil worker by virtually making the Registering Officer the de facto objector to all of them, thereby throwing the onus of satisfying the complex legal test of domicile on the mass of the Indian Tamil voters.

The Indian Tamils have been reluctant to obtain "certificates of permanent settlement" in order to exercise the franchise as they were liable to be treated as inferior to those registered under the standard domiciliary test and thereby afford justification for the acts of legislative and administrative discrimination to which they have been subjected.

It is surprising that in the face of the declared intentions of Sinhalese leaders to eliminate the Indian Tamils from Ceylon and the series of legislative and administrative measures adopted by them, the Soulbury Commission should feel sure that there is a desire to assimilate the Indian Community and make it part of a single nation.

*The Tamil submission* is that the Sinhalese objections to the enfranchisement of the Indian Tamil workers have been inspired by communal and political motives and not by economic consideration. *The Soulbury* Commission rightly points out that:—

> "the franchise itself is only a means to an end and the end is to give people such a share of political power as may enable them to redress their grievances themselves."

The Commission goes on to observe that:—

> "the distribution of political power between the various communities is determined by the extent of the franchise (with which is connected the question of emigration)."

It may be noted that the question of emigration is totally irrelevant, and the issue is in respect of Indians already lawfully admitted into Ceylon under governmental assistance and encouragement and on assurances of equality of civic and political status with the rest of the population of the Island.

The Commission also points out that:—

> "any decision of the Government of Ceylon upon the conditions of the enfranchisement of the Indian unskilled worker will have an important effect on our recommendation regarding the terms of reference of the Delimitation Commission."

The *Commission has failed* to offer a just or reasonable solution even to this limited problem which has been a fruitful source of annoyance to the peoples of India and has resulted in the progressive deterioration of the relations between India and Ceylon for the last fourteen years.

*The Tamil demand* is that the Indians should be allowed to qualify for the Franchise on the same terms as the rest of the population especially as recruitment of labour from India has been discontinued for over ten years and India herself has placed a bann [sic] on the emigration of unskilled workers since 1939.

*The public & judicial services*

For Self Government to be good government the purity of the Judiciary and the efficiency and impartiality of the Public Service must be ensured; this can be achieved only by the complete independence from political control and influence of these services.

*The Soulbury Commission* has *found* that under the present Constitution:—

> "the Ministers have used their influence . . . in support of candidates for public appointments where they could."

The Commission also appreciates the realities of the situation when it says of the future Public Services Commission that:—

> "it will be doubly necessary that the deciding authority in Ceylon should be immune from accusations of partisanship."

*The Tamil Complaint* is that the Commission accepts the Sinhalese demand that the Governor in appointing the members of the Public Services and Judicial Services Commissions shall do so after consulting the Prime Minister whose advice he is not bound to accept.

Any advice that the Prime Minister may give to the Governor about these appointments will inevitably lead to the loss of public confidence in the independence of these Commissions and to a suspicion of political patronage.

*The Tamil demands* are:—

a. that the Governor shall appoint the members of the Public Services Commission in his absolute discretion and that two out of the three members shall have held high administrative office for a minimum period of ten years under the Crown,

b. that the Judges of the Supreme Court shall be appointed on the advice of the Judicial Committee of the Privy Council,

c. that the Judicial Services Commission shall consist of the Chief Justice and two Judges of the Supreme Court acting annually in rotation.

*Safeguards for minorities*

The Soulbury Commission contemplates two kinds of safeguards in respect of legislation that may adversely affect the minorities.

(A)  By prohibition under the Order in Council of any legislation discriminatory of persons of any community or religion.

It may be noted that this provision exists under the present Constitution; nevertheless over a period of nearly ten years the machinery of the State has been utilised and the general taxpayers money expended on the administration of the affairs of Buddhist temples. On this question being raised as an act of discrimination the Commission came to the conclusion that prima facie "it affords evidence against the Sinhalese majority in the Council of partiality".

(B)  By reservation by the Governor for His Majesty's assent, of any bill which has evoked serious opposition by any racial or religious community, and which in the opinion of the Governor, is likely to involve oppression or serious injustice to any such community.

It may be noted that this provision also exists under the present Constitution but has been of no avail when some or all of the minorities seriously opposed such Bills as the Land Development and Alienation Ordinance, the Village Communities Ordinance, the Anuradhapura Preservation Ordinance.

*The Tamil submission* is that the first safeguard will be totally ineffective in practice unless the Supreme Court is empowered to adjudicate upon such legislation as ultra vires; and that the second safeguard will be even of less avail in the future than it has been in the past and that it would be placing a constitutional Governor in an invidious and embarrassing position if he is called upon to interpose himself against a united communal Ministry supported by a substantial majority in the Legislature.

*Conclusion*

The Donoughmore Commission after investigating the political situation in Ceylon in 1928 recognised the heterogeniety [sic] of the population and the suspicion and distrust of the various elements that composed it. The complete absence of a Party System and the fear that communal and racial parties would emerge convinced it that the English Parliamentary system of Government would be totally unsuitable to conditions in Ceylon. By abolishing communal representation and forcing the people into a single territorial electorate it felt assured that the "canker of communalism" would disappear. The result has been a complete miscarriage of its good intentions. Its aim of devolving on the people responsibility for the management of their internal affairs has resulted in all the transferred power and authority being concentrated in the hands of one race. Instead of the evolution of democratic government, the Constitution has brought into being an undesirable oligarchy based on race and religion.

The Constitution has failed because it rested on vain hopes and expectations instead of providing proper remedies for the realistic requirements of a plural society.

The *Soulbury Commission* investigated the position after the Constitution had been in operation for fourteen years. It frankly admits that the hopes of the

Donoughmore Commissioners that communal tension would eventually disappear have so far not been realised, and that contrary to the Donoughmore Commission's expectations the electors vote on racial grounds. It has found that the fears of the Donoughmore Commissioners were well founded and that communal parties have actually come into existence. In short, it must have realised that all the conditions and prerequisites which the Donoughmore Commission thought would be necessary for the successful functioning of English Parliamentary institutions are still non-existent. It professes to appreciate the difficulty of applying the principles of Western Democracy to Ceylon. It also admits that the prospect of transplanting British institutions to Ceylon with success may appear remote. Nevertheless because it fears that modifications of the British form of Government may not prove any more successful it recommends for Ceylon a method of Government of which it "knows something about" and which is a "result of very long experience". The obvious reply to this is that the British method of Government today is the result of the experience of centuries of its working by the British people and adapted to their particular and peculiar genius. To recommend such a Constitution for Ceylon in the face of the experience of the minorities for the last fourteen years in the anticipation that certain hopes and expectations will be realised will amount to the handing over of the future welfare of a large section of the people of the Island to the unfettered control of a permanent communal majority.

The recommendations of the Soulbury Commission might have proved more acceptable to all sections of the people of Ceylon if it had realised and proceeded on the footing that:—

> "representative institutions of the world have reached no final or definite form, that conditions vary from country to country and from continent to continent imposing each in their own sphere special and peculiar limitations on the Parliamentary system, and the history of modern constitutional development is one continuous record of attempts to adjust accepted Parliamentary practice to the realistic requirements of social and economic progress."

## 323   CO 54/987/1, no 97                              5 Nov 1945
## [Soulbury Report]: letter from H M Desai to Mr Hall urging HMG to reconsider on the issues of the franchise and the status of Indians in Ceylon

I am much obliged to you for your kind letter of 26th ultimo, and I feel grateful to you for your good sentiments wishing me a happy voyage back to Ceylon. I will convey to my friends and Associations which I represent your courtesy and warmth of reception with which you received me during my stay in London.

Before I leave the shores of England, I feel I should not conceal from you my feelings on the decisions reached by His Majesty's Government as published on 31.10.45. in the statement "Ceylon—Policy on Constitutional reform."

These decisions will be received by nearly one million Indians in Ceylon with utter disappointment and despair and they will be justified in feeling that the two vital questions—viz—Franchise and Status—which concern them have been totally ignored and left in cold-storage by His Majesty's Government. Franchise and status have been in the past source of constant friction between the Governments of India and Ceylon and the two peoples, and judging from the past attitude of the Government of Ceylon, these two issues are not likely to be settled by Ceylon in a spirit of goodwill and amity. The homogenous [sic] Board of Ministers in Ceylon have consistently pursued a policy of reducing and liquidating the numbers of Indians in Ceylon, and I feel almost sure this policy will now be pursued more vigorously than before in view of the fact that power will be centralised in the hands of the Sinhalese politicians after the proposed reforms are inaugurated. Absorption and assimilation of *Indians already in Ceylon* and making them "part and parcel of a single nation" will, in the circumstances, never be achieved. This is bound to result in creating in Ceylon a depressed class of floating and homeless people existing on the suffrance of the Sinhalese Ministers.

While the Indian Community in Ceylon has always supported the demand for full measure of self-government, and while it concedes the principle of giving Ceylon the right to determine the composition of its people, it demands that the issues of absorption and assimilation of Indians *already* in Ceylon, enfranchising them on terms of equality and conferring full citizenship rights on those who make a declaration of having made Ceylon their permanent home, should have been considered and settled. The question of future immigration is an altogether independent issue and need not be mixed up with the questions of *Indians already in Ceylon*. It is a pity that the Soulbury Commission mixed up these two issues, and I was hoping that His Majesty's Government would see the issues clearly.

I believe in a short letter like this, I can not say more than what I have stated above which merely outlines the feelings and views of the Indian Community in Ceylon.

I would, therefore, once again earnestly appeal to you and through you His Majesty's Government to reconsider the decisions reached in so far as they concern the franchise and status of nearly one seventh of the population of Ceylon. In the interests of the welfare of the Indian Community that has contributed in a large measure towards the successful prosecution of war, the questions of their franchise and status, I hope, will be reviewed sympathetically before the reforms are inaugurated.

Thanking you, Sir, once again for your courtesy.

## 324 CO 54/986/6/3, no 211                9 Nov 1945
## [Soulbury Report]: letter from Sir H Moore to G E J Gent on the reforms debate in the State Council

The Reforms Debate is still in progress; it is hoped to conclude it by this evening if all goes according to plan. I enclose some newspaper cuttings[1] of the speeches up to date. Senanayake, in a carefully prepared speech, which he read, went out of his way to allay the fears of the minorities and I think you will agree approached the subject in a statesmanlike manner.

There has been tremendous activity behind the scenes with the result that he is now assured of a large majority—if not a unanimous vote. With the possible

---
[1] Not printed.

exception of Dahanayake it is unlikely that there will be any Sinhalese votes cast against the motion since, as you will see, Bandaranaike, though he does not really like it, has not felt strong enough to take an independent stand. A solid Muslim vote was assured some time ago and the Europeans—despite their cabled protests—have as a result of various conferences decided to come in provided they can secure reasonable assurances from Senanayake on the subject of immigration later in the Debate. The Ceylon Tamils are divided though they all realise that Ponnambalam and his 50/50 cry are now dead; it remains to be seen, in the absence of Ponnambalam, how Rajakulendram will vote. It is possible that there will be no Ceylon Tamil vote cast against the motion, but in any case it is certain that there will be no solid Ceylon Tamil vote against it. The attitude of the Indian National Congress is still in doubt; it will be difficult for I.X. Pereira to retract, but Mahadeva told me this morning that Aney himself is now counselling them not to oppose the motion since he realises that they are not going to get any support in Whitehall and, that being so, the best tactics for them to pursue are to make the best terms they can with the enemy within their gates.

All this is somewhat remarkable—just another example of the highly volatile nature of so-called public opinion in Ceylon. The real moral I think to be drawn from it is that since at long last H.M.G. has made up their mind for them—a thing which they have been quite incapable of doing for themselves—they feel they had better accept the award at once with a good grace since in fact it gives them as much or more than they could have hoped to agree upon if left to themselves.

Before you get this letter I shall have sent you a wire as to the actual results of the voting and an analysis of the votes cast.

# 325 CO 54/986/6/3, no 212 10 Nov 1945
## [Soulbury Report]: letter from Sir H Moore to G E J Gent on the reforms debate in the State Council

In continuation of my letter of yesterday[1] the Debate ended last evening and I enclose Press cuttings[2] of the remaining speeches that have appeared in the Press to-day.

The Debate was shortened by the arrangement made behind the scenes that there should be only one principal speaker on behalf of each party and also that the moving of any detailed amendments on particular parts of the White Paper would be regarded as tantamount to rejection of the proposals.

You will see that my forecast of the voting[3] as made in yesterday's letter has proved substantially correct, indeed I am informed that I.X. Pereira certainly, and possibly Natesa Iyer were also going to vote for the motion but at the last moment Aney, who was sitting in the gallery, sent them down a note telling them not to do so. I have this direct from Senanayake who assures me that it is correct. If this is so, it seems to me not only improper, but a most stupid piece of interference on the part of Aney, who, as Representative of the Indian Government here, ought to be particularly careful not to identify himself so openly in our local politics.

Naturally Senanayake is in great heart and he has every reason for being so.

I am having a Conference early next week with the three Officers of State to settle

---

[1] See 324.    [2] Not printed.    [3] See 326 for the result.

on the procedure which we should now recommend for adoption and you will be hearing about that officially very shortly.[4]

---

[4] On 19 Nov, in Gent's absence, Sidebotham acknowledged Moore's letters of 9 and 10 Nov and commented: 'What a very improper step on Aney's part, if what Senanayake tells you is correct. The latter seems to have handled the whole business exceedingly well and, as you say, has every right to be satisfied with the results. Ponnambalam is still on our doorstep. He will go back a sadder and, I hope, a wiser man' (CO 54/986/6/4, no 213).

## 326   CO 54/986/6/3, no 203                                    12 Nov 1945
## [Soulbury Report]: inward telegram no 2112 from Sir H Moore to Mr Hall transmitting the result of the vote in the State Council

[On 10 Nov, Hall sent through Moore a personal message to Senanayake congratulating him on the result which he described as 'a great tribute' to the 'statesmanship and wisdom' displayed by Senanayake and his colleagues. Senanayake for his part sent brief personal messages of gratitude to Layton, Caldecott, Hall, Gater and Trafford Smith. His message to Hall, sent through Moore on 12 Nov, read: 'White Paper paragraph 12 was unnecessary. Majority was nine-tenths. New constitution has been accepted with determination so to work it that, in comparatively short space of time, Dominion status will be evolved. Most grateful courtesy and personal interest especially in accelerating White Paper.' The secretary of state also paid tribute to the work of the commissioners in a letter to Lord Soulbury on 12 Nov. Soulbury replied on 14 Nov: 'I think that what "did the trick" was the assurance that you were able to give in regard to Dominion status, coupled with the elimination of the Governor's Special Ordinances dealing with Defence and External Affairs. Judging from a cable which Senanayake sent to me yesterday he is jubilant . . .' (CO 54/986/6/4, nos 200 & 215). Hall informed the Cabinet of the result in CP(45)280, 13 Nov 1945 (CAB 129/4.)]

My telegram No. 2096.
Senanayake's motion.
Analysis of voting by communities as follows:—

(a) = total number in Council
(b) = number present
(c) = voted for
(d) = voted against.

*Low country Sinhalese*
(a) 32
(b) 32
(c) 31
(d)  1

*Kandyan Sinhalese*
(a)  7
(b)  7
(c)  7

*Ceylon Tamils*
(a)  7
(b)  5 and Speaker
(c)  5

*Europeans*
(a)  4
(b)  4
(c)  4

*Muslims*
(a)  3
(b)  3
(c)  3

*Indians*
(a)  3
(b)  3
(c)  nil
(d)  2

*Burghers*
(a)  1
(b)  1
(c)  1

**327**  CO 54/986/8, no 67                                13 Nov 1945

[Soulbury Report]: inward telegram no 2115 from Sir H Moore to Mr
Hall transmitting a message from the joint secretary, All-Ceylon Tamil
Congress, on the vote in the State Council[1]

Following sent at request of Mr. S. Sivasubramaniam, Honorary Joint Secretary All
Ceylon Tamil Congress. *Begins.* White Paper re Ceylon's future Constitution
paragraph 12 states [His] Majesty's Government will take into account views
expressed by State Council and number voting. Wish submit voting in State Council
on motion by Leader for acceptance proposals provides correct index of Council's
opinion regarding advance towards Dominion Status, but not regarding minority
safeguards considered domestic matter between communities, as indicated by views
expressed. Views expressed by Tamil members that Tamils have not been given
effective share in Government criticising Soulbury Report and White Paper merit
your careful consideration. Tamil public opinion very strong against Soulbury
Report and White Paper. Issue of second White Paper necessary giving modifications
to do justice to Tamil community. Making suitable modifications without retarding
constitutional progress and without prejudicing claims of Sinhalese community
possible, for example, by indicating minimum number of Tamil ministers and
making provision Statutory or through Instrument of instructions for consulting
Tamil Councillors in selection of Tamil ministers, and thus giving effect to emphatic
enunciation of principle advocated by Soulbury Commission in final sentence of
paragraph 261 of Report. Important witness late Speaker, Mr. Molamure, giving
evidence before Soulbury Commission, was prepared to accept composite cabinet. If
Majesty's Government not disposed to grant suitable modifications, appointment of
Parliamentary Committee and dissolution of present State Council requested. Wish
invite attention to statement of policy of one of your predecessor's made in
November, 1937, in letter to Governor Ceylon "Selected changes could not be
expected to produce good results unless adopted with general consent of all
important interests in Ceylon". Opposition of Tamil community to Soulbury
recommendations and White Paper completely nullifies essential condition of policy
above referred to. *Ends.*

---

[1] On 4 Nov 1945, the All-Ceylon Tamil Congress convened a special session in Colombo Town Hall and
condemned the Soulbury Report and the white paper. The meeting urged a joint parliamentary committee
to consider Ceylon's future constitutional proposals, an immediate dissolution of the existing State
Council and fresh elections (CO 54/986/8, no 57, inward tel no 2085 from Moore, 8 Nov 1945).

**328**   CO 54/986/8, no 94A                                    13 Nov 1945

[Soulbury Report]: letter from W Dahanayake[1] to R W Sorenson,
T E N Driberg and T Reid[2] stating the case for a general election

You are probably aware that the Soulbury Constitution, as amended by the White
Paper of the 31st ultimo, was accepted by the State Council of Ceylon by 51 votes
to 3.

I was one of the members who opposed acceptance. In the course of the debate I
raised a fundamental issue, among other objections, and I trust that it will interest
you.

The present State Council of Ceylon came into being in March 1936, that is, two
and a half years before the start of World War II. A General Election was due to be
held not later than January, 1941. In June, 1940, however, the Secretary of State for
the Colonies announced a postponement of the general election. His reason for doing
so was that "the problems of franchise and the delimitation of Constituencies"
needed to be carefully examined. His reason had no reference to the war situation.
Subsequently, in 1942 and again in 1944, postponements of the general election a
second and a third time were authorised by the Secretary of State.

Although all hostilities ended three months ago, the people of Ceylon are now no
nearer the day of a general election than they were while the war was on.

When the Secretary of State was questioned on this matter on 17th ultimo in the
House of Commons, he is reported to have said that there had been no request from
Ceylon for a dissolution of the State Council. It is obvious that Mr. Hall was wrongly
informed about public opinion in Ceylon. I am able to testify to the fact that during
the last six months there have been over 150 public meetings held in different parts
of the country at which an immediate dissolution of the State Council has been
unanimously demanded by resolution. The British Government's ignorance of these
happenings is certainly not the fault of the people of Ceylon.

It is also pertinent to inquire what the status of the present State Council is to
have decided the question of a future constitution. Is a stale institution which has
forfeited the confidence of the people capable of arriving at a correct decision? Nay
more, should it be allowed to arrogate to itself a sovereign right that should rest with
the people?

The present Board of Ministers and their yes-men in the State Council are a
tenacious team of limpets, and it serves their interests to postpone the day of
reckoning by every means at their command. And they have done so in right royal
fashion, for the amazing position is that a *general election cannot be held till about
the middle of 1947, that is, two years after the end of World War II!* I should explain
this position in detail.

The Soulbury Constitution provides for 95 electoral areas as against the present
50. The Soulbury Commissioners indicate how the constituencies should be divided,
in the following words:—

"Recommendation 7: The Delimitation Commission so appointed shall divide

---

[1] Member of State Council representing the Bibile constituency.
[2] The recipients of this letter were Labour MP's in the UK. Reid was formerly mayor of Colombo,
1919–1924, labour controller, Ceylon, 1925–1929, and a member of the Ceylon legislature, 1926–1931.

each Province into a number of electoral divisions . . . so that, whenever it shall appear to the Commission that there is a substantial concentration in any area of a Province of persons united by a community of interest, whether racial, religious or otherwise, but differing in one or more of these respects from the majority of the inhabitants of the area, the Commission shall be at liberty to modify the factor of numerical equality of persons of the Province into electoral districts as may be necessary to render possible the represensentation of that interest."

It will be obvious that the delimitation of electoral areas upon the above basis requires that the distribution of population by race and religion should be available to the Delimitation Commissioners and the witnesses who appear before them. The most recent figures available for such purpose are the census figures of 1921, which, of course, are out-of-date. The next full census takes place in April, 1946, which will be the starting point in the ushering in of the Soulbury Constitution. Three months for the sittings and finding of the Delimitation Commission, and six months for the preparation of the new electoral lists, provided that all these steps are carried out with the maximum expedition, will take us on to the middle of 1947, which is the earliest date when a general election may be expected.

Such is the position that confronts the people of Ceylon. Can you acquiesce in it? The plain request of the people here is that the present State Council should be dissolved immediately, and a general election held upon the existing Constitution, so that consequentially the new Constitution offered in the White Paper may be placed before the country for a decision by the people. Any other course of action would, I can assure you, be construed as a gross violation of the principles of democracy which the British Government professes.

# 329   CO 54/986/6/4, no 217                                   13 Nov 1945
## [Soulbury Report]: letter from Mr Senanayake to Mr Hall on the vote in the State Council and the drafting of the new constitution

I trust you received my cable on the acceptance of the New Constitution by the State Council of Ceylon.[1] As you are aware, the decisions of His Majesty's Government were available here only on the 31st October but I found it possible to introduce in the State Council on the 8th November a motion for the acceptance of the Constitution offered in the White Paper. This motion was debated on for two days (on the 8th and 9th November) and representatives of all communities and parties took part in the debate. On the 9th evening the motion was passed by a majority of 89%. Of the 57 members of the State Council, 54 were present and, except for one Sinhalese member of the Communist Party and two Indian members, the rest voted for the motion. I enclose, for your perusal, copies[2] of the Ceylon Daily News of the 9th and 10th November which give an account of the proceedings in the State Council. I am sure they will be of interest to you.

It is indeed a matter of great personal satisfaction to me that, after all the criticism since the issue of the 1943 Declaration, all communities, except the Indian Tamils,

---

[1] See 326, note.                                                  [2] Not printed.

should have rallied round me and supported me at this critical juncture. I am deeply conscious of the confidence they placed in me when they accepted the motion with such a convincing majority, and it shall always be my endeavour to put aside communal and other considerations and act in the best interests of the country.

There is still a considerable amount of work to be done before we could give effect to the decision of the House, chief among them being the appointment of a Delimitation Commission and the drafting of the Order-in-Council. I am anxious that the drafting should now be pushed on with all possible speed in order that we may not unduly delay matters. I have already written to His Excellency the Governor asking that the Legal Secretary be persuaded to go to London as soon as possible in order that the preparation of the final draft Order-in-Council may not be delayed due to correspondence.

In 1931, when the Order-in-Council under the Donoughmore Scheme was drafted, considerable difficulties arose, as the draft did not in all respects give effect to the intentions of the unofficial members of the Legislative Council. I am anxious that such a situation should not arise this time, and I should be grateful if you could keep me informed of the drafting of the Order-in-Council under the New Constitution. I shall always be ready to give you my views if you care to have them. I wish it were possible, even at this stage, to get His Majesty's Government to agree to the transfer of the general responsibility for Ceylon to the Dominions Office and admit us to Imperial and other conferences even as observers in the first instance.

Let me take this opportunity of thanking you once again for all you did especially in accelerating the decisions of His Majesty's Government on the Soulbury Report. Your courtesy and personal interest will be remembered with gratitude by all of us in Ceylon. I hope it will not be long before we are in a position to invite you to the opening of the Parliament of Ceylon.

# 330  CO 54/986/6/4                                    14 Nov 1945
## [Constitution]: note by J B Sidebotham to Sir G Gater on the drafting of the new constitution

I have been thinking about what machinery can be devised to get a new Constitution for Ceylon drafted quickly and with the least possible amount of friction between ourselves and the Board of Ministers. The Donoughmore Constitution was drafted in Ceylon, but if we were to adopt this procedure in the present case the chances are that the Board of Ministers would plump for their own original draft Order-in-Council, with a few modifications to meet the amendments now proposed. This document, Mr. Roberts Wray says, would be quite useless as a Constitution, despite the fact that it was drafted by Dr. Ivor Jennings and I am in entire agreement with Mr. Roberts Wray's views on that point. Mr. Roberts Wray's view is that the drafting of this new Constitution must be started *de novo* in the light of up to date Colonial precedents, with certain special modifications, of course, to suit the more advanced position in Ceylon.

There is, moreover, a further difficulty in having a Constitution drafted in Ceylon. The drafting will presumably have to be done by the Legal Secretary, Mr. Nihill. Now the Legal Secretary is a member of the State Council and, I think I am correct in saying, its legal adviser as well as the Governor's legal adviser, and I feel that Mr. Nihill's position might be a very difficult one, since there are a number of difficult points of a political character which will arise in the drafting and to which some solution agreeable to all parties will have to be found. Mr. Nihill will, no doubt, be under pressure from Ministers while he may be under very different pressure from our end of the picture. This is not a position in which I think he should be placed.

The ideal solution would perhaps be to send out a legal draftsman to Ceylon, well seized with our views, and with him someone who could tackle the political issues involved, and let the drafting be done by our legal draftsman out there. But that, I fear, is beyond the realms of possibility in view of the staff position here.

The next best alternative would seem to me to be to ask Ceylon to send someone home here to do the drafting in consultation with our Legal Advisers, and when a draft had been prepared, for that person to go back to Ceylon in company with someone who could go and endeavour to reach a compromise on the more vexatious political points and who would have had an opportunity of discussing those points at this end as they arose in the drafting.

Whether the Ceylon Government would be prepared to accept that is, of course, open to question. They may say firmly that they want the drafting done out there, and if they do I think it is going to be rather difficult to resist that request. I feel, however, that it would be very unfortunate for a draft to be prepared out there which was "wide of the mark", for it to be sent back here and then for us to have to turn it down and start all over again. It would be not only a waste of time, but also just the kind of proceeding which would make the Board of Ministers suspicious of H.M.G.'s good intentions etc., etc.

I think that it could be argued in favour of Ceylon sending someone home to draft here that this would probably greatly expedite the preparation of the new draft instruments and it could be explained (if it is agreed) that the intention was that when he returned someone would accompany him to explain various points which had arisen in the course of the drafting and to discuss them locally with a view to reaching final agreement on the drafts.

In view of the volume of Constitutional drafting on hand here it seems doubtful, I understand from Mr. Roberts Wray, whether anyone could possibly undertake the drafting of a new Constitution for Ceylon at the present time without putting back still further other Constitutions which, from many points of view, are equally urgent. We cannot afford to delay a new Constitution for Ceylon and I feel that it should be pressed on with as soon as possible. Whether the Ceylon Government would be prepared to release Mr. Nihill or Sir Robert Drayton to come back to this country (Mr. Nihill has only just returned there, and Sir Robert Drayton is about to go out if he has not already started) is another matter.

I think that our first course should be to consult the Governor of Ceylon in the light of whatever is decided to be the best course at this end, and see what he thinks Ministers' reactions will be. In doing so, I think we ought to make it abundantly clear that any draft which followed the lines of the Ministers' draft would be quite unacceptable as a new Constitutional instrument, and that we feel that it is essential that drafting should commence *de novo*.

I pass this through Mr. Roberts Wray in case he has any comments.

Perhaps you will wish to discuss.

P.S. One of the important things at the Ceylon end of the picture will be to get the

Delimitation Commission for new constituencies going as soon as possible. You will remember that the Government of India has pressed for certain definite instructions to be given to that Commission and we shall certainly want, I think, to see the Commission's terms of reference before the Commission is constituted.

# 331  CO 54/986/8, nos 79 & 80                                    18 Nov 1945
# [Indian labour]: inward telegrams from K Natesa Aiyar[1] and S Thondaman[2] to Mr Hall protesting against the white paper

Indian Estate labourers quite upset decision White Paper stop Feel have been let down by His Majesty's Government despite specious promises of protection safeguards and equality of status political and otherwise stop White Paper proposes hand them over to Sin Halese [sic] Leaders to be dealt with as slaves stop Sinhalese Leaders have shown their dislike of Indian workers last fifteen years when in power stop They do not demand special protection or privileges but demand rights promised them these hundred years when recruited to enrich Ceylon and British Capitalists stop Further feel repatriation India more honourable than live as slaves here stop Demand incorporation of their rights in Order in Council stop Failing please arrange repatriation with one months wages for every years service in Ceylon Estates stop Have lost all confidence in promises stop Failing settlement workers prepared take action by peaceful and lawful means to make the Governments and Investors regret their ingratitude stop This is a last effort obtain understanding honourable lines [stop] NATESA AIYAR PRESIDENT CEYLON INDIAN WORKERS FEDERATION AND MEMBER STATE COUNCIL HATTON LARGEST PLANTING CONSTITUENCY.

Ceylon Indian Congress Labour Union representing three quarter million Indian workers in Ceylon is daily receiving protests from all over the island against the injustice done to illiterate labourers with abiding interest in Ceylon in denying them fundamental right of Franchise on simple residential basis stop Protests signed by over eighty thousand estate labourers already received are being handed over to the Governor stop[3] Over two hundred protest telegrams have been sent to him by meetings held on various estates stop Your recent reply in Parliament indicates inadequate appreciation of difficulties of certificate of permanent settlement fully explained to Soulbury Commission and demonstrated by negligible number who

---

[1] President, Ceylon Indian Workers' Federation.          [2] President, Ceylon Indian Congress Labour Union.
[3] On 7 Dec 1945 Moore informed Hall that he had received a petition bearing 83,832 signatures. The petition described the Soulbury recommendations on the franchise, status and citizenship rights of Indians in Ceylon as 'unjust and unfair' and demanded 'full unrestricted adult franchise and rights of citizenship on ascertainable test of a residence of five years'. By way of explanation, on 8 Dec Moore informed Hall that the signatures had been obtained by canvass through local district organisations. The governor had been informed by S Vytilingam, member of State Council and joint honorary secretary of the Ceylon Indian Congress, that they had been collected 'largely to meet criticism of the younger and more violent members of the Congress, who had been pressing for energetic and direct action, such as a general strike'. Vytilingam had been in India contacting Indian politicians when Senanayake's motion was passed in the State Council but Moore believed that he would probably have voted in favour, his present protest being directed only against the franchise and citizenship recommendations of the Soulbury Commission (CO 54/986/8, nos 90 & 91).

have taken it in practice stop Compilation of electoral register under new Constitution would it is feared result in elimination of even those already registered under domicile qualification due to further tightening of procedure stop Reference in your reply to settlement of grievance regarding Franchise by direct negotiations overlooks unlikelihood of such settlement in foreseeable future stop Mr Senanayake recently said in state council that no settlement is possible until there is third party and the countries are independent stop In view of the foregoing it is essential that provision for Indian Franchise on simple residential basis should be incorporated in Order in Council stop Betrayal of the labour cause by the British Labour Government will cause disillusionment and widespread unrest stop THONDAMAN PRESIDENT.

**332**   CO 54/986/8, no 78                                20 Nov 1945
**[Tamils]: inward telegram no 2149 from Sir H Moore to Mr Hall transmitting a message from the joint secretary, All-Ceylon Tamil Congress, repudiating the action of Tamil members in the State Council in voting for the white paper**

Following sent at request of Sivasubramaniam, Joint Secretary All-Ceylon Tamil Congress. *Begins.* All-Ceylon Tamil Congress Committee met 15th November resolved unanimously repudiating action Tamil Members in Council voting for Mr. Senanayake's motion accepting White Paper proposals. Further declared votes of Members in Council for motion inconsistent with own views expressed during Debate on motion and opposed to election pledges and ad hoc views of constituents conveyed to them. Voting in Council, though correct index of Council's opinion regarding constitutional advance, does not represent Tamil public opinion regarding safeguards for Tamils. Tamil people greatly dissatisfied with proposals owing to failure to provide them with effective share in Government and franchise for Indian Tamils. Motion introduced with unwarranted haste, giving no time for country to express views. Unrepresentative character of Council and discrepancy between voting and views expressed in Council by Tamil Members indicate imperative need for dissolution of present Council and new election on definite issue of constitutional proposals. If modifications not contemplated demand dissolution new election and Parliamentary Committee. Representative character and strength of Tamil Congress acknowledged on 30th March this year during Soulbury Commission stay Ceylon by Sinhalese owned paper, Daily News, in special article on parties next election to State Council, though paper is opposed to Tamil Congress policy. Also predicted Tamil Congress capturing many seats Northern and Eastern electorates. These statements confirm Congress view that dissolution Council and new election will ensure Congress policy strongly represented new Council and justify demand for dissolution and Congress claim to represent Tamil opinion. Leader Council refused request of All-Ceylon Tamil Congress Joint Secretary for postponement introducing motion to enable considering terms for agreed settlement. Mr. Senanayake's speech might make pleasant reading to those not conversant with realities of Ceylon's present political situation but offers no concrete proposals for safeguarding Tamil position. His political antecedents and past attitude towards Tamils do not warrant Tamils accepting his goodwill speech as substitute for effective constitutional safeguards for future security of Tamils and other minorities. His speech refers to fact of Sinhalese being governed by Kings of Tamil people and to Tamil civilisation as most ancient of our civilisations. Contrast irremovable Sinhalese Buddhist domination of Tamils with immutable succession of Sinhalese Buddhist Prime Ministers imposed by British authority under proposed Soulbury constitution. Satisfactory constitution still possible within the framework of Soulbury recommendations without retarding constitutional advance or prejudicing Sinhalese claims if

(1) Statutory provision made regarding minimum number of Tamil Ministers and selection of Tamil Ministers by Tamil Members.
(2) Indian franchise question settled.
(3) Suitable instrument of instructions to Governor.
(4) Suitable directions to Delimitation Commission with view to give weightage Tamils and other minorities. *Ends.*

## 333  CO 54/986/8, no 84                              [Nov 1945]
## [Ceylon Association]: briefing note by Trafford Smith for Mr Hall's interview with a deputation from the Ceylon Association in London

The points which the Deputation will wish to discuss with the Secretary of State are summarised at the end of their memorandum flagged at (66) on the file. Dealing with them in order:—

1. *That provision be made in the Order in Council to preclude legislation prohibiting or restricting the re-entry of persons normally resident in the Island, or the free entry of British subjects domiciled in the United Kingdom*
The present position under the Soulbury Report is that the Governor is instructed to reserve legislation prohibiting or restricting the re-entry of persons normally resident in Ceylon. The Association wish this prohibition to be inserted in the Order in Council. The effect of this change would be that the Ceylon Government could not introduce or discuss a measure designed to restrict the re-entry of normal residents. Under the Soulbury recommendation, they would be able to introduce such a measure, and to pass it, unless the Governor decided that "in his opinion the provisions regarding the right of re-entry of persons normally resident in the Island at the date of the passing of the Bill by the Legislature are unfair or unreasonable".

It will be remembered that in his closing speech on the motion accepting His Majesty's Government's White Paper, Mr. Senanayake gave an undertaking that no Government with which he was associated would enact a message restricting the re-entry of Europeans. To incorporate the safeguard proposed by the Commission in the body of the Constitution as desired by the Ceylon Association, would undoubtedly be interpreted by M. Senanayake as expressing doubts felt by His Majesty's Government as to his good faith. It would represent a retraction from the position taken up by His Majesty's Government in the White Paper and, as such, would be unacceptable in Ceylon. Moreover the proposal shows an excessive suspicion on the part of the Ceylon Association, who can surely rest content with the instruction to the Governor to safeguard their interests as regards re-entry, if the Ceylon Government show signs of restricting them unfairly or unreasonably.

No provision safeguarding the free entry of British subjects domiciled in the United Kingdom appears in the Soulbury recommendations, as the Commission felt that it would be derogatory to the Ceylon Government's power to determine the composition of the population of Ceylon. Here again, Mr. Senanayake's undertaking in his closing speech should go some way to satisfy the Ceylon Association. The European members of the Council were satisfied to the point of enabling them to vote *for* the motion. The Deputation will of course argue that Ceylon residents have the right of entry into the United Kingdom and that such right should be reciprocal. It could be pointed out to them that, if any question arose of the Ceylon Government restricting the right, His Majesty's Government would be in a position to retaliate.

### 2. *That the conditions of enfranchisement for Indian Tamils should be five years residence*

We have already been fully into this question of the Indian franchise. The Soulbury recommendation is that the present franchise provisions should stand till they can be changed by direct negotiation between the Governments of India and Ceylon. After full consideration of the pros and cons and after hearing the views of the Government of India on the subject, His Majesty's Government have decided to accept the Soulbury recommendation. The co-operation of the Sinhalese majority community in the introduction of the new Constitution would not be forthcoming if His Majesty's Government were to decide otherwise. Now that the State Council have formally accepted the White Paper, and His Majesty's Government have announced their intention to proceed accordingly, any second thoughts on this question of the Indian franchise would be regarded in Ceylon as a breech [sic] of faith, especially by Mr. Senanayake. His Majesty's Government have every hope that the negotiations between the Governments of India and Ceylon will be resumed with results satisfactory to both sides.

### 3. *That safeguards for planting and commercial interests against discriminatory legislation be incorporated in the Order in Council*

The principal minority safeguards are contained in sections 32 (iv), (v) and 33(a) of page 115 of the Soulbury Report.

No doubt the Ceylon Association are in doubt whether "planting and commercial interests" would come within the definition of "racial community" in paragraph 32 (v) or "persons of any community" in paragraph 33(a). Overseas planting and commercial interests would of course be safeguarded by paragraph 32 (iv) which protects "the rights and property of British subjects not residing in Ceylon". Any more specific safeguards for planting and commercial interests would be open to obvious objection.

### 4. *That members representing Europeans in the Legislature should be elected by special Communal Constituencies and not nominated by the Governor*

The Commission felt that to provide for the election of European and Burgher members on separate communal rolls would

(i) introduce an undesirable element of communalism and
(ii) depart from the principle of territorial election, which they wish to preserve.

As matters stand, though European and Burgher members will be nominated to the Council, Europeans and Burghers will of course have a vote in the ordinary way in the constituencies in which they reside. To provide a separate communal roll would, as it were, "freeze" the existing separation of the European and Burgher communities from the other communities. The Commission's hope was undoubtedly that, in the fullness of time, voters in Ceylon would be able to register their votes for party candidates in the accepted way irrespective of the race of either the voter or the candidate.

5. *That the method of securing adequate representation for the minorities in the Legislature should not be left to the Delimitation Commission but provided for specifically by the well-tried expedient of communal election in such a manner as to give them a combined strength to challenge the domination of the majority community*
This proposal amounts to the establishment of communal electoral rolls which it was the Commission's intention to avoid at all costs, as such an arrangement would perpetuate the distinction between the Communities which, it is hoped, will ultimately become less marked. The acceptance of this proposal would be tantamount to overthrowing the whole basis of the Soulbury recommendations as regards the franchise and representation which His Majesty's Government has accepted and, in view of His Majesty's Government's decisions and the State Council's acceptance of them, such a radical step clearly could not be taken now, even if it were desirable.

In general, the Secretary of State might perhaps take the line with the Deputation of stressing the decisive majority in the State Council for the acceptance of the White Paper (51 to 3), and the assurances given by Mr. Senanayake in his speech, which His Majesty's Government believes to be sincere; and pointing out that, if, in fact, the new Ceylon Government behaves in a manner seriously prejudicial to European interests His Majesty's Government will not be without the means of applying counter-pressure from here in view, for example, of the dependence of Ceylon on British markets. (This agreement should of course be used with great caution). Moreover, the further progress of Ceylon towards Dominion status is conditional on the operation of the new Constitution in such a manner that His Majesty's Government can be reasonably satisfied that the minority communities have been given a square deal. If the Ceylon Government do not give the minorities a square deal, they will, by doing so, postpone the day when Dominion status can be reached. The Ceylon Government know this and surely, out of mere self interest, may be expected to behave accordingly.

# 334  CO 54/986/8, no 85                                    27 Nov 1945
## [Ceylon Association]: note by Trafford Smith of an interview between Mr Hall and a deputation from the Ceylon Association in London

At 3 o'clock this afternoon the Secretary of State saw a deputation from the Ceylon Association in response to the request contained in (66). The deputation consisted of the persons listed in (82). The brief at (84)[1] was prepared for use as background to the discussion.

---

[1] See 333.

In addition to the Secretary of State, Mr. Sidebotham and I attended the meeting for the Colonial Office.

After a brief introductory statement by the President, Mr. Boustead, who drew special attention to the extent of British capital involved in Ceylon tea, rubber and other commercial interests, most of the talking was done by Mr Hayley[2] (who explained that he had had a good deal of experience of the Ceylon Bar). The deputation confined their representations almost entirely to the first item of the summary on page 8 of the memorandum enclosed with (66) in regard to the immigration of Europeans. This, they said, they regard as of overriding importance, and they pressed that the Constitution itself should contain a provision rendering the Ceylon Govt. not competent to prevent the re-entry of normal residents, rather than (as under the Soulbury recommendations) that the Governor should simply have a power of reservation in this respect. They pointed out that the Soulbury recommendation (32 (ii) (b) on page 115) said that the Governor "may" reserve, whereas the summary contained in the White Paper (page 5, first paragraph (c)) said that the Governor General "must" reserve. Of the two wordings they prefer the latter.

The deputation then stated the Association's case in general for safeguards for the European planting and commercial communities. The Secretary of State said that in his opinion, the safeguards provided in the Report were adequate, and that he could not foresee a situation in which any British Government would tolerate action by a Colonial administration prejudicial to important British interests. He challenged the deputation to quote an instance in which such interests as they had in mind (e.g., the entry of persons, etc.,) had been so prejudiced.

The deputation also touched on the points regarding Indian franchise and the right of Europeans to elect their members instead of having them nominated. The Secretary of State said that very careful consideration had been given to the Indian franchise question, and that His Majesty's Government could not vary the policy it had adopted. As regards the establishment of communal electorates requested by the deputation, His Majesty's Government's accepted policy was against the introduction of communalism, and it would be impossible to make any concession in that direction.

The Secretary of State promised that the Colonial Office would have in mind the points raised by the Association in regard to:—

(1) the insertion in the Constitution itself of the safeguard dealing with the re-entry of normal residents;
(2) the insertion of the words "or other" in the safeguards at present applying to any racial or religious community (see the first paragraph on page 3 of the Association's memorandum and recommendation 32 (v) on page 116 of the Soulbury Report).

My impression was that a further reply will be sent to the Association after due consideration of these points.

---

[2] F A Hayley, QC (Ceylon) 1927; formerly acting European member of Legislative Council, Ceylon, 1919–1920 and president of European Association of Ceylon, 1920–1921.

**335**  ADM 116/5546                                        13 Dec 1945

[Defence]: letter (reply) from R R Powell[1] to Admiral Layton on
defence requirements

I am to acquaint you that Their Lordships have given careful consideration to your
letter, 6787/8405/45 of 25th October, concerning Constitutional Reform in Ceylon.[2]
As you will be aware, His Majesty's Government reached certain conclusions on the
subject at about the same date, and their policy has been stated in Command Paper
6690 issued at the end of last month.

2. While the Chiefs of Staff did not collectively consider the proposals of the
Soulbury Commission, the Service Departments were most fully consulted by the
Commission in the drafting of those parts of its report dealing with defence
questions. In Their Lordships' view the extremely varied and far reaching scope of
defence interests under modern conditions, to which you rightly call attention, has
been adequately recognised, both in the Commission's Report, and in the Statement
of Policy. The decisions taken by H.M. Government and announced in the Statement
of Policy are in purely general terms, and do not specifically lay down details of the
defence organisation which will ultimately be needed in order to implement policy.
There will have to be further consultation departmentally in London and between
H.M. Government and the Ceylon Government on this whole question.

3. With regard to your remarks upon the organisation necessary to enable the
Governor-General to exercise, with full effect, the special powers proposed to be
reserved to him in relation to defence matters, you will observe that in paragraph
11(b) of Command 6690 His Majesty's Government have decided to depart somewhat
from the arrangements contemplated by the Commission. In normal times H.M.
Government in the United Kingdom will, where necessary, legislate for Ceylon on
defence matters by Order-in-Council, so that any such enactments will be drafted in
London, and the Governor will not require any special assistance in that connection.
In emergency, the Governor would, by Order-in-Council, be provided with powers to
make regulations similar to those which operated in this country during the late war.
Their Lordships appreciate that as you suggest, it might be desirable for the
Governor to have a suitably qualified officer on his personal staff to advise him upon
the drafting of regulations under these emergency powers. Their Lordships are
accordingly bringing your suggestion to the notice of the Secretary of State for the
Colonies, in order that, if he agrees, it may be borne in mind should a fresh
emergency threaten during the currency of the new constitution. On the general
question of the Governor's staff and advisers, it is unlikely that this would be referred
to in detail in the Constitutional Instruments; that, it would seem, will be a matter
for discussion between the Governor and H.M. Government in consultation with the
Ceylon Government.

4. Their Lordships agree with you that, since the ramifications of Commonwealth
Defence interests are now so wide, it is important that the Governor, under the new
constitution, should have available such advice as will ensure that these will not be
overlooked in *any* acts, whether of commission or omission, of the Ceylon
Government. Their Lordships cannot, however, on their present information

---

[1] Principal assistant secretary, Admiralty.                    [2] See 315.

understand how the Governor could be better advised on such matters than by the Service Commanders in Ceylon: the Service Commanders alone would be able to base their recommendations upon the practical experience of command of forces on the spot and on the combined needs of the three Services in connection with local defence, and their views should be the sounder for being those of the officers who would ultimately be responsible for conducting operations in the area in the event of war. The local Naval Commander would normally be the Commander-in-Chief, East Indies, since Their Lordships envisage that he will continue to have his headquarters in Ceylon. Their Lordships would moreover point out that in all matters concerning local defence, and the implementation of long-range Imperial Defence policy to which reference is made in paragraph 350 of the Commission's Report, there will exist close contact between the local Service Commanders and the Service Departments in London, who would as a matter of normal procedure, review from time to time the needs of Defence in relation to the general requirements of Imperial strategy. With regard to your fear that the Ceylon Government may resuscitate the proposal to abolish the railway, or enter upon port development in such a manner as to affect unduly the needs of defence, Their Lordships feel that the policy decided upon by H.M. Government should provide adequate safeguards. Their Lordships would welcome any further observations you may wish to offer upon this subject in the light of views expressed in this paragraph.

## 336  CO 54/986/6/4, no 233                                        14 Dec 1945
## [Indo–Ceylon relations]: letter from Mr Hall to Sir H Moore on the re-opening of negotiations. *Enclosure*: CO note of a discussion between Hall and Sir R Mudaliar

With reference to my secret and personal telegram of 14th December, I enclose a note of our discussion which speaks for itself. Sir Ramaswami Mudaliar's attitude was generally helpful and while there can, of course, be no question of dictation from the Government of India's end of the picture, I feel sure that I am correctly interpreting not only my own feelings but the feelings of my colleagues here in saying that we should welcome the reopening of direct negotiations between Ceylon and India on the question of the immigration of Indians into Ceylon and in particular the Indian franchise issue, about which I have already telegraphed.

   Senanayake's attitude on this question when he was over here did not lead me to suppose that, in the event of His Majesty's Government offering Ceylon a Constitution under which they would have the right to determine the composition of their future population—as has now been done and has been accepted by the Ceylon Government—there would be any real obstacle to the resumption of direct negotiations. I fully appreciate that it may be necessary for each side to make some concessions to enable agreement to be reached, but as I have said in my telegram, we are most anxious that if an approach is made by the Government of India it should be met from Ceylon in a friendly and forthcoming manner.

   I am confident that there could be no greater proof of Senanayake's diplomacy and persuasiveness than a very real attempt on the part of the Ceylon Government to come to terms and get this matter settled, with a consequent general easing of the future relationship between Ceylon and India.

## Enclosure to 336

The Secretary of State for the Colonies saw Sir Ramaswami, a member of the Viceroy's Council, this afternoon. Mr. Sidebotham was also present at the interview.

Sir Ramaswami opened the discussion by saying that the Indian Government was anxious to settle this matter of franchise for Indians in Ceylon on a broad basis and felt that no narrow view was any longer possible. Whatever basis was reached should be one that was fair to Indian nationals in Ceylon.

The main difficulty was Indian franchise and this fell into two parts:—

1. Franchise in so far as it concerned Indians already in Ceylon, most of whom had been in Ceylon for five years.
2. Franchise for future Indian immigrants into Ceylon, which was a matter for future negotiation.

At the moment the Indian Government were particularly anxious to discuss the question of franchise for Indians already in Ceylon.

He referred to the Delimitation proposals in the Soulbury Commission's Report, under which there will be 14 seats for Indians and said that India would be quite satisfied with this, but what was of real practical importance was the question of the actual franchise itself. He felt that this could not be left to negotiation. What India wanted was that persons with five years residence should automatically obtain the franchise or, if some certificate of some kind was necessary, a bare declaration of intention should be accepted. The present arrangement for a certificate of permanent settlement or certificate of domicile would not work. That had been amply proved. It was too complicated and the Indians themselves hesitated to use it. Sir Ramaswami stated that he was assured that under the present regime if an Indian took out a certificate in one constituency and then moved to another in search of work because he fell out of employment where he was, he had to go through the whole process over again and this discouraged him.

He admitted that in the past, when there was no ban on immigration into Ceylon from the Indian end of the picture, the Ceylon Government was rightly afraid that Indians might come in and swamp them. But he contended that now Ceylon has, or will have, the right to decide herself who should enter the Colony in the future, that fear should no longer exist on that score and that so far as those Indians already in Ceylon are concerned, there should be no difficulty about conceding the Indian Government's request for franchise on the simple condition of five years residence or a bare declaration of intention to settle in Ceylon.

The Secretary of State said that he was sorry to hear what Sir Ramaswami said about the franchise for Indians already in Ceylon not being a matter for direct negotiation between the Governments of India and Ceylon, since H.M.G. had accepted the view that it was indeed a most proper subject for such negotiation, and Mr. Hall was anxious that no possible effort should be spared in getting negotiations going again as soon as possible. It would be embarrassing to H.M.G. to have to intervene in this matter. The Soulbury Commission had, in his view, come to a wide conclusion. The matter was one in which it would be necessary for some concessions no doubt to be made on both sides. Mr. Senanayake, when he was over here last summer, had not spoken with any bitterness about it at all, and Mr. Hall felt that it was unlikely that, if the Government of India really wanted to enter on fresh negotiations, the Government of Ceylon would put difficulties in their way.

He accordingly urged Sir Ramaswami to represent this point of view to his Government with the object of getting negotiations started at once. Sir Ramaswami said it would be no use from their point of view unless these negotiations could be carried through before the new Constitution came into force. The Secretary of State contented himself with saying that he saw no reason at all why this could not be done if negotiations were begun at an early date.

Sir Ramaswami concluded by saying that he would consider an immediate approach to the Government of India with the object of reopening negotiations, and Mr. Hall undertook to inform the Governor of Ceylon of what had passed at this interview.

## 337  ADM 116/5546                                          17 Dec 1945
[Defence]: letter (reply) from Admiral Layton to Sir H Markham on the need for 'unceasing vigilance' over defence matters in peacetime

With reference to Admiralty Letter M.09782/45 of the 13th December 1945,[1] be pleased to inform Their Lordships that I much appreciate the full exposition of their views and of the action taken to ensure that the defence aspects of the new constitutional scheme for Ceylon were fully considered. This very largely satisfies the object I had in mind in representing the matter.

2. My remaining feeling of anxiety, with reference particularly to paragraph 4 of the letter under reply, is connected with the necessity for unceasing vigilance, in time of peace, if we are to secure that the local government does not, by its legislative measures, prejudice the resources or facilities of Ceylon as a base for imperial defence. There can be no doubt that the potential significance of such measures, particularly in regard to communication, was insufficiently appreciated before 1942. In the future it will be more than ever important that close contact and personal confidence should be established between the Governor and the Commander-in-Chief, East Indies, in order that the latter should be in a position to give *timely* advice in regard to the defence aspects of impending legislation. As a result of my three years' experience of Ceylon politics, I do feel that in time of peace there will be an understandable tendency for the Governor to refrain from adding to the complications of the political situation by the necessity to consult local Service Commanders, where there is any doubt, and I hope that in the Governor's instructions this point may also be stressed. While I do not doubt that Ceylon's present political leaders intend to make a sincere and loyal attempt to work the new constitution I have learnt enough of their general outlook and their resentment of Whitehall interference in matters they consider their own province to be certain that these subjects which are on the border line between local self government and imperial defence will have to be handled with the greatest tact and on the best advice obtainable.

---

[1] See 335.

**338**   CO 54/988/2, no 52                                      8 Jan 1946

[Indo–Ceylon relations]: inward unnumbered telegram from Sir H
Moore to Mr Hall conveying Mr Senanayake's position on the resumption of negotiations

I have now received a note from the Government of India proposing a resumption of
negotiations in which it is suggested that, while it is not essential to predetermine
any agreed basis, negotiations might be confined, for the purposes of canalising
discussions, to matters dealt with in joint Report. It adds that the Government of
India would have no objection to negotiations being confined to these issues only in
so far as they affect Indians already resident in Ceylon.

2.   Before communicating its terms to the Board of Ministers, I have discussed the
position fully with Senanayake in the light of your letter of 14th December and its
enclosure.[1] He is most anxious to take no action that could be construed as
unappreciative of the friendly spirit which has inspired these proposals but, at the
same time, he feels bound to point out that to enter into negotiations now, even if
confined to the franchise of Indians already in Ceylon, would not only cause
unavoidable complications and delay in drafting the necessary Order in Council, but
also arouse much local controversy at a time when he is most anxious to maintain a
united front. It would also put him in an impossible political position with his
colleagues and the State Council, all of whom have interpreted the Report as leaving
the settlement of this question for negotiation between the two Governments after
the new constitution has come into force. To do so now would be to prejudge the
views of the new Parliament on this issue.

3.   He is quite willing to give an assurance to Sir Ramaswami Mudaliar, whom he
knows personally, that it will be his first task to initiate negotiations in the most
friendly spirit as soon as the new constitution has been inaugurated. He would also
welcome your giving a similar assurance to the Secretary of State for India on his
behalf, if you so wish, but he feels quite sure that neither he nor his colleagues on the
Board would feel that the present time is opportune for resuming negotiations with
any hope of success.

4.   In these circumstances, he has asked me to defer formally submitting the note
to the Board of Ministers pending any further observations you have to make in the
light of this telegram.[2]

---

[1] See 336.
[2] Hall replied on 11 Jan expressing regret that Senanayake did not feel it possible to re-open negotiations
at this stage but appreciating his difficulties. The secretary of state welcomed the assurance conveyed in
para 3 of Moore's tel and offered to deliver it to Mudaliar if he could be furnished with the precise wording
Senanayake would wish to employ. When it had been delivered Hall also indicated that he would wish to
give an assurance to Pethick-Lawrence on similar lines on Senanayake's behalf (CO 54/988/2, no 53).

# 339   CO 54/986/9/1, no 9                                          15 Jan 1946

'The proposed constitution for Ceylon': letter from S
Sivasubramaniam[1] to Mr Attlee on behalf of the All-Ceylon Tamil
Congress

The Tamil people of Ceylon read with interest your announcement some time ago to the world that His Majesty's Government is faithfully carrying out the British political aims of the war by conferring a liberal measure of Self-Government for countries in the British Empire including Ceylon. In this connection, we wish to submit for your kind consideration a few facts and our views with regard to the New Constitution, recommended by the Soulbury Commission and approved in the White Paper announcement.

Firstly, it must be stated that the proposed constitution does not in reality grant a truly democratic form of Self-Government. It has further failed to provide for a just and equitable distribution of power among the various sections of the people on the basis of a spirit of enlightened democracy. On the contrary it sets up an irremovable communal oligarchy in perpetual power and paves the way for an immutable succession of Sinhalese Buddhist Prime Ministers. To hold that the proposed constitution confers Self Government on the Ceylonese people is, to say the least, disingenuous; it is in fact the substitution of Sinhalese rule for British rule, which is not the same as Ceylonese Self Government.

May we point out, Sir that the constitution does not conform to the principles laid down by British leaders of thought and action including yourself in several of their utterances in connection with political issues of countries with a heterogeneous population like India. The proposed constitution cannot be said to have been either formulated by the people or accepted by the people, but if adopted will be practically imposed on them.

The constitution proposed by the White paper based on the recommendations of the Soulbury Commission in spite of their investigations and findings, is a copy of the draft constitution of the Board of Ministers, consisting of six Sinhalese and one Tamil follower of theirs. This draft has no constitutional or moral weight, as the Ministers, who are merely Chairmen of Committees, derived no sanction from the people explicitly or implicitly for this function. Neither this Board nor the present State Council have a mandate from the people to accept the Soulbury recommendations. The Council is more than nine years old and has ceased to be representative of the people. Meetings held through the country demanding the dissolution of the Council are evidence of the unrepresentative character of the Council (Vide Ceylon Hansard of November 8 and 9, 1945, column 6954).

It might also be pointed out that opinion is almost universal that the present Council is stale, outworn and unrepresentative. Four years ago, the late Sir D.B. Jayatilleke the then Sinhalese Leader, described it as such. Several meetings have recently been held by various organisations asking for the dissolution of the present Council in no unmistaken terms. There has not been one meeting asking for the continuance of the Council. In the State Council itself the Members, with one outstanding exception (Mr. W. Dahanayake) are unwilling to give up their seats for

---

[1] Joint secretary, All-Ceylon Tamil Congress.

obvious reasons though some of them had spoken vehemently in favour of the dissolution of the Council, at political meetings.

It is through such a Council that the motion for the acceptance of the White Paper proposals was carried. The fact that Tamil Members in Council, (but for two) voted for the motion, in spite of their expression of opinion both outside the Council and in the Council during the debate, and against the mandate of the All-Ceylon Tamil Congress and the views of their constituents conveyed to them expressly while the debate was progressing, is proof of the unrepresentative character of the Council at least as far as the Tamils are concerned.

The opposition by the Tamils to the proposal does not, however, involve an opposition to constitutional advance or the attainment of Dominion Status. The opposition is to rule by one community, and at that by an oligarchy composed from members of that community, over all the other communities. There is widespread opposition throughout the country to the Soulbury Constitution as indicated by the holding of public meetings, and by the outspoken resolutions passed at the meetings. This is, however, not reflected in the Council, where all the members but three have succumbed to the "inevitable" feeling that there was no hope of anything better, they thought it prudent to fall in with and please the new masters.

We venture to submit that the proper procedure would be to dissolve the present State Council and the holding of fresh elections on this constitutional issue. The constitution should be examined by a Constituent Assembly or Constitution making body.

We are certain that constitutional progress of real and lasting benefit to Ceylon will be evolved by the adoption of the procedure suggested by us. The Tamils have never, as a minority, obstructed constitutional progress but on the other hand have definitely been in the vanguard of progress as publicly acknowledged by Sinhalese leaders and as a perusal of the history of constitutional reform in the Island will show.

The Labour Government is interesting itself in the welfare of small nations and peoples outside the Empire and Commonwealth, and it is as it should be. But the policy of ignoring the just and sound representations of the Tamil people of Ceylon numbering over one and half millions—a people with an ancient civilization and culture second to none of those of the progressive nations of the world, a people who have been pioneers in the promotion of political and social progress in the Island—is not in keeping with the spirit and expressed principles of the Labour Party, if I might be permitted to say so with all respect.

We may also invite your kind attention to the action taken by your Government with regard to reforms in India, where the problem [sic] are similar to ours. Fresh elections on the constitutional issue and the formation of constituent assemblies there make it possible for the people themselves to choose their own destiny. This course of self determination we have been denied.

May we venture to hope that even at this stage you will be able to cause some action to be taken to save the Tamil people from the rule of a Sinhalese oligarchy which is as disastrous to a people of the stature and culture of the Tamils as any foreign domination if not more so. No self-respecting people can eternally live under an administration depending on the "goodwill" of individuals, when they by their own right are entitled to an effective share in the administration of the country. The new constitution if adopted, will spell the political extinction of the Tamil people. It is necessary, we feel, to acquaint you with the strength and representative character of the All Ceylon Tamil Congress. We shall do so by quoting an extract from "The Daily News", a Sinhalese owned local paper bitterly opposed to the policy of the Congress, where it is openly acknowledged. Speaking of the probabilities of the next elections the paper in its issue March 30, 1945, says: "Of all parties in Ceylon, the All-Ceylon Tamil Congress will probably experience least difficulty in putting itself into shape in time for the next elections, not only because it is already well organised but also because it may hope to capture many of the seats likely to be granted to the Northern and Eastern Provinces".

We would like to remove any possible misunderstanding in your minds regarding the intensity of Tamil opposition against the White Paper and the proposed Soulbury Constitution. It is possible that the voting of the Tamil State Councillors in favour of Mr. Senanayake's motion accepting the White Paper might have misled the British people regarding the attitude of the Tamil community.

We wish in all earnestness to make the following submissions in this connection.

In the first place, it may be mentioned that the phenomenon of elected representatives of the people going against popular opinion is not confined to Ceylon or to the Tamil community. Instances of even party leaders deserting their ranks to join the more powerful side in defiance of party discipline are not unknown in political history. In England itself, where political consciousness and party discipline have reached their highest development and public opinion governs the actions of political leaders to a degree not witnessed elsewhere, instances of failure to adhere to party principles are to be found. We may be pardoned if we mention the case of the late Mr. Ramsay Macdonald, who gravely compromised the position of the Labour Party at a critical time. We might also mention the fact of the late Mr. Chamberlain's Government backed by unprecedented Parliamentary support concluding the ill-fated Munich Pact with Hitler against strong public opinion, under the threat of imminent national peril.

The Tamil members in Council on this occasion surrendered, as it [sic] were overawed by the virtual surrender of the powerful British Government to the Sinhalese with no recognisable peril in sight, except the latter's threat of non-co-operation, in the event of the New Constitution not conforming to their Ministers' draft constitution. It is not the so-called offer of goodwill and friendliness by the Sinhalese leader that made the Tamil members succumb to Sinhalese politicians, who constitute the de facto Government of Ceylon, as against a few Tamil members. They were thus led to vote for the motion by force of circumstances, despite the fact that their own views and opinions expressed in and out of Council and those of their constituents and of the Tamil people as a whole, were clearly opposed to the acceptance of the White Paper. A further circumstance that contributed to the collapse of the Tamil members is the White Paper itself, which, in purporting to convey the "decisions" of His Majesty's Government, really presented a fait accompli to them. The Tamil community however does not feel so. They (the Councillors) felt that they could not but bow to what they wrongly considered the inevitable. There was also the fear that they might be charged with obstructing the general constitutional advance of the country, if they did not vote for the acceptance of the White Paper. It is this same combination of causes that had the cumulative effect of bringing about the complete collapse of all the minorities. The minority members, particularly the Tamil Councillors, were further misled by the announcement in paragraph 12 of the White paper, into thinking that, since His Majesty's Government would take their expression of views into account, it was not quite material which way they voted.

The views of the Tamil Members and some other Members expressing dissatisfaction with the Soulbury recommendations may be seen in the Hansard of November 8th and 9th of last year.

In the Council there are eleven Tamil Members (Ceylon and Indian Tamil). Seven of them (Ceylon Tamils) represent Tamil constituencies in the Northern and Eastern Provinces. Out of these one (Sir W. Duraiswamy) is the Speaker, and another (Mr. Mahadeva) is a Minister, who owes his position to his Sinhalese colleagues and as such is a follower of theirs; two (viz: Messrs. Ponnambalam and Dharmaratnam) were absent and out of the Island when the motion was debated in Council, one (Mr. Nalliah) is unduly anti-British and has on that score earned some popularity with the Sinhalese. The other two (Messrs. Natesan and Tyagaraja) though members of the Tamil Congress had been led to vote in favour of the motion in spite of having publicly expressed views to the contrary.

Of the other four Tamil members, three represent Indian Tamils, two (viz: Messrs. Natesa Iyer and Vytilingam) having been elected by the vote of the Indian Tamils in two of the Central up-country constituencies; and the third (Mr. I.X. Pereira) having been nominated to represent Indian interests; the fourth (Mr J.G. Rajakulendran) represents a predominantly Sinhalese constituency, *though returned on the Indian Tamil vote solely as a result of a splitting of votes among the Sinhalese candidates.*[2] (Had the contest been between one Sinhalese and him he would not have had a chance of being elected). He was also a member of the Tamil Congress and had strongly supported Tamil Congress views and accepted its mandate, but like the others subsequently voted for the motion. Of these Mr. Vytilingam was absent and the other two (Messrs. Natesa Iyer and I.X. Pereira) voted against the acceptance of the White Paper.

The Indian Tamil members representing nine hundred thousand (900,000) of the population thus voted solidly against the motion. Of the seven Ceylon Tamil Councillors who represent 700,000 people four only (Viz: Messrs. Mahadeva, Nalliah, Natesan and Tyagaraja) actually voted for the motion as already pointed out. It may, however, be stated that Mr. Mahadeva dissented from his brother Ministers in the matter of representation, when they submitted their original draft constitution to the Colonial Office; and it is this Ministers' draft that forms the basis of the Soulbury recommendations. These four members (viz: Messrs. Mahadeva, Nalliah, Natesan and Tyagaraja) voted definitely in contravention of the views of their own constituencies expressly conveyed to them during the course of the debate and in defiance of Tamil public opinion. *So that on the whole it would appear that the so-called Tamil vote in favour of the acceptance of the White Paper does not have the significance it may appear to have on a superficial view. In fact only 5 out of 11 Tamil councillors actually voted for the acceptance of the White Paper, and that too in defiance of the expressed views of the Tamil community. Out of the 5, one represents a Sinhalese constituency. So that only 4 members representing Tamil constituencies voted for the acceptance of the proposed constitution.*

Furthermore the members in Council by themselves have no special authority or

---

[2] Emphasis throughout in original.

status except that they are representatives of the people; and when they cease to represent the opinion and views of their constituents their action ceases to have any moral weight or political significance. As such the action of the Tamil Councillors in voting for the motion against the express views of their constituents and in contravention of a mandate given by the sole accredited political organization of the Tamils, viz: the All-Ceylon Tamil Congress, has no significance whatsoever, especially in a matter of such vital importance affecting the future of the entire country.

We are in the unhappy position of experiencing the phenomenon, now well known in Europe, of the production of Quislings in a crisis. The Tamil Councillors, who voted for the acceptance of the White Paper, now disowned by the Tamil community, are Quislings seeking the favour of the "conquerors" to whom Britain herself had surrendered all.

The State Council which passed the said motion is nine years old and is completely unrepresentative of Ceylon public opinion, particularly of the Tamil community. Its life was extended by Order-in-Council not less than three times and against strong public opinion. Its members have thus ceased to be the mouthpiece of the Ceylon Constituencies and have become the creature of an external agency. The wisdom of the All-Ceylon Tamil Congress in asking for a dissolution of the State Council even before the publication of the Soulbury Report has now become patent.

The revelation that may result by the dissolution of a representative assembly was well illustrated by the recent Parliamentary election in England. The great Parliamentary majority enjoyed by the Conservative Party was proved to be an unreliable index of public opinion in the country. In a similar way the voting of the Councillors in the present nine year old State Council is no index of the views held by the people and is certainly contrary to the opinion of the Tamil Community. The proper procedure, it is submitted, would be to dissolve the present nine year old unrepresentative Council, hold fresh elections and place any new constitution that is proposed before a constituent assembly or constitution making body.

It is a matter for regret and great disappointment that from the beginning the introduction of the New Constitution has been at every stage hastened in an unwarranted fashion. It would appear as though a deliberate attempt was made to push the matter through speedily lest objections be raised to prevent its implementation.

In the first place, the Soulbury Report should have been submitted to the State Council for criticism and expression of views as was done in the case of the Donoughmore Report. It was only after the views of the then Legislative Council on the Donoughmore Report were ascertained that His Majesty's Government made its decisions on the matter. The present procedure of issuing the White Paper within the brief period of twenty-two days after the publication of the Soulbury Commissioners' Report, before the public could express their views on it, and of introducing a motion in the State Council for its acceptance within the ridiculously short period of eight days of its publication, before the people could hardly comprehend its implications in full, is more regretable than imposing a constitution without any consultation whatever, as it has the appearance and not the substance of such a procedure. *It has become imperative that at least the early and precipitous implementation of the White Paper proposals should be deferred*; so that modifications, if any, or further consideration of the proposals may be made possible.

May we also invite your attention to the statement made recently by His Majesty's

Government in the House of Lords regarding the future Government of British India which is as follows:—

> "Since it is the firm conviction of His Majesty's Government that it is by and in consultation with the directly elected representatives of the Indian people that decisions as to the future Government of British India should be taken, it was a necessary preliminary that elections should be held to the Provincial Legislature and the Central Assembly in India".

It is thus clear that fresh elections to test the strength and representative character of organizations like the Indian Congress and the Muslim League are considered a condition precedent to a final decision on the constitution of India. We submit that the same procedure should be followed in the case of Ceylon, where all circumstances and conditions are similar to those governing Indian Problems.

A further statement of His Majesty's Government spokesman is relevant to this point. He says:—

> "I desire to make it plain that His Majesty's Government regard the setting up of a constitution making body, by which the Indians will decide their own future and also the other proposals embodied in the announcement, as a matter of greater urgency".

Here again a second condition for a democratic method of drawing up a new constitution for India is given, viz: the setting up of constitution making body. This precedent could with advantage be followed in Ceylon and it is a procedure that would satisfy all sections of the people.

If there was a genuine desire on the part of the British Government to ascertain the views of the people of Ceylon as a whole and of the different communities on the Soulbury recommendations in an accepted democratic manner based on the principle of Self-determination, the only fair and sound method is to submit the recommendations to the test of a general election and a New Council, and not to force the issue by presenting the people of Ceylon with a fait accompli in the form of the British Cabinet's "Decision". The procedure now followed would appear to be particularly unjust in view of the predominant contribution of the Tamils to war efforts of the Island and their active policy of co-operation with His Majesty's Government in the matter of the Soulbury Commissioners inquiry as against the policy of boycott adopted by the Board of Ministers and other Sinhalese politicians.

It may also be mentioned that the future constitutional development of Ceylon and its form of Government are matters that are left entirely in the hands of the future Parliament of Ceylon by the White Paper. This Parliament with a Sinhalese majority and a Sinhalese Prime Minister are expected to effect the necessary advance to Dominion Status by "modification of the existing constitution and by the establishment of conventions" which will "grow up in actual practice". So that not only does the proposed constitution vest all power of administration exclusively in their hands but, what is worse, it relegates finally and completely to them the power to frame the future constitution of Ceylon, a power which is now exercised by the British Crown and Parliament. To this position the Tamils take great objection.

This transfer of power of far-reaching effect by Britain, though nominally into the hands of the people of Ceylon, is in reality into the hands of one particular community. That this interpretation is given to the White Paper by the Sinhalese is shown by the statement of the Hon. Mr. Senanayake in the State Council made in the course of his speech on the White Paper Debate on November 8, 1945, that the future Parliament has the power to amend the constitution, and that the new constitution goes much further than any Dominion except that of Eire, with some limitations, (Ceylon Hansard of November 8, 1945, column 6923). This is a very important reason, we urge, why the constitution should not be imposed on the Tamils.

It is maintained in certain quarters that the Tamils asked for a Commission on Constitutional Reforms and that, therefore, they are bound to accept their decision. It is must first be pointed out that the Tamils have been consistently asking from the year 1937 for a Commission consisting of personnel who had a previous and intimate knowledge of conditions in the East. It cannot be asserted that the personnel of the Soulbury Commission was acquainted with conditions in India, Ceylon and the East. On the other hand, subsequent events have shown that the anticipations of the Congress regarding the futility of a Commission with no such knowledge have proved true.

It might also be mentioned that in addition to the demand for a Commission, the Congress demanded the appointment of a Select Committee of Parliament. Therefore, even if the decisions of a Commission are to be accepted it should not be before a Parliamentary Committee had examined the recommendations.

Further, asking for the appointment of a Commission to enquire into and report on the political situation in Ceylon is one thing and unconditionally accepting their recommendations is another. It cannot be said that the first necessarily involves the second.

A further attempt at misleading propaganda consists in the Sinhalese leaders, including an Official in the person of Sir Oliver Goonetilleke, making use of the Slogan of "Ceylon's War Efforts" without revealing that the bulwark of Ceylon's war contribution in the form of tea and rubber was from the Tamil labourers. Other contributions and work in connection with "war efforts" were not confined to any particular community.

It is not possible for the Tamils to come to any fair settlement on constitutional problems with the Sinhalese Leaders. Uncompromising determination to carry out their wishes is the chief characteristic of present-day Sinhalese politicians. As an instance, reference may be made to the fact that in addition to the improper procedure and undue haste followed in pushing through the White Paper proposals the Hon. Mr. Senanayake firstly declined to the request made by one of the Tamil Congress Secretaries, Dr. E.M.V. Naganathan, for a postponement of the debate in the State Council on the White Paper with a view to explore possibilities of an agreed communal settlement being submitted to the Council. Secondly in introducing the motion Mr. Senanayake stated that he would accept no amendment thereto.

In these circumstances the inescapable obligation lies on the British Government to see that justice is done to the Tamil community; and it is possible to do so without prejudicing the claims of the Sinhalese community. Further any constitution in Ceylon to be stable, workable and successful could only be had if the Tamils are given an effective share in the Government of the country. No constitution which does not statutorily guarantee to the Tamils an effective share in the Government could be stable or be considered just.

The Tamil people refuse to believe that the British Government's policy is to impose a constitution on an unwilling people. On the contrary the statement of principle enunciated from time to time by British politicians with regard to Indian constitutional advance is clearly against the impostion of a constitution. Even so recently as last Wednesday the 8th instant, one of the members of the British Parliamentary Delegation to India, Lord Chorley in the course of his interview to the press stated as follows: "There is no question of the imposition of a decision on an unwilling people. Nobody denies that the Muslim League is very strong today". The reference was made in reply to a question about the Muslim League and its demands. The implications of the statement are to our mind as follows:—

1. that the British Government would not impose a constitution on an unwilling people.
2. that the strength of the people concerned is also a consideration.

Judged by these two tests, the proposed Soulbury Constitution should not be imposed on one million six hundred thousand Tamil people who are opposed to it, notwithstanding any contrary impression that might be created to outsiders. We are constrained to refer at page 4 of this communication to our organization (The Ceylon Tamil Congress) in the interests of our people.

It would be one of the greatest ironies of present times if the British Government ignores the just demands of the Tamils, particularly in view of (a) their contribution to the war efforts during two great world wars, (b) their suspension of political agitation immediately on the declaration of the war as opposed to the conduct of Sinhalese Leaders, (c) their co-operation with the labours of Soulbury Commission as opposed to the policy of boycott and non-co-operation followed by the Ministers and Sinhalese politicians. It will indeed be a strange requital of the invaluable services rendered by the Tamils in the past to Ceylon and the British Common-wealth.

The fundamental question [is] whether the proposed Soulbury Constitution which will set up a Government that must be predominantly Sinhalese, and in effect though not in name, a Sinhalese Government, and not a Ceylonese Government, in a contry [sic] with a heterogeneous population with diverse creeds, cultures, races, languages, and interests, must in the name of democracy and fairness be submitted in the first instance to the electorates and communities of Ceylon when Britain after nearly 150 years of rule is relinquishing her control.

It is sincerely trusted that the advent of the Labour Party to absolute power for the first time in the history of the British Commonwealth of Nations and your tenure of office as Prime Minister would not witness the political extinction of the Tamil community in Ceylon. The total Tamil population (Ceylon and Indian) in this Island is one million six hundred thousand (1,600,000) and is equal to the combined population of the Arabs and Jews in Palestine. His Majesty's Government, the British Parliament and the British people are rightly concerned with the situation in Palestine and are making attempts to solve the problem. We may be pardoned for saying that the use of force in Palestine appears to have moved the British Government, Parliament and people. We are however confident that the British Government, Parliament and people are statesmenlike and far sighted enough to appreciate the gentle methods of constitutional agitation by the Tamil people of Ceylon whose welfare is watched with interest by 40 million Tamils in India, inhabiting, along with their Ceylon brethren an almost contiguous area, separated only by a narrow strip of water 16 miles in breadth, the Palks Strait. A prominent leader of this community Sir Ramasamy Mudaliar is now leading the Indian delegation at the World Conference of Nations and is rendering yeoman service to the cause of international peace and prosperity.

We should like to submit with all the earnestness at our command that the communal problem in Ceylon cannot be solved or by-passed by ignoring it. Failure on the part of the British people and Government to apply their minds in due time to the communal problems of India and Palestine has brought unhappiness to all countries concerned including Britain. It is hoped that a similar tardiness in dealing with the communal problem of Ceylon a country, with an ancient civilization and of present strategic importance, would not be followed.

While the British people are able to look back with general pride on their past history and achievements, still it is only natural that successive British Governments in the past should have had their record of mistakes which in the light of later judgment have become regrettable. That Government by the many whcih [sic] constitutes Democracy cannot be performed through hasty decisions is a sociological fact. One of the greatest leaders of Britain of all times, Oliver Cromwell once said truly, "I wish gentlemen you might sometimes think you might make a mistake." The present decisions of British Government today too have to be interpreted in the light of the lessons of history. A point of view, however officially expressed as final cannot be final; and events between the last two wars bore out the fact. The White paper on Constitutional Reform with which the people of Ceylon were presented lately, needs to be looked in that fashion without dogmatism and in a spirit of humility and cannot be regarded as a final statement of views or decision. The whole matter of Constitutional Reform for Ceylon and the procedure for evolving a suitable scheme require reconsideration.

We urge that on grounds of equity and correct political principles the least that could now be done is (1) for the British Government to defer the implementation of the White Paper, (2) for the consideration of the whole matter by a Joint Parliamentary Committee, and (3) to hold fresh elections to the State Council following the Indian precedent and the setting up of a constituent assembly or constitution making body. Such procedure we submit will not in any way prejudice the interests of any section of the people, but will satisfy everyone that accepted constitutional methods were followed in the promulgation of the New Constitution.

# 340   CO 54/988/2, no 54                                    22 Jan 1946

## [Indo–Ceylon relations]: inward unnumbered telegram (reply) from Sir H Moore to Mr Hall transmitting a message from Mr Senanayake to Sir R Mudaliar

Your secret and personal telegram of 11th January.[1] Indo–Ceylon relations. Reference paragraph 2 of your telegram. Senanayake would be grateful if you would cause the following personal message from him to be conveyed to Sir R. Mudaliar.

*Begins.*—I appreciate the friendly spirit which has inspired the most recent proposals of the Government of India to resume negotiations with the Government

---

[1] See 338, note 2.

of Ceylon on the question of Indo–Ceylon relations, and should have liked to have been able to meet the wishes of the Government of India, but the impending political change consequent on the decision of the State Council on the award of His Majesty's Government in the White Paper of 31st October, 1945, renders that course impossible at present. The desire on all sides is that the new constitution should come into force as soon as possible. The proposed negotiations, if undertaken now, would re-introduce much local controversy at a time when very urgent post-war problems demand that the present political tranquillity continues. Furthermore, the Members of the State Council, including my ministerial colleagues, accepted the award of His Majesty's Government on the assumption that negotiations with India will not be undertaken before the new constitution comes into force, and I do not think they would now change this view. I can, however, give you my personal assurance that, so far as it lies within my power, I will do all that I can to make the resumption of negotiations one of the earliest tasks of the first Government under the new constitution.—*Ends.*

2. Senanayake agrees that a similar assurance be given to the Secretary of State for India.

3. Board of Ministers has agreed on the official reply to the Government of India, which is consistent with the above and will be delayed for one week to enable Senanayake's message to be delivered.

# 341   CO 537/1674, no 3                                    25 Jan 1946
## [Draft constitution]: letter from Sir H Moore to Sir G Gater on defence, the public services and the post of attorney-general

I had two meetings with Senanayake on 22nd and 23rd January in which we discussed the outstanding points which he wished to make on the draft Constitution which Nihill has prepared and is bring[ing] home with him. Drayton and Nihill took part in the discussions and I enclose[1] for your information a copy of the Agenda and a copy of the record of decisions taken.

As already reported in my secret and personal telegram of 23rd January no exception was taken by Senanayake to the fact that the general form of the draft departs substantially from the original Ministers' draft. This is, I know, what you wanted at your end and I hope you will find it to be in a form that will prove generally acceptable to your Legal Advisers, since any departure now from this general lay-out would inevitably lead to suspicion and further delays out here. To my layman's eye Nihill and B. P. Peiris of the Legal Draftsman's Department have done a very good job of work, while I know Drayton has been of great assistance to Nihill in settling the final form of all the more important Articles. Jennings too, has been given a free hand to make suggestions and criticisms behind the scenes, since it was clearly desirable to carry him with us as far as possible.

Senanayake is, I believe, quite satisfied now with the progress made and the way things are working, and showed no signs of taking up a last ditch attitude on any of the controversial points. The only real major question of difficulty was that of

---

[1] Not printed.

Defence. On the first day he accepted the definitions in both Articles 29 (2) and 36 (1) (a) and 36 (2). The next day, prompted, I suspect, by Jennings he wanted Defence of the Island in Article 36 (1) (a) specifically defined on the general lines of the 1943 Declaration. As you see, he has been asked to prepare a statement of his views for the information of the Secretary of State, which I have not yet seen. My general impression is that he is not disputing the right of His Majesty's Government, subject to the allocation of cost under a defence contribution agreement, to prescribe the nature of the Island's defences both in respect of service establishments, personnel and fixed defences, if any, and buildings, etc., ancillary thereto. Nor does he dispute His Majesty's Government's right under Article 29 (2) to legislate by Order-in-Council in the event of a war or sudden emergency. He is apprehensive, however, lest His Majesty's Government in normal times should be empowered to prevent the local Parliament from legislating on matters affecting the economic development of the Island on the grounds that a given policy would be detrimental to a general commonwealth defence policy which could be said to embrace the defence of the Island. He is thinking really, I believe, in terms of economic warfare and has a lurking fear of quotas and control schemes. He does not however appear able to grasp the necessity of retaining the same definition of Defence in Articles 29 (2) and 36 (1) (a), if a conflict between the powers of His Majesty's Government and the local Parliament is to be avoided. I don't see at present how this point is to be met. It may be that his promised statement of views will clarify the position.

The only other point, which he did not press *à l'outrance*, is that he would now personally prefer, despite the recommendations of the Soulbury Report and the provisions of the Ministers' Scheme that the Governor should be given a free hand to accept or reject the advice of the Public Services and Judicial Services Commissions. I have already expressed my anxieties about the Soulbury proposals and will not repeat them, but I feel that Senanayake's present proposal would sooner or later inevitably bring the Governor into conflict with Parliament, and also lay himself open to the charge that his decisions were subject to political influence, since it would be very difficult for him to prevent lobbying by the Prime Minister and other interested Ministers where important appointments were involved.

In view of the importance of the post under the new Constitution and the poor field of local candidates the selection and method of appointment of the Attorney-General is giving both Senanayake and myself some anxiety, and no final decision was taken on the point.

# 342   CO 54/988/2, no 60                                              11 Feb 1946
## [Indo–Ceylon relations]: letter from Sir R Mudaliar to Mr Creech Jones urging HMG to make a decision on the franchise question

I am in receipt of your letter of the 29th January conveying a personal message to me[1] from Mr. Senanayake regarding the negotiations which the Government of India propose should be opened with the Government of Ceylon on the question of the franchise of Indians now settled in Ceylon. While appreciating the cordial tone of the

---

[1] See 340.

message, I must express, on behalf of myself and my Government, our deep disappointment that the well-intentioned efforts of the Government of India towards an amicable settlement of this vexed question with Ceylon have not succeeded. It was in consultation with the Secretary of State for Colonies and with his approval that I suggested to my Government that the negotiations should be limited to the single question of the extent of franchise to be conferred on Indians now settled in Ceylon. I made it quite clear that all questions of the future immigration of Indians to Ceylon and their status would be the subject of future negotiations after the new constitution has come into effect in Ceylon.

In the interview which the Secretary of State was kind enough to grant me,[2] I pointed out that the whole basis of the recommendations of the Soulbury Commission regarding Indians, the abolition of communal electorates, the delimitation of constituencies, the ensuring, as far as possible, of a certain number of representatives in the State Council elected by constituencies with predominantly Indian voting strength, the avoidance of discriminatory legislation against Indians in future, was, [sic] that all these were dependent on the franchise that was granted to the Indians now resident in Ceylon. I suggested, therefore, that before the constitution was finally framed by an Order in Council, there should be some guarantee that the franchise conferred on Indians would be such as to enable them to play a leading part in certain constituencies prescribed by the Delimitation Commission.

The Secretary of State urged that the Soulbury Commission had suggested that this matter should first be the subject of negotiations between the two Governments concerned; and that it would not be appropriate for His Majesty's Government to intervene at that stage. In accordance with this view the Government of India proposed negotiations but the move has proved abortive. The crux of the matter, however, is that the question of franchise for the Indians now resident in Ceylon should be settled before the new constitution is framed. The Soulbury Commission itself says "We must point out that any decision of the Government of Ceylon upon the conditions of the enfranchisement of the Indian unskilled workers will have important effect on our recommendations regarding the terms of reference of the Delimitation Commission proposed in S.P. XIV and upon our approval of the distribution of the electoral districts outlined therein". It is on this ground that the Government of India urged that there must be a definite agreement or decision upon the conditions of enfranchisement of the Indians before the constitution is framed. The attitude of the Ceylon Government amounts to this that after the constitution has been finalized by His Majesty's Government by an Order in Council, they will be at liberty to consider the question of enfranchisement. If the entire question of the delimitation of constituencies and the number of representatives who will be the spokesmen of the Indian community is to depend upon the franchise, it seems to me quite clear that the question of franchise must be determined before the legislature is elected and before the new constitution comes into force and the new Government of Ceylon is formed.

In view of the attitude that Mr. Senanayake has taken, the only course for the Government of India now is to press His Majesty's Government to make a decision on this subject. Any other course would have a disastrous effect on the relationship between India and Ceylon. I very much hope that that the Secretary of State would

---

[2] See 336, enclosure.

give the fullest consideration to what I have stated above. I am ready to make any further explanation, personally, of the position of the Government of India, which the Secretary of State may desire. May I request you to communicate these views to the Secretary of State at a very early date?

## 343  CO 54/988/2, no 61                    15 Feb 1946
## [Indo–Ceylon relations]: letter from Lord Pethick-Lawrence to Mr Hall supporting Sir R Mudaliar

Sir Ramaswami Mudaliar has shown me a copy of his reply[1] to Creech-Jones' letter of the 29th January in which he communicated Senanayake's message on the subject of negotiations between the Government of India and the Government of Ceylon, and I write to say that I am in wholehearted agreement with everything he says.

I find it difficult to believe that Senanayake and his colleagues on the eve of the introduction of a constitution which will give the Ceylon Government the right to determine both the composition of the Island's population and the conditions of the franchise, cannot bring themselves to see that the franchise for Indians now in Ceylon should be settled by agreement between the two Governments before the new constitution is introduced. Senanayake must realize that his present attitude can only increase the doubts and suspicions which Indians feel with regard to their future position in the Island; and he cannot be so blind to the present agitation among Indians both in India and Ceylon as not to realize that failure to settle this vital problem would seriously prejudice the chances of the new Constitution starting off in communal harmony.

I accordingly write to ask you to use your personal influence to have the matter reopened, for unless you do I can only see progressive deterioration in the relations between the two countries. This indeed would be a bad augury for the new era, and it is because I am so convinced that this calamity can be avoided that I am writing not only to reinforce all that Sir Ramaswami has said, but to express my own fear that unless you intervene we may be faced with disagreeable consequences.

---

[1] See 342.

## 344  CO 537/1674, no 11                    18 Feb 1946
## [Constitution]: letter from Sir H Moore to Sir G Gater on the definition of defence and the appointment of the attorney-general.
## *Enclosure*: note by Sir R Drayton (7 Feb 1946)

Thank you for your letter of the 11th February. Nihill has written me a letter giving me an account of his first meeting with Jeffries, Roberts-Wray and the department, and I understand that in due course we shall get an omnibus telegram dealing with the different points raised in the discussions which may require further consideration at this end in consultation with Senanayake.

2. As regards "the Defence of the Island" definition your people will no doubt

have seen by this time Senanayake's Memorandum[1] which Nihill took home with him. I enclose a copy of Drayton's comments upon it with which I am in general agreement. I am still very doubtful as to how far Senanayake really appreciates the point at issue, since his (sic) Memorandum clearly reveals the hand of Jennings. If the Secretary of State could satisfy him that His Majesty's Government has no sinister designs in drawing the definition in wide and general terms but that its retention is necessary to avoid a clash with the legislative powers of the Ceylon Parliament I am hopeful that it may be possible to allay his suspicions, particularly if you get Goonetilleke to accept the position.

3. I have now had further discussions both with Senanayake and Drayton on the question of the appointment of the Attorney-General. In view of the importance of this post under the Constitution we now agree that the appointment should be made by the Governor acting in his discretion. As a corollary to this Drayton suggests that the present functions of the post might be divided between the Attorney-General and a new post of Director of Public Prosecutions or Public Prosecutor. The Attorney-General's functions would then become mainly advisory, to the Governor in the exercise of his prerogative of pardon, etc., and powers of reservation and assent to bills, and to the Government on matters requiring legal interpretation or advice. While it may be argued that under such an arrangement the Governor may be subjected to political pressure in making the appointment, I consider that on balance the advantages of his being able to go outside the Legal and Judicial Service altogether in order to get a first-rate man from the local bar or even from outside the Island outweigh the disadvantages of being tied to a routine appointment on the recommendations of the Judicial Commission. Probably a special salary will have to be attached if the post is to be made sufficiently attractive.

## Enclosure to 344

My general comment on the annexed memorandum is that it is an example of dialectics and not an argument which has a foundation and a background of reality. It proceeds on the assumption that the 1943 Declaration is sacrosanct whereas the author of the memorandum claims as his greatest political triumph the fact that he persuaded the Secretary of State to remove from the Constitution the very clause for which the definition of "defence" was invented. It is true that the definition was designed to indicate the matters in respect of which the Governor (General) could legislate by Governor General's Ordinance: it is also true that the Ministers' Scheme adopted the same definition of defence for the purpose of the clause dealing with the reservation of Bills; it is equally true that, in paragraph 353, there is ample ground for supporting the argument in the memorandum. But that argument ignores (a) the admitted inconsistency between paragraph 353 and paragraph 349—an inconsistency which is reconcileable only by substituting "includes" for "means" i.e., by treating the enumeration of matters of defence as not exhaustive, (b) the fact that the primary purpose for which the definition of defence was invented is now gone and (c) (which is most important of all) the practical difficulty—discussed at such length in N'Eliya—that, under Article 29 (2), His Majesty in Council will be able to legislate for

---

[1] Not printed but see 341, para 3.

matters of defence which are outside the scope of the proposed definition and that the Ceylon Parliament will be able to legislate for the same matters and the Governor will not be able to reserve any such Bills but will have to assent.

The memorandum seems to me therefore to be wholly unreal.

## 345  CO 54/988/2, nos 62 & 63                              26 Feb 1946
[Indo–Ceylon relations]: letter from Mr Creech Jones to Lord Pethick-Lawrence explaining why it would not be appropriate for HMG to intervene on the franchise question. *Enclosure*: letter from Creech Jones to Sir R Mudaliar (26 Feb 1946)

In Mr. Hall's absence I am writing to say that he received your note about Sir Ramaswami Mudaliar's letter to me just as the reply which he himself intended to send to him was going off.[1] The reply was held up as we wished to give your letter the fullest consideration before its despatch. I have now sent it off on Mr. Hall's behalf and enclose a copy for your information.

We are very sorry not to have been able to meet your views on this issue, but we feel that quite apart from His Majesty's Government's acceptance of the Soulbury recommendations as providing the basis for a new Constitution in Ceylon, any attempt to interfere in this matter and to force Ceylon into negotiations for an agreement with India at this juncture might jeopardise very seriously, and would certainly delay the chances of getting the new Constitution for Ceylon into being.

As Mr. Senanayake has pointed out, Members of the State Council and his Ministerial colleagues have accepted the position that the Soulbury Report did not contemplate the course for which the Government of India is pressing, and we are certain that any attempt by Mr. Senanayake to get his colleagues to agree to negotiations on this issue before the new Constitution has been granted would provide his political opponents with the very handle which they would like to have and would disrupt the united front amongst his colleagues which he has been at such pains to create.

It may be that the Government of India has read into the Soulbury Commission's Report rather more than it said, and in writing to Sir Ramaswami I have endeavoured to correct any misunderstanding of this kind. But we are in any case convinced that intervention by His Majesty's Government such as the Government of India desires could do nothing but harm and would be calculated more than anything else to prejudice the chance of an agreed solution of the matter by direct negotiation in the future as envisaged in the assurances which Mr. Senanayake has given both to yourself and to Sir Ramaswami.

We trust, therefore, that the Government of India may be content to let well alone in the common interests of the Indian Tamils in Ceylon and the future relationship between the Governments of India and Ceylon under the Constitution on the basis set out in the White Paper. I feel sure that if this course is adopted the consequences you fear are likely to be far less disagreeable than those which would be provoked by interference on the part of India or of His Majesty's Government.

---

[1] See 342 & 343.

**Enclosure to 345**

The Secretary of State had hoped himself to be able to reply to your letter to me of the 11th February but he is unfortunately unwell and will be away from the Office for a few days. I am therefore not holding up an answer to the points you make.

May I say at once that we appreciate the disappointment that both you and the Government of India feel at the attitude of the Ceylon Government towards the question of a resumption at this juncture of direct negotiations with the Government of India on the question of the future status of Indians in Ceylon.

On the other hand I am sure that His Majesty's Government would not contemplate a reversal of their decision to accept the recommendations of the Soulbury Commission's Report that the existing franchise should be maintained, and that the particular issue of the future status of Indians in Ceylon should be a matter for settlement by direct negotiation.

We do not read the particular passage of the Report to which you refer as indicating that the Commission expected or anticipated that such negotiations should necessarily precede the coming into force of the new Constitution. Rather the reverse. Their calculations as to the number of seats which the Indian Tamils might expect to secure in the first elections under the new Constitution were arrived at after a most careful consideration of the best estimates they could obtain based on the existing franchise figures, and they did not do more, I think, than point out in paragraph 240 of their Report that, if by any chance some new arrangement was reached on the question of the franchise of the Indian unskilled workers before the new Constitution came into force, in those circumstances it might be necessary to consider again the weightage arrangements which had been devised to secure fair representation for the Indian Tamil section of the population of Ceylon.

In view of the assurance which Mr. Senanayake has given, we find it difficult to understand the Government of India's suggestion that to defer a decision on this matter until after the new Constitution becomes effective would "have a disastrous effect on future relations between India and Ceylon".

It appears that one of the surest ways in which to bring about such a situation, which both His Majesty's Government and the Government of Ceylon alike would deplore, would be for His Majesty's Government to attempt to intervene in the manner which the Government of India suggests. No one is more anxious than the Secretary of State to see proper minority representation under the new Constitution, and in examining the recommendations of the Soulbury Report special attention was paid by His Majesty's Government to this question.

I think that we must now leave the issue to be decided at the polls when the new Constitution comes into existence, in the confidence that the Delimitation Commission will genuinely endeavour to give effect to the recommendations of the Commission in regard to the defining of electoral areas so as to secure the objects which the Commission had clearly in view and which His Majesty's Government have endorsed in the White Paper.

# 346   CO 537/1674                                 26 Feb–23 Mar 1946
[Constitution]: minutes by J B Sidebotham and Sir C Jeffries on the drafting of the constitution

*Sir C. Jeffries*
I think it would be convenient if at this stage I recapitulated our progress so far in regard to our examination of the Ceylon Constitution first draft, which Mr. Nihill brought with him. A copy will be found at No. 4A.

You, Mr. Roberts Wray, Sir Oliver Goonetilleke, Mr. Nihill, Mr. Peck,[1] Mr. Webber[2] and myself (with Mr. Caine's assistance in connexion with the financial clauses) have now been right through this draft. We concluded our last meeting yesterday morning. In the course of our examination some major points emerged on which we felt that it would be necessary to seek a decision by the Secretary of State. I attach at A on this file a list of these points.[3] Other matters are almost entirely matters of drafting on which Mr. Peck and Mr. Nihill are now engaged. They are dealing first with the re-drafting of what I will call the more contentious points on which reference to the Secretary of State and thereafter reference out to Ceylon will be necessary. They will then proceed with getting the document as a whole into its final form.

Our timetable is, as you know, a very 'narrow' one. While there is no question of submission of the draft Order-in-Council and other Instruments to the State Council, it is proposed that Mr. Senanayake and the Board of Ministers should have an opportunity at any rate of seeing the actual Instruments for their information before they are published. Sir Oliver Goonetilleke, who has been of great assistance to us in the discussions in explaining Mr. Senanayake's standpoint (although he does not always agree with it) is leaving for Washington very shortly and expects to be there about ten days. He then, I understand, anticipates his early return to Ceylon, and it will be of great convenience from every point of view if our despatch to Ceylon on points of difficulty can go out at the same time as he does. We may expect to have it back within ten days and then, I think, to be able to finalise the document.

The Delimitation Commission will want to get to work about the end of April, when the census results will, we understand, be available, and to enable them to do so part of the Order-in-Council has to be put in force at once, other parts being made effective at varying dates later. The Order-in-Council will therefore have to be made officially during the last week of March or the first week in April if possible, so that we have extremely little time in which to bring the whole thing into final form. Added to this, there is the question of the new Royal Instruction Letters Patent, which, although they will not have to be brought into force at present, are in themselves an essential part of the Constitution and ought to be available to be studied with the new Order-in-Council itself when it is made public. I have spoken to Mr. Roberts Wray and Mr. Nihill about this this morning. . . .

J.B.S.
26.2.46

---

[1] J A Peck, senior legal assistant, CO.                    [2] F D Webber, principal, CO.
[3] Not printed: the more contentious points concerned power of disallowance in respect of Ceylon legislation, the definition of defence and external affairs and the reservation of bills on franchise and immigration matters.

These discussions have been most useful. As will be seen from No.12 the really important points for decision by higher authority are not numerous. They will be submitted separately for consideration with the necessary material.

C.J.J.
27.2.46

I had a long talk with Sir O. Goonetilleke. I found it impossible to shake him in his view that this question of the reservation of Bills relating to the franchise and immigration is fundamental and that Mr. Senanayake will undoubtedly withdraw his support of the Constitution and revert to the demand for Dominion Status if the point is pressed.

Sir O. Goonetilleke will be available for discussions on Wednesday next if desired. But his views are clear, and the immediate question is to decide what line H.M.G. are going to take. . . .

C.J.J.
23.3.46

## 347   CO 54/986/9, no 31                                    24 Mar 1946
## [Tamils]: letter from S Sivasubramaniam to Mr Attlee suggesting that the Cabinet Mission to India should visit Ceylon

Further to previous correspondence,[1] I am addressing you on the above subject.

We are happy to learn that the British Government has decided to send three Cabinet Members of high standing to India, with a view to settling the Indian question finally. It is gratifying to us, particularly because we in Ceylon are very closely connected with India historically, culturally, and ethnologically. Ceylon is separated from South India by only 16 miles of shallow sea, and the Tamils of Ceylon form one people with the Tamils of South India. Though for administrative purposes India is under the Secretary of State for India, and Ceylon is under the Secretary of State for the Colonies, yet in matters of great concern, to wit, strategy and defence during war, the two countries have been treated as one unit. In connection with the question of food supply, Ceylon and India are, I believe, now being treated together by the International Board.

No solution of the Indian political and communal problem can be said to be complete and comprehensive until and unless the communal political problem in Ceylon is satisfactorily solved at the same time, not only because, as already indicated, the two countries have been so closely connected together in the past, but also because in the future World Order and Comity of Nations in the East, Ceylon and India will have to function not as two separate units but as *one unit*[2] for all purposes.

The political and economic conditions and problems of the two countries are in several aspects similar, though there are differences between the demands made by the Tamils in Ceylon, and the Muslims of India. In Ceylon, unlike the Muslims in India, the Tamils are not asking for a partition of the country but are only demanding an effective share in the Government of the Island and the application of the

---

[1] See 339.                                              [2] Emphasis in original.

principle of racial non-domination. The solution of the communal problem in Ceylon, however, is easier than that of the Indian communal problem and it should not be allowed to deteriorate by failure to address oneself to it in time.

A convenient opportunity for the British Parliament and Government to intervene effectively and fairly, towards the solution of Ceylon's communal problems and to establish a truly democratic form of self-government for the country is provided by the forthcoming visit of the three Cabinet Ministers to India.

It would be desirable if the Cabinet Ministers visiting India are requested by the British Parliament and Government to include Ceylon in their itinerary, in view of the great dissatisfaction prevailing here with regard to the proposed Soulbury Constitution. As statesmen already acquainted to some extent with the communal political problems of the East, they would be in a position to ascertain the fundamental realities of the situation and advise His Majesty's Government accordingly.

The peaceful and comparative calm attitude maintained by the Tamils in the face of the gross injustice perpetrated by the Soulbury Commissioners' recommendations and the White Paper is only an index of their national character, which deters them from any action or course of conduct that will be subversive of constitutional development on peaceful lines and detrimental to the maintenance of friendly feelings towards other communities. If the Tamils of Ceylon have not chosen the path of political agitation followed in Palestine and India by warring communities, such abstinence should not be wrongly construed either as a sign of weakness or acquiesence in the present state of affairs. The Tamil race which has produced leaders like Sir A. Ramasamy Mudaliar, the head of the Indian delegation to the U.N.O. and Mr. C. Rajagopalachari, the ex-premier of Madras, is by temperament disposed towards the pacific solution of political differences and the restraint shown by the Tamils in Ceylon is only an exhibition of their community's natural genius in this direction.

A visit by the Ministers to Ceylon will not in any way be derogatory to the Soulbury Commission's work, even as their visit to India will not detract from the labours of the Parliamentary Delegation that recently returned from India. On the other hand, such a visit will only be supplementing the work of the Soulbury Commissioners.

The great importance of the matter of constitutional reform to our country, the significance of Ceylon to International strategy, its vital connection with India, the part it has played in the World War, and the place the solution of political and economic problems here has in the general scheme of things for World Order and peace, all these factors, combine to make such a visit by the three Cabinet Ministers carry with it the potentialities for producing good results. This country will welcome such an event.

**348**   CO 537/1673, COS(46)79, annex                    16 Mar 1946

[Defence]: CO note for COS Committee on the definition of the
defence clause in the Ceylon constitution.[1] *Enclosure*

The Chiefs of Staff will recall that His Majesty's Government, in the declaration of the
26th of May, 1943, on the subject of Constitutional reform in Ceylon, stated *inter
alia* that under a new Constitution "His Majesty's Government will retain control of
the provision, construction, maintenance, security, staffing, manning and use of
such defences, equipment, establishments and communications as His Majesty's
Government may deem necessary for the Naval, Military and Air security of the
Commonwealth, including that of the Island, the cost thereof being shared between
the two Governments in agreed proportions".

In the course of discussions in Ceylon in relation to the drafting of the new
Constitution which is now well advanced, Mr. Senanayake, the Vice-Chairman of the
Board of Ministers in Ceylon, has pressed very strongly for the inclusion in the
Order-in-Council setting out the new Constitution of a definition of "Defence" in so
far as the term is used with regard to a class of bill which the Governor is
empowered, and indeed obliged, to reserve for the signification of His Majesty's
pleasure, and, it is understood, he would like to see that definition given in the form
adopted in the 1943 declaration which was quoted in His Majesty's Government's
Statement of Policy on Constitution Reform in Ceylon, Cmd. 6690. The Secretary of
State for the Colonies is anxious, if possible, to meet Mr. Senanayake's wishes. It is
accordingly proposed, if the Chiefs of Staff see no objection, to include in the
Order-in-Council sections which refer, *inter alia*, to Defence matters in the form
given in the enclosure to this note.

It has been borne in mind that whatever definition is adopted, it is to be
anticipated that the Ceylon Government will, under the new Constitution, demand a
strict compliance with its terms, and Mr. Hall, therefore, considers is important that
the terms of the definition should be sufficiently wide to meet all possible
requirements of the fighting services.

In this connection it should be appreciated that under Section 29 of the draft
Order-in-Council His Majesty retains full power to legislate for Ceylon by Order-in-
Council on any matter which appears to him to be necessary for the defence of the
Island and that the term "Defence" for the purposes of this Section is not limited by
definition. The legal effect of these two Sections together is that the Governor must
reserve any Bill, which in his opinion falls within the definition of defence in Section
36 and must also reserve any Bill which in his opinion is repugnant to any Imperial
Order-in-Council in relation to Defence matters made under Section 29.

Mr. Senanayake will undoubtedly view with suspicion any major departure from
the formula adopted in the 1943 declaration more particularly if he feels that this is
likely to curtail to a greater extent than the 1943 declaration the full control by the
Government of Ceylon, under a new Constitution, of all matters of internal civil
administration, as promised by His Majesty's Government.

It is contemplated that under the provision of the draft Constitution a Portfolio of

---

[1] This note was sent under cover of a letter (15 Mar 1946) from Gater requesting, as soon as possible, the
views of the COS on the draft clause relating to defence in the new constitution.

Defence and External Affairs will be held by the Prime Minister. The Ceylon Government will, in accordance with the recommendation of paragraph 353 of the Report of the Soulbury Commission, Cmd. 6677, continue to have a very special interest in the welfare and administration of the Ceylon Defence Force and the Ceylon Royal Naval Volunteer Reserve but the draft definition of defence has been drawn deliberately with the intention of enabling supervision of training and operational control of those forces to be exercised by the Imperial defence authorities. As regards Section 29(2), it is contemplated that, under arrangements which cannot properly appear in a Constitutional Instrument, the cost of the defences referred to in the definition, other than the cost of the Ceylon Defence Force and the Ceylon Royal Naval Volunteer Reserve, which would be defrayed by the Ceylon Government, will be shared between His Majesty's Government and the Government of Ceylon in agreed proportions, as proposed in the 1943 declaration.

It is further contemplated that the Governor would by separate Order-in-Council (to be brought into force locally by proclamation in the event of a defence emergency arising) be empowered to put into effect on his own authority any defence measure necessary to deal with such emergency. Such an arrangement has been discussed with Mr. Senanayake and accepted by him.

It is desired, if possible, to have the Order-in-Council enacted at the beginning of April, and the Secretary of State for the Colonies is therefore most anxious to learn at the earliest possible moment whether the Chiefs of Staff are prepared to accept draft clause 36(1)(a) in order that Mr. Senanayake's concurrence in it may be obtained before it is included in the draft Order-in-Council to be submitted for Cabinet approval.

## Enclosure to 348

*Section 29(1).* His Majesty, His Heirs and Successors, with the advice of His or Their Privy Council, may from time to time make such laws as may appear to Him or Them to be necessary:—

(a) for the defence of any part of His Majesty's dominions (including the Island) or any other territory in which His Majesty has from time to time jurisdiction; or

(b) for regulating the relations between the Island and foreign countries or any other part of His Majesty's dominions or any other territory as aforesaid.

(2). No law made in pursuance of the provisions of sub-section (1) of this Section shall impose any charge on the revenues or funds of the Island or regulate the importation of goods into or the exportation of goods from the Island, except to give effect to any agreement to which the Government of Ceylon is a party.

(3). His Majesty hereby reserves to Himself, His Heirs and Successors power, with the advice of His or Their Privy Council, to revoke, add to, suspend or amend this Order as to Him or Them shall seem fit.

*Section 36(1).* Subject to the provisions of sub-section (2) of this Section, the Governor shall reserve for His Majesty's assent any Bill which in his opinion—

(a) relates to the provision, construction, maintenance, security, staffing, manning and use of such defences, equipment establishments and communications as may be necessary for the naval, military and air security of any part of His Majesty's dominions or any territory in which from time to time His Majesty has jurisdiction.

(b) is repugnant to or inconsistent with any provision of any Order-in-Council made in pursuance of the power contained in sub-section (1) of Section 29 of this order.[2]

---

[2] When the COS Committee considered this note on 16 Mar 1946, the first sea lord (Admiral Sir John H D Cunningham) expressed the view that the 'only doubtful point' concerned the inclusion of the words 'or regulate the importation of goods into or the exportation of goods from the Island' in clause 2 of section 29. These seemed open to the interpretation that, if the Ceylon government did not agree, in war or emergency HMG would have no power to regulate the export of vital strategic commodities such as rubber. Cunningham suggested that the difficulty might be overcome if the words in question were amended to read 'or regulate the import and export trade of the Island'. The committee approved this amendment for communication to the CO (CO 537/1673, COS 79(46)13). Within the CO Sidebotham commented that the original wording had been 'very deliberately' included in the draft to meet Senanayake's fear that HMG might apply a quota system to Ceylon: 'The Ceylon Government have been very badly bitten in their view by H.M.G's control of copra in this war and their refusal to let Ceylon sell direct to India and get a much better price there than H.M.G. will give her under bulk purchase buying and Ceylon will not let herself be caught again like that.' If HMG wanted Ceylon's rubber in a future war, it would have to be by a freely negotiated agreement with Ceylon, and if the need was so urgent and agreement could not be reached, in the last event the constitution would have to be rescinded. It was, however, important that HMG should appear to be relying on Ceylon's co-operation in such matters and in the drafting of the constitution should not seem to be *'anticipating* an attitude of non-co-operation in critical times for the Empire as a whole' (*ibid*, minute by Sidebotham, 21 Mar 1946). Gater communicated this view to the COS Committee, pointing out that clause 3 of section 29 provided HMG with the means to revoke, suspend or amend the order-in-council (*ibid*, no 6, letter from Gater to Col C R Price, 22 Mar 1946). The COS Committee accepted this as an adequate safeguard.

## 349   CO 537/1674, no 35D                                    29 Mar 1946
## [Franchise]: outward unnumbered telegram from Sir G Gater to Sir H Moore on different interpretations of the recommendations of the Soulbury Commission

My secret and personal telegram No. 2 of 25th March. Following from Gater.

*Begins.* Reference point raised in paragraph 2 of your secret and personal telegram of 14th March.

(1) Position may be summarized as follows: His Majesty's Government has consistently interpreted intention of Soulbury Commission to be that bills relating to Franchise and Immigration, though not reservable within category of bills relating to External Affairs, would be reserved if containing provisions bring them within the scope of paragraph 332 (v) of the Report.

His Majesty's Government had, of course, the draft of the White Paper under consideration in relation to this very point when Secretary of State for India was authorized to give assurance to above effect to Viceroy, and it is most unfortunate that the very different interpretation put on this matter by Mr. Senanayake in his speech to the State Council on the 8th November[1] has not been disclosed until this late stage.

---

[1] For the relevant passage from the speech, see 351, para 2.

(2) It is quite impossible to harmonize these two readings of the Soulbury report, which it is admitted is not entirely free from ambiguity on this most important point, nor did publication of the White Paper resolve this ambiguity, which was not then apparent.

(3) Discussions here with Goonetilleke have made it clear that he believes that Senanayake will not accept His Majesty's Government's interpretation.[2] It is inferred from your telegrams that this is also your view. The matter is accordingly one on which Secretary of State will have to consult his colleagues before decision can be reached.

(4) Seriousness of the difficulty is fully appreciated, and it is felt that it will be essential to keep Goonetilleke here until decision has been taken. Separate telegram has been sent about this in form which will enable you to show it to Senanayake if you wish. Secretary of State has given Goonetilleke to-day an opportunity of expressing his views with Nihill on this matter to himself personally, and he has explained to him that the matter is of such fundamental importance that he will be referring it to his colleagues.

(5) Goonetilleke has represented very strongly that Prime Minister's recent speech on His Majesty's Government's policy towards India,[3] despite recent regrettable events there, will afford Senanayake strong grounds for pressing for very liberal treatment of Ceylon. He has made it clear that he personally is not prepared to press Senanayake to accept anything less than His Majesty's Government is understood in Ceylon to have offered. Secretary of State has endeavoured to explain to person named that a genuine difference of interpretation has arisen owing to ambiguity of the report, and that he must now await his colleagues' views before he can carry the matter further.

(6) In the meantime Secretary of State would be grateful for your very early personal assessment of Senanayake's probable reactions if His Majesty's Government feels that it is impossible to depart from the assurance given to the Viceroy, since having regard to the political situation in India, any other course may be left to be impracticable. *Ends.*

---

[2] See 346.                                                            [3] On which see 350, para 4.

## 350   CO 537/1674, no 37                                    30 Mar 1946
## [Franchise]: inward unnumbered telegram (reply) from Sir H Moore to Sir G Gater stressing 'the danger of throwing Senanayake over now'

Your secret and personal telegram of 29th March.[1] Following for Gater. Please repeat to Nihill and Goonetilleke.

*Begins.*—1. Your paragraphs 1 and 2. I am forwarding by fast bag a memorandum prepared by Drayton on the question of interpretation with which I am in full agreement. It deals with the amendment proposed to be made in paragraph 2 of your secret and personal telegram of 11th March but if, as would now appear, the amendment is to be limited to Franchise and Immigration Bills, the argument is

---

[1] See 349.

equally cogent. I would, however, point out that correspondence with Government of India was primarily concerned with franchise, and that the statement made by His Majesty's Government that paragraph 242 (IV) was intended to override paragraph 242 (II) (Franchise) was not repeated in regard to paragraph 242 (I) (Immigration). I do not, therefore, understand inclusion of Immigration Bills in your paragraph 1, particularly in view of repetition of paragraph 242 (I) on page 5 of White Paper.

Senanayake's speech on 8th November was naturally made without my knowledge of correspondence with Viceroy, copy of which was only posted to me on 10th November. In these circumstances and in view of the ambiguity of interpretation which you now admit, I agree that it is most unfortunate that my attention was not drawn to its inconsistency with His Majesty's Government's intentions as soon as Hansard posted on 14th November had been read in the Department. At the same time, I do not see how Senanayake, in the absence of any knowledge as to the terms of this correspondence, could have arrived at the interpretation you now suggest.

2. Your paragraph 3. Inference is correct.

3. Your paragraph 4 agreed. See my secret telegram No. 507 of to-day's date.

4. Your paragraphs 5 and 6. I have no doubt at all that reaction not only of Senanayake but of all members of the Board of Ministers and the State Council will be that His Majesty's Government has once again given way to pressure by Government of India and that, taking refuge in the ambiguity of the report, has adopted for reasons of political expediency an interpretation which may go some way to mollify Indian resentment at their failure to obtain a more favourable verdict from Lord Soulbury and his colleagues. They will not believe for a moment that, at this stage of the proceedings, there can be any room for genuine misunderstanding and will accuse the Secretary of State once again of a serious breach of faith.

Personally, I cannot stress too strongly the danger of throwing Senanayake over now. At the moment, Ceylon is perhaps the only territory in South-East Asia where, thanks to belief in the honesty of His Majesty's Government's intentions, a flickering spirit of mutual trust still prevails. Relations with Senanayake have never been more cordial than they are at present. If you destroy this confidence, not only will you be throwing him to the wolves but, in my view, all hope of proceeding under new constitution can be abandoned. The consequences of such a development at the present time would be so damaging to our prestige in the East generally, quite apart from the certainty of serious political trouble in Ceylon, that in my view they should be avoided at all costs even at the risk of causing some resentment in India. The Prime Minister, in his speech as reported in the *Times* of 16th March, stated specifically that His Majesty's Government could not make Indians responsible for governing themselves and at the same time retain ourselves the responsibility for the treatment of minorities and the powers of intervening on their behalf. I agree with Goonetilleke that his speech generally and the leader upon it will immediately be seized upon and the claim made that the same principles which underlie the whole of the Soulbury recommendations should be applied to Ceylon on the grant to her of internal self-government.

# 351   CO 537/1674, no 48                                    30 Mar 1946
## [Franchise]: outward telegram no 6566 from Sir D Monteath[1] to Lord Pethick-Lawrence requesting clarification of the Indian viewpoint

*Begins.*—1. You will recollect discussion in Colonial Affairs Committee of Cabinet about Soulbury Commission's report on Ceylon in October and your telegram 23759 of 27th October to Viceroy, which stated at end of paragraph (d)[2] as follows:—"As regards reservation of franchise Bills it is pointed out that the Commission's recommendations for provisions in new Constitution against discrimination were clearly intended to be overriding and in the light of this recommendation (ii) of paragraph 242 should be read as governed by recommenations (iii) and (iv)".

2. It has now come to light in course of drafting new Constitution that Senanayake in his speech to State Council of Ceylon of 8th November recommending adoption of White Paper (Cmd. 6690) proposals made the following statement to last sentence of which attention is now directed:—

> "Besides the power to enact Orders-in-Council for the Island there will be only one restriction on full self-government in the Constitution. It will be a power to reserve Bills relating to certain classes of matters. There will be six such classes, including Defence, External Affairs, Currency, Extraordinary Measures, Minority Discrimination and Constitutional Amendment. The House will not expect me to give a disquisition on these classes, which have been the subject of much discussion and much careful drafting. *I will mention only that, subject to minor qualifications, they do not apply to Immigration, the Franchise, Trade agreements within the Commonwealth, tariffs or Shipping.*"[3]

3. The effect of this is that if Senanayake's interpretation is accepted the words "and (iv)" in the sentence quoted from your telegram are inapplicable. The material effect appears however to be unimportant since the new constitution for Ceylon would contain a provision debarring the Parliament of Ceylon from making any law rendering persons of any community or religion liable to disabilities or restrictions to which persons of other communities or religions are not made liable, or conferring upon persons of any community or religion any privileges or advantages which are not conferred on persons of other communities or religions. (See paragraph 242 (iii) of the Soulbury Report.)

4. The Soulbury Report read as a whole is not free from ambiguity in the matter and the White Paper does not resolve this ambiguity. Senanayake's statement was in all good faith and has the support of the Legal Secretary Ceylon.

5. Secretary of State for the Colonies represents that it would be impossible to ask Senanayake to go back now on his statement on this matter without jeopardising all chance of bringing into effect a constitution based on the White Paper proposals.

6. I assume from the fact that Government of India have made no comment on

---

[1] Permanent under secretary of state for India and Burma from 1942. Pethick-Lawrence was in India at this time as a member of the Cabinet mission.

[2] Error in drafting; para (d) should read para (a), see 321, enclosure 2.

[3] Emphasis in Monteath's telegram.

Senanayake's speech that they are not exercised on this point in view of the provisions referred to in paragraph 242 (iii) of the report which will provide adequate safeguards in these matters.

7. In these circumstances Secretary of State for the Colonies is considering bringing matter to notice of Colonial Affairs Committee of Cabinet first week in April, but before doing so would be very grateful to learn whether you and Viceroy would agree that assurance given in your telegram to Viceroy quoted above may be read as not repeat not including the words "and (iv)" in paragraphs 3 (a).

# 352   CO 537/1674, no 43                                        1 Apr 1946

## [Franchise]: inward telegram no 512 from Sir H Moore to Mr Hall transmitting a personal message from Mr Senanayake to Sir O Goonetilleke

Following personal from Senanayake for Goonetilleke.
*Begins.* Your secret telegram No. 377.

Please make strongest representations to the Secretary of State that, unless draft Order in Council reflects faithfully the recommendations of the Soulbury Commission as modified by decision of His Majesty's Government set out in White Paper, which was accepted by such a large majority of members of the State Council, including my Ministerial colleagues, on the understanding that the country was to receive complete internal self-government, including Soulbury Commission decision regarding franchise, Order in Council will be quite unacceptable to the people of Ceylon. Further, it will prevent any possibility of subsequent agreement with India, and I am firmly convinced that third party interference will not in any way help to solve our outstanding problems with them. I sincerely hope that decisions which will prevent me from co-operating in the future will not be reached. *Ends.*

# 353   CO 537/1674, no 45                                        1 Apr 1946

## [Franchise]: outward unnumbered telegram (reply) from Sir G Gater to Sir H Moore on Mr Senanayake's position

Your secret and personal telegram (1) of the 30th March.[1] Following from Gater.
*Begins.* I am very grateful for your prompt assessment of Senanayake's reactions if His Majesty's Government persisted in their interpretation.

2. Your request to repeat your telegram to Nihill and Goonetilleke has placed me in some difficulty since latter has not been told of commitment to India though he undoubtedly suspects something of the kind. We have thought it undesirable to disclose commitment to him at this stage if it is possible to avoid doing so. Consultations foreshadowed in paragraph 4 of my secret and personal telegram of 29th March[2] are proceeding and we should much prefer to await their outcome in the hope that the difficulty may be overcome. It would equally, we think, place Nihill

---

[1] See 350.                                                    [2] See 349.

in a very invidious position if we were to hand the telegram to him and not to Goonetilleke.

3. In the circumstances, I propose to convey to Goonetilleke concluding part of paragraph 4 of your telegram only, commencing with the words "Personally I cannot stress . . ." down to ". . . internal self-government" with the omission of the words "even at the risk of causing some resentment in India", and to do the same in case of Nihill. Please telegraph as early as possible whether you agree to this course.

4. The point in your paragraph 1 is appreciated. It is unnecessary for me to discuss the legal aspects further at this stage. I agree that it was most unfortunate that the difference in interpretation was not detected either in Ceylon on arrival of the Secretary of State's secret and personal despatch of 10th November or here when your 3P.N. note of the 14th November covering report of State Council debate was received. We fully recognize of course that Senanayake's statement of 8th November was made in entire good faith.

The contents of your secret and personal telegram of 31st March relative to Drayton's Memorandum are noted.

5. I have just received your secret and personal telegram of the 1st April reporting your talk with Senanayake and have seen your No.512 secret.[3] *[Ends.]*

---

[3] See 352.

# 354    CO 54/986/9/1, no 33                                    1 Apr 1946
## 'All-Ceylon Tamil Congress': CO note

The All-Ceylon Tamil Congress is the most recent of a number of organisations which have from time to time emerged in Ceylon, purporting to represent the two communities of Tamils in Ceylon, and pressing for reform of the Constitution in one direction or another. There are about 700,000 Ceylon Tamils and 900,000 Indian Tamils in the Island, but from what follows it will be clear that the Congress is in no sense fully representative of this combined community. The Congress is a recent foundation. It came into being some 18 months ago during the agitation for constitutional reform which preceded the arrival of the Soulbury Commission in Ceylon in December 1944. The organisation has no deep roots in the Tamil community as such: it is largely an ad hoc body, the artificial creation of a group of Tamil politicians, led by Mr. Ponnambalam, a very able lawyer and Member of the State Council, for the purpose of presenting a united Tamil front to the Soulbury Commissioners in opposition to the Sinhalese majority community. Their representations, which included a complete Constitutional Scheme, were examined in full by the Commission. Details of their allegations, together with the considered views of the Commission, will be found in paragraphs 138 to 178 of the Soulbury Report. (Cmd. 6677). Their whole case rested on the assumption that a working compromise between the Sinhalese and Tamil communities was impossible and that by accentuating their differences the maximum concessions to minorities would be gained from the Commission. This was not borne out by events.

The Soulbury Report, and the White Paper which followed it, by reason of their treatment of the minority question in Ceylon, caused the so-called United Tamil Front against the Sinhalese majority to crumble, and it was the voting in the Debate on the White Paper in the State Council which exposed the artificial character of the organisation and finally broke up the Tamil front. There are 11 Tamil members in the State Council. Seven of these represent the Ceylon Tamils. At the time of the voting one of these was the Speaker, two were absent from the Island, and the remaining four voted *for* acceptance of the White Paper. Four members represent the Indian Tamils. Of these, one was absent, one voted for and two voted against acceptance. Those Tamil Members who had voted for the motion had clearly realised the political unwisdom of continuing to refuse cooperation with the Sinhalese and attempting to reject H.M.G.'s endorsement of the Soulbury Report, implying, as it did, that adequate safeguards would be inserted in the new Constitution to protect minority interests. Thus it is doubtful whether the many representations[1] which the All-Ceylon Tamil Congress have made over the signature of Mr. Sivasubramamian [sic], since the acceptance of the White Paper by an overwhelming majority in the State Council, reflect anything more than the still-born policy of a rump of dissatisfied politicians. It appears that Mr. Ponnambalam himself, until recently President of the Congress, has for the present at least ceased from active direction of its affairs.

These representations have been made with the objects of getting the State Council immediately dissolved, of holding a fresh General Election and of having the implementation of the White Paper deferred pending the meeting of a new Council. All such representations which have been received direct in the Colonial Office, or have been referred to the Colonial Office by Ministers and M.P.'s, have been scrutinised thoroughly. In view of the very wide acceptance of the White Paper in Ceylon and of the fact that the new Constitutional Instruments will interpret faithfully the intention of the White Paper, as representing H.M.G.'s considered policy, and since that policy has clearly taken account of the need for safeguarding minority interests, it has been felt that no useful purpose would be served by acceding to the demands of this organisation which are no longer based on practical politics. For this reason the general line taken has been simply to acknowledge the representations by asking the Governor, as occasion demands, to inform the Joint Secretary that his various communications have been received by, or referred to, the Secretary of State for the Colonies.

---

[1] See eg 339 & 347.

# 355  CO 537/1674, no 50                                    2 Apr 1946
## [Franchise]: inward unnumbered telegram (reply) from Sir H Moore to Sir G Gater

Your secret and personal telegram of 1st April.[1] Following for Gater.

*Begins.* 1. Your paragraph 2. I had not overlooked the point, but it seemed to me that a stage had been reached at which it was necessary and only fair to myself and to the two officers concerned that they should be fully apprised of my views and of the attitude I wished them to adopt. Nihill is already aware of commitment to India and he is to that extent already placed in the invidious position to which you refer. If,

---

[1] See 353.

however, there is a prospect of difficulties being resolved by consultations referred to, I agree that commitment should not be disclosed to Goonetilleke at this stage. But, if preliminary decision is adverse, it will I am sure prove impossible in practice to keep it secret either from him or Senanayake, who already suspects Indian intervention in the matter.

2.  Your paragraph 3. I agree subject to paragraph 1 above.

3.  Your paragraph 4. I am not clear whether this means that the point made in respect of Immigration Bills has been conceded, and that the attitude of His Majesty's Government to immigration, to which you refer in paragraph (1) of your telegram of 29th March,[2] is therefore based on considerations other than legal interpretation of the Soulbury Report and White Paper. But, since I was originally informed that the issue was one of legal drafting and interpretation, I consider it most desirable that Nihill and Goonetilleke should be furnished with copies of Drayton's memorandum. If all words appearing immediately after "report" in second line of preamble down to "Soulbury" in sixth line are deleted, there is no other specific reference to correspondence with India and the memorandum from that point of view would appear innocuous. *Ends.*

---

[2] See 349.

## 356  CO 537/1674, no 54                                    7 Apr 1946
## [Franchise]: inward unnumbered telegram from Sir H Moore to Mr Hall on the attitude of HMG

Your secret and personal telegram of 6th April.

1.  Since it is your considered view that it is in Ceylon's interest that person named[1] should remain until the matter comes before the Cabinet Committee, Senanayake and I both acquiesce.

2.  Earlier exchange of telegrams with Gater has indicated His Majesty's Government's attitude towards reservation of franchise and Immigration Bills—see your secret and personal telegram of 29th March[2] but has not explained whether that attitude was adopted on general grounds of policy or in the belief, which I maintain is mistaken, that it reflected the recommendations of the Soulbury Report.

3.  If it is based on policy grounds, the issue raised is of fundamental importance, namely whether reservation of these Bills is or is not compatible with His Majesty's Government's declared object on page three of the White Paper to grant Ceylon full responsible Government under the Crown in all matters of internal civil administration. In view of the admitted difficulties of interpretation of certain paragraphs of the Report the immediate criticism will be made that, if His Majesty's Government's attitude is as stated on these two points, a categorical statement to that effect should have been included in the White Paper before the State Council was invited to declare its acceptance of the constitutional reforms offered by His Majesty's Government. I suggest that, in view of recent pronouncements made by His Majesty's Government

---

[1] A reference to Goonetilleke and Hall's suggestion that he should remain in London until the franchise question had been considered by the Cabinet Colonial Affairs Committee.
[2] See 349.

in respect of India and Burma, the issues raised go far deeper than the correct interpretation of public documents, and whether or not either Mr. Senanayake or the Viceroy have been unwittingly misled.

4.  But, if that attitude was due to ambiguities in the Report itself, I trust that the further intensive study which has been given to this question will have convinced you that the recommendations of the Report not only are susceptible of the interpretation I have urged upon you, but that no one in Ceylon with full knowledge of the causation of events and of the lines on which Lord Soulbury was known to be working could have reasonably placed any other interpretation upon them.

5.  I have assumed, though I have not been so informed, that you are proposing to press before the Cabinet Committee that His Majesty's Government should reconsider its attitude despite the consideration referred to in paragraph 6 of your secret and personal telegram of 29th March. On the grounds of expediency alone, I would suggest that on the long view His Majesty's Government will be much less embarrassed if Ceylon and India are left to settle their own differences between themselves, and that His Majesty's Government would in practice have the greatest difficulty in intervening effectively without raising a political crisis that might have widespread repercussions out of all proportion to the merits of the domestic issues involved.

6.  Since I still am not clear whether Goonetilleke is to appear before the Committee and if so whether he is to be fully briefed, I am anxious that you should be fully (corrupt group)ed (? appraised) of my views and that they should be clearly represented to the Committee in whatever manner you think best.

# 357   CO 537/1673, no 15, C 2(46)                              11 Apr 1946
## 'Ceylon constitution': Cabinet Colonial Affairs Committee minutes endorsing the positions adopted by Mr Senanayake

The Committee had before them a memorandum by the Secretary of State for the Colonies (C.(46) 5) regarding three points which had arisen in preparing the draft Order in Council relating to the Ceylon Constitution.

A. *Provision for His Majesty's power of disallowance*
*The Secretary of State for the Colonies* said that no reference was made in the Soulbury Commission's report to the question whether The King should have power of disallowance in respect of Ceylon legislation. Such power existed in the case of the Dominions (other than South Africa where it had been removed by an Act of the Union Legislature) but it was not in fact ever used. The Secretary of State foresaw strong objection in Ceylon if it were introduced in the Ceylon Constitution and he recommended that it should not in fact be introduced.
*The Secretary of State for Dominion Affairs* agreed with this view, though there might be repercussions in Southern Rhodesia where the power existed and was not a dead letter.
The Committee:—
(1) Agreed that the draft Order in Council relating to the Ceylon Constitution

should not provide for the exercise by His Majesty of a power of disallowance in respect of Ceylon legislation.

B. *Definition of "defence" and "external affairs"*
*The Secretary of State for the Colonies* said that the Soulbury Commission Report had recommended that Bills relating to defence and external affairs should be Bills which the Governor must reserve for signification of His Majesty's pleasure. It was necessary to define these terms more precisely in the draft Order in Council. Definitions which had been agreed by the Chiefs of Staff and the Foreign Office respectively, were included in Annex IV to the memorandum before the Committee as Section 36 (1)(a), (b) and (c) of the draft Order in Council.
   The Committee:—
   (2) Approved the definitions of "Defence" and "external affairs" included in the draft Order in Council.

C. *Reservation of bills on franchise matters*
*The Secretary of State for the Colonies* reminded the Committee that the question of the Ceylon franchise was one of much concern to the Government of India. It had a long history. The Report of the Soulbury Commission had not been explicit on the question whether or not Bills on franchise matters should be reserved for the signification of His Majesty's pleasure. The Colonial Affairs Committee when they had considered the matter before had taken the view that the subject of franchise was not excepted from the general provision whereby the Governor was required to reserve:—
| "any Bill, any of the provisions of which have evoked serious opposition by any
X racial or religious community and which, in the opinion of the Governor, is likely
| to involve oppression or serious injustice to any such community."

Following that discussion, an assurance on the point had been telegraphed by the Secretary of State for India to the Viceroy.
   Before, however, the Committee's view had been communicated to the Government of Ceylon Mr. Senanayake had, in all good faith, made a statement to the Ceylon State Council giving a different interpretation. He had stated that the power of reservation would not extend to the subject of franchise, and there was evidence that it had been his intention to imply that the general requirement referred to at X above would not apply to Bills on franchise matters.
   The Secretary of State for the Colonies said that it was most awkward that these two different interpretations had been given almost simultaneously. He entirely appreciated the embarrassment which would be caused to the Secretary of State for India if it was necessary to qualify the assurance given to the Viceroy but he was fully satisfied that it would be most inexpedient to challenge Mr. Senanayake's interpretation. The result could only be either that he resigned or that he resorted to extreme courses. In either case all prospect of bringing into being a Constitution on the lines recommended by the Soulbury Commission would be lost and there would be an era of non-co-operation in Ceylon. It was only by a small margin that Mr. Senanayake had obtained the concurrence of the Ceylon State Council in the proposed new Constitution. The balance could easily be tipped in favour of non-co-operation. Ceylon politicians might well argue that this had earned India a promise of

independence and might do the same for them. Nor would the results be serious only in Ceylon. Failure to secure acceptance of the new Constitution in Ceylon would create an unfavourable impression in the world generally and in particular in other parts of the Colonial Empire.

Moreover, there was not in fact any great likelihood of the Ceylon Government passing franchise measures that would discriminate against minorities. It was in the highest degree desirable to engender a spirit of friendliness between the different communities in Ceylon. In recent years a good deal of progress had been made towards this end. Minorities had not in fact been unreasonably treated. Mr. Senanayake himself was most reasonable on the subject and had indeed said privately that he would endeavour to include some minority members in his Government, once the new Constitution was passed. If we now showed lack of confidence in Ceylon's willingness to deal fairly with her minorities, the good work of recent years would inevitably be undone.

For all these reasons, he was most strongly of the opinion that the balance of advantage lay in accepting the view expressed by Mr. Senanayake. The draft Order in Council had been prepared on this basis—see Section 36(2)(c) which formed part of Annex IV to the memorandum before the Committee.

The Secretary of State said that he had arranged for a telegram to be sent to the Secretary of State for India explaining the position to him, and seeking his acquiescence in this course he now proposed. The Secretary of State for India, however, after consulting the Viceroy, was not willing to withdraw the assurance already given to the Government of India. In these circumstances, the Secretary of State for the Colonies thought that it would be well if the Committee could have some discussion on the matter before it was pursued further.

*The Parliamentary Under-Secretary of State for India*[1] said that it appeared that the question must be determined on a balance of expediency. He quite appreciated the force of the arguments put by the Secretary of State for the Colonies. He must, however, point out that a definite assurance had been given to the Government of India, based on conclusions reached by the Committee after their previous discussion of the matter, and it would be distinctly embarrassing to have to withdraw from it.

In discussion, the following points were made:—

(a) There was general agreement that the Committee had had good reasons for the view they had previously taken as to the interpretation of the position but that every effort must be made to avoid a situation such as that described by the Secretary of State for the Colonies whereby it became impossible to introduce the new Constitution into Ceylon.

(b) If Mr. Senanayake's interpretation was adopted, there would still be a safeguard against discriminatory franchise legislation, for under the draft Constitution the Parliament of Ceylon would be debarred from making:—

"any law rendering persons of any community or religion liable to disabilities or restrictions to which persons of other communities or religions are not made liable, or conferring upon persons of any community or religion any privileges

---

[1] Mr Arthur Henderson.

or advantages which are not conferred on persons of other communities or religions."

If, therefore, discriminatory franchise legislation were passed, a decision of the Court could be obtained that it was null and void.

It was suggested that this did not provide an equivalent safeguard to the reserve powers of the Governor. There would be delay in obtaining a decision of the Court and no certainty what that decision would be. Against this, it was argued that if a law was in fact clearly discriminatory the Governor might well be prepared to exercise the Royal power of veto against it.

The Committee:—

(3) Invited the Secretary of State for the Colonies and the Parliamentary Under-Secretary of State for India to prepare for the concurrence of the Chairman a draft telegram to the Secretary of State for India explaining the view of the Committee that:—

(a) it was most desirable to avoid action whcih could be regarded by Mr. Senanayake as letting him down;

(b) if it was agreed that reserve powers should not be exercised in regard to franchise Bills, the remaining safeguards, as indicated in the discussion, should by themselves still provide sufficient assurance against legislation in Ceylon on franchise matters that would discriminate against minorities.

# 358   CO 537/1675, no 64                                    12 Apr 1946

## [Franchise]: outward unnumbered telegram from Mr Henderson to Lord Pethick-Lawrence reporting the recommendations of the Cabinet Colonial Affairs Committee

Following for Lord Pethick-Lawrence from Mr. Henderson. Your telegram Misc. 13 of the 17th [sic][1] April for Monteath.

1. Question of revised interpretation of Report to meet Senanayake's view was considered yesterday afternoon by Colonial Affairs Committee which I attended.[2]

2. Secretary of State for the Colonies said that he fully understood difficulties felt by you and Viceroy in revising assurance in relation to franchise given to Government of India and deeply regretted necessity for raising the question. But for Ceylon point was of crucial importance and if it was not conceded all hope of acceptance of proposed Constitution must be abandoned. Senanayake was the only moderate leader of sufficient stature to carry the new constitution through and it was politically impossible for him to withdraw from the position he had taken up and to co-operate with His Majesty's Government in maintaining interpretation on which your assurance to Government of India was based.

3. Without Senanayake's co-operation, power in Ceylon would undoubtedly fall into the hands of extremists, and all that both His Majesty's Government and Ceylon stood to gain by the success of the new Constitution would be lost. Effect on world opinion, which has been impressed by recent developments in Ceylon as an earnest

---

[1] Not printed but the date should read 7 Apr.                                    [2] See 357.

of His Majesty's Government's determination to grant self-government to dependent territories as soon as qualified, would be disastrous, as would effect on dependent territories emerging towards self-government which have looked to Ceylon as the example they should follow.

4. The Committee were impressed by the safeguards which the Constitution will in any event contain. These will be as follows: (1) A clause will give effect to paragraph 242 (iii) of the Soulbury Report, the result of which will be that laws imposing disabilities or conferring privileges on one community or religion and not on others would be invalid. (2) It would be the duty of the Governor to refuse assent under the Constitution to a bill which he was advised was invalid on the ground that it infringed the clause referred to in (1). (3) In the last resort it would be competent for His Majesty's Government if they deem it necessary to take steps for the amendment of the Constitution.

5. The Committee consider that these safeguards are sufficient to cover all reasonable requirements of the Government of India in this matter, and, while in no way minimizing your difficulties and those of Viceroy *vis-à-vis* Government of India, Committee therefore recommend that His Majesty's Government should accept Senanayake's interpretation. Committee trust that in all the circumstances you will feel able to reconsider your decision. My own personal opinion is that in the light of paragraph 4 resultant position is not unsatisfactory.

6. Shall be grateful for earliest possible reply.

## 359   CO 537/1675, no 65                                          16 Apr 1946
[Franchise]: inward telegram (reply) no Misc 19 from Lord Pethick-Lawrence to Mr Henderson on safeguards for the Indian population

Following from Secretary of State for India for Mr. Henderson.

Your telegram unnumbered of 12th April.[1]

Ceylon. If it is quite clear that provision (I) in your paragraph (4) will be included in the constitution and you are satisfied that it will be applicable to franchise and that any law prescribing different franchise for rest of population than that for Indians will thereupon be invalid I agree that position is safeguarded. It seems to me however that if this is effect of that provision it is as much at variance with Senanayake's speech as my original assurance to India. Senanayake's statement is that the "only restriction on full self government will be power to reserve bills relating to certain classes of matter which subject to minor qualification do not include franchise." I understand this to be based on 242 (II) of Soulbury Report which S. regards as overriding 242 (III) and (IV) and I should have thought that protection of Indian franchise under 242 (III) would be as inconsistent with his speech as with protection under 242 (IV). Can I be assured that Senanayake is willing to stand for provision in paragraph 4 (I) of your telegram and accepts that it is applicable to franchise? Moreover, strictly speaking 4 (I) of your telegram would not apply to a bill enfranchising all communities and religions except Indians since it applies only to legislation positively imposing a disability or a privilege on one community while case in point would be imposing a privilege on all communities except one.

---

[1] See 358.

**360** CO 537/1675, no 72                                        18 Apr 1946

[Franchise]: outward unnumbered telegram (reply) from Mr Henderson to Lord Pethick-Lawrence on safeguards for the Indian population

Following for Lord Pethick-Lawrence from Mr. Henderson. Your telegram Miscellaneous 19 of 16th April.[1]

Secretary of State for Colonies is able to assure me that provision in respect of (I)
in paragraph 4 of my telegram unnumbered of 12th April will be included in
Constitution Order-in-Council for Ceylon, since this is the main safeguard for *all*
minority communities in Ceylon and an essential provision in the Soulbury
Commission's recommendations on which the new Constitution for Ceylon is to be
based. Proposed text which has been before Colonial Affairs Committee is as
follows:—

*Legislative powers and procedure*

28 (1)  Subject to the provision of this Order, Parliament shall have power to make
laws for the peace, order and good government of the Island.

(2)  No such law shall—

(a)  prohibit or restrict the free exercise of any religion; or

(b)  make persons of any community or religion liable to disabilities or
restrictions to which persons of other communities or religions are not made
liable; or

(c)  confer on persons of any community or religion any privilege or advantage
which is not conferred on persons of other communities or religions; or

(d)  alter the constitution of any religious body except with the consent of the
governing authority of that body;

provided that in any case where a religious body is incorporated by law no such
alteration shall be made except at the request of the governing authority of that
body.

(3)  Any law made in contravention of sub-section (2) of this Section shall, to the
extent of such contravention be void.

2.  As explained in (2) in paragraph 4 of my telegram of 12th April[2] it would be the
Governor's duty to refuse assent to any Bill which he is advised is *ultra vires* the
Constitution in any respect.

3.  Colonial Office point out that portion of Senanayake's speech referred to was
directed towards the powers which the Ceylon Government would possess under the
new Constitution to enact legislation on certain matters which the Soulbury
Commission had, in his view, laid down as coming within the category of internal
affairs and he was concerned to emphasise that there would be no reservation as to
franchise and other subjects mentioned.

4.  This does not, in Hall's view, however, suggest that Senanayake contemplated
that legislation which was *ultra vires* the Constitution would have to be assented to
by the Governor and, indeed, in the record of a Conference in Ceylon at Nuwara Eliya

---

[1] See 359.                                                      [2] See 358.

on the 23rd January, it was specifically mentioned that he, Senanayake, agreed that the Governor must have power to withhold his assent if advised by the Attorney-General (see paragraph 403 of Soulbury Report) that a Bill is invalid.

5.  Hall considers however that it would be quite impossible at this stage to seek from Senanayake assurance you desire since to do so would involve disclosure to him of a commitment by His Majesty's Government to Government of India of which he is unaware on this matter which is one of the greatest delicacy in political circles in Ceylon. Such disclosure would almost certainly give rise to the same situation as that envisaged in paragraphs 2 and 3 of my previous telegram of 12th April.

6.  He hopes therefore that you will feel able to accept above assurances.

7.  To my mind to impose a disability or privilege on all communities except one would constitute a breach of either sub-clause (b) or (c) of Clause 28 (2), and this seems to meet point in last sentence of your telegram.

8.  Please telegraph reply most urgently.[3]

---

[3] Pethick-Lawrence accepted these assurances on 26 Apr (CO 537/1675, no 79).

**361**  CO 54/988/4, no 8, enclosure a                         22 Apr 1946
[Indian labour]: letter from M S Aney[1] to Sir H Moore citing the acquisition by the Government of Ceylon of the Knavesmire Estate in Kegalle district as an example of discrimination against Indian plantation labour

The Government of India desire me to bring to your notice certain matters arising out of the acquisition by the Government of Ceylon of the Knavesmire Estate, Undugoda. It is understood that the estate is to be subdivided and allotted to landless Ceylonese under the Land Development Ordinance. In pursuance of this scheme the resident labourers, almost all Indians, numbering about 400 have been given notice of discharge. It does not appear from the facts so far known to us that the action contemplated is inevitable. The acquisition is not for the purpose of relieving congestion or slum conditions in adjoining area or any such justifiable reason. It is learnt that some attempt is being made by the Department of Labour to find these labourers work on other estates.

2.  Several of the Indian labourers now under notice of discharge have been born on the estate itself and have lived there all their lives some of them have lived on this estate for over 30 years; some have no contact left with India and know no other home than Ceylon. Yet few or none of them possess or can establish by proof domicile or origin in Ceylon. It is understood that this qualification of domicile or origin is insisted upon before any person is considered for an allotment though the Land Development Ordinance itself does not appear to require any such qualification. The result is that Indian labourers resident on the estate who have an abiding interest in and have no other home than Ceylon are generally deprived altogether of all opportunity to share in the development and future working of this estate for which no one has better claims than they. This one more instance of the iniquitable and harsh manner in which narrow definitions of the word "Ceylonese" in various

---

[1] Representative of the GOI in Ceylon.

statutes in Ceylon have discriminated against the welfare of Indians permanently settled in Ceylon.

3.  The proposed measure has roused considerable resentment in Ceylon among Indians on estates and elsewhere; it has greatly agitated public opinion in India and has been the subject of references in the Indian Legislature. This measure is regarded as discriminatory in flavour and especially aimed against Indian labourers. It involves disturbing many long-settled Indian families and seeks to find land and homes for certain sections of the population by depriving other sections equally entitled to the consideration of the Government of their homes. It is even feared that it may be only a prelude to more such measures which will prove to be a convenient handle for the eviction and harrasment of Indian labourers in Ceylon and militate against their assimilation as part and parcel of the nation which the Commission on Constitutional Reforms for Ceylon found to be the desired objective of the Government of Ceylon.

4.  While pointing out the inequitable and peremptory aspects of these proceedings, the Government of India feel that particularly now when both the Governments sincerely wish for an amicable settlement by negotiation of the outstanding problems of the status of Indians in Ceylon a measure of this type is likely to prejudice the relations between the two countries and react adversely on the chances of such settlement. Even though the Government of Ceylon be anxious to proceed with its development scheme it is desirable that they select for acquisition lands and plots where the interests of the estate labourers will not be involved till the issues involving the status and rights of Indians are negotiated and settled. They trust that in view of the serious repercussions of the proposed measure the Government of Ceylon will not think it fit to pursue it.

# 362   CO 54/988/4, no 8, enclosure c                        25 May 1946

## [Indian labour]: letter (reply) from Sir R Drayton to M S Aney refuting the claim of discrimination

I have the honour to refer to the message from the Government of India which you gave to His Excellency on the 22nd April 1946.[1]

2.  I should explain that it has been the policy for several years past for Government to purchase land where Crown land is not available in Revenue Officer's districts for the purpose of allocating an economic extent of land to villagers who have no land or who have such small undivided shares of land as make it impossible for them to earn a livelihood from agricultural pursuits. The Kegalle district has no further Crown land for allocation of this purpose. On the other hand the district is one in which the sale of Crown land to estates and the sale of private land also to estates has rendered it peculiarly short of land for the genuine needs of villagers and, following the above policy of providing living space for the indigenous population, the acquisition of estates for the purposes stated above has been proceeding since 1939.

3.  Knavesmire Estate was first proposed for acquisition for village expansion on January 24, 1944. From this date up to about November 8, 1945, on which date the acquisition was completed, the Estate was visited by various Government officers and

---

[1] See 361.

the purpose of the acquisition, namely for village expansion was, it is understood, well known to the labourers employed on the Estate.

4. It is not proposed to divide the estate into allotments. It will be conducted as an estate for a short period by the Assistant Government Agent, Kegalle, and will form a training ground for the allottees selected as workers on the estate; but the ultimate intention is to run the estate on a cooperative basis for the benefit of the selected allottees.

5. Selections of allottees were made from applicants from certain prescribed villages within a definite radius of the estate and included the village in which Knavesmire is situated. Those who are eligible for selection are those whom the Land Development Ordinance contemplates both in the general principles of the Ordinance as well as in the particular reference to land for village expansion contemplated in section 8 dealing with the mapping out of a village; and it is to be noted that a Ceylon domicile of origin and permanent residence in one of the prescribed villages are necessary requisites under the law for consideration of an application. There has been no bar against an application from any one for consideration of his claim for selection as an allottee. However, even if applicants satisfied the Investigating Officer as to domicile or origin and permanent residence in a village, their claims for selection had to be considered along with other applicants who were eligible and suitable for selection and no promise could be held out that they would be given prior consideration above those villagers who were equally or more entitled to first selection.

6. On March 30, 1946, notice was given by publication throughout the estate and at muster to the labourers to quit the estate by the 1st May 1946. On further instructions issued by the Land Commissioner fresh written notice has been issued to each of the workers on the estate to quit the estate by the 1st June 1946, and work is being given to them for the extended period of the notice. They were also informed that work would be found for them on the neighbouring estates. No approach was made by the labourers to ask for such employment.

7. The estate was also inspected by an Inspector of Labour on the 12th April 1946, to register the names of Indian labourers with a view to finding them employment elsewhere. The labourers were not present although they were instructed to come to the factory office for registration. Twelve estates in the vicinity had agreed to take on between them the Knavesmire labour force and the Inspector of Labour informed the Kanganies and the Thalaivar that these estates were willing to give employment to the labourers at any time.

8. There has been no violation of the legal procedure relating to employment and discharge of labourers on estates. It is, of course, not possible to select lands for acquisition on which no Indian labour is employed. On other estates which have already been acquired, where both Ceylonese and Indian labour have been employed, the same procedure has been adopted and no claim has hitherto been put forward that the mere fact that a person was born on an estate enabled him to establish a right to preferential treatment by way of selection as an allottee under these schemes for providing land for landless villagers.

9. I trust that a perusal of the history of the matter which I have given above will satisfy you that, in the application of this well-established policy of acquiring land for landless villagers, there has been no discrimination against any labourer on the ground that he is an Indian.

**363** CO 537/2214, no 1 7 June 1946

[Constitution]: letter from Sir H Moore to Sir G Gater on proposals to inaugurate the new constitution

Senanayake and Sir Oliver Goonetilleke came to see me yesterday on the subject of local celebrations to commemorate the inauguration of the new Constitution. The matter has been considered by the Board of Ministers in a general way and it was decided that some special action should be taken to mark the event. A Sub-Committee consisting of all the ministerial members of the Board *plus* Goonetilleke has been appointed to go into details and make recommendations.

From my talk yesterday I understand that the general idea is to invite representatives from the Dominions, India, Southern Rhodesia, Burma and Malaya to attend the inauguration ceremony and simultaneously with this to stage a series of semi-official and sporting events which would spread the celebrations over anything between a fortnight and a month. For example it has been suggested that Ceylon might be the venue next year for the World Co-operative Conference and the World Press Conference. I understand the possibility of these two events is likely to be explored through semi-official channels. The possibility of arranging athletic and cricket contests, in which teams from India and Australia, and possibly even further afield, would be invited to take part, is also under examination, as also a proposal to organize a big Buddhist Rally and possibly a Food Exhibition.

Goonetilleke is the moving spirit behind this and I believe broached it to you tentatively in London. Apart from the strictly official celebrations, which would involve some Government expenditure as Government representatives would of course be the guests of the Government of Ceylon, he believes that most of the other activities I have mentioned would either finance themselves by the profits from the gates etc. or would be covered by private benefactions and hospitality or concessions made by interested business firms. I think he hopes in this way indirectly to stimulate interest in Ceylon as a post-war tourist resort.

The above should give you a general picture of the lines on which they are planning, but of course the central ceremony around which all these other activities are being planned is the formal inauguration of the new Parliament. While they hope that in any case the Secretary of State for the Colonies would be able to be their guest, they are most anxious that if possible either the King and Queen themselves, or, failing that, Princess Elizabeth and her sister should be invited to perform the opening ceremony. Failing that they wondered if the Prime Minister could possibly arrange to attend.

All this is clearly a very ambitious programme, but I am sure that if it were possible for some member of the Royal family to attend it would have an excellent political effect for Ceylon hospitality is proverbial. You know our difficulties about giving any fixed date for the meeting of the new Parliament, but the best estimate we can give at the moment would be the end of May or early June. I believe the King and Queen and the two Princesses are going to South Africa in the Spring but I am not sure what the actual dates are. I suppose it would be too much to hope that they could go Home *via* Ceylon or failing that allow the two Princesses to make a deviation. In many ways I believe their presence would make a tremendous appeal. I am afraid I am quite uninstructed as to how to set about this business and I must leave it to you to say what approach, if any, should be made. But I promised to write and put you in the picture since Goonetilleke will, on arrival, certainly want to talk it over with you and I have also undertaken, in the light of such conversations, to discuss it further personally myself with you and the Secretary of State during my leave.[1]

---

[1] In the event the UK was represented at the inaugural celebrations by the Duke and Duchess of Gloucester.

## 364    CO 54/988/4, no 26B, enclosure 1                    12 June 1946
## [Indian labour]: letter from M S Aney to Sir H Moore conveying a further representation from the Government of India on matters connected with the Knavesmire Estate

With reference to letter No. CF.17/46, dated 25th May 1946,[1] addressed by the Chief Secretary to me in reply to the message from the Government of India which I conveyed to your Excellency on the 22nd of April,[2] the Government of India have desired me to address you further.

2. Although there may be no formal irregularity in the procedure adopted as stated at paragraph 8 of the letter under reference, the Government of India do not consider this incident free from discrimination against Indians. They are unable to agree that the use of the machinery of the Land Development Ordinance in this case resulting in the eviction of hundreds of long-settled Indians from the estate is either just, fair or unavoidably demanded by circumstances. If the evicted labourers were Sinhalese with no homes other than on the acquired estate the Ceylon Government's action would be shown to result in the transfer of the difficulties from one class of its subjects, to another. The Government of India also feels that in that event the Ceylon Government would probably not have proceeded with the acquisition. The argument that estate labourers are not villagers and the insistence on domicile of origin in respect of evicted Indians as a necessary condition for becoming allottees merely beg the question which is, who among the Ceylon Indians have in fact by reason of their long residence, history and abiding interest in Ceylon, the right to be treated in every respect on equal terms with the indigenous peasantry and prejudge the very issue which is outstanding between the two countries. The Government of India cannot accept the view that the present action does not involve discrimination and serious hardship to Indian labourers, particularly to those among them who under any reasonable agreement could claim full status as Ceylonese by virtue of their long residence and abiding interest in the country.

3. The Government of India were not aware that, as the Hon'ble Mr. Senanayake is reported to have informed the press, over 2000 labourers have already been evicted from the estates by State action for reasons unconnected with the economic position of the planting industries. This makes it all the more desirable that further large-scale evictions by Government action should be postponed until the question of the status of Ceylon Indians has been settled amicably by negotiations. The Government of India trust that these negotiations are not now far off and that

---

[1] See 362.                                                            [2] See 361.

therefore the Ceylon Government would be willing to postpone action in the present case. Even from a purely humanitarian point of view, the displacement of such a large number of long-settled Indian labourers makes the scheme particularly subversive of amicable relations between the two countries at the present juncture.

# 365    CO 54/986/13, no 24           17 June 1946
## [European civil servants]: despatch from Sir H Moore to Mr Hall on conditions of service. *Enclosures* 1 and 3

I have the honour to forward, for your information, copies of a letter[1] and a note sent to the Chief Secretary by certain European Officers of the Ceylon Civil Service who do not enjoy the right to retire under Section 88 of the Ceylon (State Council) Order in Council, 1931. The note sets out the position of these officers as they see it in view of the forthcoming constitutional changes and seeks enlightenment on five specific points.

2. I also enclose a copy of a letter addressed by the Chief Secretary[2] to the chief signatory to the Note, together with a copy of the enclosure thereto in which the Chief Secretary sets out in the form of a memorandum such information as it is possible to give locally on the various questions raised in the Note.

3. Since some of the points on which information is sought by the signatories are primarily matters for the Colonial Office, I shall be grateful for your confirmation of the views expressed in the Chief Secretary's memorandum.

### Enclosure 1 to 365: note by European officers

There are eleven European Civil Servants appointed after July, 1928 (and one other who by absence and return to Ceylon now comes within the same category for retirement purposes) who are faced with the problem of deciding whether to exercise the right to retire within two years of the first meeting of Parliament under the New Constitution, *or* to remain on the new terms of Service thereby losing *any* right to retire on a pension until the age of 55 is reached. It is respectfully submitted that the Secretary of State and Ceylon Government should furnish as much information as quickly as possible to these officers to enable them to make a considered decision.

2. In the first place, the officers concerned are naturally anxious to know whether those who are likely to compose the new Government of Ceylon wish to retain their services; and, if so, for what type of work, on what terms as regards salary, allowances, passages, leave, etc., and for what period. They appreciate that a final and comprehensive answer to these enquiries cannot be given at this stage but they venture to hope that the best possible reply will be given as soon as possible.

3. Secondly, will those European Civil Servants who choose to remain in the Ceylon Civil Service retain their status as members of the "Colonial Administrative Service" on the New Constitution coming into operation? Presumably they will.

---

[1] The letter, dated 10 May, 1946, is not reproduced here. It was signed by C H Hartwell, S M Duff, A K J Henderson, A R Macdonald, C E Tilney, J W H O'Regan and D W B Baron.
[2] Drayton's letter, enclosure 2 and dated 14 June 1946, is not reproduced here.

4.  Thirdly, arising from the last point, will European Civil Servants who remain in service in Ceylon continue to be considered by the Colonial Office for appointment to other Colonies on transfer or promotion? At present a Civil Servant may reasonably aspire to many of the highest staff posts or even a governorship in other Colonies. Will such prospects be diminished, or cease entirely, on the Ceylon Government assuming full independent control of the public service?

5.  Fourthly, as a corollary to the above, will annual confidential reports continue to be furnished to the Secretary of State in respect of such officers: and, if so, by whom?

6.  Fifthly, is it proposed to offer European Civil Servants transfers to other Colonies *before* the two-year period expires? It is submitted that some indication of the intention on this point is necessary at a very early date; if the matter is left in doubt until near the end of the two-year period, it will place those Civil Servants who are faced with the necessity of deciding whether to retire in a very difficult position, for the majority of them could not contemplate retirement unless assured of other employment to supplement their pension.

7.  A number of European Civil Servants have been afforded interviews at the Colonial Office on this subject, and some of them have received the impression that the Colonial Office view is that an officer who wishes to leave Ceylon at this stage must be out of sympathy with current political developments, and is therefore not likely to prove useful in other territories, where similar evolution towards autonomy must be expected in the next ten or twenty years. It is hoped that this impression is mistaken; but it may be useful to record very shortly the reasons why many European officers desire transfer from Ceylon; they are:—

(i) The Ceylonization of the Public Service, particularly of non-technical staff, has been the declared policy of the Ministers from the inception of the present Constitution. This seems to the writers a natural and understandable policy, but it is one which necessarily implies the progressive elimination of the European Officer. Should the Ministers decide to retain them, this will be on account of the difficulty of replacing them by Ceylonese Officers in the immediate future rather than the desire to retain them indefinitely. It will be hard for European officers in these circumstances to escape the feeling that they are out of place and unwanted.

(ii) Further development towards complete autonomy must be expected with the next decade, and it is quite impossible to foresee what the conditions of public service will then be. An officer who has twenty years or so of service before him must in ordinary prudence give full consideration to this point.

(iii) Up till now the Secretary of State for the Colonies has recognized that if a European Officer is to play a proper part in the development of a Colony proceeding towards self-government, he should be assured by adequate safeguards of the preservation of his salary and conditions of service. The Secretary of State has authorized the certification of the leave passage vote year after year, when it was deleted by the State Council; and his pronouncements have made it clear that he will not permit any radical alteration in basic terms of service. It does not seem possible under the form of Constitution contemplated for Ceylon that protection of this kind can continue; and there is an evident danger that the European Officers in Ceylon will not enjoy that degree of security which exists in other Colonial territories and has always been recognized as one of the main attractions of Government employment.

8.   It will be appreciated that this memorandum implies no lack of sympathy with current political developments, which are recognized as natural and inevitable.


Enclosure 3 to 365: memorandum by Sir R Drayton

This Memorandum should be read in conjunction with the Note forwarded to the Honourable the Chief Secretary on the 10th of May, 1946, by certain European Civil Servants and any references made refer to the paragraphs of that Note.

1.   The importance of the decision which these officers have to take is fully appreciated and also their desire to have as much information as early as possible as to their future prospects before it is taken. But, as will appear from succeeding paragraphs of this Memorandum, it would not appear competent for either the Secretary of State or the Ceylon Government to give a definite answer now to some of the questions put.

2.   On the general question as to whether the new Government of Ceylon will wish to retain the services of those European members of the Ceylon Civil Service who are prepared to remain here and not exercise their option of retirement under the Order in Council, the answer in the view of the Governor and his advisers is in the affirmative. So far as their general terms of service are concerned they will, so far as can be foreseen, remain the same as at present, and in view of the duties and responsibilities of the Public Services Commission that is to be appointed under section 60 of the Order in Council and the provisions of section 29 (2) (b) of the Order in Council under which any discriminatory Bill is *ipso facto* invalid, there would not appear to be any danger of European officers who are now members of the Ceylon Civil Service as at present constituted being treated differently from Ceylonese members of the same Service. So far as their existing passage rights are concerned, to which reference is made in paragraph 7 (iii) of the Note, His Excellency has been informed on good authority that it is most unlikely that the Leave and Passage Vote will be deleted by the State Council in the 1946/47 Budget. If, as he hopes and believes, this proves to be the case it may be taken as an indication of the attitude of the new Parliament in this matter.

3.   As regards questions 2, 3 and 4 contained in paragraphs 3, 4 and 5 of the note, the answers, subject to confirmation by the Secretary of State, are in the affirmative.

4.   In reply to paragraph 5, Annual Confidential Reports will be furnished to the Secretary of State by the Governor. Whether such Reports will be furnished to the Governor with a recommendation from the Public Services Commission (which under the Order in Council is responsible for and is charged with the duty of making recommendations for local promotions, etc.) or through the Permanent Secretary of the Ministry in which the officer is serving direct to the Governor is a matter which will be further examined in the light of the administrative procedure which Mr. Collins is now drawing up.

5.   The question contained in paragraph 6 of the Note is one which can only be answered by the Secretary of State. It should, however, be appreciated that since the Colonial Office is only on rare occasions notified by the Colonial Governments concerned of impending vacancies it may be difficult, if not impossible, for the Colonial Office to formulate a forward plan for offering transfer to Ceylon European Civil Servants before the two-year period expires. Those European officers who have

applied for transfer or have been recommended for transfer on promotion will have had their names noted for consideration with candidates from other Colonies when suitable vacancies occur. There is always keen competition for vacancies at a salary of more than £1,000 a year and it is unlikely that the Colonial Office will be in a position to give the signatories any guidance at this stage as to their individual chances of success. The above statement is of course subject to official confirmation by the Secretary of State.

6. No official information has been received by the Ceylon Government of the views attributed to Members of the Colonial Office in paragraph 7. As will be observed from paragraph 2 of this Memorandum it would appear unlikely that there will be any movement under the new Constitution to eliminate European Government Servants as a class. The prospects of individual officers who are willing to remain and have the necessary ability and inclination to conform to the new conditions would therefore appear to be good. Ceylon administrative scales are generally higher than those obtaining in other Colonies and a glance at the staff list will reveal that the number of senior officers approaching the age of retirement is such that the immediate prospects of local promotion are distinctly good.

# 366 CO 54/988/4, no 31                                    1 July 1946
## [Indian labour]: report by Mr Senanayake to the State Council on the Knavesmire acquisition and related matters[1]

It is a matter of common knowledge that, for the last ten years, it has been the policy of Government that economic extents of land should be allotted wherever possible to landless peasants and large sums of money have been, from time to time, voted by the State Council for this purpose. If Crown land is not available, the necessary land is purchased either by agreement or compulsorily under the Land Acquisition Ordinance, the purchase of land for village expansion being a public purpose within the meaning of that Ordinance.

It is also a matter of common knowledge that the persons to whom land is allotted under schemes for village expansion are persons whom the Land Development Ordinance contemplates as genuine villagers, that is to say, permanent residents in a village who have a Ceylon domicile of origin. Estate labourers have never been regarded as falling within the category of villagers because they do not, in fact, take part in the life of the village as a community. This fact is recognised in the provision of the Village Communities Ordinance that a labourer (including a Kangany) employed and resident on an Estate has no vote in the election of a member of a Village Committee. The circumstances in which Indian Estate labour comes to the Island from India, the extent of the protection by the Government of India which it enjoys, the association with India which so many of the individual Indian estate labourers maintain and the right of repatriation to India enjoyed under the laws of the Island are consistent with the view that the general body of resident Indian estate labour cannot properly be considered to be genuine villagers.

2. The Kegalla District has no Crown land available for village expansion. On the

---

[1] cf 361, 362 & 364.

other hand the District is one in which the sale of Crown land to estates and the sale of private land by villagers also to estates has rendered the District peculiarly short of land for the genuine needs of villagers. On an average only 1/20th of an acre of land is available to each villager and it has been reported that there are 1,315 landless families in this area. The area is therefore one in which acquisition of estates has proceeded from 1939 and must proceed if the accepted policy is to be maintained.

3.   Knavesmire Estate in the Kegalla District was first proposed for acquisition for village expansion on the 24th January, 1944, on a proposal made by the Assistant Government Agent, Kegalla, for acquisition of estates for this purpose in the financial year 1944/45. The Estate was the property of Mr. E.L. Ibrahim Lebbe Marikkar Hadjiar, a Muslim of the Kalutara District, who owned large extents of land in various parts of the Island and had purchased this Estate two years previously from an European Company. Knavesmire Estate is 772 acres in extent and consists of tea and rubber. While the proprietor did not formally consent to the acquisition, he did not oppose it.

4.   From January, 1944, on or up to about the 8th November, 1945, on which date the acquisition was completed by reference to Court, Knavesmire Estate was visited by the Assistant Government Agent, Kegalla, and officers of the Land Commissioner's Department and other departments and the purpose of the acquisition, namely, the placing of landless villagers on the Estate was well-known to the Superintendent and Staff of the Estate and to the workers also.

5.   Possession of the estate was taken by the Assistant Government Agent, Kegalla, on the 6th December, 1945, and, pending a scheme of development for the placing of the selected landless villagers on the Estate, Knavesmire Estate was administered as an Estate with the existing staff. Subsequently the Superintendent and Assistant Superintendent were replaced after due notice by a new Superintendent and an Assistant Superintendent selected from a large number of applicants.

6.   Meanwhile the Assistant Government Agent proceeded to make selections from applicants from villages within a definite radius of the Estate. These villages were those of:—

Pilawela
Rangalla
Wiyalapitiya
Diyahitiyawela
Yatideria
Uduwa
Tungago
Kendewa          } in Three Korales
Narangala
Lawala & Yakkalla
Uruniweli
Wegolla
Welatuduwa
Punahela

Alawatura        } in Beligal Korale
Pittagama

Due notice was given of the date and time of selection and of the purpose for which selection was being made by publication in the villages concerned through the Headmen.

7. It was estimated that 275 persons should be selected. This number was determined by the number of adult workers necessary for the daily and yearly normal work on the Estate, taking into consideration that, in addition to the Head of the family, some of the wives and the older children would seek employment in addition to the selected allottees, bringing the number to about 400, the strength of the labour force on the Estate at the time of acquisition.

All these steps were taken openly and it was well known that the existing labour force would be replaced when the new allottees were placed on the Estate. 243 were selected out of the total of 275 proposed. No applications were received from Indians.

8. On the 30th March, 1946, notice was given by publication throughout the Estate and at muster to the 400 labourers on Knavesmire Estate to quit the Estate on the 1st May, 1946. They were also informed that every attempt would be made to find work for them on neighbouring estates and the new Superintendent appointed by the Crown was ready and willing to find them this employment as was disclosed subsequently by the Commissioner of Labour. Labour was in great demand and all the labour force of Knavesmire Estate could have been accommodated within the month of notice on other Estates in the vicinity. No attempt was made by the labour force to seek or ask for help for such employment. On further instructions issued by the Land Commissioner, the Assistant Government Agent, Kegalla, issued fresh written notice to each of the workers on the Estate to quit the Estate on the 1st June, 1946, and work was given to them for the extended period of the notice. The Inspector of Labour at Avissawella reported that the following estates were willing to take on the Knavesmire Estate labour force:—

| | | |
|---|---|---|
| 1. | Dehiowita | 55 |
| 2. | Kegalessa | 20 |
| 3. | Dewalakanda | 35 |
| 4. | Dabar | 25 |
| 5. | Walpella | 30 |
| 6. | Kosgahakanda | 30 |
| 7. | Udabage | 50 |
| 8. | Homingford | 50 |
| 9. | Noori | 100 |
| 10. | Gelencorse | 30 |
| 11. | Sapumalkanda | 50 |
| 12. | Ederapolla | 20 |
| | | 495 |

The total labour force on Knavesmire was 574, inclusive of infants and children. The working labour force amounted approximately to 400.

He also reported that, when he visited Knavesmire Estate on 12th April, 1946, to register the names of the Indian labourers with a view to finding them employment elsewhere, the labourers were not present although they had been instructed to come to the factory office for registration. He took down the number of labourers on the Estate and informed the Kanganies and the Thalaivar that the above estates were willing to give employment to the labourers at any time. He states that they did not appear to take any interest in this information.

9. It is not proposed to divide this estate into allotments. The estate will be conducted as an estate for a short period by the Assistant Government Agent, Kegalla, as a training ground for the allottees selected as workers on the estate, the ultimate intention being to cause the estate to be managed co-operatively for the benefit of the selected allottees.

10. There has been no violation of law or procedure relating to the employment and discharge of labourers on estates. Nevertheless the Indian labourers have refused to leave the Estate and it has become necessary to take legal proceedings for their eviction. While such proceedings are pending the Indian labourers remain in the lines on the Estate but they cannot obviously be employed or provided with food by the Estate. They have been issued with ration cards and arrangements have been made for them to draw their rations from retail dealers in the neighbourhood. Their presence on the Estate impedes the working of the Estate and prevents the fulfilment of the lawful purpose for which the Estate was acquired but, short of yielding to force, the Government is doing everything in its power to avoid being harsh in its attitude towards what is indisputably an illegal occupation.

11. Just as there has been no violation of law or procedure in regard to the employment and discharge of the Indian Estate labourers so also there has been nothing either illegal or novel in the acquisition for village expansion of the Estate in question.

12. What however, is novel is the preferential claim put forward by the Ceylon Indian Congress on behalf of the Indian labourers on the Estate which is that all families that have been on the Knavesmire Estate for more than five years should be included in the Scheme for which the Estate has been acquired. This is a claim which has never before been advanced on behalf of either Ceylonese or non-Ceylonese labour on an Estate which has been acquired for village expansion. Nor indeed has long residence or even birth on an Estate previously been asserted as the basis of a claim.

13. But the matter does not end there. Coupled with the demand in regard to the Knavesmire Estate the following demands are also made by the Ceylon Indian Congress:—

(a) franchise on a footing of equality with the rest of the population of the Island;
(b) comprehensive citizenship rights to all Indians on a test of 5 years residence and a declaration of intention to permanently settle in Ceylon;
(c) a workable arrangement for operation of such schemes as the Knavesmire Estate scheme in the future on other Estates;
(d) pending legal measures to secure franchise and civic rights, the suspension of all administrative actions that are discriminative in law or in practice against Ceylon Indians.

The Ceylon Indian Congress have informed the Government that the Hartal which they have called is direct action which they have been forced to take in order to secure these demands before the new Constitution is inaugurated and that, if it is not possible to settle the questions by negotiations, the Hartal will continue. No attempt is made (or indeed could be made) to justify the Hartal on the ground that it is in furtherance of a trade dispute.

14. Anxious as my colleagues and I are to maintain good relations with India we cannot conceal from the State Council or the Country the fact that those who claim

to be part of the permanent population of this Island are endeavouring to compel a change in the law of the land, including the new Constitution which has already been granted, by taking a course of action which must inevitably not only do injury to the economic interests of this Island as a whole and of those who take part in the Hartal in particular, but also constitute a constant threat to law and order and embitter the relations between Indians and Ceylonese.

15.  Nevertheless the Ceylon Indian Congress have informed the Government that the Hartal will continue unless negotiations are begun in regard to all their demands.

It is the desire of my colleagues and myself that negotiations with the Government of India on the question of Indo–Ceylon relations should begin at the earliest practicable opportunity. Apart however from the question of beginning any such negotiations in the atmosphere created by the action of the Ceylon Indian Congress, I do not feel that such negotiations can begin under the present circumstances. With the new Constitution imminent, it is not desirable for the present Government to bind its successors in so vital a matter nor do I think that there is a Government in India at the present moment which could give an undertaking to do so and so satisfy this Government that there was no danger of an agreement successfully negotiated being subsequently repudiated.

16.  I have found it necessary to make this Report to the State Council in order to correct, so far as possible, some of the misrepresentations which are being circulated in this country and in India and also to make it apparent why this Government is not disposed to yield to the pressure which is being improperly exerted by the Ceylon Indian Congress. I trust that everyone, having the interests of Ceylon at heart, will be patient and tolerant and will refrain from doing or saying anything to exacerbate the present difficult situation in the hope that the Ceylon Indian Congress will realise how inimical to the best interests of those whom they profess to champion is the policy of direct action on which they have so deliberately embarked.


# 367   CO 54/986/13, no 25                              30 July 1946
## [European civil servants]: despatch (reply) from Mr Hall to Sir H Moore

I have the honour to acknowledge the receipt of your despatch, confidential (2), of the 17th of June,[1] enclosing a copy of a memorandum by certain European officers of the Ceylon Civil Service regarding their position in view of the forthcoming constitutional changes in Ceylon. I confirm the general position as stated in the Chief Secretary's letter of the 14th of June and its enclosure, copies of which accompanied your despatch.

2.  With regard to paragraph 6 of the officers' memorandum and paragraph 5 of the Chief Secretary's reply, I would explain that as regards the *re-employment* of officers who have decided to retire on special terms within the two-year period, it would not be possible to give any assurance that they would be re-employed in the

---

[1] See 365.

Colonial Service or in other posts under the control of the Secretary of State for the Colonies.

3. Apart from this, whilst I agree that officers who are willing to accept transfer can be given no assurance other than that they will be considered for appointments elsewhere in the Colonial Service if they so wish, I consider that they should be informed that if any of them were selected for other Colonial appointments *on transfer*, at any time from now on, and desired to accept, the Ceylon Government would raise no objection provided that the officers concerned did not occupy key posts for which no replacement was available. I shall be glad to learn whether you feel able to convey this intimation to the officers. Since suitable vacancies which would attract officers serving in Ceylon are rare, and the competition for them severe, it is not likely that I shall be in a position to offer many of the officers transfers but I do not think that it would be fair for the Ceylon Government to stand in an officer's way in present circumstances if he wished to continue in the Colonial Service outside Ceylon.

4. With regard to the first sentence of paragraph 7 of the memorandum, while it might of course be held that an officer who was out of sympathy with political developments in Ceylon might equally find it difficult to accommodate himself to similar developments which may take place elsewhere, I note with satisfaction that there is no question of this on the part of the signatories. I can assure them that the situation in respect of transfer on promotion is as stated in paragraph 5 of the Chief Secretary's note, and I assume that individual officers will record their wishes for consideration when their position in the Ceylon Civil Service becomes clearer. I am sure that it will be understood that no officer must interpret the undertaking to consider his wishes in regard to transfer as a guarantee that they will be met.

# 368 CO 852/569, no 46                                      5 Sept 1946
## 'Purchase of Ceylon products': memorandum by Sir O Goonetilleke for Mr Hall

[Before he submitted this memo, Goonetilleke had held preliminary discussions with the Ministry of Food (on tea and copra) and the Ministry of Supply (on rubber). Caine reported that although both ministries were prepared to consider Goonetilleke's representations, there was 'no chance whatever' of their meeting his full demands, except as a result of ministerial decisions on general political rather than ordinary purchasing principles. Goonetilleke was said to be emphatic about the whole of his requests being granted and on taking the issues involved to the highest levels. He had telegraphed personally to Ceylon expressing his intention to remain in London until his demands had been met and expressing considerable optimism that he would succeed. No formal submission on these issues had been made by Ceylon ministers and Caine emphasised that they were being advanced wholly on Goonetilleke's personal initiative and responsibility. On economic and financial grounds, Caine argued that it was 'quite impossible to justify the concession of all that Sir Oliver has asked for' (see 374 for Caine's detailed response). Ceylon, according to Caine, had suffered no less during the war than other colonial territories and 'incomparably less' than the UK: 'It is impossible not to feel that on balance Ceylon has contributed only barely her share towards the true costs of the war and is lucky not to be asked to contribute more'. Goonetilleke's argument that Ceylon was entitled to more generous treatment than Malaya in relation to rubber prices because her rubber industry had been exhausted during the war, ignored the enormous damage inflicted by enemy occupation in Malaya and other Far Eastern territories. Caine did not consider himself competent to express an opinion about the political issues which formed such a large part of Goonetilleke's presentation but he argued that if the decision went against Ceylon on economic grounds, the secretary of state should make it clear that Ceylon could expect no support on the political side (CO 852/569, minute by Caine, 15 Aug 1946). Sidebotham commented on the political questions involved. Specifically referring to the difficulties over the franchise issue and to Moore's warning about the danger of 'throwing Senanayake over' (see 353), Sidebotham minuted that it would be 'a major disaster' if Senanayake were to be replaced by Bandaranaike 'whose leanings are all towards Ceylon throwing in her lot with India'. Such a development might well mean the repudiation of the new constitution and would be 'wholly at variance' with the UK's strategic and other interests in Ceylon. Although arguing therefore that it was essential for HMG to avoid a situation in which Senanayake's opponents were given an opportunity of defeating him, Sidebotham agreed with Caine that an early decision was required on Goonetilleke's representations. The time had come for the secretary of state to intervene personally in an endeavour to persuade Goonetilleke that ' "the horse which he is backing just won't run" and what is more to hint that in the last event the secretary of state himself is not prepared to "back it" on the information before him, since he cannot consider Sir Oliver Goonetilleke's presentation of Ceylon gives a reasonable one' (*ibid*, minute by Sidebotham, 16 Aug 1946).]

I have the honour to address this communication to you with the request that you may be pleased to submit it for consideration to His Majesty's Government and obtain their decision on the important questions raised therein. The issues involved will have a profound effect on the economic and financial conditions of Ceylon and on the whole of her administration.

2.  I have come to London to negotiate on behalf of the Government of Ceylon with His Majesty's Government in regard to their purchase of the three main exports of Ceylon, namely, tea, coconut products and rubber. I have already submitted to you on behalf of my Government proposals in this respect which I consider fair and reasonable, taking into account the whole economy of Ceylon as affected by the Bulk Purchase Schemes introduced during the War. I have had several preliminary discussions on the Departmental level with the ministries concerned.

3.  The terms of my proposals briefly are:—

(a)  *Tea*. The present contract which expires at the end of this year should be renewed for a further period of five years at a price of 1/- per lb. above the current price. This offer is subject to the condition that should India decide at any time during the currency of the contract to remain outside the Bulk Purchase Scheme, then Ceylon should have the right to withdraw from it.

(b)  *Coconut products*. The present contract which is from [sic] a term of five years from 1st January, 1946, should be replaced by a fresh contract for ten years as from 1st January, 1947, at a price 50% above the current price.

(c)  *Rubber*. As an interim measure, the present contract which expires at the end of September, 1946, should be extended for another year at the current price, and the Government of Ceylon should be enabled to participate in the discussions on the future arrangements for purchase of rubber, which are due to take place with the American Government towards the end of the year.

(d)  *Cost of food subsidy*. Any loss in the Food Advance Account during the period 1st July, 1946, to 30th June, 1947, as the result of maintaining food prices at their present level should be reimbursed by His Majesty's Government.

4.  An essential requirement is that my proposals should be considered together. If I am obliged to accept a reduction on any one item, I would have to ask for amendments in other items in order to make good such reduction.

5.  In regard to the prices that I have asked for, I would stress the fact that *tea* will

continue to be in short supply for several years ahead. The supply of Java tea is unlikely to regain its pre-war level for the next three years. An increasing proportion of Indian tea is being consumed within India so that exports from that source will tend to decline, thereby aggravating the shortage of supplies. On the other hand, a large latent demand for tea exists in the United Kingdom itself, where tea is still being rationed, on the Continent of Europe which has been starved of tea during the war, in the countries of the Middle East where there is a large unsatisfied demand, in the United States and in the Dominions. It is a fact that the habit of tea drinking has spread. In a free market the price of tea is certain to be above the present controlled price and will rise still higher as the short supply position develops. I submit that this important fact should be taken into account in considering the price I have proposed.

6.   The tea contract for 1940 which was the first of the series of annual contracts entered into with the Ministry of Food under the Purchase Scheme fixed the price of tea as the price prevailing immediately before the war, and contained the clause that "in recognition of the exceptional conditions likely to obtain during the period of the contract and the possibility of increased costs of production of tea per lb. f.o.b. there shall be added a sum to be agreed between the Ceylon Association in London and the Minister of Food". The contract for 1942 provided for an addition of 1¾d. per lb. on this account, and it was raised successively to 4d. and 4¾d. in 1943. This was meant to ensure that the industry earned the same profit per pound of tea manufactured as before the war. However, in 1943 there was a short-fall in the crop and consequently the aggregate profits fell below the pre-war level. Therefore, in 1944, the basis of computing the price was modified to ensure that the aggregate profits of the industry were maintained at the pre-war level. On this basis a sum of 6¾d. per lb. was added in 1944, and 9¼d. in 1945. The contract for 1946 provides for the same increase of 9¼d. as in 1945. The Ceylon Association in London which was concerned primarily with the interests of the sterling companies operating in Ceylon was indifferent to the method of computing the price so long as it yielded nominal pre-war profits. This was to be expected as profits earned in excess of pre-war level were liable to 100% Excess Profits tax in the United Kingdom. In the circumstances it is readily understandable why the Ceylon Association in London should have agreed to a method of price fixing which was satisfactory to the interests it represented but was detrimental to the true national interests of Ceylon.

7.   The method followed in computing the price on the basis of pre-war profits was itself open to objection. The price was computed at such a level that only two-thirds of the estates in a sample restricted to those of the members of the Ceylon Estate Proprietory Association could earn pre-war profits. This meant that high cost estates had to be satisfied with less than pre-war profits. As the full output of every estate was required, the correct procedure should have been to secure a more representative sample and to give proper weighting to high cost units in computing the price. As this procedure was not followed, adequate consideration was not given to the increase in production costs of low country estates whose yields are less than better placed up-country estates. Low country estates have suffered loss not only on this account, but also because they were unable to secure labour at minimum rates of wages which alone were reckoned in assessing the increase in wage costs. It should be explained that the estates represented in the sample generally employed Indian immigrant labour which was available at minimum wage rates. On the other hand low country estates employed mostly native labour which had to be paid higher

wages. The net result was that most of the estates from which the sample was drawn earned more than pre-war profits and paid duty to the British Exchequer at the rate of 100% on their excess profits as they were owned in almost all cases by companies registered in the United Kingdom, while low country estates, which were hardly represented in the sample and were mostly owned by the Ceylonese, generally earned less than pre-war profits.

8. As regards *coconut products*, namely copra and coconut oil, the Government of Ceylon at present has a contract with His Majesty's Government for a period of five years from 1st January, 1946. For reasons which I shall state presently I propose that this contract be replaced by a fresh contract for a term of ten years from 1st January, 1947. In considering the price under the fresh contract it should be noted that there is a worldwide scarcity of fats and oils, and this acute short supply position will continue to exist for several years. It is also noteworthy that the price of copra in India which used to purchase before the war almost the entire export surplus of Ceylon is almost three times the price received by the Ceylon producer under the existing contract.

9. In this connection I should explain that the Ministry of Food agreed to pay under the Bulk Purchase Scheme introduced in April 1942 a price equivalent to Rs. 236/- per ton to the producer for copra. But soon after the terms of the Purchase Scheme were concluded cost conditions underwent such a violent change as a result of the onset of the inflationary rise in prices, to which reference is made in paragraph 29 below, that producers found that profit margins were much below what they expected. Notwithstanding repeated requests for a revision of price, the Ministry of Food did not grant any redress until April 1944, when a scheme was introduced to pay a bonus of Rs. 32/- per ton of copra out of the profits realised on shipments made to the Government of India. In December, 1945, the Ministry of Food agreed to raise the price so that the producer was able to receive Rs. 368/- per ton for copra. On the expiry of this contract after the termination of hostilities, a new contract was entered into for a term of five years as from 1st January, 1946, at a price of Rs. 400/- per ton to the producer. The price of coconut oil was fixed at parity with copra, with an allowance for milling and other costs. One important condition of the Purchase Scheme was that exports of desiccated coconut should be restricted. They were fixed initially at a level not exceeding 2000 tons per annum as against a pre-war export of some 30,000 tons. The new contract provides for an initial export quota of only 10,000 tons per annum rising to 15,000 tons towards the end of the term.

10. In considering what is a reasonable price for copra, account should also be taken of the low price which prevailed since the depression of the thirties. The coconut industry in [? is] one of the few industries which did not benefit from the subsequent trade revival. In fact profits in this industry have been so low in the past that it was not found practicable to introduce until recently minimum wages to the workers engaged in it. It was only in 1945 that the Minimum Wages Ordinance was applied to the coconut industry although it had been in force in the tea and rubber industries since the twenties.

11. The low prices which prevailed have also resulted in most plantations abandoning replanting of senile and low yielding areas, which is necessary to preserve the capital value of the industry. Consequently, there has been a serious decline in output which has become increasingly evident in recent years. It is essential that the industry should be enabled to carry out a systematic programme of

re-planting spread over the next ten years. As a coconut plant takes ten years to come into bearing, the industry should be assured of some price stability during this period so that the large programme of replanting requiring to make good the accumulated arrears can be carried out with confidence. Another factor which has a bearing on the price is the loss suffered by the desiccated coconut industry as a result of restriction of exports. This is estimated at ten million Rupees taking into account the deterioration of buildings and equipment of factories, and the loss of profits, etc.

12. I am aware that some consideration was given to the factors I have urged above when the price of copra was fixed under the new contract. However, it did not take into account the loss which the industry in particular and the country as a whole, has suffered by reason of the failure in the past of the Ministry of Food to adjust the price in relation to rising costs and decline in real values which occurred between 1942 and 1944.

13. I would observe that the price of copra is fixed under the present agreement on the basis that the producer receives Rs. 400/- per ton. In the circumstances, if an export duty is levied, it would become payable eventually by the Ministry of Food. It will be necessary to impose such a duty for revenue proposals if no satisfactory settlement can be reached on the proposals I have made.

14. My proposal in regard to *rubber* stands on a somewhat different footing from the other two commodities. His Majesty's Government has recently concluded an arrangement with the Government of the United States whereby the price of rubber from Malaya has been fixed at ½d. per lb. f.o.b. in respect of purchases up to 31st December, 1946. Ceylon was not represented at the discussions. The arrangements with regard to price and purchases after that date will, I understand, be discussed by His Majesty's Government with the Government of the United States towards the end of the year. I have asked that the Government of Ceylon should be given the opportunity of being represented at such discussions. I expect them to establish Ceylon's case for special treatment in regard to rubber by reason of the vital contribution she made towards victory by supplying this essential material of war at great cost and at national sacrifice. Pending these discussions, I make the present proposal in order to avoid the immediate and complete collapse of the rubber industry which would follow, should the price for Malayan rubber be imposed on Ceylon.

15. Ceylon supplied rubber during the war at a time when she was virtually the only source of supply available to the United Nations, without seeking a price which would have safeguarded her true national interests. It was obvious to everybody that the synthetic rubber industry which the exigencies of war created in America would become a competitor of natural rubber, and that once America had established a rubber industry of her own she would endeavour to use that advantage to influence the price level of natural rubber. Had Ceylon exploited the unique position she occupied in the market at that time, she could have demanded and received a price which would have enabled her to write off the capital value of her plantations at the end of the war. She would then have had sufficient resources to finance the replantation of estates with improved strains and been in a position to meet the competition of synthetic rubber when it materialized. A price of Rs. 3.50 per lb. for rubber during the intervening period of three and a half years of war after Japan occupied the territories in South East Asia would have secured sufficient to finance replanting. Alternatively, the funds so secured could have been used by the owners in

other profitable investments. In whichever way the funds might have been invested, the national capital of the country would have been maintained.

16. But the situation Ceylon is faced with now is entirely different. She has sacrificed her rubber trees by excessive and slaughter tapping. The capital of her rubber industry which really lies in the yielding capacity of the trees has suffered serious depletion. In this respect the rubber industry in the Japanese occupied territories of Malaya and the Netherlands East Indies is in a more favourable position. While it is true that factories and equipment have suffered from neglect, the yielding power of the trees has improved significantly by the long period of enforced rest. As a result the Malayan and Dutch East Indian rubber industry will have the advantage of lower unit costs. It is ironical to contemplate that the Ceylon rubber industry which sacrificed so much during the war and contributed so generously to the material resources of the United Nations in winning the war should now find itself at a serious disadvantage in competing with Malayan and Netherlands East Indian rubber.

17. I submit for the consideration of His Majesty's Government that the case of Ceylon rubber stands on a different footing from Malayan and Netherlands East Indian rubber on the one hand and synthetic rubber on the other. Ceylon is entitled to special treatment. Her industry should not be made a victim for failing to exploit the opportunities it had during the period when she had a monopoly of natural rubber. The people of Ceylon expect that the contribution the industry made to the winning of the war by supplying rubber on terms which were fixed without regard to her national interest should be recognised by the United Nations. From Ceylon's point of view the issue I raise transcends all other issues affecting the rubber industry. A satisfactory solution to it cannot be given except by His Majesty's Government and the Government of the United States acting jointly. I am confident that consideration could be secured for the special position of Ceylon at the forthcoming discussions with the Government of the United States, at which I have asked that Ceylon should be represented.

18. Meanwhile, it is necessary that Ceylon should be protected from the loss she will suffer if the reduced price of 1s. 2d. per lb. f.o.b. is offered for Ceylon rubber. At this level the over-all price which the producer will receive is 64 cents per lb. as against 94 cents per lb. on the current price of 1/7¼d. f.o.b. The cost of production of the best yielding areas with an average of 500 lbs. per acre amounts to 56 cents per lb., but computed on the average out-turn of 375 lbs. for all estates it amounts to 65 cents per lb. This calculation does not allow for cost of replanting which the industry must carry out within the shortest possible time if it is to have any chance of competing with synthetic rubber. A scheme of replanting spread over a period of 10 years will add a further 30 cents to the cost per pound. If such a scheme of replanting should be adopted it would not be before the expiry of 15 years that Ceylon would acquire in place of existing rubber revitalised plantations in full bearing. On this basis the total cost including expenses of replantation amounts to 94 cents. This will leave no margin of profit even at the current price.

19. It is thus clear that even on the current price of 1s. 7¼d. per lb. f.o.b. the Ceylon producer is on an insecure footing; but if the price is reduced to 1s. 2d. per lb. f.o.b. his position will be disastrous. In fact, should this reduced price be enforced on the Ceylon Industry, it is certain that approximately three-forths of the acreage under rubber will find it unremunerative and will be forced out of production. The first victims will be all the small holdings of Ceylonese. The next to follow will be the

large Ceylonese owned estates. I would ask of His Majesty's Government whether this is the just reward which Ceylon has earned for the part she played in supplying rubber to the United Nations on terms which form her point of view were, in reality, suicidal.

20. The request for re-imbursement of the cost of *food subsidy* during the next twelve months is due to the fact that my proposals under tea, coconut products and rubber are based on an expectation of a steady fall in the cost of living. There is every indication that the contrary might be the case in the next twelve months. It is not unreasonable to ask that the cost of maintaining the present level of food prices should be borne by the purchases of Ceylon's produce under my proposals.

21. I have stated briefly the grounds on which I consider that the prices I have asked for in my proposals are, in themselves, justified. There are, however, still other and more cogent reasons in favour of my proposals. They arise from the facts, which I shall presently establish, that the method of price fixing adopted under the Bulk Purchase Schemes operated to the detriment of Ceylon [. The country] suffered grievous loss economically and financially as a result of the war, and that this loss is so disproportionate in relation to her resources that she will shortly have to face a grave financial crisis. Annex A to this communication which is a note on the economic conditions of Ceylon in relation to her export industries contains the relevant data in support of these propositions. Marginal references to this note will be made where necessary.[1]

22. In dealing with this aspect of my proposals I should like to emphasize two general considerations which go to the root of the grounds on which they are made:—

(i) The whole internal economy of Ceylon depends on her export trade in the three main agricultural industries, tea, rubber and coconut. During the war she entered into agreements with His Majesty's Government for the sale of these products at prices which were fixed not on the basis of what was to Ceylon's best advantage, but on certain theoretical considerations of what would at the time be considered a fair price as between His Majesty's Government and Ceylon as part of the Commonwealth. If the ordinary considerations as between a willing buyer and a willing seller had prevailed Ceylon might have exploited her position as a producer of commodities in short supply. Similarly, His Majesty's Government might have exploited the situation arising from the fact that shipping was scarce, and that Ceylon had no shipping of her own. The position was that the Commonwealth was in danger, and it behoved every member of it to play her part in securing victory. This supreme consideration over-shadowed any purely commercial considerations in regard to the transactions of selling Ceylon's produce to His Majesty's Government. Ceylon did not view these agreements from a purely commercial angle, nor could she have foreseen at that time the dire economic effects which they would have had on her. She trusted that Britain would not only give her a fair deal for the time being, but would realise the spirit in which she gave all her resources to the cause of securing victory. Rubber was a commodity essential for the winning of the war. With the loss to the Allies of other rubber producing countries, Ceylon found herself the source of 90% of this most essential war

---

[1] Annexes and marginal references not printed.

requirement. She did not pause to drive a commercial bargain out of that unique position, but hacked her trees to produce every ounce of rubber she could, regardless of consequences. She agreed to accept for her rubber, as well as for her other commodities, a price which in terms of money and on the application of a theoretical rule in relation to pre-war money values seemed to her reasonable, without pausing to reckon the true economic implications of it. Both tea and coconut products were essential commodities in short supply during the war, and Ceylon played her part in producing them to the utmost of her capacity. Owing to the scarcity and the very high cost of imported materials necessary for the proper maintenance of her tea and coconut plantations and the scarcity and high cost of labour, there was a continued depreciation in her capital assets of agricultural property. She did not fully take this factor into consideration in the agreements she made with His Majesty's Government. When she found that the cost of imported materials and the cost of feeding her labour had soared far higher than the increase in prices she got for her exports, when she found that owing to the onset of inflation as a result of the manner in which war expenditure in Ceylon was being financed the real value of what she was getting for her exports had depreciated to much less than pre-war, she did not insist that before she produced another pound of rubber or tea for the Allies she should be paid sufficient to meet these increased costs and to prepare herself to shoulder the future liability continuously accruing on her industries. To-day she finds herself with depleted resources, her economy disrupted by inflation, and her tea, rubber and coconut plantations which constitute her only capital wealth, in a state of deterioration and requiring considerable expenditure for rehabilitation. At this juncture it would indeed be a very serious matter for Ceylon if she were to be told that the war being now over, Britain is not interested in her internal economy; that the part she played during the war is a matter of the past; that it is up to her to overcome her difficulties and herself make good the grievous losses she has sustained as a result of the part she played in the war, and that if she wants to sell her produce to the United Kingdom Government she can only negotiate on a purely commercial basis as between one trader and another. I have sufficient faith in the principles of justice and fairness which have pervaded British statesmanship to be confident that His Majesty's Government will not adopt such an attitude towards Ceylon. Further, I have sufficient faith in the wisdom of British statesmanship to expect that it will be realised that such a short-sighted policy would have grave consequences for the Commonwealth in the future. Ceylon holds a unique position in the Commonwealth chain. The goodwill of her people must be of very great value to the Commonwealth.

(ii) The second aspect which I would wish to place prominently before His Majesty's Government in the consideration of my proposals is that it would be quite wrong to say that Ceylon entered into agreements for sale of her products during the war as a free agent, that those accounts are now closed, and that it is not possible to review any considerations or consequences arising out of the operation of those contract. I shall be able to prove presently that on correspondence that has gone on between Ceylon and His Majesty's Government the account is not closed. It is still outstanding. On Ceylon's behalf I claim that the settlement of the account be now gone into. I shall be able to prove that even if strict legal principles that govern commercial transactions between one party and another are applied to these agreements, the account is not yet settled. But these were not mere commercial bargains. Ceylon was not in a true sense a free agent in regard to them. A great deal was taken on trust. The ordinary principles of legal interpretation cannot be applied to them. I shall presently adduce ample evidence to show that underlying the agreements were certain reservations regarding the real economic value of prices fixed in the agreements, and that the consideration of these reservations is still open. My mission to this country is, therefore, not only to secure for Ceylon a just arrangement in regard to the future, but also to secure justice and a fair deal in regard to the past.

23.   I have said that the method of price fixing adopted under the Bulk Purchase Scheme operated to the detriment of Ceylon. The principle which underlay this method was that prices should be fixed at such levels as to give the producer the same profits as in pre-war years, allowance for this purpose being made for increase in production costs. This principle would have had some justification,

(a) if the pre-war profits in the selected period were, in themselves, reasonable;
(b) if the real value of profits was unimpaired during the term of the purchase schemes; and
(c) if full allowance had been made for the increase in expenses on current and replacement account when assessing the increase in cost of production.

In actual fact, however, none of these essential conditions was satisfied, with the result that the Ceylon producer received a price much less than what he was reasonably entitled to.

24.   Taking the first condition (a) in the last preceding paragraph, the basic period selected for assessing pre-war profits in the case of tea was the three years 1936–38. The selection of this period was most unfair to the Ceylon producer because profits then earned by the tea industry cannot strictly be regarded as normal. There is a perfectly valid reason why I say that the selection of 1936–38 as the base for determining pre-war profits was unfair. It is an important condition inherent in tropical agriculture, subject as it is to wide variations in price over a cycle of change, that profits earned during a boom must be sufficiently high to offset the losses and the abnormally low profits of the intervening periods of depression and revival. It is on the successful operation of this important economic factor that the eventual profitability of tropical agriculture depends. Since the collapse of the last post-war boom of 1929, the prices of tea, rubber and coconut products did not attain reasonably profitable levels. It is true that there was a slight recovery in 1937, but a definite recession occurred in 1938. In fact, the thirties cannot be regarded as a normal period in regard to raw material prices. Tea and rubber, for example, were subject to valorisation schemes, and their output had to be restricted to realise what prices they did attain during this period. On the other hand the price of coconut products whose output was unrestricted continued to be low. The result was that the profits of the period 1936–38, adopted as the basic period for determining pre-war profit levels, were not high enough to offset the losses and low profits since the great depression of the thirties. It is noteworthy that profits of tea and rubber companies during the war magnified as they were by an inflationary spiral, were less than the profits earned during the last pre-war boom of 1925–1929 under conditions of peace, when there was no inflation. In fact, the profits earned during the five years

1940–1944, under conditions of an inflationary boom amounted to only 71% in the case of tea, and 70% in the case of rubber, of the profits earned during the peace time boom of 1925–1929.

25. I am aware that the principle of maintaining pre-war profits has been widely adopted by His Majesty's Government in controlling the internal price structure of the United Kingdom. This principle has been applied to the United Kingdom to determine permissible profit margins in manufacturing industries and in wholesale and retail trades, and also in assessing wartime liabilities such as compensation for war damage and requisitioned property, etc. There is, however, an important difference from the point of view of equity between the effect of applying such a principle within a given country and of its application to transactions between one country and another. In applying the principle in the United Kingdom the result secured was that one section of the community had to forego anything beyond pre-war profits or compensation on pre-war basis for the benefit of the rest of the community. In other words, what one section of the community lost, the rest of the community gained, so that the community taken as a whole was not a loser. But the incidence of the loss is quite different when the parties involved are two different national entities such as the United Kingdom on the one hand and Ceylon on the other. By importing into price fixing of commodities purchased under Bulk Purchase schemes the principle of maintaining pre-war profits followed in the United Kingdom, one result has been that what Ceylon lost accrued to the advantage of the United Kingdom.

26. In regard to condition (b) set out in paragraph 23 above, the real value of exports in an economy like that of Ceylon, which is almost wholly dependent for its food, clothing and materials of industry on the imports which its exports will buy, depends on the relationship between current import and export prices. This was recognised by you in a despatch dated 31st January, 1943, which contained the important observation that it was "obviously to the disadvantage of Colonies to have prices of the bulk of their exports firmly fixed while prices of imports were free to rise;" and again that the "costs of essential imports into the Colonies were tending to rise both because of the inevitable increase in freight rates and insurance increases due to adoption of special war time routeing of supplies and because of the increase in price payable in the country of origin of imported goods". The despatch further stated that "the control of prices in countries of origin presented a very great difficulty, but that investigations were proceeding as to the possibility of some system of control." No such control was in fact established, and import prices continued to mount steeply to the great detriment of Ceylon while export prices remained firmly fixed. The unfavourable price relationship between Ceylon exports and imports is clearly illustrated by a comparison of the two sets of prices. Export prices rose by 78.5% from 1939 to 1945 while, on the other hand, import prices rose by 230.1% during the same period. The result was that while the exchange of exports against imports took place in 1939 on terms some 9% more favourable to Ceylon than in the basic years 1934–38, the exchange became increasingly unfavourable with the steeply rising import prices so that during 1934–45, it was some 45% less favourable to Ceylon than before the war. These terms of exchange were markedly in contrast with what the United Kingdom secured partly, no doubt, as a result of the very favourable transactions which His Majesty's Government were able to conclude under the Bulk Purchase Schemes. The exchange of British exports against imports

which was 19% less favourable to the United Kingdom in 1939 than in 1938 steadily improved until 1943 when it was 2% more favourable and became 6% less favourable in 1945. There is no question but that the Bulk Purchase schemes which were an essential element of the price policy of His Majesty's Government have been of substantial benefit to the United Kingdom while, on the other hand, they caused serious loss to Ceylon.

27. It is, of course, realised that the widening gap between f.o.b. prices of exports and c.i.f. prices of imports was partly due to unavoidable increases in ocean freights owing to longer voyages, the addition of war risks insurance and other factors. But the increase in import prices was a real cost to Ceylon, and from her point of view, it was necessary that prices of exports should have risen to a level at least sufficiently high to enable her to exchange them on reasonable terms for the imports she needed. The vital importance of a satisfactory rate of exchange will be appreciated when it is stated that food and clothing between them account for half of the value of the total import trade of Ceylon, and that the price of food alone rose by 118% from 1939 to 1945 and of clothing by 251% over the same period.

28. In economies in which foreign trade plays a much less important part than in Ceylon it is possible that an unfavourable price relationship between exports and imports even of the magnitude experienced by Ceylon would not be so vital. But it is quite the contrary in the case of Ceylon. Her economy has been developed entirely on an export and import basis. Two-thirds of her occupied population are engaged on export industries which account for four-fifths of her national income. Only a small proportion of food required by the people is grown locally. Being without any manufacturing industries, she is obliged to depend upon imports for all essentials of a civilized life. In a backward economy of this nature the real value of income is entirely determined by the terms on which exports are exchanged against imports. The Bulk Purchase schemes by fixing firmly the price of Ceylon's exports while the price at which she secured imports remained practically uncontrolled deprived the Ceylon producer of a fair deal.

29. The result was that even the pre-war profits, which prices fixed under the Bulk Purchase schemes were intended to maintain, eventually represented only a fraction of their real value when reckoned in terms of their capacity to purchase imports. Moreover the inflationary tendencies which developed as a result of war expenditure in Ceylon by His Majesty's Government further reduced the nominal value of pre-war profits when reckoned in real terms. The general rise in prices as reflected by the relevant financial and price statistics was severe. Bank deposits rose by 256% from 1939 to 1945, bank clearings by 236% and note circulation expanded by 640%. This general expansion was associated with rises in minimum wage rates of estate labour by 159% and cost of living by 115%. These violent changes in economic values provide ample evidence of the magnitude of the inflationary rise in prices in Ceylon. It was particularly severe from 1942 when wages registered in a single year a rise of 66% above the previous year and cost of living a rise of 43%. Thus it came to pass that in the very year in which Ceylon negotiated the sale of her produce to His Majesty's Government at fixed prices a violent change in cost conditions occurred, and the very basis of the arrangement was immediately destroyed.

30. Notwithstanding the violent rise in costs, the prices fixed under the Bulk Purchase schemes did not increase correspondingly. Fixed as they were on the principle of maintaining profits at the pre-war level, they could not keep in step with

the general rise in prices, and export prices when adjusted for the decline in purchasing power as measured by the rising cost of imports showed actually a severe fall. In the case of each commodity, the price allowed under the Purchase Scheme to offset the increase in production costs, was insufficient to discount the rise in the cost of imports. For example, the price of tea adjusted to reflect its purchasing power showed a decrease of 56% in 1945 compared with 1939 as against a nominal increase of 45%. Rubber showed a decrease of 28% as against a nominal increase of 103%. Coconut products showed a decrease of 24% as against a nominal increase of 152%.

31. In this connection I should like to lay special emphasis on the fact that the principle cause of the inflationary rise in prices in Ceylon was the manner in which His Majesty's Government financed war expenditure in Ceylon. Owing to the automatic nature of the link between the currency of Ceylon and sterling, His Majesty's Government financed such expenditure against sterling obligations created by them in London. Thus, by a simple decision to spend a given amount of money in Ceylon His Majesty's Government were able to increase the note issue automatically and this inevitably produced inflation when the recipients of the additional purchasing power were unable to convert it into the goods they needed. Had this automatic link been absent, and had Ceylon enjoyed an independent status in regard to her currency and credit, His Majesty's Government would have been compelled to procure the additional purchasing power required in Ceylon to finance war expenditure either by supplying her the goods in the kinds and quantities which her people required or by selling in the local market those investments in Ceylon which British nationals in England held. Either of these courses of action would have reduced the burden of inflation which people in Ceylon suffered owing to the way in which war expenditure in Ceylon was actually financed. Unfortunately, His Majesty's Government took full advantage of the automatic link which bound Ceylon currency to sterling with the result that the entire burden of the war expenditure incurred in Ceylon was borne in a real sense by her people without being shared, at that time, by the United Kingdom. How the people of Ceylon happened to bear this burden in this manner and the economic loss suffered by Ceylon in consequence are dealt with in some detail in Annex B to this communication.

32. Going back to condition (c) in paragraph 23 above, I would point out that the allowances for increase in production costs which were successively admitted proved to be inadequate. The increase on this account fell into two parts:—

(a) current operating expenses; and
(b) replacement costs.

The Ministries concerned did not readily admit the rise in production costs claimed, and generally it was only after repeated requests were made that an increase in price was conceded. In view of violent changes in costs and other economic values which were induced by the inflationary method of financing war expenditure pursued in Ceylon, cost conditions had often changed for the worse by the time the Ministries concerned agreed to a price increase on the basis of the last available statistics. In the sum, price increases allowed under these schemes did not catch up with the increases in costs. In view of this time lag, realised profits had perforce to be less than they should have been.

33. Apart from this consideration the fact that export prices were related to pre-war levels deprived labour of the chance of improving their position relatively to

what they might well have succeeded otherwise in achieving. Wages which account for the greater part of current operating expenses in tropical agriculture had been reduced to bare subsistence levels during the depression and were, at the outbreak of war, well below what, on a reasonable standard, a living wage should have been. There was, therefore, a considerable leeway to be made on the wages prevailing when the war broke out to bring them up to a level which would afford a reasonable standard of living. Although money wages rose by 159% from 1939 to 1945, cost of living rose by 122% so that real wages went up by 17% only. It cannot be maintained that this increase is adequate when one considers by comparison that real wages in the United Kingdom where labour enjoyed a very much higher standard of living rose by some 16%, and in the United States of America by 26% during the same period. In truth it is not extravagant to contemplate that in a free market with export prices free to move, labour would have secured under conditions of a war boom wages much higher than what they were able to obtain under the limiting conditions imposed by the Purchase Schemes. Such an improvement in wages would have not only enabled labour to secure an improved standard of living but it is also certain that labour could have been induced to save a fair proportion of the additional wage and thereby increase financial security from a national point of view.

34. In this connection it is of interest to note that as a result of designed policy of the British Government the standard of living of the poorer section of the working class in the United Kingdom has improved significantly during the war. The general conditions of the people in Ceylon, however, whose standard of living is even lower than that of the poorer section of the working class in the United Kingdom have, on the whole, worsened as a direct result of the war.

35. The other factor for which adequate allowance was not made when determining price increases under the Purchase Schemes was Replacement costs. As prices continued to rise, depreciation allowances reckoned at one price level became inadequate when prices rose to a higher level. A typical illustration of this is the sum of £45 per acre allowed in 1943 for replanting expenses under the capital compensation scheme for slaughter tapping of rubber. At current prices, it would cost about £120 per acre for replanting. Plantation industries which were encouraged to produce the maximum output as part of Ceylon's contribution to the war effort now find that the margins which were allowed for depreciation in the prices they received are inadequate to cover replacement costs. The principle that special consideration should be given to making good capital consumption which has taken place during the war has been recognised in the United Kingdom where provision is made for refund after the war of 20% of the Excess Profits Tax paid from the time it was raised to 100%. Besides, there is also provision under Income Tax relief at special rates on account of exceptional depreciation. In Ceylon, however, prices fixed under the Bulk Purchases Schemes did not contain an element to make good capital consumption or exceptional depreciation during the war.

36. When the adverse effects of rising cost of imports on export prices and on the general economy of Ceylon came under notice of the Government of Ceylon, representations in the following terms were made to you by telegram dated 27th November, 1943; "It appears probable that import prices during the period immediately after the war will show a greater rise over pre-war prices than present rise in export prices, with result that funds now being accumulated to cover cost of postponed imports and replenishment of stocks will probably be insufficient. . . . *The*

*basis originally adopted of endeavouring to secure, during the war, the same net profit per unit of Ceylon exports as pre-war is disadvantageous to Ceylon* . . . in order to purchase the same quantity of pre-war imported goods in return for specified quantity of Ceylon exports, either now or shortly after the war, the rise in price of exports should be equal to average rise in price of imports now and shortly after war, when deferred imports will be purchased". To this representation a reply was received from you by savingram dated 13th January, 1944 which observed that "actual external receipts of Ceylon from exports and from other expenditure in the Island, financed from overseas, e.g. military expenditure, is clearly a good deal more than sufficient to pay for current flow of imports; and in present conditions yielding a substantial surplus which is accumulating in the form of overseas balances held on Ceylon account. . . . As a matter of wider policy it has been the consistent endeavour of His Majesty's Government to do everything possible to avoid a general rise of all prices as would lead to wide spread inflation. . . . This general principle of avoiding unreasonable increase of price has been applied as far as practicable to exports of manufactured goods from the United Kingdom itself although it is realised that such exports to Ceylon are relatively small and that *Ceylon has suffered because the countries from whom the greater proportion of her imports is drawn have hitherto exercised less control over export prices.* . . ." The contention implied in your reply that military expenditure in Ceylon has yielded a substantial surplus balance on her account is dealt with at some length in paragraphs 40 to 42 below.

37.  As there was no abatement in the continued rise in cost of imports, the Ceylon Government made further representation to you by telegram dated 24th July, 1944, which, inter alia, observed: "There is *still grave reason to fear that excess of exports visible and invisible over cost of current imports will prove quite insufficient to finance post-war reconstruction.* . . . Ceylon is, like other countries, bearing the burden of the war in the form of greatly reduced standard . . . and has no complaint to make on that score. It is not suggested that export prices should be such as to permit post-war purchases of all the goods which would have been imported into Ceylon if there had been no war, but it is suggested that they should be sufficient to allow at least resumption of pre-war standard in Ceylon was deplorably low. . . . [sic] It cannot be too strongly emphasised that the economy of an undeveloped country like Ceylon with a very rapidly increasing population which imports the great bulk of its requirements of manufacturing goods is entirely different from that of a fully developed manufacturing country with static population. . . . There is reason to fear that the failure of export prices to rise in the same proportion as import prices . . . will result in funds accumulated during the war by abstention from normal consumption proving inadequate for minimum post war needs of Government, agricultural and commercial interests and individuals alike".

38.  After this communication, I had an opportunity of discussing with the Colonial office on my visit to this country early in 1945 the probable financial situation in Ceylon over the immediate post-war period in so far as it was affected by the prices paid for her main exports. I then stated that an adjustment of these prices would be necessary in the post-war period. The fact is that Ceylon has not received the redress she sought in representations which she repeatedly made. A fundamental condition which she assumed when accepting the prices paid for her exports was that she would be able to procure at reasonable prices the essential imports which her people needed. That condition ceased to exist during the currency of the Purchase

Schemes. I claim on behalf of the Government of Ceylon, that the financial account relating to purchases which His Majesty's Government made during the war under Bulk Purchase Schemes has not been concluded. With the victorious conclusion of the war in the prosecution of which the people and the Government of Ceylon collaborated completely with His Majesty's Government they expect a fair and just settlement of this account now. The present is opportune for this settlement. The dangers of further wide-spread inflation which you referred to in your telegram of 13th January, 1944, in reply to the first representation made by the Government of Ceylon, and which you feared might follow from price increases that were claimed, do not exist now. The proposals I have submitted to you take into consideration this unsettled account. The people of Ceylon do not expect restitution in full of the loss they suffered in a common struggle. But I do ask on their behalf that His Majesty's Government should recognise that a claim is due, and accept my proposals as the minimum of justice of which Ceylon can exist.

39. The loss suffered by Ceylon as a consequence of the unfavourable terms on which her exports were purchased by His Majesty's Government is estimated at Rs. 1970 million. I should explain, however, that this sum is a minimum. It represents the price Ceylon had to pay for selling her commodities at negotiated prices whilst being obliged to exchange proceeds of their sales at uncontrolled market prices. You would appreciate more readily the magnitude of this loss when I say that it amounts to more than three times the total value of Ceylon's export trade in 1945. This loss is, in a real sense, a measure of the indirect cost borne by Ceylon in fighting the war. But this is not the only cost. There remains the direct cost of the war which she bore. This amounts to Rs. 530 million. Thus the total cost of the war to Ceylon can be reckoned at Rs. 2500 million. It is a cost of such magnitude that it will tax her national resources to the utmost to bear this greivous burden.

40. The serious financial loss Ceylon suffered owing to the war is reflected in the pancity [sic] of her foreign balances. The amount of these balances as on 30th September, 1945, is estimated at about Rs. 1230 million, representing an increase of Rs. 1000 million over the pre-war figure. I should like to emphasize that these balances do not represent, as commonly supposed, a financial benefit which Ceylon has gained in consequence of the war expenditure incurred by His Majesty's Government in that country. Ceylon, in fact, acquired these balances by sacrifice. She had to cut down supplies from abroad to the bare minimum. In almost all cases they were not supplemented by local production, so that consumption as a whole declined. The large reduction recorded in the volume of imports bears testimony to the sacrifice the people of Ceylon suffered. The shortfall in the quantity of imports over the five years from 1941 to 1945 was as large as one and a half times annual volume received during the period 1934–38.

41. The greater part of imports foregone during the war will need replacement in the ensuing years. This applies to capital goods, replacements and other materials of industry necessary to repair capital depletion suffered in war time as well as durable and semi-durable consumption goods for the purpose of restocking. That part of imports normally used for current consumption consisting chiefly of food need not, of course, be replaced. However, in a country like Ceylon with a deplorably low standard of living, even a small reduction in current consumption has its immediate reaction on the health of the people. For example, the death rate in 1945 was the highest recorded in the last 10 years. The expenditure which the Ceylon Government

will have to incur to repair the social injury to the people as a result of this sacrifice will exceed several times the value of such current consumption. But this expenditure will be incurred at price levels prevailing now and in the future. Present trends as illustrated by price levels in manufacturing countries, such as the United Kingdom and the United States of America do not suggest that prices are likely to fall in future. In fact the indications are that they will rise further. In the circumstances it is reasonable to evaluate the sacrifice undergone by the people of Ceylon by their denial of normal imports on the basis of at least current prices. The equivalent in terms of 1945 prices of the shortfall of imports during the five years since 1941 is approximately Rs. 1,200 million. It is, indeed, noteworthy that this amount is even less than the increase of Rs. 1,000 million in the surplus balances realised during the war. It is clear, therefore, that these receipts do not represent a net gain to Ceylon. The truth is that they are only a measure of the social misery and loss of capital which she has suffered as a direct consequency [sic] of the war.

42.   However, even to restore the loss of capital, the amount of the disposable balances is barely sufficient. The full amount of the surplus balances will not, of course, be available for this purpose because a margin must be retained as a working balance. The maximum realisation under the favourable conditions will not yield more than Rs. 820 million. But imports required on account of deferred maintenance, postponed capital construction and re-stocking will amount to a sum in the region of Rs. 690 million. The balance of Rs. 130 million will be certainly inadequate to repair the social injury which the war inflicted on the people of Ceylon.

43.   To summarize, I have endeavoured to show:—

(i)   that the terms on which His Majesty's Government purchases exports from Ceylon were unfair to her;

(ii)   that Ceylon did not act in these matters entirely as a free agent, and continued to protest repeatedly against the unfair treatment she received in regard to these transactions;

(iii)   that the account relating to these transactions cannot be treated as closed but is outstanding;

(iv)   that Ceylon has suffered a grievous financial loss which, together with the direct cost to her of the war, has imposed on her a financial burden beyond her capacity;

(v)   that Ceylon as a whole did not derive any financial benefit from war expenditure which His Majesty's Government incurred in the Island, but that, on the other hand, the very manner in which this expenditure was financed produced an inflationary spiral which aggravated the loss she has suffered;

(vi)   that the surplus balances held by Ceylon are, in reality, a measure of the social misery suffered by the people of Ceylon and of the depletion of national capital; and

(vii)   that the surplus balances are inadequate to restore the national and social capital of Ceylon even to pre-war level.

I venture to think that the facts I have adduced establish these propositions.

44.   It would be sheer disillusionment to the people of Ceylon if they should have to realise that the final outcome of their war effort is that their financial resources would not permit them to revert even to their pre-war standard of living. But this is not a situation which the Government of Ceylon can accept complacently. A people

cannot march backward. They rightly expect that the future will lead them to a better way of life. It is a duty of their Government to discover the way, and help them in attaining this goal.

45. But the way to social progress in a country like Ceylon is not easy. It is an uphill one. To enable you to appreciate the magnitude of the task and its urgency, I shall set out briefly the salient features of her economy. Ceylon is predominantly an agricultural country. Only one-fourth of the available land has been developed , and two-thirds of the developed area are devoted to production for export. Concentration on production for export has been so great that 80% of the national income is derived from the export industries, while the three principal commodities, tea, rubber and coconut account for 95% of the total value of the export trade.

46. Although the value of trade has expanded in recent times, production has not kept pace with the growth of population so that the pressure of population on developed resources has continued to increase during the last 20 years. The prospects are that the pressure on resources will become greater in future as the forecasted population shows an increase of 25% in the next 25 years. The need for positive action to develop national resources is, therefore, urgent in order both to sustain the increasing population and to raise the present low standard of living. However, the funds required for such development can be secured at present only from her exports on which Ceylon will have to depend in future even more than at the present time because development will have to proceed at a greater pace. The prices realised by her exports are, therefore, of the greatest importance and it will be necessary to place the maximum reliance on exports to finance development.

47. The war has not benefited the finances of the Government to the extent commonly believed. It is true that revenue has increased during the war, but a good part of the increase is due to new taxation. Direct taxation now accounts for 20% of the total revenue or 40% of the tax revenue. The increase in revenue since the war amounts to Rs. 231 million of which Rs. 127 million represent the yield of additional taxation imposed during the war, the balance of Rs. 101 million being due to revenue bouyancy following the inflationary rise in prices. However, a reduction of revenue from the present level is inevitable partly because certain emergency tax increases, such as excess Profits Duty (which lapses at the end of this year) will disappear. Moreover, should export prices drop it is estimated that there will be an immediate fall in revenue, of the order of Rs. 5 million for every 10 cents drop in price of tea or rubber from the present level.

48. Expenditure has continued to mount up with the increase in revenue, partly owing to special liabilities directly due to the war itself, such as war allowances to Government servants. For example, such liabilities amount in the current financial year to 25% of the total budgeted expenditure. Another reason is the rising cost of social expenditure, particularly health and education. Social expenditure now accounts for 36% of the total current outlay, and expenditure on economic development 32% so that these two items absorb two-thirds of the total current expenditure.

49. However, the scale of expenditure for economic and social purposes is still inadequate to satisfy the pressing needs of development. Government has borrowed largely during the war to finance war expenditure, which was a direct liability of Ceylon, as well as such limited schemes of social and economic development as could not be postponed even during the war. The net public debt has risen to twice its value

at the beginning of the war. The net value of the surplus balances on budgetary account as at 30th September, 1945, is only Rs. 53 million. This sum is hardly adequate to meet the accumulated arrears of maintenance of roads, buildings and public utilities. The result is that Government is without resources to finance the arrears of even the normal programme of development which the war arrested, much less undertake schemes of economic improvement and social betterment which are necessary to raise the living standards of the people.

50. To carry out such schemes of development a very large capital expenditure is necessary. The Commission on Social Services recently appointed by the Government of Ceylon has recommended a scheme to provide old age pensions, children's allowances, unemployment insurance and assistance and health insurance, all of which is estimated to cost Government Rs. 100 million per annum. Furthermore, the post-war plans of Government for economic development and expansion of health and educational facilities will cost annually another Rs. 150 million. At present Government revenue amounts to 25% of the national income which is estimated at some Rs. 1600 million. It should be raised by Rs. 1,000 million if Government is to secure the additional revenue required to meet the anticipated liabilities, on the assumption that the proportion of national income appropriated for Government purposes is maintained at the high ratio of 25%. But in order to produce an additional income of this magnitude a national investment of the order of Rs. 3,000 million will be required over the next 15 years. The supreme importance of a productive investment of this scale is obvious. Unless Ceylon is in a position to undertake a programme of development of this order, there is no prospect of any improvement in the economic conditions of her people. It has been repeatedly demonstrated that her economy dominated by three export products is highly sensitive to the vagaries of world markets. Every past depression has served to underline this great weakness. The importance of diversifying her production to introduce a greater degree of economic stability cannot be over-emphasized, and it is precisely this diversification which the projected programme of national development will bring about.

51. Desirable as these schemes are, they cannot be carried out without finance. The revenue Ceylon derives is bound to decrease in the next few years because the limit of taxable capacity has been reached. A tax ratio of 25% to national income is indeed high in a poor country where the per capita income in 1938 was about Rs. 100, when even in a country like the United Kingdom with a much higher income level representing a per capita income of Rs. 1,500 per head in 1938, the tax ratio was only 23%.

52. The final outcome of her efforts during the war is that Ceylon is threatened with financial insolvency. It will surely spell financial disaster if prices of her exports decline. One primary object I had in mind in making my proposals was to seek through them a way to ward off this impending disaster. The terms I seek will give the Government of Ceylon a respite of five years within which time it should be able to order the economy of the country so as to be in a position to face the financial situation that would arise at the end of this period. As it is, without an assurance of any degree of financial stability, without reserves, either on Government or national account adequate enough to meet even the minimum post-war liabilities which are a direct legacy of the war, and with the reduction in national income and loss of Government revenue which would inevitably follow should the price of any of her

leading exports fall, the financial future of Ceylon would be desperate.

53. The economic picture of Ceylon which I have outlined above is confirmed by the following extracts culled from an article in the Economist of 22nd June, 1946: "Ceylon is generally regarded as one of the most advanced Colonies in the British Empire. . . . (The) devolution of responsibility has undoubtedly been justified in social and economic terms as well as in the general rise in the political consciousness of the people. . . . Despite considerable advances which have been made, however, Ceylon like other parts of the Colonial Empire still represents a picture of considerable ignorance, poverty and malnutrition. . . . Health services are inadequate and living conditions frequently deplorable. The war, of course, has brought all the signs of a "boom" period. Despite the outward "boom" food shortages, high prices and the black market have all meant that there has been no real change in the conditions of the mass of the people. . . . The degree to which food shortages have played a part in depressing the standard of living is reflected in the figures for the death and infant mortality rates. . . . Ceylon, therefore, although it may be well down the Dominion road is still a typical example of the situation which faces the Colonial administration to-day.

"The dominating feature of this situation is the Colony's dependence on foreign interests. On the one hand, the island plays a part in the military defence of the British Empire so that outside strategic considerations influence its development. On the other, it is obliged to regulate its economy largely according to the demand of foreign investors. . . . It is quite true that agricultural reforms should be carried out, irrigation schemes launched, modern methods of cultivation encouraged and the emphasis on production for export counteracted. But such a policy in itself will not raise the standard of living to any considerable extent. Industrialisation and the full utilisation of all the Island's economic resources must also be major points of any successful economic programme for Ceylon. Such a basic change in the economy of the Colony is no longer a problem for the future. Its immediate urgency has now become clear. . . . Even Ceylon's agricultural position is not as secure as it looks. At present the Island's exports are purchased in bulk by the Government for the Ministries of Food and Supply. Should this arrangement be stopped trouble lies ahead. There will be many difficulties in such a policy of industrial expansion. But at the same time as its inhabitants have won wider democratic rights for themselves, it is true to say that Ceylon stands a better chance of successful development than most British possessions. And the number of years which will pass before the new constitution gives way to greater independence will be largely determined by the way in which the people of Ceylon tackle the economic and social problems they now face."

54. I submit that my propsals viewed as a whole are eminently reasonable, taking into account all the circumstances surrounding these transactions and the obligations and rights of both parties concerned. I suggest that from the point of view of His Majesty's Government it is a just settlement and its financial burden is relatively insignificant. On the other hand the political value of it would be incalculable. The people of Ceylon would have the satisfaction of knowing that the loss they suffered during the war has been recognized in some measure. It is scarcely necessary to stress the value of securing the goodwill of the people of Ceylon in the wider interests of Commonwealth relations. I need not emphasize the key position which Ceylon occupies in the chain of Commonwealth defence.

55. Should Ceylon be so unfortunate as not to secure acceptance of these proposals by His Majesty's Government, she will be compelled to adopt such measures as are open to her to abate the financial crisis which must inevitably follow. The Board of Ministers of Ceylon who have hitherto collaborated completely with His Majesty's Government in all matters will be driven to unilateral action. They will be obliged to have recourse to all sorts of expedients to reduce the severity of the financial disaster which will befall Ceylon. These expedients, such as unilateral action designed to secure even a temporary advantage from the current short supply position of the commodities of which Ceylon is a leading supplier, or even a degree of devaluation, may be no better than counsels of despair. But such action the Ministers will be obliged to take. It will be a great misfortune if the complete collaboration which Ceylon Ministers have maintained with His Majesty's Government for the last fifteen years should end in mere frustration. Shortly, the people of Ceylon will, for the first time in the history of their connection with British rule, be masters of their own destiny. It will, indeed, be most unfortunate if at the time they assume the political power which the new constitution confers, they should have to face a crisis of this magnitude. World opinion will rightly judge Ceylon's capacity for self-Government by the way she discharges her responsibilities towards securing the well being of her people. But for her to assume them with financial resources impaired, would, indeed be too formidable a task. I submit that His Majesty's Government have both a political and moral obligation in this respect. The sacrifice which Ceylon made during the war entitles her to a fair settlement. I confidently hope that His Majesty's Government will consider my proposals in this light and give the people of Ceylon what I claim on their behalf as their just due.

# 369   CO 852/569, no 47                                        10 Sept 1946

**[Rubber]: outward telegram no 1068 from Mr Hall to Sir H Moore explaining the implications of a recent rapid increase in the production of rubber in Malaya and suggesting that Sir O Goonetilleke should proceed to Washington with UK representatives for discussions with the Americans**

Developments in rubber situation have affected Goonetilleke's current negotiations as follows.

H.M.G. have become increasingly concerned in the last two or three weeks at the rapid increase in production of rubber in Malaya. Very briefly the estimates of production used as a basis for the international discussions which took place in June and for arrangements which were then made for purchases in Malaya at a price of 1/2d. by the American and British Governments, have proved to be far short of actual output. It now appears that availabilities of rubber in the second half of 1946 will be something like twice the figure allowed for in the June discussions. The American Government have already completed the whole of the purchase to which they were then committed and if internal Malayan price is to be maintained at 1/2d. parity, H.M.G. will have to make very heavy purchases. Existing commitments mean that H.M.G. will be holding a stock of 200,000 tons at the end of September and if purchase continues up to the end of the year their stock holding plus commitments is then estimated at 300,000 tons. As you will realise early liquidation of this stock on the free market if that were opened on the 1st January might have very depressing effect on price, while the alternative is for H.M.G. to continue to hold the stock for some considerable period at considerable expense and risk of ultimate loss.

Other aspect of the situation is that absorption of rubber in consuming countries is restricted by the absence of a free market and the existence of fixed international allocations. It has accordingly been felt necessary to initiate further conversations with the Americans at once with a view to considering what steps, including a possible opening of the market and abandonment of allocation restrictions earlier than 1st January 1947, should be taken.

The Americans have agreed to discuss the situation and discussions are to take place in Washington in about a week's time. In accordance with promise already given Goonetilleke has been informed that we should welcome participation of a Ceylon representative in these talks and he is of strong opinion that he himself should proceed to Washington for this purpose. With this I agree and he is proceeding with arrangements to leave with other U.K. representatives on 14th September on assumption that you will approve. It is hoped that his absence from London will not be much longer than a week.

None the less this necessary absence as well as the important change in the underlying rubber position which has lead to the necessity for these talks must inevitably affect and delay Goonetilleke's more general discussions. He has asked me, therefore, to inform you that he sees little prospect of being able to return to Ceylon before the end of September, but that he has decided, if he is unable to do so, to authorise Jones on his behalf to certify the budget if passed in present form. He wishes you also to know that he is asking the Board of Trade to continue present contract for Ceylon rubber for one month longer as a breathing space, pending the result of these forthcoming discussions. Board of Trade have not yet had time to consider this and their decision may in fact have to await outcome of the talks in Washington.


**370**  CO 537/1671                                          18 Sept 1946

**[Rubber]: memorandum by G L M Clauson on Sir O Goonetilleke's discussions at the State Department in Washington**

I called at the State Department by appointment on the afternoon of Tuesday, the 17th, in order to introduce Sir Oliver Goonetilleke to the State Department and to give him an opportunity of explaining the position of the Ceylon rubber industry.

He started with a general review of the economy of Ceylon and of the rubber industry in particular. Rubber represented 40% of their total economy. While Malaya was sitting back during the Japanese occupation letting the latex accumulate in their trees, Ceylon had been going all out. They had seriously overtapped their trees. They had worked up production to as much as 110,000 tons in one year. Next year they could not hope for more than 85,000 tons. They had exhausted all their bark reserves except perhaps for some of the European estates which, deterred by the excess profits tax, had done less than they might have. They had done this not only because they thought it was the right thing to do to help to win the war but also because they had had a special message from President Roosevelt himself sent verbally through a representative, because it was too secret to entrust to the telegraphic office, saying that unless Ceylon produced the maximum amount of rubber the war might be lost. Poor little Ceylon was a casualty of the war just as much as a wounded soldier and deserved all possible consideration on that account. One of the results was that their taxation amounted to 25% of their national income. Even in the United Kingdom it was only 23%.

He had two specific requests to make. The first related to the past. During the war they had not considered price questions but had taken whatever was offered. He personally explained the position that the one important thing was to win the war. He had staked his own political reputation on it and the people had done what he asked. Rubber was quite essential and if he had asked for ten dollars a pound instead of the miserable price which he had got he felt he would have got it. He thought this was an injustice and that this injustice should be righted by the United States which had got over 90% of all the Ceylon rubber.

His second request was for a breathing space. When they had repaired the damages of war and when prices of imported goods had got back to normal, they felt that they could compete with the rest of the world. But the price which was now being talked about of only a shilling a pound was no more than double the pre-war price. The cost of the industry has gone up five times. Ceylon was not like Malaya where the small holder produced most of his own food and rubber was more or less a sideline, a means of getting a little money. The Ceylon peasant produced only rubber and had to import his food and everything else. If the price went down below the present price of one and six pence farthing f.o.b., three quarters of the industry, that is everything except the European estates, would be bankrupt and he could not possibly tolerate a situation in which all the Ceylonese went out of the industry and only the Europeans were left. There would be a disastrous fall in the standard of living and Ceylon would not be able to afford any imports except food. His concrete proposal was that the United States should give a five-year contract to Ceylon for all the rubber they could produce for one and seven pence farthing.

Mr. Kennedy's[1] reply was quite admirable, friendly and good-tempered but completely firm. He did not wish in any way to under-rate Ceylon's contribution to the war but equally Ceylon must not under-rate the United States contribution. Admittedly, Ceylon rubber was extremely important but the main bulk of the rubber which won the war was the United States synthetic rubber which had been produced only by the investment of a million dollars in the industry. Sir Oliver was ill-judged enough at this point to say that a billion dollars was nothing to the United States to which Mr. Kennedy replied that he must be under no illusions on that subject. It was a great deal of money. We had all been in the war together, it was just as important to Ceylon that the war should be won as it was to anybody else. Admittedly, Ceylon had made her contribution but so had the United States and the United Kingdom and they were bigger contributions than Ceylon's. The rubber had not been used in the United States except to a trivial extent. It had been put into the bombers and the heavy military transport and had gone all over the world, Ceylon included. United States had not made the contract with Ceylon, that had been done by the United

---

[1] US State Dept.

Kingdom and the rubber had been supplied under Lease Lend but that had been washed out. The Americans had made the Lease Lend winding-up agreement by which they had surrendered a right to billions of dollars. He regarded this agreement as a contribution to winning the peace as important as their contribution to winning the war. They did not grudge the sacrifice but the extent of it must not be under-estimated. They would accept the statistics to which Sir Oliver had referred and study them with interest but this must be entirely without prejudice because he did not see what they could do. Ceylon was part of the British Empire and must look to the U.K. for help but he could not advise the United Kingdom to give Ceylon a special price for their rubber. He did not even think it would be in the interests of Ceylon herself; a special price could not go on forever and the longer the fall was deferred the worse it would be. Even if the State Department had been anxious to help it would be quite impossible to persuade Congress to put up money either to reopen a war-time transaction which they considered to have been definitely closed by the Lease Lend settlement or to pay fancy prices for Ceylon rubber for sometime to come. Apart from anything else, they anticipated that the Government would get out of the rubber trade in the near future and no machinery could possibly be devised which would make American manufacturers pay more money for Ceylon rubber than for other kinds.

The idea for which the United States and he thought the United Kingdom were working was more trade and more efficient production. Ceylon's difficulties seemed to arise more from the high price of their imports than from their difficulties over rubber itself. If anything was to be done it seemed to him that it should be done in other directions. They ought to become less dependent on imports of food and they ought to improve the efficiency of their productive machinery in every respect. To ask for a special price for rubber and to interfere artificially with their import program, if they could not get that special price, was directly contrary to everything that the United States stood for.

The meeting which lasted for rather over an hour closed with mutual expressions of goodwill which perhaps did not ring entirely true. I have not, of course, set out in this memorandum everything that was said. I felt it would be difficult to take notes and in any case a memorandum which included everything that was said would be far too long but what I have said above sets out, I think, accurately the gist of the discussion and the conclusion.

## 371   CO 852/569, no 49                                    18 Sept 1946
## [Purchase of Ceylon products]: memorandum by S Caine on Sir O Goonetilleke's proposals[1]

Sir Oliver Goonetilleke's proposals are:—

(a) *Tea*. The present contract which expires at the end of this year should be renewed for a further period of five years at a price of 1/- per lb. above the current price. This offer is subject to the condition that should India decide at any time during the currency of the contract to remain outside the Bulk Purchase Scheme, then Ceylon should have the right to withdraw from it.

---

[1] See 368.

(b) *Coconut Products*. The present contract which is for a term of five years from 1st January, 1946, should be replaced by a fresh contract for ten years as from 1st January, 1947, at a price 50% about [sic: above] the current price.

(c) *Rubber*. As an interim measure, the present contract which expires at the end of September, 1946, should be extended for another year at the current price, and the Government of Ceylon should be enabled to participate in the discussions on the future arrangements for purchase of rubber, which are due to take place with the American Government towards the end of the year.

(d) *Cost of Food Subsidy*. Any loss in the Food Advance Account during the period 1st July, 1946, to 30th June, 1947, as the result of maintaining food prices at their present level should be reimbursed by His Majesty's Government.

2.  He supports these requests with a great wealth of detailed argument, his main points being as follows:—

(1) In present conditions of shortage of supply, the free market price in the world free market of tea and copra would be much higher than the prices now being paid to Ceylon and they are, therefore, entitled to a substantial increase of price. If they now forego some part of the theoretical free market price, it should only be in return for an arrangement which would assure them against a serious fall in price when supplies become more plentiful in a few years' time.

(2) In the case of rubber, the conditions of shortage have already passed, but since Ceylon did not exploit the shortage period by getting a very high price she should now be protected from a fall in price for a period in order to provide a cushion for adjustment of the industry to new conditions.

(3) Ceylon is entitled to some recompense for the fact that during the war period the prices paid for her products were substantially less than their true value having regard to the scarcity of the commodities concerned. It is urged that the prices of Ceylon exports have increased very substantially less than the prices of her imports and that this is one indicator of the under-payment. It is, moreover, urged that Ceylon drew attention during the war to this under-payment and must, therefore, be regarded as having established a right to retrospective adjustment.

(4) Ceylon's internal economy has been inflated because of the means by which United Kingdom military expenditure in Ceylon was financed and this has resulted in inflated costs for her industries. The inflation is partly blamed on the special currency connection between the Ceylon rupee and sterling.

(5) In the particular case of rubber, the high rate of tapping employed during the war meant in fact that Ceylon rubber trees were being prematurely exhausted and her productive capital seriously depleted.

(6) There is a general expectation and intention that the standard of living and particularly the standard of social services in Ceylon shall be maintained and increased. In fact owing to the existence of war conditions and particularly of food shortages, social conditions have if anything deteriorated, e.g. as judged by mortality rates. In order that the Ceylon Government may have the revenue at its disposal to carry out the social reforms, it is essential that the revenue of the country as a whole from exports, which form so high a proportion of its total national income, should be maintained and increased.

3.  A point which is not heavily stressed in Sir Oliver Goonetilleke's memoran-

dum, but has been put more forcibly in conversation is the political one, that if Ceylon is not well treated in matters of this kind, those among Ceylonese politicians who look to a weakening or breaking of the imperial connection and possibly a closer link with India will be greatly strengthened.

4. The answers which I think should be made to the points referred to in paragraph 2 are as follows:—

(1) There is little dispute about the principle that Ceylon like other colonies should either be entitled to get the benefit of commercial prices today or be given a reasonably long-term contract at a price which will protect them against the slump in a few years' time. These are the principles put to and substantially accepted by other Ministers in our report on commodity prices. The Ministry of Food's offer on tea and copra is in fact their interpretation of these principles and although we may properly press for a somewhat more generous interpretation the differences are substantially quite small.

(2) The principle that rubber producers in Ceylon deserved some period of adjustment from war conditions is also not denied, but the Board of Trade would argue very forcibly that they have provided that period by the continuation of the war-time price for Ceylon rubber for over twelve months after the end of the war. That arrangement has in fact provoked the most bitter resentment from Malayan producers who neither enjoyed the good prices of the war years, nor had this special favour after the war and we have now intimated to Ceylon that the Secretary of State could not support any discrimination in her favour.

(3) (a) The suggestion of past under-payment leads, of course, to endless argument and possible repercussions. It is true that Ceylon rubber was of a value to the United Nations on which it would be difficult to put an exact monetary price (although the Ministry of Supply consistently held, in opposition to American views, that in the last resort there was no need for us to pay fancy prices for Ceylon rubber). But equally the value of the ships which carried the rubber and which carried also the food to feed Ceylon is hardly calculable in money terms. Still less is the value of the war ships which defended Ceylon from the Japanese attack in 1942 and of the troops and aeroplanes which in fact saved Ceylon from the fate of Burma and Malaya. If, therefore we once get on to a re-assessment of war-time activities in money terms, there is no end to the calculation and there is everything to be said for a complete and final closing of the account on both sides without further adjustment.

(b) On the particular point of the ratio between import and export prices, it has to be borne in mind that import prices reflected the full increase of freights and war-time insurance, whereas exports being calculated on an f.o.b. basis, included no such increases.

(c) The calculation based on the export/import price ratio completely ignores the very large benefits involved in increased output. In the pre-war years both tea and rubber were subject to quota restriction, rubber at times a very heavy restriction. Practically throughout the war years output was unrestricted and the total increase of output can hardly be put at less than 50%. There was also an increased demand for some other Ceylon products, such as graphite which was in very poor demand before the war.

(d) The calculation ignores also the very large accession to the income of Ceylon as a country due to military expenditure in the Island.

(e) It is argued that it has been unfair to continue to base prices on a formula which took account of profit increases of costs, but in effect stabilised profits at their pre-war level. This ignores, however, the fact that stabilising profits per unit of output meant substantially increased aggregate profits from the increased output already mentioned.

(f) The argument that Ceylon has a right to reopen the past contracts does not sustain examination. It is true that the point was made generally that, in view of the increase in import prices, export prices ought to be increased, but it was tacitly accepted that that was in fact taken into account in the striking of particular bargains over individual products, and Sir O. Goonetilleke does not claim that any reservation was ever made when particular prices were accepted.

(g) If it were true, which is not conceded, that Ceylon had in fact suffered by selling her products at less than their theoretical market prices, that can very reasonably be regarded as Ceylon's contribution to the war. She has made no other monetary contribution and has borne only a small fraction of the costs of her own defence. It is not unreasonable, therefore, that she should contribute in this way. In many other colonies it can equally be argued that they could have got higher prices for their products, but those other colonies in so far as they have consciously thought the matter out are willing to forego the right for any such deficit in payment as part of their war contribution. Mr. F.E.V. Smith has, for instance, stated that his own calculation is that Nigeria has lost between £60 and £70 million on her oilseeds as compared with the price she might have exacted, judged by much higher prices paid for similar oilseeds elsewhere in the world. A very similar calculation and a similar attitude has been taken by colonial sugar producers.

(4) (a) I regard the suggestion that the inflationary situation in Ceylon was aggravated by her currency position as completely unfounded. The currency position is simply that the backing for Ceylon's currency is held in sterling instead of being held in local securities or in gold. If the currency had been on a different basis, the Ceylon currency reserves would now consist of either local securities which would not be much use internationally or gold which, subject to any possible variations in the price at which it was acquired and at which it now stands, would be no more valuable than sterling. Ceylon has today a sterling asset which is in form available for expenditure. Provided no attempt is made to deprive her of that asset (which is another story) she is in no way damaged by this particular currency arrangement. What undoubtedly did cause inflation was the fact that expenditure was incurred at a level which could not be balanced by imports of consumer goods, but that would have been the position whatever the currency set-up.

(b) The inflationary situation was undoubtedly aggravated by the failure of the Ceylon Government to take the necessary measures, e.g. by taxation and by subsidisation of the cost of living, in order to secure stability of wages, to confine it. We repeatedly urged them to take such measures both in general circulars and in despatches on the annual estimates and it was the inability of the Ceylon Ministers, for political reasons, to carry out a sound financial policy which has caused the higher degree of inflation in Ceylon as compared with most other colonies.

(5) It is very dubious whether Ceylon rubber trees have suffered significantly as a result of intensive tapping during the war. The truth is that a great many Ceylon rubber estates were hopelessly uneconomic before the war. The temporary shortage of the war period saved them for the time being, but that temporary respite is over and they must now again face competitive conditions.

(6) I do not think the revenue needs of a country such as Ceylon with its claim to practically full self-government can be accepted as a reason for exceptional and in essence charitable treatment in commercial transactions. In any case the real truth is that, owing to the shortcomings of their war-time taxation policy (local E.P.T. was only 50%), the Ceylon Government have failed to accummulate the reserves they well could have done and cannot now ask H.M.G. to help them out of their difficulties.

5. Finally, as to the political argument it is not for me to weigh its value, but I am on general principle profoundly sceptical about the wisdom of attempting to secure political objects by economic means nor do I in fact believe that, if there is a genuine underlying trend towards breaking away from the Empire, any amount of economic benefits will counter-act that trend.

# 372  CO 852/569, no 81                                   22 Oct 1946
# [Purchase of Ceylon products]: CO note of a meeting between Mr Creech Jones and Sir O Goonetilleke on 14 Oct

The Secretary of State in welcoming Sir Oliver referred to the very full memorandum[1] which he submitted covering his commodity proposals and said that although he had not been able to study the memorandum in its fullest detail he was now familiar with its objectives and with the arguments used to support these objectives. We would continue to do everything possible to help. The Secretary of State then asked Sir Oliver to make a resume of his case.

Having congratulated the Secretary of State on his appointment, Sir Oliver dealt first with the *rubber* situation. Since his memorandum was written that situation had got worse. With rubber at 1/- a pound three quarters of the Ceylon industry was doomed. He had pressed the Americans for a special treatment of Ceylon rubber, but they had argued that any special assistance must come from H.M.G. The fact of the matter was that Ceylon rubber had sustained the market during the war and the industry was now like a wounded soldier—it could not compete with the Malayan industry which had lain fallow during the war. If it had to face such competition it would be the small-holders and the relatively inefficient Ceylonese estates which would suffer most. With high import costs, which increased the cost of labour—labour representing 70% of the cost of production of rubber—it was impossible to

---

[1] See 368.

make any immediate reduction in costs. Sir Oliver added that European estates must also suffer from the general collapse of the industry.

The Secretary of State asked whether the elimination of the less efficient Ceylon production was not already imminent before the war. Was it not therefore true to say that the artificially high price of rubber during the war had merely suspended a process of elimination which was an inevitable result of cheaper production in the Far East.

Sir Oliver admitted that this was so to some extent but again emphasised that the crucial factor was the rise in import costs especially cereals and textiles which now stood at two to three times above pre-war levels. Ceylon had tapped rubber during the war at several times the normal rate with consequent permanent damage to trees. Production had therefore fallen from a peak of 120,000 tons to about 80,000 tons even at the relatively high price of 1/7¼d. per pound. This price was only a fraction of the price which Ceylon could have got as monopolist under war conditions. In return for Ceylon's sacrifice during the war it was considered as H.M.G.'s moral obligation to support the industry during the period of falling post-war prices. He had now come to the conclusion that support by way of a differential price for Ceylon rubber was impossible (although he had reservations about the wisdom of the recent negotiations with the Americans) instead he was now proposing a subsidy for rehabilitation and he submitted a memorandum to the Secretary of State accordingly. This called for a replanting subsidy estimated at £45 million with an additional £21 million, making a total of £66 million, for maintaining estates during the rehabilitation period.

On the point of Ceylon's sacrifice in accepting something less than a monopoly price for rubber during the war the Secretary of State pointed out that this might be considered as part of the general sacrifice borne by all producers during the war and referred to the very heavy sacrifices which had fallen upon the U.K. Sir Oliver countered by saying that in his view Ceylon had borne a heavier and more personal sacrifice than any other country because of high costs of imports and consequent mal-nutrition—the death rate was now higher than it had ever been—financially Ceylon's balances were inadequate to meet deferred expenditure on rubber and other purposes and a subsidy was not only essential to rehabilitate the industry, but would be regarded as a just recompense to rubber producers for their war-time sacrifices. During the war the industry had had less than pre-war profits because of the rise in import prices; and during the war period the terms of trade had turned adversely against Ceylon which had previously had a favourable balance with the outside world.

The Secretary of State pointed out that Ceylon had enjoyed a high price for rubber for a year after the war and that Malayan rubber had meanwhile been sold at a much lower price. He asked whether, if the subsidy were granted, it would be used to re-organise the industry by eliminating inefficient production and in what way it would affect the proceeds of the more efficiently operated estates.

Sir Oliver replied that any scheme of subsidised re-planting would not apply to estates having reserves. *It was agreed* that Sir Oliver's revised proposals for rubber would be submitted to the Board of Trade although it was thought that a final decision on them would have to be taken by the Treasury.

As regards *copra*, Sir Oliver explained that a contract was in existence between Ceylon and the Ministry of Food, negotiated by himself in February. The price in the contract was 100 rps. per candy. The Ministry of Food bought Ceylon's total output under the contract and re-sold part to India on a cost basis. This meant incidentally that Ceylon copra was now being sold to India at ⅓rd. of the Indian domestic price.

Sir Oliver admitted that there were no particular grounds for breaking the contract; but the coconut industry was in a bad way and in view of the threatened crash in the rubber industry he felt that he was justified in re-opening the matter now. No large estates were involved. The small-holders who grew copra were in the same group as those affected by the rubber slump. He was asking for a 50% increase in price and a 10 years contract. The reason for the extension in the term of the contract was that coconut palms took 10 years to come to bearing and the industry needed assurance over this period if rehabilitation and improvement of plantations was to be undertaken.

H.M.G. was desperately short of fats and could certainly afford to pay more for this small part of her overseas imports. The Secretary of State asked how Sir Oliver would answer the point that a contract had been negotiated earlier this year, was still in existence and that there was nothing in the contract itself which would permit a revision now. Sir Oliver answered that apart from a change in the situation to which he had referred, H.M.G. presumably had an interest in Ceylon's welfare and must assist in the present industrial crisis otherwise the present administration would break down. He referred also to the various schemes which had been recently discussed (e.g. the scheme for growing groundnuts in Tanganyika) for the specific purpose of increasing in the long term the overseas supplies of fats. If present prices were maintained Ceylon production would fall because there would be no replanting.

In answer to a question from the Secretary of State as to whether an increased price or a replanting subsidy was suggested Sir Oliver said that he would prefer to deal with the situation by an increased price which was justified on current market values at least for Indian and Argentine oilseeds.

Sir George Gater intervened to ask whether if the price had gone the other way Ceylon would have agreed to a suggestion by the Ministry of Food that the contract should be revised. Sir Oliver replied that the U.K. could afford to stand a loss, whereas Ceylon could not. Additional money was desperately needed to improve the coconut industry. He was prepared to admit that the Ceylon administration had made a tragic blunder in not setting their sights higher in past price negotiations. They would certainly be regarded as having let the producers down if H.M.G. did not now come to their help.

The Secretary of State pointed out that during the war period Colonial producers in general had not pushed their advantage as monopoly sellers. What had been sacrifice in war-time should, he thought, be regarded as part of the general contribution to the war effort. He doubted whether the difficulties into which the industry had fallen had been caused by the payment of "unfair" prices by H.M.G. during the war. Prices paid to Ceylon had on the whole been reasonable and the good profits made during the war by most agricultural producers had placed them in a favourable position.

Sir Oliver took issue on this point. He did not agree that Ceylon had got fair prices during the war for either rubber, tea or copra. Producers had only got one half the price they were entitled to. True the peasantry rubber estates had done well, but local producers had done badly because of the relatively higher rise in costs of imports as compared with increases in produce prices. Local inflation had also been caused by H.M.G.'s method of financing local expenditure in Ceylon. This was a contributory factor to local mal-nutrition and to the recent alarming rise in mortality rates.

*It was agreed* that Sir Oliver would pursue this question further with the Ministry of Food. The Secretary of State did not hold out any strong hope that he would be successful in persuading them that the contract should be revised.

Sir Oliver admitted at this stage that *tea* was probably Ceylon's only hope. As substantial producers of tea they could take full advantage of the present shortage. Their contract with the Ministry of Food runs out at the end of this year, thereafter, if trade were free, the price would, he felt, go to five times the present level. He intended to make full use of this strong bargaining position, but he would require the support of the Colonial Office.

What he wanted was a long term contract, say for 5 years, at a 1/- a pound in excess of the present contract price.

In answer to a question from the Secretary of State Sir Oliver said that the Ministry of Food had made an offer which involved a possible increase of about 2d. a pound, but this was quite unsatisfactory. Ceylon's offer of a medium term contract at an increase of 1/- a pound was, he felt, reasonable. The immediate price then to Ceylon on a free market would be considerably greater.

*It was agreed* that this question should also be pursued further with the Ministry of Food.

Summing up the results of the discussion the Secretary of State thought he now understood fully Sir Oliver's objectives. He was impressed by the importance of reaching a satisfactory economic settlement on political considerations. The political repercussions of a failure to do so he did not wish to under-estimate. At the same time he saw considerable difficulties in persuading the buying Ministries to meet Sir Oliver's full demands and the Colonial Office was not of course master of U.K. import policy. Sir Oliver should therefore not be too optimistic although he could count on his full support in further negotiations. He would arrange for Sir Oliver to see Sir Stafford Cripps at the Board of Trade to talk over the rubber situation and would immediately have his alternative proposals for a subsidy on rubber examined by officials. He would also arrange an interview with Mr. Strachey, the Minister of Food, on copra and tea.

Sir Oliver thanked the Secretary of State for his sympathetic hearing of Ceylon's case. He would only like to add that he had personal instructions from Mr. Senanayake and to submit that before an official decision was reached H.M.G. should consider the importance of maintaining Ceylon's friendship and of ensuring that Ceylon remained a willing partner on the British side. That he was convinced could not be if a fair economic settlement of her present difficulties was not achieved. There was danger that opinion might swing in favour of the extremists who were anxious to find any reasonable ground for making a break with the U.K. Ceylon had not in the past asked for too much, she had, for example, made no call on Colonial Development and Welfare funds. Now was the time for practical assistance by H.M.G. Sir Oliver appreciated that viewed narrowly and only on economic grounds the Ceylon case would not stand. He ventured to hope, however, that Ministers would decide in favour of his submission on broader grounds, that such a decision would make for good Government in Ceylon and would in the long term cement Ceylon's position in the British Commonwealth.

The Secretary of State again assured Sir Oliver that he was fully alive to the political issues at stake. It was right that we should all look ahead and should not reach decisions on matters of this kind from a narrow or short term point of view. Whilst he could not commit other Ministers he felt that they would also be sympathetic to this view and he would certainly himself do what he could to ensure that Sir Oliver got a sympathetic hearing in his further talks.

**373**  CO 54/995/1, no 1                                                28 Oct 1946
[Senanayake and the public service]: minutes (item 17) of a meeting of the Board of Ministers on the strikes of Oct 1946                    [Extract]

. . . The Hon. Mr. D.S. Senanayake, Vice-Chairman of the Board of Ministers and Leader of the State Council, referred to the attitude adopted by the authorities concerned in dealing with the strikes and the consequent disturbances the previous week. He said that those responsible for the administration of the Public Service had in several instances acted in a manner which appeared to him to be calculated to create dissension in the Public Service and chaos in the country. He referred to the manner in which the Police had dealt with the situation created by the strike and particularly to the incident connected with the assault on the Mayor of Colombo. The Police, though they had issued a permit for a procession of the strikers on the day of the assault, had not taken sufficient precautions to protect the public. They have not yet even been able to trace the assailants.

He added that as he had lost faith in the administration generally and in the ability of the Police Force to provide any measure of protection to the law-abiding public against acts of lawlessness, he proposed to dissociate himself from the administration of the Public Service and to make a public statement at the earliest opportunity with regard to his attitude in this matter.

He stated that a few weeks before the strike he had brought to the notice of His Excellency the Officer Administering the Government his grave concern at the indifference shown in recent times by the officers responsible for the administration of the Public Service which was bound to result in an undisciplined Service. He had submitted to His Excellency that it was essential that an efficient and well-disciplined Public Service should be available when responsible government is to be handed over to elected representatives and the present state of affairs may give the impression that His Majesty's Government is no longer interested in the progress of this country. He had asked His Excellency to forward his representations to the Secretary of State for the Colonies. . . .

**374**  CO 852/569, no 87                                                [Oct 1946]
[Purchase of Ceylon products]: letter from Mr Creech Jones to Sir O Goonetilleke on the decisions of HMG. *Minutes* by Creech Jones and Sir G Gater

You submitted to my predecessor on the 5th September certain representations with regard to arrangements for the purchase of rubber, tea and copra from Ceylon and the general economic position of the Island.[1] These representations have been carefully considered by my predecessor and myself and by the other Ministers concerned, with whom you have had personal discussions. I am now, therefore, in a position to convey to you the decisions of His Majesty's Government, which are as follows.

1. *Tea*. You originally suggested a five year contract for the whole Ceylon exportable surplus at a price of 1/- per lb. above the current price. The Ministry of Food felt unable to accept this proposal, but have made an alternative offer for a contract extending over four years at lower prices and in the later years covering only a part of Ceylon's exportable surplus. The details of this alternative offer have already been communicated to you. After the fullest consideration, His Majesty's Government feel unable to go beyond this offer, and if the Government of Ceylon prefer in those circumstances to enter into no further contract arrangements with regard to the supply of tea, His Majesty's Government will consider in due course the necessary arrangements for purchase of their requirements of Ceylon tea after the end of this year through commercial channels. His Majesty's Government would ask that the Ceylon Government's decision on the acceptance or rejection of a further bulk contract should be signified as soon as possible.

2. *Coconut products*. You requested a replacement of the present five year contract by a fresh contract for ten years as from the 1st January, 1947, at a price 50% above the present contract price. His Majesty's Government regret their inability to agree to a departure from the terms of the present contract concluded early this year.

3. *Rubber*. You requested an extension of the contract which was due to expire on the 30th September, 1946. You have since been associated with more recent negotiations with the United States regarding the new situation which has developed in relation to rubber owing to the unexpectedly rapid recovery of production in Malaya and the Netherlands East Indies. As a result of those discussions, it is intended to bring Government bulk purchase of rubber to an end very shortly and to revert to marketing through normal commercial channels. In consequence, His Majesty's Government have been unable to arrange for any extension of the former Ceylon contract, but they have made interim arrangements for the purchase of further quantities of Ceylon rubber for shipment during October, November and December, at the price of 1/2d. per lb. f.o.b., in order to assist in the adjustment of the new situation. His Majesty's Government will also give careful consideration to outstanding questions with regard to the settlement of claims for the reimbursement of the cost of replanting rubber estates in Ceylon under the "slaughter tapping" arrangements made during the war and will transmit definite proposals to the Ceylon Government for the settlement of these questions.

4. In addition, you asked that His Majesty's Government should reimburse the Ceylon Government for any losses incurred in maintaining food prices at their present level during the period 1st July, 1946 to 30th June, 1947, and in representations made subsequent to your original submission to Mr. Hall, you made proposals for an ad hoc grant for the rehabilitation of Ceylon export industries, particularly rubber. His Majesty's Government regret that they cannot see their way to making any special grants of these kinds to Ceylon in view of the very heavy

---

[1] See 368.

burdens on the United Kingdom Exchequer and the continuing extremely difficult balance of payments situation of the United Kingdom.

I should like to express my regret that it has not been possible to meet your requests, but would ask you to accept my assurance that the above decisions have been reached only after very careful examination of the situation. I hope that the financial and economic difficulties which you apprehend in Ceylon will be found in practice to be less serious than your worst fears, but the difficulties of adjustment to post-war conditions which the Island is likely to experience will certainly be borne in mind by His Majesty's Government in discussions of the settlement of any other oustanding financial issues between His Majesty's Government and Ceylon.

**Minutes on 374**

An impassive but crest-fallen Goonetilleke saw me. I told him the Colonial Office had done its utmost to secure a more generous decision. I had hoped that with the goodwill of the Minister of Food we should be able to persuade the Chancellor of the Exchequer. But though I had used all the broad arguments, not excepting the political ones, the Chancellor because of financial problems of His Majesty's Government had felt unable to make any concession. He had hinted at possibly some contribution to a public work (e.g. an Airfield) but that was vague and not very helpful. Goonetilleke remained impassive and refused to argue. He thought the political reactions would be serious in the next few years. I told him he had our completest sympathy, but it would be useless for me to go to the Cabinet when, in present circumstances of the nation, the Chancellor of the Exchequer was in an impregnable position. He received the letter and indicated that with tea they would seek to sell in the free market. He asked that they, i.e. the Board of Trade, should take the necessary steps to return to the free market by 1st January. It was a gloomy interview.

A.C.J.
30.10.46

I saw Mr. Goonetilleke and his attitude was repressed and gloomy. He described the decision as a tragic blunder, and implied that it would end close co-operation between H.M.G. and Ceylon. I think that his personal pride has been wounded by his lack of success, and he looks forward to personal embarrassment as well as political difficulties on his return to Ceylon. In the circumstances there was nothing further to be said from my side and I did not prolong the interview.[2]

G.H.G.
31.10.46

---

[2] Despite these assessments, Howard (OAG in the absence of Moore) informed Gater that Goonetilleke was not unduly depressed upon his return and that he showed no signs of being embittered (CO 852/569, no 93, inward tel no 1764, 5 Nov 1946).

**375**   CO 54/995/1, no 1A                                           18 Nov 1946

[Police]: inward telegram no 1838 from Sir J Howard to Sir G Gater on
Mr Senanayake's campaign for the termination of the contracts of
three European police officers

With reference to fourth paragraph of Moore's personal message to me in your No.
1265 I think you should know that violent campaign has been launched by
Senanayake having for its object immediate termination of contracts of Bacon,
Waldron and Brodie, Police Officers appointed in 1943 on secondment from
Metropolitan Police. I anticipate early show-down as result of unanimous request for
such termination from ex Committee of Home Affairs. Senanayake campaign and
action of Committee purports to be based on matters arising from recent strike such
as the arrest of labour leader Dr. N.M. Perera who was released the same day on
account of error of law on part of Police, faulty Police arrangements in connection
with a procession in course on which Mayor of Colombo received injuries, and
alleged failure to take adequate steps for maintenance of law and order. Senanayake
also professes complete lack of confidence in Bacon by reason of dissensions in Police
as result of introduction of Metropolitan Police Officers in 1943 and considers that
divided loyalty amongst officers of Force will result in its inability to bear the strain
in the case of civil disturbances arising in the case of strikes or possibly during the
general election.

2.   Personally I consider the Police blundered badly on the arrest of Perera nor
was I satisfied with the arrangements for the control of the procession and no doubt
there are dissensions and a divided loyalty in the Force. But I am endeavouring to
persuade the Minister for Home Affairs to prevail upon his Committee to refrain from
any action in connection with the officers I have mentioned until report of Police
Commission now sitting has been received. This report, I understand, will be in my
hands by the end of this month.

3.   The contracts of the three officers mentioned expire towards the end of next
year. I gather that they would have no objection to the termination of their
appointments provided such action cast no stigma on their reputation. I understand
that Brindley would be proposed as successor to Bacon or possibly a civil servant. I
am doubtful if Brindley would be prepared to accept the appointment, appointment
of civil servant might be best solution to tide over period up to beginning operation
of new constitution when Cabinet would presumably reconsider. Civil servant would
have personal discords in the Force and would I think handle Minister and ex
Committee more adroitly than Policeman.

4.   Article 86 of 1931 Order-in-Council of course invests control of public service
in Governor and I do not propose to recommend premature termination of
appointments referred to, unless after consultation with Public Service Commission
I am satisfied that this is essential in interest of the Force and maintenance of
security. But situation very delicate and there is possibility of resignation of
Senanayake, Mahadeva and possibly other Ministers if they do not get their way. I will
keep you informed.

**376**   CO 54/995/1, no 1B                                          25 Nov 1946
**[Police]: inward telegram no 1866 from Sir J Howard to Mr Creech Jones on Mr Senanayake's proposal to establish a permanently mobilised Battalion of Volunteers**

My secret telegram No. 1612 and preceding connected telegrams.[1]

Senanayake has publicly stated that he thinks that a Battalion of Volunteers should be established and kept permanently mobilised and I have received a formal request from the Ministers for the establishment of such a unit, which I am advised could not be accomplished under the Defence Force Ordinance, but would require special local legislation. Reasons which Senanayake gave publicly are that such a unit would be beginning of an army of their own and that it would be a support to the police until latter are brought up to full strength and are fully trained. Lack of faith in police, which I do not share, is probably real reason. Furthermore, recent and contemplated use of military in aid of police has already been subject of public criticism and I am not altogether happy about Senanayake's or Mahadeva's views on this point. Apart altogether from the fact that it is inopportune now to raise issue of standing Ceylonese Military Forces, it is essential that Senanayake's confidence should be restored if serious mistakes are to be avoided, his own position is not to be weakened and the present deterioration in the political situation is not to be increased.

2.   Present scheme for use of military in aid of the civil power is based on the Inspector General of Police's estimate that, in worst possible conditions in Colombo, 800 would be his maximum requirement. Scheme is:—

(a)  The transfer of some 300–350 mobilised Ceylon Defence Force personnel from their existing duties. This transfer can be effected as to 200–250 within a very few hours and as to the balance within 20 hours, but this part of scheme depends on further demobilisation of Ceylon Defence Force being postponed (see paragraph 4 of my secret telegram No. 1722).

(b)  The call up of 800 non-effective Ceylon Defence Force personnel, which can be completed within 36–48 hours. Figure 800 allows margin for failure to respond to call up, etc.

3.   Reorganisation of Ceylon Defence Force following demobilisation is proceeding on basis that numbers must be determined by arms and equipment immediately available, i.e. that which Army Command is obliged to return, which is sufficient to equip approximately 3,500. Should be grateful if importance of speed in return of Ceylon Defence Force equipment and premises could be impressed on War Office.

4.   But it is decision on question of post-war Garrison which is most important. I understand that post-war Garrison should ultimately be able to provide 500 to 800 men in aid of civil power but, having regard to your secret telegram No. 1384, I cannot give Senanayake any assurance to this effect or as to the time when such personnel would be available. Meanwhile, I should like:—

(a)  Assurance that War Office will actively support paragraph 2(a) and paragraph 3.

(b)  Your views as to the reply which I should make to the Ministers request.

---

[1] cf 375.

5.   Paragraph 2 of your secret telegram No. 1384. Ministers' request in paragraph 1 above adds further complication. I should like your views as to reply to be made to this request before putting recruitment of Malayan Unit formally to Ministers. Senanayake may insist that Ceylon's needs must be met before Malaya's. I do not want to invite refusal, but I may find it possible to sound Senanayake informally.

# 377   CO 537/2213                                       16–18 Dec 1946
## [Burma and Ceylon]: minutes by J B Sidebotham on the political implications for Mr Senanayake of the impending promise by HMG of independence to Burma

*Sir C. Jeffries*
I think you will be interested to see Nos. 1–5 on this file. The position is, generally, that the Working Committee of A.F.P.F.L. (the Anti-Fascist Peoples Freedom League in Burma), which is the only responsible body of any sort in Burma apparently that H.M.G. has to negotiate with, when invited to send a Delegation to this country to discuss the next steps in the Constitutional progress of Burma proceeded to hold a pistol at H.M.G.'s head and demand, *inter alia*, an assurance that a categorical declaration would be made forthwith that Burma would get complete independence within a year, as well as acceptance of certain other equally inconvenient points as the basic principles which the Conference would proceed to turn into concrete proposals.

At the discussion of No. 1 by the Cabinet on the 10th December,[1] the Secretary of State referred to the possible repercussions on Ceylon (and Malaya) of any further promises of rapid constitutional development in Burma (see on second page of Cabinet conclusions at No. 2). Further discussions in the Cabinet[2] revealed that if, in the last event, H.M.G. refused to accede to A.F.P.F.L.'s request, there were few British troops available to cope with any widespread disorder and that more could not be provided without holding up the demobilisation scheme. It was decided to seek the views of the Governor by personal telegram (see copy at No. 5), which suggests the possible line which H.M.G. should take in paragraph 4 and asks the Governor's views on the timing of the approach etc.

All this is very important from the Ceylon end of the picture. If H.M.G. were to be forced into the position of promising Burma her immediate freedom at any time before the elections for the first new Parliament in Ceylon had been held, it might have the most serious consequences for Mr. Senanayake and his Party I think. Mr. Senanayake has pledged himself to see the new Constitution into existence in the belief that it is the best he can get for Ceylon and that, if the Ceylon Government works its *quasi* Dominion status satisfactorily, in a matter of 2 or 3 years Ceylon will attain full Dominion status.

If Ceylon were suddenly to be faced with the fact that H.M.G. had handed independence to Burma overnight, she would at once turn round, I think, and say, "We were your faithful helpers during the recent war, and what did Burma do? It evidently pays better to browbeat and threaten trouble to H.M.G. than to accept what

---

[1] For the record of which see *BSI*, vol II, 131.          [2] *ibid* 134, Cabinet conclusions, 12 Dec 1946.

H.M.G. offer quietly, although that offer may be far short of what we desire". Now that may or may not be the right way of looking at it, but I am quite convinced that that is the way Ministers in Ceylon will look at it and, if there is to be any promise of independence for Burma before the new Constitution in Ceylon comes into force, then H.M.G. must be prepared, I suggest in fairness to Ceylon, to make some further declaration as regards a similar grant of Dominion status to Ceylon and to undertake to re-open discussions for that purpose if necessary as soon as the new Constitution has become fully effective.

But the most important thing, from our point of view, is that nothing should be sprung on us overnight, that there should be no sudden declarations which might jeopardize the whole political set-up in Ceylon and that we are kept fully informed of progress in this matter of Burma. Sir George Gater spoke to me about it the other day and suggested that I might like to go over and talk to Mr. Smith of the Burma Office, and this I most certainly wish to do. I rang him up and said that I would do so when I had had an opportunity of studying the papers, but I should like you to see what is happening before I go, and I should also like authority to stress the very serious implications which decisions in this Burma matter might have vis-à-vis Ceylon and how essential it was that we should be kept fully in touch with developments.[3]

J.B.S.<br>16.12.46

I saw Mr. G. Smith at 3.15 p.m. this afternoon. I explained to him the difficulties at our end of the picture, which he quite appreciated. He had with him an advance copy of the attached "Most Immediate" telegram at (6) in reply to (5), from which it will be seen that the Governor of Burma has gone ahead with discussions with A.F.P.F.L. representative as to the outcome of which see "X" of paragraph 2 from which it is clear that A.F.P.F.L. would not take part in the Delegation unless (as Mr. Smith explained to me) some sort of statement promising independence in the immediate future was included. Unfortunately the Governor of Burma did not give the text of the formula referred to in paragraph 3 of that telegram, and the India Office had cabled asking for it and were hoping to have it before a meeting of the I.M.B. Cabinet Committee (of which I understand Lord Addison[4] is a member) at 10.0 a.m. tomorrow morning. Mr. Smith tells me that a Paper is being put up to that Committee,[5] in which the Secretary of State for India concludes that, if A.F.P.F.L. remain obdurate and demand an assurance as to independence in the immediate future, he will be compelled to give way. The alternative would probably be bloodshed in Burma, the British Forces there being insufficient to control the situation and the Police morale being low.

I emphasised how important it was, from our end of the picture, that we should have, if possible, some opportunity of preparing the ground if a decision was reached which would mean the early announcement to Burma of a promise of complete independence in the immediate future before the Delegation would consent to come

---

[3] Sir C Jeffries minuted (17 Dec): 'I agree with Mr. Sidebotham. If it is decided to make any concession to Burma I feel that it will be crucial at the same time (or before) to make a further offer to Ceylon.'
[4] Secretary of state for dominion affairs.
[5] For the record of this meeting of the Cabinet India and Burma Committee, see *BSI*, vol II, 144.

to this country, and what such an assurance to Burma might possibly involve us in in respect of Ceylon. I feel that it is most important that when the Cabinet comes to consider this matter at tomorrow's meeting, our difficulties in this matter should be strongly represented, and that it should be made clear, if the Secretary of State agrees, that yielding to Burma will, in all probability, entail some further offer to Ceylon being made if there is to be any hope of getting the new Constitution going at all. I think we further ought to warn the Acting Governor by secret and personal telegram of the situation which has developed in Burma. It would, in my view, be completely disastrous to allow a promise to Burma of this kind to be sprung at Mr. Senanayake at the outset of his election campaign without proper warning and without giving him a card to play in the way of some assurance of progress in the near future beyond the present Constitution. Unfortunately, the India Office are apparently tied by a timetable, the 9th of January, 1947, being, I think, the date that the Delegation is supposed to be coming here, so that the time at our disposal is extremely short.

J.B.S.
18.12.46

## 378   CO 54/995/1, no 1                                    4 Jan 1947
## [Public service]: despatch from Sir J Howard to Mr Creech Jones forwarding correspondence with Mr Senanayake and a memorandum by Sir R Drayton. *Annexes* I–V

I have the honour to address you at the request of Mr. D.S. Senanayake, Leader of the State Council and Vice-Chairman of the Board of Ministers regarding the discipline of the Public Service; I forward herewith:—

(1) a copy of a letter dated 28th September addressed to me by Mr. Senanayake on this subject, in the final paragraph of which he asks that the matter be brought to your notice. Annexe I.
(2) My reply to Mr. Senanayake dated the 1st October, 1946, in which I asked for further and more precise information. Annexe II.
(3) A further letter addressed by me to Mr. Senanayake on October 31st again asking for the further particulars already asked for in my previous letter. Annexe III.
(4) Mr. Senanayake's reply dated the 12th November, 1946. Annexe IV.
(5) The Chief Secretary's memorandum dated the 28th November on the preceding correspondence. Annexe V.

2.  I am in a position of some difficulty in commenting on these criticisms of Mr. Senanayake because they relate to a period of time when I was not holding any office in which I had either any responsibility in regard to the administration of the Public Service or any access to direct information regarding conditions in the Public Service.
3.  As you will observe from the date of Mr. Senanayake's original letter of criticism (i.e. the 28th September, 1946) his attitude towards the Public Service could not have been founded on the strikes within the Public Service which had not

then occurred or been seriously threatened, but must rest on events which occurred at a time when either Sir Andrew Caldecott or Sir Henry Moore was the Governor and Sir Robert Drayton was Chief Secretary. In these circumstances I forward the memorandum of the Chief Secretary which sets out the views of one of the responsible authorities. So far as my knowledge goes, I am in general agreement with those views although I might be disposed to qualify some of them.

4.  I have received the Chief Secretary's memorandum on trade unions within the Public Service (see paragraph 3 of Annexe V) and have referred it to the Board of Ministers for their advice. I hope to address you shortly on this subject.

## Annex I to 378

Further to the conversation I had with you on the 25th September regarding the deterioration of the standard of discipline in the Public Service, I wish to impress on Your Excellency the serious situation that has arisen by the encouragement given by the authorities for the formation of various associations and unions of public officers. I am informed that in certain cases free Railway Warrants have been issued for the transport of officers connected with the activities of these associations and unions, and I have no doubt that many of these activities are undertaken within office hours and in Government Offices where officers are expected to attend to their normal duties.

2.  You would no doubt have observed that the activities and demands made on Government by these bodies in recent times indicate that there is a serious deterioration in discipline among these public servants. These associations which count among their numbers both senior and junior officers of the same department tend to hamper the discharge of the duties of the senior officers in relation to their juniors, e.g. I am told that Sergeants in the Police Force who are members of Sergeants and Constables Union are finding it embarrassing and difficult to deal with Constables who are also members of the same Union. If this state of affairs were to continue longer, we would have a most undisciplined public service which would not be of any assistance to the Government.

3.  Under the Order-in-Council, Your Excellency is vested with the disciplinary control of the Public Service, which you have delegated to the Chief Secretary. With the impending constitutional changes, when responsible government is to be handed over to elected representatives, it is essential that an efficient and well-disciplined Public Service should be available, and I have much doubt that this will be the case if serious notice is not taken of the present state of affairs. It will not be to the credit of the present Government to hand over such a Public Service to the new Government, and may give one the impression that His Majesty's Government is no longer interested in the affairs and the progress of this country.

4.  I enclose for Your Excellency's perusal a copy of a telegram[1] sent by me to the Secretary of State on 17th November, 1944, when the question of public servants joining the All-Ceylon Tamil Congress was under consideration. I know that this matter was even brought up before the Board Ministers, but I am not sure whether any definite instruction had been issued to the departments by the Chief Secretary

---

[1] Not printed.

and whether they are being complied with. I do not even know whether the nature and scope of the activities of the numerous associations and unions, sanctioned by the Chief Secretary have been examined and approved by him. It is difficult to see how these associations could indulge in some of their recent activities, if this had been done. I would submit this matter is of such importance that Your Excellency should give your immediate and personal attention if a complete breakdown in this administration is to be prevented.

5.   I shall be grateful if Your Excellency would also bring these representations of mine to the immediate notice of the Secretary of State.


**Annex II to 378**

I have received your letter of the 28th September, 1946, with reference to the deterioration in the standard of discipline in the Public Service. I may say at once that I am prepared to give the matter my immediate and personal attention. I think, however, that before I bring your representations to the notice of the Secretary of State, it would be as well if you and I discussed the matter more fully. You will be in Nuwara Eliya on the 15th and we could talk things over then or before that date if possible.

2.   In connection with our discussion there are one or two matters referred to in your letter which I should like elucidated. You refer in the first paragraph to the encouragement given by the authorities for the formation of various associations and unions of public officers. Who are the authorities who have given such encouragement and in what way is the encouragement given?

3.   With reference to paragraph 4 of your letter I should like to know precisely what are the activities of the various associations to which you take exception.

4.   I may say that I am in complete agreement with you that it should be the object of the present Government to handover to the new Government a Public Service animated by the traditions of the past and a credit to the country. I feel confident that those responsible for this service are animated by this idea.


**Annex III to 378**

You will recollect that during our discussion on the 29th instant I mentioned your letter of the 28th September in which you invited my attention to what you described as a serious deterioration in discipline amongst public servants. In the first paragraph of this letter you requested that I should bring your representations to the notice of the Secretary of State. In my reply of the 1st October, I stated that before I brought your representations to the notice of the Secretary of State the matter should be discussed more fully. In particular the question raised by you with regard to the encouragement given by the authorities for the formation of various associations and unions of public authorities should be more fully elucidated. I am now proposing to address the Secretary of State in connection with matters arising out of the strike. Your representations could with convenience be included in such a despatch. Could you therefore let me know (a) who are the authorities who have encouraged associations and unions of public officers and in what way is such encouragement given and (b) what are the particular activities of these associations which you consider undesirable?


## Annex IV to 378

With reference to your endorsement No. S1/105/46 of 31st October, 1946, I shall be glad if a copy of my letter to Your Excellency, dated 28th September, 1946, containing my representations, could be forwarded to the Secretary of State.

2.   You have asked me for the authorities who have encouraged associations and unions of public officers and in what way such encouragement has been given. The authorities are those responsible for the administration of the Public Service under the present Constitution. With regard to the encouragement given, I wish to point out that till quite recently the Chief Secretary had opposed the employees of a number of departments from joining trade unions, but authority was recently granted by him for the formation of associations for reasons which I fear are not quite clear to me. I believe the Inspector-General of Police had issued instructions to his district officers to give assistance in the formation of the Sergeants' and Constables' Union.

3.   In regard to the manner in which some of these associations are run, I should be glad if Your Excellency would be good enough to read the minutes of some of the recent meetings of the Sergeants' and Constables' Union and the Public Services League. I should in this connection like to mention the resolution moved at a meeting of the League where it was suggested that three Senators should be representatives of the League in the Senate to watch their interests and the more recent resolution of the League condemning the action of the President and the Secretary in circularising the members of the League regarding their duty to the public and the necessity to render loyal, efficient and uninterrupted service to the country.

4.   The speeches made at meetings during the strike when employees made violent attacks on Heads of Departments, Officers of State and Ministers, the sabotage activities of Government employees and the efforts made by them to form a federation for the purpose of staging general strikes are some of the other matters I should like to mention.


## Annex V to 378

Mr. Senanayake's criticisms of the administration of the public service as expressed in his letters to His Excellency dated the 28th September and the 12th November appear to rest almost entirely on the attitude of the responsible authorities namely, the Governor and the Chief Secretary, towards public service associations recognised under Public Service Regulations 178–184.

2.   The principle of recognising such associations as appropriate organisations through which collective representations regarding pay and conditions of employment in a public service may be made has been so long recognised, both inside and outside Ceylon, that it is no longer capable of challenge.

3.   So far as I am aware, the principle has not been challenged in Ceylon except in

the limited respect in which it has been suggested that, among certain government employees, such associations should be replaced by some form of registered trade union but views on this restricted proposal are by no means unanimous or indeed either clear or precise and I am submitting to His Excellency almost immediately a comprehensive memorandum on this question. Until there is a final decision on the extent to which registered trade unions should be permitted within the public service, it is, I think, manifest that public service associations must not only be permitted but encouraged: if this is not done, there will be no means of collective representation by public servants who will consequently be thrown back on the right of individual representation. This is so retrograde a step as not to merit consideration.

4. The necessity for public service associations being admitted, the next point to be considered is whether the attitude of the Governor and the Chief Secretary towards the functions and activities of these associations in the past has been sound and whether the activities of the associations have been properly conducted and supervised.

5. Except for the case of the All Ceylon Tamil Congress which is referred to in paragraph 4 of Mr. Senanayake's letter of the 28th September, this letter of Mr. Senanayake constitutes the first and the only criticism of the attitude of the Governor and the Chief Secretary which is known to me.

With regard to the All Ceylon Tamil Congress, the matter was settled after reference to the Board of Ministers on lines acceptable to both Mr. Senanayake and myself, namely, by refusing permission for Government officers to join or to remain members of any association which engages in any political activities even if a separate organisation were maintained for the furtherance of cultural as distinct from political activities. This involved the withdrawal of facilities for membership by Government officers which had already been accorded in respect not only of the Congress but of other similar organisations.

6. It is unnecessary for me to state that I know of no basis for any criticism of the attitude of the Governor or the Chief Secretary to these Associations. Indeed, until recently, these Associations, as a whole, have been conspicuous more for their inactivity than their activity but, as from the latter half of 1945 they have been active in one respect, namely, their representations to the various Committees which have considered the pay and conditions of service of the public service and to the Treasury in connection with the same matters. It is not, however, suggested that, in this respect, their activities were improper.

7. One is left therefore with the question whether recently the other activities of their Associations have been properly conducted and supervised.

Mr. Senanayake refers to the activities of the Sergeants' and Constables' Association. His Excellency has reported on this matter to the Secretary of State for the Colonies in his Confidential Despatch No.HB.46/45 dated 6th November, 1946. I have nothing to add to that despatch except to say that there is, unfortunately, intrigue within the Police Force which is encouraged by politicians from outside the Force and an organisation, such as the Association in question, which is most desirable in itself may not survive such conditions. I would also add that the possibility of action having to be taken to suspend the Association had been under discussion between the Inspector-General of Police and myself before the matter was raised by Mr. Senanayake and that I withdrew recognition of the Association as soon as I had sufficient information supplied to me by the Inspector General.

8. Mr. Senanayake makes some vague references to reports in the newspapers of the activities of the Public Service League: there is no doubt that this Association needs careful supervision: its Secretary, unlike its President, is not a person who inspires confidence. Suffice it to say that the Chief Secretary's Office has not failed to draw the attention of the League to various recent breaches of Public Service Regulations: I have also interviewed the President and the Secretary on more than one occasion. The League is a Federation of Public Service Associations which claim to represent some 20,000 public servants of the Clerical Service type and, as such, is, potentially, an important influence for good or evil: every effort is being made to ensure that it is the former and not the latter. I have no doubt that the present attitude (which is one of reform and not of destruction) is wholly correct.

9. The previous paragraphs may perhaps be regarded as sufficient comment on such precise and specific criticisms as are contained in the two letters of Mr. Senanayake but I do not think that it would be right for me to leave the matter there because these letters do not represent the whole of Mr. Senanayake's attitude towards the public service. Annexed is a copy of Item 17 of the minutes of the meeting of the Board of Ministers held on the 28th October.[2] From these minutes, it will be seen that Mr. Senanayake has expressed the opinion that:—

> "those responsible for the administration of the Public Service had in several instances acted in a manner which appeared to him to be calculated to create dissension in the public service and chaos in the country. . . . he had lost faith in the administration generally . . . he proposed to dissociate himself from the administration of the Public Service and to make a public statement at the earliest opportunity with regard to his attitude. . . ."

Mr. Senanayake subsequently gave public expression to opinions of this kind in the State Council and elsewhere and it is now a matter of common knowledge and comment in the Press that he regards the public service as ill-disciplined, and the Governor and the Chief Secretary (and indeed His Majesty's Government) as indifferent on the point whether the Government under the new Constitution will receive at the hands of the present Government an efficient or an inefficient public service: indeed Mr. Senanayake has gone further: he has expressed in my presence the opinion that those responsible for the administration of the public service in Ceylon are deliberately demoralising the public service in order that the failure of the new Constitution may be ensured. I personally do not take this comment seriously but it is unfortunate that it has obtained public currency.

10. Mr. Senanayake has declared that he has no faith in the competence, loyalty or discipline of the public service. I entirely disagree with him. I have no doubt that intrinsically they are loyal, disciplined and wholly competent to bear the burden of the new Constitution, subject only to the vital qualification that they are freed from political interference. Their attitude in the recent strike proved the loyalty, discipline and competence of all public servants who did not go on strike and, as regards those who did, it must be remembered that they were largely skilled and unskilled labour who, though regularly employed, were paid at a daily rate of pay and, although the great bulk of them had no right to strike, the State Council had passed a resolution

---

[2] See 373.

in March, 1944, which indicated that the State Council thought that they should have that right.

11.  If Mr. Senanayake, instead of doubting the loyalty, discipline and competence of the public service, had said that they were very much concerned as to their future and wholly uncertain as to whether they would be less subject to political interference under the new Constitution than under the present and, if he had added that, whether or not they knew it, the public service as a whole was being made an important piece in the political manoeuvres which inevitably precede a general election, I would agree with him because I am certain that the undoubted restiveness of the public service today is due not to incompetence, disloyalty or ill-discipline and still less to deliberate demoralisation at the hands of the responsible authorities but to the activities of politicians.

12.  The background against which Mr. Senanayake's attitude must be placed is as follows:—

(a)  the fact that, under the existing constitution, Executive Committees have not only a right but a duty to take an interest in the appointment and promotion of individual public servants;

(b)  the State Council cannot be denied its competence to take an active interest in all the details of pay, allowances and other terms of service of all public servants;

(c)  the back-benchers would not pass the budget for 1945–1946 until the Board had promised an investigation into the emoluments of all public servants;

(d)  the reason for this attitude was as much consideration for the franchise potential of the public service as for their welfare;

(e)  during the debates on the proposals for improvement of salaries etc. the attitude of the back-benchers was blatant: they openly advocated the cause of certain categories of public servants e.g. teachers, stated that they had made a special study of such cases and had received representations from the particular body of public servants concerned and invariably pressed for better salaries, etc. than were recommended by the Board of Ministers;

(f)  the recent strike among railway, harbour workers etc. was undoubtedly wholly political and organised by politicians of the Left who are opposed to Mr. Senanayake and his followers;

(g)  as a consequence of (f) and notwithstanding that, with the concurrence of the Ministers, His Excellency, the Financial Secretary and I dealt with the representations of the strikers, there was the remarkable occurrence that the Minister of Communications and Works (within whose Ministry all the important strikes occurred) stated, on the wireless, that it was a matter of sorrow and concern to him that the strikers had not come to him with their grievances because he would have been able to gratify them but that, if this were not possible under the existing Constitution, he promised that it would be so under the new Constitution;

(h)  the tendency of Ministers and other politicians to condemn both publicly and privately the conduct of public officers in circumstances in which it is not possible for such officers to defend themselves or be defended. The general attitude of Ministers towards Messrs. Waldron and Brodie in regard to their conduct as police officers is a notable example: in particular, the fact that the Board of Ministers should have condemned these officers in the terms and circumstances recorded in the minutes of their meeting of the 18th November at which I was not present is a considerable shock to me and affords complete justification for the apprehension which the public service entertains.

13. The previous paragraph indicates sufficiently the deleterious activities of the politicians but it is not all: against that background must be placed the fact that Mr. Senanayake is known to be not only a stern critic of the public service over a period of years but also to be opposed to the recent generous increases in emoluments which the Budget for 1946–1947 provided. It has been openly stated that in the Board of Ministers he voted against the Budget which he himself had to introduce and it is commonly believed that, if he is the first Prime Minister, he hopes that circumstances will be such that he will be able to impose a cut on salaries. It is not surprising therefore that (as I am informed on very trustworthy authority) a large part of the public service consisting of the clerical type and skilled and unskilled workers who, in numbers, are considerable and concentrated in and around Colombo and so form a powerful voting bloc are strong opponents of Mr. Senanayake and are determined to get as much in the way of increased salary, etc. before the general election as possible in order that they may be able to stand the cut in salaries which they believe Mr. Senanayake will impose if he becomes Prime Minister. It follows, of course, that Mr. Senanayake's political opponents will make a determined bid to secure the political support of the public services.

I cannot imagine anything more demoralising to the public service. As the Financial Secretary said in the last meeting of the State Council, the public service belongs to the public of Ceylon and not to any one political party. That is an obvious truth. I trust that the Governor and the Secretary of State will be able to secure its acceptance by present day politicians in Ceylon who, if the new Constitution fails owing to the breakdown of the public service, will, in my opinion, be solely responsible for that failure.

# 379 CO 54/995/1, no 2							4 Jan 1947
## [Public service]: letter from Sir J Howard to Sir C Jeffries on Mr Senanayake's criticisms of the public service

I am writing this personal letter to accompany and supplement my Secret Despatch of today's date on the subject of Senanayake's criticisms of the administration of the Public Service.[1] The Despatch is accompanied by various documents including a note by Drayton on the subject. I am generally in agreement with Drayton, but I consider that his paragraph 12(f) calls for some comment from me. No doubt the October strike can be regarded as having been inspired by political reasons. On the other hand I am convinced that the strikers, who consisted of daily paid workers, had genuine and legitimate grievances. Copies of the records of the discussions with the representatives of the strikers indicate the nature of their grievances. These grievances are I am glad to say being remedied with the utmost speed. The grievances were exploited by Leftist politicians as stated in paragraph 5 of my telegram No. 1685 of the 24th October, 1946, and to this extent the strikes may be regarded as political.

---

[1] See 378.

2. Although Senanayake's letter of complaint about the Public Services is anterior to the strike, there is in my view no doubt that it appeared to Senanayake to be the culmination of a series of events which revealed hostility to him personally and to his political associates and his social and economic class. The Leftist politicians, whose movement is only now becoming formidable, have for years denounced him as a capitalist (the phrase "black Imperialist" is also employed), and he is aware and acutely conscious of their success among the urban labouring classes (including Government labour). Much of the criticism levelled against him, although common in election campaigns, is scurrilous in tone and language and grossly unfair in content; it appears from oral statements by Senanayake to me that it has actually reached the stage of hooligans equipped with megaphones shouting against him in the streets. It is evident in interviews with Senanayake that he has very strong feelings in regard to the campaign which is being conducted against him and which he suggests is an indication of a general disregard for law and order. Whether he really believes that public security is jeopardised, in conversation with me he assumes such an attitude which he ascribes to a deterioration in the discipline in the Public Service.

3. It is unfortunate that on the last day of the strike Mr. de Mel, the Mayor of Colombo, became entangled in a procession of strikers; his motor car driver apparently lost his head, drove through the crowd, and knocked down and injured some seventeen people: de Mel was assaulted, but not at all seriously. The Police reports of the incident show that the fault lay with de Mel's driver: but the affair made a very deep impression on Senanayake, who regards it as an instance of class hatred leading to violence, and of the incapacity of the Police to handle the situation. In fact the Police are some 700 men below strength and the Inspector General admits that the procession in question would have been more strongly covered if men had been available; but Senanayake in his present frame of mind magnifies the affair out of all proportion to its real significance.

4. Senanayake's demands for a standing mobilised battalion of the Defence Force (see my telegram No.1866 of 25th November),[2] and for the removal of Bacon, Brodie and Waldron (see my telegram No.1838 of 18th November),[3] and his criticism of the administration of the Public Service, are all the symptoms of the attitude to which I have referred in paragraph 2. My own opinion is that he exaggerates the danger of physical violence, but I think he is right in regarding the Leftist political groups as a serious threat to his own United National Party (see Sir Henry Moore's confidential despatch of 15th July in this connection).

5. There is to my mind no doubt that Senanayake, quite apart from losing the not inconsiderable electoral votes of the Public Service, will damage his own reputation, and the morale of the Public Service, if he persists in the irresponsible attacks which he has launched, and I shall do all in my power to persuade him to moderation. I suggest that in replying to my official despatch the need for mollifying Senanayake, and for convincing him (so far as possible) of the loyalty of the Public Service and the goodwill of those who administer it, be borne in mind.

[2] See 376.                                                                                   [3] See 375.

**380**   CO 323/1888/1                                          7–8 Jan 1947

[British Commonwealth Conference on Nationality and Citizenship]:
minutes by A B Acheson and G F Seel[1] on the question of Ceylon's
representation

[This conference of experts on nationality and citizenship which was held in London in
Feb 1947 arose from the Canadian Citizenship Act of 1946. Prior to the Canadian Act, it
had been accepted that there should be a single common code of British nationality
applicable throughout the Commonwealth (except Eire since 1935) under which all
member states had identical statutes on the subject. By contrast the Canadian Act was
based on the principle that each of the self-governing units of the Commonwealth (except
Eire) should have its own local separate citizenship, and that all persons possessing it
should be recognised as British subjects throughout the Commonwealth. While acknow-
ledging the merits of the Canadian system, the British government maintained that it
should not be adopted unilaterally (Canada had acted without prior consultation) but by
Commonwealth agreement. As these minutes by Acheson and Seel indicate, Ceylon was
not originally included in the countries which were invited to send representatives to the
Feb conference. The CO had previously argued that to allow Ceylon to legislate for its own
separate citizenship carrying British nationality would run the risk of placing in the
hands of the Ceylon government a powerful weapon which could be used to discriminate
against Indians. But having consulted Moore on the question of Ceylon's representation
at the London conference, the CO concluded that while the risk remained, it had to be
balanced against the 'political reactions' which would follow from drawing a distinction
between Ceylon and India, Burma and Southern Rhodesia. A briefing note by the CO
General Dept stated: 'The political atmosphere in Ceylon is deteriorating. Ceylon
ministers are exceedingly jealous of the status of the Colony under its new Constitution
and are liable to take serious offence at any attitude on the part of H.M.G. which can be
regarded as derogatory to that status. They are already drawing the parallel with Burma
and Southern Rhodesia. In all the circumstances it is felt that the balance of advantage
undoubtedly lies in placing Ceylon in this matter in the same position as India, Burma
and Southern Rhodesia' (CO 323/1881/1, no 3, note by General Dept, 15 Jan 1947).
Having accepted an invitation to attend, Ceylon was represented by L M D de Silva. India
was not represented throughout. The Indian high commissioner in London attended the
opening session as an observer but then departed. A draft scheme, prepared by British
delegates and intended as the legislative model for a new British Nationality Bill, was used
as the basis for discussion. The ensuing British Nationality Bill (which was enacted in
1948) provided that all persons who were citizens of any Commonwealth country except
Eire should, by virtue of that country's local citizenship, be British subjects. Significantly, however, the London conference did not produce a common approach to citizenship.
Burma and Ceylon especially were preoccupied with the question of their Indian
immigrants. While seeing no objection to any country linking nationality with citizenship
if it so desired and indicating that Ceylon would endeavour to follow suit if other
countries were committed to the principle of linking the two as the basis for the common
status of British subjects throughout the Commonwealth, de Silva maintained that it was
neither necessary nor desirable that all countries act accordingly. If such agreement was
deemed unnecessary, it should be avoided 'as it might cause Ceylon, and perhaps other
countries, some embarrassment'. He also stated that in future, the test for citizenship in
Ceylon would be based not on birth but on domicile. By implication, persons born in
Ceylon but not domiciled there would only exercise civil and political (especially voting)
rights if they passed certain domiciliary tests. On the question of nationality although de
Silva argued that persons born in Ceylon but not domiciled there might lose their status
as British subjects, he accepted that those concerned would retain their status as British
subjects, either by virtue of their being citizens of other Commonwealth countries or
because they would become citizens of the United Kingdom and Colonies (DO 35/3535
contains the report and proceedings of the London conference).]

---

[1] Seel was an assistant under-secretary of state with supervisory responsibility for the CO General Dept
which was responsible for nationality questions; Acheson was an assistant secretary and head of the
General Dept.

*Mr. Seel*

These papers are concerned with proposals for revising the U.K. law relating to British Nationality.

A circular telegram was sent to all Colonies in October outlining the proposals. They contemplated that the U.K. should participate in the Canadian system (which other Dominion Governments are known to favour) whereby in future British Nationality will be conferred through the gateway of citizenship; that the Dominions (except Eire), Newfoundland, India, Burma and Southern Rhodesia should provide by their own legislation for local citizenships under conditions they would themselves prescribe, which will automatically carry with it British Nationality; and that for the remaining countries in the Empire there should be established by an Act of the U.K. Parliament a common "citizenship of the U.K. and Colonies".

These proposals raise complicated questions of law, and the procedure which was approved by the Cabinet was that a Committee of Experts should meet to consider them in detail. The Committee is to consist of representatives of the U.K. and of the Dominions and of India, Burma, Newfoundland and Southern Rhodesia.

Since that time:—

(1) The conference of experts has been fixed to meet on the 3rd February.

(2) The replies from the Colonies to the Secretary of State's circular despatch have come in.

(3) An ad hoc Committee in this country on which Mr. Dale[2] represented the Colonial Office has produced a long paper containing the material for discussion by the Experts Committee.

As to (3) above the paper is on a separate file below. I have studied it, and there are a number of points arising from it which will evidently require some preliminary consideration in the Colonial Office (and possibly in consultation with Colonial Govts.) before the conference meets. I propose to discuss these points with Mr. Dale and to put up suggestions for action. As to (2) above the replies are in.

In general they indicate a large measure of agreement with the proposals, although certain points arise on which explanations will be necessary. These also I propose to consider with Mr. Dale.

But a point arises in regard to Ceylon on which an immediate decision is necessary. It was not proposed in the papers submitted to the Cabinet that Ceylon should be one of the countries which should legislate for her own separate citizenship and therefore should be represented at the Conference of Experts meeting in February. When the proposals were communicated to the Governor of Ceylon his views were particularly invited on this point. His reply was that he felt sure that Ceylon would wish to be invited to the Conference of Experts and would resent it most strongly if she were not classed with India, Burma, Newfoundland and Southern Rhodesia as one of the countries empowered to prescribe through her own local legislation for local citizenship carrying with it British Nationality.

The first question is whether the Governor's view that Ceylon should for this purpose be classed with India, Burma, Newfoundland and Southern Rhodesia should be accepted forthwith. The Department as you will see support the Governor's view. It has been realised that, if Ceylon is given power to legislate for her own local

---

[2] W C Dale, deputy legal adviser, CO.

citizenship carrying British Nationality, there is a risk that a Ceylon Government may use this power as a means of discriminatory measures against Indians. And indeed we have used Ceylon in argument (both oral and written) with other Departments and in a paper submitted to the Cabinet Committee as an example of the desirability of having a single United Kingdom Colonial Citizenship. But the Department now feel that, it having been decided that the citizenship principle should be adopted, the political difficulties which would arise from differentiating between Ceylon and other countries in the Empire with similar advanced constitutions must be regarded as overriding.

In these circumstances it is necessary to consider the implications. A Cabinet Committee was appointed last year to deal with this general Nationality issue. The members were the Home Secretary, the Lord Chancellor, the Secretaries of State for the Dominions, India and Burma, and the Colonies, the Minister of State and the Attorney General. (The last two do not appear to have attended any meetings of the Committee). The Home Secretary as chairman of the Committee put up a paper to the full Cabinet explaining the Committee proposed that India, Burma, Newfoundland and Southern Rhodesia should have the right to pass their own legislation on this subject, but that as regards all the Colonies it was proposed that there should be a common United Kingdom Colonial citizenship. The Cabinet accepted the Committee's proposals.

It would seem therefore that the Cabinet or at least the Cabinet Committee should know of and approve the proposed change of attitude towards Ceylon.

In itself that is not a matter of special urgency. But it becomes one, if the decision so to classify Ceylon necessarily carries with it an invitation to Ceylon to participate in the Conference opening on the 3rd February. The view hitherto taken is that it was desirable that all countries who would in due course pass their own citizenship legislation should be represented at the Conference. I gather from some conversation I have had with Mr. Beckett at the Foreign Office that he does not altogether share that view and thinks that the conference is already large enough for effective work. But it would clearly be logical and politically safe that Ceylon should at least be given the opportunity of participating in the Conference if she wishes.

On that basis the first action would seem to be to secure the consent of the Ministers immediately concerned, including the Lord Chancellor, to Ceylon being treated on the same basis as India etc. and being given an opportunity to send a representative to the conference if they wish to do so. Reference to the whole Cabinet hardly seems necessary, although of course the Cabinet should be informed when a convenient opportunity arises. It seems unlikely that any difficulty will arise either with Departments or with Ministers on this matter, although it will be necessary to explain why we have now reached the conclusion that Ceylon should be treated in this way when at the earlier stage in a paper submitted to the Cabinet Committee we actually quoted Ceylon as an example of a colony in which the system of separate local citizenship might lead to serious political difficulties. But there will be the further practical question whether the India Office, Burma Office, and Dominions Office will consider it necessary to consult the Indian, Burma and Dominion Governments and obtain their consent, before the Ceylon Government is actually invited to the Conference.

A possible alternative would be to take the view that it is not essential to invite Ceylon to participate in the work of the Experts' Conference, and that it would suffice to explain to Ceylon Ministers at a later stage that as the Conference was not a body constituted or authorised to reach agreements between Governments but were merely an advisory body charged with the task of considering technical questions, it was thought that the Ceylon Ministers would prefer that they should not be asked to consider this important issue in advance of the inauguration of their new constitution, when they would be in a position to deal with it with full information at their disposal both as to the considerations of policy and as to the complicated technical questions involved.

It seems to me that there may be something to be said for at least putting this alternative to the Governor for consideration.

A.B.A.
7.1.47


It is unfortunate that this has been delayed, as the Conference of Commonwealth Experts on Nationality is to open on the 3rd February.

Mr. Acheson has taken away the file with the replies to the circular telegram of the 13th October, and will deal separately with those and with the paper in the folder below, in consultation with Mr. Dale, with a view to producing a draft telegram at an early date. Apart from the Ceylon point, I understand that no major difficulty has arisen.

The Ceylon question is of first-class urgency if there is to be any question of that Colony sending a representative to the experts' conference, as the Governor . . . thinks that she is likely to claim. It is no doubt inconvenient that we should have to consider allowing Ceylon to legislate like Southern Rhodesia for her own local citizenship, after we have used as an argument against separate citizenships for Colonies the danger that such legislation in Ceylon would be used to discriminate against Indians. As far as I am concerned, having regard to the treatment of the terms offered to Burma in the Prime Minister's announcement before Christmas, I do not think that it is practical politics to try and force Ceylon into the common U.K./Colonies citizenship.

I think, therefore, that we shall have to reply to (2) telling the Governor that it is agreed that Ceylon should be placed in the same category as Burma and Southern Rhodesia. Having gone so far I think that we must offer Ceylon the opportunity of being represented at the Conference next month, although it may be possible to intimate that the Conference will really be one for experts only and that it is not considered essential that Ceylon should be represented (on the lines of the pen-ultimate paragraph of Mr. Acheson's minute).

Mr. Acheson has ascertained semi-officially that neither the Home Office nor the Foreign Office are likely to raise difficulty about the line proposed above with regard to Ceylon. It is possible that the Dominions Office will take the view that they must consult the Dominion Governments before acquiescing.

As regards immediate action, I do not think that this need be taken at ministerial level, and I suggest that Mr. Acheson should inform the Secretary of the Cabinet Committee and all the Departments interested simultaneously of the reply we propose to make to No. 1, inviting their concurrence. In doing so, it should be indicated to them that in view of the near approach of the date for the Conference we shall not be able to delay the reply beyond the 15th January.

As there is action outstanding on (2) and (3) of Mr. Acheson's minute, I should be glad if this file could be recirculated to me after action.

G.F.S.
8.1.47

# 381  CO 882/30, no 141                                    28 Feb 1947
## [Dominion status]: letter from Mr Senanayake to Mr Creech Jones asserting that Ceylon cannot accept a status lower than that of India or Burma

You are no doubt aware that we are holding a General Election in July and that active campaigning is going on all over the Island. Since the speeches are in Sinhalese and Tamil and are barely reported in the Press, you may not be aware of the effect of the pledges given to India and Burma by His Majesty's Government. As might be expected, the political opponents of the Ceylon Ministers are making much political capital of the acceptance by the Ministers and the State Council of a status for the Island much inferior to that now accorded to India and Burma. Their actions are being represented as a "surrender to British Imperialism" and as "an alliance between the black and the white capitalists designed for the oppression of the people". What is more significant, perhaps, is that our own friends are being compelled to pledge themselves in a manner which will certainly cause difficulties in the new Parliament.

The language of paragraph 10 of the White Paper on Constitutional Reform[1] does not help us because it was carefully framed to give Ceylon the maximum of encouragement and the minimum of power. What is more, it lays down a doctrine of Dominion Status by evolution which has been implicitly denied in the undertakings to India and Burma. Evolution, it is said, happens only to those who do not take part in rebellion against His Majesty. You will, I think, appreciate the danger of such assertions.

India and Burma have been offered independence within or without the British Commonwealth. I think you know that if Ceylon were offered such a choice I would do all in my power to secure independence within the Commonwealth. I believe that when India becomes independent it will be all the more desirable for Ceylon to be associated with the other nations of the Commonwealth; but it must be an association in which we can maintain our self-respect as a people and not be an object of contempt to our free and independent neighbour. If His Majesty's Government will not give us freedom within the British Commonwealth the pressure upon us to agitate for complete independence will become overwhelming. India is our motherland and the Burmese, like the great majority of the Ceylonese, are Buddhists. We cannot accept a lower status than they or be told, patronisingly, that we may possibly be fit for self-government if we behave well under the New Constitution.

I cannot say that all my colleagues in the State Council share my views: most of them desire an immediate agitation. I think something must be done if I am to

---

[1] See 317, annex.

prevent a serious deterioration of the position. If action is taken early I could still ensure that this full freedom will be within the British Commonwealth. I would earnestly request therefore that you read again my letter of 16th August, 1945,[2] a copy of which is enclosed for easy reference, to your predecessor to see if it is not now possible for His Majesty's Government to accept the proposal made in it.

Sir Oliver Goonetilleke, who has been very closely associated in the preparation of our New Constitution will be very shortly in England on furlough. I have discussed this matter with him and he is fully informed of my views. He will be able to state them personally more emphatically than I could do in a letter. I hope that you will allow him to discuss the matter with you as soon as you have had time to examine my request.

---

[2] See 266.

## 382   CO 882/30, no 142                                   7 Mar 1947
### [Dominion status]: letter from Sir H Moore to Mr Creech Jones supporting Mr Senanayake

I am forwarding by the same bag as carries this letter, a personal letter from Mr. Senanayake addressed to yourself.[1] As he sent a copy for information I asked him to come and discuss it, which he did.

2.  In that discussion he made his own position perfectly clear. He is above all things anxious that Ceylon should remain within the Commonwealth, and believes that action on the lines he now advocates is the best way to secure it.

3.  He makes no secret of his own fear and distrust of India and, as a realist, recognizes Ceylon is too small to stand on her own feet in the modern world. He would, therefore, much prefer to be a small but independent partner of the Commonwealth to being absorbed by an independent India. He knows Nehru personally and has had discussions with him. He is quite satisfied that Nehru's ambition is to make an independent India the dominant power in this part of the world with or without alliances with China and possibly Russia, so that there may be a strong Eastern Asiatic block arrayed against the Western Powers. Nehru's interest in Ceylon is in his view solely because of its strategic importance as providing a naval base in Trincomalee and air bases in other parts of the Island.

4.  His present letter and his earlier letter of 16th August, 1945,[2] which forms an enclosure, are largely if not entirely the work of Jennings, whose drafting abilities have been utilized to put the floating ideas of Senanayake and his intimates into coherent form. But if they were looking round for some method of bringing home to the general public the importance of Ceylon's strategic position to Empire Defence the solution has been provided by Air Chief Marshal Joubert's[3] lectures on the subject in London and Cambridge which have received the fullest local publicity— see cuttings enclosed. To question the desirability of such headlining of the obvious at the present time would be an implied criticism of the art of Public Relations, whose mysteries remain a closed book to the uninitiated, but the practical result so

---

[1] See 381.                                                          [2] See 266.
[3] Director of public relations, Air Ministry, 1946–1947.

far as Ceylon is concerned has been to draw the attention of our Independence Group to the feverish search for Empire bases now being conducted by the Service authorities.

5. With that general background the question arises as to what is now the best thing to do. Mr. Senanayake was the first to admit to me that there are many who do not share his views that it is in Ceylon's best interest to remain within the Commonwealth, though they are as fully alive as he is as to the importance of Ceylon to His Majesty's Government. He also appreciates that no one can prophesy the length of his own political, to say nothing of his natural, life, and that His Majesty's Government can properly expect in return for any further concessions now granted some permanent form of agreement over a period of years. This he would be prepared to negotiate, and further indicated that so far as he was concerned he would make no difficulties as to what His Majesty's Government might ask in order to meet their legitimate defence requirements; further that clauses could be added in respect of foreign relations, so as to secure that Ceylon would enter into no foreign commitments which might be embarrassing to the Commonwealth as a whole.

6. He also made it clear that apart from questions of local prestige he attaches the greatest importance to Ceylon's constitutional status being such as to entitle her to membership of the United Nations Organization. As already stated he has no doubts whatever as to the foreign policy which India will pursue and believes that the battle will be joined at the United Nations Organization. India's attitude over the South African question has filled him with alarm, as he sees in it the red light as to the sort of pressure she may try to exert over Ceylon in the settlement of her domestic differences with India on the question of the franchise. He also anticipates similar difficulties in other British Colonies and Dominions. He suggests, therefore, that Ceylon's inclusion would strengthen His Majesty's Government's hands when such controversies are revived and intensified.

7. On the general question of policy I believe that the reservations in respect of Defence and Foreign Affairs as finally incorporated in the Order in Council are such that they would be exceedingly difficult to exercise in practice without the goodwill of the Government of the day. Since my return I have been examining in more detail the actual administrative machinery necessary for the working of the defence department and it is inevitable that there will be few if any, matters from which the Prime Minister can constitutionally be excluded. I am therefore inclined to think that the defence interests of His Majesty's Government might well be better secured by an agreement of the nature now proposed. In any case we should be no worse off. In my Secret and Personal telegram of September 25th, 1945,[4] to your predecessor I advocated such an agreement at a time when it appeared that Mr. Senanayake was about to reject the Soulbury Constitution on his return from London. How narrowly that was averted is within the personal knowledge of some of your advisers, and indeed Mr. Senanayake's present difficulties are principally due to the fact that many of his own supporters now feel that, had he rejected the Soulbury Constitution as some of them had advocated, Ceylon would by this time have received the same sort of offer as His Majesty's Government has recently made to Burma. Bluntly they consider that loyalty to His Majesty's Government during the war, judged by recent developments in India and Burma, is obviously not a paying proposition, and that the

---

[4] See 295.

rate of constitutional advance is governed not by the merits of the case but by the nuisance value of the applicants.

8. I am afraid that his conclusion is inescapable. But there is still a chance of retaining Ceylon as a loyal and willing member of the Commonwealth, and I consider the most serious and urgent consideration should be given to Mr. Senanayake's proposals.

9. If you are prepared to consider them, close examination will have to be given as to how such an agreement could be made with a Ceylon, which did not constitutionally enjoy independent status, and how the safeguards necessary to secure His Majesty's Government's defence requirements could legally be enforced. These are matters of detail and Mr. Senanayake has told me that later he would be prepared to come to London if necessary to discuss them. [His general idea is that such an announcement should be made on the official inauguration of the new Parliament, and he still entertains the hope that some personage of distinction, preferably a member of the Royal Family, may be able to undertake this task. On this latter point I will address you again later.]

10. He has deputed Sir Oliver E. Goonetilleke to discuss these matters with you further, but has instructed him to make no move in the matter until he hears from you that you are ready to receive him.

# 383   CO 882/30, no 143                                      19 Mar 1947
## [Dominion status]: outward unnumbered telegram (reply) from Mr Creech Jones to Sir H Moore on Mr Senanayake's proposals

Your secret and personal letter to me of the 7th March.[1]

1. I am very grateful for the expression of your own views, which will be of great assistance to me in considering Senanayake's request.

2. I should propose, if you agree, to send him a personal acknowledgment of his letter, saying that he will appreciate that these proposals, on which I hope to have a talk with Sir Oliver Goonetilleke, will require very careful consideration not only by myself but by other Ministers, and that I will write to him again as soon as it is possible for me to do so. Please telegraph whether you concur.

3. I am not altogether clear, however, from your reference to "an announcement on the official inauguration of the new Parliament" what precisely is the programme which Senanayake contemplates. Unless some prior announcement of His Majesty's Government's conclusions was made it would not appear to be of any practical value to Senanayake in his political campaign, nor would it be possible for His Majesty's Government to reach an agreement with Goonetilleke and himself at some date considerably prior to the announcement without every risk of leakage and consequent embarrassment.

4. In a brief informal talk with the Department here Goonetilleke has given the impression that Senanayake would wish to come to this country and take back with him His Majesty's Government's decision on the request he has made, which would be announced on his return, and that, simultaneously with the inauguration of the

---

[1] See 382.

new Parliament, the Order in Council would be amended to delete the reservations in regard to defence and external affairs, a signed agreement on these matters being adopted in their place. Some such advancing of the time table which you apparently contemplated would seem more consistent with Senanayake's political needs.

5.  I shall, of course, find it necessary to consult the Cabinet in the near future and, with that in view, I should welcome your personal views as to:—

(a)  whether Goonetilleke has correctly represented what Senanayake wants;
(b)  whether, as things are at present, there is any doubt about Senanayake's Party being returned at the forthcoming elections; or
(c)  how far its return would be dependent on some indication being given before the election that His Majesty's Government were prepared to meet Senanayake's wishes for a further constitutional advance as proposed in his letter to me and represented by Goonetilleke.

6.  I should be grateful for an early reply.

# 384  CO 882/30, no 145                                    22 Mar 1947
## [Dominion status]: minute by Mr Creech Jones to Mr Attlee on Mr Senanayake's proposals

*Prime Minister*
1.  You will remember my note to you of the 21st December about the possible repercussions on Ceylon of the Government's decision on the Burma situation.

2.  As I mentioned verbally at a later date, although up to then the position in Ceylon had remained undisturbed, I did not feel confident that it would continue to do so indefinitely, and my forebodings have now been realized.

3.  A few days ago I received a personal letter[1] from Mr. Senanayake, the Vice-Chairman of the Board of Ministers in Ceylon, in which he pointed out that, as leader of the Moderate Party which is fighting the forthcoming election for the first Parliament under the new Constitution, he is seriously embarrassed by the considerable capital which his political opponents are making out of the acceptance by himself and other Ceylon Ministers of a status for Ceylon much inferior to that now accorded to India and Burma.

4.  As he bluntly puts it, "we cannot accept a lower status than they, or be told patronizingly that we may possibly be fit for self-government if we behave well under the new Constitution", when India and Burma have been offered independence within or without the British Commonwealth. It is being said in Ceylon that acceptance of the doctrine of "Dominion status by evolution" is only required of those who do not take part in rebellion against His Majesty. Mr. Senanayake says quite frankly that a considerable number of his colleagues in the State Council desire an immediate agitation, and that it is essential to take action to prevent a serious deterioration in the political situation in Ceylon, when, as he puts it, "the pressure upon us to agitate for complete independence will become overwhelming."

5.  He accordingly asks that His Majesty's Government should reconsider a

---
[1] See 381.

request which he made when he was over here in 1945 for negotiations in connection with the Constitution. This request, if accepted, will commit us to very early consideration of the grant of full Dominion status to Ceylon. Immediately, it will involve the excision from the new Constitution, which will come into force this summer, of the reservations in respect of defence and external affairs, and will necessitate the conclusion between His Majesty's Government and Ceylon of agreements in respect of these matters.

6. Mr. Senanayake confidently claims that, if early action is taken to meet his request, he will be able to keep Ceylon within the Commonwealth, which he is most sincerely anxious to do.

7. The Governor of Ceylon has also written to me endorsing Mr. Senanayake's view as to the dangers of the political situation, and supporting Mr. Senanayake's request for further concessions, which he urges, should have serious and urgent considerations.

8. Mr. Senanayake has sent Sir Oliver Goonetilleke, the Financial Secretary of Ceylon, who is a close personal friend of his, over here to conduct discussions with me on his behalf. I propose to see him and hear what he has to say. After I have ascertained from him the details of Mr. Senanayake's proposals, I will, with your approval, obtain the views of the Chiefs of Staff and other Ministers concerned upon them, and then submit a Paper to the Cabinet.[2]

---

[2] Attlee minuted: 'Noted. C.R.A. 23.3.47.'

# 385  CO 882/30, no 148                                24 Mar 1947
## [Dominion status]: inward unnumbered telegram from Sir H Moore to Mr Creech Jones conveying Mr Senanayake's views on the timing of an announcement by HMG

In continuation of my secret and personal of 20th March. I have had a further conversation with Senanayake, in course of which he made it clear that, if His Majesty's Government were prepared to grant the further advance now asked for, he hoped that any announcement made would be in a form which would imply that this was a spontaneous gesture which, in view of His Majesty's Government's declared policy in the case of India and Burma, it was only proper for His Majesty's Government to make regard being had to Ceylon's present constitutional development and war record.

2. Such an announcement would be made at the opening of the new Parliament and would go on to say that the necessary amendments of the Order in Council could not be made until the Ceylon Government of the day entered into a Defence Agreement satisfactory to His Majesty's Government, and, if full Dominion Status were granted, until the formalities necessary to secure Ceylon's inclusion in the Schedule to the Statute of Westminster had been completed.

3. He appreciated that under such an arrangement any agreement provisionally entered into by him would have to be kept secret, and that he would therefore be debarred from making political capital out of it for election purposes. While he would naturally welcome this additional ammunition he feels sufficiently confident of his

Party's return to be able to dispense with it. He feels that on balance it would be wiser to do so, since if it is known during the election that Ceylon's constitutional status is again *sub judice*, his main opponents, the Independence Groups, might gain fresh adherents on the slogan of Independence versus Dominion Status. He feels, however, that if some such announcement is not made as soon as Parliament meets there will be an immediate agitation in the new Parliament for further constitutional advance, which it would be much more difficult for him to control, and that in any case my concessions made later under pressure would have the appearance of being forced upon His Majesty's Government rather than voluntarily conceded.

4.  He appreciates the risk of leakage, but considers this could be largely obviated if arrangements could be made whereby the final draft of the agreement was settled here instead of in London with a representative of yourself. He does not want to leave Ceylon just now, and I personally consider it should be avoided if possible. He only made the suggestion because he felt such an arrangement would be more convenient to you and your Advisers.

5.  Your paragraph 5.[1]

(A) I think yes, but that probably Senanayake has now somewhat modified his ideas. I believe paragraphs 3 and 4 above correctly represent his present attitude.
(B) No.
(C) See paragraph 3 above.

6.  If there is any likelihood of the Parliamentary or Permanent Under-Secretary being able to visit us—see paragraph 4 above—I have no doubt suitable cover could be provided for the visit.

---

[1] Of Creech Jones's tel of 19 Mar, see 383.

## 386   CO 54/1001/3, no 5                                   24 Mar 1947
## [Finance]: letter from S Caine to Sir H Moore on the management of Ceylon's sterling balances

Thank you for your letter of the 7th March about the Ceylon financial position. We do not propose to send any official comments on the statement enclosed in your despatch No. 103, nor indeed do I propose to make any very lengthy comments privately.

I should, however, like to say that I am glad to see that Goonetilleke's statement is based on the assumption that although there may be some increases of expenditure, the greater part of the proceeds of the new export duties on tea and copra products will be added to reserve funds. I have no doubt that both he and you realise the necessity for caution in adding to expenditure commitments. The present good market for tea and copra certainly will not last for ever, and it will be the task of prudent finance to build up reserves while times do stay good so that Ceylon will not be without defences if and when a slump comes.

The same policy is, I think, indicated by other considerations of less direct selfish interest to Ceylon, but of very considerable importance to His Majesty's Government, i.e., the undesirability of Ceylon at present making any calls on her accumulated sterling balance. This is a subject on which I think the Treasury will want to have a talk with Goonetilleke in the fairly near future, with the idea of reaching some kind of agreement on the management of Ceylon's sterling balances, but certainly one of their main points will be to try and secure that calls on the accumulated balances are reduced to a minimum in the next few years. Accordingly it is all to the good if the Ceylon Government is itself adding to its reserves at the moment rather than calling upon them.

# 387    CO 882/30, no 150                                      4 Apr 1947
## [Dominion status]: inward telegram no 502 from Sir H Moore to Mr Creech Jones transmitting a message from Mr Senanayake to Sir O Goonetilleke on an announcement by HMG and proposals for defence and external affairs

Following for Goonetilleke from Senanayake.

*Begins.* After further discussion with Governor in the light of observations received from Secretary of State, I now consider most satisfactory procedure is that His Majesty's Government should make spontaneous announcement immediately that it has decided to grant people of Ceylon full responsible Government within the British Commonwealth at the earliest practicable date; that this will involve, in addition to the necessary amendments to the Statute of Westminster, the prior conclusion with the Ceylon Government of an agreement in respect of Defence and External Affairs; and that this agreement will be negotiated with the Ceylon Government as soon as possible after introduction of the new Constitution. Further, that in order to avoid delay, immediate arrangements should be made for a preliminary examination, by the appropriate authorities concerned, of details of such an agreement. Until agreement has been negotiated and further necessary legislation effected, the constitution provided in 1946 Order in Council will continue in force, but if by amendment Order in Council, Ceylon could be made eligible for membership of the United Nations Organization, I should like this to be done pending these further steps.

2. If procedure on these lines is acceptable to the Secretary of State, I do not consider that it will be necessary for me to go to the United Kingdom as it should be possible to agree with him by telegraph in consultation with yourself, where necessary, the actual scope of the announcement.

3. I wish, however, to stress that I regard it of the first political importance that draft agreement should be ready for presentation to the Cabinet immediately after the inauguration of the new Constitution. If preliminary negotiations over agreement are begun only after the new Parliament has come into being, it would provide time and opportunity for extremist groups to gather strength in support of their counter issue of independence outside the Commonwealth.

4. I am satisfied that, as under the present Constitution Governor is responsible for Defence and External Affairs, no reasonable objection can be raised at this end to his drawing up, in consultation with the Secretary of State and appropriate departments of His Majesty's Government, the heads of an agreement that will subsequently required to be ratified by the new Parliament and I see no reason why any secret should be made of the fact that he is doing so. Under such an agreement,

there could be no suggestion that Secretary of State was entering into a secret agreement with myself though I have no doubt the Governor would be satisfied himself by informal consultation with me, where necessary, that terms of the agreement were likely to prove generally acceptable.

5.  I should like you also to impress on the Secretary of State that if he could see his way to include in proposed announcement a statement that, on the inauguration of new Constitution, the designation of Governor will be changed to that of Governor-General and responsibility for Ceylon affairs transferred from Colonial to Dominions Office such a declaration would, in my view, convince Ceylon public that grant of full Dominion status was not likely to be long delayed and would strengthen my hand against independence group.

Please telegraph your telephone number. *Ends.*


**388**  CAB 129/18, C(47)4                                        29 Apr 1947
'Ceylon constitution': memorandum by Mr Creech Jones for Cabinet Colonial Affairs Committee recommending that HMG should support Mr Senanayake over dominion status

My colleagues on this Committee will remember our discussions leading up to the Order in Council of 15th May, 1946, which provided a new Constitution for Ceylon on the basis of the statement of policy on constitutional reform in Ceylon made by His Majesty's Government in October, 1945 (Cmd. 6690).

2.  Preparations for the introduction of the new Constitution are well advanced, and it is expected that the new Parliament will meet for the first time in October next. In the meantime, as I have informed the Prime Minister on the 22nd March,[1] I have received a personal letter from Mr. Senanayake[2] in which he explains that, as Leader of the Moderate Party which is fighting the forthcoming election for the new Parliament, he is seriously embarrassed by the considerable capital which his political opponents are making out of the acceptance by himself and other Ceylon Ministers of a constitutional status for Ceylon greatly inferior to that now accorded to India and Burma. He points out that a considerable number of his colleagues in the State Council desire immediate agitation for similar concessions to those made to India and Burma, and that, if serious deterioration in the political situation is to be prevented, action must be taken quickly. I should explain that the political opposition to his Moderate Party consists mainly of the Indian Congress Party and of the Communists, who have gained considerable ascendency in the local Trade Unions.

3.  It will be remembered that proposals which were made by Mr. Senanayake in the course of discussions with my predecessor in 1945, for the grant of Dominion status to Ceylon, were then rejected in principle by the Cabinet (see C.M.(45) 30th Conclusions).[3] Mr. Senanayake has, however, now sent Sir Oliver Goonetilleke, K.B.E., C.M.G., the Financial Secretary of Ceylon, to this country to approach His Majesty's Government with a view to securing a reconsideration of the position.

4.  Sir Oliver Goonetilleke has explained to me that the dominating factor in the

---

[1] See 384.                     [2] See 381.                     [3] See 283.

recent developments was the declaration of His Majesty's Government's intention to withdraw from India in June, 1948. Mr. Senanayake regarded it as certain that when India became independent she would bring strong pressure on Ceylon to throw in her lot with India. India would be in a position to put economic sanctions on Ceylon and, through the local Congress Party, could foment labour disturbances and gravely embarrass the Ceylon Government. He felt that it was unrealistic to suppose that His Majesty's Government would be willing to face a major clash with India in order to protect Ceylon's interests, and it was, therefore, essential that Ceylon should secure her own international status as an independent State to enable her to have recourse to the protection of the United Nations against possible Indian aggression. At the same time, Sir Oliver was able to assure me that it is the strong desire of the vast majority of the Ceylonese to achieve their independence within the British Commonwealth, and that Mr. Senanayake is confident that if the promise of independence is given there will be no effective pressure for leaving the Commonwealth.

5. Mr. Senanayake, therefore, has asked that Ceylon should be granted full independence within the British Commonwealth as soon as possible after the new Parliament comes into being. He is prepared, however, to undertake that Ceylon for her part will be willing, if His Majesty's Government so desires, to negotiate agreements with His Majesty's Government for safeguards in respect of Imperial defence and external affairs, which are at present 'reserved subjects' (see Annexure I).[4] These agreements, he suggests, should, in the meanwhile, be drafted by me in consultation with the Governor, who would in his turn consult his Ministers under the existing Constitution as to what would be likely to be acceptable to the future Government of Ceylon.

6. In putting forward these proposals on Mr. Senanayake's behalf, Sir Oliver Goonetilleke asked that His Majesty's Government should make an immediate declaration to the effect that, in the light of developments regarding India and Burma, and in view of representations made to them by Mr. Senanayake, they have reconsidered the White Paper of 1945 and have decided that, instead of Ceylon being required (as envisaged in that Paper) to achieve Dominion status by a process of evolution (see Annexure II), the people of Ceylon should be given full independence as soon as possible after the new Parliament comes into being; that, having regard to the desire of the people of Ceylon to remain within the British Commonwealth, the independence granted would be that of an independent member of that Commonwealth; and that instructions have been given for the preparation of the necessary documents to make possible the achievement of this objective.

7. Sir Oliver Goonetilleke pressed for the use of the expression "independence" rather than "Dominion status", since the latter was not used in the cases of India and Burma, but it is clear that in effect it is Dominion status which is being sought. The status of a self-governing Colony such as Southern Rhodesia would not be acceptable to Ceylon. He also contemplated that the necessary amendment of the new Constitution should be effected as soon as the agreements had been negotiated with the new Government of Ceylon, though he was anxious that the declaration should not be so framed as to make the grant of the principle of independence conditional on the conclusion of these agreements. He emphasised Mr. Senanayake's anxiety that Ceylon should be admitted to membership of the United Nations before June, 1948.

[4] Annexures not printed.

In conclusion he said that Mr. Senanayake was anxious that the title of the Governor should be changed to "Governor-General" and that responsibility in this country for the affairs of Ceylon should be transferred to the Dominions Office.

8. Sir Oliver Goonetilleke thought it was most important that this declaration should be made before the opening of the final meeting of the present State Council on the 13th May, otherwise there was a definite risk that some member of the Council would bring forward a Motion in favour of independence which could hardly fail to be passed. Mr. Senanayake, as he said, was naturally anxious to keep the initiative in his own hands and to avoid allowing the question of remaining in the British Commonwealth to become a matter of debate.

9. I have no doubt whatever that the Ceylonese desire for independence is strong and genuine. I have received communications from the Governor of Ceylon in which he urges that the most serious and prompt consideration should be given to Mr. Senanayake's proposals. Sir Henry Moore further expresses the view that the defence interests of His Majesty's Government might well be better secured by a negotiated settlement of the nature now proposed than under the procedure laid down in the Order in Council of May, 1946, which made defence a reserved subject, (see Annexure I).

10. The position as I see it may be summarised thus:—Mr. Senanayake is faced with a general public demand that Ceylon should become "independent". He is distrustful of and afraid of India and would prefer Ceylon to be an independent member of the British Commonwealth rather than be absorbed by India. He has to meet the growing criticism that Ceylon's rate of constitutional advance, despite her loyalty and assistance to His Majesty's Government during the war, is slower than that of India and Burma. He is well aware of the strategic importance of Ceylon to the British Commonwealth, and is ready, in return for the grant of independence within the Commonwealth, to meet His Majesty's Government's essential needs in the defence sphere, as well as to give undertakings not to enter into foreign commitments which might be embarrassing to the Commonwealth as a whole.

11. I am advised that an amendment of the Statute of Westminster would not necessarily be required to secure the further advance which Mr. Senanayake is seeking, but that an Act of Parliament would be needed to apply to Ceylon the principles of independence inherent in that Statute.

12. I have given anxious thought to this matter, more particularly in view of the accusation which has been made against the present Government of "scuttle" and of "squandering the Empire". It seems to me that, on the contrary, if this matter is rightly handled, we have an excellent opportunity not only of keeping Ceylon within the British Commonwealth and of securing our vital defence interests there, but of demonstrating to the world that our proclaimed policy for the Colonial peoples is not an empty boast, and that an independent status in the Commonwealth is not, in practice, reserved for people of European descent. Such a demonstration would both confound our critics and give deserved encouragement to loyal and progressive elements in the Colonial peoples. Unless, on the other hand, a positive move is made now to forestall the demand for independence which has been quickened by events in India and Burma, there is, I understand, little prospect of the 1946 Constitution being successfully inaugurated, and the most unfortunate results may well follow. My conclusion is that we should accept in substance the proposals which Mr. Senanayake, through Sir Oliver Goonetilleke, has put forward.

13.  I recognise that the outcome largely depends upon Mr. Senanayake himself, and that however much we may rely upon his good faith, and however likely it may be that he will return to power, we cannot be certain that it will be with him and not with some other leader that we shall have to deal when it comes to the point. I fear that any attempt to qualify the grant of independence, or to make it in terms conditional on the prior acceptance by the Ceylon Government of stipulations insisted upon by His Majesty's Government, would seriously damage Mr. Senanayake's chances of being returned on a platform of "independence within the Commonwealth". Nor should we, in practice, find it easy to enforce any stipulations upon a Ceylon Government committed to a policy of independence and indifferent or even hostile to the maintenance of the British connexion. The dilemma is real but I think it unlikely that our faith would prove unfounded.

14.  I should, therefore, propose, if my colleagues agree, to enter into discussions at once with Sir Oliver Goonetilleke and to consult the Chiefs of Staff and other Departments concerned, with a view to formulating an announcement substantially on the lines contemplated in paragraphs 6 and 7 above, in terms mutually acceptable to Mr. Senanayake on the one hand and to His Majesty's Government on the other. I should not, of course, at this stage involve His Majesty's Government in any final commitment, but as soon as the agreed formula had been reached I would place it before this Committee with a view to seeking Cabinet approval before making such an announcement. For the reasons given in paragraph 8 above, the matter is of some urgency.[5]

---

[5] The Colonial Affairs Committee endorsed Creech Jones's recommendations on 1 May. On 2 May Greenwood, chairman of the committee, submitted a memo to Cabinet recommending that, subject to the views of the Chiefs of Staff and the dominions, Creech Jones should be authorised to enter negotiations with Sir O Goonetilleke (CAB 129/18, CP(47)144).

# 389  CAB 129/18, CP(47)147                                    5 May 1947
## 'Ceylon constitution': Cabinet report by COS on the strategic importance of Ceylon and UK defence requirements

In accordance with the invitation of the Colonial Affairs Committee we have examined the military implications of the proposals put forward by the Secretary of State for the Colonies in C.(47) 4[1] (Annex to C.P.(47) 144).

*Strategic importance of Ceylon*
2.  The maintenance of the security of our sea and air communications is one of the basic requirements of Commonwealth strategy.

Ceylon derives its importance from the commanding position it occupies in relation to our sea and air communications in the Indian Ocean. In any future war we should require to use Ceylon as a base from which to defend these communications.

The Island forms an essential link in our cable and wireless network to Australia

---

[1] See 388.

and the Far East. It is also the centre of our Naval intelligence organisations for countries bordering the Indian Ocean.

3.   Inability to use Ceylon would deprove us of the only existing main fleet base between Malta and Singapore and would seriously weaken our control of the Indian Ocean. If in addition we were unable to use ports and airfields in India, our sea communications in the Indian Ocean and our air routes to Australia and the Far East would be gravely endangered.

*Defence requirements in Ceylon*
4.   In broad terms our defence requirements in Ceylon are:—

(a)  In peace the right to base naval and air forces in Ceylon and to maintain the necessary facilities there: the right to station limited land forces as a nucleus organisation for the defence of the Island: the retention of our cable and wireless facilities.
(b)  In war, the right to develop the above facilities.

*Ability to obtain our defence requirements*
5.   The Secretary of State for the Colonies proposes that His Majesty's Government should make an immediate announcement granting full independence within the British Commonwealth, instead of requiring her, as contemplated in the White Paper of 1945, to achieve Dominion status by a process of evolution, during which period defence matters would be reserved to the Government.

In return for this grant of independence the Secretary of State for the Colonies hopes that Ceylon would be willing to negotiate special agreements with His Majesty's Government for safeguards in respect of Commonwealth defence and external affairs. The grant of independence would, however, be made unconditional and before these special agreements had been drawn up.

6.   It is clear, therefore, that the issue of independence for Ceylon has got to be faced sooner or later—either immediately if the latest proposal is adopted, or at some future date if the policy in the White Paper of 1945 is adopted. In either case it is vital to the security of the Commonwealth that we should obtain our defence requirements in Ceylon by some form of reservation or agreement.

7.   The immediate grant of unconditional independence is admittedly a gamble on the good faith of the leader of the Moderate Party and on his chances of being returned to power. In view of the magnitude of the issues at stake, and with experience of the Egyptian negotiations fresh in our minds, we are convinced that from the military point of view this risk is unacceptable.

*Conclusion*
8.   We conclude, therefore, that the grant of independence to Ceylon, whether now or later, must be accompanied by reservations which will ensure that our defence requirements will be adequately and permanently met.

# 390  PREM 8/726, CM 44(47)2                                    6 May 1947

## 'Ceylon: constitutional development': Cabinet conclusions to the effect that a decision on dominion status should not be rushed

The Cabinet considered a memorandum (C.P.(47) 144)[1] submitted by the Minister without Portfolio as Chairman of the Colonial Affairs Committee on the constitutional position in Ceylon. They also had before them a report by the Chiefs of Staff (C.P.(47) 147)[2] on the military implications of the proposals put forward in C.P.(47) 144.

*The Secretary of State for the Colonies* recalled that, in the discussions in 1945 on the Report of the Soulbury Commission, Mr. D.S. Senanayake, the Vice-Chairman of the Ceylon Board of Ministers, had proposed the immediate grant of Dominion status to Ceylon. This proposal had been rejected by the Cabinet, but the constitution granted on the basis of the Statement of Policy of October, 1945, (Cmd. 6690) gave the Ceylon Government full control of the internal affairs of the Island in the expectation of eventual evolution to Dominion status. In view of recent developments in India and Burma, Mr. Senanayake had now reopened the matter by asking that Ceylon should be promised "independence within the British Commonwealth" as soon as possible after the inauguration of the new Constitution in October, 1947. He had undertaken that Ceylon would enter into agreements with His Majesty's Government for safeguards in respect of Imperial Defence and external affairs, but had asked that the promise of independence should not be made conditional on those agreements. Acceptance of this proposal would involve taking a risk on Mr. Senanayake's good faith and his chances of being returned to power; but refusal would strengthen the hands of the extremists in Ceylon, who were pressing for complete independence, and might prejudice the inauguration of the new Constitution. In that event, we might fail both to secure our defence requirements and to retain Ceylon within the Commonwealth. The Secretary of State therefore recommended that a statement should be made on the lines suggested by Mr. Senanayake. His proposals had the full support of the Governor of Ceylon, and had been endorsed by the Colonial Affairs Committee, subject to the views of the Chiefs of Staff and Dominion Governments.

*The Chief of the Air Staff*[3] stressed the strategic importance of Ceylon. It was an essential base for the defence of the Indian Ocean. It was also an essential link in our air, cable and wireless communications with the Far East. The Chiefs of Staff considered that the grant of independence to Ceylon should be accompanied by reservations which would ensure that our defence requirements would be adequately and permanently met.

In discussion there was strong support for the view that it would be unwise to reach a hurried decision on a question of such major importance, which was of close concern to all the Commonwealth countries. The Dominion Governments should have full opportunity for comment before any commitment was made to Ceylon; and Australia and New Zealand, in particular, should be informed of the views of the Chiefs of Staff on the military implications of the proposal. The Cabinet should not expose themselves to the criticism of acting precipitately in response to an overture

---

[1] See 388, note 5.                    [2] See 389.                    [3] Lord Tedder.

from a party leader on the eve of an election, of committing themselves without adequate consultation either within or outside Ceylon, and ignoring the position of the minorities whose interests had hitherto been carefully safeguarded. There was also a risk that an announcement on the lines proposed would be interpreted as an indication of weakness: there could be no assurance that Mr. Senanayake would keep his promise: and we should be encouraging demands for similar political concessions in Malaya and elsewhere. In any event was it not premature to agree to any further measure of constitutional reform in Ceylon? The new constitution, which had been drawn up after full investigation and consultation in the Island and embodied a scheme put forward by Ceylon Ministers themselves, had not yet come into operation. The announcement now proposed would involve abandoning this before an election had been held under it.

*The Secretary of State for the Colonies* said that a negative reply might have serious political results in Ceylon.

In discussion the following further points were made:—

(a) The implications of the term "independence within the British Common-wealth", should be carefully considered. The use of the word "independence", apart from giving Ceylon a right to apply for membership of the United Nations, might place His Majesty's Government in an embarrassing position in connection with demands for the withdrawal of troops from "independent" countries.

(b) Mr. Senanayake had suggested that it was unrealistic to suppose that His Majesty's Government would be willing to face a major clash with India in order to protect Ceylon's interests. It should be made clear to him that His Majesty's Government could not accept such an agreement.

(c) Consideration should be given to the definition of an appropriate constitution-al status for Colonial territories whose political development would soon enable them to expect some degree of independence within the Commonwealth.

(d) The arrangements agreed with the Union of South Africa for the naval base at Simonstown might provide an appropriate precedent for the agreement which would ultimately have to be made with the Ceylon Government for the safeguarding of our defence requirements on the Island.

The Cabinet:—

(1) Invited the Secretary of State for the Colonies to submit, for consideration by the Cabinet, the draft of the communication to be made to Mr. Senanayake in the light of their discussion;

(2) Invited the Chiefs of Staff to consider what arrangements for safeguarding our defence interests would have to be made with Ceylon Government, if the Island attained a position of independence within the Commonwealth."

---

[4] Creech Jones informed Moore of the Cabinet's decision by tel on 7 May. The first two paras explained the Cabinet's reasoning. The tel then continued:

'For these reasons, while Cabinet remain in full sympathy with aspiration of Ceylon to achieve full responsible self-government within the Commonwealth and fully stand by proclaimed intention of His Majesty's Government to co-operate with people of Ceylon towards that end, they must conclude that any announcement of further constitutional change before meeting of State Council this month is out of the question.

Cabinet have requested me to submit to them draft of communication to be made to Senanayake in light of these conclusions. I should be most grateful for your advice as to best way of presenting what I realize must be a disappointing decision and for your estimate of consequent effects upon local political situation.

Above is at this stage of course for your personal information only.

Draft message will be submitted to my colleagues early next week and I hope to telegraph it out immediately thereafter. Subject to your advice I should propose to give substance simultaneously to Goonetilleke. Meanwhile I shall see latter and tell him that no information as to probable attitude of His Majesty's Government can be given to him for a few days yet and I suggest that you should now inform Senanayake to same effect, assuring him that I appreciate and sympathize with his anxiety for early communication, and will give him his answer as soon as I can possibly do so, but explaining that questions he has raised have needed consideration at highest level which cannot be completed sooner' (CO 882/30, no 151).

**391**  CO 882/30, no 152                                          8 May 1947

[Dominion status]: inward unnumbered telegram (reply) from Sir H Moore to Mr Creech Jones conveying his initial reaction to the Cabinet's decision

Your top secret and personal telegram of 7th May.[1]

I fully appreciate Cabinet's reluctance to be rushed over a matter of such importance and I was unaware that Senanayake was pressing for an announcement by 13th May. This may be as a result of a telephone conversation with Goonetilleke, details of which have not been communicated to me, but while he was always anxious for as early an announcement as possible—see paragraph 3 of my secret and personal telegram of 4th April[2]—he never pressed in the conversation with me that it should be made before the Council meets again on 13th May. Duration of next Council Session may be anything from three to six weeks, dependent on the time taken over the Education Bill, and while it would no doubt be advantageous to make the announcement before the Council is finally dissolved, I would not personally consider this an overriding consideration. It is, however, most desirable that it should be made as early as possible before nomination day, 31st July. If you can assure Senanayake that the Cabinet is giving sympathetic consideration to his request, but that owing to the necessity for consultation with different authorities concerned an immediate announcement cannot be made, but that you hope to do so before 31st July, I believe that he will accept it. I strongly advise giving some definite date so as to dispel any suspicion that His Majesty's Government is temporising in the matter pending governments in India or Burma.

2.  As regards the strategic aspect, which clearly, is of first rate importance, I am not sure how far the Service Departments fully appreciate the position created by the adoption in their present form of Sections 30, 37 (1) (a) and (b) and 46 (4) of the Order-in-Council. Since the Prime Minister has been specifically made Minister of Defence and External Affairs, he must administer those departments, and I do not see how in practice the Governor could withhold from him information as to Imperial policy which might involve Legislation either under Section 30 or Section 37.

3.  As regards protection of minorities, Section 37 (2) (b) and (c) already leaves question of Indian Immigration and franchise entirely in the hands of Ceylon Government, and apart from Section 37(1)(f), the principal minority safeguards are

---

[1] See 390, note 4.                                            [2] See 387.

incorporated in Section 29 (2) and (3). I imagine these provisions would not be affected by grant of Dominion status, but in any case paragraph 178 of Soulbury Commission Report is very relevant.

4.  As already stated in paragraph 7 of my secret and personal letter of 7th March,[3] I see no reason why necessary safeguards in respect of defence and foreign affairs could not be as effectively secured under the terms of the proposed agreement. While I appreciate the Cabinet's hesitation in appearing to treat with a party leader, I suggest the point should be stressed that, if this opportunity is missed, the demand for complete independence outside the Commonwealth will become so strong that Senanayake himself may not be able to resist it. The reference to a major clash in India is not understood. I imagine it has emanated from Goonetilleke, as Senanayake has never used such an argument with me.

5.  I agree that you should inform Goonetilleke as proposed, provided sufficient time is allowed to ensure that I can deliver the message to Senanayake before Goonetilleke could telephone him.

6.  I am informing Senanayake in the sense you suggest.

---

[3] See 382.

## 392   CO 882/30, no 154                          12 May 1947
## [Dominion status]: outward unnumbered telegram (reply) from Mr Creech Jones to Sir H Moore transmitting drafts of a message to Mr Senanayake and an announcement by HMG

Top Secret and Personal 12th May.
Many thanks for your top secret and personal telegrams of 8th[1] and 10th May, which I have found extremely helpful. Pressure for announcement by 13th May was conveyed to me by Goonetilleke, who stated that it was, as you surmised, result of telephone conversations with Senanayake. The reason given was possibility that some Member might bring forward during State Council meeting a motion for independence which would be certain to be passed. It was pointed out that Senanayake would naturally wish to keep initiative in his own hands and prevent any question being raised of independence outside the Commonwealth.

2.  I am much relieved to learn from you that matter is not of such extreme urgency as had been represented, as this will give reasonable time for consultations which must precede any announcement. I will however do my best to secure early decision.

3.  I now propose to submit, for the consideration of the Cabinet, that a reply should be made by me to Senanayake's letter on the following lines.

*Begins*

*Draft of possible message to Mr. Senanayake*
My Colleagues and I are most appreciative of the co-operative spirit displayed by

---

[1] See 391.

Ceylon in war and in peace. His Majesty's Government understand the desire of the people of Ceylon to achieve full responsibility in all their affairs and recognise, particularly in view of recent developments in India and Burma, that the period envisaged by the reference to an evolutionary process in the White Paper of 1945 should be shorter and more clearly defined.

Indeed, we hope and believe that, as soon as the new Ceylon Parliament elected under the 1946 Constitution comes into being, it will be possible, without any unnecessary delay, to work out, in consultation with the Ceylon Cabinet, arrangements under which independent status within the Commonwealth can be attained. It will be our aim to shorten the process as much as possible by using the interval to clear the ground. You will appreciate how necessary it is for us, in dealing with a matter of such immense concern not only to the United Kingdom and Ceylon but to all members of the Commonwealth, to ensure that all proper consultations have been carried out and all relevant considerations taken into account.

For example, in the sphere of defence, it will clearly be necessary to formulate the essential conditions needful to secure the position of Ceylon in the arrangements for Commonwealth defence and the security of the Island itself. Again, the relationship of Ceylon to other members of the Commonwealth in the matter of external affairs will have to be thought out. Both these questions will involve not only careful study by United Kingdom Ministers and their advisers but also consultation with the other Commonwealth Governments. Moreover, in view of the obligations of His Majesty's Government towards the minorities in Ceylon, some assurance as to their future position under an independent government would be expected. Finally, any transfer of power to an independent Government in Ceylon must, to be fully effective, be authorised by an Act of the United Kingdom Parliament. (It will be within your knowledge that Acts of Parliament are necessary in the case of India and Burma). It is obvious that Parliament would not be in a position to pass such an Act until it was satisfied that all necessary agreements had been arrived at.

While, therefore, as I have said, we can and will at once institute preliminary work on these subjects, my colleagues feel that it is impracticable for them to give an unconditional promise of independence now. We realise that you for your part had quite understood the need for consultation and negotiation, but had hoped that an assurance from you of Ceylon's willingness to enter into agreements would enable such a promise to be made. We are grateful for and gladly accept your assurance, but you will, we are sure, understand that we are bound at the moment to regard it as given in your personal capacity, and that we cannot publicly involve ourselves in an advance commitment which would tie our hands in negotiating with whatever government may be in power in Ceylon when the time comes.

The main reason emphasised to me by Goonetilleke for taking immediate action was distrust of India. He said that it was unrealistic to suppose that His Majesty's Government would be willing to face a major clash with India in order to protect the interests of Ceylon. The Cabinet wish to make it clear that they cannot accept any such assumption.

Taking all these matters into consideration, His Majesty's Government propose, at a suitable date to be decided in consultation with the Governor but in any case not later than the 31st May, to make an announcement to the following effect.

*Begins*

*Draft announcement*
The new Constitution of Ceylon is about to come into force, and it is anticipated that the newly elected Parliament will assemble in October. In their statement of policy of October, 1945, which followed on the Report of the Soulbury Commission and led to the grant of the new Constitution, His Majesty's Government declared their anxiety to co-operate with the people of Ceylon in their advance to Dominion status, and expressed the hope that in a comparatively short space of time such a status will be evolved. Meanwhile political developments in India and Burma of immense importance have occurred, and these changes have quickened the desire for the realisation of full self-government in Ceylon. His Majesty's Government have consequently reviewed the programme of constitutional advance contemplated at the time of the Soulbury Commission.

As they have already made it clear, His Majesty's Government are in sympathy with the desire of the people of Ceylon to achieve an independent status within the British Commonwealth. They have decided that, as soon as the new Parliament has been elected and the new Government of Ceylon has taken office, they will be prepared to enter into discussion with the Ceylon Government in the hope that agreements with regard to the matters reserved under the 1946 Constitution can be concluded in such terms as to make possible the advance of the Island to full self-governing status at the earliest practicable date. In the meantime His Majesty's Government have given directions that the matters to be included in such agreements should be studied by the competent authorities in order to obviate delay. *End* of Draft announcement. *End* of proposed message to Senanayake.

4.   I shall be most grateful for your early comments on these proposals as I hope to bring the matter before the Cabinet during next few days. You will appreciate that the above are at the moment tentative drafts which may have to be modified after consideration by Cabinet.

# 393   CO 882/30, no 155                              14 May 1947
## [Dominion status]: inward unnumbered telegram (reply) from Sir H Moore to Mr Creech Jones suggesting amendments to the message and the announcement

Your top secret and personal telegram of 12th May.[1]
   Your paragraphs 1 and 2 noted.
   2.   Your paragraph 3. I suggest the omission of

   (a)   Sentence beginning "Indeed we hope", ending "attained", and substitution of the following therefor:—"In order, therefore, to accelerate the steps by which Ceylon can qualify for full and independent membership of the United Nations Organization, we propose to present to the Ceylon Cabinet for their consideration as early as is practicable after the new Ceylon parliament elected under the 1946 Constitution has come into being, the heads of an agreement covering the subjects at present reserved

---

[1] See 392.

under the Soulbury Constitution, which on ratification would enable Ceylon to attain full independent status within the Commonwealth, as soon as the necessary act of United Kingdom Parliament had been passed."

(b) Sentence beginning "Moreover", ending "expected". This would now be covered, if the terms of the amendment proposed in (a) above are adopted. I feel it would be a mistake to press the point specifically with Senanayake, particularly in view of His Majesty's Government's attitude towards the minority question in India and Burma, unless it is also to be reproduced in official announcement. If it is to be so reproduced, the form and nature of the required assurance should be stated.

3. *Draft announcement*

For the penultimate sentence beginning "They have decided", ending "practicable date", suggest substitution of text suggested in paragraph 2 (a) above with consequential substitution of the words "they have decided" for "we propose" immediately before "to present". But if you are in a position to announce now that formal agreement will be confined to defence and external affairs, I would strongly recommend your doing so in substitution for the phrase "subjects at present reserved", etc.

4. I have made the above suggestions because I am sure that it is essential that statement should be unequivocal and make it quite clear that His Majesty's Government has accepted the grant of Dominion status in principle, and that His Majesty's Government, having laid down policy, it rests with Ceylon to play her part by ratifying the terms of the proposed agreement. The phrase "discussions in the hope that" will, I fear, not be regarded as sufficiently convincing.

5. I note that no reference is made to the proposed transfer to the Dominions Office. I have already stated that I personally realize the practical advantages of not making too distinct a change, but I should be failing in my duty if I did not again repeat the very great importance which is somehow attached to such a transfer, as a definite gesture indicative of His Majesty's Government's determination to implement her declared policy at a very early date. Since in any case the transfer cannot now be long delayed there may be practical advantages in making the change a gradual one, and I do not know if you would see any serious objection to announcing something on the lines that though the Secretary of State for the Colonies will naturally be responsible for negotiating the agreement on behalf of His Majesty's Government, it is proposed after the date of the first meeting of the new Parliament, to initiate the necessary steps to transfer responsibility for Ceylon affairs from the Colonial to the Dominions Secretary.

# 394   CO 882/30, no 156                                    16 May 1947

[Dominion status]: outward telegram (reply) no 544 from Mr Creech Jones to Sir H Moore suggesting further amendments to the message and the announcement

Your top secret and personal telegrams 14th May.[1] Constitution.

---

[1] See 393.

I am very grateful for your suggestions which I will incorporate in draft to be submitted to Cabinet subject to following variations:—

(a) Question of membership of United Nations involves certain complications from point of view of general foreign policy, and it would not be acceptable to put this forward as the primary objective of the proposed constitutional change. I realize, however, desirability of making reference to the point and propose to deal with it by adding paragraph to draft announcement as follows:—
    *Begins.* His Majesty's Government will lend their full support to any application by Ceylon for membership of United Nations as soon as Ceylon's constitutional position makes it possible for such an application to be entertained. *Ends.*
    This is taken from corresponding text of Burma declaration, see paragraph 6 of Cmd. 7029.
(b) The second paragraph of draft letter to Senanayake would then read:—
    *Begins.* In order, therefore, to accelerate the steps by which Ceylon can achieve the full responsibility desired by its people, we propose to present, etc. *Ends.*
(c) Corresponding sentence in draft announcement would read:—
    *Begins.* In order, therefore, to accelerate the steps by which Ceylon can realise this aim, His Majesty's Government have decided to present, etc. *Ends.*
(d) I feel sure that my colleagues will not agree to omit specific mention of minorities. I propose, therefore, to re-insert sentence as previously drafted in letter to Senanayake and to add following words in brackets to draft announcement after the reference to subjects at present reserved under the Ceylon Constitution.
    *Begins.* (Namely defence external affairs and the safeguard of minorities). *Ends.*
    This would mean that safeguarding of minorities would be one of the matters to be dealt with in negotiating the proposed agreement. For example, Ceylon Government might be invited to undertake not to pass legislation which would be *ultra vires* under 1946 Constitution.
(e) There are difficulties about entering into specific public commitment at this stage regarding transfer of Ceylon affairs to the Dominions Office. For your own information general question of future arrangements for handling affairs of newly enfranchised countries is under consideration. I will raise the point in Cabinet, but I doubt whether they will feel able to agree to any public announcement, such as you envisage at the present juncture.

2.   If you have any further observations on the above proposals I shall be grateful if you will let me have them as soon as possible. If necessary consultations can be completed in time, I hope to put the matter before the Cabinet early next week and, if they approve, it should be possible to give Senanayake his reply immediately after and then make the announcement on a date agreed with you as mutually convenient. I appreciate his anxiety for earliest information as to possible date of my reply, but you will see that in the circumstances I cannot say more now than that I hope to be in a position to communicate with him by the end of next week. I am informing Goonetilleke to this effect.[2]

---

[2] Bevin, the foreign secretary, was especially unhappy with the wording of the declaration. See his letter to Creech Jones, 20 May, and the latter's reply, 23 May (CAB 118/29), reproduced in BDEEP series A, vol 1, R Hyam, ed, *The Labour government and the end of empire 1945–1951*, part I, 26 & 28. As in the case of India's independence, Bevin's concern over Ceylon was dictated by his opinion that there would be adverse repercussions for Britain's position in the Middle East.

# 395    PREM 8/726                                     1 June 1947
'Ceylon constitution': Cabinet memorandum by Mr Creech Jones on the message to Mr Senanayake and the announcement by HMG. *Annexes*

At the meeting of the Cabinet on 6th May (C.M.(47) 44th Conclusions, Minute 2)[1] I was asked to submit a draft of a communication regarding the future of Ceylon which might be made to Mr. Senanayake. I now submit this draft (Annex I), together with the draft (Annex II) of an announcement which might be made by His Majesty's Government. I submit the second draft as I feel that my message to Mr. Senanayake should contain the text of an announcement which His Majesty's Government could reasonably make at this stage. The Foreign Secretary and the Secretary of State for Dominion Affairs agree with the drafts. I have also consulted the Minister without Portfolio.

2.   The Governor (Sir Henry Moore, with whom I have been in close consultation) has done his best to relieve the local pressure for an immediate statement and the State Council has been adjourned until 10th June. It will then sit for a few hours only and the Governor very strongly recommends that my reply to Mr. Senanayake should arrive in time for an announcement to be made on that day.

3.   The drafts in their present form fall short of what has been urged upon me by Mr. Senanayake with the support of the Governor, who recommended that the most serious and urgent consideration should be given to Mr. Senanayake's representations. Mr. Senanayake clearly contemplated that Ceylon should now be promised independence within the Commonwealth as soon as the new Parliament met, on the understanding that specific agreements would be made between Ceylon and His Majesty's Government to safeguard our vital defence interests and to secure that Ceylon would enter into no Foreign commitments which might be embarrassing to the Commonwealth as a whole.

4.   The main difference between the present drafts and Mr. Senanayake's proposals is that we do not use the word 'independence' and we make it clear that the 1946 Constitution must be brought into force and actually function before any agreements involving further constitutional changes can be entered into.

5.   The Governor has represented that the inclusion of safeguards for minorities in the subjects specified for formal agreement to be made between the two Governments may cause some difficulty. In view of the feeling evinced by my colleagues on this point when the subject was last discussed I informed Sir Henry Moore that I considered that a specific mention of minorities must be included.

6.   Another point to which considerable importance is attached in Ceylon is the transfer of responsibility for its affairs from the Colonial Office to the Dominions Office. I appreciate that there may be difficulty in committing ourselves specifically at this stage to such a transfer, seeing that the future handling of Indian and Burmese affairs has not been settled, and that the implications of such a transfer, from the point of view of the Dominions, would have to be gone into. I feel, however, that it is important to do something to satisfy Ceylon's natural desire to see any change in her status reflected in our administrative arrangements, and for this

---

[1] See 390.

reason I have added what I consider to be an appropriate sentence at the end of the draft announcement.

7. Finally, considerable importance is attached in Ceylon to the change of the Governor's title to Governor-General. This was recommended by the Soulbury Commission but the Government decided not to make the change during the operation of the 1946 constitution. A reconsideration of this decision now would have an excellent psychological effect in Ceylon, and would help to soften any disappointment which may be caused by our inability to meet their wishes in other respects. The change is one which could be made without difficulty by a simple amendment of the Order-in-Council. I recommend that we should meet Ceylon over this. If this is agreed, a paragraph can be added to the draft announcement.

## Annex I to 395: communication to Mr Senanayake

1. In response to your representations, my colleagues and I have reviewed the constitutional position of Ceylon as it now stands as a result of the Soulbury Commission Report and the White Paper of 1945. We are most appreciative of the co-operative spirit displayed by Ceylon in war and in peace, and we recognise that recent events in India and Burma have quickened the desire of the people of Ceylon to achieve full responsibility in their affairs within a more clearly defined space of time than was envisaged in the White Paper of 1945.

2. We have therefore sought means of accelerating the evolutionary process to which reference was made in that Paper. We do not feel that the present time, when the 1946 Constitution has not yet come into force and the elections for the new Ceylon Parliament have not yet been held, is opportune for making further pronouncements with regard to possible changes in that Constitution. We are, however, prepared to undertake that, as soon as the new Ceylon Parliament has come into being and is functioning, we shall be ready to enter into discussions with the Ceylon Government with regard to the matters now reserved under the 1946 Constitution, that is to say defence, external affairs and the position of minorities. If as a result of these discussions it is possible (as we hope and believe it will be possible) to draw up agreements satisfactory to both parties covering all these matters, we shall be prepared to proceed with the necessary action to amend the present Constitution so as to advance the status of Ceylon within the British Commonwealth of Nations.

3. Further, in order to obviate any avoidable delay in the negotiation of the agreements, we are arranging for the competent authorities to proceed at once to examine the detailed subjects which should be included in the proposed agreements. You will appreciate how necessary it is for me, in dealing with a matter of such immense concern, not only to the United Kingdom and Ceylon but to all members of the Commonwealth, to ensure that all proper consultations have been carried out and all relevant considerations taken into account.

4. For example, in the sphere of defence, it will clearly be necessary to formulate the essential conditions needful to provide for the security of Ceylon itself and its position in relation to the strategic needs of the Commonwealth. Again, in the field of external affairs, the relationship of Ceylon to other members of the Commonwealth will have to be thought out. Both these questions will involve not only careful

study by United Kingdom Ministers and their advisers but also consultation with the other Commonwealth Governments. Moreover, in view of the obligations of His Majesty's Government towards the minorities of Ceylon, some assurance as to their future position in new conditions would be expected. Finally, the effective realisation of another constitutional advance might well involve not only amendment of the Order-in-Council but also an Act of the United Kingdom Parliament. It is obvious that Parliament would not be in a position to pass such an Act until it is satisfied that all necessary agreements have been arrived at and would remain in force after any constitutional change.

5.  While, therefore, as I have said, we can and will at once institute preliminary work on these subjects, my colleagues feel that it is impracticable for them to give an unconditional promise of independence now. We realise that you for your part had quite understood the need for consultation and negotiation, but had hoped that an assurance from you of Ceylon's willingness to enter into agreements would enable such a promise to be made. We are grateful for and gladly accept your assurance, but you will, we are sure, understand that we are bound at the moment to regard it as given in your personal capacity, and that we cannot publicly involve ourselves in an advance commitment which would tie our hands in negotiating with whatever government may be in power in Ceylon when the time comes.

6.  The main reason emphasised to me by Goonetilleke for taking immediate action was distrust of India.[2] He said that it was unrealistic to suppose that His Majesty's Government would be willing to face a major clash with India in order to protect the interests of Ceylon. The Cabinet wish to make it clear that they cannot accept any such assumption.

7.  Taking all these matters into consideration His Majesty's Government propose, at a suitable date in the near future, to be decided in consultation with the Governor, to make an announcement to the following effect.

## Annex II to 395: draft announcement by HMG

1.  The new Constitution of Ceylon is about to come into force, and it is anticipated that the newly elected Parliament will assemble in October. In their statement of policy of October, 1945, which followed on the Report of the Soulbury Commission and led to the grant of the new Constitution, His Majesty's Government declared their anxiety to co-operate with the people of Ceylon in their advance to Dominions status, and expressed the hope that in a comparatively short space of time such a status will be evolved. Meanwhile political developments in India and Burma of immense importance have occurred, and, although it will be noted that there are many difficulties to overcome there, these changes have quickened the desire for the realisation of full self-government in Ceylon. His Majesty's Government have consequently reviewed the programme of constitutional development contemplated at the time of the Soulbury Commission.

2.  As they have already made it clear, His Majesty's Government are wholly in sympathy with the desire of the people of Ceylon to achieve a fully responsible status within the British Commonwealth of Nations. In order, therefore to accelerate the

---

[2] Attlee sidelined this sentence and commented 'Good lord'.

steps by which Ceylon can proceed towards a further constitutional advance, His Majesty's Government will be prepared to discuss with Ceylon, as early as is practicable after the new Ceylon Parliament elected under the 1946 Constitution has come into being and is functioning, the possibility of drawing up an agreement covering the subjects at present reserved under the Soulbury Constitution (namely defence, external affairs and the safe-guarding of minorities). If a satisfactory agreement can be reached on these matters, the way will be open to consideration of amendment of the Constitution. In the meantime, His Majesty's Government have given directions that the matters which might be included in such an agreement should be studied by the competent authorities in order to obviate delay.

3. His Majesty's Government will lend their full support to any application by Ceylon for membership of United Nations as soon as Ceylon's constitutional position makes it possible for such an application to be entertained.

4. Any future change in the constitutional status of Ceylon will naturally involve reconsideration of the present arrangements by which Ceylon affairs are the responsibility of the Colonial Office.[3]

---

[3] T L Rowan, Attlee's principal private secretary (1945–1947) commented on the two annexes to Creech Jones's memo: 'The wording of the documents is verbose, the thought underlying them is not clear and in certain passages the draft seems to be wholly objectionable' (PREM 8/726, minute to Attlee, 2 June 1947). Attlee agreed and sent a minute to Creech Jones on the same day: 'I have read your Memorandum on Ceylon. Its wording is one of the worst examples of turgid jargon that I have ever seen. The draftsman seems afraid to use words of less than five syllables. There must be a revised draft written in plain straightforward terms' (ibid).

Cabinet considered the memo on 3 June and made the following points. (1) The draft contained only a 'perfunctory reference' to the problem of adequate protection for the minorities and to the other 'difficult issues' involved in the grant of further powers to the Ceylon Govt. The announcement should not suggest that further constitutional progress in Ceylon was free from practical difficulties. (2) It was inadvisable to suggest that the development of events in India and Burma had been responsible for HMG's willingness to consider the possibility of speedier constitutional progress in Ceylon. (3) No reference should be made to HMG's willingness to lend support to an application by Ceylon for UN membership. (4) It was inadvisable to make any reference to the possibility that the present arrangements by which Ceylon affairs were the responsibility of the CO might be reconsidered.

Creech Jones pointed out that in its discussion on 6 May (see 390), the Cabinet had taken the view that Senanayake should be informed that HMG did not accept his assumption that the UK would be unwilling to face a major clash with India in order to protect Ceylon's interests. The secretary of state asked whether this point should be included in the formal communication which was to be sent to Senanayake. Cabinet decided that it would be inexpedient to make such a statement in a written document which would no doubt achieve wide publicity. The governor, however, might make the point in discussion with Senanayake. Creech Jones was instructed to revise the drafts in accordance with the Cabinet's recommendations (ibid, CM 51(47)4).

# 396   CO 537/2217, no 3, JP(47)63(Final)                    3 June 1947

## 'Ceylon defence requirements': report by the Joint Planning Staff for COS Committee *Annex*: draft report from COS to Cabinet

It will be recalled that at a recent meeting of the Cabinet[1] the Chiefs of Staff were invited to consider the arrangements which will have to be made with the Ceylon

---

[1] See 390.

Government for safeguarding our Defence Interests if the island should attain independence within the Commonwealth. As instructed we have examined these arrangements and have prepared, at Annex, a draft report from the Chiefs of Staff to the Cabinet. We have consulted the Colonial Office.

*Future status of Ceylon*
2.  The status of a country enjoying 'independence within the Commonwealth' has not yet been defined and there is, as yet, no precedent on which to establish mutual defence obligations. We have, therefore, examined our defence requirements in Ceylon on the assumption that this status carries with it no inherent obligations.

*Strategic importance of Ceylon*
3.  We have already emphasized in J.P.(47) 58 (Final) the stratefic importance of Ceylon. The island is and will remain essential to us as the base from which to control all communications which traverse the Indian Ocean.

*Our military requirements in Ceylon*
4.  In broad terms our military requirements in Ceylon are:—

(a) In peace, the right to base forces and to maintain the necessary facilities in the island: and to retain our necessary telecommunications and signal intelligence facilities.
(b) In the event of a threat to Commonwealth security, the right to introduce additional forces and to develop and add to existing facilities as necessary.

5.  In defining our military requirements below we have borne in mind the possibility of concentrating our somewhat dispersed installations and facilities, in case such a suggestion arose in the course of our negotiations with the Ceylonese.
We have come to the conclusion, for the reasons given below, that we can do little in this direction without heavy financial expenditure and some loss of efficiency and of the advantages of dispersion.

*Naval requirements*
6.  The principal naval requirements are:—

(a) The continued use of the main fleet base at Trincomalee with all its facilities, including an airfield in the port area and three outlying establishments situated up to 25 miles from the port.
(b) The occasional use of repair facilities in Colombo in peace time so as to maintain the value of that port as a subsidiary to Trincomalee, for which purpose it would be repaired in war.
(c) The retention of four store depots, including the Admiralty constructed cold storage at Colombo itself. The retention of three stores/depots and two wireless stations all within 25 miles and one store depot within 60 miles of Colombo.

The outlying facilities at Trincomalee and at Colombo are required to enable stocks to be kept available for the expansion of the fleet in time of war and to effect dispersal. None of them could be moved without considerable expenditure of labour and time and in some cases loss of efficiency. In particular the wireless stations at Colombo constitute the largest naval wireless station to be constructed abroad and, together with the smaller one near Trincomalee, control the Indian Ocean Traffic and are the main link between U.K., Singapore and Hong Kong. To move them would involve great expense and the task would take some years to complete.

*Air Force requirements*
7.  In peacetime the requirements of the R.A.F. in Ceylon are as follows:—

(a) A flying-boat base.
(b) An airfield for a land based maritime-strike Squadron.
(c) An Air Staging Post on the Trunk Route to Australia and the Far East.
(d) Signals facilities.
(e) Miscellaneous units (Air H.Q., and supporting maintenance units).

8.  Plans have already been made to make *Kogalla*, at the South end of the island, into the permanent flying boat base. The only alternative area in the island from which flying boats can be operated is China Bay, at *Trincomalee*, but there is not room for this and the fleet anchorage.

9.  The land based maritime strike squadron and the Air Staging Post are at present located at *Negombo*, 20 miles North of Colombo. Alternative airfields, large enough for these tasks, exist at *Minneriya*, about 50 miles S.W. of *Trincomalee*, and at *Kankesanturai*, at the extreme north of the island. The runways of these two airfields are believed still serviceable but all living accommodation has been handed over to civil authorities. In addition *Kankesanturai* is a bad location administratively while *Minneriya* is in an unhealthy inland area.

10.  Ceylon is at present being developed as an essential link to take the place of *Delhi* in the R.A.F. Signals point to point system to the Far East. The transmitting station is operating at *Negombo* and the receiving station at *Gangodwila*, both in the Colombo area. To move and reinstal the equipment, besides involving rebuilding the stations, would however take about two years to complete, and would be dependent upon suitable alternative sites being found.

11.  The R.A.F. Wartime reserve of bombs is located in a bomb dump at *Karunegala* [sic]. Any removal would involve considerable expense.

12.  Air H.Q. is at present located at *Katukurunda*, South of Colombo. Any decision to move R.A.F. Operational units to the northern part of the island would involve the move and re-accommodation of Air H.Q., and maintenance units.

*Army requirements*
13.  The role of the Army in Ceylon would be the defence of the facilities required by the other services against external threat or internal disorder. Although at the moment we do not plan to locate a combatant unit other than A.A. and C.D. in the island in peacetime, we require the right to move in such forces as we may deem necessary. The location of these forces would then be dependent upon the role they were called upon to perform.

In war we require the right to develop and expand our defensive arrangements.

*Requirements common to all three services*
14.  We would require to retain our Tele-communications facilities for the Empire Cable system and for the Empire integrated wireless chain; and to extend them if necessary.

15. It is also essential that we retain the use of the Signals Intelligence Centre which has recently been established in Ceylon. This station which is now located near Colombo could only be moved if a technically suitable alternative site in the Island could be found. Such a move would be extremely costly.

16. We shall require leave, recreational and hospital facilities at least to the standard we now enjoy. We shall in addition require the use of port facilities in Colombo for the maintenance of our forces.

### The integrity of Ceylon

17. The comparatively small size of the Island and the unavoidably dispersed pattern of the military facilities and installations which we require in Ceylon makes it necessary for us to concern ourselves with the security of the whole Island. Ceylon's value to us as a base would be lost were any substantial portion of the island to be overrun by a hostile power, or were the local Government to be unable to maintain internal security.

We must therefore add to our requirements:—

(a) The security of Ceylon against external aggression.
(b) The maintenance of internal order within the Island.

### External defence

18. A threat to the territorial integrity of Ceylon is likely to come only from India, although a full scale attack from that country is only likely to occur if she were overrun by, or had thrown in her lot with a hostile power.

19. It is unlikely that Ceylon will ever be able to raise and train forces of her own capable of securing her coasts, and it appears, therefore, that our defence requirements in Ceylon will only be met if we continue to accept responsibility for the security of the Island from external aggression. By shouldering this responsibility we should not be incurring any new commitment, since Ceylon is only likely to be threatened in the event of a major war and under these circumstances we should wish, in any case, to preserve our essential defence interests in the country.

### Internal security

20. The danger of *India* (particularly Congress India) interfering with Ceylonese internal politics and provoking dissension among the powerful Indian minority is a real one. The extent of this danger cannot accurately be assessed until the future constitutional set-up in *India* is known. This danger is superimposed on the problems of racial differences, anti-European feeling, communism and labour unrest, which by themselves are liable at any time to cause internal disorder.

21. It seems to us that the agreements between the United States and the Philippine Republic might in some respects provide a better example of the method of approach to this problem.

The extensive military facilities enjoyed by the Americans in the Philippines were established and developed before the Philippines were granted independence. Moreover, the Philippines are an important outpost in the American defensive system. The facilities the Americans now have in the Islands are widely dispersed, and dependant upon the port of Manila and internal communications. In all these respects, there is a close similarity with the problem of Ceylon, but most important of all, the Filipinos before being granted independence were made to see that, without American support, their independence would be little more than nominal.

*Conclusions*

22. We conclude that, if Ceylon were to attain independence within the Commonwealth:—

(a) Her continued integrity would be of vital importance to us and we must continue to accept responsibility for her defence.

(b) Our defence requirements would be:—

(i) In peace-time the right to station armed forces and the continued use of extensive facilities throughout the Island.

(ii) In the event of any threat to her integrity the right to introduce additional forces to take action necessary to protect our interests and to extend and add to existing facilities.

(iii) The development of Ceylonese forces under our supervision and with our assistance.

(c) Although our continued responsibility for the defence of Ceylon would mean that the last word on defence matters would rest with us an Anglo–Ceylonese civil and military body to co-ordinate defence matters would be necessary.

(d) Since our requirements in Ceylon are long term, any agreement reached with an independent Ceylon must be lasting, and such an agreement must therefore be based on goodwill and understanding of our common interests.

(e) The agreements between the U.S.A. and the Philippine Republic appear to provide a precedent more appropriate to Ceylon than does the Simonstown Agreement.[2]

## Annex to 396

We have examined the arrangements which would have to be made with the Ceylon Government to safeguard our defence interests, if the Island attained a position of independence within the Commonwealth.

*Military requirements*

2. In view of the strategic importance of Ceylon our military requirements in the Island are:—

(a) In peace, the right to base forces and to maintain the necessary facilities in the island; and to retain our necessary telecommunication and signal intelligence facilities.

---

[2] Under the Simonstown agreement of 1921, the responsibility for the land defences of the Cape Peninsula, including those of the naval dockyard at Simonstown, were transferred from the British to the South African government on the condition that the latter would maintain the naval station in such a state of defence that it would at all times be able to discharge its functions as a naval link in the sea communications of the British empire. By contrast, under the Military Bases Agreement of March 1947 between the United States and the Philippines, the former received a ninety-nine year lease of twenty-three bases in the Philippines, with full legal jurisdiction over them. The editor is grateful to Dr P J Henshaw for information about the Simonstown agreement.

(b) In the event of a threat to Commonwealth security, the right to introduce additional forces, and to develop and add to existing facilities as necessary.

3.  The requirements which we consider are essential to the three Services in peacetime are given below.

*Navy*
    4.  (a) The continued use of the main Fleet base at Trincomalee, with all its facilities, including an airfield.
    (b) Three associated establishments situated within 25 miles of the port.
    (c) The occasional use of repair facilities in Colombo.
    (d) The retention of four store depots at Colombo itself. The retention of three store Depots and two wireless stations within 25 miles and one store depot within 60 miles of Colombo.

*Air Force*
    5.  (a) A flying boat base for one squadron at *Kogalla*.
    (b) An airfield at *Negombo* for a land based maritime strike squadron, and for an Air Staging Post on trunk routes.
    (c) Wireless transmitting and receiving stations in the vicinity of *Colombo*.
    (d) Storage facilities at *Karunegala* [sic] for wartime reserves of bombs.
    (e) Air H.Q. and a few small miscellaneous units in the Colombo area.

*Army*
    6.  Although at present we do not plan to locate a combatant unit other than A.A. and C.D. in the Island in peacetime, we require the right to move in such forces as we may deem necessary for the defence of the facilities required by the other Services against external threat or internal disorder.

*Requirements common to all three services*
    7.  (a) The continued use of our Tele-communication facilities for the Empire Cable system and for the Empire integrated wireless chain and their extension if necessary.
    (b) The continued use of the Signals Intelligence Centre near Colombo.
    (c) Leave, recreational and hospital facilities to the existing standard.
    (d) The use of port facilities in Colombo for the maintenance of our forces.

*Conclusion*
    8.  The requirements shown above for the three Services are the minimum necessary for the satisfaction of our strategic responsibilities. Any attempt to concentrate them in one area of the island would result in heavy expenditure, some loss of efficiency and of the advantages of dispersion.

### The security of Ceylon

9.  All the above will be of no effect unless the integrity of the Island is fully preserved. We must therefore concern ourselves with:—

(a) The security of Ceylon against external aggression.
(b) The maintenance of internal order within the island.

*External defence*

10.  As it is unlikely that Ceylon will be able to provide forces capable of defending the Island against aggression we must assume responsibility for its defence. This is no new commitment since Ceylon is only likely to be threatened in the event of a major war, and under these circumstances we should wish, in any case, to preserve our essential defence interests in the country.

While we must retain the ultimate responsibility we suggest that the co-ordination of defence matters with the local authorities would be made easier by the establishment of some form of Joint Defence Committee.

*Internal security*

11.  There is always a danger of *India* (especially Congress India) interfering in Ceylonese internal politics and promoting discontent among the powerful Indian minority. The extent of this danger depends upon the future constitutional set-up in *India*. This danger is superimposed upon the problems of racial differences, anti-European feeling, Communism and labour unrest which by themselves are liable at any time to cause internal disorders. Such disorders, however provoked, would have a serious effect upon the working of our service establishments.

Although the Ceylon Government should be responsible for internal security, in the event of the situation becoming beyond her capacity to control and our defence interests being threatened, we should reserve the right to introduce forces, and to take action as necessary to protect our interests.

*Locally raised forces*

12.  With a view to improving the standard of locally raised forces so that they can maintain internal order and assist in the defence of the island we should wish them to be developed and expanded with our assistance and under our direction.

### Method of obtaining our defence requirements

13.  The decision as to the method of approach to the Ceylon Government must be a political one. Our military requirements would however be satisfied if an agreement for as long a period of years as possible were concluded with Ceylon, whereby, in return for the use of facilities and installations as outlined above, we guaranteed the integrity of the Island.

We would suggest that any such agreement might be modelled on the bilateral agreement concluded between the United States and the Philippine Government. There is no satisfactory analogy with the Simonstown agreement which deals with one isolated area, whereas our requirements in Ceylon are dispersed throughout the Island.

**397** CO 537/1940, no 6 4 June 1947

[Strikes]: inward unnumbered telegram for Sir H Moore to Sir C Jeffries on the attitude of the Board of Ministers to the possible introduction of emergency powers

For to-day's strike situation see my secret telegram No. 746[1] which I have transferred to secret series in view of procedure proposed if situation further deteriorates.

2. Attitude of Board of Ministers as reflected therein is highly encouraging and I hope Secretary of State will support it. Their inactivity during the last few days was deliberate as they were anxious to make the Chief Secretary and myself carry the baby. Press comment has left them in no doubt that the public are fully aware of its true paternity, and they have been much criticized for not taking more active steps to combat the present challenge to established authority.

3. At the last two Galleface meetings, the Sama Samajist and Communist leaders have made violent attacks on the Board of Ministers, the Chief Secretary and myself, and Dr. Colvin de Silva is reported as saying openly that every blow aimed against the Board of Ministers was a blow against the introduction of the Soulbury Constitution.

4. The Board of Ministers, if belated, have now appreciated the force of my arguments that by timidity in coming out into the open they are seriously influencing electoral prospects of all those who are anxious to make the Soulbury Constitution a success, and that by trying to shelter behind the Governor's emergency powers they will forfeit such respect in the country as they can still command.

5. I am of course fully alive to the danger of using emergency powers such as detention or restriction orders against leaders of political parties that are in opposition to the Board of Ministers. But fortunately I believe Senanayake is equally sensitive on the point and would be most reluctant to advise such a course except in the very last resort.

6. There are already signs of manoeuvrings behind the scenes and, if we can stave off a crisis within the next day or two, it would be in accordance with local political traditions to produce some face-saving formula which might or might not be acceptable so far as the clerical service is concerned. There are unsubstantiated rumours that Ponnambalam and 50–50 party are not as innocent as they would appear to be. Certainly—Tamil clericals have been conspicuous in the revolt.[2]

---

[1] Tel 746 read: 'Board of Ministers now propose to invite State Council to pass a bill giving general powers on the lines of Emergency Powers Order-in-Council. Bill has been already drafted by Acting Legal Secretary and copy is being sent by bag so that there may be no unavoidable delay in securing assent. I would telegraph any amendments made in State Council.

Procedure proposed is that, on state of emergency arising, I should immediately bring Emergency Powers Order-in-Council into force by proclamation and take any necessary action thereunder so as to retain element of surprise. Immediately thereafter State Council would be invited to pass legislation referred to in paragraph one, on enactment of which I would withdraw Order-in-Council by proclamation.

All are agreed situation to-day does not warrant immediate proclamation and I hope we may get through without recourse to extraordinary powers at all' (CO 537/1940, no 5).

[2] In tel 624 of 7 June, Creech Jones informed Moore: 'I am much appreciative of attitude which Ministers have adopted in regard to strikes, and trust that this, together with force of public opinion, may bring the present unhappy situation to an end. I have no objection to adoption of procedure in your telegram if you consider the circumstances require it' (ibid, no 7).

**398**   CO 882/30, no 158                                    6 June 1947

[Dominion status]: outward unnumbered telegram from Mr Creech Jones to Sir H Moore on the Cabinet's amendment of the terms of the announcement

Reference your top secret and personal telegram of 2nd June.

1.  Cabinet have carefully considered the terms of the announcement to be made by His Majesty's Government in reply to Senanayake's representations, and have shortened the drafts previously communicated to you, without, however, materially altering their substance.

2.  Please now convey to Senanayake message in the terms of my immediately following telegram No. 620[1] saying that I am writing in the same sense in reply to his personal letter.[2]

3.  It may be that Senanayake may not regard this message as fulfilling all his hopes but I must emphasize that His Majesty's Government have given the most careful consideration to the representations made and are genuinely anxious to help him in meeting, as far as they feel possible, the political difficulties with which he is faced.

4.  I propose that announcement should be made in reply to a question in the House of Commons about 15.00 hours D.B.S.T. on Wednesday, the 11th June, and shall be grateful if simultaneous publication can be arranged in Ceylon in such manner as is most convenient. I need not emphasize that publication in Ceylon should in no circumstances precede my statement in the House here. Until then Senanayake will I am sure understand that text of announcement is given to him for strictly personal information.

5.  I propose to inform Goonetilleke on Monday of contents of message on similar understanding.

6.  You will see that final draft of message omits mention of Goonetilleke's suggestion that His Majesty's Government might not be prepared to face clash with India if necessary in order to protect Ceylon's interests. Cabinet considered that it would be inexpedient to refer to this in a document of this kind. You are however authorised if question is raised by Senanayake in discussion to make it clear to him that His Majesty's Government could not (repeat not) accept any such assumption.

[1] See 399.                                                      [2] See 381.

**399**   CO 882/30, no 159                                    6 June 1947

[Dominion status]: outward telegram no 620 from Mr Creech Jones to Sir H Moore transmitting a message to Mr Senanayake and the text of an announcement approved by Cabinet

Please convey to Senanayake following reply to his personal letter to me of 28th February.[1]

[1] See 381.

I am writing personally in the same sense by early mail.

*Message begins.* His Majesty's Government have considered your request that Ceylon should now take a further step towards fully responsible status within the British Commonwealth. They value highly the co-operative spirit displayed by Ceylon in war and peace and recall the hope which they expressed in the White Paper of October, 1945. They understand the desire of the people of Ceylon to take this further step as soon as possible. The new Constitution, however, is only now coming into operation and the new Parliament has yet to be elected. His Majesty's Government undertake, when the new Ceylon Government is fully functioning, to consult with them on the important matters now reserved under the 1946 Constitution. Such questions as defence, external affairs and the safeguarding of minorities must be effectively provided for by an agreement satisfactory to both parties before His Majesty's Government can go on to an amendment of the Constitution giving Ceylon fully responsible status in the Commonwealth.

His Majesty's Government cannot assume an advance commitment which would tie their hands in negotiating with whatever government may be in power in Ceylon when the time comes. They are, however, ready to do all they can to clear the way and are, therefore, putting in hand at once the study of these matters. As for defence, it is essential that provision should be made for the security of Ceylon itself and its position in relation to the strategic needs of the Commonwealth while in external affairs the relationship of Ceylon to other members of the Commonwealth must be worked out. His Majesty's Government have obligations towards minorities and they will therefore desire a satisfactory assurance on the position of these communities under responsible government. Constitutional changes may also involve legislation in the United Kingdom and Parliament will have to be satisfied that agreements on all these matters have been concluded and will remain in force after the constitutional advance has been made.

Meantime, in order to make the position clear to all concerned, His Majesty's Government propose, on a date to be fixed in consultation with the Governor to make the following announcement.

*Begins.* Announcement.

In 1945 His Majesty's Government affirmed their willingness to co-operate with the people of Ceylon in their advance to Dominion status, and expressed the hope that within a comparatively short space of time such a status would be achieved. Elections are about to be held under the constitution granted to Ceylon in 1946 and a new Parliament will assemble in October.

His Majesty's Government recognise that the people of Ceylon wish to see their country attain a fully responsible status within the British Commonwealth of Nations. Therefore His Majesty's Government will be ready, when the new Ceylon Government is fully functioning, to consult with them about an agreement satisfactory to both Governments dealing with defence, external affairs and the safeguarding of minorities. This will prepare the way for the further stage of constitutional advance.

In the meantime, to avoid delay, His Majesty's Government have begun a study of these matters. *End of Announcement. End of Message.*

Until Announcement is released for publication Senanayake will I am sure, understand that text is given to him for strictly personal information.

**400**   CO 882/30, no 160                              8 June 1947
[Dominion status]: inward telegram (reply) no 760 from Sir H Moore
to Mr Creech Jones reporting Mr Senanayake's surprise at the
'retrograde nature' of the announcement

Your telegram No. 620.[1]

I have conveyed to Senanayake text of the telegram. He expresses great disappointment with your reply and is surprised at the retrograde nature of the announcement.
He considers that the country would regard such an announcement as indicating
that His Majesty's Government now intends to impede the attainment of Dominion
status by reopening matters already settled. For example publication by His Majesty's
Government of your proposals safe-guarding of minorities would be taken as a
definite attempt to re-agitate this question. Senanayake considers that this
announcement would cause grave discontent in the country, particularly in view of
the recent decision to grant Dominion status to India almost immediately. He is
opposed to your making announcement, and insisting on an unequivocal declaration
of Dominion status as the next step.

---

[1] See 399.

---

**401**   CO 882/30, nos 161 & 162                         8 June 1947
[Dominion status]: inward unnumbered telegram (reply) in two parts
from Sir H Moore to Mr Creech Jones supporting Mr Senanayake's
concern and transmitting an amendment to the announcement

[*Part 1*]
Your top secret and personal telegram of 6th June.[1]

I discussed with Senanayake the text of proposed announcement. For his reply, see
my secret telegram No. 760.[2] While he accepts your assurance that the Cabinet's
intention is to grant the substance of his desiderata, he feels, and I entirely agree
with him, that an announcement in the terms proposed would not only be of no
assistance to him in the particularly difficult times with which we are faced to-day,
but also be positively damaging to the cause of Dominion status which he has at
heart, but which independence groups are openly out to sabotage. There can,
therefore, be no question of the announcement being made in its present form with
his consent, and I am strongly of the opinion that it would be a grave mistake for His
Majesty's Government to press him to reconsider his attitude.

I feel sure, however, that you and your colleagues would be very sorry to see the
whole matter go by default and I therefore, in my immediate following telegram,
have attempted an alternative draft which Senanayake would accept. You will observe
that it omits reference to minorities for the reasons already stated in my top secret
telegrams of 8th May[3] and 17th May. In conversation, Senanayake made it clear that
he would have no objection to the retention of Section 29 (2) of the Order-in-Council

---

[1] See 398 & 399.                    [2] See 400.                    [3] See 391.

which constitutes the only statutory safeguard to minorities at present, but, as stated in his telegram, he takes strong exception to the suggestion in proposed draft that grant of Dominion status should be made contingent on a formal agreement as to minority safeguards, since, except for the section referred to above, no statutory safeguards are provided by the Soulbury Constitution, nor are they compatible with Dominion status which connotes full powers of internal self-government. I am, of course, unaware whether such safeguards are being insisted upon for the two new Indian Dominions, but if they are not, Senanayake's case would appear unanswerable.

As I have previously stated, His Majesty's Government will, in my opinion, be making serious blunder if it fails to exploit to the full Senanayake's present attitude of goodwill. Quite apart from his inaccessible prospects, he makes no secret of his fears lest in the absence of an acceptable announcement, his own supporters will take early advantage, as happened immediately on the promulgation of the Donoughmore Constitution, of the provisions of Section 29 (4) (a) of the Order-in-Council to press for further amendment of the Constitution, particularly as His Majesty's Government are already committed by the White Paper to co-operate in such constitutional advance. He referred in the conversation to personal assurances given him in London that Dominion status would be granted within three years, i.e., two years from now—and, therefore, is clearly apprehensive lest the announcement in its present form is intended to impede such an evolutionary development.

In present circumstances, both Senanayake and I consider that the Cabinet text should not (repeat not) be given to Goonetilleke on Monday if, as I hope, the text is to be reconsidered.

*[Part 2]*

For all words in the proposed announcement after sentence "elections are about to be held . . . in October" substitute the following "His Majesty's Government appreciate the desire of the people of Ceylon to attain Dominion status and to qualify for membership of the United Nations. In order to accelerate this process, His Majesty's Government, are prepared to discuss with the new Cabinet, as soon as it has been constituted under the 1946 Constitution, the heads of an agreement covering Defence and External Affairs. In order that there may be no unnecessary delay, His Majesty's Government will give the necessary instructions at once to the competent authorities to undertake the work necessary for determination of the issues involved. On conclusion of an agreement acceptable to both His Majesty's Government, and Ceylon, His Majesty's Government will take the necessary steps to secure Dominion status for Ceylon".

**402**   CO 882/30, nos 163 & 164                                    9 June 1947

[Dominion status]: outward telegrams (reply) nos 636 and 637 from
Sir C Jeffries to Sir H Moore explaining that the governor's amendments would be unacceptable to Cabinet and transmitting the text of
points suggested by Sir O Goonetilleke

*No. 636*

*Begins.* Your telegrams[1] received over week-end made it clear that no announcement on Wednesday will now be possible, and arrangements for question have been
cancelled.

2.  I fear that your draft would not be acceptable to Cabinet in certain important
respects. As I had appointment to see Goonetilleke this morning I gave him, with
Secretary of State's approval, a confidential outline of present position without
actually communicating texts of any drafts, and we discussed a tentative redraft
which Secretary of State is now considering.

3.  Goonetilleke requested that Senanayake should be given text of suggestions
originally made by Goonetilleke as to points to be included in proposed announcement. This text is contained in immediately following Secret telegram. *Ends.*

*No. 637*

Following is text of points which were originally suggested by Goonetilleke for
inclusion in proposed announcement.

*Begins.*

### Notes by Sir Oliver Goonetilleke

(A)  In the light of these declarations, i.e., Burma and India, and in response to
representations from Mr. Senanayake, the Vice-Chairman of the Ceylon Board of
Ministers, His Majesty's Government have given further consideration to the
statement of policy referred to above, and have reached the conclusion that it is no
longer reasonable that Ceylon should be required to achieve Dominion status by a
process of evolution. His Majesty's Government have, therefore, decided to satisfy at
the earliest possible date the desire for full independence on the part of all sections of
opinion in Ceylon.

(B)  His Majesty's Government are also aware of the desire of the people of Ceylon
to exercise this independence as a member of the British Commonwealth of Nations.
His Majesty's Government, on their part, fully reciprocate the wish that, despite the
proposed constitutional change, the close association of the British with the people
of Ceylon will continue.

(C)  In order that both the matters referred to in (A) and (B) above may be finally
determined, His Majesty's Government have given instructions that preparatory
action should be taken by the authorities concerned with a view to the necessary
arrangements to establish the new relationship being concluded as soon as possible
after the new Parliament of Ceylon has come into being. Various technical questions,
including matters relating to defence, will arise out of this transfer of power to the

---

[1] See 401.

representatives of the people of Ceylon, and His Majesty's Government will negotiate agreements with regard to these with the new Government of Ceylon when it has taken office.

(D) His Majesty's Government have also decided that, as from the date of the opening of the new Ceylon Parliament, the designation of Governor will be changed to that of Governor-General and the responsibility for Ceylon affairs will be transferred from the Colonial to the Dominions Office.

(E) His Majesty's Government will lend their full support to the application by Ceylon for membership of the United Nations Organization as soon as the proposed constitutional changes have been made. In the meantime His Majesty's Government will explore with the Secretary General how far it is possible for Ceylon to be represented at any meeting of, or under the auspices of the United Nations Organization. They will also approach such other international bodies as the Government of Ceylon may desire, with a view to ascertaining whether Ceylon can be associated with the work of those bodies as a member nation or otherwise. *Ends.*

**403**   CO 882/30, no 166                                     10 June 1947

**[Dominion status]: inward unnumbered telegram (reply) from Sir H Moore to Sir C Jeffries explaining that Mr Senanayake is anxious for an early announcement and emphasising the two points of overriding importance**

Following for Jeffries.

*Begins.* Your telegram No. 636.[1]

I have explained the position to Senanayake and passed him copy of your secret telegram No. 637.[2] His reply is contained in my immediately following secret telegram No. 770.

2. Owing to the situation here, he is most anxious that a very early announcement should be made, as it would strengthen his hand enormously in dealing with the present strike situation the political nature of which is universally recognized and openly admitted by the strike leaders.

3. Council is likely to adjourn to-morrow till 24th June, but, if an agreed announcement can be made before then, as he hopes, I would call a special meeting of the Council, if necessary, to deliver it. I would earnestly stress the necessity for very early action. I am sure that the only two points of over-riding importance are:—

(a) That the announcement should give unequivocal assurance of His Majesty's Government's intention to accelerate the pace of advance to Dominion status, subject to the necessary safeguards for His Majesty's Government's own interests.

(b) That there should be no suggestion that His Majesty's Government is re-raising the minority controversy which is locally regarded as having received its quietus by State Council vote on the Soulbury Constitution. It would be particularly dangerous to do so at the present time. *Ends.*

---

[1] See 402.                                                    [2] See *ibid.*

# 404  PREM 8/726                                    10 June 1947

## [Dominion status]: minute by Mr Creech Jones to Mr Attlee explaining the case for a revised announcement. *Minute* by T L Rowan[1]

*Prime Minister*

I have now heard from the Governor of Ceylon and I regret to have to report that the draft announcement recently approved on the Ceylon constitution is unacceptable to Mr. Senanayake. He feels that it would be regarded in Ceylon as retrograde, and even as suggesting an intention to impede the attainment of Dominion status by re-opening matters already settled, e.g., the safeguarding of minorities. He asks for an unequivocal declaration of our intention to confer Dominion status, and says that the announcement as approved would cause grave discontent in Ceylon, particularly in view of the recent decision to grant Dominion status to India almost immediately. It would increase rather than relieve his political difficulties.

The Governor advises that it would be a serious blunder for His Majesty's Government to fail to exploit to the full Mr. Senanayake's present attitude of goodwill. He feels also that it would be unwise to let the matter go by default and make no announcement at all.

Discussions between my officials and Sir Oliver Goonetilleke suggest that from the Ceylon point of view the essential point is to assure Ceylon that she will not have to wait for Dominion status until an indefinite process of evolution has been gone through, but that once satisfactory agreements have been reached the grant of Dominion status will follow at once.

I think that a revised statement in the terms attached[2] might resolve the difficulty. You will see that it avoids mentioning specifically the subjects on which agreements will be necessary. This leaves us free to state our requirements in discussions without arousing public controversy at this stage.

I should like, if you agree, to get the Governor's opinion on this.

## Minute on 404

*Prime Minister*

It is difficult to follow the Secretary of State's arguments. For example, he says the safeguarding of the minorities is already settled. If so, I cannot understand how the Colonial Office put into the draft letter to Mr. Senanayake that we would desire "a satisfactory assurance on the position of these communities *under responsible Government*".[3] But the point is that it must be clearly understood by all involved that the subjects which will have to be covered by the Agreement are those mentioned earlier. Provided this is understood, I cannot see any objection to the revised draft announcement. In fact it is the first decently drafted announcement on this subject which has been produced.

I know Bridges[4] has in mind the suggestion that these constitutional developments in the Colonies should be dealt with by a Committee as strong as the India and

---

[1] See 395, note 3.                          [2] See 405 for the revised announcement.
[3] See 399, emphasis in Rowan's minute.      [4] Sir E Bridges, Cabinet secretary.

Burma Committee, indeed perhaps by that Committee itself with a changed name and certain additional Ministers. The Colonial Affairs Committee have certainly not handled this matter well and it seems wasteful to have two Committees working on very similar problems. I think this aspect of the matter might be pursued.[5]

T.L.R.

10.6.47

---

[5] Attlee minuted: 'I have no objection to announcement now proposed. C.R.A. 10.6.47.' The prime minister also signified his agreement with the last sentence of Rowan's minute. As a result, officials in the Cabinet Office reviewed the Cabinet committee arrangements for dealing with constitutional and other problems arising in various parts of the Commonwealth, including the colonial territories. It was decided at the end of June to amalgamate the Colonial Affairs Committe with the India and Burma Committee (under the title of the latter), an arrangement which continued until Oct 1947 when a new Commonwealth Affairs Committee was appointed. CAB 21/1739 contains the background papers.

# 405   CO 882/30, no 169        12 June 1947
## [Dominion status]: outward telegram (reply) no 651 from Mr Creech Jones to Sir H Moore transmitting the text of a revised announcement

Reference your secret telegram No.760.[1]

Please inform Senanayake that, in the light of his representations, His Majesty's Government have given further consideration to matter and are ready to make announcement in the following terms.

*Begins.*  1.  In 1945 His Majesty's Government affirmed their willingness to co-operate with the people of Ceylon in their advance to Dominion status and expressed the hope that within a comparatively short space of time such a status would be evolved.

2.  His Majesty's Government recognize that the people of Ceylon are anxious to see this aim realized as quickly as possible and are eager to know how soon they may expect this to come about.

3.  Elections are now being arranged under the Constitution granted to Ceylon in 1946, and a new Parliament will assemble in October. Clearly no further constitutional change can take place before a new Ceylon Government is in office and fully functioning. Agreements will then have to be negotiated on a number of subjects. When such agreements have been concluded on terms satisfactory to His Majesty's Government and the Ceylon Government, immediate steps will be taken to amend the Constitution so as to confer upon Ceylon fully responsible status within the British Commonwealth of Nations.

4.  To avoid delay in opening negotiations with the future Ceylon Government, His Majesty's Government have directed that preparatory work should be put in hand for drawing up the heads of the necessary agreements. *Ends.*

This, it is considered, meets the points which he has made. Question generally has been discussed with Goonetilleke, and he is being given text of proposed announcement.[2] I need not emphasize further point made in my concluding

---

[1] See 400.

[2] In outward tel no 652 (12 June) to Moore, Creech Jones transmitted the following message from Goonetilleke to Senanayake:

'*Begins.* I have seen the revised draft announcement which is being communicated to you by His

sentence of my telegram No. 620 secret.[3]

___

Excellency. I am satisfied that there are very good reasons for His Majesty's Government not being able to make a detailed announcement on the lines of my original draft. I recommend very strongly that you should accept proposed announcement. It is very important that Wijewardene should assist with full press publicity as in case of 1945 White Paper. *Ends*' (CO 882/30, no 170).
[3] See 399.


# 406   CO 882/30, no 171                                           13 June 1947
## [Dominion status]: inward telegram (reply) no 783 from Sir H Moore to Mr Creech Jones transmitting a message from Mr Senanayake suggesting alternatives to the phrase 'fully responsible status within the British Commonwealth of Nations' in the announcement

Reference to your telegrams Nos. 651 and 652[1] which I have shown to Senanayake. Following from Senanayake. *Begins*. I am personally satisfied with the text of the proposed announcement, since I appreciate that it means that, once agreements have been made as indicated in paragraph 3, His Majesty's Government will confer full Dominion status upon Ceylon. I wish to point out, however, that the phrase "fully responsible status within the British Commonwealth of Nations" in paragraph 3 would probably be both misunderstood and misrepresented as something less than Dominion status. I would, therefore, be very grateful if you would substitute for the words "fully responsible status within the British Commonwealth of Nations" either "full dominion status" or the phrase "independence within the British Commonwealth of Nations". *Ends*.[2]

___

[1] See 405 & 405, note 2.
[2] Moore sent a further tel on 13 June which explained that Senanayake had spoken to Goonetilleke over the telephone and instructed him to make clear that if the secretary of state were unable to accept either of the two alternatives suggested, he would accept the draft proposed in Creech Jones's tel of 12 June. The governor added that Senanayake would really prefer 'Independence within the British Commonwealth of Nations'. Jennings had told Senanayake that in his opinion all three phrases meant the same thing. Moore ended: 'I think you should realize that his [Senanayake's] personal acceptance of the draft is based on the belief that Dominion status in the popularly accepted sense of the term will be offered on completion of the agreements' (CO 882/30, no 172).


# 407   CO 882/30, no 173                                           14 June 1947
## [Dominion status]: outward telegram (reply) no 660 from Mr Creech Jones to Sir H Moore on the wording of the announcement

Your telegram No. 783.[1] Following for Senanayake.
  *Begins*. I am glad to learn that you are personally satisfied with terms of proposed announcement. As regards your suggestion for amendment, I appreciate your difficulty but the expression "independence within the British Commonwealth of

___

[1] See 406.

Nations" would be open to the objection that it might be taken to signify some new and unprecedented form of relationship.

On the other hand we have avoided the expression "Dominion status" for the following reasons:—First, it was originally urged on us by Goonetilleke that the expression was not desired in Ceylon and might cause misconception there. Secondly, it is true that the expression has recently been revived in relation to India, but it is not self-explanatory and its meaning is not entirely clear in the absence of statutory definition.

For these reasons I am sure that the phrase we have used is preferable as stating as precisely as possible what was meant by the final stage of constitutional advance for Ceylon foreshadowed in the White Paper of 1945. I do not therefore feel able to amend the announcement but I should have no objection to your making it clear at your own discretion to all concerned in Ceylon that the announcement means that, when the agreements have been concluded and the necessary legislative action has been taken, Ceylon will enjoy that full degree of self-government within the British Commonwealth of Nations which the term "Dominion status" is generally understood to connote. *Ends.*[2]

---

[2] On 14 June Goonetilleke sent through Creech Jones a message to Senanayake which explained that it would not be possible to attempt any variation of the wording of the announcement without the risk of 'great delay' in reaching a fresh decision. The message continued: 'I am satisfied that, in view of Secretary of State's reply to you, no repeat no variation of announcement is necessary. The agreements and legislative enactments which have to be approved by the new Government of Ceylon will make it quite clear that Ceylon has secured her final goal of full national status within the British Commonwealth' (CO 882/30, no 174). The announcement was made on 18 June.

# 408   CO 882/30, no 179      19 June 1947
## [Heads of agreement]: inward telegram no 811 from Sir H Moore to Sir C Jeffries on the issues to be decided

Following for Jeffries.

*Begins.* Your telegram No. 676.

Senanayake considers that advantage should be taken of Goonetilleke's presence in London to represent Ceylon in the proposed negotiations, at any rate in the initial stages, but before he is officially instructed to do so, he would like more precise information as to the heads of agreement which His Majesty's Government has in mind.

2. So far as Defence is concerned, I have already had informal conversations with Admiral Palliser,[1] who has left to-day for the Singapore Defence Conference and intends to raise the matter informally not at the Conference but in private discussion with Army and Air Force Service Chiefs. My preliminary view, which he shared, was that if I were to receive a general directive on broad lines as to Service requirements for communication to local Service Commanders, details could probably be filled in locally. In view of the general instructions received by the Services for economy during the next two years, it is obvious that the Services would have difficulty in formulating detailed desiderata, and the most important point would seem to be to

---

[1] C-in-c, East Indies Station, 1946–1948.

secure general undertaking that land required for Defence purposes present or prospective, is not alienated or allotted for other purposes.

3. I foresee more difficulty in respect of external affairs and the minority question, if the latter issue is to be revived, and find difficulty in suggesting procedure until His Majesty's Government's general attitude on both of them is more clearly defined.

4. While I have not discussed this with Senanayake, I have no doubt he would favour my making a flying visit to London at a time you considered appropriate, if it is considered this would expedite matters. Some time in July would probably be the most favourable time locally. *Ends.*[2]

---

[2] Moore visited London in July 1947 to participate in the discussions.

## 409    CO 537/2220, no 1                                      9 July 1947
## [Draft agreement on minorities]: CO note of a discussion with Sir H Moore

It is not clear what form any agreement relating to the minorities would take. Sir Henry Moore explained that the minority problem as such was the problem of securing full franchise rights and full representation in Parliament for all communities, large or small. Franchise was a matter which was wholly within Ceylon's competence, and the question of representation had already been dealt with both in the Order in Council (creation of Senate, and continuance of nomination system) which had followed the Soulbury recommendations, and by the Delimitation Commission which had adopted several devices to secure adequate minority representation. Sir Henry Moore indicated that there was no suggestion that Section 29 of the 1946 Order in Council would be removed although, for his part, he was not clear that this section represented a minority safeguard. He felt that to re-raise the minority question by insisting on an agreement would be very dangerous indeed. It certainly seemed impracticable to make an agreement in which Ceylon undertook to keep Section 29 in being for a specified length of time. Sir Henry Moore added that he would, with Mr. Mulhall,[1] prepare a note setting out the minority problem and explaining what safeguards would continue to exist.

On receipt of this a paragraph would be drafted (to form part of the Cabinet Paper submitting all the agreements) explaining the situation vis a vis the minorities in Ceylon and that it seemed impracticable, unnecessary and even dangerous to ask Ceylon to sign a special agreement. Mr. Paskin[2] suggested however that, in view of the time factor, a draft agreement calling for a general undertaking by Ceylon to protect minorities should be drawn up for consideration in case the Secretary of State felt that the Cabinet would require a special agreement.

---

[1] J A Mulhall, secretary to the governor.
[2] J J Paskin, assistant secretary, head of CO Eastern Dept.

# 410    CO 537/2226, no 1                              14 July 1947

## [Order-in-Council]: minute by K O Roberts-Wray[1] on the changes proposed by Sir O Goonetilleke. *Annex*

Sir Oliver Goonetilleke came to my room this afternoon thinking that the meeting was here. I explained that it was in Mr. Sidebotham's room, but he took the opportunity to leave with me the attached notes which I went through very rapidly with him with the following results:—

1.  I gather that this means merely that section 30 of the Order in Council will be revoked.

2.  I said I assumed that this was accepted, but that it would not, I thought, be appropriate to put anything in the Constitution to this effect.

3.  Here again I said I understood that this was correct, but I was not sure whether any formal action was necessary. I thought it probably was not.

4.  I suggested that "Ceylon" alone would suffice and that it was now usual to refer to "Canada" and "New Zealand" and that I thought that this practice was reflected in some Act of Parliament or other instrument recently enacted. Sir Oliver said that they would very much like "Kingdom of Ceylon". I did not say so but this seems to be quite inappropriate.[2]

5.  Sir Oliver's point was that he wished to stress his view that the power of disallowance should go. He murmured something to the effect that Ceylon might, if necessary, deposit a sum of money by way of security. I reiterated that the whole question must be discussed with the Treasury.

6.  Here Sir Oliver wished to raise a point which I was surprised was not mentioned in Mr. Senanayake's letter—namely that the Constitution should be amended so that where under the present Order in Council the Governor is to act in his discretion, the Governor-General will act on the advice of Ministers.

7.  I am not sure why this is included. Sir Oliver mentioned that the allegiance to the Crown is the only visible bond of unity between the members of the British Commonwealth—a fact of which we are all aware.

Annex to 410: notes by Sir O Goonetilleke

1.  Order in Council will expressly withdraw H.M.'s powers to make laws by Order in Council.

2.  Governor-General should be approved by H.M. on advice of P.M.

3.  Relations with Ceylon will become concern of Secretary of Commonwealth Relations.

4.  Dominion of Ceylon or Kingdom of Ceylon.

5.  Sec 39.[3]

---

[1] CO legal adviser.

[2] Mr Thomas, parliamentary under-secretary of state at the CO, commented in the margin: 'May I suggest "Realm of Ceylon".'

[3] The reference is to section 39 of the Ceylon (Constitution) Order-in-Council of 1946. This section dealing with laws relating to Ceylon Government stocks had been introduced because neither the

6. Crown acts only on advice of the Ministers of the Dominions.
7. Allegiance to Crown only. General bond of unity.

---

constitution of 1946 nor the original ministers' draft constitution had provisions to disallow legislation. There were four sub-sections in this of which the first applied to sterling loans. The existing sterling loans became trustee securities on the basis that any laws which interfered with the securities could be disallowed. Sub-section 2 applied to loans subsequently raised in the UK and included in the trustee list at the request of the Ceylon government.

# 411  CO 537/2226                                    14–16 July 1947
## [Commonwealth]: minutes by J B Sidebotham, K O Roberts-Wray, J J Paskin, Sir C Jeffries and Sir T Lloyd on Ceylon's right to secede

*Mr. Roberts-Wray*
*Mr. Paskin*
In the course of the preliminary examination this morning with Mr. Roberts-Wray, at which Sir Henry Moore and Sir Oliver Goonetilleke were present, the question arose whether certain words at present appearing in the 1946 Order-In-Council should be retained. Their retention would remove from Ceylon, when fully responsible status within the British Commonwealth of Nations was granted, the right to secede.

Sir Oliver Goonetilleke counselled very strongly against raising this issue at all in the amended Instrument. He said that to do so would just give the Opposition in Ceylon the very handle they were seeking. When H.M.G.'s announcement was made they had all taken the line, "Oh, wait and see, there is a catch in this". Sir Oliver referred to the Resolution of the 1926 Imperial Conference in which the words "a free association" occurred. That freedom could only imply the ability of a member of the British Commonwealth to secede from that association if it so desired. Sir Oliver went to far as to say that, if there was any doubt on this subject, we might as well terminate our discussions at once and leave it to Ceylon to 'come again' with a request for full self-government at a later date. He further pressed the point that no such tie had been insisted on in the case of the new Indian "Dominions", who would almost certainly claim the ability to secede at a later date.

Sir Henry Moore referred to the statement made on this matter by the Prime Minister, the concluding words of which (Columns 2458–2474 of the Hansard attached as flagged)[1] refer to "welcoming two new Dominions into that full partnership, hoping that they will long remain with us . . .", which certainly suggests, at any rate, that they might decide not to do so, in which case they would be free to go out.

My own view has always been that, in conferring fully self-governing status within the British Commonwealth of Nations on Ceylon, we cannot in fairness attach to that new status any bond which does not obtain in the case of the other members of the British Commonwealth, and if we have not, in fact, put any such tie on India, it would be most unreasonable to do so in the case of Ceylon, whose request for Dominion status has been pressed on the ground that she wishes to remain within

---

[1] During the debate in the House of Commons on the Indian Independence Bill, *H of C Debs*, vol 439, 10 July 1947.

the British Commonwealth partly, of course, out of fear of her very large neighbour, India. But it is important, I think, to relieve Sir Oliver Goonetilleke's anxieties on this matter at the very earliest opportunity. If we do not he will merely start upsetting Mr. Senanayake, and we should wish to have the Secretary of State's authority, I think, to tell him at once that no provision would be included in the new Constitution which would debar Ceylon from breaking away from the British Commonwealth if, eventually, it was her desire to do so.

J.B.S.
14.7.47

The question was not actually whether certain words should be retained (if we were merely to leave the clause alone it might attract little attention), but whether certain words should be inserted (which might be more difficult). I think it is necessary to explain more fully the point at issue.

At present there is no limitation under section 29 of the Order in Council upon the power of the Parliament of Ceylon to amend the Constitution, except that under Section 37 the Bill must be reserved for His Majesty's pleasure, from which it follows of course that if the amendment were one which H.M.G. could not approve assent would not be given.

When Ceylon attains the status of a dominion Section 37 would, of course, be repealed, and although in theory under Section 36 the Governor could refuse assent, presumably it would not be constitutional for him to do so, whatever the nature of the Bill. If that is not so Ceylon would enjoy a degree of independence less than that of the present dominions.

H.M.G.'s statement and the telegram sent to Ceylon saying that Mr. Senanayake was free to state that Ceylon was being given the same degree of independence as the other dominions,[2] were carefully framed for the express purpose of excluding from Ceylon's powers, the right to secede.[3] I may add, for what it is worth, that my impression was that this would be acceptable to Mr. Senanayake, on the ground that he would not wish his political opponents, if they came into power, to take any steps for the removal of Ceylon from the British Commonwealth.

What I had in mind as an amendment of the Order in Council to give effect to H.M.G.'s decision was that Section 29 should be amended so as to except from Ceylon's power to amend the Constitution the provision in Section 45 that the executive power of the Island should continue vested in His Majesty. The discussion at yesterday's meeting arose when I enquired whether this should be done.

This is, in fact, the "catch" which the opposition in Ceylon anticipate. The question whether my proposal should be adopted is, of course, one of first importance. The decision of the Cabinet I understand was quite definitely that Ceylon should be given independence within, and not without, the British Commonwealth. If the amendment I have proposed, or some modification on the same lines is not made, then there would be nothing to prevent Ceylon having the same right to secede as any other members of the British Commonwealth. (The question of how far they have that right is one upon which I sent the Department a note a few weeks

---

[2] See 407.
[3] Paskin noted in the margin: 'It has been understood by Mr. Senanayake in precisely the contrary sense'.

ago—but it is more a matter of metaphysical interest than of practical importance.)

K.O.R-W.<br>15.7.47

The line taken by Sir O. Goonetilleke in the course of our discussion may be summarized as follows:

In the White Paper of 1945 the goal promised to Ceylon was that of "Dominion status".

In the recent statement the words "Dominion status" have not been used but there has been another description of the status which Ceylon is acquiring.

The opponents of the present regime in Ceylon, and indeed various Indian politicians in public speeches, have seized upon this as meaning that the status which Ceylon is now about to achieve is something less than that of "Dominion status".

It has always been understood in Ceylon that the right of secession is inherent in Dominion status.

Whatever the strictly legal (or metaphysical) position may be as regards the old Dominions, there is certainly no explicit obstacle to their seceding from the Commonwealth.

If, therefore, in the Amending Order in Council, words are introduced which explicitly debar Ceylon from seceding, the opponents of the present regime in Ceylon will be presented with an opportunity, almost beyond your dreams, of being able to say, "There you are. We told you so. There *was* a catch in it".

Sir Oliver Goonetilleke felt confident that, rather than have to face this situation, Mr. Senanayake would wish to drop the whole idea of acquiring this new status at the present time in the circumstances now contemplated.

I must say that I fully share Sir O. Goonetilleke's reactions on this point. Throughout our discussions with him we have taken our cue from the Secretary of State's statement in Parliament that 'For all intents and purposes, under the status thus achieved, Ceylon will enjoy that full degree of self-government within the British Commonwealth of Nations which the term "Dominion Status" is generally understood to imply'. It is important that we should avoid any words or action which would imply any overt differentiation between the status of Ceylon and that of the old Dominions. As I have pointed out above there is no *explicit* bar to the old Dominions seceding from the Commonwealth. It is I think therefore very important indeed that there should not be introduced into the Amending Order in Council any words which will explicitly debar Ceylon from the power of seceding.

J.J.P.<br>15.7.47

The last thing we want is to arouse an unrealistic controversy over this matter of "secession".

I had hoped that a provision, leaving the King as King of Ceylon, without the power of amendment, might have gone through without comment. But as the question has been raised, I am clear that we cannot place Ceylon in this matter under a formal disability which would give disaffected people a claim to say that this is not real Dominion status but that there is a catch in it. I therefore agree with Mr. Paskin.

C.J.J.<br>15.7.47

*Secretary of State*

You may wish to discuss this either before or immediately after the meeting at 3 p.m. tomorrow, when the Department are to have a talk with you about the draft paper for the India Burma Committee. Sir O. Goonetilleke will be present for the discussion on that paper, and the particular point at issue is clearly unsuitable for debate in his presence. If, however, it were discussed in advance and some decision reached favourable to his view, you might wish to tell him of that in the course of the subsequent talk.

On the merits I entirely agree that nothing should be introduced into the Order in Council which would limit or even give the impression of limiting, Ceylon's right of secession. To do that would not only be open to the objection that it would be invaluable as a source of ammunition to Mr. Senanayake's political opponents, but it would also in my view be unrealistic, seeing that the use of force to prevent a determined Ceylon from seceding is unthinkable.

The decision on this point is of the first importance since clearly the issue whether the new arrangements will or will not permit secession by Ceylon is likely to be raised whenever the new Constitution comes up for discussion in the House, which will expect a plain answer to that question. The answer in my judgment would in substance have to be that Ceylon will in this respect be placed in exactly the same position as any other member of the British Commonwealth.

T.I.K.L.
16.7.47

# **412** CO 537/2216, no 13                                    15 July 1947

## [Defence agreement]: CO note of a discussion with Sir H Moore and Sir O Goonetilleke on the third draft

Mr. Paskin explained that in view of the time factor this draft was already on its way over to the Chiefs of Staff Secretariat with a view to its being considered by the Directors of Plans on the afternoon of Tuesday the 15th July. He wished it to be quite understood, however, that the persons present at the meeting were not precluded from freely discussing the draft and raising any points.

Sir Oliver Goonetilleke wished to know whether the agreement as it stood would preclude Ceylon from raising her own Army. It was pointed out, in reply, that Ceylon would be quite free to raise her own forces and indeed the terms of the draft contemplated the existence of such forces.

Sir Oliver's only other point was in regard to the bracketed portion Clause 2.[1] At first he felt that it would be desirable not to particularise in this manner. Mr. Paskin explained that the Colonial Office were generally in favour of leaving out this sentence and that appropriate representations had been made to Mr. Mallaby of the

---

[1] Clause 2 of the draft, with its bracketed portion, read: 'The Government of Ceylon will grant to the Government of the United Kingdom all the necessary facilities for the objects mentioned in Article 1 as may from time to time be mutually agreed between them. These facilities will include the use of naval and air bases and ports and the use of telecommunication facilities. [The Government of the United Kingdom will in particular retain the use of the fleet base and air field and other establishments at Trincomalee, the flying boat base at Koggala and the air field at Negombo.]'

Chiefs of Staff Secretariat. After further discussion Sir Oliver Goonetilleke felt that there might be some point in keeping this particular sentence in the draft. It might give to critics the useful impression that H.M.G.'s defence requirements were of a restricted character. Sir Henry Moore was in favour of leaving this sentence out of the draft although he did not wish to press the point strongly. It was agreed that the Colonial Office would have to be bound by what the Directors of Plans decided.

Sir Oliver Goonetilleke was not, however, in favour of using the words "retain the use of". It was generally agreed that it would be much better if the sentence could be turned round to give the impression that Ceylon was granting the use of these places as opposed to H.M.G. retaining it. A form of words was agreed on and Mr. Paskin immediately communicated this to the Chiefs of Staffs Secretariat.

Sir Henry Moore wondered whether the use of the word "and" in the third line of Clause 2 was necessary. It was agreed to refer this to Mr. Dale[2] for advice.

---

[2] See 380, note 2.

# 413    CO 537/2221, no 3                                15 July 1947
## [Reciprocal treatment of nationals]: CO note of an inter-departmental[1] discussion with Sir H Moore and Sir O Goonetilleke

During the course of his introductory remarks Sir G. Clauson agreed that Sir Oliver Goonetilleke had a reasonable point in that the agreement now contemplated would form a precedent for a similar agreement with India. On the other hand, although there were more Indian than U.K. nationals in Ceylon, there was certainly more U.K. than Indian property, and it might be felt desirable to secure some protection for U.K. nationals and property at this stage.

Sir Henry Moore wanted it to be explained how the question arose. He indicated that in the course of the negotiations leading up to H.M.G.'s statement on the 18th June, this topic had never been broached. He wished to know whether Ministers had raised this issue now or whether the question had arisen at the departmental level. He indicated that Ceylon could not accept the proposition that a trade agreement of this nature must form one of the heads of agreement as a condition precedent to the grant of full responsible Government. Sir Oliver Goonetilleke said that this was quite the wrong time to raise the issue as there was only a caretaker Government in power in Ceylon. In any case the matters concerned, rights of entry, residence etc., were essentially internal matters which, if they were in doubt, should have been settled by H.M.G. two years ago before the Order in Council was made. Ceylon had the unrestricted right to decide the composition of her population and if H.M.G. now wanted to lay down conditions they would be fighting a battle they had already lost.

Sir G. Clauson said that the question had been raised because the Colonial Office had to anticipate Ministerial enquiries. Furthermore there was a case for considering the question as an essential part of external relations.

Mr. Beckett[2] explained that the draft clause in question was based on only one of several alternative drafts which were being considered in relation to India. The basic

---

[1] The other departments represented were the FO, CRO and Board of Trade.
[2] Representing the Foreign Office.

idea was to have some temporary understanding, to tide over the confused period in India coinciding approximately with the transfer of power.

Sir Henry Moore pointed out that the fact that only a temporary undertaking was envisaged rather distinguished this agreement from the external affairs and defence agreements. He pressed strongly that it should not be made one of the agreements precedent to the grant of the new status.

Sir Oliver Goonetilleke could not accept the proposition that the matters involved were an integral part of external affairs. He felt that there would be no advantage to H.M.G. in urging Ceylon to sign such an agreement. At the moment U.K. nationals had to be subjected to certain restrictions in order to prevent Ceylon from being swamped by Indians. If it came to the point, Ceylon would prefer not to have any rights in respect of trade etc. in the U.K. rather than be forced into the position of opening her doors to India. In the last resort Mr. Senanayake would be likely to say that, at the price of such an agreement, Dominion Status would be too expensive and that he would rather stay on the present basis. Sir Oliver saw no objection to the second part of the provision although he felt that it might be regarded as casting a slur on Ceylon's loyalty. He urged that any discussions should not be started now but that they should be deferred until Ceylon had settled with India. Meanwhile there would certainly be no danger to H.M.G.'s interests in Ceylon. Mr. Senanayake was emphatic that Ceylon wished to stay within the Commonwealth and one of his reasons was that H.M.G. was Ceylon's best customer. There was no question of British Capital being invited to quit Ceylon. Ceylon's record in the past justified her being trusted in this respect.

Sir Henry Moore took the opportunity to explain that outstanding questions relating to franchise and citizenship rights of Indians were, with H.M.G.'s concurrence, left to be settled by direct negotiation between the Governments of India and Ceylon.

Mr. Beckett referred to an alternative approach which had been considered for India and read out a draft provision which made U.K. treatment of nationals etc. as the yardstick by which Indian practice in relation to U.K. nationals etc. should be regulated as an interim measure. Sir Oliver Goonetilleke indicated that much of Ceylon's practice was necessarily dissimilar to British practice. He wondered why, if there was no such agreement with Australia, H.M.G. should require to have one with Ceylon. Mr. Beckett on this point, agreed that there was no similar agreement with Australia but, talking broadly, the matters in question were already secured by Australian law. Mr. Beckett wondered whether Ceylon would agree to a draft on the lines that for a fixed period Ceylon undertook to make no change in the present legal position relating to the matters under discussion. Sir Oliver Goonetilleke indicated that even this would be embarrassing to Ceylon. Moreover he could not see the necessity for it, particularly as we had never asked Australia, for instance, to do the same.

Sir Henry Moore said that he had heard no suggestion that British commercial interests either in Ceylon or in London were at all worried about the transfer of power. In this connection he referred to the Constitutional safeguards in Section 29 of the 1946 Order in Council.

Mr. Hooper[3] felt that the discussion had been very useful as a preliminary

---

[3] Representing the Board of Trade.

exchange of views but considered that the Board of Trade would want to give much more thought to the question whether any agreement on the lines envisaged between Ceylon and H.M.G. was really necessary.

Mr. Paskin, after saying that from the political standpoint he fully sympathised with Ceylon's case as presented by Sir H. Moore and Sir O. Goonetilleke, explained the very restricted time table to which the Colonial Office were working. Mr. Paskin intimated that a decision would have to be made one way or the other before Wednesday the 16th of July.

Summing the meeting up, Sir G. Clauson affirmed that there could be no question of making this particular agreement one of the conditions precedent to the grant of full responsible status to Ceylon. It was, however, desirable for some such understanding to be arrived at between the two Governments so that people concerned should know where they were. Sir G. Clauson suggested a form of words which might be inserted in the Cabinet paper submitting the draft Agreements to higher authority. This would embody the Office view that this Trade Agreement should not be one of the Agreements to be negotiated in advance, and explain that the competent Departments were now looking into the question of whether an understanding would be required at a later stage between the two Governments on matters relating to Trade etc., and if so what form it might take.

# 414   CO 537/2226, no 2                                    17 July 1947
## [Draft agreements]: CO note of a discussion between Mr Creech Jones and Sir H Moore and Sir O Goonetilleke

The Secretary of State opened the discussion by referring to various anxieties which he understood were felt by Ceylon in regard to the implementation of the promise of full responsible government within the Commonwealth.

(1) *The avoidance of the term dominion status*
The Secretary of State explained that this was an unpopular term, although there had been no alternative to its use in the case of India. He would, however, attempt to clear away any doubts on Supply Day as to what was meant by the term "fully responsible status within the British Commonwealth". Sir Henry Moore and Sir Oliver Goonetilleke hoped that the matter would be clarified. Sir Henry Moore mentioned the various imputations which were being made locally and in India that Ceylon was getting rather less than dominion status.

(2) *The question of secession*
The Secretary of State made it clear that this point had not been specifically considered in the Cabinet, the reason being that the discussions in regard to Ceylon had all been on the basis of the grant to Ceylon of full independence *within* Commonwealth. He gave it as his personal view that dominion status carried with it the right of self-determination in a matter such as secession. He felt that it was alien to the spirit of the Commonwealth to force a member to stay in against its own wish. He thought that the point should be left untouched. If the question were raised the answer must be, in the Secretary of State's opinion that if Ceylon is a member state

of the Commonwealth she is entitled to all the privileges that such membership carries with it. Sir Oliver Goonetilleke agreed that it would be preferable that there should not be any public reference to this issue. He explained that the matter had arisen as a drafting point when the Colonial Office had started their preliminary examination of the necessary amendments of the Constitution Order in Council. He hoped that Section 45 would not be singled out as being the one section which Ceylon could not amend without the consent of His Majesty's Government.

(3) *Minorities*
The Secretary of State affirmed that this point had been raised in Cabinet. He fully appreciated Ceylon's desire not to re-raise the issue and he was inclined to think that Ceylon's intention not to amend Section 29 would provide a basis of complete understanding as between His Majesty's Government and Ceylon in the matter. He agreed that, if possible, the matter should not be made a public issue. In this connection Sir Oliver Goonetilleke informed the Secretary of State that so far as he was aware there had been not one single representation from the minority communities in opposition to the recent statement. Sir Oliver also referred to what the Prime Minister had said about the inherent right of India and Pakistan to settle their own minority questions.

(4) The three draft Agreements were then considered.

(a) *Public officers*
Sir Charles Jeffries took the opportunity to mention that certain representations had been put forward in an informal way with the object of securing the continuing option to retire on special terms for "Soulbury" officers. This matter was discussed at some length but it was felt that the agreement provided very fair safeguards. Sir Henry Moore explained that the younger officers probably could not afford to retire within the next two years. In fact it was not the first five years which gave anxiety but the next five. Sir Oliver Goonetilleke considered that the present proposed change in the Constitution was not one which affected specifically European officers. The momentous change for them had come when the 1946 Order in Council was made. On this point Sir Charles Jeffries observed that we had to bear in mind that while the Order in Council is still in being His Majesty's Government have quite substantial residual powers and that to that extent the change now contemplated was substantial. Sir Henry Moore also mentioned that some pensioners were anxious to lead a delegation to him and possibly to the Secretary of State. They wanted His Majesty's Government to underwrite the Ceylon Government's pension liability. It was generally agreed that there was no case for this and Sir Henry Moore said he was not inclined to bother the Secretary of State with such a delegation. Mr. Roberts Wray pointed out that the draft did not make provision completely covering Section 64 (1) of the Order in Council. It was agreed to deal with this point before the draft was shown to Mr. Senanayake.

(b) and (c) *Defence and external affairs*
Mr. Paskin explained the general principles by which the Colonial Office had been guided in drawing up these agreements. With the exception of Clause 6 of the External Affairs Agreement, no points were raised. On this Clause Mr. Roberts

Wray pointed that in the draft clause transferring treaty obligations we were implicitly committing foreign governments to accepting Ceylon in place of His Majesty's Government. It was pointed out that Mr. Beckett of the Foreign Office had drafted the Clause and it was felt that the point need not be pursued at this stage.

During the course of the discussion several references were made to the Legislative action required and the following points emerged.

(1) Ceylon would agree to retain in the Order in Council that section which provided that the Constitution could be amended only by a two thirds majority, and to preserve this position the United Kingdom Act should contain a section on the lines of section 8 of the Statute of Westminster.
(2) The United Kingdom Act would be a short act containing about 6 to 8 clauses. The Secretary of State hoped that it would be as non-controversial as possible but said that he could not make any firm promise in the matter of expediting its course through Parliament. He added that notice of the Bill should be given forthwith.

Finally, Mr. Paskin outlined the action which had been taken in regard to the treatment of nationals etc clause in order to give the background to the advice embodied in the draft Cabinet Paper.

## 415  PREM 8/726, IB(47)44                                21 July 1947
## 'Ceylon constitution': memorandum by Mr Creech Jones for Cabinet India and Burma Committee on the draft agreements

Since my announcement on 18th June that Ceylon in due course would be given fully responsible Government within the British Commonwealth, but that certain Agreements on matters of mutual concern must first be entered into with the new Ceylon Government as soon as it was fully established under the 1946 Constitution, my Office has studied the subjects on which agreement should be obtained. We have also been able to consult the Governor and to prepare draft agreements which, to judge from conversations with Sir Oliver Goonetilleke and correspondence with Mr. Senanayake, are likely to prove acceptable to a new Ceylon Government. In preparing these drafts my Office has consulted the Foreign Office and the Department of Commonwealth Relations.

2. In drafting these Agreements we have tried to keep in mind—

(a) that they will be published, and indeed, probably registered with the United Nations Organisation,
(b) that no words should be used which would suggest that the new status of Ceylon will be inferior to that of any of the old Members of the Commonwealth, or
(c) which would endanger the success of Ceylon's application (which cannot, however, be considered until September, 1948) for admission to the United Nations, or
(d) which would imply any precise undertaking as to the conduct of the other Members of the British Commonwealth in their relations with Ceylon.

*Defence* (see draft Agreement at Annex I)[1]

3. As a result of a discussion with Sir Henry Moore it was agreed that it would be preferable, from the point of view of His Majesty's Government's own security requirements, to avoid giving publicity to the details of the various *desiderata* specified in the Chief of Staff's Report C.P. (47) 179[2] of 9th June (which is now also before my colleagues), especially as the information available here on some of the details is not fully complete or up to date. In any case, the precise method of giving effect to some of the *desiderata* (*e.g.*, the ownership of land or the basis of our "user" of land or other facilities required for defence purposes) will clearly have to be negotiated on the spot.

The conclusion was accordingly reached that, if the Chiefs of Staff were agreeable, the Agreement should be formulated in very general terms, and any necessary details should be left to be negotiated later with the new Ceylon Government. The draft Agreement has now been examined by the Joint Planning Staff, by whom it has been provisionally agreed on behalf of the Chiefs of Staff.

Since the draft was prepared, however, it has been suggested that the absence of a time limit for its operation may be regarded as such a derogation from the sovereign status of Ceylon as seriously to jeopardise her application for admission to the United Nations. On the other hand, if a time limit were inserted, it might be argued that her admission should be deferred until that time limit had expired.

A third possible course would be that there should not be any specific time limit for the duration of the Agreement, but that it should contain a provision by which it could be determined by either party on giving [five] years' notice. This course might obviate the disadvantages referred to in the preceding paragraph and would be more in line with the recommendation of the Chiefs of Staff that the Agreement should be on a permanent basis. I personally am disposed to favour this course but I should be glad to have the views of my colleagues on this important point.

*External affairs* (see draft Agreement at Annex II)

4. The Foreign Office and other interested Departments have been consulted as to the matters to be covered by this Agreement, in the drafting of which the considerations referred to in paragraph 2 above have been kept in mind. It will be noted that provision has been made for Ceylon to take over all existing Treaty obligations which have been entered into on her behalf.

*Public officers* (see draft Agreement at Annex III)

5. The provisions of this Agreement are designed to continue the provisions of the 1946 Constitution in regard to retirement terms for certain classes of officers. It also preserves the pension rights of all officers and the conditions of service of officers who continue in the service of the Ceylon Government and their eligibility for transfer to other Colonial service.

*Minorities*

6. I have discussed how best to safeguard the interests of minorities on the transfer of power to the Ceylon Government. The Governor strongly advises against any reopening of this matter in Ceylon where it is regarded as settled by the 1946

---

[1] Annexes not printed; see 436 for the final texts of the agreements.
[2] Not printed but see 396, annex.

Constitution Order-in-Council. Mr. Senanayake has also emphasised how strongly discussion of this matter would be resented and Sir Oliver Goonetilleke confirms this view. The present Constitution contains important safeguards against discriminatory legislation; it also provides for the establishment of a Second Chamber and a Public Services Commission; and it is Mr. Senanayake's intention that these clauses in the Order-in-Council shall be retained when that Order-in-Council is amended to give effect to this new constitutional development. The Ceylon Legislature will, of course, have the power to amend the Constitution by a two-thirds majority but with the emergence of parties in the political life of Ceylon and the decline in public feeling in the matter I am assured that the situation need arouse no apprehension.

*Treatment of nationals*
7. The question has also been raised whether any agreement for the treatment of nationals, companies, and shipping is required. The Governor has pointed out that the conclusion of such an agreement has not been in the mind of Mr Senanayake, and that any agreement made with His Majesty's Government would immediately be seized upon by the Government of India as a basis for requesting identical treatment for Indian nationals in Ceylon. This would prejudice the position of Ceylon most seriously, particularly in relation to the negotiations which will have to be opened between the Governments of Ceylon and India in regard to the future status, &c., of Indians in Ceylon as soon as the new Government under the 1946 Constitution becomes fully effective. My colleagues will remember that His Majesty's Government decided that that issue was one for direct settlement between the Governments of Ceylon and India in accordance with the recommendations of the Soulbury Commission, and that the right of the Government of Ceylon to determine the composition of the population of the Island was recognised in the Order-in-Council of 1946, which provided that any Bill relating solely to the prohibition or restriction of immigration, and not containing any provision relating to the re-entry into Ceylon of persons normally resident there at the date of the passing of the Bill, which, in the opinion of the Governor, was unfair or unreasonable, should not be reserved for the signification of His Majesty's Pleasure. These arguments appear to me very cogent, and I do not consider that the conclusion of an agreement regarding trade and establishment matters even of a temporary character, should be required before the conferment on Ceylon of full self-government within the British Commonwealth of Nations. The present position in these matters is satisfactory so far as the interests of United Kingdom nationals and companies are concerned. I propose, however, that the competent departments should consider in due course whether it will be desirable at some future date to suggest the negotiation of an agreement on these matters with the Government of Ceylon when she becomes a full member of the British Commonwealth.
8. If my colleagues endorse the above views and the draft agreements, it is proposed that those relating to Defence and External Affairs (Annexes I and II) should be communicated to the Governments of the other Members of the Commonwealth. After that, it is suggested that all three drafts should be discussed in confidence by the Governor with Mr. Senanayake with a view to ensuring that they are likely to be acceptable to the new Ceylon Government. The drafts would be submitted to the new Ceylon Government when established. When agreement is reached it will be necessary for a short Bill to be passed here.

9.   Ceylon is entering upon this new chapter in her history in a spirit of great friendliness to this country. She is not merely an acquiescent but an eager candidate for full Membership of the British Commonwealth. But there are elements in Ceylon which would prefer that she should attain independence outside the Commonwealth. It seems to me to be overwhelmingly in our interest to avoid giving these elements an opportunity to embarrass the new Ceylon Government.

**416**   CO 882/30, no 182                                                21 July 1947

**[Commonwealth]: outward telegram Z no 52 from Lord Addison to UK high commissioners in the dominions on the draft agreements and consultation with dominion governments**

My telegrams D. Nos. 529 and 530 of 16th of June.
Announcement made on 18th of June indicated in effect that Ceylon would in due course be given fully responsible status within British Commonwealth, but that certain agreements on matters of mutual concern must be first entered into with the new Ceylon Government as soon as it was fully established under 1946 Constitution. In letter to Mr. Senanayake (see my telegram D. No. 506 of 7th June) it was pointed out that provision would have to be made in respect of, *inter alia*, defence and external affairs. Since date of announcement these questions have been under examination and have been discussed in London with the Governor of Ceylon, who is fully aware of Mr. Senanayake's views.
   2.   As a result draft agreements have been drawn up, relating to (a) defence and (b) external affairs, which appear to provide the necessary safeguards and are thought also to be of nature likely to prove acceptable to a new Ceylon Government. Texts of these drafts are contained in my two immediately following telegrams Z. Nos. 53 and 54.
   3.   It is contemplated that when these drafts (together with a draft agreement dealing with retirement, pensions, etc., of certain classes of officers) have been approved by Ministers here, they should be discussed in confidence by Governor with Mr. Senanayake with view to ensuring that they are likely to be acceptable to new Ceylon Government. Drafts would be submitted to that Government when it is established (i.e., in October).
   4.   In drawing up draft agreements those concerned have had in mind—

(a) that Ceylon is entering upon this new constitutional step in spirit of great friendliness and with every desire for full association in British Commonwealth;
(b) that there are nevertheless certain elements in Ceylon who would prefer independence outside the Commonwealth and to whom no opportunity should be given to embarrass new Ceylon Government;
(c) that any terminology should be avoided which would endanger success of Ceylon's eventual application for admission to United Nations (which cannot, in any case, be considered until September 1948).

   5.   Draft defence agreement has been examined by Joint Planning Staff by whom it has been provisionally agreed on behalf of Chiefs of Staff. This agreement has been formulated in somewhat general terms, partly in order to avoid giving publicity to

details of various defence desiderata, intention being that necessary details should be left to be negotiated later with the new Ceylon Government. Question whether draft agreement should contain a time limit, or whether it should contain provision whereby it could be terminated by either party on giving some period (e.g., five years) of notice, remains for consideration.

6. Draft agreement on external affairs embodies *inter alia* unilateral declaration by Ceylon to conform to resolutions of past Imperial Conferences as these are followed by existing members of the Commonwealth, while Government of United Kingdom, in relation to Ceylon, and Ceylon Government itself will in regard to external affairs generally, and particularly in regard to communication of information and consultation, observe the existing Commonwealth principles and practice.

7. Please communicate substance of above to Dominion authorities and inform them that present intention is that these drafts should be submitted to Ministers here for consideration on 24th July. You should add that if they wish, at this preliminary stage, to offer any observations on their terms, it would be most helpful if these could be received before that date.

# 417   CO 537/2216                                               22 July 1947

## 'Ceylon—defence agreement': minute by J S Bennett[1] to J B Sidebotham on the responsibility for the maintenance of internal security

You will remember that during our discussions on the text of the Defence Agreement a point came up about the responsibility for the maintenance of internal security in Ceylon after the new regime has come into force. I understand that the Chiefs of Staff wanted to maintain, at least in reserve, the right to intervene in matters of internal security in Ceylon if in their judgment a situation was developing which would threaten U.K. strategic interests; and that they would contemplate using British troops for this purpose if the occasion ever arose. We discussed the merits of providing for this in the Defence Agreement and reached the conclusion on a number of grounds that it was much better not to mention it. Nevertheless, the wording of the relevant Article in the draft Defence Agreement has, I believe, been left sufficiently vague to cover the possibility; and I suppose it is always possible that when the draft is discussed with the Ceylon Ministers they will ask for the vague passages to be interpreted and we shall have to make our position clear one way or the other.

In this morning's "Times" I notice the following extract from the short discussion in the House of Commons yesterday which followed the Prime Minister's statement about the situation in Burma following the assassination of Aung-San[2]:—

> "*Mr. Eden*—While sharing the right hon. gentleman's sentiments about this outrage, may I ask him if he can give us any information as to what is now the position and responsibility of any British troops in Burma?
> *Mr. Attlee* replied that the responsibility for maintaining internal security rested with the Governor of Burma, and the troops were available for that

---

[1] Assistant secretary, head of CO International Relations Dept.
[2] President, AFPFL, 1945–1947; member of Burma Executive Council and counsellor for defence, 1946–1947; assassinated with five of his council colleagues, 19 July 1947.

purpose. They were under British command, and were under the control of the Governor. Burma was not yet a Dominion Government, and therefore we had our responsibility for law and order. Every step was being taken to provide for reinforcements if they were needed, and a request had been made to India for the use of Indian troops if that should prove necessary. So far it had not".

Mr Attlee's statement seems to imply very clearly that if and when Burma did become a Dominion Government, the U.K. would have no responsibility for law and order in Burma, and that British troops could have no functions in relation to the maintenance of internal security. I do not know whether this can be taken as a firm doctrine on the subject, but it certainly reflects what is so far as I know normal practice with the existing Dominions, and it shows what is in the Prime Minister's mind about the new ones. It is also quite possible that the Ceylon Ministers may read this statement by Mr Attlee; they are, of course, very interested in what happens in Burma, and they might therefore quote it against us in the course of the negotiations about the Ceylon Defence Agreement if the U.K. were attempting to leave any loop-hole for the exercise of responsibility by the U.K. Government and the U.K. troops in relation to internal security.


# 418   CO 537/2223, no 8A                          28 July 1947
[Commonwealth]: letter from F Strahan[1] to UK high commission in Australia communicating the views of the Australian government on the agreements for defence and external affairs and suggesting that relations between Ceylon and the UK and the dominions should be discussed at a Commonwealth meeting

I am directed by the Prime Minister to refer to your letter of 22nd July on the subject of the future constitutional position of Ceylon.[2] In general, the Australian Government agrees that a country, before admission to the British Commonwealth, should undertake certain obligations. Among the questions which have been considered by the Government are first, whether such obligations should be stated in contractional form and second, whether, particularly where the obligations involve the Commonwealth as a whole, they should be discussed at a Commonwealth Meeting rather than negotiated solely between the Governments of the United Kingdom and Ceylon.

The Australian Government agrees that the Defence obligations to be undertaken by the Government of Ceylon should be stated in the form of an Agreement. While such an agreement is a matter for concern to the Dominions, it is appropriate, since the United Kingdom Government is undertaking full responsibility in the matter, that this Agreement should be negotiated and signed by the Governments of the United Kingdom and Ceylon, on completion of the normal intra-Commonwealth consultation.

In regard to the terms of the Draft Agreement on Defence, it is noted that it has been cast in general terms and that military facilities to be granted to the United Kingdom, including the use of naval and air bases, ports, military establishments and

---

[1] Cabinet secretary, government of Australia.                          [2] cf 417.

telecommunications are to be such "as may from time to time be agreed". In the light of the above, it is considered that, as far as the United Kingdom is concerned, the Agreement is generally in accord with the strategic requirements of Australia. It is noted that the question whether the draft Agreement should contain a time limit or whether it should contain a provision whereby it could be terminated by either party on giving some period (e.g. 5 years) of notice is still to be considered by the United Kingdom Government. It appears desirable that the Agreement should remain in force as long as possible, preferably indefinitely, and that this might best be achieved by omitting all reference to the time factor. Further, it is assumed that existing defence arrangements in Ceylon would remain in force pending the conclusion of a satisfactory mutual agreement between the United Kingdom and Ceylon Governments regarding the details of future defence arrangements.

The obligations which might be undertaken by the Government of Ceylon in regard to External Affairs appear different from those in regard to Defence. Whereas the latter do not involve any commitments on the part of other Dominions, the very fact of the admission of Ceylon to the Commonwealth may involve all other Dominions in obligations. In particular, the Dominions may feel obliged to keep the Government of Ceylon informed of their intentions in the field of foreign policy, in accordance with the normal practices now in use, and they may wish to receive similar benefits from that country. It is noted that the draft Agreement on External Affairs as between the United Kingdom and Ceylon makes no reference to the obligations to be undertaken by Ceylon in regard to the other Dominions and by the other Dominions in regard to Ceylon. Further, in the absence of consultation with other Dominions, the Australian Government is not convinced that such obligations would most suitably be expressed in contractual form. At this preliminary stage it appears that an appropriate procedure might be for the relations of Ceylon with the United Kingdom and the other Dominions to be discussed at a Commonwealth meeting at which representatives of the new Ceylon Government would be present. Such a meeting could conveniently be held in London, the Dominions being represented by their High Commissioners. The undertakings mutually agreed could be formulated in the type of statement usually issued on conclusion of British Commonwealth meetings.

Should such a procedure be adopted, the points stated in the draft Agreement on External Affairs would, in general, be those which the Australian Government would wish to have discussed. As the Agreement stands at present, its terms do not sever the undertakings which Dominions such as Australia might expect from the Government of Ceylon and those which they in turn would wish to give to the Government of Ceylon. The first five paragraphs would appear to need redrafting to make them applicable within the Commonwealth as a whole.

Consideration has also been given to the fact that should such a procedure be adopted for the admission of Ceylon to the Commonwealth, it should also be adopted for the admission of other countries. The case of India and Pakistan is not however an exact parallel. The Government of India has been in practice regarded as a member of the Commonwealth, and the Australian Government for its part has in general included India in its intra-Commonwealth consultation. It would not therefore expect of India or Pakistan prior undertakings similar to those which might be asked of Ceylon or any other country which is entering the Commonwealth for the first time as a fully self-governing community.

# 419 PREM 8/726, IB 43(47)1					28 July 1947

## 'Ceylon constitution': Cabinet India and Burma Committee minutes on the draft agreements

The Committee had before them a memorandum by the Secretary of State for the Colonies (I.B.(47) 144)[1] covering the drafts of three Agreements to be made with the Ceylon Government after the inauguration of the new Constitution in October, 1947.

*The Secretary of State for the Colonies* recalled that he had announced in the House of Commons on 18th June that Ceylon would, in due course, be given fully responsible government within the British Commonwealth, but that certain Agreements on matters of mutual concern must first be entered into with the new Ceylon Government. Drafts of three Agreements relating to Defence, External Affairs and Public Officers, respectively, had now been prepared in consultation with the Foreign Office and the Commonwealth Relations Office, and had been discussed with the Governor of Ceylon and Sir Oliver Goonetilleke. The draft Agreement relating to Defence (Annex I to I.B.(47) 144) had been formulated in general terms, since it had been thought advisable to avoid giving publicity to the details of the various desiderata specified by the Chiefs of Staff in C.P.(47) 179; any necessary details could be negotiated later with the Ceylon Government. The Chiefs of Staff had raised no objection to this procedure. Since the draft was prepared, however, it had been suggested that the absence of a time limit for its operation might be regarded as such a derogation from the sovereign status of Ceylon as seriously to jeopardise her application for admission to the United Nations. This objection might be met by the insertion of either a time limit or a provision under which the Agreement might be determined by either party on giving appropriate notice.

*The Prime Minister* said that the Chiefs of Staff had urged that there should be no question of imposing or suggesting a time limit to the provision of our defence requirements in Ceylon. While they realised that the question was one primarily for a political decision, they were doubtful of the wisdom of providing in the Agreement for either of the alternatives suggested by the Secretary of State for the Colonies. They felt that the inclusion of a time limit would merely encourage the Ceylon Government to regard that as the terminating date of their obligations under the Agreement; on the other hand, if a period of notice was specified, the impression would be given that we expected that the Agreement would in due course come to an end. Their view was, therefore, that either provision might act as a goal towards which the Ceylon Government might strive with the object of throwing off the last remaining evidence of British control. They saw nothing inconsistent in an Agreement on the lines suggested in Annex I in I.B.(47) 144 with full membership of the United Nations; it differed in no essentials from, for example, the Anglo–Iraqi Treaty of 1930, which had not been regarded as derogating from the sovereignty of Iraq.

In discussion, the following points were made:—

(a) It was suggested that there was a risk that the prospects of reaching agreement might be prejudiced if too much was asked of the Ceylon Government.

---

[1] See 415.

*The Secretary of State for the Colonies* said, however, that the Ceylon political leaders had shown themselves anxious to meet our defence requirements in full; they recognised that this was a matter of mutual interest. Their only anxiety was that Ceylon's sovereignty should not be jeopardised.

(b) It was suggested that an agreement which imposed a permanent obligation on the Ceylon Government to permit, for instance, the United Kingdom Government to base naval, air and land forces in Ceylon might be regarded as inconsistent with full independence. It had been argued that a similar agreement with the Transjordan Government constituted a bar to the latter's membership of the United Nations. Moreover, there was no precedent for a formal agreement of this nature between the United Kingdom Government and a Dominion Government.

As against this, the *Lord Chancellor*[2] pointed out that there was ample precedent for Defence Agreements of the nature proposed for Ceylon which were not held to imply any derogation for sovereignty; such, for instance, were the Agreements relating to the lease of bases to the United States Government in Bermuda and the West Indies. The insertion of a reference to a time limit or to notice of termination would in his view needlessly open His Majesty's Government to the risk of embarrassing pressure from the Ceylon Government.

(c) *The Secretary of State for Commonwealth Relations*[3] said that the Australian Government, who had been consulted, were opposed to the inclusion of any reference to a time limit in the proposed Agreement.[4]

(d) The Committee considered that the phrase "and as may from time to time be mutually agreed" in paragraph 1 of the draft Defence Agreement was ambiguous and open to misunderstanding. It was agreed that, for these words, there should be substituted the words "and as may be agreed".

(e) *The Lord Chancellor* pointed out that the detailed Agreements relating to defence matters, which would in due course have to be concluded with the Ceylon Government, would raise many difficult problems such as the provision of powers for the maintenance of discipline among the British forces stationed in the Island. He would like to be consulted in due course regarding the terms of the drafts of those Agreements.

(f) It was agreed that paragraph 1 of the draft Agreement relating to External Affairs (Annex II to I.B.(47) 144) should be amended by the omission of the words "as these are followed by the existing Members of the Commonwealth".

(g) *The Secretary of State for the Colonies* said that he had not overlooked the question whether special steps should be taken by agreement to safeguard the interests of minorities on the transfer of power to the Ceylon Government. The Governor had, however, advised strongly against re-opening this matter in Ceylon, where it was regarded as settled by the 1946 Constitution Order-in-Council. The present Constitution contained important safeguards against discriminatory legislation; it provided for the establishment of a Second Chamber and a Public Services Commission; and it was Mr. Senanayake's intention that these clauses in the Order-in-Council should be retained. The Ceylon legislature would, of course, have the power to amend the Constitution by a two-thirds majority but, with the emergence of parties in the political life of Ceylon and the decline in public feeling in the matter, he was assured that the situation need arouse no apprehension. In view

---

[2] Lord Jowitt.                          [3] Lord Addison.                          [4] See 418.

of the confidential nature of the discussions which had so far taken place, it had not been possible to consult the minority leaders on this question.

The Committee felt that no useful purpose would be served by an attempt to provide by treaty or agreement for the safeguarding of minorities. It was possible, however, that the new Ceylon Government might be prepared to make a declaration on the subject. The Governments of India and Pakistan could have no ground for complaint, since no requirements regarding the future treatment of minorities under their control had been imposed on them in connection with the transfer of power.

(h) The Committee agreed that the question of the negotiation of an agreement on the treatment of nationals, companies and shipping should be deferred until Ceylon has become a full member of the Commonwealth.

The Committee:—

(1) Approved the draft Agreements annexed to I.B.(47) 144, subject to the amendments suggested in discussion, and invited the Secretary of State for the Colonies to arrange for their submission in due course to the new Ceylon Government.

(2) Invited the Secretary of State for the Colonies to consult the Lord Chancellor regarding the terms of the arrangements which would have to be made with the Ceylon Government in order to give detailed effect to the Defence Agreement set out in Annex I to I.B.(47) 144."

# 420   CO 537/2216, no 18                    29 July 1947
## [Defence agreement]: CO note of an inter-departmental[1] discussion with Sir H Moore

Mr. Paskin referred briefly to the proceedings of the India and Burma Committee on 28th July.[2] He mentioned that the Committee had agreed that there should be no time limit to the Defence Agreement. He also indicated that, in deference to the Lord Chancellor's views, some addition might have to be made to the Defence Agreement to provide for the exercise of jurisdiction over members of H.M. Forces stationed in the Island. Sir Henry Moore said that he hoped both he and Sir Oliver Goonetilleke would have a chance of seeing what was envisaged in this connection before he left the country.

Mr. Paskin also mentioned that the Lord Chancellor had intimated that he would like to see the subsidiary agreements which should be consequential on the general Defence Agreement. He said that the Colonial Office would try to find out what exactly the Lord Chancellor had in mind.

Mr. Price[3] said that the agreements would now have to be put formally to the Dominion Governments. He was agreeable that reference to the Dominion Governments should be on the basis that any points now raised by the Dominions would have to be settled within three weeks. Sir Henry Moore pointed out that he would like to be in a position to show the drafts to Mr. Senanayake before August 24th i.e. the date on which the general elections will commence in Ceylon.

---

[1] The Chiefs of Staff and the CRO were also represented.                    [2] See 419.
[3] Representing the CRO.

As regards action to be taken in Ceylon vis-à-vis the Defence Agreement, Sir Henry Moore envisaged two stages. First, he would consult with the Service Chiefs and find out what their desiderata were to implement the Defence Agreement. When these were agreed either at Singapore or in Whitehall, as may be necessary, the Ceylon Government would in consultation with the local Service Chiefs work out the detailed arrangements under which land, buildings etc. would be used by the three forces. Mr. Mallaby[4] saw no objection to this course of action and agreed to arrange for the local Commanders-in-Chief, who were already in possession of the Chiefs of Staff's desiderata, to be informed of Sir Henry Moore's impending return and to be advised that they must be prepared for stage 1 accordingly. He also agreed to arrange for Sir Henry Moore to be sent a copy of the joint planners' submission to the Chiefs-of-Staff in respect of defence desiderata in Ceylon.

Mr. Paskin took the opportunity to refer to the question of H.M.G.'s rights to introduce troops into Ceylon for the purpose of safeguarding H.M.G.'s installations. He pointed out that the India and Burma Committee had not examined the Chiefs of Staff's paper in detail and had relied on the fact that the Chiefs of Staff accepted the terms of the Defence Agreement. Mr. Mallaby confirmed that he understood that constitutionally H.M.G. would not be able on their own initiative to introduce forces into Ceylon for internal security purposes.[5]

It was agreed:—

(a) to let Sir Henry Moore have copies of the three draft Agreements in the form in which they had been submitted to the India and Burma Committee, straight away, and

(b) to forward by fast air-mail a copy of the Defence Agreement as amended in the light of the decisions of the India and Burma Committee.

Subsequently, any further amendments rendered necessary after consultation with the Dominion Governments would be telegraphed.

---

[4] Secretary to Chiefs of Staff Committee.								[5] cf 417.

# 421   CO 882/30, no 185								2 Aug 1947
## [Commonwealth]: outward telegram Z no 67 from Lord Addison to UK high commissioner in Australia transmitting a reply to the views of the Autralian government

Addressed to Ukrep Canberra repeated to Ukreps Ottawa, Wellington and Pretoria. My immediately preceding telegram.

*Ceylon*
1. We have not yet received text of Australian Government's communication sent by air-mail but in view of urgency we should be glad if you would convey to them following observations on their comments as summarized in your telegram No. 520 of 28th July.[1]

(a) As regards Australian Government's doubts about setting out obligations of

---

[1] Tel 520 of 28 July was a summary of Strahan's letter of the same date, see 418.

this nature in regard to external affairs in a contractual form, we too in general feel that matters of the kind are best expressed more informally. Case of Ceylon is however a very special one. As Australian Government know we are anxious to get substantial agreement on this and other matters before (repeat before) new Ceylon Government takes office in October, and to have reasonable assurance that necessary safeguards will then be immediately agreed to by new Ceylon Government as preliminary to any legislation here to amend Ceylon Constitution. Failing immediate conclusion of such agreements between the United Kingdom and new Ceylon Government, it is doubtful how far progress can be made in Parliament here with any legislative steps to confer on Ceylon full responsible status within British Commonwealth.

(b) Procedure suggested by Australian Government for London meeting after (repeat after) new Ceylon Government has been formed would lead to delay and would deprive us of assurance which we hope to obtain in advance from Mr. Senanayake that, if he is returned to power, he will recommend the draft agreements on defence and external affairs to his Cabinet for acceptance.

(c) Special procedure suggested by Australian Government for dealing with external affairs might prejudice possibility of obtaining advance acquiescence in terms of defence agreement also to be entered into—Mr. Senanayake might take line that he would like latter subject deferred to a Conference also.

(d) Draft agreement as between United Kingdom and Ceylon was purposely so worded as to involve no commitment, expressed or implied, on part of Members of the British Commonwealth other than the United Kingdom as to their relations with Ceylon in field of external affairs. United Kingdom Government is at present, and will remain until constitutional change is made, responsible for Ceylon's external affairs, and for this reason we feel that bilateral agreement between United Kingdom and Ceylon before that responsibility is surrendered is appropriate method of procedure. There is no reason to believe however that Ceylon would not be ready, if that were the desire, to enter into similar understandings with the other Members of the British Commonwealth, and conclusion of bilateral agreement would not in our view preclude later meetings on the lines and for the purpose suggested by the Australian Government if this should be agreeable to the other Commonwealth Governments concerned.

2.  Please convey these comments urgently to Australian Government and express the hope that in the light of them they will see no objection to our proceeding with the draft Agreement. Other United Kingdom High Commissioners may find above comments of use if any similar points are raised by other Dominion authorities.[2]

---

[2] The response of the Australian government was forwarded by the UK high commission in tel 606 on 19 Aug:

'Australian Government notes view expressed in first sentence of paragraph (d) of your telegram Z. No. 67 and having regard to circumstances attending the negotiations is not disposed to raise any objection to United Kingdom Government proceeding with draft agreements.

2.  Australian Government hopes however that, bearing in mind attainment by Ceylon of Dominion status would be a matter of especial interest to Australia and other Dominions, United Kingdom Government will give very full consideration to calling together in London, after conclusion of agreements but before Ceylon's actual admission to Commonwealth, representatives of the several Dominion Governments and of the new Ceylon Government for purpose of discussing their relations with one another and with United Kingdom' (CO 882/30, no 188).

**422**   CO 822/30, no 190                                    3 Sept 1947

[Commonwealth]: outward telegram no 1011 from Mr Creech Jones to Sir H Moore on the Australian proposal for a Commonwealth conference on Ceylon

My telegram No. 945.

Arising out of transmission of text of draft agreements to other members of Commonwealth, Government of Australia has expressed hope that, as Australia and other members of British Commonwealth will be specially interested in attainment by Ceylon of membership of Commonwealth, His Majesty's Government in the United Kingdom will consider arranging for a meeting in London of representatives of other Commonwealth Governments and of Ceylon with object of discussing their relations with one another and with His Majesty's Government in the United Kingdom. Government of Australia suggests that Conference should meet after agreements have been concluded, but before Ceylon's actual admission to the Commonwealth.[1]

2.   It is noted from your telegram No. 1100 that new Parliament is not now likely to be able to meet before 25th November, and, as you know, it is hoped that United Kingdom Bill will have been passed and Order-in-Council amended by end of December. The effect of the above would be to give full self-governing status to Ceylon with effect from date (presumably in February) to be fixed.

3.   But if inauguration ceremony is to be arranged for February, timetable will be very compressed, and I should like before considering what reply should be made to Australian Government to have your personal views on the probable practicability from this point of view of meeting their request. As that request has not yet been referred to other Commonwealth Governments, Senanayake should not be consulted at this stage.

---

[1] See 418 & 421.

**423**   CO 882/30, no 191                                    5 Sept 1947

[Commonwealth]: inward telegram (reply) no 1146 from Sir H Moore to Mr Creech Jones arguing against the Australian proposal for a Commonwealth conference

Your telegram No. 1011. Secret.[1]

I had always assumed that Ceylon's actual admission to the Commonwealth would follow automatically on passage of United Kingdom Bill and promulgation of Order-in-Council at the end of December, the only other formality necessary being the issue of official Royal Instructions and Letters Patent to the Governor-General.

2.   I had not contemplated any suspending clause being inserted which would delay admission to the Commonwealth to a date to be fixed in February so as to enable the Duke of Gloucester actually to inaugurate the new Constitution. Date in

---

[1] See 422.

February was agreed to meet His Royal Highness's personal convenience and, in the circumstances, celebrations would take the form of Royal recognition of the status so recently assumed. I believe the above to be Senanayake's own conception too, though I have not discussed the matter with him. On such a timetable it would be quite impracticable to arrange any meeting with representatives in London.

3.  But in any event, I consider Australia's suggestion should be politely but firmly discouraged. It will inevitably create impression here that despite the conclusion of agreements, Ceylon is to be subjected to yet another test imposed by other Commonwealth Governments before His Majesty's Government carries out her pledge to grant her the promised status and the fact that Pakistan and India have been subjected to no such test but would now be free to take part in applying it to Ceylon would most certainly be resented.

4.  The elections are going very badly for the United National Party and while it seems likely that Senanayake will obtain a majority over any other single party, it is almost certain that he will have to win over some Independents and form some kind of coalition if he is to secure a working majority in the House. It is, therefore, of first importance that nothing should be done which would give further ammunition to his opponents who are still openly suggesting that there is a catch somewhere in the status we are being promised.

5.  Australia has her own Commissioner here who can make local representations which the Australian Government wants and possibly invitations might be sent to other Commonwealth representatives to attend the February celebrations, in which case a conference as to procedure once the new Constitution was safely launched could take place in Colombo, though I do not advocate it.

6.  As things are going, I am sure Senanayake could not afford to leave Ceylon in the next few months and he would not trust Corea to represent him in London on so important a question.

## **424**  CO 882/30, no 192                                      17 Sept 1947

**[Commonwealth]: outward telegram no 643 from Lord Addison to UK high commissioner in Australia transmitting a reply to the Australian government's proposal for a conference on Ceylon**

Your telegram No. 606 of 19th of August[1] and your despatch No. 263 of 20th of August.

*Ceylon*

We have carefully considered Australian Government's suggestion in last paragraph of enclosure in despatch No. 263 for meeting in London between representatives of the several British Commonwealth Governments and representative of new Ceylon Government.

2.  Since we expressed tentative view in last sentence of paragraph 1 (d) of my telegram N. No. 67 of 2nd August, consultation with Governor of Ceylon and further examination of the question has indicated that timetable and other factors would

---

[1] See 421, note 2.

render it virtually impossible in practice and undoubtedly embarrassing politically, to hold a meeting of nature suggested in the interval between the formation of new Ceylon Government and the coming into effect of necessary United Kingdom legislation.

3.  These factors are as follows:—

(a)  Ministers of new Ceylon Government will not now assume full functions until 25th November. It would be impossible for Senanayake (if he becomes Prime Minister) to leave Ceylon during next few months, and Governor is clear that Senanayake would not be ready to entrust attendance at such a meeting to anyone else.

(b)  Summoning of such a meeting would create impression in Ceylon that despite conclusion of defence and external affairs agreements with United Kingdom, it was desired to impose on Ceylon yet another test of her suitability for her new status before that status was finally conferred. Such an impression would provide, at inopportune moment politically, dangerous ammunition for opponents of Senanayake.

(c)  If meeting envisaged by Australian Government were to be called, it appears inevitable that Governments of India and Pakistan should participate. This would be likely to be most embarrassing in more ways than one. In the first place it would be much preferable from point of view of United Kingdom, and no doubt from that of other British Commonwealth countries, that questions of consultation and information regarding foreign affairs should not be raised in detail in discussions with representatives of India and Pakistan for the time being. In the second place Ceylon Government would almost certainly find it embarrassing to discuss with representatives of India and Pakistan at so early a stage matters of external affairs or defence, and are likely much to prefer to wait until arrangements of this nature between India and Pakistan on the one hand and other Members of the British Commonwealth on the other, have been more fully defined.

4.  Although these difficulties seem to rule out the idea of meeting at time suggested by Australian Government there is no reason whatever to believe that at more convenient opportunity after Ceylon has obtained her new status, Ceylon Government would not be very ready, if this were considered necessary or desirable, to enter into similar understandings either individually or collectively with Governments of Canada, Australia, New Zealand, and South Africa, to those contained in draft external affairs agreement with the United Kingdom.

5.  Please explain matter to Australian authorities on above lines and express hope that in the circumstances they will not wish to press their suggestion. It is important that you should keep the Secretary of State informed of this correspondence as soon as he is available but this need not delay your communication to the Australian authorities.

6.  Please see also my immediately following telegram.

# 425 CO 54/993/4, no 21                    24 Sept 1947
## [General election]: inward unnumbered telegram from Sir H Moore to Mr Creech Jones on the election results

Following are final election results:—

| | |
|---|---:|
| United Nationalist [sic] Party .. .. .. .. .. .. | 42 |
| Independents .. .. .. .. .. .. .. 21 | |
| Lanka Sama Samaj Party .. .. .. .. .. .. 10 | |
| Bolshevik–Leninist Party .. .. .. .. .. .. 5 | |
| Communist Party .. .. .. .. .. .. .. 3 | |
| Tamil Congress .. .. .. .. .. .. .. 7 | |
| Indian Congress .. .. .. .. .. .. .. 6 | |
| Labour .. .. .. .. .. .. .. .. 1 | |
| Total .. .. .. .. .. .. .. .. | 95 |

2. I am inviting Senanayake to-morrow to form a Ministry and will report what coalition he prefers in order to obtain working majority.

3. Twenty-two former members including three Ministers, Mahadeva, Kannangara and Hewavitarne, have lost seats and election petition against fourth, George de Silva, is rumoured. Senanayake may, therefore, have some difficulty in forming a strong Ministry, but I see no reason to suppose that he will not obtain necessary support for his declared policy of fully responsible status within the Commonwealth.

4. It is most satisfactory that the elections throughout have been orderly, without any serious public disorder.

# 426 CO 537/2222, no 19                    6 Oct 1947
## [Civil service]: letter from Sir C Jeffries to Sir H Moore on British practice in respect of the control of permanent secretaries

[In Sept 1947 Moore informed the CO that Senanayake wanted control over the appointment, disciplinary control and dismissal of all permanent secretaries to be removed from the Public Service Commission and vested in the governor-general acting on the advice of the prime minister. Senanayake's real objective was said by Moore to be to secure the right to remove a permanent secretary who could not get on with his minister; an officer would not be dismissed on disciplinary grounds without a full independent enquiry. Moore anticipated the difficulty that once an officer had been appointed to a permanent secretaries grade, any transfer back to grade 1 of the civil service would automatically involve loss of emoluments. The governor was therefore proposing to explore the possibility of probationary appointments and to discuss the matter further with Senanayake. In the meantime he requested information as to home practice in respect of permanent secretaries (CO 537/2222, no 9, tel 1181, 17 Sept 1947). On 26 Sept Moore reported that Senanayake adhered firmly to his view that the prime minister should have the power to advise the governor-general to transfer, within the permanent secretary grade, an officer who had failed to work harmoniously with his minister and, in extreme cases where officers had shown themselves to be 'misfits' as permanent secretaries, to advise that they be transferred (with consequent loss of emoluments) back to the service or grade from which they were appointed to be permanent secretaries. Subject to this, Senanayake agreed that disciplinary control of permanent secretaries, including dismissal from the public service, should remain vested in the Public Service Commission (*ibid*, no 12, unnumbered tel.]

I am writing for Lloyd who is on leave.

We are sorry not to have replied sooner to your request to him in paragraph 3 of your secret and personal telegram No. 1181 of the 17th September, in which you asked for information as to the practice here in respect of disciplinary control, etc., in relation to Permanent Secretaries.

In view of the decision notified in your telegram of the 26th September and as the position here may not be of any great guide in the case of Ceylon, I am not telegraphing the information but sending it to you by fast air mail.

Briefly, the position here is that a Permanent Secretary in the Home Civil Service is appointed by the Minister of the Department concerned, with the approval of the Prime Minister. One of the duties of the Permanent Secretary to the Treasury is to tender advice to the Prime Minister on the making of these appointments. The position of a Permanent Secretary in the United Kingdom Civil Service is constitutionally precisely the same as that of any other servant of the Crown, that is to say, that he is technically liable to dismissal at any time "at pleasure"; in practice, he is only liable to be removed from the Civil Service for misconduct or to be retired before reaching the normal retiring age for serious inefficiency. There is, therefore, in practice, no such power in this country as that which Mr. Senanayake was seeking, i.e., the right to remove a Permanent Secretary who cannot get on with a Minister. Such cases in this country are, in any case, very rare, and when they do arise they are handled according to circumstances and not by reference to any practice which has ever been publicly defined.

As regards the suggested possibility of a probationary period, probation does not seem to us altogether appropriate for an officer of this rank and might undermine his authority. Moreover, the possibility of a Permanent Secretary not getting on with his Minister would not necessarily be overcome by such a period of probation, as he might already have served such a period satisfactorily under some other Minister.

The whole question was dealt with in a speech made by Lord Simon, when Lord Chancellor, in the House of Lords on the 25th November, 1942 (Hansard, Col. 233 et seq.). If you think there is any occasion now to pursue the matter further and have not got a copy of the Hansard available, please let me know and I will have an extract made and send it to you.

## 427  CO 882/30, no 317                          17 Oct 1947
[Citizenship]: inward telegram no 68 from Sir H Moore to Mr Creech Jones transmitting a message from Lord Addison[1] to Mr Attlee on citizenship negotiations with India and the British Nationality Bill

Following for the Prime Minister from the Lord Privy Seal.

*Begins.* I had a useful conversation yesterday afternoon with Mr. Senanayake and there were two matters arising out of it that affect the Parliamentary programme which should be borne in mind, although perhaps the Colonial Secretary may have already mentioned them. He has arranged for negotiations with the Indians on the citizenship question and was aware of the possibility of our introducing legislation

---

[1] Addison (now lord privy seal) visited Ceylon in Oct 1947.

affecting Commonwealth citizenship in the near future. He anticipates that Indian negotiations will be successfully concluded before the end of this year and thinks that they might be prejudiced by a previous introduction of our Bill. It would, therefore, seem helpful to him if our Bill could be deferred until the New Year or until Ceylon–Indian negotiations are complete. So far as can be gathered, the inauguration of the Parliamentary Institution here has gone smoothly. On this you will, no doubt, be otherwise informed. *Ends.*[2]

[2] From within the CO, Jeffries requested clarification of this message in tel no 29 of 29 Oct:

'We are not clear on what grounds Senanayake considers the United Kingdom Nationality Bill might prejudice negotiations with Government of India since the Bill would leave it to Ceylon and India to settle their own citizenship law. As Prime Minister may raise matter with Lord Privy Seal within next few days should be glad to know immediately whether Senanayake has anything particularly in mind' (CO 882/30, no 318).

# 428   CO 537/2223, no 30                                    24 Oct 1947
## 'Ceylon Bill—armed forces': letter from A H Stainton[1] to J A Peck[2] on the legal position of UK forces in Ceylon

I understand that we must so far as possible put Ceylon in the position of a Dominion in all Forces matters in view of the susceptibilities of Ceylon.

The main thing we have to secure is that the legal position of U.K. Land Forces remaining in Ceylon is unassailable.

In view of Ceylon susceptibilities we must, I think, start with an amendment making Ceylon a Dominion for the purposes of the Army Act. This in itself will exclude the Government of Ceylon from having any say in the confirmation of a court martial or other matters (cf. e.g. s.54(4) s.122 and s.189(2) of the Army Act). It will be necessary to consider whether any transitional provisions are required in respect, for instance, of court martial proceedings pending when the Bill comes into operation.

If Ceylon Forces are to come under command of U.K. Forces I apprehend that Ceylon must make an enactment corresponding to s.179 B of the Army Act in order that s.175(13) and S.176(12) of the Army Act may apply.

These are matters of minor importance but there remains a much more weighty question of what authority under the Law of Ceylon is given to U.K. Forces exercising their powers in Ceylon. That is to say, what is the defence to an action by a U.K. soldier against his C.O. for unlawful imprisonment brought in the Courts of Ceylon? The answer to this is that the Army Act is itself, probably even with the amendment treating Ceylon as a Dominion, part of the Law of Ceylon. This, however, will no longer be the case when the existing Army Act expires next year. The re-enactment will certainly, having regard to the general provisions of the Bill, not extend to Ceylon. Accordingly Ceylon must have legislation corresponding to the Visiting Forces Act of 1933 at least before the expiry of the Army Act. The Imperial Visiting Forces Act has been extended to Ceylon but only as respects the Forces of other Dominions.

[1] Office of the Parliamentary Counsel.                    [2] Deputy legal adviser, CO.

The main trouble in practice will no doubt arise from the U.K. soldier who runs down a Ceylon civilian. S.41 of the Army act may be amended, as was done in relation to India, so as to ensure that the U.K. Forces can themselves try the soldier. This, however, will not avail after the current Army Act expires and could, of course, always be repealed by Ceylon. I apprehend that a U.K. soldier who runs down an Australian civilian in Canberra will be tried in the Courts of Australia for manslaughter. Presumably Australia has a Visiting Forces Act with a provision corresponding to s.1 of the Imperial Act. Would you be satisfied that such a provision would entitle the U.K. Forces in Australia themselves to try the soldier, instead of handing him to the Australian civil power?

You have already rejected the suggestion that we should in the Bill provide a Ceylon Visiting Forces Act for the benefit of U.K. Forces in Ceylon. It would only be by such a provision that we could secure a wider field in which U.K. Forces in Ceylon would be immune from the civil power. Even if we were to make such a provision it would, of course, be amendable by Ceylon at any time. But you may be able to persuade Ceylon to produce something wider than s.1 of the Visiting Forces Act.*

*Naval Forces*
I think that the principles with which this letter starts involve legislation for the Naval Forces of Ceylon on the lines of clause 3 of the draft Bill in your possession. I understand, however, that South Africa has not adopted the Dominion Naval Forces Act of 1911 and gets on quite well under the Colonial Naval Defence Act, 1931. My information on this point may be out of date.

* Cf. the U.S.A. Visiting Forces Act of 1942.

---

# 429   CO 882/30, no 319                              27 Oct 1947
## [Citizenship]: inward telegram (reply) no 33 from Sir H Moore to Sir C Jeffries transmitting a statement by Mr Senanayake explaining the grounds upon which he considers that the British Nationality Bill might prejudice his negotiations with India

Following for Jeffries.

*Begins.* Your personal and secret telegram No. 29.[1] Following is statement by Senanayake of grounds on which he considers that Bill might prejudice his forthcoming negotiations with India.

*Begins.* The principal matter in the negotiations with India will be the determination of the citizenship of about 600,000 Indians now resident in Ceylon. A considerable section of these Indians will fall outside the pale of Ceylonese citizenship if domicile is adopted as the basis for Ceylonese citizenship. If, on the other hand, India adopts birth as the basis, it is likely that some of these Indians will also fail to obtain citizenship of India and only the operation of Sub-Section 2 of the Section 13 of the Draft Bill will enable them to be British subjects. The passing at this juncture of the United Kingdom Nationality Bill recognising birth as the basis of

---

[1] See 427, note 2.

citizenship will enable India to urge that Ceylon should adopt the same basis for citizenship. It may also be urged that departure from the United Kingdom model and the introduction of the basis of domicile are discriminatory. Moreover, the grant of British nationality through Ceylon citizenship without conferring civic rights on all these citizens is also likely to be objected to as discriminatory. The passing of the United Kingdom Bill now will therefore prejudice the stand that Ceylon is likely to take up on this matter during the negotiations. Public opinion in Ceylon is decidedly in favour of adoption of domicile and not birth as basis for citizenship. *Ends.*

**430**   CO 537/2223, no 35                                        28 Oct 1947

**[Defence]: inward telegram no 37 from Sir H Moore to Sir C Jeffries on the provisions to be made for UK service requirements in the Ceylon Independence Bill**

Following for Jeffries.
   *Begins.* Your secret and personal telegram No. 28.[1]
   I frankly do not fully appreciate what the desiderata of the services are which they wish incorporated in Act. Ceylon conditions are, as you point out, quite different from those of India, and it is of course contemplated in the Draft Defence Agreement itself that Imperial services will be allowed to continue to operate here and that Service Commanders will exercise same control and jurisdiction over members of said Forces as they exercise at present.
   2.   How exactly Ceylon Defence Force and Ceylon Royal Naval Volunteer Reserve will be controlled and administered cannot be definitely settled before Defence Agreement itself is signed, but existing Ordinances do not raise the same disciplinary difficulties as Sections referred to of Indian Independence Act are designed to remove, and there would therefore appear to be no grounds for legislating in the United Kingdom Act to remove a difficulty which does not at present and perhaps may never arise.
   3.   On general political grounds, I think it most unwise to include anything in Act which might at this stage give rise to suspicion that United Kingdom forces are being given a privileged position, though my private belief is that once Agreement has been signed the Ceylon Parliament would be willing to pass any necessary legislation to meet service requirements. *Ends.*

---

[1] In tel no 28 of 23 Oct, Jeffries explained that a question of policy might arise if the UK service departments pressed for the insertion of provisions in the Ceylon Independence Bill on the lines of sections 11(2), 12(2a) & (4) and 13 of the Indian Independence Act which governed jurisdiction over UK military and naval forces in India after independence (CO 537/2223, no 26).

**431**   CO 537/2223, no 33                                        29 Oct 1947

**[Ceylon Independence Bill]: inward telegram no 106 from Sir H Moore to Mr Creech Jones explaining that the Ceylon Cabinet is anxious to have the bill passed on or before 20 Nov**

Senanayake informs me that Cabinet has authorised him to sign Agreements on

External Affairs, Defence and Public Officers, after he has seen the Draft U.K. Bill or a complete summary of it and has satisfied himself that it contains only what was understood it would contain in the London discussions as well as the points subsequently indicated by telegram.

Cabinet decided further that Senanayake should ask you to give the Bill the title of Ceylon Independence Bill, following the Indian precedent. Cabinet is most anxious to have Royal Assent to Bill on or before 20th November, in order that arrangements may be made for debate in Ceylon Parliament which meets on 25th November.

## 432    CO 537/2223, no 38                                          29 Oct 1947
### [Ceylon Independence Bill]: inward telegram no 39 from Sir H Moore to Mr Creech Jones explaining Mr Senanayake's views on the timetable

Reference my secret telegram No. 106.[1]

I am sure you will be most gratified that Senanayake has succeeded so rapidly in obtaining Cabinet approval of his signature. I therefore urge that text of U.K. Bill be telegraphed out immediately—see my secret and personal telegram No. 38 to Jeffries.

2.  Senanayake has explained to me privately that Bandaranaike gave him most difficulty in raising all sorts of questions of detail and interpretation suggestive of suspicions as to the bona fides of H.M.G. It is for this reason, and because he is most anxious that the Opposition here should not be in a position to raise all sorts of similar questions while the U.K. Bill is being debated in London, that he presses that Royal Assent should be given before 20th November. He has, however, explained that he would be quite satisfied if Bill had been read three times in both Houses by that date. I have no doubt the suggested title "Independence Bill" is a similar concession to Opposition sentiment.

3.  I appreciate that these requests may perhaps cause you some inconvenience, but in view of the issues at stake I trust you will do your very best to meet his wishes. I open Parliament on 25th November.

---

[1] See 431.

## 433    CO 537/2223, no 40                                          30 Oct 1947
### [Ceylon Independence Bill]: outward telegram (reply) no 36 from Mr Rees-Williams to Sir H Moore on the timetable

Your Secret and Personal telegram No. 39.[1]

Following from Rees-Williams. *Begins.*

We are most gratified at news in your Secret telegram No. 106 and we fully appreciate reasons why Senanayake is unable to sign Agreements until he has seen copy or full summary of Bill. As at present drafted Bill contains long Schedule of amendments to United Kingdom Acts consequent on Ceylon's new status, which

---

[1] See 432.

would be difficult to summarise. We feel therefore that best course will be to send you copy of Bill by fast air mail as soon as printed copies are available which we hope will be by end of this week. We can then telegraph any amendments made in the further course of drafting. Schedule requires consideration by all United Kingdom Departments concerned and in particular by Service Departments. It is therefore certain that final text of Bill will not be ready for Ministerial approval here before a meeting to be held on 11th (eleventh) November.

I regret therefore that it will be quite impossible for Bill to have passed all stages by 20th November. I am however urgently exploring possibility of introduction in the House of Lords and completion of all stages there by that date. This is the best I can hope for and while I will do my best to achieve it I cannot promise that it will be possible. [*Ends*].

## **434**  CO 882/30, no 320                                        4 Nov 1947
## [Citizenship]: outward telegram (reply) no 43 from Mr Creech Jones to Sir H Moore on the British Nationality Bill

Your telegram No. 33.[1] British Nationality Bill. Senanayake's views are under urgent consideration and a reply will be sent as soon as possible.

2.  Meanwhile I should be glad to learn whether he is in a position to give any indication as to the intention of the Ceylon Government in regard to legislation on similar lines (see my despatch No. 400 of the 17th September). I appreciate that it may not be possible for Ministers to furnish observations on the details of the Bill at this stage: but it would be of assistance to the United Kingdom Government if they could be informed whether the main principle embodied in Clause I of the Bill (namely that of adopting citizenship as the common basis for British nationality) is acceptable to Ceylon Ministers, and whether it is their intention to give effect to this principle in any Ceylon legislation regarding Ceylon citizenship. As explained in Lloyds' letter of the 11th September it will be possible to adopt this principle even if it is desired to adhere to the proposal to adopt domicile as the basis for Ceylon citizenship.

3.  Please communicate with your Prime Minister in the above sense. It would be convenient if his reply, together with any observations you may have to make, could be sent by telegram as soon as possible.[2]

---

[1] See 429.
[2] Moore replied in tel no 58 on 8 Nov:

'Senanayake sees no objection to the principle of adopting citizenship as the common basis for British nationality, and is of the opinion that the Ceylon Government would be prepared to give effect to this principle in Ceylon legislation after Ceylon has been able to define "Ceylon Citizenship". The definition of "Ceylon Citizenship" however, will not (repeat not) be undertaken until after an attempt has been made to reach an understanding with India on the status of Indians in Ceylon. It is proposed that a meeting between the Prime Ministers of India and Ceylon should take place towards Christmas' (CO 882/30, no 321).

# 435   CO 537/1994, no 64                                      6 Nov 1947

## [Sterling balances]: outward telegram no 102 from Mr Creech Jones to Sir H Moore expressing grave concern over the extent of the proposed further reduction of Ceylon's sterling balances

[Caine minuted Rees-Williams on this tel: 'You should see this telegram before it goes. There is a good deal of past history which I can explain orally if you wish, but the present situation is quite simple. Ceylon has for the last year or so been running an adverse balance of trade and drawing on her sterling balances at a quite startling rate. Indeed, in proportion to the actual size of the balances, Ceylon has drawn them down a great deal more rapidly than any other overseas country. The Treasury feel that this cannot be allowed to continue either in our own interests or (and here we cannot but agree with them) in Ceylon's own interests as the country is headed straight for bankruptcy.[1] The position has been repeatedly brought to the notice of the Ceylon Government by telegram and by discussion, e.g. with Sir Oliver Goonetilleke, formerly financial secretary and now Minister for Home Affairs, during visits to London, but so far no real steps have been taken towards redressing the situation.[2] The present admittedly stiff telegram is intended to shock them into doing something. It implies a threat to block the remaining balances, which is a serious step to take towards a member of the Commonwealth but I am afraid it is a necessary threat in the circumstances. The suggested Private and Personal telegram is intended to make clear that we are not now speaking as the Colonial Office controlling the affairs of the Colony, but as bankers for the sterling area. The same line has, of course, been taken with such countries as Egypt and Iraq' (CO 537/1994, minute, 5 Nov 1947).]

Your telegram No. 31.

Sterling Balances.

His Majesty's Government have examined import/export forecast and are gravely concerned with extent of proposed further reduction of sterling balances. From information available here, it appears that Ceylon's balances (including Commercial Banking funds and holdings of Dominion and Colonial Securities) have declined from £73,200,000 at 31st December, 1946 to £48,300,000 at 30th September, 1947. In particular, during this period currency reserve has fallen from £22,300,000 to £19,600,000 and Government funds not allocated to sinking funds or other specific purposes from £20,400,000 to £1,200,000.

2.   It had been hoped that import restrictions outlined in your telegram No. 1124 would greatly curtail drawings on Ceylon's reserves. Your forecast, however, contemplates further large scale withdrawals on sterling balances, and seriousness of adverse balance of payments positions is emphasised by your telegram No. 45.

3.   I must most earnestly suggest that further drastic steps should be taken to rectify balance of payments position, as continuance of present trend cannot fail to have serious effect on Ceylon's stability.

4.   As you will be aware the economic crisis has rendered it necessary for His Majesty's Government to place limitations on the withdrawals of sterling held here by other countries. In pursuance of this policy and on the basis of the information at present available it is the view of His Majesty's Government that Ceylon's sterling

---

[1] For the view of the Treasury, see the letter from E Rowe-Dutton (third secretary) to Caine, 27 Oct 1947, which declared: 'The fact is that Ceylon is just about broke, and must be made to realise it' (CO 537/1994, no 63).

[2] Goonetilleke attributed Ceylon's heavy deficit on current account to high prices for food imports coupled with the fall in the return from Ceylon rubber (*ibid*, minute by J B Williams, assistant secretary, head of CO Finance Dept, 16 July 1947).

balances should not (repeat not) be reduced from the present total by more than £8 million sterling between now and 30th June, 1948; an amount very considerably less than that suggested in your telegram under reference. His Majesty's Government are prepared to discuss the whole position with a fully authorised representative of your Government, and at an early date if you should so desire. But in the absence of fuller details His Majesty's Government consider that withdrawals of £8 million should be regarded as an effective limit.

5. Regarding your paragraph 4, I would refer to Colonel Stanley's confidential despatch No. 33 of 31st January, 1945, which elaborated reasons against any appreciable investment in local funds of currency reserves. Reasons suggested are perhaps even more relevant today in view of adverse balance of payments. Local investment of currency funds weakens external backing of currency and basis of public confidence. It would, I consider, be a most serious step in present circumstances. Similar considerations of public confidence apply also to Savings Bank funds investment.

# 436 PREM 8/726                                          11 Nov 1947

## 'Proposals for conferring on Ceylon fully responsible status within the British Commonwealth of Nations': text of white paper (Cmd 7257). *Appendices*: I–III

*Constitutional development in Ceylon*

1. In a statement in Parliament on the 18th June, 1947, it was indicated that when Agreements on a number of subjects had been concluded on terms satisfactory to His Majesty's Government in the United Kingdom and the Ceylon Government, steps would be taken to amend the Constitution so as to confer upon Ceylon fully responsible status within the British Commonwealth of Nations.

2. Agreements (of which the texts appear in Appendices I, II and III of this paper) have now been concluded on the following matters of mutual concern:—

(a) Defence;
(b) External Affairs;
(c) Certain matters affecting Public Officers.

3. The steps necessary to confer upon Ceylon the new status mentioned above are:—

(a) the enactment of an Act of Parliament on the lines of the Bill the text of which has now been published; and
(b) the amendment of the Ceylon (Constitution) Order in Council, 1946, so as to bring it into a form suitable for a fully self-governing member of the British Commonwealth.

4. The principal alterations proposed in the Order in Council are as follows:—

(a) in place of the Governor, there will be a Governor-General who, in the exercise of his powers and functions, will, generally speaking, act in accordance with the constitutional conventions applicable to the exercise of similar powers and functions in the United Kingdom by His Majesty;

(b) the powers reserved to His Majesty to make laws for Ceylon in matters relating to Defence and External Affairs, and to amend and revoke the Order in Council, will be abolished;

(c) the provisions for the reservation of bills for His Majesty's pleasure will be revoked.

## Appendix I to 436: United Kingdom–Ceylon defence agreement

Whereas Ceylon has reached the stage in constitutional development at which she is ready to assume the status of a fully responsible member of the British Commonwealth of Nations, in no way subordinate in any aspect of domestic or external affairs, freely associated and united by common allegiance to the Crown;

And whereas it is in the mutual interest of Ceylon and the United Kingdom of Great Britain and Northern Ireland that the necessary measures should be taken for the effectual protection and defence of the territories of both and that the necessary facilities should be afforded for this purpose;

Therefore the Government of the United Kingdom and the Government of Ceylon have agreed as follows:—

(1) The Government of the United Kingdom and the Government of Ceylon will give to each other such military assistance for the security of their territories, for defence against external aggression and for the protection of essential communications as it may be in their mutual interest to provide. The Government of the United Kingdom may base such naval and air forces and maintain such land forces in Ceylon as may be required for these purposes, and as may be mutually agreed.

(2) The Government of Ceylon will grant to the Government of the United Kingdom all the necessary facilities for the objects mentioned in Article 1 as may be mutually agreed. These facilities will include the use of naval and air bases and ports and military establishments and the use of telecommunications facilities, and the right of service courts and authorities to exercise such control and jurisdiction over members of the said Forces as they exercise at present.

(3) The Government of the United Kingdom will furnish the Government of Ceylon with such military assistance as may from time to time be required towards the training and development of Ceylonese armed forces.

(4) The two Governments will establish such administrative machinery as they may agree to be desirable for the purpose of co-operation in regard to defence matters, and to co-ordinate and determine the defence requirements of both Governments.

(5) This Agreement will take effect on the day when the constitutional measures necessary for conferring on Ceylon fully responsible status within the British Commonwealth of Nations shall come into force.

Done in duplicate, at Colombo, this 11th day of November, 1947.

Signed on behalf of the Government of the United Kingdom of Great Britain and Northern Ireland.

HENRY MOORE

Signed on behalf of the Government of Ceylon.

D.S. SENANAYAKE

## Appendix II to 436: United Kingdom–Ceylon external affairs agreement

Whereas Ceylon has reached the stage in constitutional development at which she is ready to assume the status of a fully responsible member of the British Commonwealth of Nations, in no way subordinate in any aspect of domestic or external affairs, freely associated and united by common allegiance to the Crown;

And whereas the Government of the United Kingdom of Great Britain and Northern Ireland and the Government of Ceylon are desirous of entering into an agreement to provide for certain matters relating to external affairs;

Therefore the Government of the United Kingdom and the Government of Ceylon have agreed as follows:—

(1) The Government of Ceylon declares the readiness of Ceylon to adopt and follow the resolutions of past Imperial Conferences.

(2) In regard to external affairs generally, and in particular to the communication of information and consultation, the Government of the United Kingdom will, in relation to Ceylon observe the principles and practice now observed by the Members of the Commonwealth, and the Ceylon Government will for its part observe these same principles and practice.

(3) The Ceylon Government will be represented in London by a High Commissioner for Ceylon, and the Government of the United Kingdom will be represented in Colombo by a High Commissioner for the United Kingdom.

(4) If the Government of Ceylon so requests, the Government of the United Kingdom will communicate to the Governments of the foreign countries with which Ceylon wishes to exchange diplomatic representatives proposals for such exchange. In any foreign country where Ceylon has no diplomatic representative the Government of the United Kingdom will, if so requested by the Government of Ceylon, arrange for its representatives to act on behalf of Ceylon.

(5) The Government of the United Kingdon will lend its full support to any application by Ceylon for membership of the United Nations, or of any specialised international agency as described in Article 57 of the United Nations Charter.

(6) All obligations and responsibilities heretofore devolving on the Government of the United Kingdom which arise from any valid international instrument shall henceforth insofar as such instrument may be held to have application to Ceylon devolve upon the Government of Ceylon. The reciprocal rights and benefits heretofore enjoyed by the Government of the United Kingdom in virtue of the application of any such international instrument to Ceylon shall henceforth be enjoyed by the Government of Ceylon.

(7) This Agreement will take effect on the day when the constitutional measures necessary for conferring on Ceylon fully responsible status within the British Commonwealth of Nations shall come into force.

Done in duplicate, at Colombo, this 11th day of November, 1947.

Signed on behalf of the Government of the United Kingdom of Great Britain and Northern Ireland.

HENRY MOORE

Signed on behalf of the Government of Ceylon.

D.S. SENANAYAKE

## Appendix III to 436: United Kingdom–Ceylon public officers agreement

The Government of the United Kingdom of Great Britain and Northern Ireland and the Government of Ceylon have agreed as follows:—

(1) In this Agreement:—

"officer" means a person holding office in the public service of Ceylon immediately before the appointed day, being an officer—

(a) who at any time before the 17th day of July, 1928, was appointed or selected for appointment to an office, appointment to which was subject to the approval of a Secretary of State, or who, before that day, had entered into an agreement with the Crown Agents for the Colonies to serve in any public office for a specified period; or

(b) who on or after the 17th day of July, 1928, has been or is appointed or selected for appointment (otherwise than on agreement for a specific period) to an office, appointment to which is subject to the approval of a Secretary of State; or

(c) who, on or after the 17th day of July, 1928, has entered or enters into an agreement with the Crown Agents for the Colonies to serve for a specific period in an office, appointment to which is not subject to the approval of a Secretary of State, and who, on the appointed day, either has been confirmed in a permanent and pensionable office or is a European member of the Police Force;

"the appointed day" means the day when the constitutional measures necessary for conferring on Ceylon fully responsible status within the British Commonwealth of Nations shall come into force;

"pension" includes a gratuity and other like allowance.

(2) An officer who continues on and after the appointed day to serve in Ceylon shall be entitled to receive from the Government of Ceylon the same conditions of service as respects remuneration, leave and pension, and the same rights as respects disciplinary matters or, as the case may be, as respects the tenure of office, or rights as similar thereto as changed circumstances may permit, as he was entitled to immediately before the appointed day, and he shall be entitled to leave passages in accordance with the practice now followed; but he shall not be entitled to exemption from any general revision of salaries which the Government of Ceylon may find it necessary to make.

(3) Any officer who does not wish to continue to serve in Ceylon, being an officer described in paragraph (a) of the definition of "officer" in Clause 1, may retire from the service at any time; and in any other case may retire from the service within two years of the appointed day. On such retirement he shall be entitled to receive from the Government of Ceylon a compensatory pension in accordance with the special regulations made under Section 88 of the Ceylon (State Council) Order in Council, 1931, in force on the appointed day; but an officer who leaves the Ceylon service on transfer to the Public Service in any colony, protectorate or mandated or trust territory shall not be entitled to receive such a pension.

(4) Pensions which have been or may be granted to any persons who have been, and have ceased to be, in the public service of Ceylon at any time before the appointed day, or to the widows, children or dependants of such persons, shall be

paid in accordance with the law under which they were granted, or if granted after that day, in accordance with the law in force on that day, or in either case in accordance with any law made thereafter which is not less favourable.

(5) The Government of Ceylon will comply with any reasonable request which may at any time be made by the Government of the United Kingdom for the release of a public officer for employment in the public service elsewhere.

(6) This agreement will take effect on the appointed day.

Done in duplicate, at Colombo, this 11th day of November, 1947.

Signed on behalf of the Government of the United Kingdom of Great Britain and Northern Ireland.

HENRY MOORE

Signed on behalf of the Government of Ceylon.

D.S. SENANAYAKE

# 437   CO 537/2224                                      19 Nov 1947

## 'External Affairs': editorial comment from the *Times of Ceylon* on the Ceylon Independence Bill

The article[1] published on this page analyses in detail the implications of the Ceylon Independence Bill. In most countries, certainly those which claim to be democratic, so vital a measure would be presented to the public in a manner which would enable the country's legislature to study it carefully and for public opinion equally to subject it to the most searching scrutiny. Any attempt to hustle the Government and its works would rightly be regarded with suspicion. Yet these are precisely the tactics which the Island's Cabinet are adopting. Not only are the Government attempting to hustle public opinion, but they are trying to stampede the country's legislature into accepting something on their own valuation.

It would seem that a mood of careless rapture seized Ceylon's Government when it appended its signature to the Heads of Agreement. Yesterday we pointed out certain deficiencies in the Defence Agreement. The Agreement relating to External Affairs, although not so vital, is worthy of close study. The writer of the article on this page draws attention to clause 2 which stipulates that in regard to External Affairs generally and in particular to communication of information and consultation, Ceylon will follow the principles and practice *now* observed by the members of the Commonwealth. It is possible, as the writer suggests, that the limitation imposed by the word 'now' may embarrass future Ceylon–British relationships if by convention or agreement the present forms of communication and consultation are altered. An even more intriguing clause is clause 1, whereby the Government of Ceylon "declares the readiness of Ceylon to adopt and follow the resolutions of past Imperial Conferences." If clause 2 is unnecessarily restrictive, clause 1 is needlessly expansive. There is no constitutional enactment which makes it imperative for a Dominion to adopt and follow the resolutions of any Imperial Conference, and why the Ceylon

---

[1] The reference is to an article entitled 'Secret pacts do not give Ceylon freedom', by S.N. It was known at the time that the initials stood for S Nadesan who had just been elected to the Senate. Nadesan was a Tamil lawyer with ties to the Marxist left. See also 438.

to suggest that His Majesty was not King of Ceylon. He is, however, likely to be subjected to some pressure on the matter and before coming to a decision would like to know if the Clerk of Parliaments or other appropriate authority considers it would be undesirable on constitutional grounds, regard being had to Dominion usage elsewhere.

5. I think the introduction of the throne has really been suggested as a piece of added pagentry but Senanayake himself appreciates that its presence may be resented by the Tamils and he would of course have to satisfy himself as to this should the proposal be regarded as otherwise unobjectionable.

**442** CO 537/1994, no 74                                                      20 Dec 1947
[Sterling balances]: inward telegram (reply) no 280 from Sir H Moore to Mr Creech Jones explaining that the Ceylon government cannot accept the proposed limit on sterling withdrawals

Your confidential telegram No. 102.[1]
Sterling Balances.
Your paragraph 1. Request detailed statement of items comprising balance as at 31st December, 1946 and 1947. Computation made on data available locally does not agree with amount mentioned.

2. Your paragraphs 2 and 3. Increased import duties introduced 2nd December, 1947, with 1947–48 Budget. Comparative statements showing previous and new duties are being despatched by air mail. New duties not only discriminate severely against semi-essentials and luxuries, rate on several items being so high as to be virtually prohibitive, but also affect especially inessential items imported from dollar and other hard currency areas, thereby discriminating indirectly against imports from these areas.

Difficult to estimate at this stage to what extent new duties would check imports, but have reason to believe, in light of public trade reactions to duty increase, that reduction of imports would be larger than originally anticipated.

3. Your paragraph 4. Ceylon Government regret cannot agree limit £8,000,000 proposed to be imposed on sterling withdrawals up to 30th June, 1948. Am agreeable hold discussions earliest possible but, in view of heavy Parliamentary business connected with the Budget and assumption shortly of Dominion status, not possible to send delegation before first week in March, 1948. Presume discussions will not last more than fortnight.

4. Your paragraph 5. Observation noted. Government of Ceylon contemplates establishing shortly reserve bank and so providing organised currency and banking system. Would observe that operation of the kind proposed are not different from these ordinarily undertaken by other countries where reserve banks have established organised currency and banking systems.

---
[1] See 435.

**443**   DO 35/3268, no 1                                     21 Jan 1948

## [Maldives]: letter from Mr Gordon Walker to Mr Creech Jones on administrative arrangements for the Maldive Islands

[The Maldive Islands had long enjoyed the protection of the British Crown, and this was formally recorded in an exchange of letters between the sultan and the governor of Ceylon in Dec 1887. There was no British representation in the islands themselves and communication was maintained through a Maldivian representative in Ceylon. At the end of 1947, Creech Jones had written to the CRO suggesting that, in view of the importance of the UK's defence interests and the status of the islands as a protected state, the CO should continue in its responsibility for matters relating to the Maldives, with the new UK high commissioner in Ceylon serving as the channel of correspondence and acting as the agent for the CO in this matter. He added that a new treaty which it was hoped to negotiate with the sultan to secure UK defence requirements would leave unchanged the arrangement whereby the British government did not concern itself with the internal affairs of the islands (DO 35/3268, no 2, Creech Jones to Mr P Noel-Baker (S of S for Commonwealth relations, 1947–1950), 30 Dec 1947). For the reasons explained in the letter reproduced here, Gordon Walker (parliamentary under-secretary of state for Commonwealth relations, 1947–1950) argued that it would be better for the CRO to assume responsibility. At first the CO did not accept these arguments. Creech Jones emphasised that, from the political standpoint, it was 'important to avoid the possibility of any suggestion being made, and, still more, any risk of it actually happening, that the needs of the less important territory, the Maldive Islands, were subordinated to the needs of the more important territory, Ceylon' (*ibid*, no 6, Creech Jones to Gordon Walker, 27 Jan 1948). The issue was finally resolved at a meeting in Colombo in Feb 1948 between Moore, as governor-general of Ceylon, Lord Listowel, minister of state at the CO and Sir Walter Hankinson, the newly arrived UK high commissioner to Ceylon. Moore and Hankinson indicated their preference for the CRO assuming responsibility. Listowel maintained that if at any time an emergency arose and it became necessary to administer the Maldives in any way, the CO were better equipped to undertake such administration. It was finally agreed to recommend that responsibility for Maldivian affairs should be transferred to the CRO on the understanding that it would be re-transferred to the CO if at any time an emergency occurred which necessitated the administration of the islands by HMG. It was also agreed that local responsibility for Maldivian affairs should be transferred from the governor-general to the high commissioner as soon as possible (*ibid*, no 18, record of meeting, 17 Feb 1948). These recommendations were accepted and a new agreement was signed with the sultan in Apr 1948. This provided that the islands should remain under the protection of the Crown, that their external affairs should be conducted by, or in accordance with the advice of, the British government, that the latter should refrain from any interference in the affairs of the islands, and that the sultan should afford such facilities to British forces as were necessary for the defence of the islands or of the Commonwealth.]

In Noel-Baker's absence at New York I am answering your letter to him of 30th December about the Maldive Islands. I am sorry for the delay, but it was necessary for us to obtain some information about the Islands. I have now discussed the matter with my advisers and we have had the advantage of conferring with Mr. Sidebotham of your Department who has explained the position to us fully.

Since it will no longer be possible for the Governor (Governor-General) of Ceylon to act as agent for His Majesty's Government in the United Kingdom in relation to the Maldives, and as Ceylon will obviously, as hitherto, be the most convenient channel of correspondence, we are agreeable to let our High Commissioner in Ceylon take this function over. We think, however, that before this is finally settled, Sir Henry Moore should be asked to explain the position to Sir Walter Hankinson who is due to arrive at Colombo any day now and make sure that he sees no objection. Could this be done without delay?

But if this is arranged, we do feel somewhat strongly that the logical and sensible arrangement would be for the Commonwealth Relations Office instead of the Colonial Office to be responsible in future for our relations with the Maldives. It is always unsatisfactory when an officer is responsible to two Departments, and we are anxious to avoid this in the case of our High Commissioner at Colombo. We understand that there is (according to the Agreement of 1887) no question of any *administration* of the Maldives, which might be regarded more as a function of the Colonial Office than of our Department. On the other hand, our defence requirements in the Maldives which, as you say, are an important current question at present, are the type of question with which the Commonwealth Relations Office is already dealing (or will shortly be dealing) in relation to Ceylon, India and Pakistan, and there are obvious advantages in dealing with the area as a whole. Finally, trade and other questions between the Maldives and Ceylon are, we understand, apt to arise, and the Commonwealth Relations Office would be responsible for any approach to Ceylon. Altogether, it seems to us that there is every practical reason for correlating this business under the Commonwealth Relations Office, and we hope that, if we agree to the United Kingdom High Commissioner at Colombo being the United Kingdom Government's agent, you will acquiesce in our having the ultimate responsibility, though we shall, of course, always be ready to avail ourselves of the advice and experience of the Colonial Office in the matter.

## 444   CO 537/1994, no 79                                    26 Jan 1948
## 'Ceylon sterling balances': briefing memorandum by CO Finance Department for Mr Gordon Walker explaining the current position

1. The sterling balances of Ceylon have declined rapidly during the past two years. The figures are as follows:—

30th June, 1946   –   £78.9 million
30th June, 1947   –   £55.1 million
30th Sept, 1947   –   £49.4 million
31st Dec, 1947    –   £50.1 million

2. When the Financial Secretary to the Government of Ceylon came to London last summer, it was put to him that this rate of drawing was excessive and called for drastic tightening of Ceylon's import controls. He returned to Ceylon with the intention of making further cuts in imports and of overhauling Ceylon's exchange control machinery.

3. In September we realised that the drain on the balances was continuing steadily and telegraphed urgently to Ceylon for forecasts of the import and export position during the next nine months. At the same time we asked the Governor privately whether he thought that the Government of Ceylon would be willing to send a delegation to London to negotiate an agreement providing for a limitation of further drawings on the sterling balances. The Governor replied that he saw no prospect of anybody being available for this purpose before Christmas.

4. Meanwhile, the import and export forecasts became available and they revealed that during the nine months ending in June, 1948, Ceylon would incur an overall

deficit in her balance of overseas payments of some £14 million this being the result of a dollar deficit of £16 million (largely on account of food) offset by a small surplus in other directions. It was expected that under the present system of international food allocations all of the grain import requirements of Ceylon would have to come from dollar sources.

5.    This, by itself was a serious outlook, but it was made graver by the intimation we received from Ceylon that the Government were making plans to amend the currency law so as to replace up to half of the sterling backing with Ceylon rupee securities, thus releasing additional sterling for the purchase of capital goods. We accordingly decided to bring matters to a head by sending a telegram[1] to Ceylon saying that we could not contemplate a continued drawing down of sterling balances at this rate; that the amount which we would feel able to release for Ceylon's current requirements up to the middle of 1948 would be not more than £8 million; and that we wished to discuss the whole matter in London with representatives of the Ceylon Government at the earliest possible opportunity. After a silence of six weeks the Ceylon Government have replied that they could not agree to our suggestion and that there would be no opportunity for discussion until early March.[2]

6.    Since the end of September, Ceylon's sterling balances have not further decreased, (they had already exhausted their "disposable funds") and although this altered trend may be partly seasonal our immediate anxieties have been somewhat allayed. We are at the present moment considering whether to accept the Ceylon Government's suggestion that negotiations should be deferred until March. In the meantime, if the subject is referred to in discussion, it would be desirable to let it be known that we are very disquieted at the extent to which Ceylon's prospective adverse balance of payments seems likely to lead to a further drain upon her sterling reserves; that in our own exceedingly difficult position we cannot possibly afford this continued drain, which involves both a loss of dollars and the sending of "unrequited exports" to Ceylon; and that we are anxious for further discussions at the earliest possible date.

7.    In this context, it would be very desirable to remind Ministers and officials that since the Sterling Area Conference held in London last September (at which Ceylon was directly represented), all the Governments of the Sterling Area have been asked to co-operate in adopting measures for the protection of the monetary reserves of the Sterling Area during the critical period ahead. We hope that Ceylon will also co-operate in this and not seek to delay further discussion with us on their external financial position during the coming year, the development of which bears closely upon the fortunes of the Sterling Area as a whole.[3]

---

[1] See 435.                                                                    [2] See 442.

[3] Referring to Ceylon's tel of 20 Dec, the CO also wrote to the Treasury in Jan 1948 explaining that so long as Ceylon did not significantly run down her balances 'we are rather inclined to lie low'. Complete figures for 31 Dec 1947 were not yet available and therefore no information existed about commercial banking funds at that date. However, from preliminary figures received from the Crown Agents, it seemed that Ceylon's disposable funds had increased by about £1.6 million since Nov. During that month, total balances had increased by £0.9 million. The CO's letter also explained that the setting up of a Reserve Bank was under consideration in Ceylon. (The first speech from the throne of the new government in Sept 1947 promised that the government intended to seek expert advice with regard to changes in the country's financial structure which might be necessitated by the transition from a colonial to a free economy. This item in the speech had been contributed by J R Jayewardene and it was known that he was intent on establishing a Reserve or Central Bank). The CO reminded the Treasury that when this had been discussed

with Goonetilleke in June 1947 he had agreed with UK officials that a Reserve Bank would prove far too expensive. More would be heard of this during discussions on sterling balances but in view of the constitutional position the CO felt that it would be 'useless and undesirable to comment at this stage'. Regarding the discrepancy in figures to which the tel from Ceylon referred, Goonetilleke had been asked in June both orally and by letter, for his figures, but without result. According to the CO, the discrepancy might be explained by the difference between nominal and market values of investments (CO 537/1994, no 78, letter to E Rowe-Dutton, 23 Jan 1948).

# **445** DO 35/2402                                                              Mar 1948
## 'Ceylon defence contribution': War Office memorandum

*Pre-war*

1. Before the 1939–45 war the cost of the Imperial garrison fell on Army funds, but the colony paid an annual contribution equal to three-quarters of the cost of the garrison (or 9½% of the assessable revenue of the colony, whichever was the less) and was responsible for capital expenditure on military works and lands outside Trincomalee. The Ceylon Defence Force, a locally raised unit, was the complete responsibility of the Colonial Government.

*During the war*

2. These arrangements continued after the outbreak of war, and as the threat of Japanese invasion developed the C.D.F. was mobilised and the small regular garrison reinforced by other Imperial forces. Under arrangements laid down in the local defence scheme, pay and accounting services for the C.D.F. were taken over by the Command Paymaster, subject to financial adjustment, but as the war progressed, the setting up of military establishments unconnected with the defence of the island and the despatch of considerable reinforcements made it impossible to calculate the cost of the garrison for the purpose of fixing the military contribution, and added to the difficulties of carrying out adjustments for the C.D.F. It was ultimately agreed that the W.O. should assume complete financial responsibility for the C.D.F. with effect from 1st October, 1941, in return for an annual contribution of Rs 27,000,000 (£2,025,000) (a contribution of Rs 3,000,000 (£225,000) was also made to the Admiralty in respect of the Ceylon R.N.V.R.). The previous contribution had more recently (on the basis of three-quarters of the cost of the Imperial garrison) been in the neighbourhood of £200,000 to £230,000, but in addition Ceylon had then paid the full cost of the C.D.F.

*From V.J. Day to 30th September, 1946*

3. This arrangement continued to V.J. Day, from which date (it was subsequently agreed) the undertaking to pay the higher rate of contribution ceased to have effect, but the Ceylon Government were asked, nevertheless, to consider continued payment at the existing (higher) rate pending decisions as to the post war composition and strength of the garrison in Ceylon. The Ceylon Government indicated that they were prepared to contribute with effect from 15th August, 1945, only at the rate of Rs 5,000,000 (£375,000) of which the Army share was Rs 4,500,000 (£337,500). Payment of the Army share has continued at that rate up to and including 31st December, 1947, but it is understood that the naval contribution of Rs 500,000 ceased on 1st April, 1946, when the Ceylon R.N.V.R. reverted to the control of the colony.

4.  Meantime, discussions with the Colonial Office and the colony continued. The basis of the War Office case was that, the wartime arrangement having been declared at an end as from 15th August, 1945 (although the C.D.F. remained an Army responsibility), it was necessary to review the position in the light of pre-war practice so as to provide a reasonable basis for the defence contribution during the interim period until the shape and size of the post war garrison, and the basis of colonial contributions for the future, were decided. In this connection it was established at the end of 1945 that 9½% of the colony's assessable revenue for the Colonial year October 1945 to September 1946 would be approximately Rs 28,000,000 (£2,100,000) whereas the average strength of forces maintained, and to be maintained, in Ceylon during the same period (excluding the C.D.F.) was such that three-quarters of their cost would far exceed that figure. It was recognised, however, that there would be practical difficulties in the way of securing a higher rate of contribution than that which obtained during the war, but it was felt that any smaller figure would not be equitable to the Department or the British taxpayer.

5.  The matter was discussed with Sir Oliver Goonetilleke on 14th February, 1946, when it emerged that (1) he erroneously assumed the War Office figure of Rs 27m to have been put forward as a bargaining figure, and that (2) the Rs 5m suggested by the Ceylon Ministers was similarly regarded by them and was not their considered view of an equitable contribution for the year in question. Even so, it was clear that there was little or no chance of the higher figure proving acceptable and that some compromise figure would have to be reached. To this end the War Office indicated that they would be prepared to accept a sum of Rs 20m (£1,500,000) for the colonial year 1945/46 without prejudice to subsequent years. The Colonial Office returned to the charge on the grounds that according to Sir Oliver Goonetilleke the maximum amount which could be expected was Rs 12m (£900,000) although the Colonial Office felt that something more substantial might be expected. Later, in a further effort to compromise, the War Office proposed a contribution of Rs 16,000,000 (£1,200,000).

6.  No definite reply to the War Office proposal for a contribution of Rs. 16,000,000 for the period from 1st October, 1945 to 30th September, 1946, has ever been received from the Colonial Office. It would follow that payment at the same rate should be made for the period from 15th August, 1945 to 30th September, 1945 and the War Office claim in respect of the whole period therefore stands at Rs 13,000,000 (£975,000), i.e. Rs 18,000,000 less the contribution already paid of Rs 5,000,000. The cost of the troops in Ceylon (including the C.D.F.) during the period was of the order of Rs 170,000,000 (i.e. £m13). A contribution of the size proposed by the War Office would, therefore, cover only 10% of the cost of the Forces in Ceylon, and it would yet enable the colony to enjoy a substantial saving in expenditure following the end of the war. Furthermore, this contribution would represent little more than half the amount payable under the pre-war formula of 9½% of assessable revenue.

*1st October, 1946 to 31st March, 1947*

7.  The War Office has put forward no specific proposals relating to the period from 1st October, 1946 to 31st March, 1947, in view of the failure to make any progress in respect of the earlier period. The cost of the troops in Ceylon during this period was of the order of £800,000. A contribution at the rate of Rs 16,000,000 a year (£600,000 in a half year) proposed for 1945 to 1946 would, therefore, be

consistent with the pre-war formula and could be regarded as acceptable. Rs 2¼ million have been paid, leaving Rs 5¾ million (£430,000) to be claimed on this basis.

*1st April, 1947 to 31st December, 1947*

8. In addition to their contribution at the rate of Rs 4½ million (£337,500) the Ceylon Government have recently agreed in principle to bear, with effect from 1st April, 1947, the cost of that part of the C.D.F. retained in being for internal security purposes (which has remained a charge on Army Votes), although this is understood to be subject to ratification by the Ceylon Parliament. Recoveries in respect of the period involved (1st April, 1947 to 31st October, 1947) are expected to be in the neighbourhood of £85,000. The Ceylon Defence Force was dis-embodied by 1st November, 1947, apart from a small number of personnel retained for Imperial purposes. From 1st April, 1947 to 31st December, 1947, the cost of troops in Ceylon has been some £600,000 (excluding expenditure relating to the recruitment of Ceylonese for employment in Malaya), towards which Ceylon will have contributed some £350,000, provided that they pay the amount due in respect of the Ceylon Defence Force. This is rather less than the pre-war basis, but can be regarded as reasonable, bearing in mind the fact that many of the troops in Ceylon perform functions not directly connected with the defence of the Island. It is therefore suggested that no further claim should be raised in respect of this period but that the delegation should be asked to confirm that the amount to be claimed in respect of the C.D.F. will be paid in addition to the general contribution.

**446**  CAB 129/26, CP(48)91                                    17 Mar 1948

**'Report on Ceylon': Cabinet memorandum by Mr Gordon Walker on the independence celebrations and the political situation in Ceylon**

[Gordon Walker (see 444, note 1) represented the UK government at the independence celebrations in Ceylon. In the absence of Mr Noel-Baker, secretary of state at the CRO who was in New York, he circulated this report to members of the Cabinet, explaining in a prefatory note that the practical questions touched upon were all receiving consideration inter-departmentally.]

*General*

1. Ceylon is settling down as a genuine Dominion. Present Ministers are extremely friendly and want to maintain and deepen the British connexion. They want, for instance, to preserve English as the official language in Parliament and courts. They do not want Ceylon to be a Republic: in looking for a name to describe themselves they are inclined to favour "Kingdom of Ceylon." Senanayake is in the genuine tradition of Dominion Prime Ministers: deeply committed to the British connexion.

2. The present Administration is firmly in the saddle and has, I think, been strengthened by the transfer of power. To quite an extent we can help the present Administration if we preserve the right approach to them. It is hardly too much to say that if we treat them strictly as a Dominion, they will behave very like a loyal colony: whereas if we treat them as a Colony we may end in driving them out of the Commonwealth. For some time the tone in which we conduct our various

negotiations will be extremely important. I think that all such negotiations should, therefore, be conducted by our High Commissioner or through the Commonwealth Relations Office.

*The celebrations*

3. Two somewhat contradictory themes ran through the celebrations. First, there was real rejoicing at independence peacefully won in co-operation with Britain. (This revealed itself in the official flying of the Union Jack side by side with the Lion Flag: the unofficial flying of quite a number of Union Jacks; the emphasis on royalty in the celebrations; the good will of the crowds towards the Duke; passages in the Prime Minister's speeches.) Simultaneously the other theme was developed that indepenence was the outcome of a struggle for liberty: there was even an undertone of talk about martyrs (evidence: the three versions of my broadcast published in the papers all left out the passage about Ceylon's independence being the mutual achievement of Ceylon and Britain; some young officials made remarks like "the only permanent benefit from the Duke's visit is that the roads have been improved"; fairly widespread criticism about the cost of the celebrations—6 lakhs of rupees).

4. The celebrations put royalty and the Duke right in the centre, and opposition to the Royal visit was limited. One man in the crowd produced a placard "Go back Gloucester": one village in the north flew black flags: a few slogans were stencilled on walls: "Real, not fake, independence." I talked with all the opposition leaders and all of them said they were content to boycott the celebrations and did not want to try and disorganise them or protest against them. The Communist M.P.s and the M.P.s of the two Trotskyite Parties stayed away from the opening of Parliament but took up the seats allotted to them for their friends and relatives.

*Defence*

5. Of the two contradictory themes the one of loyalty and rejoicing was far the more emphatic and dominant. The friendship of Ceylon for Britain, which was always strong, became stronger after 4th February. There is, however, a subdued note of doubt that is still to be overcome. It seemed to me that the root cause of this is the military agreement that was made a condition precedent of Dominion status. Why, it is asked by the opposition, was this insisted upon if it does not diminish independence? And Ministers do not find this easy to answer.

Our defence relations with Ceylon will depend upon mutual friendship and confidence: this cannot be written into a document and certainly cannot be forced out of Ceylon as the result of a document. On balance the Prime Minister favours as early talks on defence as possible. His motives are:—

(a) Doubt whether the existing Defence Agreement, which was agreed to by Ceylon before its independence, may not prejudice Ceylon's entry into the United Nations Organisation; and

(b) His desire to get a firm defence agreement that will allay his fears about excessive Indian influence in the affairs and future of Ceylon.

It was not my intention to bring up this subject but it was immediately raised on their side. The chief points are:—

(a) Ceylon will insist on the formal preservation and assertion of its sovereignty and would prefer unpublished agreements and assurances to a Formal Treaty.

(b)  Ceylon is eager to get an extremely close military tie-up with us and will in fact give us all we want, if the forms of sovereignty are preserved.

(c)  We may have some bargaining to do about rent, &c., for ground we use: but I do not think they will try and pinch us too far.

(d)  They are not prepared to spend very much themselves on their own defence: and we may need to push them in this matter. They want an independent force of their own but are thinking of a force only 1,000 strong.

(e)  They want us to train Ceylonese in our military bases and to raise Ceylon units of the Imperial forces which can serve outside Ceylon. They want the Pioneer Corps in Malaya to be continued.

I am sure we can get all we want in the way of facilities for ourselves if we make the right approach. Everything could be spoiled if we talked to Ceylon as if it were a colony or dependency or as if we had rights in its territory. Any defence agreement we may make will depend upon the good will of the Government and people of Ceylon: we must assume this and can count on it. We must not attempt to substitute for it cast-iron concessions or extra-territorial rights.

Confidential defence talks should, I am sure, be conducted very soon and by our High Commissioner to whom the military should act as expert advisers.

## Admission to the United Nations Organisation

6.  The successful entry of Ceylon into the United Nations Organisation is of paramount importance, and is largely bound up with the Defence Agreement. The Prime Minister impressed this on me several times. If Ceylon fails and Burma succeeds in getting into the United Nations Organisation the present Government might be seriously shaken and might even be compelled, with the utmost reluctance, to leave the Commonwealth. Ceylon Ministers are alarmed about Russia's possible attitude and use of the Veto.

7.  The Ceylon Government is eager for us to give all possible advice and help to them about the best procedure for applying for membership of the United Nations. It will ease their minds if we can do this as fully, quickly and continuously, as possible.[1]

---

[1] In anticipation that Russia would use its veto to oppose Ceylon's application for UN membership—the Russian argument being that the defence agreement with the UK indicated that Ceylon was not really independent—a revision of the defence agreement was discussed with Goonetilleke in London in Apr 1948. A new defence declaration was drawn up, explicitly stating that it had been freely negotiated between the two countries and naming the places and purposes for which defence facilities had been granted to the UK. The UK assumed that the new declaration would be agreed and published before Ceylon applied for UN membership but in the event the Ceylon government did not consult the UK before it made its application to the secretary-general. When asked by the UK what it now intended to do about the defence declaration, the Ceylon government replied that it preferred to put it to one side for the present, first because a study of the draft could not be completed within the short time available, and secondly because the new declaration would give rise to discussion in the Ceylon parliament which would be more prejudicial than advantageous to the UN application. In Aug 1948, the CRO forecast that if Ceylon did not succeed in its application, the mainly communist opposition in the country would argue that responsibility rested with the defence agreement and membership of the Commonwealth. Burma had by this time succeeded in gaining admission to the UN. Given that Burma had left the Commonwealth, the CRO anticipated that there might be pressure on Ceylon to follow suit (PREM 8/725, CP(48)204, memo on Ceylon by Noel-Baker, 17 Aug 1948). With the UK and its western allies using the veto to block the admission of Outer Mongolia and Albania to the UN on the grounds that they were Soviet satellites, Russia used its veto

*India*

8.  Relations with India play a leading part in Ceylon's policy. The Prime Minister told me that he regarded the Indian problem as one of the two dangers facing Ceylon (the other is the Left opposition).

In part Ceylon fears Indian pressure and for this reason wants a close military tie-up with us. They want to be treated on their merits and do not wish to come too closely within the Indian orbit.

In part Ceylon fears economic and social pressure by Tamil immigration. This underlies the problem of Ceylon citizenship. India wants all the immigrant Tamils from Madras to be full Ceylon citizens: there are some 800,000 of them and they are liable to increase. Ceylon wants to limit the number of these Tamil citizens to about 400,000.

Senanayake and Nehru have had conversations on this. They have agreed "in principle" but in fact left all the real issues to be settled as "details". Senanayake has the impression that he and Nehru are pretty close in their ideas. I very much doubt it and I think that when Ceylon publishes its proposals there may be quite sharp tension with India. Senanayake feels strongly on this matter.

*The Opposition*

9.  The opposition in Ceylon consists of two quite distinct sections.

One is the Tamil Congress, which represents the resident Tamils (not to be confused with the immigrant Tamils described above) and is strong in the north of the island. It is not against Senanayake on social or economic issues, but is against him as a Sinhalese. I was told that there are good chances that the Tamil Congress will join the Government, getting two seats in the Cabinet.

The other section of the opposition consists of three Marxist parties or Leftists as they are commonly called.

There is a Communist party with 3 seats (out of 95) and two Trotskyite parties (one with 10 seats, one with 5). All are led by ex-officers of the Oxford or Cambridge Union. I talked with the leaders of these parties. The differences between them are very subtle and theoretical. The Communist party of course follows Russia over the Marshall Plan, but its detailed local policy is really indistinguishable from that of the two Trotsky parties:—they speak for the poor against the rich; demand land reforms; put forward constant claims for wage increases; and stand for "genuine" independence. The only difference that I could detect between the two Trotsky parties (apart

---

to block the admission of Ceylon. The Ceylon government was much concerned and Senanayake raised the issue at the meeting of Commonwealth prime ministers in Oct 1948. He wanted from the meeting (a) a statement to the effect that Ceylon really was independent (this was forthcoming), and (b) Commonwealth support for an Argentine proposal that new countries would be admitted if they received seven supporting votes in the Security Council (this was rejected). Cabinet discussed the issue again at the end of Nov 1948, specifically in response (a) to Gordon Walker's views that because Britain's defence interests were at stake, the UK should reconsider its policy on UN admissions, and (b) to Goonetilleke's claim that he had been told by Ernest Bevin, the foreign secretary, that the UK would trade Ceylon's admission for that of Outer Mongolia and Albania. The FO denied that Bevin had made such a remark and the Cabinet refused to reconsider policy on UN admissions on the grounds that any concession would be incompatible with the general principles established in May 1948 by the International Court of Justice on conditions for UN membership (*ibid*, CM 76(48)3, 25 Nov 1948). Ceylon was not admitted to the UN until 1955 when the Soviet veto was finally withdrawn. Two years later the bases acquired by the UK under the 1948 agreement were transferred back to the government of Ceylon.

from acute personal differences) is that the smaller of the two accepts the lead of the Trotsky party in Madras, whilst the other refuses to. It seems probable that the two Trotsky parties will one day unite. The differences with the Communist party are of course unbridgeable and a serious source of weakness to the Left. There are a few Bikkhus or Buddhist priests associated with the Trotsky parties; but this is not an important factor.

10.   These Left parties do represent and reflect a serious social problem. They are a danger in the sense that if Ceylon comes a cropper it would take the form of very serious social upheaval; just as if India came a cropper it would reveal itself in communal anarchy. I do not think the Left parties are an imminent danger though they will continue for a considerable time, as the causes of the social discontent that has given rise to them are deep-rooted.

*Social and economic problems*

11.   Socially, Ceylon is a mixture of feudalism and Eighteenth Century landed aristocracy. There is relatively little caste and practically no communal tension. In the middle of the island, especially in the old kingdom of Kandy, something very close to feudalism has survived.

Apart from the Left leaders, every politician is an extremely rich landowner with local power and influence comparable to a Whig landlord in George III's time. They have much the same attitude towards politics. Public life is riddled with affable and open corruption, moral and otherwise.

These Whig landlords have honestly led a political campaign for independence but they have very little idea of social progress. They tend to be terrified by the Left opposition which they do not understand; they regard it as a monstrous and wicked violation of the natural order and, if it grew, would be tempted to suppress it. Their spontaneous reaction is to combat Marxism with Buddhism and they are spending a good deal on this propaganda. Buddhism (and the Catholicism in the coastal area north of Colombo) are indeed very powerful barriers to the advance of the parties of the Left. Nevertheless it is in just these areas that they have won their successes; they have some influence amongst the Tamil immigrants (who are however run by powerful and unscrupulous bosses of their own who are also money-lenders); they have made no impression at all on the resident Tamil population of the north.

Fairly elaborate programmes of social reform have been launched by the Government—especially in education, hospitals and the like. Indeed these schemes may well be beyond the economic resources of the island. Such measures will not however remove the real causes of social discontent. The standards of cleanliness, education and village housing are already considerably higher than in India; but social discontent is also more serious than in India.

The main cause of discontent is the fragmentation of the ownership of land which has gone to fantastic lengths. Eight people will have a share in one acre of paddy-field or in a handful of coconut trees. Three separate families will have the right to cultivate a given field in successive years. The result is either a reluctance to work the land at all because so many people have contingent claims upon the produce or feverish exploitation to get out as much as possible during the year of cultivation.

For this there is no remedy but to make more land available and to give it in compensation for loss of present rights in parcels of land. Under the stimulus of the Prime Minister considerable progress is being made in reducing jungle to paddy-field by digging irrigation canals (all this jungle was rich land a thousand or two thousand years ago). The work is held up by lack of bulldozers, scoops, etc. Half-a-dozen more would enable the work to be greatly speeded up. Colonisation, as it is called, of these new settlements is said to be very corruptly done; but the essential thing is that new families are being settled.

12.    Jungle-clearance, however, cannot do the trick fast enough. Some lands will have to be expropriated and resettled if the causes of social discontent are to be removed. Over this there is likely to be a sharp division in the Cabinet. The chief leader of a forward policy is Bandaranaike, commonly talked of as Senanayake's successor and another product of the Oxford Union. Himself a lawyer, he will find it hard to convince his land-owning colleagues. He talked to me about the possibility of resignation if he does not get his way.

13.    A further cause of social discontent is a certain amount of unemployment. The ultimate remedy can only be the development of some simple secondary industries. Some remedy might be found in a reduction of the Tamil immigrant population and this is one of the main motives behind Bandaranaike's extreme anti-Indian policy. The unemployment problem doubtless underlies the eagerness that we should raise Ceylon units of the Imperial Forces. If, as seems likely, there is not enough money both for large land reform and re-employment measures and for major social reforms Ceylon should give preference to the first. The removal of economic discontent is her most pressing problem.

14.    A great need in Ceylon is a genuine radical Labour Movement based on proper Trade Unions. Anything we could do to forward this would be in our interests. I put forward the suggestion that batches of workers might come from Ceylon to England to learn about modern Trade Unions and industrial practice. The idea was welcomed and any proposal we could make would be eagerly taken up.

15.    If no serious land reforms are undertaken the Left Parties will remain of some importance, though I doubt whether they will make electoral headway. The United National Party is beginning for the first time to take local organisation seriously. Buddhism and Catholicism will become increasingly stubborn obstacles to Marxism. If reforms were undertaken, the Marxist opposition would cease to be serious: but this would be a slow process.

16.    I was impressed by the keenness and efficiency of a number of young Government officials I met. These should in due course somewhat improve the standards of administrative morality in the island.

17.    I was also deeply impressed by the good start made by the High Commissioner and his skeleton staff. They have immediately hit off the right tone for a Dominion and have won the confidence of the key officials and civil servants.

# Biographical Notes: parts I–II*

Aluvihara, B, 1902–1961
Lawyer and politician; after his education at Oxford, he went to India and was drawn into the political struggles there; jailed during *satyagraha* campaigns of the late 1920s; member of State Council from 1936; in House of Representatives, 1952–1956; minister of education and cultural affairs, 1960.

Aluvihara, Richard, 1895–1976
Kt 1948; elder brother of B Aluvihara (qv); served in European war, 1914–1918; Ceylon Civil Service from 1920; inspector-general of police, 1947–1953; high commissioner of Ceylon in India, 1957–1963

Attlee, Clement Richard (1st Earl cr 1955) 1883–1967
MP (Lab) from 1922; member of Indian Statutory Commission, 1927; leader of Labour Party in House of Commons from 1935; S of S for dominion affairs, 1942–1943; lord president of the Council, 1943–1945; deputy prime minister, 1942–1945; prime minister 1945–1951 and minister of defence to 1946; leader of the Opposition, 1951–1955

Bandaranaike, Solomon West Ridgeway Dias, 1899–1959
Oxford-educated lawyer; joint secretary, Ceylon National Congress, 1927–1930, president, 1932; member of State Council from 1931; minister of local administration, 1936–1947; founded Sinhala Maha Sabha, 1936–1937; assisted in formation of the United National Party, 1946; aspirant to leadership of nationalist movement from the early 1940s; minister of health and local government and leader of House of Representatives, 1947; resigned from government in 1951 to form his own political party; prime minister, 1956–1959; assassinated, 1959

Batuwantudawe, U, 1910–1982
Member of State Council, 1940–1947, as member for Kalutara; there was some controversy attaching to his election because he had earlier served a term of imprisonment on a criminal charge

Blaxter, Kenneth William, 1895–1964
Malvern College and Magdalene, Cambridge; Home Civil Service, 1920; Ministry of Transport, 1920–1922; CO, 1924–1956; assistant secretary from 1942 (acting head of Eastern Dept, 1941)

Caine, Sydney, 1902–1991
KCMG 1947; Harrow County School and London School of Economics; transferred from Inland Revenue to CO, 1926; secretary, West Indies Sugar Commission, 1929; financial secretary, Hong Kong, 1937; CO assistant secretary from 1940 (head of Economic Dept, 1940–1942); member, Anglo–American Caribbean Commission, 1942; financial adviser to S of S for colonies, 1942; CO assistant under-secretary of state from 1944; joint deputy under-secretary of state, 1947–1948; 3rd secretary, Treasury, 1948

Caldecott, Andrew, 1884–1951
KCMG 1937; Uppingham and Exeter, Oxford; Malayan Civil Service from 1907; chief secretary, Federated Malay States, 1931–1933; colonial secretary, Straits Settlements, 1933–1935; OAG, Straits Settlements, and high commissioner, Malay States, 1934; gov, Hong Kong, 1935–1937; gov, Ceylon, 1937–1944

Chelvanayakam, S J V, 1898–1977
Teacher and distinguished lawyer; his entry into national politics was stimulated

---

* An asterisk indicates that the date of birth, death or both are not known.

by G G Ponnambalam (qv) with whom he was associated from 1942; joined Tamil Congress on its formation in 1944; in House of Representatives, 1947–1952, 1956–1977; founder president of Federal Party, 1949; and of Tamil United Front, 1972; and of Tamil United Liberation Front, 1975–1977

**Clauson, Gerard Leslie Makins, 1891–1974**
KCMG 1945; Eton and Corpus Christi, Oxford; oriental scholar; CO from 1919 (from Inland Revenue and army); assistant secretary from 1934 (head of Economic Department, 1934–1940); assistant under-secretary of state, 1940–1951; chairman, International Wheat Conference, 1947, and International Rubber Conference, 1951; retired, 1951; chairman, Pirelli Ltd, 1960–1969

**Coomaraswamy, C, 1892–1968**
Ceylon Civil Service from 1913; registrar-general and director of commercial intelligence, 1936; food controller and controller of prices in addition to his duties; commissioner of food purchases, 1942; government agent, Eastern Province, 1943; government agent, Western Province, 1945–1946; representative of Ceylon government in Malaya, Nov 1945; permanent secretary, Ministry of Home Affairs and Rural Development

**Corea, (George) Claude (Stanley), 1894–1962**
KBE 1952; practised as lawyer from 1916; left Bar for politics, 1930; president of Ceylon National Congress on three occasions; member of State Council as member for Chilaw from 1931; minister for labour, industries and commerce, 1936–1946; established Bank of Ceylon and Industrial and Agricultural Credit Association; Ceylon government representative in London, 1946–1948; ambassador for Ceylon in US, 1948–1954; high commissioner for Ceylon in UK and minister for Ceylon in France and Netherlands, 1954–1957; chairman, GATT, 1956–1957; ambassador and permanent delegate for Ceylon to UN, 1958–1961

**Cranborne, Viscount,** *see* **Salisbury, 5th Marquess of**

**Creech Jones, Arthur, 1891–1964**
MP (Lab) 1935–1950; executive member, Fabian Society; member, CO Education Advisory Committee, 1936–1945; chairman, Fabian Colonial Bureau and Labour Party Imperial Advisory Committee; vice-chairman, Higher Education Commission to West Africa, 1943–1944; parliamentary under-secretary of state for colonies, 1945–1946; S of S for colonies, 1946–1950

**Dahanayake, W b 1902**
Teacher turned politician; member of Galle Municipal Council, 1939–1959; mayor of Galle, 1939–1942; won election to State Council at by-election in 1944 and quickly established a reputation there for his radical views and anti-establishment attitudes; one of three members of State Council who voted against the acceptance of the Soulbury reforms; minister of education, 1956–1959; prime minister, 1960; minister of home affairs, 1965–1970; minister of co-operatives, 1980–1988

**de Silva, Dr Colvin R, 1907–1989**
Lawyer, politician and historian; founder member of LSSP and active trade unionist; jailed in 1940, escaped 1942; in House of Representatives, 1947–1952, 1956–1959, 1960–1965, 1968–1977; minister of constitutional affairs and of plantation industry, 1970–1975

**de Silva, G E, 1878–1950**
Lawyer and politician; began career as member of Kandy Municipal Council; member of the Ceylon National Congress from its inception and president on five occasions, the last of these being between 1945 and 1951; member of the State Council from 1931; minister of health, 1942; elected to first parliament in 1947 and minister of industries, industrial research and fisheries, 1947–1948; unseated by election petition, 1948

**de Silva, L M D, 1893–1962**
Legal luminary; educated at Cambridge; called to English Bar, 1916; lucrative private practice in Ceylon for a decade

before joining the official Bar in 1925; successively solicitor-general, acting attorney general, acting legal secretary and acting puisne justice of Supreme Court; confidant and legal adviser to D S Senanayake; consulted on all important political and constitutional issues of transfer of power; chairman in 1946 of Delimitation Commission which demarcated constituencies for new parliament

de Silva, M W H, 1886–1960
Lawyer; joined official Bar as additional district judge, Colombo; deputy solicitor general, 1935; solicitor general, 1940; King's Counsel, 1941; acting legal secretary, 1945; puisne justice, 1946; attorney-general, 1947; minister of justice, 1956–1959

de Silva, Dr W A, 1869–1942
Philanthropist, businessman and politician; member of Ceylon Legislative Council from 1924; member of State Council from 1931 as member for Moratuwa; minister of health, 1936–1942

Drayton, Robert Harry, 1892–1963
Kt 1944; Exeter School; solicitor, 1918; solicitor-general and subsequently legal draftsman, Palestine, 1920–1943; called to Bar, 1934; attorney-general, Tanganyika, 1934–1939; legal secretary, Ceylon, 1939–1942; chief secretary, Ceylon, 1942–1947; chief draftsman, Pakistan Constituent Assembly, 1950–1953

Eastwood, Christopher Gilbert, 1905–1983
Eton and Trinity, Oxford; CO from 1927; seconded as private secretary to UK high commissioner, Palestine, 1932; secretary, International Rubber Regulation Committee, 1934; principal, CO, 1935; private secretary to S of S for colonies, 1940–1941; seconded as principal private secretary, Cabinet Office, 1945; assistant under-secretary of state, CO, 1947–1952 and 1954–1966; commissioner for crown lands, 1952–1964

Fonseka, M b 1896*
Lawyer; acting legal draftsman, 1932; legal draftsman from 1933; associated with W I Jennings in preparation of ministers' draft constitution of 1944

Gater, George Henry, 1886–1963
Kt 1936; Winchester and New College, Oxford; local government from 1912; CO permanent under-secretary of state, 1939–1947 (seconded to Ministry of Home Security and Ministry of Supply, 1940–1942)

Gent, Gerard Edward James, 1895–1948
KCMG 1946; King's School, Canterbury and Trinity, Oxford; CO from 1920; assistant secretary, Indian Round Table Conference, 1930; assistant secretary from 1939 (head of Eastern Dept, 1939–1942); assistant under-secretary of state, 1942–1946; gov, Malayan Union, 1946–1948; high commissioner, Federation of Malaya, 1948; killed in air crash

Goonesinha, A E, 1891–1967
Pioneer trade unionist and politician; member of Ceylon National Congress from its inception; reached height of influence in national politics in the late 1920s; established Labour Party in 1928; elected to State Council in 1931 and 1936, by which time he had lost his working class base to LSSP, and with it much of his influence in politics; in House of Representatives, 1947–1952; minister without portfolio, 1948–1952

Goonetilleke, Oliver Ernest, 1892–1976
KCMG 1948; entered public service as an accountant; assistant auditor for railways, 1921; assistant colonial auditor, 1924; colonial auditor, June 1931; auditor-general, July 1931; member of War Council and civil defence commissioner and food commissioner, 1942–1945; financial secretary, 1945–1947; minister of home affairs and rural development and leader of Senate, 1947–1948 and 1951–1952; high commissioner for Ceylon in UK, 1948–1951; minister of finance, 1953–1954; gov-gen, Ceylon, 1954–1962

Goonewardene, L S, 1909–1983
Lawyer; founder member of LSSP and active trade unionist and politician from 1930s; only one of LSSP leadership to evade arrest and imprisonment in 1940; in House of Representatives, 1947–1952, 1956–1977; minister of communications, 1970–1975

Greenwood, Arthur, 1880–1954

MP (Lab) from 1922; minister of health, 1929–1931; deputy leader of Labour Party, 1935; member of War Cabinet and minister without portfolio, 1940–1942; lord privy seal, 1945–1947; postmaster-general, 1946–1947

Gunawardena, D B Robert, 1904–1971

Left-wing politician and trade unionist; brother of Phillip Gunawardene (qv); founder member of LSSP and one of its principal trade unionists, especially active in organising dock workers; in House of Representatives, 1947–1965

Gunawardena, D Phillip R, 1901–1972

American-educated socialist, trade unionist and politician; pioneer Marxist in Ceylon and one of founders of LSSP; led struggle to capture trade union movement from A E Goonesinha (qv); elected to State Council in 1936 along with Dr N M Perera (qv); together they wielded influence out of all proportion to their numbers (the LSSP was set for greater political success in the early 1940s when the outbreak of the Second World War interrupted its progress); jailed in 1940 upon proscription of LSSP; escaped to India in 1942; in House of Representatives, 1947–1948, 1956–1970; minister of agriculture and food, 1956–1959; minister of industries and fisheries, 1965–1970

Hall, 1st Viscount cr 1946 (George Henry Hall) 1881–1965

MP (Lab) from 1922; parliamentary under-secretary of state for colonies, 1940–1942; financial secretary to Admiralty, 1942–1943; parliamentary under-secretary of state for foreign affairs, 1943–1945; S of S for colonies, 1945–1946; first lord of Admiralty, 1946–1951

Hewavitarane, R, 1898–1958

Wealthy businessman; educated at Dulwich School; returned to Ceylon in 1923 and joined family firms; active in Buddhist associations; member of State Council as member for Matara from 1936; minister for labour, industries and commerce, 1946–1947

Howard, John Curtois, 1887–1970

Kt 1942; Uppingham and Clare, Cambridge; called to Bar, 1913; served in European war, 1915–1920; attorney-general, Cyprus, 1924–1926; solicitor-general, Nigeria, 1926–1933; attorney-general, Gold Coast, 1933–1936; attorney-general, Ceylon, 1936; legal secretary, Ceylon, 1936–1939; chief justice, Ceylon, 1939–1949

Jayah, T B, 1890–1960

Educationist and politician; principal, Zahira College, Colombo, 1921–1948, the premier Muslim educational institution in Ceylon; member of Legislative Council, 1924–1930; made unsuccessful bids to win election to State Council in 1931 and 1936; nominated to State Council in 1936 and remained a member until 1947; elected to parliament in 1947 and appointed to Cabinet as minister of labour and social services

Jayatilake, Don Baron, 1868–1944

Kt 1932; scholar, lawyer and politician; called to Bar in UK, 1913; founder member of Ceylon National Congress; member of Ceylon Legislative Council, 1924–1931; vice-chairman of Board of Ministers, minister for home affairs and leader of State Council, 1931–1942; Ceylon government representative in India, 1942

Jayewardene, J R, 1906–1996

Lawyer and politician; joined Ceylon National Congress in 1938, joint secretary, 1940–1942; together with young colleagues like Dudley Senanayake (qv), succeeded in infusing new life into Congress and converting it into a political party with a coherent programme and a network of branches; elected to State Council in 1943; supported decision to merge the Congress in UNP in 1946 and became one of the joint treasurers of the new party; retained Kelaniya seat in election to new parliament in 1947; minister of finance, 1947–1953, 1960; minister of agriculture and food, 1953–1956; leader of House of Representatives, 1953–1956, 1960; minister of state, 1965–1970; leader of the Opposition, 1970–1977; prime minister,

1977–1978; executive president, 1978–1988

**Jayawardena, N U b 1908**
Public servant who rose from the ranks to an important position in the executive grades; deputy commissioner of commodity purchases from 1942, acting commissioner, 1945; moved into areas of government activity relating to public finance, 1947–1948; rose to be governor of the Central Bank, 1953–1954

**Jeffries, Charles Joseph, 1896–1972**
KCMG 1943; Malvern and Magdalen, Oxford; CO from 1917; assistant secretary from 1930 (establishment officer and head of personnel, Colonial Service, 1930–1939); assistant under-secretary of state from 1939; joint deputy under-secretary of state, 1947–1956

**Jennings, (William) Ivor, 1903–1965**
Kt 1948; Bristol Grammar School and St Catherine's, Cambridge; called to Bar, 1928; reader in English law, University of London, 1930–1940; professor of political science, University of British Colombia, 1938–1939; principal, Ceylon University College, 1940–1942; deputy civil defence commissioner, Ceylon, 1942–1945; vice chancellor, University of Ceylon, 1942–1955; chairman, Ceylon Social Services Commission, 1944–1946; member, Commission on Ceylon Constitution, 1948; president, Inter-University Board of India, 1949–1950; constitutional adviser and chief draftsman, Pakistan, 1954–1955; member, Malayan Constitutional Commission, 1956–1957

**Kannangara, C W W, 1884–1969**
Teacher, lawyer and politician; member of Ceylon Legislative Council from 1923; member of State Council and minister of education, 1931–1947 (the longest such tenure of office in Ceylon's history and by far the most momentous in terms of the changes in education introduced); minister of local government, 1952–1956

**Kotelawala, John (Lionel), 1897–1980**
KBE 1948; member of State Council from 1931; minister of communications and works, 1936–47; minister of transport and works from 1947; prime minister of Ceylon and minister of defence and external affairs, 1953–1956

**Layton, Geoffrey, 1884–1964**
KCMG 1945; Royal Navy from 1903; vice admiral commanding 1st Battle Squadron and second-in-command, Home Fleet, 1939–1940; c-in-c, China, 1940–1942; c-in-c, Ceylon, 1942–1945; admiral, 1942; c-in-c, Portsmouth, 1945–1947

**Lloyd, 1st Baron of Dolobran cr 1925 (George Ambrose Lloyd) 1879–1941**
MP (Unionist, 1910–1918; Conservative, 1924–1925); gov of Bombay, 1918–1923; high commissioner for Egypt and the Sudan, 1925–1929; S of S for colonies, 1940–1941

**Lloyd, Thomas Ingram Kynaston, 1896–1968**
KCMG 1947; Rossall, Gonville and Caius, Cambridge; transferred from Ministry of Health to CO, 1921; secretary, Palestine Commission, 1929–1930; secretary, West India Royal Commission, 1938–1939; assistant secretary, CO, from 1939 (head of Colonial Service Dept, 1941–1942, Defence Dept, 1942–1943); assistant under-secretary of state from 1943; permanent under-secretary of state, 1947–1956

**Macan-Markar, Hadji Mohammad, 1879–1952**
Kt 1938; wealthy businessman; first Muslim member of Legislative Council, 1924–1931; member of State Council as member for Batticaloa South from 1931; minister of communications and works, 1931–1936; entered Senate in 1947 and remained a highly respected Muslim leader

**MacDonald, Malcolm John, 1901–1981**
Son of J Ramsay MacDonald; MP (Lab) 1929–1931, (Nat Lab) 1931–1935, (Nat Govt) 1936–1945); parliamentary under-secretary of state for dominion affairs, 1931–1935; S of S for dominion affairs, 1935–1938 and 1938–1939; S of S for colonies, 1935 and 1938–1940; minister of health, 1940–1941; UK high commissioner in Canada, 1941–1946; gov-gen, British territories in South-East Asia, 1946–1948; commissioner-general in South-East Asia,

1948–1955; subsequently gov/gov-gen/UK high commissioner, Kenya, 1963–1965

**Mahadeva, Sir Arunachalam, 1885–1969**
Member of Ceylon Legislative Council from 1924; member of State Council as member for Jaffna from 1934; succeeded Sir D B Jayatilaka as minister of home affairs, 1942–1947

**Molamure, Alexander Francis, 1888–1951**
KBE 1949; returned uncontested to State Council, 1931; elected speaker and held post until 1935; lost seat when he was jailed for contempt of court arising from a dispute over a will; returned to legislature at a by-election in 1943 and elected to House of Representatives, 1947; first speaker of post-independence legislature until his death in 1951, felled by a massive stroke while presiding over a debate

**Moore, Henry Monck-Mason, 1887–1964**
KCMG 1935; King's College School and Jesus, Cambridge; Colonial Service in Ceylon, Bermuda, Nigeria and Kenya, 1910–1934; gov of Sierra Leone, 1934–1937; assistant under-secretary of state, CO, 1937–1939; deputy under-secretary of state, 1939; gov of Kenya, 1939–1944; gov of Ceylon, 1944–1948; gov-gen of Ceylon, 1948–1949

**Motha, G R, 1892–1949**
Lawyer; active interest in politics of Indian labour movement in Ceylon and member of Board of Immigrant Labour from 1932; secretary of Ceylon Indian Association; secretary, Ceylon Indian Congress; in London in 1945 to petition on behalf of Indians in Ceylon; elected to parliament in 1947

**Moyne, 1st Baron cr 1935 (Walter Edward Guiness) 1880–1944**
MP (Unionist) 1907–1931; minister of agriculture and fisheries, 1925–1929; Financial Mission to Kenya, 1932; chairman, West India Royal Commission, 1938–1939; parliamentary secretary, Ministry of Agriculture, 1940; S of S for colonies, 1941–1942; deputy minister, Cairo, 1942–1944 (Jan); Cabinet minister-resident in Middle East, 1944 (Jan–Nov); assassinated by Stern Gang

**Natesa Aiyar, K \***
Trade unionist and journalist; represented Indian community in Ceylon Legislative Council, 1924–1931; member of State Council as member for Hatton, 1936–1947; president of Ceylon Federation of Workers, active in unionising plantation workers; opposed Soulbury reforms and voted against 1945 white paper

**Nihill, (John Harry) Barclay, 1892–1975**
Kt 1948; Felsted and Emmanuel, Cambridge; called to Bar, 1919; Colonial Service, Hong Kong, 1921; legal secretary to High Commission, Baghdad, 1927–1933; solicitor-general, Uganda, 1934; acting chief justice, Uganda, 1935; attorney-general, British Guiana, 1937; puisne justice, Ceylon Supreme Court, 1938; legal secretary, Ceylon, 1945–1947; chief justice, Kenya, 1947–1950; president, Court of Appeal for East Africa, 1950–1955

**Nugawela, E A, 1898–1972**
Lawyer and politician; member of State Council, 1936–1947; served on the Executive Committee on Education; minister of education, 1947–52

**Panabokke, Sir Tikiri Banda, 1879–1963**
Lawyer and politician; member of State Council from 1931; minister of health, 1931–1935; defeated in 1936 but retained considerable influence in the politics of the Kandyan areas; succeeded Sir D B Jayatilaka as Ceylon government representative in New Delhi, 1944

**Parkinson, Arthur Charles Cosmo, 1884–1967**
KCMG 1935; entered Admiralty, 1908, transferred to CO, 1909; assistant secretary from 1925; assistant under-secretary of state, 1931; permanent under-secretary of state, 1937–1940; permanent under-secretary of state, DO, 1940; acting permanent under-secretary of state, CO, 1942–1944; seconded for special duty in colonies, 1942–1944; retired, 1944, re-employed as adviser on reorganisation of Colonial Service, 1945

**Paskin, Jesse John, 1892–1972**
KCMG 1954; King Edward's, Stourbridge and St John's, Cambridge; transferred

from Ministry of Transport to CO, 1921; assistant secretary from 1939 (head of Eastern Dept, 1942–1947); assistant under-secretary of state, 1948–1954

**Pereira, I X, 1888–1951**
Prominent businessman; elected to represent Indian community in Ceylon Legislative Council, 1924–1931; nominated to State Council to represent Indian community, 1931–1936 and 1936–1947; active role in agitation against Soulbury constitution; voted against acceptance of 1945 White Paper

**Pereira, R L, 1880–1960**
Lawyer and member of Ceylon Legislative Council in 1931; one of Ceylon's leading criminal lawyers in 1920s; leader of unofficial Bar on criminal side over next three decades

**Perera, Dr N M, 1905–1979**
Socialist politician and founder member of LSSP; elected to State Council in 1936 where he became an influential back bencher; jailed along with other LSSP leaders in 1940 and organised a successful jail break; elected to parliament in 1947 and after a few years became leader of Opposition, 1956–1959; minister of finance, 1964, 1970–1975

**Ponnambalam, G G, 1901–1976**
Cambridge-educated lawyer; returned to Ceylon in 1927 and developed a lucrative practice as one of the outstanding criminal lawyers of his day; member of State Council as member of Point Pedro from 1934; assumed leadership of the Tamil cause; retained his seat in 1936 and led the Tamils over the next eleven years in their demand for weighted representation as the price of their support for the transfer of power; established Tamil Congress in 1944; at general election his party swept the polls in Tamil constituencies in the north of Ceylon

**Rajakulendran, J G b 1907 ***
School teacher turned politician; member, Urban Council, Nawalapitiya, 1938–1942; member of State Council from 1943; member, Executive Committee on Communications and Works

**Rajapakse, L A, 1900–1976**
Lawyer and politician; KC, 1942; founder member of the UNP and first secretary of the party's propaganda section; resigned from UNP in May 1947 on brief appointment as commissioner of assizes; appointed to Senate and to Cabinet as minister of justice, 1947

**Ranasinha, A G, 1899–1976**
Civil servant and diplomat; graduated from Cambridge and entered Ceylon Civil Service, 1921–1922; worked with D S Senanayake during the latter's first and perhaps most creative phase as minister of agriculture and lands, 1932–1936; public trustee and superintendent of census, 1944–1946; organised and prepared 1946 census report; one of D S Senanayake's small team of advisers in London in July 1945 to negotiate transfer of power

**Ratnayake, A, 1900–1977**
Teacher, lawyer and politician; member of State Council as member for Dumbara from 1931; made his mark in field of education, most notably through his membership of the Education Commission of 1943; member of S W R D Bandaranaike's Sinhala Maha Sabha; minister of food and co-operatives, 1947; minister of home affairs and rural development, 1952–1956; president of Senate, 1965–1971

**Roberts-Wray, Kenneth Owen, 1899–1983**
KCMG 1949; Royal Military Academy, Woolwich and Merton, Oxford; called to Bar, 1924; assistant legal adviser, CO/DO, 1943; legal adviser, 1945

**Salisbury, 5th Marquess of 1947 (Robert Arthur James Gascoyne Cecil) 1893–1972**
Viscount Cranborne 1942; MP (Unionist) 1929–1941; parliamentary under-secretary of state, FO, 1935–1938; paymaster-general, 1940; S of S for dominion affairs, 1940–1942 and 1943–1945; S of S for colonies, 1942; lord privy seal, 1942–1943; leader of House of Lords, 1942–1945; S of S for Commonwealth Relations, 1952; lord president of the Council, 1952–1957; resigned over Conservative colonial policy

Saravanamuttu, Mrs N, 1897–1941
Entered State Council in 1932 for Colombo North when her husband, Dr R Saravanamuttu, was unseated by an election petition; unseated herself on a technicality but was re-elected later in 1932 and held the seat until her death in 1941; second woman to be elected to the national legislature under universal suffrage

Senanayake, Don Stephen, 1884–1952
Planter and politician; member of Ceylon Legislative Council, 1924–1931; made agriculture and irrigation his main interests; member of Land Commission appointed in 1927 (the commission's pathbreaking reports constitute a major landmark in Sri Lanka's recent history); active member of Ceylon National Congress; entered State Council in 1931 without a contest; minister for agriculture and lands, 1931–1947; succeeded Sir D B Jayatilaka in 1942 as vice-chairman of Board of Ministers and leader of State Council; founded the UNP in 1946; prime minister from 1947–1952; killed in riding accident, 1952

Senanayake, Dudley Shelton, 1911–1973
Elder son of D S Senanayake (qv); lawyer and politician; member of State Council as member for Dedigama from 1936; joint secretary of Ceylon National Congress with J R Jayewardene (qv), 1939–1942; re-elected to the Dedigama seat at 1947 general election; minister of agriculture and lands, 1947; prime minister and minister of defence and external relations, 1952–1953, Mar–Apr 1960, 1965–1970

Shuckburgh, John Evelyn, 1877–1953
KCMG 1922; Eton and King's, Cambridge; India Office, 1900–1921; CO from 1921; assistant under-secretary of state, 1921–1931; deputy under-secretary of state, 1931–1942; appointed gov of Nigeria in 1939 but did not assume office owing to outbreak of war; retired, 1942; narrator, Historical Section, Cabinet Office, 1942–1948

Sidebotham, John Biddulph, 1891–1988
King's School, Canterbury and Gonville and Caius, Cambridge; CO from 1921

(from Inland Revenue); principal, 1930; assistant secretary from 1941 (head of Ceylon and Pacific Dept, 1943–1948)

Sittampalam, C, 1898–1964
Educated Cambridge and Middle Temple; Ceylon Civil Service from 1923; held various judicial and administrative positions (assistant government agent, district judge and magistrate in Mannar and Vavuniya, acting government agent of North Central Province); resigned from CCS and practised as an advocate; elected to Mannar seat in parliament of 1947; minister of posts and telecommunications, 1947

Smith, Trafford, 1912–1975
Leicester School and Trinity, Cambridge; CO from 1935; seconded to Fiji, 1938; served in British Solomon Islands, 1940, and Gilbert and Ellice Islands, 1941; secretary, Soulbury Commission on Constitutional Reform in Ceylon, 1944–1945; assistant secretary, CO, 1945; lieutenant-gov, Malta, 1953–1959; assistant under-secretary of state, CRO, 1959–1967; UK ambassador to Burma, 1967–1970

Soulbury, 1st Viscount cr 1954 (Herwald Ramsbotham) 1887–1971
1st Baron of Soulbury 1941; Uppingham and University College, Oxford; called to Bar, 1911; served in European war, 1914–1918; MP (Con) 1929–1941; parliamentary secretary, Board of Education, 1931–1935; parliamentary secretary, Ministry of Agriculture and Fisheries, 1935–1936; minister of pensions, 1936–1939; first commissioner of works, 1939–1940; president, Board of Education, 1940–1941; chairman, Commission on Constitutional Reform, Ceylon, 1944–1945; gov-gen, Ceylon, 1949–1954

Sri Pathmanathan, R *
Oxford-educated lawyer; member of State Council from 1936 as member for Mannar-Mullaitivu; played active role in Tamil politics at national level

Stanley, Oliver Frederick George, 1896–1950
MP (Con) 1924–1950; parliamentary under-secretary of state, Home Office, 1931–1933; minister of transport, 1933–

1934; minister of labour, 1934–1935; president of Board of Education, 1935–1937; president of Board of Trade, 1937–1940; S of S for war, 1940; S of S for colonies, 1942–1945

**Suntheralingam, C, 1895–1985**
Educationist, lawyer and politician; returned to Sri Lanka from Oxford and Gray's Inn in 1920 and entered Ceylon Civil Service; resigned in 1922 and became vice-principal of a leading school in Colombo; professor of mathematics, University College, 1922–1940; after two unsuccessful attempts at entering the State Council through by-elections, resigned from university and began practising as a lawyer; elected to parliament in 1947 and appointed minister of trade and commerce

**Thondaman, S b 1913**
Planter, trade unionist and politician; entered politics as a trade unionist, organising Indian plantation workers; one of founders of Ceylon Indian Congress or Ceylon Workers' Congress as it came to be known later and led agitation on behalf of that body during negotiations on the transfer of power; won the Nuwara Eliya seat in the first parliament of 1947–1952

**Vytilingam, S P, 1903–1984**
Landowner; elected to State Council as member for Talawakelle; served on Executive Committee of Labour, Industry and Commerce; actively interested in affairs of Indian community and plantation work-

ers; agitated against Soulbury recommendations along with S Thondaman (qv)

**Wedderburn, Maxwell MacLagan, 1883–1953**
KBE 1941; George Watson's College, Edinburgh and Edinburgh University; Ceylon Civil Service from 1906; chief secretary, Ceylon, 1937–1940

**Wickremasinghe, Dr S A, 1901–1981**
After a medical education in Ceylon and England, established a lucrative private practice in Matara, in south Ceylon; member of State Council for Morawaka, 1931, lost seat, 1936; founder member of LSSP; left for Britain in 1936; broke with LSSP on his return and established United Socialist Party which became the Ceylon Communist Party in 1943; won the Morawaka seat again at a by-election in 1947 during last days of State Council but was debarred on a technicality from contesting a seat to the new parliament; in national legislature, 1956–1977

**Wijewardene, Don Richard, 1886–1950**
Cambridge educated barrister; Sri Lanka's most successful and most influential newspaper magnate who owned the Lake House group, or the Associated Newspapers of Ceylon Ltd, as it came to be known officially; supported D S Senanayake's claims to political leadership in 1940s when his political influence reached its peak; his association with Senanayake and Sir O Goonetilleke was a notable feature of the negotiations on the transfer of power

# Bibliography 1: Public Record Office sources searched

The documents reproduced in this collection constitute only a minute proportion of the official records which relate to Sri Lanka in the period 1939–1948. The following classes were searched in arriving at the preceding selection.

## 1. Cabinet

(i) *Cabinet committees*
War Cabinet committees: Miscellaneous & General series
    Ceylon constitution (Gen 3): CAB 78/5 (1943)
    Ceylon constitution (Gen 99): CAB 78/39 (1945)
General series from 1945
    Colonial Affairs Committee: CAB 134/52 (1945–1947)
    India and Burma Committee: CAB 134/341–346 (1945–1947)

(ii) *Cabinet Office*
War Cabinet conclusions (minutes): CAB 65/1–57 (1939–1945)
War Cabinet memoranda: CAB 66/1–67 (1939–1945)
Cabinet conclusions from 1945: CAB 128/1–12 (to 1948)
Cabinet memoranda from 1945: CAB 129/1–24 (to 1948)
Cabinet Office registered files: CAB 21/1739 (proposed amalgamation of Cabinet India and Burma and Colonial Affairs Committees, 1947)

## 2. Colonial Office

(i) *CO original correspondence, 1939–1948: geographical classes*
Ceylon: CO 54/964/1–1004/1 (1939–1948)

(ii) *CO original correspondence, 1939–1948: subject classes*
Colonies, general: CO 323/1881/1 (British Nationality Bill, effect on citizenship of colonies: Ceylon, 1946–1947)
Colonies general supplementary ['secret']: CO 537/1671–1676, 1909–1910, 2211–2228, 3377, 3768–3770 (1946–1948)
Economic: CO 852/452/2, 497/12, 497/13, 514/14, 515/10, 515/11, 515/12, 516/4, 516/5, 516/6, 516/7, 569/2, 605/6, 605/9, 605/10, 605/11, 608/1 (1942–1946)

(iii) *Confidential print, 1947: Eastern*
Constitution of Ceylon: CO 882/30 (1943–1948)

3. *Dominions Office and Commonwealth Relations Office*

> *DO original correspondence: DO 35*
> DO 35/2400–2402 (Ceylon–UK defence negotiations, 1948)
> DO 35/3268 (Maldive Islands: future position when Ceylon attains full status, 1947–1948)
> DO 35/3535 (report on British Commonwealth Conference on Nationality and Citizenship, 1947–1948)
> DO 35/3777 (Ceylon's application for UN membership, 1948)

4. *Foreign Office*

> *FO original correspondence, political: FO 371*
> FO 371/63556 (constitutional changes in Ceylon, 1947)

5. *Admiralty*

> *Admiralty and Secretariat cases: ADM 116*
> ADM 116/5546 (constitutional reform in Ceylon: Admiralty discussions on Soulbury Report and statement of government policy on Ceylon, 1945–1946)

6. *War Office*

> (i)  *WO registered files, general series: WO 32*
>      WO 32/9629 (Ceylon: military contribution towards defence, 1941–1950)
>      WO 32/1099 (Ceylon constitution, 1942–1947)

> (ii) *War of 1939–1945, military headquarters papers, Far East: South-East Asia Command: WO 203*
>      WO 203/5540 (Ceylon Defence and Planning Committee papers: correspondence on defence matters, 1942–1945)
>      WO 203/5832 (Ceylon War Council meetings, 1942–1945)

7. *Prime Minister's Office*

> (i)  *Confidential papers, 1940–1945: PREM 4*
>      PREM 4/50/16 (Ceylon, 1942–1944)

> (ii) *Correspondence and papers, 1945–1951: PREM 8*
>      PREM 8/725 (question raised by Mr Senanayake about status of Ceylon; Ceylon application for UN membership, 1948)
>      PREM 8/726 (Report of Soulbury Commission; Ceylon Independence Bill, 1945–1948)

# Bibliography 2: Official publications, unpublished official material, unpublished private papers, published documents and secondary sources

1. *Official publications*

   (a) *United Kingdom*
   *Report of the Special Commission on the Constitution* (Donoughmore Report) Cmd 3131, 1928
   *Correspondence Relating to the Constitution of Ceylon* Cmd 5910, 1938
   *Report of the Commission on Constitutional Reform* (Soulbury Report) Cmd 6677, 1945
   *Ceylon: Statement of Policy on Constitutional Reform* Cmd 6690, Oct 1945
   *Ceylon: Proposals for Conferring on Ceylon fully Responsible Status within the British Commonwealth of Nations* Cmd 7257, Nov 1947
   *British Nationality Bill, 1948: Summary of Main Provisions* Cmd 7326, 1948

   (b) *Ceylon*
   *Correspondence between the Ministers and the Governor regarding the Ceylon Constitution, March–May 1937* SP XI, 1937
   *The report of the Bracegirdle Commission* SP XVII, 1938
   *Report of a Commission appointed to inquire into the shooting at . . . Mool Oya Estate, Hewaheta* SP XV, 1940
   *Governor's despatch dated 13th June, 1938 and Secretary of State's despatch dated 10th November, 1938, regarding the Ceylon Constitution* SP XXVIII, 1938
   *Indo–Ceylon Relations Exploratory Conference: Report of Ceylon Delegation* SP VIII, 1941
   *Statement by the Ministers on Undertakings given to the Government of India* SP XIV, 1941
   *India–Ceylon Relations* SP XXVIII, 1941
   *India–Ceylon Relations* SP III, 1943
   *Correspondence of the Board of Ministers with the Secretary of State and the Governor, 1941–1943* SP XIII, 1943
   *Reform of the Constitution* SP XVII, 1943
   *Reform of the Constitution* SP XII, 1944
   *Reform of the Constitution* SP XIV, 1944
   *The Ceylon (Constitution) Order in Council* in the *Ceylon Government Gazette Extraordinary* 17 May 1946
   *The Independence of Ceylon* SP XXII, 1947

*The Constitution of Ceylon* SP III, 1948
*Correspondence Relating to the Citizenship Status of Indians Resident in
    Ceylon* SP XXII, 1948

2.  *Unpublished official material*

    *United Kingdom: Foreign and Commonwealth Office Library*
    *Special Commission on the Constitution, 1928* (Donoughmore Commission):
        written and oral evidence
    *Commission on Constitutional Reform, 1944–1945* (Soulbury Commission):
        oral evidence

3.  *Unpublished private papers in the UK*

    *Institute of Commonwealth Studies, London*
    *Papers of Sir Ivor Jennings*
    Files B/111/4, B/111/5: letters and drafts of documents on negotiations on the
        transfer of power, 1945–1947
    Files B/111/7, 1943–1945: drafts of letters prepared by Jennings for D S
        Senanayake, 1948–1960
    File C IX: *Donoughmore to independence: a contribution to the constitutional
        history of Ceylon, 1931–1948* 129 pp (with appendix of 13 pp) unpublished
        typescript
    File C XIV: *Road to Peradeniya* 163 pp, unpublished typescript of Jennings's
        autobiography

4.  *Published selections of documents and speeches*
    S R Ashton & S E Stockwell, eds, BDEEP series A, vol 1, *Imperial policy and
        colonial practice 1925–1945* in 2 parts (London, 1996)
    S W R D Bandaranaike, *Towards a new era: selected speeches* of Bandaranaike
        made in the legislatures of Ceylon 1931–1954 (Colombo, 1961)
    S W R D Bandaranaike, *Speeches and writing* (Colombo, 1963)
    R Hyam, ed, BDEEP series A, vol 2, *The Labour government and the end of
        empire 1945–1951* in 4 parts (London, 1992)
    W S Muttiah & S Wanasinghe, eds, *Britain, World War 2 and the Sama
        Samajists* (Colombo, 1996)
    A N Porter & A J Stockwell, *British imperial policy and decolonization,
        1938–1964* vol 1  *1938–1951* (London, 1987)
    M W Roberts, ed, *Documents of the Ceylon National Congress and nationalist
        politics in Ceylon, 1929–1950* in 4 vols (Colombo, 1978)

5.  *Select list of published books*
    S W R D Bandaranaike, *Remembered yesterdays* (London, 1929)
    S W R D Bandaranaike, ed, *The handbook of the Ceylon National Congress
        1919–1928* (Colombo, 1929)
    C H Collins, *Public administration in Ceylon* (London, 1951)
    K M de Silva, ed, University of Ceylon *History of Ceylon* vol III (Colombo &
        Kandy, 1973)

K M de Silva, ed, *Sri Lanka: a survey* (London, 1977)

K M de Silva, ed, *Universal franchise, 1931–1981: the Sri Lankan experience* (Colombo, 1981)

K M de Silva, ed, *Managing ethnic tensions in multi-ethnic societies: Sri Lanka, 1880–1985* (Lanham, Md, 1986)

K M de Silva & H Wriggins, *J R Jayewardene of Sri Lanka: a political biography* vol I (London, 1993) vol II (London, 1994)

K N O Dharmadasa, *Language, religion and ethnic assertiveness: the growth of Sinhalese nationalism in Sri Lanka* (Ann Arbor, 1992)

L Goonewardene, *A short history of the Lanka Sama Samaja Party* (Colombo, 1961)

H A J Hulugalle, *The life and times of D R Wijewardena* (Colombo, 1960)

H A J Hulugalle, *British governors of Ceylon* (Colombo, 1960)

H A J Hulugalle, *The life and times of Don Stephen Senanayake* (Colombo, 1975)

V K Jayawardena, *The rise of the labour movement in Ceylon* (Durham, NC, 1972)

Sir Charles Jeffries, *Ceylon: the path to independence* (London, 1962)

Sir Charles Jeffries, *O E G: a biography of Oliver Ernest Goonetilleke* (London, 1969)

Sir Ivor Jennings, *Comments on the constitution* (Colombo, 1947)

Sir Ivor Jennings, *Comments on independence* (Colombo, 1948)

Sir Ivor Jennings, *The constitution of Ceylon* 3rd ed (Oxford, 1953)

Sir Ivor Jennings & H W Tambiah, *The dominion of Ceylon: the development of its laws and constitutions* (London, 1952)

S U Kodikara, *Indo–Ceylon relations since independence* (Colombo, 1965)

Sir John Kotelawala, *An Asian prime minister's story* (London, 1956)

G J Lerski, *Origins of trotskyism in Ceylon* (Stanford, 1968)

J Manor, *The expedient utopian: Bandaranaike and Ceylon* (Cambridge, 1989)

V L B Mendis, *British governors and colonial policy in Sri Lanka* (Dehiwela, Sri Lanka, 1984)

S Nadesan, *A history of the upcountry Tamil people* (Colombo, 1993)

S Namasivayam, *The legislatures of Ceylon, 1928–1948* (London, 1951)

G StJ Orde Browne, *Labour conditions in Ceylon, Mauritius and Malaya* (London, 1943)

A G Ranasinha, *Memories and musings* (Colombo, 1972)

M W Roberts, ed, *Collective identities, nationalisms and protest in Sri Lanka during the modern era* (Colombo, 1978)

R R Ross & A M Savada, eds, *Sri Lanka: a country study* (Washington DC, 1991)

J Russell, *Communal politics under the Donoughmore constitution, 1931–1947* (Colombo, 1982)

D R Snodgrass, *Ceylon: an export economy in transition* (Homewood, Illinois, 1966)

S Thondaman, *Tea and politics: an autobiography* vol II *My life and times* (Delhi, 1994)

H Tinker, *Separate and unequal: India and the Indians in the British Commonwealth, 1920–1950* (London, 1976)

H Tinker, *The banyan tree: overseas emigrants from India, Pakistan and*

*Bangladesh* (London, 1977)

I Ɖ S Weerawardena, *Government and politics in Ceylon, 1931–1946* (Colombo, 1951)

G Wijekoon, *Recollections* (Colombo, 1951)

A J Wilson, *S J V Chelvanayakam and the crisis of Sri Lankan Tamil nationalism, 1947–1977: a political biography* (London, 1993)

C Woodward, *The growth of a party system in Ceylon* (Providence, RI, 1969)

P Ziegler, *Mountbatten* (London, 1985)

P Ziegler, ed, *The personal diary of Admiral Lord Louis Mountbatten, 1943– 1946* (London, Collins, 1988)

6. *Select list of published articles*

R L Brohier, 'D S Senenayake as minister of agriculture and lands' *Ceylon Historical Journal* vol V (1955–1956) pp 68–80

K M de Silva, 'The formation and character of the Ceylon National Congress, 1917–1919', *Ceylon Journal of Historical and Social Studies* vol X (1967) pp 70–102

K M de Silva 'The Ceylon National Congress in disarray, 1920–21: Sir Ponnambalam Arunachalam leaves the Congress' *Ceylon Journal of Historical and Social Studies* new series vol II (1972) pp 97–117

K M de Silva 'The Ceylon National Congress in Disarray II: the triumph of Sir William Manning 1921–24' *Ceylon Journal of Historical and Social Studies* new series vol III(1) (1973) pp 16–35

K M de Silva, 'The history and politics of the transfer of power, 1931–1948' in K M de Silva, ed, University of Ceylon *History of Ceylon* vol III (Colombo & Kandy, 1973) pp 489–533

K M de Silva, 'The transfer of power in Sri Lanka: a review of British perspectives' *Ceylon Journal of Historical and Social Sudies* new series vol IV(1&2) (1974) pp 8–19

K M de Silva, 'The model colony: reflections on the transfer of power in Ceylon' in A J Wilson & D Dalton, eds, *The states of South Asia* (London, 1982) pp 77–88

K M de Silva, 'The high politics of the transfer of power in Sri Lanka: 1943–1946' *Sesquicentennial Commemorative Volume of the Royal Asiatic Society of Sri Lanka, 1845–1995* (1995) pp 487–520

B H Farmer, 'The social bases of nationalism in Ceylon' *Journal of Asian Studies* vol XXIV (1965) pp 431–439

V K Jayawardena, 'Origins of the left movement in Ceylon' *Modern Ceylon Studies* vol 11(2) (1971) pp 195–221

W I Jennings, 'The appointment of the Soulbury Commission' *University of Ceylon Review* vol III (1945) pp 11–28

W I Jennings, 'The evolution of the new constitution' *University of Ceylon Review* vol V (1947) pp 1–20

W I Jennings, 'The Ceylon general election of 1947' *University of Ceylon Review* vol VI (1948) pp 183–195

W I Jennings, 'Notes on the constitutional law of colonial Ceylon' *Journal of the Royal Asiatic Society* (Ceylon branch) new series vol I (1950) pp 51–72

W I Jennings, 'Nationalism and political development in Ceylon: the background to self-government' *Ceylon Historical Journal* vol III (1953–1954) pp 62–86, 99–114, 197–206

W I Jennings, 'D S Senanayake and independence' *Ceylon Historical Journal* vol V (1955–1956) pp 16–22

W I Jennings, 'The making of a dominion constitution' *The Law Quarterly Review* (October 1949) pp 456–479

M W Roberts, 'Elites, nationalism and the nationalist movement in Ceylon' in M W Roberts, ed, *Documents of the Ceylon National Congress and nationalist politics in Ceylon, 1929–1950* vol 1 (Colombo, 1978) pp xxix–ccxxii

J Russell, 'The dance of the turkey-cock: the Jaffna boycott of 1931' *Ceylon Journal of Historical and Social Studies* new series vol VIII(1) (1978) pp 47–67

A J Wilson, 'Minority safeguards in the Ceylon constitution' *Ceylon Journal of Historical and Social Studies* vol 1(1) (1958) pp 73–95

A J Wilson, 'The development of the constitution, 1920–1947 in K M de Silva, ed, University of Ceylon *History of Ceylon* Vol III (Colombo & Kandy, 1973) pp 359–380

# Index of Main Subjects and Persons

This is not a comprehensive index, but a simplified and straightforward index to document numbers, together with page references to the Introduction in part I, the latter being given at the beginning of the entry in lower-case roman numerals. It is designed to be used in conjunction with the summary lists and chapter headings of the preliminary pages to both parts of the volume. A preceding asterisk indicates inclusion in the Biographical Notes at the end of part II. Where necessary (e.g., in particularly long documents), and, if possible, paragraph numbers are given inside round brackets. The following abbreviations are used:

N – editor's link note (before main text of document)
n – footnote

Documents are divided between the two volume parts as follows:

nos   1–239   part I
nos 240–446   part II

Abrahams, Sir S   93
Acheson, A B   380
Addison, Lord   307, 317, 377, 416, 421, 424, 427
* Aluwihare, B   34, 57, 236
* Aluwihare, R   xxix
Amarasuriya, H   255
Amery, L S   xxi, lvii, lxxxvii n 15, 52, 70, 130, 137, 159, 162, 202, 233 (1, 2)
Aney, M S   xxviii, lxxv, lxxxviii n 58, 177 n 2, 183, 230 N, 233 (1, 2), 234, 243 (2)
Anti-Fascist People's Freedom League (AFPFL) 377, 417
* Attlee, C R   xxi, xxii, xxix–xxxiv, lxxiv, lxxviii, 278, 281, 339, 347, 384, 404, 427, 439
on draft statement on constitutional reforms in the island   317
criticisms of Colonial Office text on proposed announcement on future of Ceylon, 1947 lxxx, 395 n 3
agrees to new draft statement, 1947   404
on defence agreement, 1947   417
Aung San   xxix, lxxviii, 417
Australia
views on admission of Ceylon to Commonwealth lxxxii, 418, 421–424

Bajpai, Sir G   liv, xciii, 33, 74, 75, 84, 89, 105, 251
Bandaranaike, Mrs (Miss Ratwatte)   72, 80 (5), 96

* Bandaranaike, S W R D   xxiii, 1, 37, 45, 46, 75, 87, 90, 91, 105, 183, 191, 231, 247, 251, 261, 262, 289, 303, 320, 324, 446
anti-Indian speech of, 1940   33, 34
Ceylon Independence Bill   432
Free Lanka Bill   lxvi, lxvii, 236, 253, 255, 300
marriage   72, 80 (5), 96
preparations for his dismissal from office, 1940 92–95
Sinhala Maha Sabha   xl, 67
Banks, P N   28, 31
* Batuwantudawe, U   97
Bennett, J S   417
Bevin, E   lxiv, 394 n 2, 446 n 1
* Blaxter, K W   xxii, lii, 34, 53, 57, 67, 71, 80, 81, 126, 128
Board of Ministers   xxxi, xxxvi, xxxix, xli, xlviii, lii, lv, lvi, lxi, lxiii, lxv, lxvi, lxxvii, lxxviii n 12, 2, 3 (2, 9), 5, 6 (3, 4), 9, 11, 14, 21 (7), 22, 23, 24 (4), 25, 32, 34, 35, 36, 43, 45, 46, 48, 49, 52, 54, 58, 62, 68, 69, 71, 73, 76, 78, 81, 86, 87, 90, 91, 104, 105, 106, 107, 109, 111, 113, 114, 115, 124, 125, 138, 139, 150, 151, 153, 155, 160, 161, 169, 170, 171, 175, 177, 178, 179, 183, 185, 193, 201, 207, 208, 209, 210, 211, 215, 216, 220, 221, 224, 225, 230, 231, 233, 235, 236, 243, 249–253, 255, 259–260, 262, 266–267, 270, 272–281, 283–284, 286, 292, 296, 298, 300–302, 304, 309, 312, 322–323, 328, 330, 338–340, 346, 348, 350, 363, 369, 373, 378, 384, 390, 397, 402

Board of Trade    xiii, xxxvi, 87, 158, 161, 260, 274, 317, 369, 371, 374, 413, 438
Bolsher, G F    50
Bracegirdle, M A    xli–xlii, lxxxvii n 16, 1, 42, 46, 53
    Bracegirdle affair    332
Bridges, Sir E    xxii, 281
British Nationality Bill    xxxiv, lxxxiii, 380, 427, 429, 434
Buell, R L    189
Burrows, F J    lxiv, 318
Burghers    lxxxvii n 26, 106, 161, 226
Burma    vi, x, xi, xii, xv, xvii, xxi, xxix, xxx, xxxiv, xxxv, lvii, lviii, lix, lxvii, lxviii, lxix, lxxii, lxxiii, lxxviii, lxxix, lxxxiv
    constitutional development    9, 11, 16, 81, 102
    influence on Ceylon negotiations    377, 380–383, 388, 402, 404, 417, 446
    Japanese invasion of    106
    promise of self-government to    377, 380–383, 388
    self-government for    149, 150, 159, 191, 199, 200, 212, 266, 268, 270, 278, 380
    white paper on, 1945    303–305, 308, 322
Bushe, Sir G    53, 90, 93, 101


Cabinet/War Cabinet    xlii, lv, lvii–lix, lxiii, lxix–lxx, lxxiii–lxxiv, lxxix–lxxx, 155, 156, 398, 399
    minutes & memoranda    106, 146, 161, 169, 202, 270, 271, 273, 280, 283, 312, 316, 317, 389, 390, 395, 396, 446
Cabinet/War Cabinet committees    xxxiii–xxxiv
    Ceylon Committee    260
    Ceylon Constitution Committee    161 n 5, 164, 165
    Colonial Affairs Committee    lxix, lxxiii, lxxiv, lxxvi, lxxix, lxxx, 270, 304, 306, 312, 357, 358, 388, 404 n 5
    India & Burma Committee    404 n 5, 415, 419
* Caine, S    lxi, lxxvii, 162, 371
* Caldecott, Sir A
    constitutional reform, 1937–1939    xlii–xliv, xlvii, xlviii, 1, 2, 4, 9, 13, 14, 332
    constitutional reform, 1940–1943    xlviii, liv–lix, 23, 32 (6), 36, 44, 47, 54, 67, 78, 81, 87, 90–93, 95, 97, 100, 101, 102, 103, 104, 107, 108, 109, 110, 111, 112, 113, 119, 120, 124, 125, 141, 142, 143, 144, 145, 148
    Indo–Ceylon negotiations    intro l–liv, 5, 10 (5), 7, 8, 10, 15, 17, 18, 19, 20, 21 (7), 22, 25, 33, 34, 37, 38, 39, 40, 41, 45, 49, 52, 54, 58, 59, 64, 65, 68, 70, 72 (8), 73, 76, 77, 79, 82, 83, 84, 86, 88, 94, 96 (5), 98, 99, 105 (12), 121, 122, 123, 130, 131, 132, 134, 135, 136, 137, 139, 140, 156, 157, 177 n 2, 230
    ministers' draft constitution, 1944    lxi–lxii,

148, 149, 150, 152, 153, 154, 155, 159, 161, 163, 164, 165, 166, 168, 169, 170, 171, 173, 174, 199 (Appendix A), 201
    Mool-oya crisis    27, 28, 29, 30, 31, 32, 35, 46, 66
    opposition to 'fifty-fifty' demand    xliv–xlvi
    postponement of general election, 1940    42, 51
    Soulbury Commission    xiii–lxiv, 203, 204, 205, 206, 207, 208, 209, 210, 211, 212, 213, 214, 216, 217, 218, 219, 220, 221, 224, 225, 226, 227, 231, 326
    'Things Ceylonese' series    1, 3, 6, 16, 21, 24, 32, 34, 46, 57, 64, 72, 89, 96, 105
Campbell, I M R    248
Carstairs, C Y    370
Ceylon Association    5, 19, 22, 41, 46, 52, 55, 63, 151, 172, 192, 333–334, 368
Ceylon Civil Service    105, 265, 300, 365, 367, 378, 379
Ceylon Citizenship Act 18 of 1948    lxxxiii
Ceylon Daily News    1, 16, 21, 25, 32, 33, 34, 82, 136, 171, 206, 303, 320, 331, 339
Ceylon Defence Force (see also defence)    21, 50, 83, 128, 129, 183
Ceylon Independence Bill    xxv, lxxxii, 430–433, 437–438, 440
Ceylon Indian Congress (later Ceylon Workers Congress)    xvii, lxxxiv, 16, 19, 34, 41, 49, 65, 72, 81, 89, 98, 154, 168, 179, 199, 210, 215, 309, 331, 332, 339, 366, 425
Ceylon National Congress    16, 20, 23, 34, 64, 70, 73, 79, 81, 82, 96, 111, 125, 154, 168, 183, 191, 199, 207, 292, 301, 322
Ceylon Observer    32, 46, 64, 67
Chamberlain, N    339·
Churchill, W S    xi, xxi, xlvii, lx, lxxvii n 41, 120, 169, 178, 200
* Clauson, G L M    370, 372, 413
Clyde, W M    175
coconut    lxxvii, 72, 87, 368, 371–372, 374, 446
    (see also copra)
Collins, C H    xxiii, xxiv, 72, 87, 238, 240, 253, 255, 261
Colombo    xxvii, xxviii, xxx, xxxii, xxxiii, xlvii, xlix, lii, liii, liv, lvi, lx, lxiii, lxiv, lxxi, lxxv, lxxvii, lxxx, lxxxii, lxxxiv, lxxxvi, 12 N, 21, 37, 46, 72, 83, 87, 89, 96, 105, 120, 129, 199, 208, 231, 258, 261, 307, 315, 327, 373, 375–376, 378–379, 396, 423, 436, 438–439, 443, 446
Commission on Social Services    368 (50)
Commission (also British Commonwealth)    viii, ix, xii, xiii, xvii, xxxiii, xxxiv, lvii, lviii, lxiii, lxvii, lxxi, lxxvii, lxxviii, lxxix, lxxx, lxxxi, lxxxii, lxxxiii, lxxxiv, lxxxv, lxxxvi, 266, 298, 300, 305, 308, 310, 312, 317, 339, 372, 380, 382, 384, 387, 388, 389–390, 392, 395, 399, 402, 405–407, 410–411, 414–415, 416, 418, 419, 421–422, 424, 436, 438

constitutional development/constitutional reform
(*see also* declaration of 1943; Donoughmore
Commission; Donoughmore Constitution;
Donoughmore Report; ministers' draft
constitution, 1944; Soulbury Commission;
Soulbury Constitution; Soulbury Report; white
paper of 1945) xv, xlii–intro l, xlvi, liv–lix, xliii,
lxxiv, 7, 9, 12, 27, 29, 34, 45, 54, 69, 133, 149,
150, 152, 228, 261, 270, 273, 276, 280, 281, 292,
293, 294, 304, 312, 315, 316, 317, 322, 335, 339,
347, 377, 390, 415, 436
* Coomaraswamy, C 87
copra xxxiii, lxxvii, 58, 74, 75, 156, 199, 200, 266,
298, 348, 368, 371–372, 374, 386
* Corea, G C S xxiii, liii, lxvi, 6, 16, 32, 34, 37,
45, 46, 52, 64, 70, 72, 73, 87, 89, 105, 138, 231,
253, 272, 308
* Cranborne, Lord (later Lord Salisbury) xxi,
xxii, liv, lv, lvi, 115, 116, 117, 118, 121, 122,
123, 124, 125, 126, 127, 134, 140, 141, 142, 143,
144, 145, 147
* Creech Jones, A lxxix–lxxxi, 274, 284, 342–343,
345, 372, 376, 378, 382–383, 388, 390–395, 397
n 2, 398–401, 404, 405, 406, 407, 414, 415, 422,
427, 431–435, 439, 440, 441, 442, 443
Cripps, Sir S lvi, 125
    Cripps scheme 153


* Dahanayake, W lxxv, 253, 255, 324, 328, 339
Dalton, H xxi, 158 n 2, 161 n 5
declaration of 1943 lxii, lxiii, lxv, lxvii, lxx
    origins of 140–145
    role of Caldecott and Layton in drafting 148–
        150, 152, 153, 154, 155, 161, 163, 164, 165,
        166, 168, 169, 170, 171, 173, 174, 175
de Mel, R F S 379
* de Silva, Colvin R 46, 50, 60, 127
*de Silva, George E xxiii, lxxv, lxxxviii n 57, 34,
46, 73, 87, 105, 115, 207, 231, 255, 292, 308,
425
* de Silva, L M D 380 N
* de Silva, M W H xxiv
* de Silva, W A xxiii, 34, 45 n 1, 46, 86, 105
de Zoysa, A P 34, 255
Davies, T W 74, 75, 87
defence 1, 3, 16, 21, 26, 34, 56, 57, 60, 72, 83,
102, 105, 114, 115, 117, 122–129, 131, 138, 143,
146, 149, 150, 153, 159, 161, 164, 166, 168, 169,
170, 176, 178, 179, 183, 186, 188, 189, 190, 191,
197, 199, 200, 237, 239, 242, 246, 248, 260–261,
263, 265–266, 270, 274, 279–280, 285–286, 290,
292, 295–296, 298, 300, 304, 306–307, 312,
315–316, 318, 322, 326, 335–337, 341, 344,
346–348, 357, 368 (53), 371 (4), 376, 379, 382,
383, 384, 388, 389, 390, 391, 392, 396, 399, 401,
402, 407, 412, 413, 414, 415, 416, 417, 418, 419,

420, 428, 430, 436 (Appendix 1), 437, 438, 446
(5)
defence agreement xv, lxxxi, lxxxii, 280, 330,
346, 351, 354, 356, 366, 367, 417, 419–420,
436
defence expenditure 16, 105, 296
defence force 266, 279, 296, 298, 348, 376,
430, 445, 446 (5)
defence regulations 21, 46, 52, 53, 57, 63, 71,
106, 125, 135, 196, 296
Delimitation Commission, 1946 xlix, lxii, 259–
260, 265, 300, 310, 312, 322, 328–330, 332–333,
346, 348, 409
Desai, H M 267, 288, 323
Devonshire, Duke of xxii, 237
dominion status for Ceylon xxix, xxxii, lv, lvii,
lviii, lix, lxvii, lxviii, lxix, lxx, lxxi, lxxii, lxxiii,
lxxvi, lxxviii, lxxix, lxxx, lxxxi, lxxxii, lxxxiv,
lxxxv, 111, 112, 149, 150, 152, 261, 280, 283,
288
Donoughmore Commission 7, 9, 12, 27, 29, 34,
45, 54, 69, 133, 270, 282, 322
Donoughmore Constitution 266, 270, 274, 282,
285, 292, 298, 300, 310, 322, 329–330, 401
Donoughmore Report xxxvi–xxxix, xlii, xliii,
intro l, lxxii, 69, 228, 280, 339
* Drayton, Sir R xxii, xxiii, xxiv, 24 n 1, 25, 38,
105, 183, 233, 235, 239, 240–241, 243, 251, 254,
258, 261–262, 268, 272, 282, 330, 341, 344, 350,
353, 355, 365, 378, 379
Driberg, T E N 328


* Eastwood, C G 58
Eden, A xxi, 417
elections xxix, xxxix, intro l, li, lii, lxvii, lxviii,
lxxix, lxxx, lxxxiii, 9, 14, 20, 25, 37, 96, 149, 154,
185, 199, 200, 201, 202, 218 (6), 266, 282, 290,
300, 322, 328
    elections, 1947 339, 345, 337, 383, 395, 399,
        425
    postponement of general election, 1940 42,
        44, 46, 64, 71, 72, 78, 81, 87
executive committees xxxvi, lxxxvi n 4, 1, 2, 3, 6,
9, 24, 27, 28, 30, 32, 34, 41, 43, 46, 48, 57, 69,
70, 71, 81, 90, 91, 97, 100, 102, 115, 133, 154,
157, 160, 182, 193, 236
emergency powers 1, 46, 65, 102, 114, 117, 119,
239, 257, 303, 306, 312, 335, 397
external affairs 62, 115, 135, 161, 166 (b), 168,
170, 186, 199, 200, 260, 263, 266, 268, 270, 274,
279–280, 282, 286, 290, 292, 298, 300, 306, 312,
318, 322, 326, 346, 348–349, 351, 357 (B), 384,
387, 388, 389, 390, 391, 392, 393, 395, 396, 399,
401, 408, 413, 414, 415, 418, 419, 421, 431,
436–437, 443

Fennelly, R D   192
fifty-fifty campaign   xliv–xlv, lxxxvii n 18, 303
* Fonseka, M   xxiv
franchise (see also India; Indo–Ceylon relations
    and negotiations)   xxxvii, xxxviii, xliv, xlv, intro
    l, li, lxix, lxxiii, lxxiv, lxxv, lxxvi, 44, 45, 46, 47,
    49, 54, 58, 67, 76, 79, 84, 87, 88, 100, 113, 133,
    151, 153, 154, 181, 183, 201, 209 (8), 210, 215,
    230, 258, 259, 265, 266, 274 (1), 282, 284, 290,
    295, 298, 300, 309, 310, 312, 321–323, 331,
    333–334, 336, 338, 342, 343, 345, 346, 349–350,
    352–353, 355–356, 357–360, 382, 409, 413
Free/Sri Lanka Bill   lxv, lxvi, 236, 247, 253, 255,
    259, 264, 266, 268, 293


* Gater, Sir G   xxii, 76, 150, 238, 240, 253, 262,
    264, 273, 274, 279, 282, 287, 288, 292, 330, 341,
    344, 349–350, 355, 363, 372, 374–375
* Gent, G E J   xxii, 3, 9, 21, 40, 42, 46, 48, 49, 52,
    59, 63, 65, 67, 71, 80, 81, 88, 90, 101, 113, 120,
    143, 150, 151, 183, 186, 256, 258, 261, 265, 272
    n 2, 274, 279, 282 n 1, 297, 307, 311, 318,
    324–325
Gibson, P J   321
Gilchrist, R N   276
* Goonesinha, A E   xxxix, xl, xlii, lii, 1, 19, 89
* Goonetilleke, Sir O   xxix, lxx, lxxi, lxxvii, lxxxviii
    n 53, 53, 64, 138, 170 N, 175, 238, 339, 435,
    438, 444 n 3, 445, 446
    as member of negotiating team, 1945–
        1946   lxx, lxxi, 240, 253, 261–262, 264, 303,
        346, 349, 350, 352, 353, 355, 356, 363
    role in drafting new constitution, 1947   381,
        383, 387, 388, 390 n 4, 392, 394, 402, 404,
        407 n 2, 410, 411, 412, 413, 414, 415
    drafting agreements on defence, external affairs
        and public officers, 1947   419, 420
    plans for post-war reconstruction   lxxvii, 368,
        369, 370, 371, 372, 374
* Goonewardene, L S   50, 60, 85
Gordon Walker, P   443, 444, 446
* Greenwood, A   lxix, 270, 304 n 1, 312, 317 n 1,
    388 n 5
* Gunawardena, D P R   xl, 21, 50, 53, 57, 60


Halifax, Lord   xxi
* Hall, G H
    constitutional reform in Ceylon, 1945–
        1946   lxvii, lxix, lxx, lxxiv, lxxvi, lxxxv, 47,
        101, 300, 302, 303, 306, 308, 309, 314, 317 n
        1, 318, 319, 320, 322, 323, 326, 327, 329,
        331, 332, 333, 334, 336, 338, 340, 345, 352,
        356, 360, 365, 367, 368, 369, 374
    discussions with Senanayake, September
        1945   lxix, lxx, 266–268, 270, 272–274, 278,

        280, 284, 292, 293, 294, 295, 298
    discussions with Ponnambalam   284
    with representatives of Indians   288, 291, 299
Hambro, Sir C   221
Henderson, A   361
House of Commons   47, 87, 169, 205, 208, 211,
    250, 252, 261, 278, 311, 328, 398, 411, 417, 419,
    437, 438
* Howard, J C   xxiv, 23, 25, 87, 92, 93, 113, 261,
    374 n 2, 375, 376, 389–379
Huxham, C J   xxiv, liii, 64, 72, 74, 75, 77 n 1, 87,
    89, 105


Illangakoon, J W R   xxiv
immigration/immigration policy   xxxi, 3, 7, 8, 41,
    49, 59, 64, 67, 71, 74, 75, 76, 84, 86, 87, 88, 89,
    94, 98, 99, 121, 131, 134, 189, 258
    Immigration Bill   88, 90, 99, 132
    Immigration Ordinance   130, 131
independence day   440–441
India   vi, viii, x, xi, xii, xv, xviii, xix, xxi, xxiv, xxvii,
    xxviii, xxix, xxxii, xxxiii, xxxiv, xxxv, xxxvii,
    xxxviii, xxxix, xlii, intro l, li, lii, liii, liv, lv, lvi,
    lvii, lviii, lix, lx, lxi, lxiii, lxiv, lxvii, lxviii, lxx,
    lxxii, lxxiii, lxxiv, lxxv, lxxvi, lxxvii, lxxviii, lxxix,
    lxxx, lxxxi, lxxxiii, lxxxiv, lxxxv, lxxxvii, lxxxviii n
    58, 23, 33, 38, 39, 40, 42, 46, 52, 64, 70, 71, 72,
    74, 75, 76, 77, 79, 81, 82, 84, 86, 87, 89, 90, 98,
    99, 100, 101, 102, 115, 151, 154, 157, 162, 167,
    192, 196, 199, 223, 229, 230, 243, 251, 258, 259,
    261, 265, 266, 268, 270, 274, 275, 276, 277, 280,
    281, 282, 283, 284, 286, 288, 289, 291, 293,
    295–300, 305, 310, 312, 313, 321, 322, 323,
    331–332, 339, 340, 342, 345, 346, 349, 351, 353,
    355, 356, 357, 358, 359, 360, 361, 362, 364, 366,
    371, 372, 377, 380, 381, 382, 384, 385, 388, 389,
    396 (20 & Annex), 402, 404, 413, 414 (1), 415
    (7), 418, 419, 427, 429, 434
Indian labour   xxxvii, xxxviii, xliv, intro l, li, lii,
    liii, liv, lxix, lxxvi, 1, 19, 34, 37, 38, 40, 41, 46,
    49, 50, 52, 65, 66, 68, 89, 96, 106, 115, 116, 122,
    123, 130, 132, 226, 236, 251, 300, 313, 331, 361,
    362, 364, 366
Indian National Congress   xvii, liii, 6, 21, 41, 64,
    72, 73, 81, 98, 154, 179, 199, 210, 215, 255, 324,
    339, 342, 396
Indo–Ceylon relations & negotiations (see also
    Indian labour)   xv, intro l–liv, 3, 5, 6, 8, 10, 15,
    17, 18, 19, 20, 22, 33, 37, 38, 39, 40, 45, 54, 58,
    59, 62, 70, 72, 73, 74, 75, 76, 77, 79, 83, 84, 86,
    87, 88, 89, 96, 97, 114, 121, 122, 123, 130, 131,
    132, 134–137, 139, 151, 153, 156, 157, 160, 162,
    164, 166, 177, 183, 230, 233, 234, 243, 251, 258,
    340

* Jayah, T B   21, 22, 108, 125 n 1, 144, 255
* Jayatilake, Sir D   xxiii, xxviii, xl, xlii, xliv, xlix,
  intro l, 1, 3, 6, 24, 34, 46, 87, 105, 106, 266, 298,
  339
* Jayewardene, J R   xxx, lv, lxxv, 20 n 2, 255, 444
  n 3
* Jeffries, Sir C   lxxvi, lxxxv, 344, 346, 377, 379,
  402–403, 408, 426, 429
* Jennings, W I   xxviii, lxxii, lxxiii, lxxv, lxxxiv
  prepares ministers' draft constitution of
    1943 lxi, lxii, lxiii
  in London as advisor to Senanayake, August
    1945 lxii, lxix, lxx, 170 N, 175, 183, 208 n 6,
    266 N, 268, 290 N, 344, 382
  helps in drafting new constitution, 1945–
    1947 330, 341, 406
  principal, University College, Colombo   lxxiv,
    69
  vice-chancellor, University of Ceylon   lxxxiv
Jones, C E   xxiv, 87, 369


Kandy   lxii, lxxxvi n 7, 20, 34, 45, 46, 50, 69, 73,
  79, 85, 87, 89, 105, 127, 133, 161, 178, 179, 199,
  226, 228, 256, 282, 446
Kandyan throne   441
*Kangany/kanganies*   xxv, 34, 41, 49, 52, 220, 362,
  366
Kankesanturai   396
* Kannangara, C W W   xxiii, 32, 34, 45, 54, 67,
  87, 89, 133, 206, 231, 253, 308, 425
Katukurunda   396
Kegalle/Kegalle district   133, 361, 362, 366
Knavesmire estate   361, 362, 364, 366
Knox, Sir A   26
Koggala   396, 412 n 1
* Kotelawala, Sir J   xxiii, lxvi, lii, 1, 21, 22, 32, 34,
  45 n 1, 46, 67, 87, 89, 226, 247, 253, 308
Kurunegala   133, 396


Lake House   26, 55, 82, 106, 109, 149, 150, 303,
  320
* Layton, Sir G   xxvii, xxviii
  commander-in-chief, Ceylon   lv, 119, 120, 124,
    129
  presides over War Council   lvi
  supports constitutional reform   lvii, lviii, 149,
    152, 169 n 3 & 4, 183, 190, 199 (Appendix B),
    200, 203, 222
  expresses concerns over defence, 1945–
    1946 lxxv, lxxvi, 263, 307, 315, 326 N, 335,
    337
* Lloyd, Lord   xxi, liv, 45, 46, 47, 51, 52, 54, 55,
  56, 57, 58, 59, 60, 61, 62, 63, 64, 66, 67, 68, 73,
  76, 77, 78, 82, 83, 84, 86, 113
* Lloyd, Sir T   411, 434

Lee, F G   167
Lennox Boyd, A T   50
Linlithgow, Lord   xxiv, 70
Lyttelton, O   192, 229


* Macan-Markar, Sir M   60, 87
* MacDonald, M J   xxi, xliii, xlvi, xlviii, liv, 2, 4, 5,
  7, 8, 9, 10, 13, 14, 15, 20, 22, 26, 27, 28, 29, 30,
  31, 38, 39, 40, 41, 42, 43, 44, 71, 81, 106, 113,
  250, 339
Machtig, Sir E   439
Madras   251, 322, 347, 446
Mahadeva, Sir A   xxiii, xxviii, lvii, 108, 143, 145,
  148, 182, 209, 220, 236 N, 253, 255, 308, 324,
  339, 375–376, 425
Maldive Islands   443
Markham, Sir H   315
Manila   396
Minimum Wages Ordinance   368
ministers   1, 2, 3, 14, 17, 23, 25, 26, 28, 29, 30,
  31, 32, 34, 35, 36, 46, 62, 73, 82, 86, 95, 97, 103,
  104, 105, 107, 109, 111, 112, 115, 116, 124, 128,
  138, 139, 140, 141, 142, 143, 147, 148, 157, 161,
  165, 168, 169, 170, 171, 173, 174, 181, 183, 184,
  185, 186, 197, 202, 204, 208, 209, 210, 212, 213,
  214, 215, 216, 217, 218, 219, 220, 224, 230, 236
ministers' draft constitution, 1944   xv, xxviii, lxi–
  lxiii
  Caldecott & Layton support appointment of
    commission to examine   190, 191, 195, 196,
    197, 198, 199, 200, 204, 205
  Colonial Office response   187
  minority opposition to   188, 193, 194
  minority views on   201
  ministers oppose terms of reference of
    commission   210, 211, 216, 217, 219, 221,
    222
  origins of   173–175
  submitted to Caldecott   181–186
Minneriya   396
minorities   xxxvii, xxxix, xl, xli, xliv, xlvi, xlvii,
  xlviii, xlix, li, lvi, lviii, lxi, lxii, lxv, lxvii, lxx,
  lxxiii, lxxv, 11, 13, 71, 101, 106, 144, 145, 149,
  150, 161, 164 (4), 165 (4), 180, 182, 183, 194,
  195, 209, 212, 213, 215, 226, 232, 249, 255,
  259–261, 265–266, 270, 273, 279, 281, 283–284,
  290, 292, 295, 298–300, 303–304, 309, 312, 316,
  322, 324, 332–333, 339, 350, 354, 357, 390–392,
  394–395, 399–401, 404, 409, 414–415, 419
Molamure, F   327
Monteath, Sir D   351
Mool-oya   xlix, xxvii, intro l, lxxxvii n 25, 24, 26,
  32, 34, 42, 46, 322 (*see also* Senanayake, D S)
* Moore, Sir H (*also* Monck-Mason Moore, Sir
  H)   xxii, xxviii, xxx, lxiv, lxvi, lxvii, lxix, lxx,
  lxxiii, lxxiv, lxxv, lxxvi, lxxix, lxxxi, lxxxii, lxxxiii,

3, 12 N, 232, 233, 234, 235, 236, 238, 240–241,
    243–247, 249–254, 265, 267–269, 272, 297,
    302–303, 306, 308–309, 313–314, 319–320,
    324–327, 331–332, 336, 338, 340, 350, 352–353,
    355–356, 361, 363–365, 367–369, 374 n 2,
    378–380, 382–383, 385–388, 390 n 4, 392, 394,
    395, 397–403, 405–409
  argues case for 'generous and spontaneous
    gesture' to Sri Lanka   295
  at Colonial Office   409, 411–415, 420, 422,
    425–427, 429–436, 439–443
  draft constitution, 1946–1947   341, 344, 349
  on publication of Soulbury Report   286, 289
  personal views on Soulbury Report   259, 261
  supports Senanayake on dominion status   382,
    383, 385, 387, 391
Morrison, H N   248
* Motha, G R   291, 299
Mountbatten, Lord Louis   xxviii, xxix, xxxiv, xxxv,
    lxiii, lxxxvii n 36, 178, 199, 200, 203, 222
* Moyne, Lord   xxi, liv, xcvi, xcvii, xcviii, 91, 92,
    94, 95, 97, 98, 100, 102, 103, 104, 106, 107, 108,
    109, 110, 111, 112, 114
Mudaliar, Sir R   lxxvi, 146, 321, 336, 338–339,
    340, 342–343, 345, 347
Muslims (also Moors)   lxii, 1, 36, 106, 133, 159,
    161, 226, 256, 259, 261, 265, 270, 300, 322, 326,
    347


Nalliah, V   255, 339
* Natesa, Aiyar K   16, 19, 21, 34, 50, 325, 331,
    339
navy   46, 72, 87, 125, 202 n 3, 296, 307, 396
Negombo   396, 412
Nehru, J   lxxix, lxxxiii, 16, 34, 49, 64, 65
  visit to Sri Lanka, 1939   16, 49, 65
* Nihill, J H B   xxiv, xxix, lxxv, 183, 236, 261–
    262, 279, 282, 292, 330, 341, 344, 346, 349–350,
    353, 355


Pakistan   xxix, lxxx, lxxxiv
* Panabokke, Sir T   228, 251, 258
* Parkinson, Sir C   xxii, xxxv, 9, 12, 18, 19, 47,
    101, 120
* Paskin, J J   xxii, 409, 411–414, 420
Passfield, Lord   lii, 31, 45, 54, 79, 322
Peck, J A   428
* Pereira, I X   ix, 13, 45, 108, 126, 182, 240, 250,
    255, 325, 339
* Pereira, R L   21, 144
* Perera, N M   xi, 46, 50, 53, 57, 60
Pethick-Lawrence, Lord   lxxvi, lxxvii, 305, 310,
    321, 345, 359
Philippines   xxviii, lxxxi, 396
planters/plantations   xlix, 41, 52, 72, 87, 105, 243,
    322, 361, 368

police   lxxxiv, 21, 199, 200, 373, 375–378, 436
* Ponnambalam, G G   xxxix, 21, 255, 339, 354,
    397
  at Colonial Office, 1945   lxix, 249, 250, 252,
    256, 284, 320 n 1, 322, 325 n 1
  constitutional reform, 1939   lxvii, 1, 4, 11, 13,
    14, 32
  constitutional reform, 1942–1944   144, 182,
    188, 208, 209, 210 (13), 215 (8), 236 N, 237,
    240 (V)
  fifty-fifty campaign   xliv, xlv, lxii, lxvii, 302,
    325
  opposition to constitutional reform, 1940   19,
    36
  protests against Soulbury Report and white
    paper of 1945   lxxiii, 322
  supports Indian agitation for voting
    rights   intro l, li
Ponniah, S   223
Powell, R R   335
Preston, G E   158
Public Security Act   lxxxii
Public Services Commission   lxxxvi, 87, 257, 259–
    261, 270, 322, 419, 426


Quebec Conference, 1943   xlvii


* Rajakulendran, J G   324, 339
* Ranasinha, A G   274, 279, 292 n 1
* Ratnayake, A   64, 255
Rees, J F   lxiv
Rees Williams, D R   434
Reid, T   328
Reserve Bank (also Central Bank)   442, 444 n 3
* Roberts-Wray, K O   93, 265, 279 n 1, 282, 330,
    344, 346, 410, 411, 414
Rolleston, W L   128
Rowan, T L   395 n 3, 404
Royal Air Force (RAF)   396
rubber   xv, xxxiii, xxxviii, xlvii, lix, lx, lxxvii, 19,
    22, 41, 81, 87, 151, 160, 162, 167, 172, 180, 189,
    192, 195, 196, 199, 200, 202 n 3, 229, 234, 243,
    266, 285, 292, 298, 299, 309, 322, 334, 339, 348
    n 2, 366, 371, 372, 373, 435 n 2


Sabben-Clare, E E   296
Samarakkody, E   16, 50, 60, 128 N
Sama Samajists (also Lanka Sama Samaj
    Party)   xviii, xxvii, xxviii, xl, xliii, xliv, xlviii,
    lvi, 1, 19, 21, 32, 41, 46, 49 (3), 50, 52, 53, 55,
    56, 57, 60, 63, 70, 71, 72 (11), 85, 120, 127, 272,
    292, 303, 397, 425
second chamber/Senate   xliv, lxvii, lxviii, lxix, xxx,
    lxxxii, 37, 181, 182, 193, 236, 253–254, 257,

259, 260, 261, 265, 266, 268, 273, 274 (3), 279, 290, 312 (11a), 317 (10), 322, 378, 409, 415 (6), 437, 438

Seel, J F 380

* Senanayake, D S 12 N, 16 (3), 24 (3), 25, 69, 87, 128, 198 n 5, 253, 262, 306, 309, 339, 348 n 2, 364, 366, 368 N, 373, 425, 426, 446

and Soulbury Commission Report lxiii, 204, 206, 208 n 6, 209, 211, 222, 226, 232, 236, 237, 245, 246, 261

at Colonial Office, 1945 lxvi, lxvii, lxx, 238, 240, 241, 247, 249, 250, 252, 255, 256, 257, 264, 265, 266, 268, 269, 270, 271, 272, 273, 274, 275, 276, 279, 280, 282, 283, 284–286, 287, 290, 292, 293, 294, 295, 298, 300, 301, 302, 303, 304, 311

Burmese independence 377, 381, 393

constitutional reform, 1937–1938 xliv, lv, 1, 3

constitutional reform, 1941–1943 lvii, lix, lx, 81, 154, 156 n 1, 168, 170 N, 181

debate on white paper, Nov 1945 lxxv, 312, 313, 316, 318, 319, 320, 324, 325, 326, 333

defence agreement lxxxi, lxxxii, 387, 416, 421, 424, 433, 436, 438

drafting of new constitution, 1946–1947 341, 344, 346, 349, 350, 352, 353, 357, 363, 382, 383, 384, 385, 388, 390, 391, 392, 395, 398, 399, 400, 401, 402, 403, 404, 405, 406, 407, 408, 410, 411, 414, 415, 419, 432, 439, 440

labour agitation and strikes lxxviii, 373, 375, 376, 378, 379, 397

ministers' draft constitution, 1944 lxi, lxiii, 175, 181 N, 183, 191, 203

Mool-oya crisis 24, 26, 32, 34, 42, 46, 322

negotiations on constitutional reform lxxi, lxxii, lxiii, lxxix

negotiations with India lxxxiii, 7, 37, 45 (1), 64, 72, 73, 75, 76 n 1, 79, 82, 83, 89, 96, 105, 116, 122, 139, 151, 243, 251, 291, 297, 338, 340, 342, 345, 429, 434

* Senanayake, Dudley 1, 87

Shaw, A P 239

* Shuckburgh, Sir J xxii, 378

* Sidebotham, J B xxii, lxiv, lxxviii, 162, 172, 175, 229, 258 n 2 & 4, 265, 274, 276, 279, 299, 325, 330, 334, 336, 346, 348 n 2, 368, 377, 410, 411, 417

Simonstown/Simonstown agreement lxxxi, 390, 396

Singapore, fall of xxxiii, 114–116

Sinhala Maha Sabha xxxix, xxlv, xliv, lxvii, 32, 34, 45, 46, 67, 72, 89, 90, 100, 199, 206, 301, 322

Sivasubramaniam, S 347, 357

* Smith, Trafford lxiv, lxxiii, 229, 239, 242, 257, 265, 274–275, 279, 282, 299, 304, 311, 317, 326, 333, 334

Sorenson, R W 328

* Soulbury, Lord 186

and dominion status for Ceylon 381–388, 390, 391, 392, 393, 394, 395, 399, 400, 401, 402, 403, 404, 405, 406, 407, 408, 409, 410, 411, 412, 413, 414–415

discussions on Soulbury Report with Colonial Office 276, 277, 297, 305, 310, 321, 342, 343, 351, 358, 359, 360

argues case for more advanced reforms than those recommended in his report 300, 311, 318

Soulbury Commission, appointment of lxiii, lxvi, lxxix, 202–205, 206, 210, 211, 212, 213–220, 221, 222, 224, 225, 226, 227, 231, 232, 237, 239

Soulbury Report 244–246, 248, 251, 253–254, 256–257, 259, 260–277, 278–287, 289, 290, 291, 292–295, 298, 299, 301–304, 306, 307, 308, 309, 312–317, 319–320, 322–326, 328, 329, 332–335, 337, 339, 347

Soulbury Report and framing of new constitution 330, 341, 344, 345, 346, 348, 349, 350, 352, 353, 357

Southern Rhodesia lvii, 101, 150, 158, 161, 164, 165, 166, 168, 181, 261, 266, 282, 357, 363, 380, 388

* Sri Pathmanathan, R 13, 73

Sri Lanka Freedom Party xl

Stainton, A H 428

Stanley, Sir H xxxviii, lii, 31, 45, 54, 79, 274 (1), 282

* Stanley, O xxi, liv, lv, lviii, lxiii, lxv, 147–150, 152, 153, 154, 155, 156, 159, 160, 161, 163, 164, 165, 166, 168, 169, 170, 171, 173, 174, 182, 184, 185, 186, 187, 190, 195, 196, 197–198, 201, 202

South-East Asia Command xxviii, xxxiv, xlvii, lxiii, lxxvii, 176, 178, 190, 195 (2), 198, 199, 200, 202 (8), 213, 266, 298

State Council xxviii, liv, lv, lviii, lxiii, lxv, 1, 3 (iv), 6, 9, 14, 16, 18, 19, 20, 21, 22, 25, 26, 28, 29, 31, 32, 35, 39, 40, 43, 45, 46 (4), 48, 51, 53, 55, 68, 69, 71, 72, 79, 81, 84, 86, 87, 89, 94, 96, 97, 100, 103, 105, 106–108, 110, 113, 114, 115, 124, 133, 148, 150, 151, 153, 154, 156 n 1, 157, 160, 161, 170 N, 173, 179, 182, 183, 185, 187, 193, 194, 196, 198, 199, 200, 201, 202, 203, 207, 208, 211, 213, 214, 215, 216, 219, 222, 226, 231, 232, 236, 237, 245, 249, 253, 255, 256, 258–260, 262, 266, 267, 270–273, 275, 276, 280, 282, 284, 290, 292, 296–298, 300, 301, 312, 316, 317, 320, 322, 324, 331, 332, 338, 339, 342, 345, 346, 349, 350, 354, 357, 378, 381, 403

Stubbs, Sir R xli, xliii, 322

Stewart Sandeman, N 11

Strahan, F 418

sterling balances lxxxii, 386, 435, 442, 444

strikes 331, 373, 375, 378, 379, 397

Supreme Court  lxxxiv, 183, 260, 261, 265, 266, 274, 322

Tamil Congress (*see also* Ponnambalam, G G) xviii, lxviii, lxxv, 209, 299 n 1, 303, 327, 339, 354
Tamils  249, 260, 265, 284, 297, 300, 310, 312, 321, 322, 324, 327, 332–339, 347, 354, 442, 446
tappers (rubber)  157 n 2, 172, 180
tea  xxxiii, xxxviii, xli, lxxvii, 19, 21, 22, 26, 34, 46, 50, 52, 72, 81, 87, 90, 99, 105, 128, 130, 195, 196, 199, 200, 266, 285, 298, 299, 309, 322, 334, 339, 365, 366, 371, 374, 386
*thalaivars*  361, 366
* Thondaman, S  331
Thornley, C H  284, 305
Thorogood, C F  438
Thiagaraja, J  255
*Times of Ceylon*  xlix, 21, 25, 30, 32, 34, 46, 51, 56, 57, 64, 72, 113, 141, 142, 303, 320, 437, 438
trade  xxi, xxv, xxxiii, xxxix, xl, xli, xlviii, xlix, lii, liii, lvii, lxi, lxxvii, lxxviii, lxxxii, 8, 17, 19, 21, 25, 26, 34, 46, 50, 52, 57, 58, 72, 74, 75, 77, 87, 89, 106, 122, 151, 158, 161, 163, 166, 169, 171, 212, 258, 260, 266, 270, 274, 279, 292, 298, 299, 310, 312, 317, 348, 366, 368, 370, 372, 378, 413, 415, 435, 438, 442, 444
  trade agreement  351, 413, 414

trade unions  378, 388, 446
Treasury  xxxiii, lx, lxxxi–lxxxii, 167
Trincomalee  xxviii, xlvii, lvi, 6, 169 n 3, 199, 200, 255, 266, 298, 322, 368, 371, 382, 387, 388, 390, 393, 395, 401, 402, 415, 418, 419, 436, 446
Turnbull, F F  305

United Nations  266, 298, 322, 368, 371, 382, 387, 388, 390, 393, 395, 401, 402, 415, 416, 419, 436, 446

* Vytilingam, S P  13, 331, 339

War Council  137
War Office  248, 296, 376, 445
Wavell, Lord  234, 273, 275–276, 321
* Wedderburn, M M  xxiii, 13
white paper of 1945  xv, 266, 291, 298, 300, 305, 312, 316, 317, 320, 322, 325–326, 329, 331–333, 339, 340, 345, 349–350, 356, 381, 388, 389, 392, 395, 401, 405 n 2
* Wickremasinghe, S A  lxxxvii n 62, 50
* Wijewardene, D R  46, 87 n 3
Wodeman, C S  xxii, xxiii